Financing Public Schools

Financing Public Schools moves beyond the basics of financing public elementary and secondary education to explore the historical, philosophical, and legal underpinnings of a viable public school system. Coverage includes the operational aspects of school finance, including issues regarding teacher salaries and pensions, budgeting for instructional programs, school transportation, and risk management. Diving deeper than other school finance books, the authors explore the political framework within which the schools must function, discuss the privatization of education and its effects on public schools, offer perspectives regarding education as an investment in human capital, and expertly explain complex financial and economic issues. This comprehensive text provides the tools to apply the many and varied fiscal concepts and practices that are essential for aspiring public school administrators who aim to provide responsible stewardship for their students.

Special Features:

- "Definitional Boxes" and "Key Terms" throughout chapters enhance understanding of difficult concepts.
- Coverage of legal, political, and historical issues provides a broader context and more complex understanding of school finance.
- Offers in-depth exploration of business management of financial resources, including fiscal accounting, school facilities, school transportation, financing with debt, and the nuances of school budgeting techniques.

Kern Alexander is Excellence Professor of Educational Administration at the University of Illinois, Urbana-Champaign, USA.

Richard G. Salmon is Professor Emeritus of Educational Leadership at Virginia Polytechnic Institute and State University, USA.

F. King Alexander is Professor in the College of Human Sciences and Education, Louisiana State University (LSU), USA.

Financing Public Schools

Theory, Policy, and Practice

Kern Alexander, Richard G. Salmon, and F. King Alexander

Routledge
Taylor & Francis Group

NEW YORK AND LONDON

First published 2015
by Routledge
711 Third Avenue, New York, NY 10017

and by Routledge
2 Park Square, Milton Park, Abingdon, Oxon, OX14 4RN

Routledge is an imprint of the Taylor & Francis Group, an informa business

Library of Congress Cataloging-in-Publication Data

Alexander, Kern.
   Financing public schools : theory, policy, and practice / Kern Alexander, Richard G. Salmon, F. King Alexander.
      pages cm
   Includes bibliographical references and index.
   1. Education—Finance.   2. Education and state.   3. School management and organization.   4. Educational leadership.   5. Education—Philosophy.
I. Salmon, Richard G., 1938–   II. Alexander, F. King (Fieldon King)
III. Title.

   LB2824.A45 2014
   379.1′3—dc23
   2014009877

ISBN: 978-0-415-64534-8 (hbk)
ISBN: 978-0-415-64535-5 (pbk)
ISBN: 978-0-203-07401-5 (ebk)

Typeset in Aldine401BT
by Apex CoVantage, LLC

SFI Certified Sourcing
www.sfiprogram.org
SFI-00453

Printed and bound in the United States of America
by Edwards Brothers Malloy

Brief Contents

Contents

13 Analyzing Equity and Adequacy of State School Finance   347

17 School Budget Development and Administration 437

18 Risk Management, Student Transportation, and School Food Services 450

Preface

The central theme of this book concerns the necessity for the general diffusion of knowledge throughout society and the financing of the public school as the principal mechanism to achieve that end. Centuries of human experience in many lands has taught that only government has the capacity to address this embracing obligation that is owed to the citizenry. The aspect most essential to fulfilling the social contract is that government commit itself to the adequate and equitable financing for the public schools of the youth of a nation. When this responsibility is properly discharged the duality of happiness of the individual and viability of the democratic state is achieved.

Public schools are best defined as a system of "public entities that provide public instruction and are of the body politic, possessing state sovereignty controlled by publicly elected officials, governed by the people, free and common to all children and youth for the ages set forth in law."[1] A *public school* is "not merely a function of government; [rather] it is of government."[2] The "power to maintain a system of public schools is an attribute of government in much the same sense as is the police power or the power to administer justice or to maintain military forces or to tax."[3] Public schools were, in fact, created not merely to convey value-free knowledge geared to the pursuit of private economic interests, but rather were founded primarily for the inculcation of the values and understanding of the principles of virtuous government.

Thus, children are educated with the goal of creating citizens who will value democracy, a particular form of government that is best able to ensure that the affairs of state will be conducted in the most virtuous manner possible. Montesquieu early observed that all forms of government require education, that monarchies require education to instill deference and politeness, that despotisms require education to teach excessive obedience, and that the republican form of government requires education to instill a desire for freedom and equality, a preference for public over private interests, and an appreciation of the expansion of knowledge.[4] Montesquieu therein captures the essential nature of the republic and the key ingredients of the public common school system: liberty, equality, and community purpose buttressed by the limitless expansion of knowledge. It is now acknowledged by all advanced nations and societies that free schooling furnished by government is not merely a "right granted to pupils as [but] a duty imposed upon them for the public good."[5] Public expenditure must be provided to effectuate the ends of that public or common good, whether that good is for public instruction, defense of the nation from invasion of foreign enemies, health care, or financial support for the poor and benighted.[6] In a pure economic sense, the public expenditure for public instruction is justified because a large measure of fiscal outlay for education is an investment that yields high social rates of return for progress and a rising standard of living. As this book indicates, the more advanced nations of the world expend much greater percentages of their gross domestic product on education than do underdeveloped nations. Development and education are part and parcel of each other. It is a settled maxim that public provision of education is the principal foundation stone of more economically advanced nations.

The issue of inequality of opportunity in American society reverberates through-out this book and is almost certainly one of the most urgent issues of our time. Later in this book we shall see how Piketty and Saez have shown that inequality between rich and poor in the United States is now the most severe since Woodrow Wilson was president. Equality is desirable not only because it is moral and just in all societies, but also because inequality is economically inefficient and generally deleterious to good government. Equality fuels economic growth and stimulates the overall standard of living of a country.[7] As if one would find it necessary to document the ill effects of inequality in a society, various studies[8] have done so primarily because some conservative economists, who oppose progressive taxation and positive redistribution, have gone to great lengths in attempting to prove the perverse position that inequality is a necessary attribute of positive economic growth.[9]

Rebecca Blank, in her book, *Changing Inequality*, enumerates the baneful economic consequences of inequality that should be known and resisted by government policy-makers. *First*, rising inequality usually indicates a declining economic position of those at the bottom of the income ladder, more families and individuals falling into poverty, and an increase in the relative economic difference between the haves and have nots. *Second*, inequality reduces economic mobility, creating a stagnation of movement upward in economic class, sealing in a permanent underclass. *Third,* inequality is harmful to economic growth. The absorption effect of an economy is reduced if a high percentage of the population is frozen in poverty. Though quantitative economic analyses give mixed results, it can be reliably concluded, per Bowles and Gintis, that "under favorable circumstances egalitarian outcomes are not incompatible with the rapid growth of productivity or other valued economic outcomes."[10] *Fourth*, inequality will almost certainly have injurious effects on political processes and democracy. The great Justice of the U.S. Supreme Court, Louis D. Brandeis, summed the issue when he said, "We can have democracy in this country, or we can have great wealth concentrated in the hands of a few, but we can't have both."[11] Stiglitz in his 2012 book, *The Price of Inequality*, explains that one of the most important costs of inequality is that "our democracy is being put in peril."[12]

When the voice of the affluent individual and the *speech* of their corporations are backed with such fiscal strength that the nation's political system is dramatically skewed in the direction of their interests, and inequality, then democracy may well be endangered.[13] Such distortion is readily observed as banks and other large corporations are financially protected by government while the middle and lower classes are denied services for health, education, and welfare. The popular and highly instructive book, *The Spirit Level: Why Greater Equality Makes Society Stronger,* by Wilkinson and Pickett, cites an imposing array of malevolent consequences of inequality, including infant mortality, low life expectancy, crime and incarceration, physical and mental health problems, and reduction in educational performance.[14]

There is no conflict between equality and efficiency. The most efficient economic systems are those that are supported by wide-ranging equality of opportunity. Equality of education is economically efficient because it systematically develops intellectual capacities throughout society and the wastage attributable to underdeveloped human capabilities is kept to a minimum. The most thoughtful philosophers of political economy acknowledge the importance of educational opportunity as a public enterprise to undergird economic growth.[15] John Stuart Mill, the great utilitarian and archetypal champion of privatization, singled out education as one of the few exceptions that should be publicly governed to assure that imperfections in private demand and lack of aspiration would not be permitted to stifle individual intellectual development and thereby reduce the economic capability of the nation as a whole. According to Mill, equality of educational opportunity is essential to a utilitarian government because without it members of the community would "suffer seriously from the consequences of ignorance and want of education in their fellow citizens."[16] It is, thus, a false thesis that postulates that equality is detrimental to social utility. In fact, current thinking regarding economic development strongly supports the theory that greater income equality is compatible with economic growth and that heavy emphasis on universal education results in higher growth rates and lower inequality.[17] If equality is both economically productive and utilitarian, it can hardly be rationally maintained that equality is subversive to quality or that schools in the United States cannot be both equal and excellent. Decisions with regard to school financing that deprive some children of equal opportunity in the name of quality education for a few are sustained on assumptions that are erroneous and socially and economically injurious. The discussions throughout this book implicitly assume that equality, efficiency, and quality of education are complementary and mutually supportive.

The organization of this book is envisaged as an inverted pyramid, general to the specific, broad to the narrow, federal to the state, and state to the local school district. In keeping with that rough design, we begin by defining the public schools as a legacy of *The Enlightenment*, move to the international view of the fundamentality of education, and consider from that broad perch the theoretical questions of equality and liberty. Finally, we span a series of more pointed issues ranging from politics, taxation, teacher compensation, vouchers and charter schools, equity measures down to the specific fiscal considerations of state school financing, distribution procedures, and, at last, to the more mundane but vital aspects of local school district financial management, including financial accounting, budgeting, school infrastructure, debt, risk management, the financing of pupil transportation, and school food services. The line-up of the overall content of the eighteen chapters is briefly as follows.

The initial chapters of the book are devoted to the essential nature of the public school in achieving a virtuous society. The first chapter reminds the student of the watershed era of *The Enlightenment*, that arose principally in the United States and

France, in removing the cloud of myth and superstition that had previously been so detrimental to the progress of mankind.

Chapter 2 examines the entitlement of the human being to knowledge and the right to know, whether education is a fundamental right of each individual, and how that right is perceived as a natural liberty. This chapter considers both the moral sentiments of such fundamental liberty and its sanctification and inviolability by statutes and constitutions in the United States, the United Nations, and the European Convention on Human Rights.

Chapter 3 explains the problem of poverty within states and other nations. Of most importance in this chapter is the concept that poverty is the result of a "system" of private human social and economic interaction that drives some into an underclass of social and economic immobility and the failure of government to play a transcending role in extricating persons from that underclass.

Chapter 4 is concerned with the morality of equality, the philosophical justifications, and the divergent views regarding poverty and inequality. This chapter explains the dichotomy of views from the "selfish gene" of self-interests, as theorized in Social Darwinism, and Adam Smith's "invisible hand," to the charitable spirit of Reinhold Niebuhr's "moral man and immoral society" and John Rawl's "difference principle."

Chapter 5 explores in some depth the idea that education is a highly productive investment in human capital that benefits both the individual and the state. Considerable attention is given to John Stuart Mills' views on gender equality and the economic benefits to the state derived in providing women with equal educational opportunity as well as equality in the workplace. Also important to this chapter is the methodology of how rates of return are calculated and, in particular, McMahon's unraveling of the complexities of the measurement of the external nonmarket benefits to investment in education.

Chapter 6 provides an overview of various political issues that bear on the provision of education in the United States. The chapter attempts to relate the various aspects of political reality to the funding of education. Of particular interest in this chapter is the political power of business corporations in influencing governmental decision making and the overall effect on public schools as a common good. At its base, this chapter attempts to identify the various aspects of political reality as evidenced by the politics of race and religion in America.

Chapter 7 explains the realities of the financial circumstances of states and nations as measured by their fiscal capacity and fiscal effort to support government and education. The various most common barometers of wealth and income are defined and comparability of government units by such measures are set forth. Considerable discussion is devoted to property wealth as a common source of public school funding within states of the United States. Another feature of this chapter is the concept of "fractionalization" of society by race, religion, and ethnicity, and the effects that it may have on tax effort for public services in general, and public schools in particular.

In Chapter 8, the book proceeds into the realm of taxation. Herein we are reminded of the words of Justice Oliver Wendell Holmes regarding taxes: "I like to pay taxes. With them I buy civilization." With taxes for public schools one can easily see what Justice Holmes had in mind. The taxation chapter begins by reviewing the "tax maxims" advanced by Adam Smith in 1776 and Joseph Stiglitz in 2002. From that point the chapter proceeds to define the various types of taxes used by states and the Federal government. A portion of the chapter is utilized to identify new types of taxes that are popular in European countries but are not common to the United States. In addition, this chapter cites a host of tax exemptions that tend, in the most part, to drain resources away from worthy public functions and favor individual or corporate enterprises that may or may not be for the public good.

The federal role in the financing of education is examined in Chapter 9. The chapter begins with the constitutional justification for federal spending on education and the major programs that have historically been a staple of educational activities in states. This chapter enters into the controversial waters of the federal debt, and the current lively debate over the merits or demerits of federal fiscal austerity versus stimulus. Figures and tables are provided that show the effects of federal austerity on the funding of major federal education programs such as ESEA and IDEA and unfunded mandates.

We devote Chapter 10 to the most important educational budgetary consideration, the compensation of the public school teaching force. Teachers' salaries in the United States are compared with other developed countries, teacher pensions and, generally, the relative financial condition of the teaching force.

Chapter 11 is wholly devoted to the recent rise of charter schools, as corporate entities, in the delivery of educational services as a parallel system with the traditional public school. This chapter also discusses the public funding of church schools by means of the voucher in the United States, a phenomenon that was put into play by the present United States Supreme Court in 2003 when it largely nullified the Establishment Clause of the United States Constitution.

Chapter 12 discusses the production function research question of "whether money matters" and the difficulty of relating the quantum of money directly to school performance and productivity. The measurement of the equity and adequacy of school funding is the thrust of Chapter 13. Here we provide specific explanations of the statistical methods that are most commonly used by finance experts in determining the fiscal effects of state school funding formulas.

A key chapter of the book is found in Chapter 14 wherein the principal methods of state school funding are set forth. This chapter has the practical value of relating in simplified form the fiscal procedures utilized by states in distribution funds to local school districts. Basic to the various methodologies are the extent and degree of fiscal equalization employed by state funding in mitigating the disequalizing effects of the local property tax.

The final part of the book, Chapters 15 through 18, is devoted to the business management of local school district financial resources. These chapters explain in considerable detail fiscal accounting, school facilities, financing with debt, and nuances of school budgeting techniques. The book concludes with a thorough explanation of fiscal management considerations in safeguarding the school district against liability and the methodologies for school district provision of pupil transportation and school food services.

In sum, this book pays attention to foundational fiscal issues regarding public schools and at times expresses evaluative opinions in keeping with the principles and processes enunciated herein. Regardless of the technical discussions undertaken in this book, the underlying values of public common school ideals emerge as evaluative criteria. Whether taxpayers are treated equitably, whether tax burdens are properly apportioned, whether equal distributions are achieved, whether the finance system supports the common good and deters ill-gotten privilege, and whether the educational needs of all children are addressed equitably are all relevant to the determinations of how public funds for education should be distributed.

As with any project involving three professors, uniformity of agreement is not necessarily a foregone state of affairs. This is especially true when the topics under discussion involve a multiplicity of issues that bear on theory and policy, and political philosophy. Several chapters in this book have to do with matters of perception on which we have general agreement, but may, when further explicated, discover nuanced issues that can lead to divergence of thought, or even dissent. Writing assignments in this book were divided equitably, but not evenly, amongst we three professors, and in some instances the majority opinion may represent the dominant view, but not unanimity or concordance. The book is dissimilar from a judicial panel in that we do not publish our concurrences and dissents. The author of the chapter quite naturally has the weight of persuasion on his side.

There is a most compelling issue on which the three authors are in complete accord and sing in unison the praise and appreciation for Mrs. Shari Hall. We express our great indebtedness and profound thanks to Mrs. Hall for her research, coordination, editing, and transcribing of this entire project. Without her dedication to the task the authors could not have possibly brought it to fruition.

We also wish to extend our appreciation to Ms. Karla Walsh for her timely assistance in completing the preparation of the manuscript and for her assumption of the onerous task for obtaining permissions from sources utilized in the text.

Finally, we must give our sincere thanks to Ms. Heather Jarrow, our Routledge editor, who was most gracious and understanding as we extended, and extended again, the timetable for the submission of the manuscript.

Kern Alexander, Urbana, Illinois
Richard G. Salmon, Blacksburg, Virginia
F. King Alexander, Baton Rouge, Louisiana

NOTES

1. Newton Edwards, *The Courts and The Public Schools* (Chicago: The University of Chicago Press, 1955), p. 29.
2. Ibid.; *City of Louisville v. Commonwealth,* 134 Ky 488, 121 S.W. 411.
3. Ibid.
4. Montesquieu, *The Spirit of Laws, 1748,* ed. David Wallace Carrithers (Berkeley: University of California Press, 1977), pp. 126–130.
5. Edwards, *op. cit.*, p. 26. *Fogg v. Board of Education*, 76 N.H. 296, 82 A. 173 (1912).
6. David Miles, Gareth Myles, and Ian Preston, *The Economics of Public Spending* (Oxford: Oxford University Press, 2003), p. 1.
7. Janet C. Gornick and Markus Jäntti, *Income Inequality: Economic Disparities and the Middle Class in Affluent Countries* (Stanford: Stanford University Press, 2013), p. 3.

8. Rebecca M. Blank, *Changing Inequality* (Berkeley: University of California Press, 2011).
9. The following researchers have reviewed and discussed these studies: Philippe Aghion, Eve Caroli, Cecelia Garcia-Penalosa, "Inequality and Growth: The Perspective of the New Growth Theories," *Journal of Economic Literature*, 37:4, pp. 1615–1660; Sarah Voitchovsky, "Does the Profile of Income Inequality Matter for Economic Growth," *Journal of Economic Growth,* 10:3, pp. 273–296.
10. Samuel Bowles and Herbert Gintis, "Recasting Egalitarianism: New Rules for Communities, States and Markets," edited by Erik Olin Wright (London: Verso Books, 1999).
11. http://izquotes.com/author/louis-d.-brandeis/3.
12. Joseph E. Stiglitz, *The Price of Inequality: How Today's Divided Society Endangers our Future* (New York: Norton, 2012), p. 117.
13. Gornick and Jäntti, *op. cit.*, p. 4.
14. Richard Wilkinson and Kate Pickett, *The Spirit Level – Why Greater Equality Makes Societies Stronger* (New York: Bloomsbury Press, 2009).
15. John Stuart Mill, *Political Economy, Vol. II* (London: Colonial Press, 1900), pp. 454–456.
16. Ibid., p. 455.
17. Sylvia Nasar, "Economics of Equality: A New View," *New York Times*, January 8, 1994.

CHAPTER 1

The Nature and Theory of the Public School

TOPICAL OUTLINE OF CHAPTER

- The Theory of Public Schools
- Virtues of Public Schools
- The Public School Philosophy
- *The Enlightenment* and Public Schools
- The French Connection
- Adam Smith and Public Instruction
- Economic Development and Public Instruction
- Common Schools for Public Instruction
- A System of Schools
- Public School Precepts

INTRODUCTION

An understanding of public school finance requires some basic knowledge of the nature of public schools and how they developed in both their philosophical and historical contexts. To know only the mechanisms of how public tax dollars are distributed by governments for the purpose of education without knowing the purpose for which they are distributed is to know the means but not be aware of the rationale for the ends to be achieved. This book will go into substantial detail about the technicalities of the allocation of funds for public schools, but first it is appropriate that a few words in this chapter be devoted to the philosophy and purpose undergirding the idea of public schools.

THE THEORY OF PUBLIC SCHOOLS

Public schools are an organized means to educate the citizens of a republic, schools of a republic. Public schools were not created merely to teach persons to read and write but, importantly, to provide universal education for the purpose of maintaining a republican form of government. It is a tenet of public school philosophy that a knowledgeable people will reject tyranny, and if the people understand their options, they will recognize and revere liberty and equality. Yet, learned people do not choose a republican form of government in the abstract; rather, they adopt such a government to acquire and maintain a government of virtue. A virtuous government holds freedom, liberty, and equality in the highest regard and dispenses social justice to achieve that end. A government without virtue is not worth preserving. It is believed that an educated populace is a condition precedent to achieve virtue in government. Sustaining a virtuous government requires a people of sensitivity and compassion willing to act for the commonweal. Knowledge elevates persons above the state of nature. In an uneducated world without governments to regulate and without "Knowledge of the face of the Earth," Hobbes' language in *Leviathan*, citizens cannot discern between the individual liberties that must be subordinated to the mutual benefit of society and those that should not.

A virtuous government must be buttressed by an educational system that instills ideals reflecting the social justice that should be fostered in society. The system of public common schools as envisaged by the American founders and their contemporaries in France represents society's best effort to broadly diffuse knowledge to effectuate the end of a desirable government. The United States is still involved in the public common school experiment, started less than two centuries ago, that seeks to achieve these ideals.

VIRTUES OF PUBLIC SCHOOLS

In a 2008 book of remarkable scholarship, Goldin and Katz,[1] two Harvard economists, capture the unique historical essence of the American public school. They assert that the twentieth century could be appropriately called either the "American Century" or the "Human Capital Century" in which great strides were taken toward worldwide mass education, and at its base in all of the developed nations was the American concept of public schools. Other countries that had become economically developed with high standards of living had emulated or adopted the American model of public schools. Goldin and Katz tell us that from about 1830 to 1900 the United States set out on a path of public universal education of which European philosophers had dreamed, but America implemented. This "American Century was an era of long-term economic growth and declining inequality."[2] At the heart of this undiminished progress, "the secret of American success," was the system of public schools.[3] Following the American lead, the now advanced nations of the world adopted, with slight variations, the concept of public schools. That which was unique about American education were attributes that Goldin and Katz identify and group into seven categories of *virtues*.[4]

These *virtues,* Goldin and Katz say, are "a set of characteristics that originate in basic democratic egalitarian principles" unique to a new nation unshackled by old world culture and mores. The virtues they discern as inimitable and peerless elsewhere among nations produced a rapid pervasive unparalleled diffusion of knowledge.[5] The virtues of American public schools are these:

1. Public funding
2. Public instruction
3. Secular control
4. Open access
5. Lay-controlled independent districts
6. Gender neutrality
7. Forgiveness

Goldin and Katz summarize these virtues to be basically a common system of equality of opportunity.[6] Briefly, these may be elaborated as follows: *Public funding* means "free," no fees for the children, all costs are paid by the public collectively. *Public instruction* is "public provision,"[7] meaning that children are instructed by publicly employed teachers certified by the state who teach a publically, democratically approved curriculum. *Secular control* refers to separation of church and state as standard; sectarian ideologies and religious dogma are not a part of the curriculum and are left to home and church. *Open access* is an implicit virtue, but at times it is easily overlooked or desensitized as with issues of nationality, race, culture, ethnicity, disability, etc. The virtue of *lay control* is an unexcelled earmark of the American public school. Systems in Europe were by and large controlled by a state central authority, certainly France, England, countries of northern Europe, and arguably Germany, after Bismarck. In America, local control pervaded; control was vested in 50 states composed of thousands of school districts, run by a hundred thousand or more democratically elected lay persons. Goldin and Katz recognize that the downside of the American system was a high degree of fiscal inequality, yet it had a compensating and contrasting attribute of being of the local community, non-elite, and close to the people.[8] Of singular importance is the virtue of *gender neutrality.* American public schools, from the origins, rejected the idea of separate schools for boys and girls, as had been practiced in the private systems of Europe, primarily religious schools that had prevailed for centuries. In America, the "[h]igh school entering classes in 1900 . . . contained an almost equal number of boys and girls. Considerably more girls than boys were in attendance in the upper secondary school grades, and a larger proportion of females than males eventually graduated."[9] Finally, the last virtue expounded by Goldin and Katz is that of *forgiveness.* Unlike most education in European countries, the American public school system has the quality of tolerance, indulgence, and pardon. It offers at various levels a second chance for children or youth who at some point in their education did not attain a requisite level of performance. The system has extended allowance to those who for some personal or societal reason have not mastered or cleared a particular educational hurdle.

In various ways most of these virtues have been emulated, in some measure, by advanced countries of the world; yet, in no instance have such virtues been as pervasive as they have been in the American public school system. Today, however, there is a tendency in the United States to question the efficacy of certain of these virtues with centralizing legislation, reducing lay local democratic control, decreasing public funding, practicing unequal fiscal distribution, and reducing government funding of public instruction in favor of private instruction.

THE PUBLIC SCHOOL PHILOSOPHY

The public schools were formed from philosophical reasoning that aspired to betterment in government through commonality, mutuality, and harmony of interests. The common school followed the idea of community as opposed to that of "individual self-interest" and elevation of self over the interests of the state. The public school's philosophical foundation is found early in Aristotle's *Politics*[10] wherein he says that each citizen is pledged in allegiance to the state to place the interests and common good of all above those of self and separate interests. Aristotle maintained that the impulse of man, a "political animal," is to increase individual pleasure and reduce personal pain by the elevation of the condition of the entire community. The state, according to Aristotle, "has a natural priority over the household and over the individual among us. For the whole must be prior to the part."[11] This pursuit of the common good through political association enables liberty and justice for the individual to prevail.

BOX 1.1

Aristotle on Education

. . . it is manifest that education should be one and the same for all, and that it should be public, and not private . . . Neither must we suppose that anyone of the citizens belongs to himself, for they all belong to the state, and are each of them a part of the state, and the care of each part is inseparable from the care of the whole.

Source: Aristotle, *The Politics, Book VIII*, in *Aristotle, The Politics and The Constitution of Athens*, edited by Stephen Everson, translated by Benjamin Jowett (Cambridge: Cambridge University Press, 1996), p. 195.

The Aristotelian argument simply maintained that all are better served by the "wisdom of collective judgments" than by determinations of individuals.[12] In Aristotle's view, popular judgment was also more efficient simply because in the long run decisions made in consideration of self-interest will only consider a part and not the whole. The vagaries of decision by many parts without considering the common good will inevitably result in an inefficient government. Public schools are no different. Decisions to advance the conditions of all people are more likely to be effective and efficient if made by the many rather than the few. It is said that Canning, the prime minister of England, in 1827, once pithily commented, "The House of Commons, as a body, had better taste than the man of best taste in it . . ." This view was very much prevalent in the mid-nineteenth century when the public schools were formed in the United States. The *common will* is a more reliable standard for social conduct than individual caprice and is an underlying assumption of democratic governments.

This was the view of the French philosopher Condorcet who, in his 1792 Report on the General Organization of Public Instruction to the National Assembly of France, argued that "only through universal education could citizens be taught effectively to enjoy their rights and fulfill their responsibilities."[13] The need for an educated citizenry to act in common to advance the republican form of government was best expressed by James Madison when he explained, "A people who mean to be their own Governors must arm themselves with the power which knowledge gives and must act in concert for the common good."[14]

THE ENLIGHTENMENT AND PUBLIC SCHOOLS

The idea of schooling the masses owes its origins to *The Enlightenment, The Age of Reason* of the eighteenth century. *The Enlightenment* was the period in human progress when the most significant steps were taken to remove the shackles of myth and superstition that had bound the human mind to darkness in all prior times. From the early seventeenth century, a steady progression in thought ensued that led to the concept of universal education. There is no date certain as to when *The Enlightenment* or *The Age of Reason* began, but thereafter until today, it has marked a rising realization of people that knowledge is the most basic condition required to ensure liberty and happiness.

The first sprouts of *The Enlightenment* emerged with Francis Bacon's *Novum Organum Scientiarum* in 1620 and René Descartes' *Discourse on Method* in 1637, both prescribing thought processes of a scientific method of reasoning. That human beings could study natural phenomena and discover their causes was a new idea in an age dominated by ignorance, myth, spiritualism, and religious dogma. This benighted time of a thousand years after the decline of the Roman Empire saw kings and ecclesiastics suppress learning in order to maintain control over the mind of man, restraining progress and denying liberty and equality to most human beings except for a privileged few. We know that a light of learning was emerging by the time of Isaac Newton's *Principia Mathematica* in 1687 and John Locke's *The Second Treatise of Government* in 1689. Newton's great genius was a foremost example in the world's history of man's ability to reason. Newton's works were probably a watershed and the most important indicator of a new *Age of Reason*. Locke was the first to clearly elucidate that the rightful condition of all human beings is one of freedom and equality, limited only by their own ability to reason. Citing a couple of major players such as Newton and Locke, however, does not capture the growth of learning for which that age formed the foundation in contributing to individual autonomy, liberty, and equality that was to emerge so dramatically in *The Age of Reason*.

As Ulrich Im Hof, the German historian, wrote, learning in that era had begun "removing all of 'veils and screens' from men's minds and had rid the world of 'slavery and superstition' and dispel[ed] the 'shadows' . . ."[15] The progress of light and liberty owes much to the states of northern Europe where there was freedom from government and church censorship; where authors with new ideas could be relatively safe from criminal prosecution or retribution by the King and Church. Indeed, Descartes,[16] the great mathematician and philosopher mentioned above, was forced to flee north to live in Sweden until his death, and Locke escaped the wrath of Charles II of England to live and write in Holland. France, however, ultimately withstanding church and state censorship and pervasive obduracy toward progress, became the European leader of the greatest remonstrance against ignorance and repression the world had known to that time as its people rose up in violent revolution.

As Anthony Pagden puts it in his acclaimed treatise, *The Enlightenment and Why It Still Matters,*[17] in the world before *The Enlightenment* man had not acquired "sufficient knowledge"[18] to inspire him to quest for more knowledge. Until *The Enlightenment* there was no developed concept of *public instruction* to elevate man from ignorance, intolerance, and myth of all the ages before. The intellect of man was frozen, or as Pagden writes, "marooned in time,"[19] and there was no real conception of "equality before the law,"[20] the public good, or the public interest.[21] All of these things were the consequences of knowledge and *public instruction*.[22]

THE FRENCH CONNECTION

The intellectual ferment generated by *The Enlightenment* took hold in Europe on both sides of the Atlantic, primarily in France, and to the greatest degree in the new American Republic. In these two places the idea of universal education was founded. Jefferson proposed the first system of free public elementary schools for all children in 1779. In Jefferson's system, all youth would attend free public schools and the costs were to be borne by all citizens of the state.[23]

Schools of the republic, in comparable degree to Jefferson's, took place, also, in France. Furet, the eminent French historian, stated the view of the Revolution best: "If the citizens were enlightened, and therefore reasonable, they could not desire other than the public good, which was also their own."[24] According to Furet, public schools "became the essential means of regenerating citizens, which was indispensable to the foundation of the Republic."[25] When French and American revolutions were fought, the emergent leaders were imbibed in the philosophy of republican government, the prerequisite for which was an educated people who could read well enough to escape poverty and ignorance. Woloch explains that in France, during the Revolution, 1791–1793, "Education quickly assumed an unparalleled ideological . . . importance. The revolutionaries came to regard universal primary schooling as the hallmark of a progressive nation and as a key to the future prospects of the French people."[26]

Condorcet, the strongest voice for public schooling during the French Revolution, maintained that the poor and oppressed lower classes could not become functioning citizens in a republic unless they had the freedom to obtain education.[27] Roche, an eminent French historian today, explains that *The Enlightenment* brought a spotlight upon "The people [who were] ignorant, inarticulate, and systematically deceived ('coddled with myths') – lived in prejudice and were lulled by preaching that kept superstition alive. Oppressed by work, they had no opportunity to learn."[28] The great revolutionary leader, Danton, averred that, "In the Republic no one is free to be ignorant,"[29] and more directly he made clear that the child ultimately "belongs to the Republic."[30]

What limited education there was in France before the Revolution was only for boys.[31] Neither parents nor the church usually found it desirable to educate girls. This general disregard for the value of education had produced a largely illiterate population on the eve of the Revolution.[32] In the late 1780s only 27 percent of the brides and 47 percent of the grooms could sign their names on parish marriage registers,[33] which meant that most of them were illiterate; they were counted as literate simply because they could place their mark on the marriage registers. In wide swaths of France a vast majority of the men and women were completely illiterate. The same was true of the United States. The problem was so severe in both countries that it was realized that intergenerational remediation could only be addressed by a system of public instruction with a huge public commitment of labor and capital as its foundation. The supply of qualified teachers was nonexistent, requiring the state to first create training schools to certify teachers and in doing so develop a force of trained teachers for primary schools, the costs to be provided at state expense.[34]

BOX 1.2

Science, Progress, and Myth

If the society's world view encourages the belief that humans have the capacity to know and understand the world around them, that the universe operates according to a largely decipherable pattern of laws, and that the scientific method can unlock many secrets of the unknown, it is clearly imparting a set of attitudes tightly linked to the ideas of progress and change. If the world view explains worldly phenomena by supernatural forces, often in the form of numerous capricious gods and goddesses who demand obeisance from humans, there is little room for reason, education, planning, or progress.

Source: Lawrence E. Harrison, "Underdevelopment Is a State of Mind" in *Development and Underdevelopment: The Political Economy of Global Inequality*, 4th Edition, edited by Mitchell A. Seligson and John T. Passe-Smith (Boulder: Lynne Reinner Publishers, 2008), pp. 231–232.

Certain principles emerged from the revolutions in America and France that formed the nature of public schools: (1) society must do everything possible to favor the progress of public reason, (2) instruction must be secular and should not be under the control of priests, (3) primary education must be universal and free to all children, (4) the costs must be borne by the state, (5) instruction in the public schools must be conveyed by trained, state-certified teachers, and (6) the decision to educate children must not be optional for parents.[35]

ADAM SMITH AND PUBLIC INSTRUCTION

A principal aspect of *The Enlightenment* philosophy was that education should be universal and that education should be formed and effectuated by public instruction.[36] Public instruction, formal instruction, is not simply parental instruction, and not merely ecclesiastical instruction, but, rather, instruction that is free to all, taught by public school teachers with a curriculum designed by the people in the state to foster freedom and independence of mind. Adam Smith, the father of economics, a pillar of *The Enlightenment*, the author of *The Wealth of Nations* (1776),[37] wrote that school instruction should be without religious superstition,[38] and, importantly, children should be taught to be "incredulous," with inquiring minds that separate the child from the limits of parental mind control, religious inculcation, or government propaganda. Smith said,

> There seems to be in young children an instinctive disposition to believe whatever they are told . . . Their credulity accordingly, is excessive, and it requires long and much experience of the falsehood of mankind to reduce them to a reasonable degree of diffidence and distrust.[39]

Accordingly, Smith argued that neither the parent nor the church was capable of teaching "incredulity" in children. The parents innocently instill in their children their own beliefs, right or wrong, and generally demand that their children adhere to those beliefs without question. Homeschooling was rejected by Smith as was the English residential "public" school. The English "public" school remains today a private elite school for children of the wealthy. It is an interesting paradox that Adam Smith's philosophy of economic competition has been relied upon to justify the public funding of private schools in America. Smith had much to say in his rejection of private schools, especially clerical schools that had dominated and limited education to his time by the Church of England and the state church of Scotland.

Condorcet, cited above, writing immediately before the French Revolution, referenced Adam Smith in his first proposal for "true public instruction"; he concluded that free universal public instruction is the "only effective remedy"[40] to adequately redress the condition of illiteracy of the people of France.[41] Emma Rothschild, in her recent important work, *Economic Sentiments: Adam Smith, Condorcet and The Enlightenment,* cites the connection between Smith and Condorcet, who both called for public instruction to alleviate poverty and to form the foundation for a republic. Condorcet cites Smith, saying: "Instruction is the only remedy for this ill . . . The laws proclaim an equality of rights, and only institutions for public instruction can make this equality real."[42] Condorcet encapsulated the importance of public instruction when he said that the ultimate objective should be for individuals to understand their rights in the acquisition of ultimate happiness.[43]

Rothschild writes that the "efficiency" of society and the economy, to Smith and Condorcet, were dependent on equality of public instruction "which would lead in turn to greater equality of industry and wealth,"[44] and that, according to Smith, a system of public instruction would "ensure that no one was obliged to depend blindly on others in the ordinary business of life or in the exercise of individual rights."[45] We know, as Rothschild observes, that Thomas Jefferson's own views regarding public schools may well have been influenced by Smith and Condorcet. When Jefferson compiled his "course on reading" in 1799, he included Locke's *Essay Concerning Human Understanding*, Smith's *Wealth of Nations*, and Condorcet's *Esquisse D'un Tableau Historique Des Progress De L'espirit Humain.*[46]

BOX 1.3

Public Instruction Drives Total Education

The history of mass primary and secondary schooling is dominated by the rise of public, not private, supply. No high-income OECD country has relied solely on private demand and supply in education, least of all in primary schooling.

Source: Peter H. Lindert, *Growing Public: Social Spending and Economic Growth Since the Eighteenth Century, Vol. I* (Cambridge, UK: Cambridge University Press, 2004), p. 88.

ECONOMIC DEVELOPMENT AND PUBLIC INSTRUCTION

Peter H. Lindert, in one of his remarkable books, *Growing Public: Social Spending and Economic Growth since the Eighteenth Century,*[47] chronicles the progression of public schools from about 1820 into the twentieth century. He documents that initially, from 1833 to 1850, "no country collected even as much as one-half of one percent of national income in taxes for education."[48] He shows that even though funding in the mid-nineteenth century was minimal, it was much better than before *The Enlightenment* took hold in the late eighteenth century.[49] Lindert theorizes that the dearth of investment at this early stage was not due to the lack of intellectual leadership but, rather, is to be attributed to the opposition of mostly powerful persons who for self-indulgent and pietistic reasons blocked public school creation and public financing.[50]

Lindert further writes that "[I]n fact, both Adam Smith in Britain and Thomas Jefferson in colonial America supported the government's collection and allocation of taxpayers' dollars to pay for the education of 'other people's children.'"[51] The expressed views of Smith and Jefferson are worth noting, even though their opinions were strongly opposed by controlling persons who generally objected to taxes for schools, as well as other social spending. Social spending for welfare at that time was referred to as "poor relief," and in reference to education, at least in England and some states in the United States, public school funding was justified as aid for only "paupers' children."

Progress toward tax funding of public schools was led by the United States, France, and countries of northern Europe. Leadership in the expansion of state schooling was also developed in Prussia and Scandinavian countries that had moved forward at a slower, but with an increasingly competitive, pace. German education progressed dramatically under Bismarck, 1870 to 1890, but lost ground with the calamity of World War I.

Thus, some countries were more directly influenced by *The Age of Reason* than others as they, in different measure, absorbed new learning. Those countries that progressed more rapidly, according to David S. Landes, in his bestseller, *The Wealth and Poverty of Nations*,[52] had two special characteristics. "First, their stress on instruction and literacy for girls as well as boys"[53] resulted in "greater literacy and a larger pool of candidates for advanced schooling. The education of girls ensured a continuity of literacy from generation to generation."[54] According to Landes, "Literate mothers matter."[55] Landes' second rationale for educational and economic progress was what he calls "unobtrusive evidence of the importance of time."[56] Learning had led to a reliance on clocks which were manufactured and used to govern the efficient use of the individual's days. Landes also explains that countries with an educated labor force were more advanced in scientific measurement and commerce. He argues persuasively that countries controlled by the clergy that remonstrated against *The Enlightenment,* constrained new knowledge, censored literature, and repressed scientific works were the same countries that resisted public schooling. As a result, the same countries were relegated to a future of lower standards of living.[57] Landes cites for corroboration Hugh Trevor-Roper, the famous British historian, who maintained that because of religion and anti-learning the countries of southern Europe and Central and South America sealed their fate of lingering for centuries as underdeveloped countries.[58]

America adapted to mass public education with greater alacrity than most countries of Europe because the people in America were unburdened from centuries of control by princes and priests. Prussia, under Bismarck,[59] had stimulated peripheral awakening in Austria. Bismarck's grand design for the modernization and unification of Germany had been, to a large degree, dependent on economic development and, particularly, mass education in the face of rigid opposition by both Protestant and Catholic churches.[60]

The Enlightenment did not reach Africa, India, or the Far East, primarily because of geography, but it did not reach Latin America for other reasons. The western hemisphere was first accessed by Spain and Portugal, but both had rejected the ideals of public instruction for its secular overtones and had thereby been denied the benefits of the progress that had ensued. The result was a stagnation that negatively affected both Iberia and its influences throughout Central and South America of which it controlled and exploited.

Angus Maddison conjectures that Latin America lagged behind Western Europe and North America because it was dominated by Iberian institutions that "were less propitious to capitalist development than those of North America."[61] Also, he speculates that Spain and Portugal did little to elevate the indigenous people of Central and South America; they allowed a large economic and social underclass to persist and, moreover, public schools were founded in the face and opposition of the interests of Iberian institutions which were hampered by economic control of religious traditions and culture. Thus, "over the long run the rise in per capita income was much smaller than in North America."[62] Daron Acemoglu and James A. Robinson set forth the theory that the "institutions" there were "absolutist," politically controlled by King and Church, and were economically "extractive,"[63] not "inclusive" economic systems that were "narrowly monopolized," unequal with an immobilized underclass, and made no provision for a secular broad-based education system. Absolutist regimes, whether state or church, are obstacles to entrepreneurial activity and equality.[64]

COMMON SCHOOLS FOR PUBLIC INSTRUCTION

The use of the word *common* invokes special meaning in economic, historical, and constitutional contexts. Common schools in the United States were created as institutions where all children, regardless of economic or social condition, could obtain public instruction free of charge. The costs were to be shouldered by the public through taxation. The instruction was to benefit all in common, and the costs were to be shared by all in common. Use of the term *common* as an adjective implies that the schools are free and open to all. The great educational debate of the late eighteenth and nineteenth centuries was whether schools should be free to all children and the costs borne by the citizenry from revenues gained from taxation.

The framers of the various state constitutions in the United States in using the term *common* evidenced an unmistakable state role for the general diffusion of knowledge. Importantly, the intent was to create state-operated schools that were free to all. Early, as it became clear that private schools had failed to meet the general educational needs of the people, some states experimented with public academies, but it soon became apparent that they were ineffectual in educating the masses. Though academies and pauper schools proliferated, they failed to enroll a significant segment of the youth and soon disappeared; thus, public schools became dominant.

As the private and quasi-private forms of schooling were unable to meet the needs of an expanding nation, an awakening educational consciousness called for a government-maintained system of schools for all children. This philosophy generally followed the ideas of eminent thinkers of *The Enlightenment* who sought to build republican forms of government on the foundation of a more literate and homogeneous mass of people. Specifically, the common schools were designed to remedy three major shortcomings: (1) The private schools did not constitute a system but were created and funded by different means by various initiatives for private objectives. (2) The private schools were not normally free. Poor families struggled financially in order to enroll their children. (3) The private schools had special motivations of religious, social, ethnic, economic, and sometimes racial separation.

When the common school system was finally established in the United States, the recurrent theme enunciated by the earlier proponents encompassed certain elements that distinguished public common schools from their forerunners. These common schools were based on certain *a priori* considerations:

1. Each child was equally important to the republic.
2. Education benefitted all, not just the person being educated.
3. All should pay in common.
4. All should receive the educational benefits in common.

The word *common* as it relates to schools has special and significant meaning. The common school system as envisioned by the policymakers during its formative years is a stark contrast with its educational antecedents. The common school was unique because it was:

1. A free school where the levy of tuition or fees could not impose a burden on poor children.
2. A school open to all, not just the poor but a cross-section of the population where all classes could mingle and learn together.
3. A school supported by taxation of all the people of the state.
4. A school that provided public instruction and was governed as a public secular entity, free from sectarian or special interest control.
5. A school that was part of a system where a high degree of uniformity existed throughout the state.

A SYSTEM OF SCHOOLS

In the late eighteenth and early nineteenth centuries the word *system* in state constitutions in the United States held a special connotation emanating from the earlier discussed revolutionary enlightenment republicanism. The idea that public instruction of the masses was the key to the formation of the new political order and general happiness of the people was a pervasive theme as it became clear that tutorials, home instruction, private schools, and other limited devices such as the pauper schools were inadequate to support a new and thriving nation. Only a state system could meet the needs of a growing nation.

The new concept of mass public education was premised on four beliefs: (1) that education was vital to the republic; (2) that a proper education consisted of the general diffusion of knowledge; (3) that virtue and civic responsibility were essential; and (4) that public schools and colleges were the best means of providing mass education on the scale required.[65] Two important and distinguishing characteristics of this new concept of education were that it was a system and that it was of the polity. Cremin observed, "What was fresh in the republican style was the emphasis on 'system,' on a functional organization of individual schools and colleges that put them in regular relationship with one another and with the polity."[66]

The historical discussion of *system* usually employed terms such as *machine* as well as *harmony* and *uniformity*. The educational system was to be likened to a machine, which would function smoothly and efficiently in the general diffusion of knowledge. An efficient system demanded the balance and harmony of its working parts.

The term *system* was used in at least four different but related senses.

1. A vertical incremental pattern of institutions which permitted progress from one level of educational attainment to another (primary, secondary, and college).
2. A related curriculum of standard subjects which would provide a firm knowledge base for all persons.
3. A uniformity of offerings which would assure that all persons received the education necessary to carry out civic responsibilities.
4. An aspect of the polity, or extra-familial, as opposed to familial. It was necessary to fashion a system in which education was not dependent on the private sector or the family, but instead was dependent on the public.

Thus the term *system* assumes a coordinated curriculum and allows for a progression of educational achievement. Uniformity, equality, and harmony of function are implicit features of a system and are essential to the efficient diffusion of knowledge throughout the population.

PUBLIC SCHOOL PRECEPTS

The discussion of the philosophical and historical bases for public schools may be summarized in a list of precepts or principles that form the rationale for the creation and maintenance of public schools in the United States. The principles given were adapted from a statement provided by a select committee in the landmark case of *Rose v. Council for Better Education, Inc.*[67] that held in 1988 the system of public school education in Kentucky unconstitutional. The principles were accepted and were reflected in the standards adopted by the Kentucky Supreme Court.

1. *The schools are to be public, of the body politic, and are to be governed and controlled by the people.* Early experimentation showed that quasi-private and semi-public schools would not suffice to educate the masses. Control by private interest groups, regardless of their nature, always placed limitations that reduced public participation and prevented full access of the people. To assure openness to all, the system must be controlled by the polity.
2. *The schools are to be established as a system, an organic whole, arranged with interdependent parts.* The word *system* requires a measure of orderliness and uniformity regardless of the number of school districts. The state system must form a cohesive whole and cannot be merely a conglomeration of local independent initiatives.
3. *The schools are to be free and common to all with no charges to limit access.* Reluctance on the part of the people to finance schools from the public treasury was a primary hindrance to the establishment of a viable common school system. Early attempts to create an educational system failed partially because of user charges, usually in the nature of tuition and fees, which limited attendance to those who could afford to pay the requisite costs of operating the schools. The public schools are to benefit all the people and all of the people must pay for them.
4. *The schools are to be secular and free from sectarian religious control, and public funds should not be expended for religious or parochial schools.* Public schools should exemplify toleration, and the power of the state should not be used to promote or inhibit the free exercise of religion. Strict religious neutrality should be maintained in the public schools. Public tax monies should not be used to establish religion by preferring one religion over another nor by aiding a "multiple establishment" of more than one religion.
5. *The schools are to be financed by tax resources which are distributed in such a manner as to ensure that the quality of a child's education will not be dependent on the fiscal ability of the local school district.* The quality of a child's education in virtually all the states is determined by the financial ability of the community in which the child attends school. A system of schools cannot be efficient if some children are denied educational programs and services because their local communities do not happen to have wealth or income to sustain school revenues that are available to local communities that possess larger and more lucrative local tax bases.

6. *The schools are to provide equitable educational treatment to all children in the accommodation of their educational needs.* All educational programs and services cannot be precisely uniform. School districts in different areas of a state may have children with varying educational needs. For example, every school district will not have precisely the same percentage of children with disabilities or culturally deprived children. Children having such special needs may require particular educational programs which cost more than regular programs. Equity requires that additional funds be expended if the state's moral and legal obligation of an efficient system is to be met.

7. *The schools shall be financed in a manner which will prevent the quality of a child's education from being dependent on the vagaries of local tax effort.* Whether a local school district has high or low tax effort to support the schools may be determined by conditions quite unrelated to education. The social, political, and economic structure of each community is different and each community, for various reasons, may respond differently to entreaties to support the schools. This may be true even if the people, from community to community, have the same desire and aspiration for the education of their children. Because the schools of a state exist as a unified system, the caprice of local political conditions cannot be permitted to harm the educational opportunity of a child. No community has a right to impose an inferior education on its children.

8. *The schools shall be properly managed to ensure the most effective and productive use of tax funds.* The Constitution contemplates the utilitarian use of public school funds and in so doing the schools are accountable to the people. In creating a state school system, the framers of the Constitution sought to capture the advantages and utility of educating the masses in the most efficient manner possible. If aspects of the school system's management hinder efficiency of operation, they must be revised and more acceptable alternatives must be incorporated and enforced.

9. *The General Assembly of each state is to bear the responsibility for the enactment of laws to govern the common schools.* The establishment and maintenance of the common schools is not a matter of local discretion. Neither is it primarily a federal function. While the time-honored concept of local control is desirable and should be assured and safeguarded, the ultimate discretion over the schools, within the bounds of the state and federal constitutions, rests with the state legislatures. Responsibility for taxation in support of public schools falls upon the state legislature and cannot be delegated away.

SUMMARY

In summarizing and concluding this chapter, it should be noted that singular progress toward universal free education was made as a result of the ideals of *The Enlightenment*. Yet even today we have not developed satisfactory systems of tax support for the public schools in many countries and in states in the United States, and the struggle for satisfactory levels of financial support continues. As will be shown later, the public schools in the United States are still involved in what Huxley called a "struggle for existence,"[68] and the battle for tax-supported public schools is a continuing battle for survival and growth. In a rapidly changing world, there must be improvement in the public schools or it, as an institution fundamental to democracy, may be harmed or permanently impaired. This in turn will threaten liberty, equality of opportunity, and ultimately the republican form of government.

The public common school concept rests on the belief that a knowledgeable people will be better able to perpetuate a republican form of government than will persons of little or marginal knowledge. The object and interest of the people is to have a virtuous government that will protect liberty and advance equality. This is best accomplished in a republican form of government that rests on the foundation of an informed citizenry. Public common schools are the principal vehicles fashioned by the people to maintain a knowledgeable electorate.

The term *common schools* envisages free schools which all persons rich and poor attend and from which all benefit in common. The common school concept further requires that all persons pay in common through general taxation to support the schools.

Public instruction was a response to the recognized limitation and inadequacies of private schools to meet the needs of a modern nation. In creating public schools, the people of the United States implicitly decided that all children were children of the republic with equal rights and opportunities. The meaning of the word *common* encompasses all the presumptions necessary to provide mass universal education.

The term *system* is an important aspect of public common schools. Early in this country, states employed piecemeal approaches to the provision of education, utilizing inadequate devices such as rate bills, pauper schools, and quasi-public academies in endeavoring to redress a prevailing cognizance of the need for universal education. These methods failed because they were not systems of incremental education. Moreover, they failed to provide uniformity or thoroughness across the state.

As envisaged by the American founders, a system of public schools has the attributes of uniformity, thoroughness, and equality. Moreover, the founders saw universal public education as a great machine which operates with harmony and efficiency in the conveyance of knowledge and prosperity. Public schools were seen as a vehicle to reduce inequalities in society and to make the foundations of the social system rest on merit rather than privilege.

Public school precepts may be summarized as follows: to be of the public; to be a system, an organic whole; to be free and common to all; to be secular; to be financed from general taxation; to be equitable; to be equal regardless of location; to be efficient; and to be the responsibility of the state.

KEY TERMS

- Public education
- Public schools
- Public instruction
- Public school virtues
- *The Enlightenment*
- Public reason
- Common schools

- System of schools
- Public school precepts
- Polity
- Body politic
- Sectarian schools
- Secular schools
- Private schools

NOTES

1. Claudia Goldin and Lawrence F. Katz, *The Race Between Education and Technology* (Cambridge, MA: Harvard University Press, 2008), pp. 2–8.
2. Ibid., p. 3.
3. Ibid., p. 5.
4. Ibid., p. 130.
5. Ibid.
6. Ibid.
7. Ibid.
8. Ibid., p. 133.
9. Ibid.
10. Aristotle, *Politics*, translated by T.A. Sinclair, revised and represented by Trevor J. Saunders (London: Penguin Books, 1981), p. 60.
11. Ibid.
12. Ibid., p. 201.
13. R. Freeman Butts and Lawrence A. Cremin, *A History of Education in American Culture* (New York: Henry Holt and Company, 1953), p. 190.
14. James Madison to W.T. Barry, August 4, 1822, *The Writings of James Madison Comprising His Public Papers and His Private Correspondence, Including Numerous Letters and Documents Now for the First Time Printed,* ed. Gaillard Hunt (New York: Putman, 1910), vol. IX, p. 103.
15. See Ulrich Im Hof, *The Enlightenment,* translated from the German by William E. Yuill (Oxford: Blackwell Publishers, Ltd., 1997).
16. Descartes: *Key Philosophical Writings*, translated by Elizabeth S. Haldane and G.R.T. Ross, and edited by Enrique Chavez-Arviso (Ware, Hertfordshire: Wordsworth Editors, 1997), p. xxii. It should be noted that Descartes' works were placed on the *Index of Forbidden Books*, by the Roman Catholic Church.
17. Anthony Pagden, *The Enlightenment and Why It Still Matters* (Oxford: Oxford University Press, 2013).
18. Ibid., p. 154.
19. Ibid., p. 143.
20. Ibid., p. 254.
21. Ibid., p. 260.
22. Ibid.
23. Carl F. Kaestle, *Pillars of the Republic, Common Schools and American Society, 1780–1860* (New York: Hill and Wang, 1983), pp. 8–9.
24. Francois Furet, *Revolutionary France 1770–1880* (Oxford: Blackwell Publishers, Inc., 1995), p. 193.
25. Ibid.
26. Isser Woloch, *The New Regime: Transformation of the French Civic Order, 1789–1820s* (New York: W.W. Norton & Company, 1994), p. 177.
27. Daniel Roche, *France in the Enlightenment*, translated by Arthur Goldhammer (Cambridge, Mass.: Harvard University Press, 1998), p. 339.
28. Ibid.
29. Ibid., p. 180.
30. Ibid., p. 179.
31. Ibid., p. 186.
32. Ibid., p. 174.
33. Ibid.
34. Ibid., p. 188.

35. Ibid., pp. 179–181.
36. Emma Rothschild, *Economic Sentiments: Adam Smith, Condorcet, and The Enlightenment* (Cambridge, Mass.: Harvard University Press, 2001), pp. 10–11.
37. Adam Smith, *The Wealth of Nations, Books I–III*, first published in 1776 (London: Penguin Books, 1999).
38. Adam Smith, *The Theory of Moral Sentiments*, first published in 1759 (Indianapolis: Liberty Finance, 1984), edited by D. D. Raphael and A.L. Macfie, pp. 333–336.
39. Ibid.
40. Rothschild, *op cit.*, pp. 225–256.
41. Ibid.
42. Ibid.
43. Condorcet's *Sur l'instruction Publique*. See: Rothschild, *op. cit.*, pp. 227 and 335.
44. Rothschild, *op cit.*, p. 11.
45. Ibid. Citing Adam Smith, *An Enquiry into the Nature and Causes of the Wealth of Nations*, referenced. Edited R.H. Campbell and A.S. Skinner (Oxford: Clarendon Press, 1976).
46. Rothschild, *op cit.*, p. 4.
47. Peter H. Lindert, *Growing Public: Social Spending and Economic Growth Since the Eighteenth Century* (Cambridge: Cambridge University Press, 2004), p. 9.
48. Ibid.
49. Ibid.
50. Ibid.
51. Ibid.
52. David S. Landes, *The Wealth and Poverty of Nations* (New York: W.W. Norton & Company, 1999), p. 178.
53. Ibid.
54. Ibid.
55. Ibid.
56. Ibid.
57. Ibid., pp. 179–180.
58. Hugh Trevor-Roper, "Religion, the Reformation and Social Change," a collection of essays of the same title, delivered at Fifth Irish Conference of Historians in Galway, 1961. Also see Landes, *op cit.*, p. 548.
59. Woloch, *op. cit.*, p. 21.
60. Karl A. Schleunes, *Schooling and Society: The Politics of Education in Prussia and Bavaria, 1750–1900* (Oxford: Berg, 1989).
61. Angus Maddison, "The World Economy: A Millennial Perspective," in *Development and Underdevelopment: The Political Economy of Global Inequality,* 4th Edition edited by Mitchell A. Seligson and John T. Passe-Smith (Boulder: Lynne Rienner Publishers, 2008).
62. Ibid.
63. Daron Acemoglu and James A. Robinson, *Why Nations Fail: The Origins of Power, Prosperity, and Poverty* (London: Profile Books, Ltd., 2012), pp. 220–221.
64. Lawrence E. Harrison, "Underdevelopment is a State of Mind," in *Development and Underdevelopment: The Political Economics of Global Inequality*, 4th Edition, edited by Mitchell A. Seligson and John T. Passe-Smith (Boulder: Lynne Rienner Publishers, 2008), p. 232.
65. Lawrence A. Cremin, *American Education, The National Experience, 1783–1876* (New York: Harper & Row, 1980), p. 148.
66. Ibid., p. 118
67. 79 S.W. 2d 186 (1989).
68. Aldoux Huxley, *Brave New World* (New York: Perennial Library, 1989).

CHAPTER 2

Fundamental Rights and State School Finance Litigation

TOPICAL OUTLINE OF CHAPTER

- Fundamental Rights
- Knowledge and Right
- Education as a Positive or Negative Right
  - The Price Tag
- Fundamental Right of Education and the U.S. Constitution
- State Constitutions in the United States
  - Entitlements and Prescriptions
- State Education as a Fundamental Right
- States Where Education Is Not a Fundamental Right and Plaintiffs Prevailed
- National Access Network
- Universal Declaration of Human Rights
- European Convention on Human Rights

INTRODUCTION

What is a fundamental right? What does it mean to have a fundamental right to education? What has state financing to do with a fundamental right? These are basic issues that have been addressed by legislatures and the courts in different ways and constitute illusive fiscal and legal concepts. Foremost, however, with regard to education finance, the recognition that acquisition of knowledge is of primary worth to the human being is "a value for its own sake, a basic value, and should be funded liberally by the government."[1] The right of the human being to knowledge is self-evident. Knowledge is peremptory of other rights, for without knowledge there can be no understanding as to the meaning of important human rights such as liberty and equality. Without knowledge one is unable to determine truth, and matters of human worth cannot be judged correctly.[2] Obviously, to reason without knowledge is a futile exercise, and that which is reasonable cannot be ascertained in a shade of ignorance. This chapter will explain the rationale for holding that for the acquisition of knowledge, education is fundamental and, as such, requires public funding as a principle of *positive* law. Further, the chapter will identify and classify those states in the United States where education is a fundamental right.

BOX 2.1

Self-Evidence of Knowledge as a Good in Natural Law

The basic practical principle that knowledge is good need hardly ever be formulated as the premise for anyone's actual practical reasoning . . . Is it not the case that knowledge is really a good, an aspect of authentic human flourishing, and that the principle which expresses its value formulates a real (intelligent) reason for action? It seems clear that such, indeed, is the case, and that there are no sufficient reasons for doubting it to be so. The good of knowledge is self-evident, obviously. It cannot be demonstrated, but equally it needs no demonstration.

John Finnis

Source: John Finnis, *Natural Law and Natural Rights* (Oxford: Clarendon Press, 1980), p. 64.

FUNDAMENTAL RIGHTS[3]

A fundamental right is a "good," a "basic good," for human well-being. A sentient being is, by definition, alive; thus, self-preservation, or the value of "life," is first among basic human goods, values, and rights.[4] Knowledge is second only to life.[5] It is beyond argument that life and knowledge are fundamental. Education to procure knowledge is the means for a person to gain "capacity" in order to exercise liberty. Nozick explains that "only a person with the capacity to so shape his life can have or strive for a meaningful life."[6] According to Henkin, in his book *Human Rights*, a fundamental right is inherent in the individual and constitutes a protected claim that need not be earned; rather, it is immanent in the human being as an entitlement;[7] its foundation is found in moral law. Since education is a fundamental right, everyone is entitled to obtain it by virtue of being human. As Henkin has written, "When a society recognizes that a person has a right, it affirms, legitimates, justifies that entitlement, and incorporates and establishes it in the society's system of values, giving it important weight in competition with other societal values."[8]

Individual or human rights that carry the appellation of "fundamental" are therefore basic and essential to the life and dignity of each individual.[9] Yet, even fundamental rights are not absolute and can be abridged; but to override them requires special circumstances by which the government must show that society at large is in some way enhanced by the denial of an individual's right.

A fundamental right enjoys a special place in the social contract between the individual and the state. Standing at the nexus of the social contract, a right enjoys a *prima facie* or presumptive inviolability, and by its nature "trumps" other less important public goods.[10] Individual human rights cannot be denied or sacrificed merely because the majority of society is inconvenienced or has preference or a disposition to deny the right; a fundamental right can only be denied for a compelling reason.

According to Ronald Dworkin, fundamental human rights are claims on society.[11] Where education is elevated to the level of a fundamental human right, there are accompanying obligations for the government and society to satisfy.

KNOWLEDGE AND RIGHT

Jefferson, among political philosophers, best explains that knowledge is an incontrovertible rule of liberty, in his Preamble to his Virginia "Bill for the More General Diffusion of Knowledge," 1779, where he expresses *The Enlightenment* ideal that education is not only a natural right but that it is the *a priori* condition for liberty and freedom. Pointedly, he says in his *Bill* that to "illuminate as far as practical the minds of the people at large, and more especially to give them knowledge" is the best safeguard against tyranny; knowledge as a first principle promotes "publick happiness." Importantly, for Jefferson, the ultimate goal of all human beings is "happiness."

Condorcet, in 1791, as we noted in Chapter 1, wrote extensively on the necessity of "public instruction" to instill "public virtues,"[12] on the road to happiness, maintaining that universal public instruction is the "only effective remedy" for the ills of society. Condorcet reinforced the idea that public instruction is necessary for achieving freedom and equality of the individual. He said in his memoirs that "public instruction is the only viable means to achieve the 'equality of rights,' and it is only public instruction that can make equality real."[13]

One can easily see the "close kinship"[14] among the three seminal documents, the American Declaration of Independence (1776), the French Declaration of the Rights of Man (1789), and the United States Bill of Rights (1791), from the American Revolution and the French Revolution – documents that were the epitomes of *The Enlightenment's* legacy of individual rights, democracy, and happiness.

Horace Mann, the first Secretary of Education in Massachusetts, 1837, often referred to as the father of public education in America, wrote that education is an "absolute right," or a "natural right."

> We can cite no attributes or purpose of the divine nature, for giving birth to any human being, and then inflicting upon that being the curse of ignorance, of poverty and of vice, with all their attendant calamities.[15]

Mann argued that natural ethics requires the creation of public common schools in fulfillment of a state's duty to pass along to each succeeding generation all the knowledge and wealth of the preceding generation.[16] The paramount law of nature requires that children should come into possession of all knowledge of the earlier generation.[17]

It was Mann's view that knowledge was the property and wealth of each individual. To Mann, the public schools were the means by which the state ensures the efficient and just transfer of knowledge to the next generation: "[t]he claim of a child, then, to a portion of the preexistent property begins with the first breath he draws . . . He is to receive this, not in the form of lands, or of gold and silver, but in the form of knowledge and training to good habits."[18]

Mann believed natural ethics required that the state has an obligation to every child to enact a code of laws establishing free public schools. These laws governing education become "the fundamental law of the State."[19] Mann's rationale for fundamentality of education and the duty of the state are:

1. The successive generations of men, taken collectively, constitute one great Commonwealth.

2. The property of this commonwealth is pledged for the education of all its youth, up to such a point as will save them from poverty and vice, and prepare them for the adequate performance of their social and civil duties.
3. The successive holders of this property are trustees, bound to the faithful execution of their trust, by the most sacred obligations . . .[20]

The obligations under these inviolate propositions that form the philosophical foundation for the intergenerational transfer of knowledge require the establishment of a system of public instruction in public common schools.[21]

EDUCATION AS A POSITIVE OR NEGATIVE RIGHT

The Bill of Rights and the Fourteenth Amendment to the U.S. Constitution enunciate *negative* rights or *negative* liberties that the government "shall not" deny. The Constitution alone does not provide for *positive* rights or liberties. However, if either the federal or state government decides through legislation to provide for education, it, thereby, creates a "claim"[22] for all persons similarly situated, an entitlement of benefit, creating a liberty and property interest, a *positive* right that cannot be taken away without procedural due process. To understand education as a right or liberty requires reliance on moral philosophy as much as law and economics.

Isaiah Berlin has best explained the two concepts of rights or liberties, *negative* rights and *positive* rights. Berlin writes that education is fundamental to individual freedom in that a world of options may be wide open to an individual yet that individual may be restrained by ignorance or poverty and thereby have no freedom to exercise those options.[23] This lack of capability to access liberty emanates, in fact, in nearly all instances, from a deficiency in knowledge. Berlin asks "What is freedom to those who cannot make use of it? Without adequate conditions for the use of freedom, what is the value of freedom?"[24] Berlin first elaborated his concept of *positive* and *negative* rights in 1958,[25] the same idea of which was subsequently applied to legal theory by Charles Reich in a *Yale Law Journal* article in 1964,[26] and was given judicial recognition in the U.S. Supreme Court's landmark decision in *Goldberg v. Kelly*.[27] But the U.S. Supreme Court has since rejected any affirmative or *positive* right to government aid for education[28] or welfare.[29]

Thus, Berlin, in his essay, *Two Concepts of Liberty*,[30] identifies two kinds of liberty, *negative* and *positive*. Negative liberty or freedom means that a person "should be left to do or be what he is able to do or be, without interference of other persons,"[31] freedom *from*. Negative liberty is the liberty that John Stuart Mill defined in his classic work, *On Liberty*,[32] where he analyzed the social and political world in terms of "a struggle between liberty and authority."[33] The authority for which Mill was most concerned was the government and organized religion, both of which had historically exercised "dominion," temporal and spiritual, over human beings in body and mind.[34] Protection against these two powers is the "negative freedom" that Berlin calls "keeping authority at bay."[35] This is "liberty *from*" that Mill concludes is "The only freedom which deserves the name is that of pursuing your own good in your own way."[36] Such liberties are frequently termed *civil* and *political* rights. These are the rights against government usurpation that are enshrined in the *Bill of Rights* of the United States Constitution, rights to freedom *from* government interference, freedom of religion, speech, association, privacy, etc. Such rights are also found in the French *Rights of Man* and in various provisions of the *Universal Declaration of Human Rights of the United Nations,* the *Preamble to the Universal Declaration,* and the *European Convention on Human Rights,* each of which ensures the liberties of speech and belief.

Negative liberties are also the rights expounded by Locke and Jefferson, freedom from government interference. As Henkin writes, Locke and Jefferson apparently did not contemplate *positive rights,* "that the social contract between the people and government might include an obligation on government to help people meet their basic needs if they were unable to satisfy them from their own resources."[37]

Berlin encapsulates it best. *Positive* liberty concerns the issue of "what can I do with my freedom?" Thus, accordingly, "the *positive* conception of liberty is not freedom *from,* but freedom *to*";[38] freedom to form a particular of life, freedom to become an autonomous human being, freedom to have equal prospects in life. This *positive* conception of liberty, the responsibility of government to enhance and secure the general welfare of the people, is credited in the philosophical sense to Kant in his *The Metaphysics of Morals.*[39] He explains that *rights* are divided in two parts. The first, *natural rights,* moral rights, or innate rights; these are Berlin's "negative rights, freedom from government, the 'shalt nots,' rights that government cannot invade or abrogate. This 'innate' right belongs to everyone by nature."[40] The second are *civil rights* that are given to all persons by a social contract as expressed in government legislative acts.[41] Encompassed within this meaning of right is the idea of *duty,* that is, duty to oneself and *duty* to others.[42] Kant's classification of rights comes down to this: a right in the state of nature is the *private right* of autonomy; and the second is, according to Kant, the right to benefits in *civil society* that "secure what is mine or yours by public laws."[43] Civil rights, therefore, are the *positive rights* of economic and social benefits that are deemed necessary to ensure human dignity "and to make negative rights meaningful."[44]

Positive rights were set forth best by Jefferson in his Virginia *Bill for the More General Diffusion of Knowledge* (1779), and later in the Land Ordinance of 1785 and Northwest Ordinance of 1787, under the old Articles of Confederation, to allocate lands in the public domain for education. In France, these same rights were recognized by Condorcet in his plan for compulsory primary education paid for by the state and implemented during the French Revolution in 1793.[45] Later, the *positive* rights of social security, first provided in Germany by Bismarck in 1884, and a few years later for national health care, equipped disability health care insurance in 1889.[46] Bismarck's old age pension programs created "the first modern welfare safety net in the world, which still forms part of modern Germany's 'social security' system."[47]

Explained another way, a *positive right* is the opportunity to protect human dignity, the right to be respected by others, usually thought to include personal security, work, and a means of earning a reasonable wage – an adequate standard of living, including shelter, food, clothing, health care, and, of course, education. Dignity, worth, and respect, in being human, cannot be fulfilled without the essentials that all humans owe to each other, and governments are obligated by their authority and power to provide for these *positive* or *dignity* rights by creating legislation for the essentials of human existence. The idea that the state must help fiscally to provide for the essentials of human welfare was not fully developed until the twentieth century, at which time it was realized that, as a matter of morals and ethics, human worth and dignity are implicit in the social contract, requiring more of the state than to merely leave people alone.

Positive rights, therefore, define a basic moral imperative encompassing the individual's opportunity to succeed in life, which should not be denied simply because the state will not provide sufficient fiscal resources. Jeremy Waldron clearly explained the economic and social aspects of this *positive* right:

> It is no longer widely assumed that human rights must be pinned down to the protection of individual *freedom*. Humans have other needs as well related to their health, survival, culture, *education*, and ability to work. We all know from our own case how important these needs are . . . It is now widely (though not universally) accepted that material needs generate moral imperatives which are as compelling as those related to democracy and civil liberty. If we want a catalogue of what people owe each other as a matter of moral priority, we should look not only to liberty but also to the elementary conditions of material well-being . . . Everyone has a right to a standard of living adequate for health and well-being of himself and his family. [emphasis added][48]

The Price Tag

Accommodation of dignity rights have a *price tag* that government may be unwilling to bear. Governments cannot legitimately justify denial of such rights on the grounds that they are too cumbersome, too administratively difficult, or too costly. This is especially true in the case of *positive* or *dignity rights* related to economic well-being for the reason that large governmental programs such as mass public education are major budget items. In this regard, Dworkin sees denial of adequate government funding for a *positive* right as "a grave injustice," and essential to human happiness.

> So if rights make sense at all, then the invasion of a relatively important right must be a very serious matter. It means treating a man as less than a man, or as less worthy of concern than other men. The institution of rights rests on the conviction that this is a grave injustice, and that it is worth paying the *incremental cost* in social policy or efficiency that is necessary to prevent it. [emphasis added][49]

FUNDAMENTAL RIGHT OF EDUCATION AND THE U.S. CONSTITUTION

Whether education is a fundamental right in the United States has been a contentious and litigious issue in school finance since 1973 when the U.S. Supreme Court rendered a decision in the case of *San Antonio Independent School District v. Rodriguez*[50] holding that education is not a fundamental right under the First and Fourteenth Amendments to the U.S. Constitution. The Court said, "Education . . . is not among the rights afforded explicit protection under our federal Constitution. Nor do we find any basis for saying it is implicitly so protected." In so holding, the Court rejected the essential reasoning of plaintiff children from a property poor school district where the quality of education was directly related to property wealth disparities. The plaintiff's case hinged on the reasoning that knowledge is a prerequisite to the exercise of other rights. The Court rejected this "nexus" argument:

> They [plaintiffs] insist that education is itself a fundamental personal right because it is essential to the effective exercise of First Amendment freedoms and to intelligence utilization of the right to vote. In asserting a nexus between speech and education, appellees urge that the right to speak is meaningless unless the speaker is capable of articulating his thoughts intelligently and persuasively . . . That the corollary right to receive information becomes little more than a hollow privilege when the recipient has not been taught to read, assimilate and utilize available knowledge.[51]

The Court, in rejecting this rationale of the peremptory force of knowledge, bifurcated the question saying that this is not a complaint that the legislature "has unconstitutionally denied or diluted anyone's right . . . but rather that the legislature violated the Constitution by not extending the relief " available to others.[52] The Court, therefore, rejected the argument that there was a nexus between education and the exercise of other fundamental rights or liberties, and in so doing implicitly separated individual rights into two categories, the first being that government "shalt not" deny a person's acquisition of education, and the second, that government "shalt" affirmatively extend a benefit in some corrective way that mitigates inequalities or corrects "imperfections" in the distribution of a state's financial resources.[53]

Foremost in the mind of the Burger Court in *Rodriguez* were two issues, neither directly related to a right: *first*, federalism and the *second*, taxation. Regarding the former, the Supreme Court said that "the maintenance of the principles of federalism is a foremost consideration" in examining state action. Concerning the latter, the Burger Court made it clear in *Rodriguez* that it would not intervene to correct inadequacies in state systems of school financing where "fundamental constitutional rights or liberties" were not at stake,[54] and that, therefore, the Court would not "nullify statewide measures for financing public services merely because the burdens or benefits thereof fall unevenly depending upon . . . relative wealth."[55]

After *Rodriguez*, the Supreme Court found it necessary to hedge and explain its position in another Texas case, *Plyler v. Doe*,[56] where the state, by law, absolutely denied public education to undocumented immigrant children. With Justice Brennan writing for the majority, the Court ruled that while education is not a fundamental right neither is it "merely some government 'benefit' indistinguishable from other forms of social welfare legislation. Both the importance of education in maintaining our basic institutions and the lasting impact of its deprivation in the life of the child mark the distinction."[57] Justice Brennan, who had earlier dissented in *Rodriguez*, but writing for the majority in *Plyler*, could not garner the votes to hold that education is fundamental, but he made a valiant effort by holding that even though education is not a "fundamental right,"[58] it, nevertheless, "has a pivotal role in maintaining the fabric of our society,"[59] and, further, that to deny education to children will attach a "stigma of illiteracy" that will "mark them for the rest of their lives."[60]

Importantly, Brennan's reference to "stigma" takes the issue into the realm of constitutional questions regarding substantive due process of law, another aspect of constitutional law which the Court later expounds on in the case of *Goss v. Lopez*.[61] In *Goss*, the Court had said that for government to attach a "stigma" to one's reputation involves the denial of a "liberty" interest, and to take away educational benefits of a public education is to also deprive the student of a "property interest," under the Due Process Clauses of the Fifth and Fourteenth Amendments of the U.S. Constitution. The Court in *Goss* relies on an earlier precedent, *Board of Regents v. Roth*,[62] in which the Court's concept of the "penumbras" of liberty and property rights "relate to the whole domain of social and economic fact" and that to "impose a stigma" is a denial of liberty without due process.[63] Citing a much earlier precedent that expanded the implication and the meaning of liberty and property, the Court reached back to a 1923 case, *Meyer v. Nebraska*, where it had held that liberty is "not merely freedom from bodily restraint but also the right of the individual to . . . acquire useful knowledge" [emphasis added].[64]

What, then, does this all mean regarding the issue of whether education is a fundamental constitutional right under the U.S. Constitution? The answer is this: *First,* education is not a fundamental right under the Equal Protection Clause. This means that for a state not to provide education at all to anyone would not violate the Equal Protection Clause. *Second,* the Equal Protection Clause is not offended if a state, in providing for public education, permits funding disparities because of variations in local wealth or uneven economic conditions. To do so would require that the Court hold that education is a *positive* right. *Third,* where a state provides for education, it cannot arbitrarily deny such benefit to some children while providing it for others. The Due Process Clause prohibits the federal or state governments in provision of education to deny education to some children while permitting it for others. To do so would stigmatize the disadvantaged child in violation of a liberty interest and would also deny a property interest by deprivation of useful knowledge, and as such would ignore a constitutionally protected *negative* right.

STATE CONSTITUTIONS IN THE UNITED STATES

Berlin's *negative* and *positive* constructs of rights and liberties help explain the shortcoming of the U.S. Constitution with regard to education. Concerning the denial of education *per se*, *sans* race, the U.S. Constitution does not set forth *positive* requirements concerning education. Any *positive* law entitling a person to education at the federal level must come about through statutory law of Acts of Congress pursuant to the authority vested in it in the Spending Clause or, possibly, through the Commerce Clause of the Constitution.

However, the federal system in the United States creates another broad dimension to school funding via the state in that the states have their own constitutional requirements, structured provisions that are unique to the particular state. These constitutions have both Berlin's *negative* provisions, "the shalt nots" and *positive* provisions, "the shalts" that when invoked by courts set forth conditions for the funding of public schools.[65] The state constitutions include in their structural provisions language of *positive* law that requires states to establish and finance public school systems. The enunciations of state *positive* law are usually found in the body of the state constitutions requiring that a system of public schools be established, normally accompanied by an adjective, such as *efficient*,[66] although the words *thorough, quality, uniform,* and others may have also been used by the framers of the state constitutions.

State constitutions are different from the Federal Constitution in that they include various levels of explicit requirements, *positive* and affirmative, mandates for state legislatures to create systems of education with prescriptions for state legislative implementation.

Entitlements and Prescriptions

Elazar, in his book, *The American Constitutional Tradition*, writes that "state constitutions are important determinants of who gets what, when, and how in America because they are conceptual and at times very specific statements of who should get what, when, and how."[67] Rodriguez, writing in a law review article in 1998, elucidated on *positive* rights and explained that state constitutions create *entitlements*: "state constitutions resemble regulatory statutes because they prescribe social and economic policies expressed in the language of *positive* rights while, according to the legislature, have instrumental discretion to carry out the constitutional mandate."[68] These constitutional requirements "commit the state to explicit public goals, state constitutions compel state legislatures to enact policies that carry out these goals, and, thus, alter the terms of political discourse."[69]

Hershkoff, too, explains that these state constitutional provisions for education are not negative governmental prohibitions against government intrusion on individual rights, liberties, and freedoms, but are rather quite different in that they are obligations that require legislatures to take action to provide for education: "These *positive* rights are not simply structural limits on governmental power, they are also *prescriptive duties* compelling government to use such power to achieve constitutionally fixed social ends" [emphasis added].[70]

For example, the Supreme Court of the State of Washington ruled in 2012 that Article IX of that State's Constitution "confers on children in Washington a *positive* constitutional right to an amply funded education" [emphasis added].[71] And the Wyoming Supreme Court reads that state's constitution as a *positive* right to education declaring that education in that state is a "fundamental right"[72] and that the legislature must make "adequate" fiscal provision for the public schools,[73] and, further, the court has required that the level of spending cannot be a function of the wealth of the local school district.[74]

Prescriptive *positive* constitutional language is found in most state constitutions.[75] Montana is a representative example of states with very clear constitutional requirements of educational goals and duties for the legislature. It reads in part, "It is the goal of the people to establish a system of education which will develop the full educational potential of each person. Equality of educational opportunity is guaranteed to each person of the state."[76] In 1989, the Montana Supreme Court approved the language of a state district court that had ruled that "Public education is, without doubt, a fundamental and most important function of the state of Montana and its political subdivisions."[77] This constitutional language enabled a state district court in *Columbia Falls Elementary School District No. 6 v. State of Montana*, after an intensive evidentiary analysis of the nuances of the state funding system, to rule that "there is no question that the current funding system is not reasonable,"[78] and that "school funding system violates the Article X, Section 1 of the Montana Constitution in that it fails to provide *adequate* funding for Montana's public schools" [emphasis added].[79] The legislature had failed to live up to the *positive* constitutional language. The Court further, in elaboration of the implications of the *positive* constitutional mandate, held that to satisfy the constitution the school finance system must be based on the "needs and costs of the public school system," and the funding factors in which it is based must be "educationally relevant."[80]

These recent cases in Washington, Wyoming, and Montana are illustrative of judicial interpretations that follow the intent of the people as expressed in constitutional language. These constitutional provisions prescribe certain funding requirements that must be addressed in the allocation of tax monies for children in local school districts. Such *positive* constitutional language invokes judicial discretion in the determination of adequacy of funding.

STATE EDUCATION AS A FUNDAMENTAL RIGHT

State high courts in at least fifteen states, at one time or other, have held that education is a fundamental right.[81] See Table 2.1. Even though the Alabama Supreme Court held in *Opinion of the Justices,* 1993, that education is a fundamental in that state, the court revisited the issue in *Alabama Coalition v. Ex Parte Governor Fob James*, 2002, and, while not fully recanting, nevertheless, said that it would not intervene to see that the legislature lived up to its constitutional obligations. The state high court

Table 2.1 States Where Education Is a Fundamental Right

State	Case	Citation	Year	Ruling
Alabama	*Opinion of the Justices*	624 So. 2d 107	1993	For Plaintiff
Arizona	*Shofstall v. Hollins*	515 P.2d 590	1973	For Defendant
California	*Serrano v. Priest (I)*	487 P.2d 1241 96 Cal.Rptr.601	1976	For Plaintiff
	Serrano v. Priest (II)	557 P.2d 929 135 Cal. Rptr. 545		For Plaintiff
Connecticut	*Horton v. Meskill*	376 A.2d 359	1977	For Plaintiff
Kentucky	*Rose v. Council for Better Education, Inc.*	790 S.W.2d 186	1989	For Plaintiff
Minnesota	*Skeen v. Minnesota*	505 N.W.2d 299	1993	For Defendant
Montana	*Helena Elem. School District No. 1 v. Montana*	236 Mont. 44, 746 P.2d 684 as mod. 784 P.2d 412	1989	For Plaintiff
	Columbia Falls Elem. School Dist., No. 6 v. Montana	326 Mont. 306, 109 P.3d 257	2005	For Plaintiff

New Hampshire	Claremont School Dist. v Governor (II)	142 N.H. 462, 703 A.2d 1353	1997 For Plaintiff
	Opinion of the Justices (School Financing) (III)	142 N.H. 892, 712 A.2d 1080	1998 For Plaintiff
	Claremont School Dist. v. Governor (V)	144 N.H. 210, 744 A.2d 1107	1999 For Plaintiff
	Opinion of the Justices (School Financing) (VI)	145 N.H. 474, 765 A.2d 673	2000 For Plaintiff
	Claremont School Dist. V Governor (VII)	147 N.H. 499, 794 A.2d 744	2002 For Plaintiff
North Dakota	Bismarck Public School Dist. v. North Dakota	511 N.W.2d 247	1994 For State
	Williston v. State	Pending	
Tennessee	Tenn Small School Systems v. McWherter (I)	851 S.W.2d 139	1993 For Plaintiff
	Tenn Small School Systems v. McWherter (II)	894 S.W.2d 734	1995 For Plaintiff
	Tenn Small School Systems v. McWherter (III)	91 S.W.3d 232	2002 For Plaintiff
Virginia	Scott v. Commonwealth of Virginia	247 Va. 379, 443 S.E.2d 138	1994 For State
Washington	McCleary v. State of Washington	Supreme Court Case No. 84362-7	2012 For Plaintiff
West Virginia	Pauley v. Kelly	255 S.E.2d 859	1979 For Plaintiff
Wisconsin	Kukor v. Grover	436 N.W.2d 568	1989 For State
	Vincent v. Voight	614 N.W.2d 388	2000 For State
Wyoming	Washakie Co. School Dist. No. 1 v. Herschler	606 P.2d 310, cert den. 449 U.S. 824	1980 For Plaintiff
	Campbell Co. School Dist. v. Wyoming (I)	907 P.2d 1238	1995 For Plaintiff
	Campbell Co. School Dist. v. Wyoming (II)	19 P.3d 518	2001 For State

Notes:
1. Does not include rulings related strictly to capital or facilities financing.
2. Does not include high court procedural rulings.
3. Does not include intermediate court rulings.

Sources: ACCESS, Education Finance Litigation (http://www.schoolfunding.info/states/state_by_state.php3); Education Law Center, State Laws Relating to Pre-K (http://www.startingat3.org/state_laws/index.html); Gormley, Ken. 2006. "Education as a Fundamental Right: Building a New Paradigm," *Forum on Public Policy* 2(2), 207–229, http://forumonpublicpolicy.com/vol2no2.edlaw/gormley.pdf. Also: Sean P. Corcoran and William N. Evans, "Equity, Adequacy and the Evolving State Role in Education Finance," in Helen F. Ladd and Edward B. Fiske, editors, *Handbook of Research in Education Finance and Policy* (New York: Routledge, 2008), pp. 332–356.

concluded that enforcement of the fundamental right was not the responsibility of the judiciary, but rather "rested squarely upon the shoulders of the Legislature."[82] Thus, without judicial enforcement, the fundamentality standard would, of course, not be enforceable if the legislative branch itself chooses not to adhere to the standard. The Alabama situation is the "Achilles heel" of all fundamentality cases. Education may be declared a constitutional right under a state constitution, but if the court does not enforce the constitutional mandate it will be of little consequence in the funding of education.

The Supreme Court of Virginia earlier set the non-enforcement pattern since followed by the Alabama court. The Virginia court ruled that education is a constitutional fundamental in that state, but then decided that the judiciary would not enforce the provision.[83] Such a determination by a state court leaves the constitutional provision unenforceable. A *positive* constitutional mandate is merely a hollow gesture if the courts are unwilling to enforce such enunciations of the will of the people.

STATES WHERE EDUCATION IS NOT A FUNDAMENTAL RIGHT AND PLAINTIFFS PREVAILED

A state constitution does not necessarily need to be classified by the state high court as fundamental for plaintiffs to win in school finance litigation. Neither does the state constitution need to bestow a *positive* right to education for a plaintiff to win. Table 2.2 shows those states where plaintiffs were successful even though education was not held to be fundamental.

Table 2.2 States Where Education Is Not a Fundamental Right and Plaintiffs Prevailed

State	Case	Citation	Year	Ruling
Arkansas	*DuPree v. Alma School District No. 30*	279 Ark. 340, 651 S.W.2d 90	1983	For Plaintiff
	Lake View School District No. 25 v. Huckabee (III)	351 Ark. 31, 91S.W.3d 472	2002	For Plaintiff
	Lake View School District No. 25 v. Huckabee (V)	210 S.W.3d 28	2005	For Plaintiff
Kansas	*U.S.D. 229 v. State*	256 Kan.232, 885 P.2d 1170	1994	For State
	Montoy v. State (II)	278 Kan.769, 102 P.3d 1160	2005	For Plaintiff
	Montoy v. State (IV)	138 P.3d 755, 761	2006	For Plaintiff
Massachusetts	*McDuffy v. Sec. of Exec. Office of Educ.*	415 Ma.545, 615 N.E.2d 516	1993	For Plaintiff
	Hancock v. Driscoll	443 Ma. 428, 822 N.E.2d 1134	2005	For State
New Jersey	*Robinson v. Cahill (I)*	62 N.J. 473, 303 A.2d 273	1977	For Plaintiff
	Robinson v. Cahill (II)	69 N.J. 449, 355 A.2d 129	1976	For State
	Abbott v. Burke (II)	100 N.J. 269, 405 A.2d 376	1990	For State
	Abbott v. Burke (III)	136 N.J. 444, 643 A.2d 575	1994	For State
	Abbott v. Burke (IV)	149 N.J. 145, 693 A.2d 417	1997	For State
	Abbott v. Burke (V)	153 N.J. 480, 710 A.2d 450	1998	For State
New York	*Levittown v. Nyquist*	57 N.Y.2d 27, 439 N.E.2d 359, 453 N.Y.S.2d 643	1982	For State
	Campaign for Fiscal Equity, Inc. v. New York	100 N.Y.2d 893	2003	For Plaintiff
North Carolina	*Britt v. North Carolina Bd. of Education*	86 N.C.App.282, 357 S.E.2d 432 *affd. mem.*, 320 N.C. 790, 361 S.E.2d 71	1987	For State
	Hoke County Board of Education v. North Carolina (Leandro II)	599 S.E.2d 365	2004	For Plaintiff

Ohio	Board of Education v. Walter	58 Ohio.2d 368, 390 N.E.2d 813, cert. den. 444 U.S. 1015	1979	For State
	DeRolph v. Ohio (I)	78 Ohio.3d 193, 677 N.E.2d 733, as clarified 78 Ohio.3d 419, 678 N.E.2d 886	1997	For Plaintiff
	DeRolph v. Ohio (II)	89 Ohio.3d 1, 728 N.E.2d 993	2000	For Plaintiff
	DeRolph v. Ohio (III)	93 Ohio.3d 309, 754 N.E.2d 1184	2001	For Plaintiff
	DeRolph v. Ohio (IV)	97 Ohio.3d 434, 780 N.E.2d 529	2002	For Plaintiff
Texas	Edgewood Ind. School Dist. v. Kirby (I)	777 S.W.2d 391	1989	For Plaintiff
	Edgewood Ind. School Dist. v. Kirby (II)	804 S.W.2d 491	1991	For Plaintiff
	Carrolton-Farmers Branch ISD v. Edgewood Ind. School Dist. (III)	826 S.W.2d 489	1992	For Plaintiff
	Edgewood Ind. School Dist. v. Meno (IV)	893 S.W.2d 450	1995	For State
	West Orange-Cove Consolidated ISD v. Neeley	176 S.W.3d 746	2005	For Plaintiff
Vermont	Brigham v. Vermont (I)	166 Vt. 246, 692 A.2d 384	1997	For Plaintiff
	Brigham v. Vermont (II)	179 Vt. 525, 889 A.2d 715	2005	For Plaintiff

Notes:

1. Does not include rulings related strictly to capital or facilities financing.
2. Does not include high court procedural rulings.
3. Does not include intermediate court rulings.

Sources: ACCESS, Education Finance Litigation (http://www.schoolfunding.info/states/state_by_state. php3); Education Law Center, State Laws Relating to Pre-K (http://www.startingat3.org/state_laws/index. html; Gormley, Ken. 2006. "Education as a Fundamental Right: Building a New Paradigm," *Forum on Public Policy* 2(2), 207–229, http://forumonpublicpolicy.com/vol2no2.edlaw/gormley.pdf. Also: Sean P. Corcoran and William N. Evans, "Equity, Adequacy and the Evolving State Role in Education Finance," in Helen F. Ladd and Edward B. Fiske, editors, *Handbook of Research in Education Finance and Policy* (New York: Routledge, 2008), pp. 332–356.

NATIONAL ACCESS NETWORK

The National Access Network, www.schoolfunding.info, Teachers College, Columbia University, is the best current and most comprehensive source for following state school finance litigation. The purpose of the site is to "provide up-to-date information on equity issues and school finance and to promote meaningful educational opportunities for all children."[84] In addition to citation of historic and current case law, the site is also a good source of relevant state school finance studies.

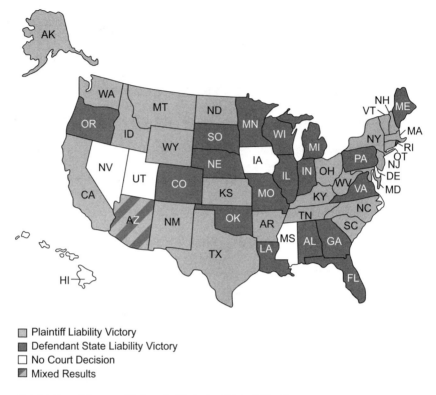

☐ Plaintiff Liability Victory
■ Defendant State Liability Victory
☐ No Court Decision
▨ Mixed Results

Figure 2.1 National Access Network, State by State Litigation

Source: National Access Network, www.schoolfunding.info. Reprinted by permission.

UNIVERSAL DECLARATION OF HUMAN RIGHTS

On December 10, 1948, the United Nations General Assembly adopted and pro-claimed the *Universal Declaration of Human Rights*[85] that set forth fundamental rights. Such a declaration was deemed to be of special importance after the atrocities that stained humanity during World War II. Several passages of the *Declaration* are rele-vant to *knowledge* and *education*; in the *Preamble* that states, "*Whereas* the peoples of the United Nations have in the Charter reaffirmed their faith in fundamental human rights, in the dignity and worth of the human person and in equal rights of men and women . . ." member nations "shall strive by *teaching* and *education* to promote respect for these rights and freedoms and by progressive measures, national and inter-national, to secure their universal and effective recognition" [emphasis added].[86] And *Article 26(1)* states that "Everyone has the right to education. Education shall be free, at least in the elementary and fundamental stages. Elementary shall be compulsory."[87] Subsection (2) elaborates further saying that education "shall be directed to the full development of the human personality and the strengthening of respect for human rights and fundamental freedoms."[88] These are all averments of *positive* rights that are fundamental.

Thus, importantly, the *United Nations' Declaration* establishes education as a fundamental right. Nations that are signatories to this treaty commit themselves to these objectives. In interpreting the U.N. obligations, Henkin writes that "such human rights as enunciated derive from natural rights theories and systems harking back through English, American, and French constitutionalism to John Locke et al., and earlier natural rights and natural law theory."[89]

In viewing the provisions of the *United Nations' Declaration* through the lenses of Isaiah Berlin's liberty rights, one sees both the *negative* and *positive* rights implicated. The *negative* aspects are found in the prohibition that government encroachment on individual liberties, Article 8, ensures all persons the right of *due process* of law against acts of government that violate "fundamental rights granted . . . by the constitution or by law."[90] In this Article we find Berlin's *negative* liberty protecting a *fundamental right*, and education and acquisition of knowledge are therefore protected.

EUROPEAN CONVENTION ON HUMAN RIGHTS

The *European Convention for the Protection of Human Rights and Fundamental Freedoms* drafted by the Council of Europe, signed in Rome on November 4, 1950, entered into force on September 3, 1953,[91] and was ratified by the eight original members of the Council of Europe: Denmark, the Federal Republic of Germany, Iceland, Ireland, Luxembourg, Norway, Sweden, and the United Kingdom. The number of nations has now increased to forty-one. The requirements of the Convention are implemented by the European Court of Human Rights and the European Commission on Human Rights located in Strasbourg. Janis et al. point out that "What is extraordinary about the Convention is Strasbourg's enforcement machinery."[92] The Commission has three primary functions to serve as a screen for judicial actions by filtering complaints, mediating disputes, and fact finding.[93] The Court itself sits as a tribunal rendering legally binding decisions that must be followed by the courts of the member nations. The provisions of the Convention include Protocol No. 1, Article I, March 20, 1952, a *negative* right, "No one shall be deprived of his possessions except in the public interest . . . subject to the conditions provided by law."[94] This provision is the equivalent of the *due process* clauses of the Fifth and Fourteenth Amendments of the U.S. Constitution, i.e., property cannot be taken by government without due process of law. Article 2 of the Convention is the Right to Education stating that: "No person shall be denied the right to education. In the exercise of any functions which it assumes in relation to education and to teaching, the State shall respect the right of parents to ensure such education and teaching in conformity with their own religious and philosophical convictions."[95] Other protocols include the guarantees of free elections and freedom of movement and prohibit discrimination as to sex, race, color, language, religion, political opinion, and the death penalty.

The Right to Education of Protocol 1, Article 2, of the Convention is in the *negative* form, "no person shall be denied the right to education," rather than the *positive*, "every person has the right to education."[96] Several countries have entered reservations to this Right to Education, Protocol 1, Article 2, including the United Kingdom. The United Kingdom's qualification reads "the principle affirmed in the second sentence of Protocol 1, Article 2, is accepted by the United Kingdom only so far as it is compatible with the provision of efficient instruction and training and the avoidance of unreasonable *public expenditure*" [emphasis added].[97] Therefore, the United Kingdom makes it quite clear that the provision providing a "Right to Education" does not commit or compel the signatory state to any particular level of public education funding to fulfill the "Right."[98] Thus, what the provision means to the United Kingdom is the *negative*, that government cannot deny education to the citizenry. It does not mean that the government must fund education in any particular way or at any specified level.

The European Court of Human Rights has interpreted the "Right to Education" Protocol, although stated in the *negative*, to, in fact, enshrine education as a right; however, the Court has explained that the *negative* formulation does not establish the right so as to require signatory states to "establish at their own expense or to subsidize education of any particular type or at any particular level."[99] The Court has further held that the *negative* formulation of the right to education provision does not imply that the state is required to allocate resources at any particular level or for any particular educational provisions.[100] Further, the Court has held in *Family H. v. United Kingdom* that the state may at its discretion require education for all children at the elementary and secondary levels in public school, private school, or educate them at home. The state may allow private education and private schools, but the state has "no obligation to fund or subsidize these arrangements."[101]

The European Convention on Human Rights' concept of education as a right can best be explained by Isaiah Berlin's categorization of rights and liberties into those that are *negative*, the *shalt nots* and those that are *positive*, the *shalts*. That is, government cannot deny a *negative* right, but it has discretion in the extent of provision and the level of funding of *positive* rights. In the case of the European Convention on Human Rights, all the member states at the time of signing the Education Protocol[102] already had state systems of education so there was no question with regard to requiring them to provide for education. All of the states provided for education at the elementary and secondary levels; thus, they had met the criterion of the *negative* right in that no child or youth was denied education. Also, they had met the *positive* criterion in that a system of public education was provided to all children and youth. What is not guaranteed by either the *negative* or the *positive* right is a predicate level of public expenditure for the education.

SUMMARY

This chapter explores the issue of fundamental rights as applied to education in the United States, the *Universal Declaration of Human Rights*, and the *European Convention on Human Rights*. Fundamental rights are defined as an individual's right to acquire knowledge as the key to other rights, primarily liberty and equality. The discussion relies to a great extent on the thoughts of Isaiah Berlin and his famous essay titled, *Two Concepts of Liberty*. Those two concepts, both *negative* and *positive* liberties, are utilized in an attempt to explain the reasoning of both state and federal courts in their garbled and inexact attempts to explain the nature of fundamentality as it applies to education. Berlin explains that *negative* rights or liberties are enunciations of what government cannot do, the "thou shalt nots" of political philosophy and law, and he further makes it quite clear that there are also *positive* liberties and rights, those things that governments are required by the people to do, "thou shalts."

For example, a *negative* liberty prohibits government from taking one's property or life without due process of law. And a *positive* liberty, or right, is illustrated in the case of those state constitutions in the United States that declare states must establish systems of public schools to which children and youth must have access. Ronald Dworkin, the political and legal philosopher, identifies the limitations of such constitutional requirements as the reality of the "price tag," whether governments will pay for the realization of liberties and rights.

Considerable discussion is devoted to the U.S. Supreme Court's rulings that deny that education is a fundamental right under the Equal Protection Clause of the Fourteenth Amendment, but bestows a liberty interest under the Due Process Clause for children and youth who may be denied access to education.

The fundamentality issue is treated at the state level by showing the vicissitudes and unpredictability of some courts as they meander and misapprehend the meaning of fundamentality of education. Cases are cited where child plaintiffs may lose in their quest for equal or adequate education even though fundamentality of education is the constitutional standard, and, in some cases, plaintiff children may win their cases where education has not been declared by the courts to be fundamental.

The chapter concludes with an explanation of the right to education as viewed by the main international convention and courts.

KEY TERMS

- Fundamental rights
- Negative rights
- *Due process* liberties
- Liberty as a right
- Positive rights
- Equal protection rights
- "Penumbras" of liberty
- Stigmas and liberty
- Constitutional entitlements
- Dignity rights
- Human rights
- Public expenditures and rights

NOTES

1. John Finnis, *Natural Law and Natural Rights* (Oxford: Clarendon Press, 1980), p. 64.
2. Ibid., p. 59.
3. Parts of this section are taken from Kern Alexander and M. David Alexander, *American Public School Law*, 8th Edition (Belmont, CA: Wadsworth/Cengage Learning, 2011).
4. Finnis, *op. cit.*, pp. 86–87.
5. Ibid., p. 92.
6. Robert Nozick, *Anarchy, State and Utopia* (New York: Basic Books, 1974), p. 31.
7. Louis Henkin, Gerald L. Newman, Diane F. Orentliches, and David W. Leebron, *Human Rights* (New York: Foundation Press, 1999), p. 4.

8. Ibid.
9. Ibid.
10. Ibid. *See also*: Ronald Dworkin, *Taking Rights Seriously* (Cambridge, Mass.: Harvard University Press, 1977).
11. Dworkin, *op. cit.*, pp. 190–195.
12. Emma Rothschild, *Economic Sentiments: Adam Smith, Condorcet, and The Enlightenment* (Cambridge, Mass: Harvard University Press, 2001), p. 235.
13. Ibid., p. 225.
14. Mark Janis, Richard Kay, and Anthony Bradley, *European Human Law*, 2nd Edition (Oxford: Oxford University Press, 2000), p. 12.
15. Lawrence Cremin, *American Education: The National Experience, 1783–1876* (New York: Harper & Row, 1980), p. 125.
16. See: Alexander and Alexander, *op. cit.*, p. 33.
17. Cremin, *op. cit.,* pp. 133–142.
18. Ibid., pp. 124–125.
19. Ibid.
20. Ibid.
21. Alexander and Alexander, *op. cit.*
22. See: Dworkin, *op. cit.*
23. Isaiah Berlin, "Two Concepts of Liberty," in *Four Essays on Liberty* (Oxford: Oxford University Press, 1991), pp. 122–123.
24. Ibid., p. 124.
25. Isaiah Berlin's Inaugural Lecture delivered at the University of Oxford on October 31, 1958, and published by Clarendon Press, Oxford in the same year.
26. Charles A. Reich, The New Property, 73 Yale L.J. 733 (1964).
27. *Goldberg v. Kelly*, 397 U.S. 254 (1970).
28. *San Antonio Independent School District v. Rodriguez*, 411 U.S. 1 (1973).
29. *DeShaney v. Winnebago County Department of Social Services*, 489 U.S. 189, 196 (1989).
30. Isaiah Berlin, *Four Essays on Liberty* (Oxford: Oxford University Press, 1969).
31. Ibid., pp. 121–122.
32. John Stuart Mill, *On Liberty*, 1869, cited in *The Basic Writings of John Stuart Mill* (New York: Random House, 2002), pp. 3–4.
33. Ibid.
34. Ibid., pp. 9–16.
35. Berlin, *op. cit.,* p. 126.
36. Mill, *op. cit.* See Berlin, *op cit.*, pp. 126–127.
37. Henkin et al., *op. cit.*, p. 82.
38. Berlin, *op. cit.,* p. 131.
39. Immanuel Kant, *The Metaphysics of Morals*, first published in 1797 (Cambridge: Cambridge University Press, 1991), translated by Mary Gregor, p. 63.
40. Ibid.
41. Ibid.
42. Ibid.
43. Ibid.
44. Henkin et al., *op cit.*, p. 82.
45. Francois Furet, *Revolutionary France 1770–1880* (Oxford: Blackwell, 1995), p. 193.
46. Jonathan Steinberg, *Bismarck: A Life* (Oxford: Oxford University Press, 2011), p. 417.
47. Ibid.
48. Jeremy Waldron, "Nonsense Upon Stilts" (1987), pp. 157–159, in Henkin et al., *op. cit.*, pp. 83–85.

49. Dworkin, *op cit.*, p. 199.
50. *San Antonio Independent School District v. Rodriguez*, 411 US. 1, 93 S Ct. 1278 (1973).
51. Ibid.
52. Ibid.
53. Ibid.
54. Ibid.
55. Ibid.
56. *Plyler v. Doe*, 457 U.S. 202, 102 S. Ct. 2382 (1982).
57. Ibid.
58. Ibid.
59. Ibid.
60. Ibid.
61. *Goss v. Lopez*, 419 U.S. 565, 95 S. Ct. 729 (1975).
62. *Board of Regents v. Roth*, 408 U.S. 564, 92 S. Ct. 2701 (1972).
63. Ibid.
64. *Meyer v. Nebraska*, 362 U.S. 390, 43 S. Ct. 625 (1923).
65. See: Alexander and Alexander, *op cit.*, pp. 80–81 and pp. 1057–1062.
66. At least twenty states use the term "efficient." See Texas, Article VII, Section I and Constitution of Kentucky, Section 183.
67. Daniel J. Elazar, *The American Constitutional Tradition* (Lincoln: University of Nebraska Press, 1988).
68. Daniel Rodriguez, "State Constitutional Theory and Its Prospects," 28 N.M.L. Rev. 271 (1998).
69. G. Alan Tarr, "Understanding State Constitutions," 65 Temp. L. Rev. 1169, 1181–83 (1992).
70. Helen Hershkoff, "Positive Rights and State Constitutions: The Limits of Federal Rationality Review," *Harvard Law Review,* Vol. 112, No. 6, April 1999, pp. 1155–1156.
71. *McCleary v. State of Washington, En Banc*, No. 84362–7, January 5, 2012.
72. *Washakie County School District v. Herschler*, 606 P.2d 310 (Wyo. 1980).
73. *Campbell County School District v. State of Wyoming*, 97 P.2d 1238 (Wyo. 1995).
74. See: Campbell I (1995), Campbell II (2001), Campbell III (2004), and Campbell IV (2008).
75. National Education Access Network, www.schoolfunding.info.
76. Montana Constitution, Article X, Section I.
77. See: *Helena Elementary School District No. 1 v. State*, No. ADV-85–370, at 10–11 (Mont. 1st Jud. District, January 13, 1988); *Helena Elementary School District No. 1 v. State*, 236 Mont. 44, 769 P. 2d 684 (1989), modified by 236 Mont. 44, 784 P.2d 412 (1990).
78. *Columbia Falls Elementary School District No. 6 v. State of Montana*, Cause NO. BDV-2002–528.
79. Ibid.
80. Ibid.
81. Ken Gormley, "Education as a Fundamental Right: Building a New Paradigm," *Forum on Public Policy* 2:2, p. 219.
82. *Alabama Coalition for Equity, Inc. v. Ex Parte, Governor Fob James* , May 31, 2002.
83. *Scott v. Commonwealth of Virginia*, 247 Va. 379, 443 S. E. 2d 138 (1994).
84. *National Education Access Network,* www.schoolfunding.info.
85. G.A. Res, 217A U.N. Doc A/810, at 71 (1948).
86. Henkin et al., *op cit.*, pp. 287–288.
87. Ibid.
88. Ibid.
89. Henkin, "The Age of Rights" in Louis Henkin, Gerald L. Newman, Diane F. Orentlichen, and David W. Leebron, *Human Rights* (New York: Foundation Press, 1999), pp. 281–282.

90. Ibid., p. 289.
91. Janis et al., *op cit.*, p. 3.
92. Ibid, p. 23.
93. Helen Fenwick, *Civil Liberties*, Second Edition (London: Cavendish Publishing Limited, 2000), p. 20.
94. Ibid., p. 74.
95. Ibid., Protocol No. 1, 20 March 1952.
96. John Wadham and Helen Mountfield, *Blackstone's Guide to the Human Rights Act 1998*, Second Edition (London: Blackstone Press Limited, 2001), p. 135.
97. Ibid.
98. Ibid.
99. Ibid., p. 136. See: Belgian Linguistic Case (No. 2) IEHRR 252 (1968).
100. Ibid., p. 136.
101. Ibid.; citing *Family H. v. United Kingdom*, 37 DR 105 (1984).
102. Ibid.

CHAPTER 3

The *System* and Public Schools

INTRODUCTION

Universal education of all youth is today perhaps the most important calling of all nations: those nations that are already considered post-industrial in their economic development as well as those that are aggressive aspirants to a higher level of economic condition. All nations, both developed and developing, are faced with the reality of creating and institutionalizing measures that are most conducive to such development. A condition precedent is the recognition that mass education is the lynchpin of success. Implementation of education policy is, however, dependent to a large degree on the economic *system* in which the people, at their inception, find themselves. Several political and economic systems are not as fertile for growth as others. Some systems are extractive, unequal, and exploitive of the people, while others are inclusive, more egalitarian, redistributive, and receptive to human capital development. In extractive systems education has been generally denied to the masses and a wide divergence of income and wealth exists among the population. The idea, of course, is to influence and shape the system through education and redistributive policies that will foster growth and welfare of all the people. This chapter addresses the ongoing matter of the nature and improvement of the *system* by means of education.

RESPONSIBILITY OF GOVERNMENT

Government has two basic responsibilities to its citizenry: one is an affirmative obligation to take measures to correct imbalances in opportunity that evolve from human interaction. Such interactions, cultural, religious, economic, or social, are caused by the *system* of human relationships that may elevate some to the detriment of others. Only government is equipped to mitigate the natural state of man to pursue his own welfare even though such pursuit may reduce liberties of others. That is, government is obliged to create, enhance, and stimulate a social system in which man's self-preservation and liberty is controlled in order to preserve the interests of others.[1] As Thomas Hobbes explained, man is not likely to relinquish his advantages unless he finds himself advantaged by a mutual transferring of rights and liberties to others. It is the role of government to stimulate these transfers and redistributions.

BOX 3.1

Man will always be imaginative enough to enlarge his needs beyond minimum requirements and selfish enough to feel the pressure of his needs more than the needs of others.

Source: Reinhold Niebuhr, *Moral Man and Immoral Society* (New York: Charles Scribner's Sons, 1932), p. 196.

Second, government is obliged to not create, exacerbate, or magnify man's natural tendencies to acquire personal liberties at the expense of the rights of others. Government itself must not, by its own affirmative acts, cause to be created disparities that may be worse than exist in the state of nature. Rather, it is the duty of government to redistribute rights and liberties in a way that is consistent with the greatest happiness of all.

Compared with those of other developed countries, U.S. poverty rates are extraordinarily high, as are the odds of remaining in poverty over several generations. No longer do immigrants from Europe desire to come to America; the social and economic policies of their countries are superior, their public schools are better funded, and their overall standard of living is higher. The weight of poverty in America places a heavy burden on public schools as the most important agents of poverty remediation. The results of this burden are manifested in a prevailing view that the public schools are failed institutions. Taken alone, international test comparisons appear to show that America's public schools are inefficient and unsuccessful, yet such comparisons are misleading. This chapter clarifies the factors that must be considered in viewing the totality of effort and the effect of comparative international educational performance. The principal factor is the level of child poverty in the United States compared with other developed countries. The *system* in the United States breeds poverty, with marginal hope of escape. For the vast majority, there is little reason to believe that children in poverty today can expect a better tomorrow.

THE *SYSTEM*

Public schools in the United States operate in a national economic *system* that not only permits substantial economic disparities among individuals and families but by its very nature tends to exacerbate division between the rich and poor. Muhammed Yunus, Nobel Peace Prize winner in 2006, has observed that "poverty has not been created by poor people. The *system* has created them."[2] The *system* consists of the social and economic institutions that governments permit, establish, and nourish.

BOX 3.2

The *System* and Poverty

My position has been that poverty has not been created by poor people. The *system* has created them. The *system* being institutions, the concept or framework of living. That's where the seed of poverty is.

Source: Muhammed Yunus, Nobel Peace Prize winner, 2006, *The New York Times*, Sunday, December 8, 2006, p. 34.

Even *The Wall Street Journal*, the bastion of conservative economic thought, has noticed the extent and magnitude of the disparities in income and wealth of the American system. In a revealing issue, *The Journal*, using U.S. Bureau of Census data, noted that the gap between the poorest 20 percent of the population and the richest 20 percent had increased substantially since 1970.[3] However, *The Journal* concluded that the issue of rich versus poor has not materialized into a viable issue that is likely to have an effect on national politics.[4] The *system* in the United States is characterized by inadequate funding of education, rising health care costs, rising energy prices, and a decline in the value of the dollar compared to currencies of other developed countries. Globalization has made middle class Americans realize that their standard of living has declined when measured against counterparts in Europe and other OECD economies.[5] Without government intervention to remediate the effects of globalization, inequality has continued to increase in the United States[6] and has resulted in a permanent and expanding underclass.

The relative decline in the standard of living is visited most harshly upon the poor and lower middle class and hardly enters the consciousness of the upper 10 percent of the U.S. income class. The public schools are attended largely by the children of the middle and lower income classes, and the situation worsens as the more affluent remove their children to private schools, parochial schools, and to suburban public schools.

GOVERNMENT AND PRIVATE INTERESTS

The *system* that prevails in the United States, the United Kingdom, and other developed countries, and to a distressing degree in developing countries, is one in which government does not sufficiently mitigate the Hobbesian self-interest, but rather aligns public policy in a way that may tend to further harm the least advantaged. Holmes and Sunstein maintain that the U.S. system is one in which the government is employed and public costs are incurred primarily for the purpose of protecting property rights, the rights of those who already hold the vast majority of the wealth of the nation. They say that "protection of property rights is a government service that is delivered to those who currently own property, while being funded out of general revenues extracted from the public at large."[7] In short, taxes are principally used to protect the property rights of wealthy individuals.[8] Corroboration of the Holmes and Sunstein thesis is easily found in the daily press reports of many sectors of the economy, energy, banking, health care, insurance, etc. The right to the protection of private property is well established and is generously encouraged by government.

As Holmes and Sunstein point out, even though private propertied interests gain the lion's share of government advantage through subsidies, tax expenditures, tax deductions and credits, the propertied class argue most vehemently against social transfers to help the least advantaged. Bentham early identified the issue as an inherent aspect of not only government but of human nature in general: "It is the principle of self-preference. Man, from the very constitution of his nature, prefers his own happiness to that of all other sentient beings put together."[9] It was this self-preference that Adam Smith turned into an economic philosophy. Adam Smith's metaphor of the invisible hand, "By pursuing his own interest he frequently promotes that of the society more effectively than when he really intends to promote it,"[10] is the prevailing view for economic policy that bears heavily on the underclass.

This credo encapsulates the economic doctrine that, if unrestrained, feeds inequalities and gives incentive for self-preference. Smith's invisible hand has been exploited to harness government for the benefit of some and the misery of others. In fact, this doctrine has served as a convenient palliative for the upper class who wish to justify their disregard for the needs of the underclass. Niebuhr best explained that "man will always be imaginative enough to enlarge his needs beyond minimum requirements and selfish enough to feel the pressure of his needs more than the needs for others."[11] The system that produces government-insulated advantage for the upper class and perpetuates inadequate treatment for the underclass is thereby justified. The system that freezes into poverty a large segment of the population provides its own satisfaction by conjuring rationale that to the undiscerning eye appears to be rational and moral. That the poor are content and happy is convenient exculpation for the haves who object to social transfers and redistribution for the have-nots. John Kenneth Galbraith probably put it best in his essay on poverty when he satirically commented, "People are poor but happy. Why stir them up, cause discontent? They are loved by God, which is why there are so many of them."[12]

SEEDING POVERTY

The *system* described by Muhammed Yunus seeds poverty, growing the numbers of the underclass at a more rapid rate than can be extricated by education and other social transfers. Negative social and economic forces, aided and abetted by failed and inadequate government programs to assist the poor, combined with government stimuli favorable to the upper classes, increase their economic hegemony and persistently rejuvenate inequality. Such inertia is fed by government omissions and commissions that guarantee social and racial exclusion, such as *de facto* segregation of zoning laws, gated communities, regressive taxes, tax benefits for for-profit business enterprises, government graft, government deception in seizing upon ignorance in diversion and control of the collective interest by use of myth, superstition, and destructive religion. These combined forces, if unmitigated by government action, seed and cultivate poverty, pulling down and retaining a large segment of the population in poverty. The positive redistributive social transfers in the United States that can generally be classified in government programs of health, welfare, and education, as well as progressive taxation, have insufficient overall effect to reverse the down draft caused by market forces that are aided and abetted by government policy, or at least government omissions and failures (see Figure 3.1).

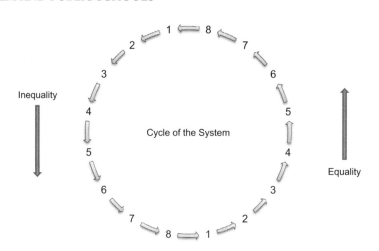

The System

Institutions: Seeding Poverty	Institutions: Remediating Poverty
Extractive Economic Systems	**Inclusive Economic Systems**
Extractive Political Systems	**Inclusive Political Systems**
1. Regressive Taxation	1. Progressive Taxation
2. Unregulated Capitalism	2. Income and Wealth Redistribution
3. Social Stratification	3. Social Mobility
4. Private Schools	4. Common Schools
5. Racial Segregation	5. Racial Integration
6. Myth and Superstition	6. Enlightenment and Reason

Figure 3.1 Applying Yunus' System: Institutions that Seed and Remediate Poverty

Note: This list is merely illustrative and by no means exhaustive.

WHY NATIONS FAIL

There are various theories as to why some nations are well-developed economically and others are underdeveloped, why the standard of living is high in some and low in others. Landes theorizes in his *The Wealth and Poverty of Nations*[13] that there are several interactive factors that have contributed to the great wealth disparity among nations, including a fertile condition for expansion of knowledge, access to trade routes, government ideology, exploitation of comparative economic advantage, weather proximity to the equator (hot climates have been slow to develop), and, importantly, the belief in modernity, progress, commitment to scientific and technological knowledge, and a rejection of myth, magic, superstition, and religious enthusiasm.

Jeffrey Sachs attributes the failure of nations to policies that contribute to inequality among its people and to imbalances between the private sector economy and government control of the economy. Sachs maintains that the most productive nations have well-established balances between government regulation and market capitalism. The most viable combination of the two he calls the "mixed economy" that has five core elements:

1. Efficient institutions for allocating society's economic resources,
2. Fairness and justice in the allocation of incomes,

3. Government redistribution policies that keep income and wealth in motion, reallocating resources from the rich to the poor,
4. Provision for "public goods" such as education, scientific research, infrastructure, and environmental regulation, and
5. Government policies that actively regulate private financial institutions for the direction and redirection via monetary and fiscal policy.[14]

With regard, specifically, to the prosperity of the United States, Sachs says that the most serious threat is the lack of investment in its human capital – the falling behind of "America's public schools."[15] In this regard Sachs warns that the intellectual capital, once the pride of America, has begun in recent years to be ceded to China and other countries that are investing in science and technology.[16]

INCLUSIVE VERSUS EXTRACTIVE SYSTEMS

A compelling argument as to the reasons for the vast wealth of some nations and the failed economies of others is explained by Acemoglu and Robinson in their book, *Why Nations Fail: The Origins of Power, Prosperity and Poverty.*[17] It is their conclusion that rich nations are characterized by economic institutions that shape fiscal incentives, provide incentives to become educated, stimulate new technologies, and, importantly, have at their foundations political institutions that ensure "stability and continuity."[18] It is their theory that prosperity arises with "inclusive economic institutions," that is, institutions that advance and protect economic activity and productivity. Among such institutions are property rights, due process of law, sanctity of contracts, appropriate government regulation, and an education system. Such

> inclusive economic institutions create inclusive markets which not only give people freedom to pursue the vocations of life that best suit their talents, but also provide a level playing field that gives them the opportunity to do so, and [i]nclusive economic institutions also pave the way for . . . the engines of prosperity: technology and education.[19]

Today, technological change requires education both for the innovator and the worker buttressed by economic institutions that have equitable foundations for the acquisition of knowledge and access to opportunity to engage the knowledge for technological advancement.[20]

On the other hand, nations that are poor and benighted are those with "extractive economic institutions." Extractive political institutions "concentrate power in the hands of a narrow elite and place few constraints on the exercise of this power."[21] The economic institutions in such countries enrich the few elites at the top of the economic ladder and systematically deny and block social mobility. In contrast, "inclusive economic institutions . . . create a more equitable distribution of resources, facilitating the persistence of inclusive political institutions."[22] A principal aspect of extractive systems is their failure to redistribute income and wealth, to minimize the scope of the common good, and to restrict the benefits of economic growth. The result is that economic growth is not self-generating and has little ability or possibility to gain internal stimulation.

Fiscal deprivation of education and a limited diffusion of knowledge are endemic to extractive systems. According to Acemoglu and Robinson, inclusive systems are by their nature "linked to technology – by education, skills, competencies, and know-how of the workforce, acquired in schools, at home, and on the job . . . It is education and skills of the workforce that generate the scientific knowledge upon which our progress is built."[23]

ABSOLUTE AND RELATIVE POVERTY

Any discussion of poverty and the system that harbors it needs to first define "poverty" and understand how it is measured. Most researchers see poverty in two forms: *absolute poverty* and *relative poverty*. *Absolute poverty* is the lack of basic subsistence.[24] Subsistence is that which is required to maintain life, the minimum necessary required to stay alive. At the bottom, those in absolute poverty do not live long, or at least as long as normal life expectancy. These are the ones who during the night live in cardboard boxes on the streets of Los Angeles or sleep over the sidewalk grates in winter of every big city in America or, until recently, have no health care. Many of these persons are older and die of hypothermia because they either have no homes or live in homes that are not heated.

Absolute poverty is defined differently from *relative poverty*. Alcock explains that *relative poverty* rests on a comparison between the "standard of living of people who are poor and the standard of living of other members of society who are not poor."[25] Atkinson observes that the War on Poverty in the United States in the Johnson years and a corresponding liberal concern in Britain in the same period came to an end in the 1980s when the "pendulum swung to the other extreme."[26] He said, "The Thatcher government in Britain and the Reagan administration in the United States . . . cut social security and other programs in a way"[27] that continues today to worsen the plight of low income groups (reference the Yunus system above). The Reagan, Bush, and Thatcher conservative governments resisted programs for people in relative poverty and argued that government should intercede only if people were starving or entirely without shelter. A good example of the Thatcher view was expressed in a Thatcherite study by Joseph and Sumption who asserted that "a family is poor only if it cannot afford to eat."[28]

Amartya Sen, a Nobel Laureate in economics, has attempted to define *poverty* in terms of capabilities. *Capability* to Sen is the ability to achieve. Presumably, Sen would say that government should attend to the basic needs of persons to acquire the capability to exist in society.[29] This existence is probably best explained in measurable terms by Townsend who has argued that the best assumption would be to relate poverty to *sufficiency*.[30] Accordingly, sufficiency to live should be measured in terms of the "average rise (or fall) in real incomes."[31] Townsend developed the most generally acceptable definition of poverty that comes close to combining the *absolute* and the *relative* measures:

> Individuals, families, and groups in the population can be said to be in poverty when they lack the resources to obtain the types of diet, participate in the activities and have the living conditions and amenities which are customary . . . in the societies to which they belong.[32]

This definition is normally reduced and quantified in terms of the income that an individual or a family would need to exist, and function[33] with some minimal level of dignity, in the society in which they find themselves.

Relative poverty defined with actual measurements of poverty that are amenable to use in government formulae normally include some dimension of income. The most common and acceptable approach was developed by Mollie Orshanksy in 1965 for the American Social Security Administration whereby she followed the concept originated by Ernst Engel, a nineteenth century German researcher, who analyzed family expenditure patterns and compared them to income levels. Engel found that as income rose, the proportion of income spent on necessities declined. Orshanksy adapted the Engel approach to determine that persons should be classified in poverty if they spent more than 30 percent of their income on food.[34] It is this measure or some close derivation thereof that is used by most countries to determine the numbers and percentages of persons and families who live in poverty, and is the basis for the income estimates used by the federal government to determine those school children who are entitled to free and reduced price lunches.[35]

CARAVAN OF INEQUALITY

The metaphor of the caravan has been used in the London press to describe the persistent rise of poverty in the United Kingdom.[36] As the trek across the desert proceeds, the poor stragglers increase in number and distance from the main body, thus, they are left farther behind. The caravan is an ironic but apt metaphor for the United States where the federal government titles a program "No Child Left Behind," while the overall "system" actually leaves large numbers of children behind as the caravan moves on. By most measures the numbers of poor stragglers have increased dramatically in the United States. Income separation has risen in both quantity and distance from the mean. In the United States today, the top 10 percent has 42 percent of the total income. Piketty points out that "Not since World War II have the top 10% of the earners in the U.S. had such a large share of total income."[37] The disparity in wealth is as striking as with income; in 2001, "the richest 1 percent of Americans held 32 percent of the nation's wealth,"[38] and Bush tax and social policies worsened the condition. More recently in 2012, Chrystia Freeland reported that 20 percent of Americans own 84 percent of the wealth of the nation.[39]

Emmanuel Saez has shown that the disparity between rich and poor, high income and low income families, was the greatest in 2012 than in any year dating back to 1917. The Great Recession of 2008–2012 resulted in a widening gap in an already widely disparate economic system in the United States.[40] In 2012 the income of families in the top decile held 50.4 percent of the total income of the nation, "higher than any other year since 1917 and even surpasses 1928, the peak of the stock market bubble in the 'roaring' 1920s."[41]

HIGH POVERTY RATES IN THE UNITED STATES

In the United Kingdom, the Blair government policy was to permit the rich to become as rich as they desired so long as the poor did not fall further behind. Though making some inroads on poverty, the Blair policy did not have the dramatic effect for the poor that was promised. *The Economist* noted that the richest have returned to the dominating income position that they held 60 years ago.[42] The nadir of the fortunes of the rich occurred just before Thatcher took office, and during her tenure the distance between rich and poor began to separate and has continued to increase ever since. The Cameron government has lately felt the dire effects of unemployment and poverty in the London riots of 2011.

Inequality within countries is most commonly measured using the Gini Coefficient. As explained in more detail later in this book, the Gini, named after an Italian mathematician, measures the proportion of income or wealth that is owned or received by various percentages of the population. If the percentage of income is precisely shared by the same percentage of the population, then the Gini Coefficient would be zero. In other words, if the bottom 10 percent of the population receives 10 percent of the income, the bottom 20 percent of the population receives 20 percent of the income, and if the population and income remains symmetrical to 100 percent, then you have perfect equalization. If, on the other hand, all the income belongs to the one richest person, then there is "perfect" inequality or a Gini of 1.0.

As Figure 3.2 indicates, the United States has grave income inequality. Among the 35 OECD countries, the United States ranks 31st, very low when compared to

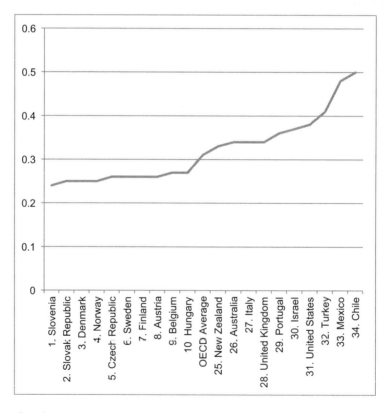

Figure 3.2 Gini Coefficient, Late 2000s

Source: Based on SOCIETY AT A GLANCE 2011: OECD SOCIAL INDICATORS. Provisional data from OECD Income Distribution and Poverty Database (www.oecd.org/els/social/inequality). http://dx.doi.org/10.1787/888932381874.

major economically developed European nations. The countries that are worse than the United States – Chile, Mexico, and Turkey – are not really of the caliber with which the United States has traditionally aspired to keep company. Chile is a bit of an embarrassment to OECD and probably should not even be included in its membership. Mexico and Turkey, though better than Chile, are not countries that the advanced nations wish to emulate.

The implications of these data for education are quite clear. The *system* in the United States that pulls people down into poverty and keeps them there is much more pronounced than in other developed countries. Problems of relative poverty in the United States cannot be ameliorated solely by education. To change such a disparate system requires not only equal educational opportunity but an array of social programs armed to redress poverty and the employment of a more progressive system of taxation. Disparities in income and wealth among individuals and families, of course, translate into greater poverty among the children who attend the public schools.

BOX 3.3

Static Society

Never has the accident of birth mattered more. If I am born to educated, supportive parents, my chances of doing well are totally different than if I were born to a single parent or abusive parents.

Source: James J. Heckman, winner of Nobel Prize in Economics, 2000, quoted in Alexander Stille, "Grounded by an Income Gap," *New York Times*, Nov. 15, 2001 as cited in James J. Heckman and Alan B. Kruger, *Inequality in America* (Cambridge, MA: The MIT Press, 2003), p. 11.

TRAPPED IN THE UNDERCLASS

The United States is not the land of opportunity that it was once believed to be. More than the citizens of Europe, the underclass in the United States tends to be stuck in poverty. Alesina and Glaeser have noted "the mobility of the poor is lower in the United States than in Europe . . . The American poor seem to be much more trapped than their European counterparts."[43] Society in the United States is both more disparate and fixed than in European countries. In the United States, social mobility is far more perceived than real. Thomas Piketty concludes in his book *Capital in the Twenty-First Century* that education, over time, in the United States has not increased social mobility: "the available data suggest that social mobility has been and remains lower in the United States than in Europe."[44] Krueger encapsulates the issue: "The United States has become a more polarized and static society, one in which children have become comparatively more disadvantaged."[45]

The United States as a rags-to-riches country has been much misrepresented, at least since 1835 when Alexis de Tocqueville wrote in *Democracy in America* that in the

United States, "wealth circulates with astonishing rapidity, and experience shows that it is sure to find two succeeding generations in full enjoyment of it."[46] This conclusion regarding intergenerational economic and social mobility in the United States may have been true 200 years ago, but the reality today is that prospects of children rising above the economic status of their parents are less likely in the United States than in most advanced countries. Corak, professor of economics at the University of Ottawa, in a 2013 *New York Times* article "Who's Your Daddy?" indicated that the large inequalities of incomes in the United States now tend to increase the chances that the children of the top 1.0 percent income group will themselves be in that same top group due to their parental investments in superior educational opportunities while the children of poor parents "have a higher chance of being stuck in poverty."[47] The unlikelihood of poor children moving up the economic and social ladder is now well documented. Gottschalk's studies have shown that "nearly half the people who were in the low income quintile in 1968 remained in the same quintile in 1991."[48] Thus, the saying first given wide publicity at the 1988 Democratic National Convention when Jim Hightower, Texas Agriculture Commissioner, famously said that George Bush, Sr., had been "born on third base [and] thought he had hit a triple." Such is equally applicable to many offspring of the more affluent families in America today.

Intergenerational mobility is influenced by many variables that can be roughly categorized into two groups: *first*, "human capital investment," including, most importantly, education and health, and *second,* "endowments," which include genetic capabilities, learning environment, skills, goals, "and other 'family commodities' acquired through belonging to a particular family culture."[49] Overall, a child's future income as an adult will depend on the returns to and the amount of her/his total attributes of human capital.[50] Thus, it is obvious that many factors are in play, and there is much room for intergenerational research; however, the evidence now extant is summed by Alesina and Glaeser, referred to above, in their book titled *Fighting Poverty in the United States and Europe: A World of Difference,*[51] which shows that the United States falls below Europe in prospects for the poor to improve their economic and social prospects. They conclude that in the United States, the poor are subject to more prolonged entrapment in the basement of the country's economic structure. Alesina and Glaeser show that, "the mobility of the poor is lower in the United States than in Europe . . . [and] the American poor seem to be much more trapped than their European counterparts."[52]

What this means is that the European systems of government, society, and economic condition "are much more generous to the poor relative to the U.S. level of generosity,"[53] and redistribution is more vigorous. As to causes, Alesina and Glaeser show that the United States has greater social fractionalization than European societies. The principal fractures are built primarily around "racial animosity" that militates against income "redistribution to the poor, who are disproportionately black."[54] We refer to fractionalization in more detail later in this book.

Longitudinal studies also indicate that the underclass in the United States has less upward mobility than the low income persons in most other developed countries.[55] Solon has determined that the correlation between earnings of fathers and sons is .40 or higher in the United States, whereas in Canada the correlation is .23, Germany, .34, and Sweden, .28.[56] This means that sons tend to more frequently track fathers in the United States rather than move up the economic scale. In other analyses, Solon showed that if one calculates the amount of income needed relative to basic survival, producing an income-to-needs ratio for both fathers and sons, the correlation between fathers and sons is .50. From this he concluded that society in the United States is much less mobile than previously thought, and sons are apt to be as poor as their fathers.[57] Not surprisingly, less mobility is found in the lowest income quartiles. Children who are unlucky enough to be born into the lowest quartile stand a 40 percent chance of remaining in that bottom quartile throughout their lives.[58]

MOBILITY AND RACE

Moreover, the immobility of the underclass of Americans has important racial overtones. Rodgers has shown that whites are more likely to escape poverty than are nonwhites.[59] She concluded that not only are nonwhites more likely to remain stuck in poverty, but that the overall perception of the United States as an upwardly mobile society is inaccurate. She observes that claims of social and economic mobility in the United States are exaggerated and that, in actuality, greater persistence in poverty across generations exists than is commonly believed.[60]

BOX 3.4

Race and the *System*

Racial prejudice is a major reason for the absence of a functioning system of welfare for the poor. A system of redistribution that helps the poor "requires a degree of mutual trust and understanding greater than that common in the United States. When trust is absent it is very hard to establish widespread support for a system . . ." You have to see your fellow humans as like you in order to support such a system. If you see them as a different kind of human being, following different kinds of motivation, perhaps as lazier than you, not as clever as you think you are, or as upright or as moral, then you may be less likely to back systems of mutual support. Seeing groups of others as generally lazy, immoral and stupid is usually social status related; it is part of seeing them as beneath you.

Source: Daniel Dorling, *Injustice: Why Social Inequality Persists* (Bristol, U.K.: Polity Press, 2011), pp. 186–187. See also: Paul Krugman, *The Conscience of a Liberal* (New York, NY: W. W. Norton, 2007), p. 178.

Keister concluded from her own simulations of social mobility and the review of other studies that poverty tends to be passed along from parents to children and that the belief of equality so revered in the United States falls far short of reality.[61] Keister verified the conclusion of Rodgers, showing that where escape from poverty does transpire, it happens in far greater percentages and with more favorable odds among whites than among nonwhites.[62]

CHILDREN IN POVERTY

The numbers and percentages of children in poverty correspond closely with the income disparities across age groups. Child poverty rates in the United States compared to other developed countries are reflective of the income disparity. As observed elsewhere in this book, the United States has a high percentage of children who live in poverty. The poverty rate which is a percentage of children in poverty under the age of 18 years, compared to the total population, finds the United States among OECD countries to rank very low. Figure 3.3 shows poverty rates for children relative to the total population. The *child poverty rates* shown here represent the "share of all children living in households with an equalized disposable income of less than 50% of the median for the total population." Children of ages less than 18 years are considered as sharing the household income earned by other members of the household.[63] Throughout the OECD countries the child poverty rate of all children was about 13 percent. The highest poverty rates were in Chile, Israel, Mexico, Turkey, and the United States, as one can see from Figure 3.3. It is, thus, better to be a child in an array of other countries than in the United States. Said another way, the United States is not a good place to be a child if one considers the odds. Children of sole parent households have a much higher chance of being in poverty.[64]

THE *SYSTEM* AND THE EDUCATIONAL OVERBURDEN

Berliner has pointed out that a primary problem facing the public schools of the United States is the daunting task of educating such great numbers of children in poverty.[65] He rightly argues that the public schools of the United States are blamed for achievement test shortcomings when the real culprit is not inefficient educational programs but rather the socioeconomic system that persistently drives children into poverty. Poverty places a costly educational overburden on the schools.[66] Berliner says that poverty is the "600 pound gorilla in the school house." It condemns the public schools to always play the lonely game of achievement test catch-up.[67]

The *system* that produces child poverty in the United States, cited above in this chapter, is a much stronger and a more formidable force than inadequately funded public schools are able to handle. The *system* described by Yunus is the same as that which was documented by Richard Rothstein in his book *Class and Schools,*[68] wherein he concluded that reform of public schools alone is insufficient to raise children out of poverty. He argued that the schools must be aided by a broader social and economic restructuring of redistribution mechanisms if there is to be effective remediation of child poverty. Public schools are the essential government mechanism for ameliorating poverty, and to underfund them is to undermine any overall governmental strategy to raise people out of poverty.[69] Keister and others[70] have well documented that education "markedly" increases the odds for "upward mobility."[71]

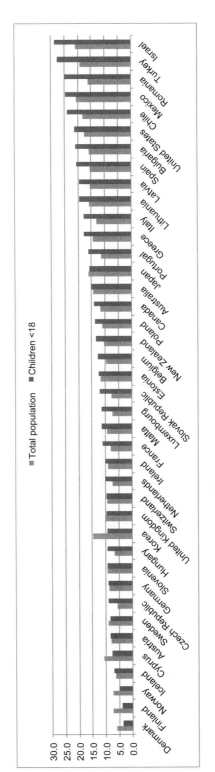

Figure 3.3 Poverty Rates for Children and the Total Population, 2010

Source: Based on OECD Family Database, www.oecd.org/social/family/database, CO2.2.A.

U.S. SAFETY NET SYSTEM

The U.S. *system* does have a "safety net" for families and children in poverty; however, it is at a much lower level than such provisions in most OECD countries. The total effect of federal assistance to families, including children, was to lift 40 million people out of poverty in 2011.[72] Figure 3.4 shows the positive effects of the social transfers, or safety net, that we now have in the United States. Social Security, the same type of program that Bismarck implemented in Germany in 1889,[73] lifted 26 million people out of poverty in the United States in 2011.[74] The federal Earned Income Tax Credit, EITC, kept 6.1 million Americans out of poverty in 2011, a number that included 3.1 million children.[75] EITC and the Child Tax Credit, CTC, raised 9.4 million people, including 5 million children, out of poverty in 2011.[76] Further, among these social transfers, SNAP (food stamps) kept 4.7 million people, including 2.1 million children, out of poverty. Food stamps kept 1.5 million children out of abject poverty.[77] Both EITC and SNAP are "means tested." In spite of these and other programs to assist families and children in poverty, substantial evidence indicates that the number of U.S. families with children who exist on cash income of less than $2 per person per day, the level used by the World Bank as the measure of absolute

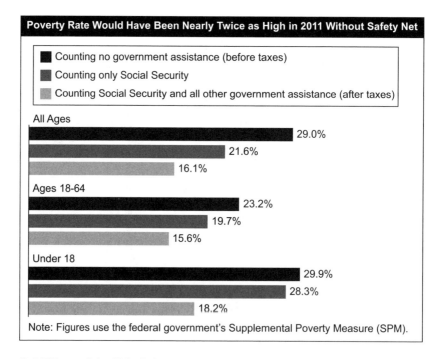

Figure 3.4 Effects of the U.S. Safety Net

Source: Center on Budget and Policy Priorities, "Various Supports for Low-Income Families Reduce Poverty and Have Long-Term Positive Effects on Families and Children," by Arloc Sherman, Danilo Trisi, and Sharon Parrott, July 30, 2013, www.cbpp.org/cms/?fa=view&id=3997, Figure 1. Reprinted by permission.

poverty for underdeveloped countries, has risen by 15 percent during the period from 1996 to 2011.[78] Also, in computing the extent of poverty in the United States, Shaefer and Edin have shown that extreme poverty increased between 1996 and 2011.[79] Thus, in the United States the main federal government transfers have steadily fallen behind and, while doing much to stem the effects of the *system* that drives people into poverty, the United States is losing ground.

INEQUALITY AND LOW TAX EFFORT

Moving people out of poverty requires that government establish programs that keep income and wealth from becoming permanently lodged with the upper classes. Taxation is the most effective redistributive mechanism for the movement and cycling of income and wealth in a nation's economic quiver. The collection of taxes and redistribution through social transfer programs and public education has traditionally been viewed as a critical part of social and economic systems of modern countries.

REDISTRIBUTION BY TAXATION

An analysis of taxation in the United States actually shows two important facts: Citizens of the United States do not bear heavy tax burdens when compared to their peers in other developed countries, and the taxes that are paid bear more heavily on the poor than on the rich. Taxation in the United States as a device to remediate poverty is much less effective as a redistributive mechanism than in European countries. Alesina and Glaeser clearly explain the situation: "Because of the smaller emphasis on policies that redistribute toward the poor, the bottom decile of the income ladder in the United States is less well off than the bottom decile in European countries. In America, poor are really poor."[80] Moreover, they show that the public policies to help those in poverty in the United States are much more limited than in Western Europe.[81] In this regard, federal and state policies in the United States are less likely to support social transfers, including expenditures for education, than are western European countries.

The overall redistributive effect is less favorable to the poor and those in poverty in the United States than in Europe, and Alesina and Glaeser show that there is greater pretax inequality in the United States than in Europe. Using the Gini Coefficient as their equality measure they concluded that "The Gini coefficient measured on pretax income for the United States is 38.5, whereas the average for European countries is 29.1, which means that Europe has lower before-tax inequality."[82]

Thus, the United States has greater pretax inequality than does Europe, and the redistributive effect of the system does not correct the inequalities. In Europe, government spending policy favors the poor to a greater degree than in the United States. The cycle for both pretax and post-tax equality in Europe is superior to that of the United States.

Not only does the United States have more pronounced inequality than countries in Europe and in most other OECD countries, in the United States tax effort to support governmental services is among the lowest in developed countries. McIntyre, in an analysis of the tax effort of 30 OECD countries, shows that in 2005 the overall total taxation in the United States, federal, state, and local, amounted to 25.8 percent of the gross domestic product.[83] This ranked the United States 28th with only Korea and Mexico registering lower overall tax effort.

In 2000, the tax effort for the United States was 29.6 percent, ranking it 27th among the 30 OECD countries. The relative position of the United States among the OECD countries was considerably less in 2005 than in earlier years, falling from 13th in 1970, to 27th in 2000, and then to 28th in 2005.[84] In their 2004 citizens' guide to taxation, Slemrod and Bakija noted that the tax cuts by the Bush government have lowered U.S. tax effort even further.[85]

THE *SYSTEM'S* LACK OF REDISTRIBUTION

The *system* of a country that drives people into poverty and has no economic or social dynamism to extricate them creates a static caste and class. Desirable government policies are such that redistribution occurs and the poor are given the opportunity to improve their condition. Two basic measures of the effectiveness and viability of redistribution are: (a) social spending as a percentage of the gross domestic product and (b) the extent and progressivity of the taxation structure. Later in this book we discuss the attributes of taxation; here, however, we can see that the United States does not compare favorably with other OECD countries as to social spending or in its use of its tax system to redistribute.

With regard to social spending, we see, using OECD data, that social spending in the United States is low compared to major developed nations of Europe. See Figure 3.5.

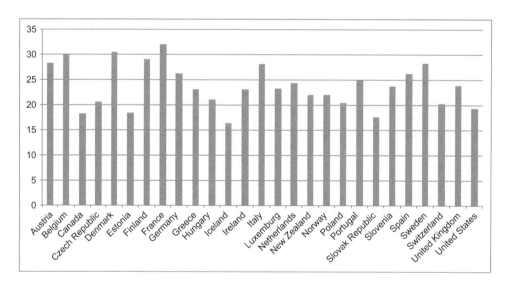

Figure 3.5 Total Public Social Expenditure as a Percentage of GDP, Selected OECD Countries

Source: Based on OECD Social Expenditure Statistics (database), November 16, 2012.

The 2012 Total Public Social Expenditure as a percentage of the gross domestic product is quite low in the United States, is less than the OECD composite total, and ranks near the bottom of OECD countries. Social expenditures are defined by OECD as comprised of cash benefits, direct in-kind provision of goods and services, and tax break with social purposes.[86] The three largest categories of social transfers are pensions, health, and income transfers to the working age population.[87] Social spending by government as a percentage of GDP is 19.4 percent compared to Denmark at 30.5 percent or Belgium at 30.0 percent; among the larger European countries, France is 32.1 percent, Germany is 26.3 percent, and the United Kingdom is 23.9 percent.

The other main part of the *system* concerns how much the government collects in its coffers as tax revenue which may be used in some part for social transfers to effectuate redistribution.

POVERTY AND EDUCATIONAL ACHIEVEMENT TESTS INTERNATIONAL

In recent years, the OECD has instituted the PISA international student performance project that compares test scores in mathematics, reading, science, and problem solving. PISA provides test score comparisons among the 30 OECD countries for each of these categories.

In the United States, these test scores have been used both to assist public school reform efforts and to deride the public schools as an institution. Comparisons of national test scores have generally placed the mean scores of students in the United States near the middle of the rank of the 30 OECD countries. However, Berliner has pointed out that the heterogeneity of the student population in the United States requires that the various ramifications and limitations of international comparisons be considered with appropriate *caveats*.[88] He said, "In a country as heterogeneous and as socially and ethnically segregated as ours, mean scores of achievement are not useful for understanding how we are really doing in international comparisons."[89]

In 2013 the National Center for Education Statistics (NCES) released a study that linked National Assessment of Education Progress (NAEP) test data for math and science with TIMSS (Trends in International Mathematics and Science Study) data. These data showed not only national averages, but test data for individual states in the United States. The TIMSS data were for 60 countries (2011), 500,000 students, including 20,000 students in the United States who attended over 1,000 schools.[90] The linked TIMSS and NAEP reports show that the states of Massachusetts, Vermont, Minnesota, New Hampshire, and a host of other states exceed most countries; however, several of the states, Alabama, Mississippi, Tennessee, Oklahoma, West Virginia, California, New Mexico, and Georgia score rather low. Yet, the average for the United States public schools exceeds Great Britain, Australia, and some of the educationally highly regarded countries of Norway, Sweden, New Zealand, and Australia, which do not have the degree of poverty overburden of the United States. From these data it would appear, at the macro levels, that most of the states in the United States are operating quite effective public school systems. This means, of course, that there is a wide disparity of educational opportunity in the United States, but importantly, by and large the schools of the United States are performing quite effectively in spite of high percentages of low income children and a substantial degree of racial segregation.

Racial prejudice in the United States has undeniably contributed to a system wherein African-American children receive, on average, a lower-quality education, especially in rural areas of the South and the core cities of the North.[91] Alesina and Glaeser show that states fractionalized by racial and ethnic diversity are less generous in overall social welfare spending.[92] They calculated that the effect of racial fractionalization on welfare spending constitutes about 50 percent of the gap between the United States and Europe.[93] In other words, the racial heterogeneity or diversity of the population in the United States is accompanied by a backlash in government policy that provides less support for minorities in the United States than in Europe.[94]

What this all means is that the public schools in the United States do a good job of educating white children, but that because of the failure of contingent government policies, Hispanic and African-American children tend to be left behind. Berliner's disaggregation for international comparisons for PISA scores shows that the differences between white students compared to Hispanic and African-American students are even more pronounced.[95]

The obvious conclusion that must be drawn is that public schools in the United States are very effective and efficient mechanisms for mass education when they are not overwhelmed with the extraordinary educational overburden of children who are poor and live in the harsh environment of poverty and are funded at levels sufficient to remediate the educational problems resulting from poverty. These two qualifying factors, poverty overburden and inadequate fiscal resources, appear to be at the heart of the mediocre performances of U.S. schools as measured by comparisons of international test scores.

SUMMARY

It is very difficult to believe that there is some intrinsic failure in the public schools of the United States, as an institution, in their inability to produce high achieving individuals if one considers the educational overburden borne by those schools. The *system* described by Yunus cycles into the schools such great numbers of poor children that international expenditure and test score comparisons are highly problematic; yet, even then, this shows a high degree of effectiveness of the U.S. public schools. This is particularly true if one considers the additional costs of educational programs necessary to extricate a generation of children from the doldrums of an immobile social and economic underclass. In the face of heavy educational needs and costs, gross spending comparisons are largely irrelevant as material measures of the success or failure of the nation's schools.

In sum, the *system* and its heavy weight of educational need due to poverty tends to add a perspective to international comparisons that is not revealed with simple per pupil or per capita data.

KEY TERMS

- The *system* and Muhammed Yunus
- Absolute poverty
- Seeding poverty
- Relative poverty
- Cycle of the system
- Caravan of inequality
- The Great Recession
- Extractive economic systems
- Extractive political systems
- Gini coefficient
- Inclusive economic systems

- Inclusive political systems
- Economic underclass
- Intergenerational mobility
- Social mobility
- Children in poverty
- Poverty rates
- Educational overburden
- U.S. safety net
- Redistribution of income
- Poverty and school achievement

NOTES

1. See: Thomas Hobbes, *Leviathan*, first published 1651 (New York: Penguin Classics, 1985), Part I, Chapter XIV, p. 189.
2. Muhammed Yunus, *The New York Times*, Sunday, December 8, 2006, p. 34.
3. D. Solomon, "Political Divide – Democrats' Risky Strategy: Trumpeting the Wealth Gap," *The Wall Street Journal*, October 2, 2006, pp. A1, A9.
4. Ibid.
5. Ibid.
6. B. Davis and J. Lyons, "Wealth of Nations, Globalizations Gains Come With a Price," *The Wall Street Journal*, May 24, 2007, pp. A1, A12.
7. S. Holmes and C. R. Sunstein, *The Cost of Rights: Why Liberty Depends on Taxes* (New York: W.W. Norton, 2000), p. 29.
8. Ibid., p. 25.
9. Jeremy Bentham, *Works of Jeremy Bentham*, Vol. X (New York: Russell and Russell, 1962), p. 80.
10. Adam Smith, *An Enquiry into the Nature and Causes of the Wealth of Nations*, ed. R. H. Campbell, A. S. Skinner, and W. B. Todd (1776; Oxford University Press, 1976), p. 75. See also: Adam Smith, *The Theory of Moral Sentiments*, ed. D. D. Raphael and A. L. Macfie (1759; Indianapolis: Liberty Fund, 1984), p. 184.
11. R. Niebuhr, *Moral Man and Immoral Society* (New York: Charles Scribner's Sons, 1932), p. 196.
12. J. K. Galbraith, *The Nature of Mass Poverty* (London: Penguin Books, 1979), p. 83.
13. David S. Landes, *The Wealth and Poverty of Nations: Why Some Are So Rich and Some So Poor* (New York: W. W. Norton & Company, 1999).
14. Jeffrey D. Sachs, *The Price of Civilization: Reawaking American Virtue and Prosperity* (New York: Random House Trade Paperbacks, 2012), pp. 28–29.
15. Ibid., p. 19.
16. Ibid.
17. Daron Acemoglu and James A. Robinson, *Why Nations Fail: The Origins of Power, Prosperity and Poverty* (London: Profile Books, Ltd., 2013), pp. 42–43.

18. Ibid.
19. Ibid., pp. 76–77.
20. Ibid., p. 78.
21. Ibid., p. 81.
22. Ibid., p. 82.
23. Ibid., p. 78.
24. P. Alcock, *Understanding Poverty*, 3rd edn. (Houndmills, U.K.: Palgrave MacMillan, 2006), p. 64.
25. Ibid., p. 65.
26. A. B. Atkinson, *The Economics of Inequality*, 2nd edn. (Oxford: Clarendon Press, 1983), p. 254.
27. Ibid.
28. K. Joseph and J. Sumption, *Equality* (London: John Murray Publishers, 1979). See Alcock, *op. cit.*, p. 65.
29. G. Hawthorn (Ed.), *Amartya Sen: The Standard of Living* (Cambridge: Cambridge University Press, 1987), pp. 24, 36.
30. P. Townsend, *Social Security Research: The Definition and Measurement of Poverty* (London: HMSO, 1979), p. 31. See Hawthorn, *op. cit.*, p. 17.
31. Townsend, *op. cit.*, p. 31.
32. Ibid.
33. Sen speaks of "functioning" as an achievement, or the wherewithal to achieve. Individual capabilities and functionings help define the condition of poverty. See: Hawthorn, *op. cit.*, p. 37.
34. Alcock, *op. cit.*, pp. 72–73.
35. See Chapter 18, Risk Management, Student Transportation, and School Food Services.
36. David Cameron, Tory leader in the House of Commons, adopted the caravan metaphor to emphasize the importance of ensuring that the poorest kept pace with the rest of the travelers. See "Income Inequality: Dividing Up the Cake," *The Economist*, March 31, 2007, p. 40.
37. T. Piketty, cited by A. Bernasek in "Income Inequality and Its Cost," *The New York Times*, June 25, 2006, p. 4.
38. Federal Reserve Survey of Consumer Wealth as reported in *The New York Times*, December 6, 2006. The percentage of wealth held by the top 1 percent excludes billionaires on the *Forbes Magazine* list who control another 2 percent of the nation's wealth.
39. C. Freeland, *Plutocrats: The Rise of the New Global Super Rich and the Fall of Everyone Else* (New York: Penguin Books, 2012).
40. Emmanuel Saez, "Striking It Richer: The Evolution of the Top Incomes in the United States" (updated with 2012 preliminary estimates), updated version of earlier article in *Pathways Magazine*, Stanford Center for the Study of Poverty and Inequality, Winter 2008, pp. 6–7.
41. Ibid.
42. "Income Inequality," March 31, 2007. p. 40.
43. A. Alesina and E. L. Glaeser, *Fighting Poverty in the U.S. and Europe: A World of Difference* (Oxford: Oxford University Press, 2002), p. 4.
44. Thomas Piketty, *Capital in the Twenty-First Century* (Cambridge, MA: Belknap Press, 2014), pp. 483–484.
45. A. B. Krueger, "Inequality, Too Much of a Good Thing," in *Inequality in America*, ed. J. J. Heckman and A. B. Krueger (Cambridge, MA: MIT Press, 2003), p. 11.
46. Alexis de Tocqueville, *Democracy in America* (London: Saunders and Otley, 1835); *Democracy in America* (New York: Doubleday, 1959), p. 53.
47. Miles Corak, "Who's Your Daddy?," *The New York Times*, Sunday, July 21, 2013, p. 7.

48. P. Gottschalk, as reported in Michel Bernstein and Schmitt, *The State of Working America, 1996–1999* (Armonk, NY: Sharpe, 1997) and as reported in J. Slemrod and John Bakija, *Taxing Ourselves: A Citizen's Guide to the Debate over Taxes*, Third Edition (Cambridge, MA: The MIT Press, 2004), p. 67.

49. Anders Björklund and Markus Jäntti, "Intergenerational Income Mobility and the Role of Family Background," in Wiemer Salverda, Brian Nolan, and Timothy M. Smeeding, *The Oxford Handbook of Economic Inequality* (Oxford: Oxford University Press, 2011), p. 493.

50. Ibid.

51. Alesina and Glaeser, *op. cit.*, p. 4.

52. Ibid.

53. Alberto F. Alesina, Edward L. Glaeser, and Bruce Sacerdote, "Why Doesn't the U.S. Have a European-Style Welfare State?," Harvard Institute of Economic Research Disc Paper No. 1933, November 8, 2001.

54. Ibid.

55. Ibid., p. 10.

56. G. Solon, "Cross-Country Difference in Intergenerational Earnings Mobility," *Journal of Economic Perspectives* 16(3) (2002), pp. 59–66.

57. G. Solon, "Intergenerational Economic Mobility in the United States," *American Economic Review* 82 (1992), pp. 393–408.

58. E. Peters, "Patterns of Intergenerational Mobility in Income and Earnings," *Review of Economics and Statistics* 24 (1992), pp. 456–466.

59. J. Rodgers, "An Empirical Study of Intergenerational Transmission of Poverty in the United States," *Social Science Quarterly* 76 (1995), pp. 178–194.

60. Ibid.

61. L. A. Keister, *Wealth in America: Trends in Wealth Inequality* (Cambridge: Cambridge University Press, 2000), p. 250.

62. Ibid., pp. 240–243.

63. OECD Family Database, www.oecd.org/social/family/database.

64. Ibid.

65. D.C. Berliner, "Our Impoverished View of Educational Reform," *TC Record*, August 2, 2005, p. 4.

66. Ibid.

67. Ibid., p. 4.

68. R. Rothstein, *Class and Schools: Using Social Economic and Educational Reform to Close the Black-White Achievement Gap* (Washington, DC: Economic Policy Institute, 2004).

69. Keister, *Wealth in America*, p. 245.

70. Krueger, *op. cit.*, p. 41.

71. Keister, *Wealth in America*, p. 245.

72. Arloc Sherman, Danilo Trisi, and Sharon Parrott, "Various Supports for Low-Income Families Reduce Poverty and Have Long-Term Positive Effects on Families and Children," Center on Budget and Policy Priorities, July 30, 2013, www.cbpp.org/cms/?fa=view&id=3997.

73. Jonathan Steinberg, *Bismarck: A Life* (Oxford: Oxford University Press, 2011), p. 417.

74. Ibid.

75. Ibid.

76. Ibid.

77. Ibid.

78. Ibid.

79. H. Luke Shaefer and Kathryn Edin, "Rising Extreme Poverty in the United States and the Response of Federal Means-Tested Transfer Programs," National Poverty Center, Working Paper 13–06, May 2013.

80. Alesina and Glaeser, *op. cit.*, p. 47.
81. Ibid., p. 1.
82. Ibid., p. 58.
83. R. McIntyre, *United States Remains One of the Least Taxed Industrial Countries* (Washington, DC: Citizens for Tax Justice, April 2007), p. 1.
84. Ibid., p. 2. Note: Data for 2005 are for 23 OECD countries with reported information plus the 2004 figures for the 7 other countries.
85. J. Slemrod and J. Bakija, *Taxing Ourselves: A Citizen's Guide to the Debate Over Taxes*, 3rd edn. (Cambridge, MA: MIT Press, 2004), p. 15.
86. "Social Expenditures," in OECD Factbook 2013, *Economic, Environmental and Social Statistics*, OECD Publishing.
87. Ibid.
88. Berliner, *op. cit.*, p. 11; citing: M. Lemke, A. Sen, E. Pahlke, L. Partelow, D. Miller, T. Williams, D. Kastberg, L. Jocelyn, *International Outcomes of Learning in Mathematics Literacy and Problem Solving: PISA 2003, Results from the U.S. Perspective*, NCES 2005–003 (Washington, DC: U.S. Department of Education, National Center for Education Statistics, 2004).
89. Ibid., Table III, p. 12.
90. National Center for Education Statistics: International Association for the Evaluation of Educational Achievement as reported in *Education Week*, October 30, 2013, *In Math and Science, Most States Surpass the Global Average*, www.edweek.org/links.
91. See L. F. Katz, "Comments," in *Inequality in America*, ed. J. J. Heckman and A. B. Krueger (Cambridge, MA: MIT Press, 2003), pp. 276–277.
92. Alesina and Glaeser, *op. cit.*, p. 134.
93. Ibid.
94. See also Keister, *op. cit.*, pp. 98–100.
95. Berliner, *op. cit.*, pp. 12–14.

CHAPTER 4

Equality of Opportunity: The Rationale

INTRODUCTION

In this chapter we discuss the inequality of opportunity that is visited on children in the public schools. Inequality of fiscal resources to fund the schools has to do with the fiscal capacity of the nation, the states, and the local school districts. Inequality is not new, having plagued the human condition throughout history. It is about distributive principles and how a good is divided among people.[1] It is about the principle of justice, to treat people as equals "except where there are relevant differences between them."[2] In that sense this chapter is about social justice; it concerns the "distribution of benefits and burdens" in society and especially the financial benefits of public schools among children.

INEQUALITY OF LIFE PROSPECTS

Inequality is now an unfortunate fact of life in the United States. The separation between rich and poor is among the worst of the developed countries. A social class of excluded persons, an *underclass*,[3] now exists in a perpetuating system of poverty. As Stiglitz points out in his book, *The Price of Inequality,* "inequality is, to a very large extent, the result of government policies that shape and direct the forces of technology and markets and broader social forces."[4] Stiglitz explains that "the United States has become a society in which there is less equality of opportunity, less than it was in the past, and less than in other countries."[5] As discussed earlier, the issue concerns the *system* of government that acts in concert with private markets to drive some persons to the bottom of the social and economic ladders and then fails to provide corrective or remedial mechanisms to extricate them. It is this reality that led Yunus, the Nobel Peace Prize winner in 2006, to posit that it is the *system* that creates poverty, not those who themselves are in poverty.

BOX 4.1

Equality of Opportunity and Equality of Result

Equality of Opportunity . . . is to allow persons to compete on equal terms for successes and rewards yet to come . . . [It] contemplates that some persons will succeed and others will not because of their differential characteristics . . . *Equality of result* accepts that persons will have done different things and have become different things and have become different from one another in any number of respects other than the one(s) in which they are to be equal . . . Equality of opportunity and equality of result refer to the substantive qualities that make persons different individuals one from another.

Source: Lloyd L. Weintraub, *Natural Laws and Justice* (Cambridge, MA: Harvard University Press, 1987), pp. 180–181.

Public schools are one of the most critical of governmental functions that can be engaged to help rectify inequality. The world's richest countries have well-educated people while the poorest countries have much lower school attendance rates and are plagued by a surfeit of ignorance. Countries with low levels of schooling have inordinately high levels of population growth and are particularly identifiable by the denial of educational opportunity to female children.[6] Nagel writes that, "We are so accustomed to great social and economic inequalities that it is easy to become dulled to them."[7] Such is the case both among and within nations. The problem is not the great spread between the relative levels of income and wealth, but rather that there is poverty at such great levels of pervasiveness that families are trapped at the bottom of the economic ladder, even in developed countries, with little hope of emerging, even over several generations. Poor families lack access to "cultural goods, quality health care, education, and other perquisites for upward social mobility."[8] Such inequality holds serious moral implications for government, but it also means, as Stiglitz says, that these are "unequal societies [that] do not function efficiently, and their economies are neither stable nor sustainable in the long term,"[9] and education is a condition precedent to an efficient economy. Stiglitz makes this quite clear that "When little money is invested in education for lack of revenues, schools do not produce the bright graduates that companies need to prosper."[10]

A tenet of public common schools is equality of educational opportunity. Society may rationally classify children in many ways in order to effectuate reasonable educational objectives; however, to create a system that classifies and confines children to educational disadvantage due to cultural, social, and economic conditions has no moral or ethical justification.

Inequality of educational opportunity is a term much confused by inaccurate discourse and poor definition. Many times inequality of funding is defended by oblique arguments that interject discussions of outputs, measures of efficiency, production functions, and achievement tests. We will say more about these later, but here it is important to note that the question of inequality of opportunity must be clarified and must not be confused with complex and poorly designed econometric analyses of outputs and outcomes. The state is responsible for the provision of substantial uniformity in courses, programs, facilities, and personnel, and above all, it must not create inequalities by state action that favors some children over others. In this regard it is helpful to speak in terms of equal prospects and equal resources rather than equal gain[11] or equal ends. The state is responsible to provide for equal prospects, but it cannot assure equal outcomes.

TYPES OF INEQUALITY

For our purposes, inequality in opportunity can best be explained by reference to four types of inequality:

1. *Luck*. The secret workings of providence: Some people are lucky and some just happen to be in the wrong place at the wrong time.
2. *Natural inequality*. Nature creates differences among all individuals: no two have the same native intelligence, height, weight. Some have inherent disabilities that

cause disadvantages in competing with others and may overlap with luck under certain circumstances.

3. *Environmental inequality.* The social and economic environment permits or creates inequalities, results of human interaction.
4. *State-created inequality.* The state itself by its own laws causes inequality of treatment.

Luck is an ever-present cause of inequality. Bad luck, of course, is undesirable and damaging to a person's prospects in life but cannot be avoided. Ronald Dworkin divides luck into two subcategories. The *first* is "brute luck" or the "birth lottery,"[12] the condition in which some people are born into circumstances of penury and poverty with no feasible means of escape. The *second* is "option luck" wherein a person is subjected to a condition from which she/he can be extricated by choices and decisions. With "option luck" the person may have the opportunity to insure her/himself against poverty and inequality and rise from the underclass. By definition, "brute luck" is unjust but can be ameliorated by positive government action, and even in some circumstances be almost neutralized, whereas "option luck" is not unjust.

Natural inequality is what nature decides, and it may overlap with Dworkin's explanations of luck. Perhaps Darwinian natural selection fits this category best. This is the base unfeeling and unseeing effects of Richard Dawkin's "selfish gene."[13]

The *third* type, *environmental inequality,* emanates from conditions that are largely caused by the interaction of human beings in cultural and social contexts. Environmental inequality is, as Nagel calls it, "negative equality of opportunity,"[14] where one suffers from discrimination such as racial, gender, ethnic, religious, or perhaps an educational disadvantage due to intergenerational effects.

The *fourth* type is best explained as *state-created* disadvantage. It is *state-created* inequality of resources to which much of the discussion of this book is directed. It is not nature created. This type is created by state action, state laws that, themselves, cause inequality.

Presently, widely disparate tax bases cause substantial variations in per-pupil revenue available in states and nations. Such disparities are state created. Historically, the public schools have been tied primarily to local property taxes with the potential availability of several smaller taxes for supplemental revenue. For most of the less fiscally able school districts, supplemental property tax revenues have remained either unavailable or negligible in yield. Where nonproperty tax resources are available the disparities in tax bases and yields usually do little to create greater equality. Therefore, reliance on local taxation to support the schools has usually had a detrimental effect on the equality of school funding. This reliance has contributed to the problems of a system that has both inadequate resources and an unequal distribution of those limited resources. Because of these disparities in fiscal capacity, most school finance systems require taxpayers in the less fiscally able school districts to exert several times more tax effort than that of the more fiscally able districts if they are to provide equal resources for their children. Reform has been glacial, and students in the poor school districts remain at a substantial educational disadvantage because of underfinanced educational programs and services. This common variety of inequality emanating from unequal capacity is largely due to the failure of governments to take measures to address tendencies of human beings to act primarily in their own self-interest.

THE MORALITY OF EQUALITY

Problems of inequality will always be a political question of paramount importance to states and nations. How much of the wealth is to be shared and how much is to be held aside by individuals for their own use is of profound importance to all societies. The issue though is not merely theoretical or philosophical, but is one of the most persistent and pervasive moral questions with which a state or nation must wrestle. Rousseau best and most succinctly captured the essence of inequality and its origins in his famous first line of *A Discourse on the Origin of Inequality*, "The first man who, having enclosed a piece of ground, bethought himself of saying 'This is mine,' and found people simple enough to believe him, was the real founder of civil society."[15] From this beginning, inequality proceeded and has been justified in various ways, by both individual acquiescence and laws of civil society. The economic interests encompassing property and possessions created the conditions of inequality that still persist today. In the vein of Rousseau's *Discourse*, Niebuhr observed that the inequality of privilege that we experience in our society today is due chiefly to disproportion of power, and "the power which creates privilege need not be economic but usually is."[16] As this economic and propertied power influences government, the conditions of inequality have become exacerbated and woven into the fabric of the social, economic, and political systems.

BOX 4.2

The Bosom of Equality

Public education, therefore, under regulations prescribed by the government, and under magistrates established by the Sovereign, is one of the fundamental rules of popular or legitimate government. If children are brought up in common in the bosom of equality; if they are imbued with the laws of the State and the precepts of the general will; if they are taught to respect these above all things; if they are surrounded by examples and objects which constantly remind them of the tender mother who nourishes them, of the loves she bears them, of the inestimable benefits they receive from her, and of the return they owe her, we cannot doubt that they will learn to cherish one another mutually as brothers, to will nothing contrary to the will of society, to substitute the actions of men and citizens for the futile and vain babbling of sophists, and to become in time defenders and fathers of the country of which they will have been so long the children.

Source: Jean Jacques Rousseau, *A Discourse of Political Economy,* 1758, translation and introduction by G.D.H. Cole, in *The Social Contract and Discourses* (London: J.M. Dent & Sons, 1973), p. 149.

OF CAKES AND SHARES

The basic premise of egalitarian philosophy is that similar cases should be accorded similar treatment.[17] Persons should be treated in a uniform way unless there is sufficient reason not to do so.[18] Departure from equality requires reasons and justification. Isaiah Berlin explains it simplest and best: "society in which every member holds an equal quantity of property needs no justification; only a society in which property is unequal needs it."[19]

BOX 4.3

Of Cakes and Shares

If I have a cake and there are ten persons among whom I wish to divide it, then if I give exactly one tenth to each, this will not, at any rate, automatically call for justification; whereas if I depart from this principle of equal division, I am expected to produce a special reason.

Source: Isaiah Berlin, "Equality," *Concepts and Categories* (New York: Viking Press, 1978), p. 84.

One can see how readily this aphorism applies to public school finance and most notably to the school finance litigation discussed earlier. Legislatures would not be challenged and required to justify allocation of state and local revenues among school districts if fund distributions were equal. Explanation is only required when funds are distributed unequally. What is the reason for the state giving twice the resources to some children for their education as for others?

SELF-EVIDENT TRUTH

The concept of equality as a basic tenet of human interaction found little basis in political reality until the philosophers of the new American republic accorded it the status of a "self-evident truth." It was not that the idea was not known, it had been discussed by Aristotle and *The Enlightenment* philosophers; but any modern notion of practicality or applicability had not been advanced to the level of governmental consideration until the Declaration of Independence, the American Revolution, and later the French Revolution.

BOX 4.4

Equality in America

America differed from Europe: Differences of wealth and rank and social style it did indeed have – but these were not built on laws of privilege. No one claimed that colonial society was composed, like that of Europe, of different "estates" or upon legally implanted hierarchy of rights. In America, as John Adams remarked, there was "but one order."

Source: J.R. Pole, *The Pursuit of Equality in American History* (Berkeley: University of California Press, 1978), p. 36.

Commager, in his classic work *The Empire of Reason*, discusses "how Europe imagined and America realized *The Enlightenment*,"[20] and he explains how governmental leaders, statesmen, bishops, judges, generals, and admirals in the old world were chosen from the upper one-tenth of the population, a social and economic elite, on the basis of birth, wealth, or religion.[21] The lower classes of Europeans dreamed of rectifying this system of privilege, but only in America was that dream to come to fruition. It was such antecedents of European inequality that caused Jefferson to so stoutly argue for universal public instruction. Jefferson maintained that through education, those individuals possessing talent and merit, not those of birth and social advantage, could rise to govern the new republic. Jefferson most directly related the ideal of equality to the desirability of public school in his education plan for Virginia in 1779 in which he proposed that "By that part of our plan which prescribes the selection of youths of genius from among the classes of poor, we hope to avail the State of those talents which Nature has sown as liberally among the poor as among the rich, but which perish without use."[22]

SELF-INTEREST

Equality and liberty must be delicately balanced in such a way that government fosters equality but does not dampen the competitive spirit of individuals. Equality and economic freedom are ultimately intermingled and highly interdependent. The role of the state in fostering care, protection, and equality as balanced against individual freedom and liberty forms the primary ground on which political philosophy is argued and tested at the polls, in the legislatures, and in the courts of the nation. Few can argue against man's innate propensities to help himself in preference to others. "What man," said Helvetius, " . . . if with a scrupulous attention he searches all the recesses of his soul, will not perceive that his virtues and vices are wholly owing to different modifications of personal interests?"[23]

BOX 4.5

The Invisible Hand

Adam Smith's historic reference was to the innate guiding force of man's self-interest that drives economic development. The concept, introduced by Adam Smith in *The Wealth of Nations* in 1776, described the paradox that society is made better off economically if government does not interfere with the private pursuit of self-interest because by each person pursuing his own interest the good of all society is enhanced. The whole process is guided by a benevolent invisible hand.

ADAM SMITH AND THE INVISIBLE HAND

Adam Smith, cited and discussed earlier, described this self-interest in terms of the "invisible hand" to advance commerce, economic growth, and man's general betterment. As noted previously, it was Smith's view that an unimpeded pursuit of individual self-interest would ultimately improve society, generally.[24]

BOX 4.6

Political Democracy and Market Capitalism

Political democracy and market capitalism exist in an uneasy marriage. The democratic state proclaims equality. The market generates inequality. The ideological champions of the market *celebrate* inequality. In the *civic realm*, the first democratic freedom is citizenship – membership in a political community, which implies security and an equal voice in governance. In the *market realm*, the first freedom is freedom of exchange – the liberty to achieve personal economic success or failure. Absolute freedom of exchange thus creates extremes of social inequality. By market standards, inequality is not a regrettable necessity, but a virtue. In theory, the dynamism of the market and its unequal outcomes are logically inseparable. And the dynamism supposedly makes up for the social imbalance.

The conflict between polity and market is most acute with respect to the distribution of wealth and income. In a democracy, the rights of citizenship are supposed to be equally distributed and broadly diffused. They necessarily exist in a realm beyond the reach of personal economic differences. But the gross inequality generated by the market, at some point, compromises the ideal of political equality for citizens who cannot enjoy an equal political voice when they live at vastly different standards of material security. At some point, unequal wealth purchases unequal influence.

Source: Robert Kuttner, *The Economic Illusion, False Choices Between Prosperity and Social Justice* (Philadelphia: University of Pennsylvania Press, 1984), pp. 10–11 [emphasis added].

Smith's great thesis provided a salve and justification for those who wanted to help only themselves, but felt they needed some moral justification. To learn that "in pursuing his own interest, the individual pursues that of the community, and in promoting the interest of the community he promotes his own"[25] was a philosophy that led to the altogether satisfying conclusion of opponents of public common schools that by pursuing one's own individual self-interest the needs of society are resolved.

HARMONY OF INTERESTS

A "harmony of interests" was thus produced that strengthened all, yet no one needed to be particularly and directly concerned with the common good or the good of the whole. It was contribution enough to be concerned only with one's self.

By this rationale, proponents of unfettered laissez-faire economics claim that their policies of self-interest will ultimately lead to greater equality as the benefits "trickle down" to the less able. Kuttner, wryly commenting on this economic justification for the lack of governmental attention to inequalities in society, observed: "Thus do the defenders of inequality seek legitimacy for their approach by invoking the egalitarian ideal."[26] Sociologist Philip Green terms this logical twist "the homage that vice self-confidently pays to virtue."

SOCIAL DARWINISM

This philosophical justification for economic and social inequality found reinforcement in Darwin's *The Origin of Species*, 1859, for after Darwin, survival of the fittest, the stronger, and more privileged could justify their advantages by resorting to the biological laws of nature, the "perpetual struggle for life and the elimination of the unfit."[27] The struggle for existence among organisms leads to a strengthened species. Social organisms that gained strength and trod down the weak were justified in this biological context. This philosophy, of course, had a most attractive and natural appeal to nations that sought hegemony over their less powerful neighbors. At the turn of the century, Social Darwinism provided a satisfying justification for European control and colonization of Africa and Asia. "The harmony of interests was established through the sacrifice of 'unfit' Africans and Asians."[28] It later provided much of the philosophical justification for the aggressions that caused the two World Wars.

The rationale was conveniently clear that inequality was a fact of life or even a plan of nature, and if it was *ipso facto* natural then it was morally justifiable. Accordingly, not only was inequality justified, it was essential if stronger human beings, social systems, and nations were to progress and advance. "The doctrine of progress through elimination of unfit nations seemed a fair corollary of the doctrine of progress through the elimination of unfit individuals."[29]

It is this kind of reasoning that we too often discover is used to justify inequality of educational opportunity between rich and poor nations, rich and poor states, and rich and poor school districts. Yet even today a strong consciousness of equality lies at the heart of many of our public policy considerations, though the arguments are replayed with each generation.

MORAL MAN

Several contemporary moral and legal philosophers give cogent arguments against various forms of inequality. It is Niebuhr's thesis that man is innately moral, but his actions are corrupted by society. Niebuhr, in his *Moral Man and Immoral Society*,[30] observed the fallacies of the many justifications for inequalities by the privileged in society, and he identified the "specious proofs" that they used to justify their advantaged positions. Most prominent among the justifications for inequality is faulting the victim. This has been practiced in different ways, but usually culminates in a rationale that attempts to give moral superiority to the leisured classes and philosophical justification for disparities in opportunity. Thus, the moral justification for inequality may be found in the assertion that advantage is desirable because it emanates from thrift and good habits. It is said that the rich are virtuous because they are diligent and frugal, while the disadvantaged are deserving of their plight because they are lazy and improvident.[31] Niebuhr cites a typical puritanical justification for inequality espoused by Timothy Dwight, early president of Yale and a champion and leader of the New England upper class. Dwight said that the poor and underprivileged had caused their own misfortune because they are "too idle, too talkative, too passionate, too prodigal, and too shiftless to acquire either property or character."[32]

It takes an innate counterbalance of human character to prevent a thesis such as the one proffered by Dwight to prevail. Equality has its own visceral appeal to most people. The general goal of equality is that each person should have no less than an equal share of the community's resources.[33] Equality of treatment is *prima facie*[34] just as Rawls who observes that, "injustice, then, is simply inequalities that are not to the benefit of all."[35] Inequality is only morally justified if it benefits all or if the distribution is made in favor of the least advantaged.[36]

The theory of equality of treatment by government is based on the social contract theories of Plato, Hobbes, and Rousseau. Plato's contract of citizenship between the citizen and the state calls implicitly for equal treatment of citizens. Where there are obligations and responsibilities as well as benefits and detriments under a social contract, the citizen does not contemplate receiving less or inferior treatment from the state; and, in theory, one who does not receive a fair share is justified in withdrawing from the social contract.[37] Both Hobbes and Rousseau recognized this contract, but they differed as to whether the citizen can withdraw if maltreated. Hobbes believed that the citizen is stuck with the relationship and Rousseau argued that everyone had a right to withdraw, even by revolution if necessary.

BOX 4.7

Equally Undeserving

Although we come unto the world at different times, and somebody was always there before us, we enter in the same way, without any more right to the bounty of nature than anyone else who sees daylight for the first time. It therefore seems sensible to ask how the world should be carved up among people who are equally able but equally underserving . . . The presumption must therefore be that people are entitled to equally valuable shares, unless some difference between them justifies a departure from equality.

Source: Eric Rakowshi, *Equal Justice* (Oxford: Clarendon Paperbacks, 1993), p. 65.

EQUAL SHARES AND FAIR SHARES

Equal shares may not always be fair shares. Justice may not be done by giving everyone equal amounts. Equity is roughly equivalent to justice, but equality may not necessarily result in equity.[38]

Strict equality requires that equals be treated as equals, but equity, fairness, or justice may require that unequals be treated as unequals. Raphael explains that *"fair shares* depend on merit, need, and capacity, which of course are not equally distributed."[39] This view emanates originally from Aristotle who pointed out that equity is a matter of proportionate distribution and is not confined to strict equality.[40] "Equity allows, or rather, requires discrimination by reference to morally relevant differences and forbids discrimination in the absence of such difference."[41] "The rule is to treat like cases alike and unlike cases differently."[42] It is fair to discriminate in favor of the needy, but unfair and inequitable to discriminate in favor of the privileged and advantaged. This rule is explained in more detail regarding state school funding formulas in a later chapter of this book.

RELEVANT DIFFERENCES

Only morally relevant differences should be taken into account in departure from strict equality. Where legislative allocations of funds for public schools often go astray is the provision of greater resources for *irrelevant* differences. Differences in allocations among children based on their economic, social, or family conditions may be relevant to good education. Similarly, natural learning capacities or physical disabilities may be relevant criteria for departure from mathematical equality in the distribution of resources. Property wealth, however, is not relevant to educational needs. The state cannot remain within the bounds of equity and justice while providing more funding to favored children in more affluent school districts.

What is relevant and legitimate becomes the primary issue. Can we give more to the most advantaged, to the intellectually gifted? The school finance cases require that the legislature give reasons as to relevancy. The danger, of course, lies in the justifications of relevancy by those who seek to retain their advantages. As noted earlier, Niebuhr has observed that human kind is very adept in conjuring justifications for inequality and generating specious proofs to justify social and economic privilege. Representatives and residents of affluent communities and school districts have proven both adept and creative in justifying their financial preeminence. Niebuhr says that,

> Man will always be imaginative enough to enlarge his needs beyond minimum requirements and selfish enough to feel the pressure of his needs more than the needs of others.[43]

Examples of imaginative defenses by affluent school districts in attempting to give relevancy to irrelevant factors supporting discrimination, and to justify and explain their privilege in having greater financial resources, include: (1) the sanctity of insularity; we have a separate community and it is our property wealth that produces the advantage and we get to keep it; (2) it is not a state system, it is a local one; (3) the children in rich districts have higher aspirations and thus should have a more enriched curriculum; (4) the costs of living are greater in our district; therefore, we need more money than others; (5) ours should be a *lighthouse* district that will illuminate the way for the others to follow; (6) local control is our right, and state efforts toward equality will erode that right; and (7) the poor districts in which others live are less efficient and will merely waste additional resources. The inventiveness and ingenuity of those justifying advantage is almost endless.

But possibly the most common response of the privileged is to blame the victim and argue that those in poor school districts do not try hard enough, have little regard for education, and put forth lower tax effort to support their own schools than do persons from the more affluent school districts. Ryan has said that "we cannot comfortably believe that we are the cause of that which is problematic to us; therefore, we are almost compelled to believe that they – the problematic ones – are the cause" of the problem.[44] Educationally relevant criteria justifying departure from fairness thus become difficult to discern. What is relevant to achieve equity and is not merely an excuse to justify inequality? This is a complex dilemma made more difficult by the clouded lenses of self-interest through which the problem is most frequently observed.

THE LEAST ADVANTAGED

John Rawls' *A Theory of Justice*[45] (cited above) is commonly acknowledged as the pre-eminent work of political and legal theory of this century and may rank him with the great political philosophers of earlier eras. Nozick, a highly regarded political philosopher, has said that Rawls'

> *A Theory of Justice* is a powerful, deep, subtle, wide-ranging, systematic work in political and moral philosophy which has not seen its like since the writings of John Stuart Mill, if then. It is a fountain of illuminating ideas, integrated together into a lovely whole. Political philosophers now must either work within Rawls' theory or explain why not.[46]

Rawls maintains that natural duties among moral persons require mutual respect and treatment. Accordingly, justice presumes equality. This is to say that among human beings, "none are entitled to preferential treatment in the absence of compelling reasons"[47] to justify inequality. Importantly, Rawls maintains that "the burden of proof favors equality: it defines a procedural presumption that persons are to be treated alike."[48] Where the rationale is not sufficient to support a clear finding that deviation from strict equal division of goods will foster greater equity and justice, then the departure is not justified. Departures from equal treatment must be defended and "judged impartially by the same system of principles that hold for all."[49] The deviation that is permissible may only be for the needs of the least advantaged.

BOX 4.8

Rawls' Principle of Fair Equality of Opportunity

Assuming that there is a distribution of natural assets, those who are at the same level of talent and ability, and have the same willingness to use them, should have the same prospects of success regardless of their initial place in the social system, that is, irrespective of the income class into which they are born. In all sectors of society there should be roughly equal prospects of culture and achievement for everyone similarly motivated and endowed. The expectations of those with the same abilities and aspirations should not be affected by their social class.

Source: John Rawls, *A Theory of Justice* (Cambridge, MA: Harvard University Press, 1971), p. 302.

It is in this regard that Rawls' *difference principle* is propounded; his general conception is that,

> All social primary goods – liberty and opportunity, income and wealth, and the bases of self-respect – are to be distributed equally unless an unequal distribution of any or all of these goods is to the advantage of the least favored.[50]

His principle encompasses education, and he rejects the idea that at times the whole society may benefit from certain restrictions on equality of opportunity.[51] He places a priority on fair opportunity and assumes that all will benefit from particularized attention to the least advantaged. Further, he argues that equality "requires equal life prospects in all sectors of society for those similarly endowed and motivated."[52] While he indicates that fair opportunity may require greater assistance to children of deprived circumstances, if the family is a barrier to equal prospects, he acknowledges that equal outcomes cannot be assured.[53] Thus, Rawls advances and justifies the concept of *need* in education. Social justice requires that each person be affected by fiscal distribution based on neediness.[54] The principles of justice and equality have a symbiotic relationship with the concept of educational need. Miller reasons that the relationship is based "first, in the fact that the equal satisfaction of needs is the most important element in bringing about full equality; and second is the fact that the premise which underlies distribution according to need also underlies equality in the broader sense."[55]

BOX 4.9

The Principle of Needs

Because people have varied needs . . . physical resources such as food, medicine, and *education* should not be assigned in equal quantities to each man, but in different proportions to different people, according to their peculiar characteristics. No serious egalitarian has thought otherwise.

David Miller, *Social Justice*

INEQUALITY AMONG COUNTRIES

The hope and optimism that the income and wealth gaps between rich and poor nations will narrow over the decades, the convergence theory, has not come to fruition, as we have seen the disparity actually widen in recent years. Seligson observed in 2008 that the disparities between rich countries and poor countries, in both income and wealth, increased in the 50 years between 1950 and 2001, and the trend continues.[56] From 1960 to 2005 the data show, unfortunately, that poor countries are not closing the income gap with rich countries. As Passé-Smith bleakly writes, "the absolute gap . . . seems to suggest that no matter how well countries perform economically, they can never catch up to the rich."[57] Passé-Smith, however, qualifies his statement by pointing out that some underdeveloped countries could, possibly, close the gap with certain high-income countries over a period of many years; for example, China could close the gap in 64 years, but it would take Chile 511 years and Pakistan 1,152 years and India a practically insurmountable 1,272 years to close the gap.[58] This picture of possible gap closing of incomes between countries is probably accurate since the absolute gap between rich and nonrich countries has not closed but has become worse in recent years.[59] More about inequality of nations will be found in later sections of this book.

As to causes for continuing inequality, factors have to do with overpopulation, ongoing debt, technological change, etc. However, there is general agreement that education intersects with all other reasons and that knowledge is the ultimate foundation of progress, income, and wealth—the cornerstone, according to Harrison,[60] who explains why Latin American and African countries have lagged and are not likely to make significant strides has to do with the "society's world view" that is undergirded by the "availability of educational opportunities"[61] by means of an "effective and accessible education system: one that provides basic intellectual and vocational tools, nurtures inquisitiveness, critical faculties, dissent and creativity; and equips people to solve problems."[62] And at its root is the "idea of equality," a basic tenet of the tradition and culture that requires a *mindset* of a people that embraces the "idea of equality."[63]

Despite a general awareness that education is important to economic development and individual attainment, the underdeveloped countries of the world continue to fall farther behind the developed countries in educational investments. The disparity in educational opportunity between the *haves* and the *have-nots* becomes greater yearly and there is apparently no end in sight.

Coombs in his perceptive analysis entitled *The World Crisis in Education* has shown that the great diversity in ability and aspiration for education between the rich and poor nations of the world has manifested itself in a crisis of major proportions.[64] He writes that "disparity – taking many forms – between educational systems and their environments is the essence of the worldwide crisis in education."[65] These disparities are evidenced by inequalities that may be subdivided into four categories: *First*, there is a great gulf in the level of aspiration for education; those with little education have less aspiration, and a downward spiral of low aspiration feeding poor educational quality drives people toward poverty. *Second*, there is a scarcity of financial resources and wide variances in fiscal capacity for education. The countries with less education have lower wealth and income and are therefore able to pay for only inferior education. *Third*, an inherent intellectual momentum exists in countries that have more educated people than in countries with underdeveloped human capital. People in better developed countries are more efficient as both producers and consumers, and the result is a separation between rich and poor that increases geometrically. *Fourth,* the societies themselves have built-in features that either enhance or retard the effects of investment in education. "[T]he heavy weight of traditional attitudes, religious customs, prestige and incentive patterns, and structures – has blocked them from making the optimum use of education and of educated manpower to foster national development."[66] We have all observed how the society of Japan values and enhances educational achievement and how the opposite conditions exist in underdeveloped countries.

Disparities and inequalities between underdeveloped and developed countries may be viewed in yet another way. Coombs notes that the disparities are most notably a result of three types of inequalities that must be overcome in order to provide equality of educational opportunity. All three are associated with financial ability and economic circumstance, but each highlights an overlay of inequality that is readily discernible. They are (1) geographic disparities, (2) sex disparities, and (3) socioeconomic disparities.

First, the geographic disparities are, of course, obvious between developed and underdeveloped countries, but within countries the difference may be as great. A common earmark of an underdeveloped country is internal inequality, particularly between urban and rural areas. Most urban areas have relatively better education than the usually benighted rural areas.

Second, disparities in the way the sexes are treated create inequalities of opportunity that are often the products of primitive social mores and religious beliefs, both fostering subjugation of women to near or actual abject poverty. The World Bank has shown in an interesting but not firmly conclusive analysis that there is a strong correlation between economic development, civil liberties, and female education. The World Bank says that, "controlling for income growth and regional effects, liberties appear to be strongly and positively associated with measures of welfare improvements such as women's education, overall education, and infant mortality declines."[67]

The World Bank, in its new strategy statement for 2020 titled *Learning for All,* has observed that the poorest countries in the world have two main characteristics, large percentages of out-of-school children and very high ratios of girls who are not in school. Though these percentages are improving, there still remain daunting numbers of uneducated in developing countries.[68]

As Jeffrey Sachs correctly points out in his book, *The End of Poverty,*[69] improving the education of girls is one of the most important, if not the most important, element for economic development of countries. Overpopulation is at the base of most of the world's problems. Most of the developed world has experienced decline in fertility rates in recent years.[70] In the developed world where girls are well educated, births per woman are quite low; but in poor countries where girls are deprived of public education, births per woman remain very high. In such circumstances, the population of the poorer countries doubles every generation, and the detrimental effect on economies and the environment is proportional. In those poorest of countries where fertility rates have fallen, the one factor that is most apparent is the education of females. Sachs says that "girls' literacy has translated rapidly and dramatically into the desire for fewer children,"[71] with the result that women are empowered by their education to more easily join the labor force and increase their earning power and options in their livelihood.

Third, disparities associated with socioeconomic conditions emanate from social caste and class of various types, including conditions of economic incapacity associated with property wealth and income, and racial and ethnic differences.[72] These, of course, underlie geographic and sex inequalities discussed above and are pervasive. Advantages of social status and money are usually associated with better educated parents who themselves had the advantage of privileged treatment. The more underdeveloped are the countries, the greater the likelihood that the inequalities will be pronounced. Coombs notes that many studies suggest "that children whose parents are at the bottom of the socioeconomic hierarchy are not as inclined to seek or gain access to available educational facilities as are children from families located at the middle or top of the hierarchy."[73]

This is, of course, no great revelation as we have observed the positive effects of parental advantage on the educational attainment in not only underdeveloped countries, but in the United States as well.

INEQUALITY WITHIN COUNTRIES

The United States ranks near the bottom of the OECD countries in income inequality among its people. The disparities within countries were illustrated in Chapter 3 using the Gini Coefficient as a statistical measure. Emmanual Saez and Thomas Piketty, economists from the University of California, Berkeley, and the University of Paris, document, further, the rise of inequality in the United States.[74] As shown in Figure 4.1,

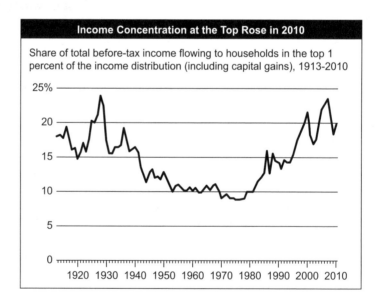

Figure 4.1 Income Concentration at the Top Increased in 2010

Source: Center on Budget and Policy Priorities, "Incomes at the Top Rebounded in First Full Year of Recovery, New Analysis of Tax Data Shows Top 1 Percent's Share of Income Starting to Rise Again," by Hannah Shaw and Chad Stone, March 7, 2012, www.cbpp.org/cms/index.cfm?fa=view&id=3697. Reprinted by permission.

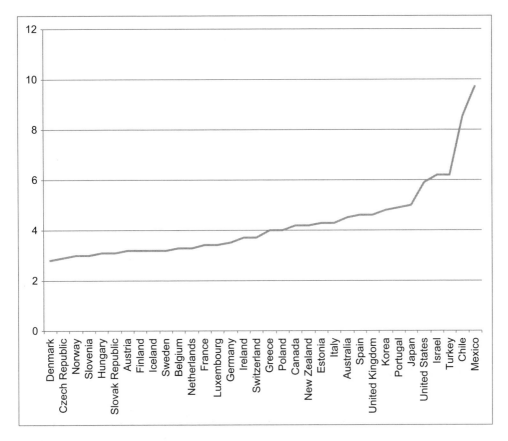

Figure 4.2 Income Inequality

Source: Based on OECD Factbook 2013.

the share of total before-tax income to households in the top 1 percent of the income distribution, including capital gains, rose dramatically from 1970 to 2010, with 2010 showing the greatest disparity since just before the Great Depression in 1930.

A helpful way to look at inequality is to compare the level of income at the 10th decile with the 90th decile. Figure 4.2 indicates that in the United States the 9th decile is nearly six times as great as the 1st decile, ranking it 30th among 34 OECD countries.

Figure 4.3 shows the magnitude of inequality between rich and poor within OECD countries. The United States ranks 4th from the bottom of 34 OECD countries in poverty rate and 3rd from the bottom of the 34 countries in the poverty gap between rich and poor. As shown here and in Chapter 3, the U.S. separation between the *haves* and the *have-nots* far exceeds that of the average of the OECD countries. Gross inequalities and inadequate opportunities for people of all ages have undoubtedly had a detrimental effect on the development of the nation. The price of indifference and neglect has exceeded the cost that would have been necessary to ensure adequate and equitable opportunities for everyone.

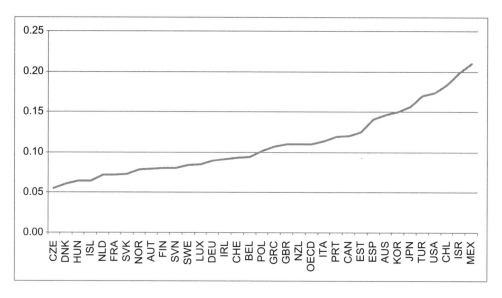

Figure 4.3 Poverty Rates (Ratio)

Source: Based on OECD Factbook 2013. StatLink http://dx.doi.org/10.1787/888932707059.

INEQUALITIES AMONG STATES

While the international trend in economic disparities does not present a sanguine picture of *convergence*, the picture among states in the United States does not present a dissimilar picture at this point in history. Although the absolute position of the underclass in the United States is not nearly as bad as in other countries, the relative disparities within the nation persist and are not improving. Bernat[75] has shown that there was a convergence between states in per capita income from 1950 to 1979, but since that time there has been little convergence,[76] and in recent years the disparity has been growing.

The income of the citizens of a state affects their potential expenditure for education and other governmental services. The expenditures for education on a state-wide basis relate to the quality of education provided or as a minimum have a positive correlation with selected indicators of quality. The fiscal capacity of states is discussed more fully in Chapter 7 of this book.

Complicating factors in any interstate analysis arise from (1) the mobility of the population within the United States, (2) migration and concentrations of ethnic and racial groups, and (3) the composition of the population in each of the states – rural and urban dwellers, whites, nonwhites, and so on.

INEQUALITIES WITHIN STATES

The evidence indicates rather clearly that the range in educational opportunities available within most states is considerably greater than the interstate differences indicated by the averages among states. In a few states, a majority of children seem to have reasonably adequate educational opportunities. Generally speaking, the states with the greatest extremes are states that are organized into many small districts in which only limited state support supplements local funds. In some of the small poverty-stricken districts and the urban ghetto areas, educational opportunities are tragically inadequate. The fact that African-American and other minority children who have attended schools in the South, in the urban ghettos, and in many other impoverished areas have had inadequate educational opportunities has been widely publicized during the past few years and as a result some improvements have been made, but the problem remains unresolved. The opportunities for many other children, regardless of race or similar factors, also continue to be far from satisfactory even in many of the more financially able school districts and states.

Enclaves of Affluence

Economic power and influence are at the root of the problem traditionally faced by state legislatures in providing fiscal resources for education.[77] Initially, in the formation of public schools, legislatures were reticent to accept responsibility for imposing taxes at the state level, and to avert this obligation they delegated substantial taxing authority to localities. The local tax bases included extreme disparities in property wealth, and the revenue yields from the tax bases resulted in great differences in educational funding. By allowing local taxing power, the legislatures created nearly insurmountable problems of inequality.

Persons in enclaves of wealth have been adept in convincing legislatures that their advantageous position is in some way justified and indeed necessary for the maintenance of a quality educational system. Such justifications, mostly defensive afterthoughts, have been successful enough to perpetuate wide revenue disparities between rich and poor school districts in many states.

These disparate conditions have led some to observe that the public school system of the United States is not public at all, but rather a quasi-private or a quasi-public system with a sense of "solidarity and community" based upon economic conditions and affluence formed around small school districts.[78] The interests of the parents and children in these districts are insular, particularized, and geographically defined. Moreover, their insularity and educational privilege are protected by the state legislatures which continue to enact school funding laws that yield disparate financial results. Parents and neighbors in these advantaged districts are driven by two primary objectives: maintaining the educational advantage for their children, and "a near obsessive concern with maintaining or upgrading property values."[79] State legislatures have in many cases reflected and fortified the insularity of these compounds of wealth through state school financing schemes.

Legislatures influenced by special interests as well as traditional anti-tax forces often stand against educational finance reform. Educational equity falls prey to self-interest, and state legislatures composed of competing political fiefdoms are unable to provide for quality of educational opportunity. The fact that this situation prevails in many states is the reason that advocates of school finance reform have turned to the courts to intervene in an effort to force legislatures toward greater educational equity.

Intrastate School District Disparities

Studies of funding disparities in individual states, as measured by various equity statistics such as Salmon's and Driscoll's comprehensive analysis of Virginia reported in the *Journal of Education Finance* in 2013, finds increasing disparities in school district expenditures in years 2003, 2005, and 2011.[80] The Gini Coefficient and the Coefficient of Variation (CV) measurements reflect the macro effects of the Great Recession of 2008 as well as an historical retrogressive attitude toward public schools found mostly in states with lower levels of adult educational attainment and, as is observed in another chapter of this book, cultural conditions that militate against investment in education. The Salmon and Driscoll approach is an inclusive and thorough method for reliable individual state equity analysis.

Regarding multistate equity analysis of financial equity, Riddle and White earlier established a within-state baseline for fiscal disparities analysis among school districts.[81] In 1991–1992 they found that states with the greatest disparities in unified school district expenditures, as measured by the Coefficient of Variation (CV), not counting Alaska, were Missouri, Ohio, Massachusetts, New York, and Michigan, with Pennsylvania, Tennessee, and Illinois not far behind. The states with the least disparities were West Virginia, Delaware, Rhode Island, Iowa, and Florida. Notice that the states with the greatest disparities were those with high numbers of school districts and those with greater intrastate equality were states with few school districts, indicating that the level of equalization among school districts has much to do with not only the percentage of state funding to offset the weight of the disequalizing local property tax, but the number of school districts as well. As to whether the situation is improving with disparities among school districts in all states, the data must be analyzed over a number of years or decades.

There is some evidence that throughout the country it appears that states have gradually improved the equality of distribution of state and local funding among school districts. Corcoran and Evans show that using the four measures of equality, the Gini Coefficient, the Coefficient of Variation, a 95-to-5 ratio, and the Theil Index (these measures are explained in detail in Chapter 13), there was a discernible improvement in equality of distribution from 1972 to 2004.[82] Table 4.1 shows the values for the two most common of these measures, the Gini Coefficient and the Coefficient of Variation (CV), for the three decades. The larger the Gini and the CV the greater the inequality. As the table indicates, between 1972 and 1982 equality increased rather sharply and then receded during the 1980s but then equality again increased after 1990 until 2000; however, inequality increased from 2000 to 2004, with the Gini rising from 12.3 in 2000 to 13.7 in 2004 and the CV increasing from 1.98 in 2000 to 2.24 in 2004.[83] We don't have comparable data for the years from 2004 through the Great Recession to present, but one can be reasonably certain that inequality in state school funding increased after the onset of the Recession in 2008. State funding in many states declined as state revenues fell; local school districts' only reliable fiscal source was the local property tax, a regressive but more stable tax, which was increasingly relied upon to maintain the schools.

Probably the most sophisticated model for the measurement of school funding disparities within states has been developed by Bruce Baker, David Sciarra, and

Table 4.1 Inequality in Per-Pupil Current Expenditures, United States, 1972 to 2004

School Year Ended	Gini (×100)	Coefficient of Variation (×100)
1972	16.2	30.57
1982	13.7	25.53
1990	15.7	30.02
1992	14.9	28.81
1994	14.5	26.45
1996	13.5	26.45
1998	12.5	24.59
2000	12.3	24.52
2002	12.9	25.58
2004	13.7	27.51

Note: Unified districts only in all years, excluding Alaska, Hawaii, Montana, Vermont, and the District of Columbia.

Source: Sean P. Corcoran and William N. Evans, "Equity, Adequacy and the Evolving State Role in Education Finance," in *Handbook of Research in Education Finance and Policy*, edited by Helen F. Ladd and Edward B. Fiske (New York and London: Routledge, 2008), pp. 336–337.

Danielle Farrie, titled, *A National Report Card*, first issued in 2010, with a second edition published in 2012.[84] The principal value of this model in evaluating state school finance systems is that it is constructed of four fairness measures:

1. *Funding level* measures the overall state and local revenue that flows to school districts, comparing each state's average per-pupil revenue with that of other states. This revenue for each state is adjusted to reflect differences in regional wages, poverty, economies of scale, and population density.[85]
2. *Funding distribution* measures the distribution of state and local funds across local school districts taking into consideration the degree of student poverty in the school districts.[86]
3. *Effort* is the measure of state spending on public schools relative to the state's fiscal capacity. Fiscal capacity is the state's per capita share of gross domestic product (GDP) of the nation.[87]
4. *Coverage* measures the proportion of school-age population attending public schools as compared with those not attending public schools, primarily those children attending Catholic schools, other private schools, or homeschools.[88]

The *Effort* and *Coverage* measures are readily calculated from extant descriptive data, and the states are ranked accordingly. The *Funding Level* and *Funding Distribution* involve the use of variables such as teacher salaries, school district size, population density, and several student characteristics such as child poverty, to control for variations and create comparable comparisons. Regression analyses predict the outcomes against which the state numbers are evaluated. States are then ranked by each of the four measures.

Regarding the *Funding Level* criterion, the analysis ranks Wyoming at the top and Tennessee at the bottom.[89] With regard to *Funding Distribution*, the most progressive states were Utah, New Jersey, and Ohio. There were 17 states adjudged to be progressive in their funding under this criterion. Sixteen states were found to have regressive funding systems, with Illinois, North Carolina, Alabama, and Texas to "show clearly regressive funding patterns."[90] In applying the fairness measure of *Effort*, it was shown that the states with the lowest effort were Delaware, South Dakota, Louisiana, and Tennessee and the states with the highest effort were Vermont, New Jersey, and New York.

The fourth measure of fairness, *Coverage*, is an important evaluation aspect of the model in that it takes into account two important elements. *First*, it determines the number and percentage of children who actually attend public schools in each state. This percentage varies considerably in that, for example, only 78 percent school-age children attend public schools in Washington, DC, and 80 percent in Delaware, while 93 percent attend public schools in Wyoming and Utah.[91] *Second*, the *Coverage* part of the model determines the household income of public school students in contrast with private school students. For example, Baker et al. observed that in Washington, DC, private school students in 2010 had a median household income of $195,651, and that year the median household income for public school students was only $55,993. Importantly, stability of the model is enhanced by use of three-year medians or averages on each of the fairness criteria. This Baker-Sciarra-Farrie model of analyzing fiscal fairness provides a unique and comprehensive view of state systems of school finance which can be of much value yielding valuable guidance for educators and legislators as they endeavor to improve public school funding.

In addition to the Baker-Sciarra-Farrie model, there are other sources that may assist in analyzing state school finance systems. The National Center for Education Statistics (NCES) is a reliable source for determining state and local revenue per pupil. For many years the National Education Association has published the *Rankings of the States & Estimates of School Statistics*.[92] *Education Week*, the education newspaper, annually publishes school finance data and calculates the deployment of state funding within states.[93] This is a valuable source of state school finance information that is published 37 times a year. The U.S. Department of Education in 2011 published the *Education Dashboard* that provided valuable state fiscal data measuring the differences in per-pupil expenditures among school districts, with information for high- to low-poverty districts throughout the country. Yet another valuable source is the *Education Trust*, a Washington, DC, education advocacy organization that periodically publishes studies of state education funding taking into account regional wage variations, adjustments for children in poverty, limited English proficiency, and children with disabilities.[94]

In a report to the United States Secretary of Education titled *For Each and Every Child* (2013), a commission of education experts identified intrastate school funding disparities as a major impediment to equal opportunity in the United States.[95] The Report pointed out that across school districts in most states the expenditure per pupil between affluent and property-poor school districts is about two to one. In some states, California and Illinois, for example, affluent school districts expend well over three times the amount per pupil as do districts with less fiscal capacity. Moreover, the rate of poverty among school children is not uniform among districts of a state, and in many states the high-poverty school districts receive less state and local funding per pupil than districts with lower percentages of children in poverty.[96] "[In] Illinois, the high-poverty districts typically spend one-third less than low-poverty – $8,707 per pupil – as compared with $11,312 per pupil," even though the high-poverty districts have greater concentration of children with needs.[97] Moreover, the districts with high concentrations of poverty have increasing enrollments accumulating their percentages of low-income children.[98] The Report made the general recommendation to the Secretary that each state should "ensure that funding is equitable and publicly reported . . . while taking into account school characteristics such as size, geography, demographics, and student need."[99]

Further, the commission recommended that the federal government provide "appropriate incentives" to implement state school finance systems that will (a) provide sufficient resources effectively and efficiently fund state content and performance standards, (b) ensure that state "dollars are not used to perpetuate or exacerbate inequities," and (c) ensure "equitable distribution of state and local resources among schools within school districts" in addressing the educational needs of children from low-income families.[100]

REASONS FOR INEQUALITIES IN OPPORTUNITY

Why are serious inequalities in educational opportunity permitted to exist year after year in a country in which a majority of the people seem dedicated to the concept of equality? Some of the background factors involved are:

1. Many people do not realize the extent or implications of inequalities.
2. Some people have become accustomed to the existing situation and accept it as normal.
3. Substantial numbers seem to be more concerned about their own personal problems and the rising costs of living and government than about variations in educational opportunity that do not seem to affect them immediately.
4. Until comparatively recent years, the procedures needed to solve certain aspects of the problem had not been satisfactorily developed or understood.
5. Self-interest often overcomes common interest and mutuality of concern for others.
6. There are wide differences among local school districts in fiscal capacity per pupil.

SUMMARY

In this chapter we have sought to give a perspective on inequality, in general, which, of course, affects equality of educational opportunity. Much of any discussion of public school finance is devoted to issues pertaining to equality because it is an ever persistent social and economic problem that greatly influences the kind and quality of education that every child receives. We attempted to show that inequality is not merely perceived but is real among nations, states, and within states. It is a philosophical and moral issue that has invoked the concern of politicians and moral philosophers worldwide. The following main points were emphasized in this chapter.

Inequality of privilege emanates from disproportionate distribution of economic power.

The concept of equality as a basic concern of human interaction was never realized in Europe until after the American Revolution had established its practical importance to the republican form of government. Before Jefferson's Declaration in 1776, equality was an intuition without form that allowed practical political consideration.

The importance of public, mass, universal education as an essential element of freedom and liberty was first and best enunciated by Rousseau's reference in 1758 to public education as the vehicle to nurture children in the "bosom of equality."

Human self-interest is a fact of life that Adam Smith recognized as the driving force of the *invisible hand* that advances society but leaves inequality in its wake. Laissez-faire economic philosophy eschews equality and warns of damage to economic growth by governments' efforts to reduce or eliminate inequalities.

The doctrine of *harmony of interests* sought to justify economic inequality by maintaining that unfettered pursuit of one's own self-interest would ultimately raise the economic condition of all in society. This theory has recently been referred to as *trickle-down* economics.

Unfettered pursuit of self-interest was justified on the biological theory of "survival of the fittest" advanced by Darwin, commonly entitled "social Darwinism." The United States followed this philosophy and it pervades the context in which we think about school finance, competition for school fiscal resources, school districts as *lighthouses*, and so on.

The basic premise of egalitarian philosophy is that similar cases should be accorded similar treatment, equal treatment of equals. There is a difference between equality and equity. Equality means all are entitled to equal shares while equity means that all are entitled to fair shares.

Departure from equal shares is not justified unless it can be shown that greater justice is served by unequal shares. Such a departure from equality is only justified for *educationally relevant* reasons intended to elevate the least advantaged. Contrived reasons that provide more to the more affluent, advantaged, or privileged cannot be relevant reasons for departure from equal distribution.

Inequality in fiscal resources is evident among nations. Great gulfs of disparity exist between developed and underdeveloped countries and the differences are broadening rather than diminishing. Inequality in income follows inequality in education and vice versa. Inequality in education among and within nations is always associated with economic and financial disability, but is particularly discernible in socioeconomic disparities.

Inequalities in educational opportunity in the United States are particularly severe between rich and poor states, cities and suburbs, rural areas, and among racial and ethnic groups that cluster in these particular geographic areas.

Grave inequalities in educational opportunity exist within states. Many school districts have three or four times the fiscal resources to expend per pupil as other districts. These per-pupil differences amount to differences of many millions of dollars between the rich and poor school districts in most states each year.

Inequalities persist within school districts and are most apparent in many large school districts. This is particularly true in large urban areas that have enclaves of fiscally advantaged and disadvantaged communities that influence the quality of educational opportunities provided.

KEY TERMS

- Laissez-faire school of economic thought
- Income disparity
- The invisible hand
- Inequality of educational opportunity
- Harmony of interests
- Wealth inequality among school districts
- Social Darwinism
- Revenue inequality among school districts

- Egalitarian philosophy
- Equal shares
- Fiscal ability
- Equitable shares
- Fiscal effort
- Relevant differences
- Rawls' difference principle
- Least advantaged
- Liberty as connected with equality
- Disparity in educational opportunity among countries

NOTES

1. David Miller, *Social Justice* (Oxford: Clarendon Press, 1976), p. 19.
2. Ibid., p. 21.
3. Pete Alcock, *Understanding Poverty* (New York: Macmillan, 2006).
4. Joseph E. Stiglitz, *The Price of Inequality* (New York: W. W. Norton & Company, 2012), p. 82.
5. Ibid., p. 75.
6. Jeffrey D. Sachs, *The End of Poverty: Economic Possibilities for Our Time* (New York: The Penguin Press, 2005), p. 64.
7. Thomas Nagel, *Equality and Partiality* (Oxford: Oxford University Press, 1991), p. 64.
8. Sachs, *op. cit.,* p. 20.
9. Stiglitz, *op. cit.,* p. 83.
10. Ibid., p. 84.
11. Brian Barry, *Theories of Justice* (Berkeley: University of California Press, 1989), p. 109
12. Ronald Dworkin, *A Matter of Principle* (Oxford: Oxford University Press, 1986), p. 206.
13. Richard Dawkins, *The Selfish Gene* (Oxford: Oxford University Press, 1976).
14. Nagel, *op. cit.*, p. 102.
15. Jean Jacques Rousseau, "A Discourse on the Origin of Inequality," *The Social Contract and Discourses*, translation and introduction by G.D.H. Cole (London: J.M. Dent and Sons, 1973), p. 84.
16. Reinhold Niebuhr, *Moral Man and Immoral Society* (New York: Charles Scribner's Sons, 1932), p. 114.

17. Isaiah Berlin, *Concepts and Categories* (New York: Viking Press, 1978), p. 82.
18. Ibid.
19. Ibid., p. 84.
20. Henry Steele Commager, *The Empire of Reason* (New York: Anchor Press/Doubleday, 1978).
21. Ibid., p. 135.
22. Thomas Jefferson, *Notes on the State Virginia*, Query XIV, p. 206 (Philadelphia: H.C. Carey and I. Lea, 1825).
23. Helvetius, *De L'Espirit*, or *Essays on the Mind*, Essay II (1970), Ch. 2.
24. Adam Smith, *The Wealth of Nations* (New York: Modern Library, 1937). Originally published in 1776. See Paul A. Samuelson and William Norelhaus, *Economics*, Fourteenth Edition (New York: McGraw-Hill, 1992), pp. 40, 739.
25. Ibid., p. 423.
26. Edward Hallett Carr, *The Twenty Years' Crisis, 1919–1939* (New York: Harper Torchbooks, 1939), p. 42.
27. Robert Kuttner, *The Economic Illusion* (Philadelphia: University of Pennsylvania Press, 1991), p. 12.
28. Carr, *op. cit.*, p. 47.
29. Ibid.
30. Niebuhr, *op. cit.*, p. 123.
31. Ibid.
32. Ibid.
33. Ronald Dworkin, *A Matter of Principle* (Oxford: Oxford University Press, 1986), p. 206; Brian Barry, *Theories of Justice* (Berkeley: University of California Press, 1989), p. 230.
34. Brian Barry, *op. cit.*, p. 226.
35. John Rawls, *A Theory of Justice* (Cambridge, MA: Harvard University Press, 1971), p. 62.
36. Ibid.
37. Plato's Dialogue, *Crito*, in D.D. Raphael, *Problems of Political Philosophy* (London: Macmillan, 1976), p. 86.
38. D.D. Raphael, *Problems of Political Philosophy* (London: Macmillan, 1976), p. 172.
39. Ibid.
40. Ibid., p. 173.
41. Ibid.
42. Ibid.
43. Niebuhr, *op. cit.*, p. 196.
44. William Ryan, *Blaming the Victim* (New York: Vintage Books, 1976), p. 13.
45. Rawls, *op. cit.*
46. Robert Nozick, *Anarchy, State, and Utopia* (New York: Basic Books, 1974), p. 183.
47. Rawls, *op. cit.*, p. 507.
48. Ibid.
49. Ibid.
50. Ibid., p. 303.
51. Ibid., p. 301
52. Ibid.
53. Ibid.
54. David Miller, *Social Justice* (Oxford: Clarendon Press, 2002), p. 125.
55. Ibid., p. 149.
56. Mitchell A. Seligson, "The Dual Gaps: An Overview of Theory and Research," in *Development and Underdevelopment: The Political Economy of Global Inequality*, 4th Edition, edited by Mitchell A. Seligson and John T. Passé-Smith (Boulder, CO and London: Lynne Rienner Publishers, 2008), pp. 1–2.

57. Excerpted from *Development and Underdevelopment*, John T. Passé-Smith, "Characteristics of the Income Gap Between Countries," pp. 20–21.
58. Ibid., p. 22.
59. Ibid., pp. 27–28.
60. Lawrence E. Harrison, "Underdevelopment Is a State of Mind," in Seligson and Passé-Smith, *op. cit.*, pp. 227–233.
61. Ibid., p. 230.
62. Ibid., p. 232.
63. Ibid.
64. Philip H. Coombs, *The World Crisis in Education, The View from the Eighties* (New York: Oxford University Press, 1985).
65. Ibid., p. 5.
66. Ibid.
67. World Bank, *World Development Report 1991, The Challenge of Development* (Oxford: The World Bank and Oxford University Press, 1991), p. 50
68. World Bank, *Learning for All: Investing in People's Knowledge and Skills to Promote Development, 2020, Executive Summary* (New York: World Bank), p. 2.
69. Jeffrey D. Sachs, *The End of Poverty: Economic Possibilities for Our Time* (New York: The Penguin Press, 2005), pp. 64–65.
70. Ibid., p. 64.
71. Ibid., p. 65.
72. Coombs, *op. cit.*, p. 230.
73. Ibid.
74. Thomas Piketty, *Capital in the 21st Century* (Cambridge, MA: Belknap Press, 2014).
75. G. Andrew Bernat, Jr., "Convergence in State Per Capita Personal Income, 1950–99," *Survey of Current Business*, June 2001, pp. 36–48.
76. Ibid., p. 36.
77. Adapted in part from Kern Alexander, "The Common School Ideal and the Limits of Legislative Authority: The Kentucky Case," *Harvard Journal on Legislation* 28:2 (Summer 1991), pp. 348–349.
78. Robert Reich, "Secession of the Successful," *New York Times* Magazine (January 20, 1991), pp. 16, 42.
79. Ibid.
80. Richard G. Salmon and Lisa Driscoll, "Challenges Confronting Public Elementary and Secondary Education in the Commonwealth of Virginia," *Journal of Education Finance*, 38:3, Winter 2013, pp. 230–254.
81. Wayne Riddle and Liane White, "Expenditures in Public School Districts: Estimates of Disparities and Analysis of Their Causes" (Washington, DC: Congressional Research Service, 1996), pp. 25–35.
82. Sean P. Corcoran and William N. Evans, "Equity Adequacy and the Evolving State Role in Education Finance," in *Handbook of Research in Education Finance and Policy*, edited by Helen F. Ladd and Edward B. Fiske (New York and London: Routledge, 2008), pp. 336–337.
83. Ibid.
84. Bruce Baker, David Sciarra, and Danielle Farrie, *Is School Funding Fair? A National Report Card*, Second Edition, June 2012 (Rutgers, NJ: Education Law Center, 2012).
85. Ibid., p. 10.
86. Ibid., p. 13.
87. Ibid., p. 23.
88. Ibid., p. 25.
89. Ibid., pp. 11–12.

90. Ibid., p. 13.
91. Ibid., p. 25.
92. National Education Association, NEA Research, Washington, DC, www.nea.org.
93. *Education Week*, www.edweek.org.
94. Carmen G. Arroyo, "The Funding Gap," *The Education Trust*, January, 2008.
95. The Equity and Excellence Commission: A Report to the Secretary, *For Each and Every Child: A Strategy for Education Equity and Excellence* (Alexandria, VA: Ed Publications Center, http://www.edpubs.gov.
96. Ibid., p. 18.
97. Ibid.
98. Ibid.
99. Ibid., p. 19.
100. Ibid., p. 19.

Education as an Investment in Human Capital

INTRODUCTION

Today, knowledgeable leaders of nations are well aware that in the end, the people with the greatest wealth of human capital will lead all other nations. Jeffrey Sachs in his best seller, *The Price of Civilization* (2011), has pointed to the slippage of human capital as a major emerging problem of America: America is ceding its "technological leadership to China and to other countries."[1] The decline in the quality of American human capital is readily evident in the lacking capabilities of the labor force[2] and the financial neglect and underfunding of public schools. Further, the human capital problem in the United States is exacerbated by contradictory policies on human capital retention and development. For example, immigration policies of the U.S. government require nearly all Chinese and other Asians of high academic attainment, educated in American universities, to return to their native countries after they receive their graduate degrees. The United States leads the world in the exporting of valuable human capital.

BACKGROUND

Historically, human beings have been valued primarily for their physical, rather than their mental, capabilities as soldiers, serfs, or slaves. For example, throughout the centuries, the labor of individuals has shaped markets, whether that labor was provided by freemen, serfs, or slaves.[3] The market value of the human, however, changes dramatically with fluctuations in the supply of workers. As Tuchman observed, a decline in population caused by the bubonic plague of the fourteenth century placed such a premium on labor that the value of the individual was reflected in wage reforms which swept Western Europe and affected commerce for centuries.[4]

In earlier eras, valuation of people was based on their physical productivity as hewers of wood and drawers of water, not necessarily as philosophers, scientists, teachers, or physicians. According to this method of valuing the individual, the nation with the greatest population had the greatest human capital value. However, the fallacy in this approach became apparent in the nineteenth and twentieth centuries as the world's work force became less *labor intensive* and more *brain intensive*. The country with the greatest population was not necessarily the most productive or influential. If sheer numbers had been the measure of human value, England would have been a dependent of India rather than vice versa.

It was not until the 1960s that full awakening to the real value of human capital actually occurred. We should point out that while it was in the 1960s that the idea of an education as an investment took root and flowered, the idea was first advanced by S. G. Strumilin, who studied the economic value of education in Russia in 1925. His work *Ekonomiski Truda* was not published and translated to English until 1960 in a UNESCO publication titled, *Readings in Economics of Education* (Paris, 1968). Guided by Theodore W. Schultz, later to win the Nobel Prize in 1979 for Economic Science, economists and educators began to recognize the economic importance of the human being in the production process and to begin to seek ways to measure the magnitude of human capital.[5]

EDUCATION AND ECONOMIC GROWTH

Today there is a plethora of empirical research throughout the world that shows the primacy of human capital investment for economic development. For example, a Development Report of the World Bank summarizing studies in 60 countries concluded the importance of education to economic development: "sustained development in many countries, notably the Scandinavian countries after 1870 and the East Asian economies after World War II, can be largely explained by education . . ."[6]

Reasons for the unprecedented economic growth of the Pacific Rim countries referred to as the economic tigers, China, South Korea, Taiwan, Hong Kong, Singapore, Indonesia, and Malaysia, were foretold in an article in *The Economist* magazine titled, "Where Tigers Breed, A Survey of Asia's Emerging Economies," the prescience of which was well-proven by 2013. *The Economist* article noted several lessons to be learned from them, but concluded: "The last lesson is probably the most important: investing in education pays in spades. The tigers' single biggest source of comparative advantage is their well-educated workers."[7]

Importantly, the debate over how to best stimulate economic growth has reached a new plane. In earlier generations it was obliquely recognized that human capital investment led the way to more productive economies. Today, however, the issue tops national agendas because it has become vastly more apparent that the new technological demands of the age require a much higher level of knowledge of the people. "There is nothing new in the triumph of brain over brawn. The richer countries have long found that ever larger proportions of their populations are employed in jobs that require mental power rather than muscle power."[8] What is new is that the unremitting progress of innovation and technology has created an even greater premium on education and a highly skilled workforce. The shift toward the "smarter jobs,"[9] i.e., Google, Facebook, and Twitter, of the information age has placed requirements on all economies to educate and train the masses for advanced learning.

CLASSICAL ECONOMIC VIEW

Mark Blaug summarized the view of classical economics as follows: "The classical economists did not conceive a mass education as an investment in economic growth, but they recognized that it might contribute indirectly to growth by promoting civic peace and population control."[10]

Adam Smith

The mainstreams of thought of the classical school of economists are best summarized by reference to Adam Smith and John Stuart Mill; the views of both are also discussed at other places in this book. Early economists differed on the issue of whether or not to recognize people in their overall definition of wealth or capital. Adam Smith in 1776 did conceive of human capital in his definition of fixed capital saying it consisted

of the acquired and useful abilities of all the inhabitants or members of society. The acquisition of such talents by the maintenance of the acquirer during his education, study or apprenticeship, always costs a real expense, which is a capital fixed and realized, as it were, in his person.[11]

Yet, even though Smith never related the value of human capital to economic growth, he nevertheless advanced the idea of public education for the *common* people who could not be fortunate enough to be instructed to the level of "people of rank and fortune."[12] Smith pointed out in *The Wealth of Nations* that for a

very small expense the public can facilitate, can encourage, and can even impose upon almost the whole body of the people the necessity of acquiring those most essential parts of education . . . The public can facilitate this acquisition by establishing in every parish or district a little school where children may be taught . . . [13]

However, Smith's political philosophy was obviously limited by the realities of the world in which he was surrounded in 1776. That world was one of English and Scottish private ecclesiastical schools for the affluent.

Yet Smith never really related the educational function of government to the development of human potential nor did he attempt to measure it. Basically, Smith was unable to perceive of a man in any terms other than that of an "expensive machine," a position fundamentally adhered to by other nineteenth century economists such as Alfred Marshall.[14] The idea that education was a human capital investment did not occur to Marshall.[15] He did not see that there was, in fact, a "capital market for labor," that is, human capital could not be traded in the marketplace in the same way that is the case for physical capital.[16] Marshall, an economist of great prestige, maintained that while humans were certainly capital from an abstract point of view, it was impractical to include them as an element when analyzing national investment and development.[17]

John Stuart Mill

The great John Stuart Mill, long remembered for his treatise, *On Liberty*, 1859, did not define wealth as including human capital. He did, however, see human learning as the principal catalyst for creating productive economic growth. "In propriety of classification, the people of a country are not to be counted in its wealth . . . They are not wealth themselves, though they are means of acquiring it."[18]

Mill, while in nearly all respects progressive in his thinking, suffered from a myopic view of the value of mass public education. Mill's limited view of *public* had been influenced by the lack of separation between church and state in England; therefore, he believed that government could not escape church intolerance in the provision of state education.[19] To Mill, religious influence on the state created "moral repression" of the individual. This observation was reflected in his own educational experience where he was kept from formal education and was reared and tutored in privilege at his father's great country house in England.

He, therefore, did not approve of public schools because he did not believe that public instruction could be secular and separated from the Church of England. Moreover, his distrust of government education was based on the history of education in Europe as well as in England, specifically where religious sects controlled or influenced the sovereign. Thus, to Mill, if the state were controlled by a church, the public schools would *ipso facto* be so controlled. He points out that state schools could not avoid converting subject matter "into a mere battlefield for sects and parties causing the time and labour, which should have been spent in educating, to be wasted in quarrelling about education."[20] Mill would, apparently, have accepted secular public schools, but he knew of no such system and thought that such was unattainable. Thus, he could not see clearly the value of mass universal public secular education as an institution and, even further, could not conceive of its value for economic development of a nation.

MILL AND GENDER EQUALITY

Mill, however, more than anyone else of his day, saw educational deprivation of women as a profound economic loss to a nation. Women who were not educated constituted a great loss of productive human capital. Even though Mill had an outmoded view of public instruction, he nevertheless believed that government had the sovereign power to require compulsory education for the general economic benefit of society. The arena in which Mill best enunciated the relationship between education and economic growth was his rationale for the educational equality of women for their inclusion in productive occupations. Mill clearly understood that the bottom line of gender inequality was inefficiency in the development and use of human capital. In his seminal women's manifesto, *The Subjection of Women*, 1869, Mill makes his best and most decisive commentary on the value of investment in human capital when he observes what today is obvious, that permitting women to have education and equal social status with men can possibly double the productive economic capacity of a state or nation. He said,

> giving to women the free use of their faculties, by leaving them free choice of their employments, and opening to them the same field of occupation and the same prizes and encouragements as to other human beings, would be that of doubling the mass of mental faculties available for the higher service of humanity. Where there is now one person qualified to benefit mankind and promote the general improvement, as a public teacher, or an administrator of some branch of public affairs or social affairs, there would be a chance of two."[21]

A more compelling reasoning regarding the value of human capital had not been written before Mill. Thus, Mill, as one of the great classical economists, clearly conceived that to waste "one-half of what nature proffers"[22] in human capabilities is a formidable inefficiency and a deterrent on the economic development of a nation.

Mill, however, did not carry the idea further and did not have the formal economic training or insight to reduce his human capital equation to a rate-of-return or cost-benefit analysis. He understood the concept, but the details and the qualifications did not materialize until 1960 with modern human capital economists. Mill, thus, never connected the dots. To his credit, though, he saw the value of the education of women to a nation's economy as evidenced in his tract on women. Such equality with men would inevitably lead to better education which in turn would result in rational population growth limitations to reduce overpopulation. In this light, Mill was an ardent student of Thomas Malthus' view of the dire effects of uncontrolled population growth, and the lack of capacity of the uneducated women to practice voluntary family planning and birth control. The education of women was the solution.[23]

Horace Mann

Smith and Mill and other economists of their day did not fully grasp the economic value of human capital to both the individual and to society. Smith was of an earlier era than Mill, but Horace Mann was a contemporary of Mill, and Mann understood the value and the means by which that value could be enhanced. Horace Mann in his 1848 education report persuasively observed that:

> Our *means of education is the grand machinery* by which "raw material" of human nature can be worked into inventors and discoverers, into skilled artisans and scientific farmers, into scholars and jurists, into the founders of benevolent institutions, and the great expounders of ethical and theological science. By *means of early education*, these embryos of talent may be quickened, which will solve the difficult problems of political and economic law. [emphasis added][24]

In these statements, Mann took to task the limited views of Adam Smith and others whose thoughts of political economy failed to recognize the condition of the poor uneducated workers of the industrial revolution, and asserted that the true wealth of a nation lay largely in the intelligence of its people – *intelligence* meaning the intellectual storehouse of knowledge possessed by all the people. In this regard Mann said,

> For *creation of wealth*, then – for the existence of a wealthy people and a wealthy nation – intelligence is the grand condition. The number of improvers will increase as the intellectual constituency, if I may so call it, increases. In former times, and in most parts of the world even at the present day, not one man in a million has ever had such a development of mind as made it possible for him to become a contributor to art or science. Let this development proceed, and contributions, numberless, and of inestimable value, will be sure to follow. *That Political Economy, therefore, which busies itself about capital and labor, supply and demand, interest and rents, favorable and unfavorable balances of trade, but leaves out of account the element of a wide-spread mental development, is nought but stupendous folly.* The greatest of all the arts in political economy is to change a consumer into a producer – an end to be directly attained by increasing his intelligence. [emphasis added][25]

With few exceptions, Mann's perception of the thinking of political economists of the nineteenth century was accurate; their efforts were spent almost entirely on matters of fiscal and physical capital with little concern for human capital. As observed above, the balance sheet of political economy did not include entries for the store of human potential or lack of it.

Despite the efforts of Mann, however, only sporadic recognition of his views was given in the literature until Theodore Schultz measured the value of human capital over 100 years later.[26]

HUMAN CAPITAL APPROACH

Theodore Schultz, as noted above, observed that the classical economists had "put us on the wrong road" of economic thought.[27] What Schultz actually noticed was the heterogeneity of capital, and he saw that the individual human was a form of capital that could be developed. Schultz's important contribution was the assertion that skills and knowledge are complementary forms of capital.

> Although it is obvious that people acquire useful skills and knowledge, it is not obvious that these skills and knowledge are a form of capital, that this capital is in substantial part a product of deliberate investment that has grown in Western societies at a much faster rate than conventional [nonhuman] capital, and that its growth may well be the most distinctive feature of the economic system.[28]

Schultz and other modern economists noted that the income of the United States and other countries had been increasing at a much higher rate than could be accounted for by combining the amount of land, number of hours worked, and stock of reproducible goods used to produce this income. As the discrepancy between the two amounts became larger, economists, without knowing its nature, called the difference *resource productivity*. Schultz said that to call this discrepancy "a measure of *resource productivity* gives a name to our ignorance but does not dispel it."[29]

With Schultz's work as an impetus, a reform of thinking occurred in the 1960s with many economists attempting to measure the effects of human capital on the economy. Educators eagerly sought evidence to support their assertions that greater investment in the public schools would yield higher economic returns. Within a few years the volume of research was so great that the question of the value of human capital became an important subspecialty of both economic and social science. As noted above, the ultimate acknowledgment of the importance of human capital research was given in 1979 when the Nobel Prize for Economic Science was awarded to Theodore W. Schultz and Sir W. Arthur Lewis for their efforts in this area.

HUMAN RESOURCES AND THE WEALTH OF NATIONS

The importance of human resources to economic development is richly illustrated in a book by Frederick H. Harbison, in which he maintained "that human resources – not capital, nor income, nor material resources – constitute the ultimate basis for the wealth of nations."[30] As this quotation indicates, Harbison took to task those economists of the Adam Smith school who largely ignored human resources in their theories of political economy. Harbison pointed out that capital and material resources are *passive* factors of production which can only be activated by the catalyst of human resources.

> Human beings are the active agents who accumulate capital, exploit natural resources, build social, economic, and political organizations, and carry forward national development. Clearly, a country which is unable to develop the skills and knowledge of its people and to utilize them effectively in the national economy will be unable to develop anything else.[31]

Accordingly, Harbison, as Horace Mann before him, maintained that the wealth of nations should not only be measured in terms of gross national product, national income, and gross domestic product, but should also reflect what ought to be the primary objective of national economic policy, the stock and condition of human capital. The strength of national economies would therefore be more accurately judged by whether human resources were adequately developed and appropriately used. Education, he noted, is a primary instrument for resolving economic problems related to both underdevelopment and underutilization of human resources.

Absorption Effect

Research and writing in the area of human capital and economic development has ranged from the broad sociological aspects to precise mathematical measurements. Much work was conducted internationally to analyze the importance of education and new knowledge acquisition in underdeveloped countries. W. Arthur Lewis, working extensively in non-industrialized countries, observed that the level of literacy and the type of social conditions combined to either enhance or retard technological development. Societies with rigid class systems tended to withhold education from the masses, thereby retarding economic growth.[32] Also, it was observed that a certain "absorption effect" was at work wherein the masses had to have a minimum level of education in order to become intelligent consumers.[33] An illiterate populace could not appreciate or take advantage of technological advances.

Because the knowledge of the people must be of such quality to allow absorption of technological advances, the educational underpinnings of a national system of education must be firmly established. Investment in elementary and secondary schools provides this foundation. A government that invests too lavishly in higher education while denying resources to lower levels of education builds its house upon the proverbial sand. The World Bank study by Tan and Mingat show that the malapportionment of fiscal resources – giving inordinately greater amounts to higher education to the detriment of primary education – is an earmark of poorer countries.[34] Moreover, such an imbalance in educational investment harms the equity of a nation. The authors note, "If a government allocates most of its spending on education to the higher levels to benefit a few people, leaving few resources for primary school pupils, it achieves a lower level of structural equity in the education system than a government that pursues the opposite policies."[35] Education is important not only as a direct investment in output but also as a consumer good to enable people to enjoy life and to understand their environment better.[36]

Formal Education and Skill Acquisition

Beyond the absorption or consumption aspect, a nation's economic output "is a function of the infrastructure it has developed and the skill of its people."[37] Skills and competence in the workforce are acquired primarily through formal educational systems designed to transmit acquired knowledge, skills, and techniques. Ginsberg explained that formal education is the primary source of the skill acquisition necessary for economic development.

> [M]any years of exposure to didactic instruction in the classroom, supplemented by reading assignments on the outside, result in young people's acquiring a considerable stock of knowledge that helps inform their judgments about private and public issues on which they must act . . . The schools are not solely responsible for these horizon-stretching, comprehension-deepening efforts, for the media play important complementary roles. But the contribution of the formal education system is primary.[38]

Of course, it would be inaccurate to attribute all acquisition of knowledge and skill to formal school processes. Knowledge and skill formation actually come about from many sources of learning and experience, but three modes are the heart of the process:

1. General formal schooling.
2. Formal vocational education which extends from early high school through graduate professional schools.
3. Learning opportunities provided by employers through on-the-job training or in special industry-financed programs, which usually take the form of short intensive seminars and institutes for management and white-collar workers.

All combine to constitute the total of a nation's educational investment. More broadly, investment in human resources should not be viewed as limited to knowledge and skill acquisition, but must also include the health of the nation. It goes without saying that a nation of people suffering from hunger and poor health will not be economically productive. Politics – and indeed the political economy of any society – is first and foremost "bread politics," a set of measures founded on a nutritional determinant.[39] When basic nutritional needs are met, the individual can then turn thoughts and actions to higher levels of economic considerations that ultimately enhance overall productivity. Advancements in health generally extend the productivity of individuals and make any investment in education longer lived and more rewarding.[40]

EDUCATION AND LABOR

The production process may be regarded as the transformation of resources into goods and services. Transformation is generally more efficient if the process utilizes educated workers, even though the precise nature of the interaction between education and economic productivity is not known. Bowen lists six ways in which worker productivity is increased by education:

1. *Quantity of product.* Workers with higher levels of education produce more goods and services in a given time period because of their greater skill, dexterity, and knowledge.
2. *Quality of product.* The more educated produce better goods and render services with greater skill and/or sensitivity to human conditions.
3. *Product mix.* Educated workers may be able to produce goods and services which are more highly prized by society than those produced by workers with less education.
4. *Participation in the labor force.* Educated workers are less susceptible to lost time from unemployment and illness, and are usually characterized by higher aspirations.
5. *Allocative ability.* Workers, through education, may be better able to assess their own talents; to achieve greater skills; and to be more receptive to new technologies, new products, and new ideas.
6. *Job satisfaction.* The educated may have greater job satisfaction because they tend to acquire jobs with greater psychic rewards.[41]

Employers believe that the education of their employees improves the financial potential of the firm. There is a definite positive relationship between the amount of formal education of employees and the amount of on-the-job training they received.[42] Firms apparently find that greater productivity can be achieved with less cost by investing in the more educated employees. Greater benefits can be obtained by grafting job training to the knowledge already acquired from formal schooling.[43] It may also be that the employer responds in part to the worker's own willingness to invest in himself or herself, since employer investment in the worker appears to increase in about the same proportion as the worker's self-investment in schooling. The less educated experience greater unemployment. On the average, "job losers" have almost a year and a half less education than "job keepers."[44] Labor turnover and unemployment are related to consumer demand for goods and services. Although the correlation is rather weak, the more educated, being more generally employed in service jobs, have greater employment stability.[45] Evidence also shows that in certain areas of the economy, physical capital is more likely to be substituted for unskilled than for skilled labor. Consequently, the less educated labor force is more susceptible to layoffs due to advances in technology and fluctuations in types of goods produced and methods of production. The *Economist* notes,

> People who leave school early rapidly run out of rungs on the earnings ladder; university graduates not only find plenty of rungs, they also discover that each step upwards is increasingly remunerative. One reason for this is that the well-educated land jobs that provide them with more training, while the uneducated are locked out of opportunities to improve their skills.[46]

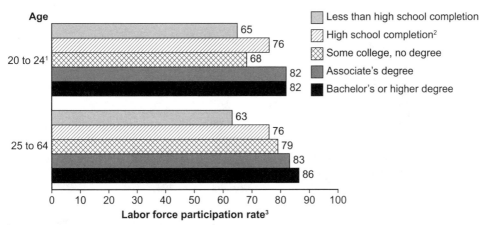

¹ Excludes persons enrolled in school.
² Includes equivalency credentials, such as the General Educational Development (GED) credential.
³ Percentage of the civilian population who are employed or seeking employment.

Figure 5.1 Labor Force Participation Rate of Persons 20 to 64 Years Old, by Age Group and Highest Level of Educational Attainment: 2009

Source: U.S. Department of Labor, Bureau of Labor Statistics, Office of Employment and Unemployment Statistics, unpublished 2009 annual average data from the Current Population Survey (CPS).

Thus, education may be viewed as a type of private (and social) hedge against technological displacement. Weisbrod called this the "hedging option," the value of which is difficult to quantify.[47] Further, inexperienced and uneducated workers who earn less than minimum wage have higher unemployment. Better educated workers may well have the edge in communication, discipline of the mind, flexibility, and adaptability. Also, as illustrated in Figure 5.1, the more educated the worker, the more likely he or she is to be receptive to new ideas and knowledge.[48] Figure 5.2 shows the difference that schooling has on the unemployment rate. In the post-recession period immediately following the Great Recession of 2008, when the overall average unemployment rate was at about 8.0 for all education levels, those persons with bachelor's degrees or higher had only a 4.6 unemployment rate while those with less than high school completion had an unemployment rate of 14.6.

Machlup has summarized the effects of education on increased productivity as follows:

It is with regard to . . . improvements in the quality of labor, that education can play a really significant role. Positive effects may be expected on five scores: (a) better working habits and discipline, increased labor efforts, and greater reliability; (b) better health through more wholesome and sanitary ways of living; (c) improved skills, better comprehension of working requirements, and increased efficiency; (d) prompter adaptability to momentary changes, especially in jobs which require quick evaluation of new information, and, in general, fast reactions; and (e) increased capability to move into more productive occupations when opportunities arise. All levels of education may contribute to improving the quality of labor.[49]

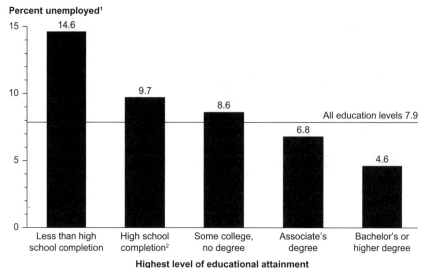

Figure 5.2 Unemployment Rates of Persons 25 Years Old and Over, by Highest Level of Educational Attainment: 2009

Source: U.S. Department of Labor, Bureau of Labor Statistics, Office of Employment and Unemployment Statistics, unpublished 2009 annual average data from the Current Population Survey (CPS).

Education differs in a basic way from most other social or public services in that it constitutes an investment in knowledge and skills that yield economic and social benefits in the future. It differs materially from governmental welfare or health expenditures, which may be characterized as maintenance of human capital rather than development.

While it is true that benefits from these public services cannot be completely self-contained, it is obvious that the provision of public education is quite different from that of other social services. Education, therefore, should not be treated in the same light by legislators. There is a fundamental difference between the mere maintenance of human capital and the development of human capital.

MEASURING THE BENEFITS OF EDUCATION

The benefits of education may be broadly defined as anything that,

1. Increases production through enhancement of the capacity of the labor force;
2. Increases efficiency by reducing costs, thus reserving or releasing resources for other productive pursuits;
3. Increases the social consciousness of the community so that the standard of living is enhanced.[50]

Beyond these generalizations, though, the actual measurement of the benefits of education becomes more difficult. Since the early 1960s, literally hundreds of research projects have been undertaken which have sought to quantify the benefits of education, all supplying pieces to a complex puzzle but none truly achieving the desired precision of measurement. Most of the analyses can be categorized into four basic approaches:

1. Simple relationship analysis
2. Residual
3. Cash value or direct monetary return
4. Cost-benefit or rate of return.[51]

Relationship Analysis Approach

One approach to measuring the benefits of education is simply to compare levels of educational attainment with other socioeconomic indicators. For example, the years of schooling for persons in certain age groups can be compared to their annual incomes.[52] *The Economist* has pithily stated: "The educated are different: they earn more money."[53] One can also compare the relationship between the income of certain wage earners by their education level, between their economic attitudes and their education levels, or the number of high school dropouts and their annual loss in dollars by simply comparing employment.[54] The Great Recession of 2008 highlighted the connection between education level and unemployment. Shown in Figure 5.3 is the effect of educational attainment on unemployment rates. This figure also shows the wide differences in median weekly earnings by degree level of education.

On a macroeconomic scale, such analysis may relate an index of educational attainment to the GNP per capita, national income per capita, or any other broad economic measure. For example, enrollment ratios have been found to have a positive correlation with GNP per capita.[55]

While helpful, these studies are far from definitive because they do not show cause-and-effect relationships between education and economic growth. Other important factors which relate to both may be present, influencing the positive relationships.

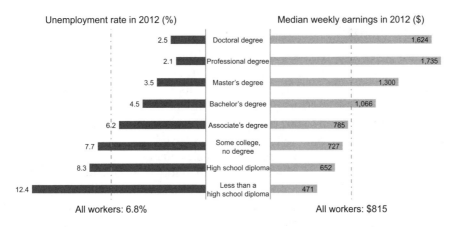

Figure 5.3 Earnings and Unemployment Rates by Educational Attainment

Source: U.S. Department of Labor, Bureau of Labor Statistics, "Employment Projections," www.bls.gov/emp/ep_chart_001.htm.

Residual Approach

This approach is also known as the growth accounting method and is based on the concept of an aggregate production function using multiple regression analyses that link outputs (growth) to inputs of physical capital and labor.[56] Recognition that the classical inputs of land, labor, and capital were not the sole determinants of a nation's economic advancement is the basis for other macroeconomic analyses which have sought to ferret out the various contributors to economic growth. As indicated earlier, economists found that even after all physical inputs were considered, a persistent and unidentified residual remained. Kendrick examined this phenomenon in 1961 and estimated that for the period between 1889 and 1957 a combined index of inputs increased 1.9 percent annually while the nation's output index increased 3.5 percent annually, leaving an unexplained discrepancy of 1.6 percent.[57] He found that about 80 percent of the increased output per unit of labor input was attributable to a residual – something other than land, labor, and capital. That other growth he suggested came from investments in education, research and development, and other intangible capital.

Schultz in 1961 and Denison in 1962 set out to explain this residual and to determine what portion of it was attributable to education.[58] Schultz estimated that 44 percent of the increase in earnings of labor could be attributed to additional education from 1929 to 1957.[59] Schultz's methodology, although giving quite a range of results depending on the rate of return used, nevertheless was a major contribution because it constituted the first attempt to treat education as a separate production function in a nation's economic growth.

The residual approach continues to be a useful tool in the measurement of education's contribution to real national income growth. Studies using similar methodology have been conducted for other countries, with widely varying results. However, all of these studies made one overall conclusion quite clear: "Increased education of the labor force appears to explain a substantial part of the growth of output in both developed and developing countries."[60]

Cash-Value Approach

Educational benefits can also be measured by relating earnings to the educational level of individuals. Individuals with a high school education will, on average, have higher earnings than those with only a tenth-grade education, and college graduates will earn more than high school graduates. This pattern has held for many years. We show the median weekly earnings in Figure 5.3. You will also notice in Figure 5.4 and Figure 5.5 that median annual full-year, full-time earnings have been consistently higher over the years as one moves upward in education degree attainment.

The monetary benefits to education are, therefore, well documented. A person progressing through the educational system can be comforted by the knowledge that he or she, on the average, stands a better chance of having a higher income throughout a lifetime. This does not, of course, assure that every individual will earn more with a higher degree than if he or she had only completed, say, the tenth grade. Our history is replete with examples of "self-made" persons who without formal education

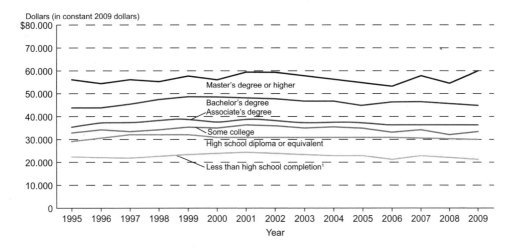

Figure 5.4 Median Annual Earnings of Full-Time, Full-Year Wage and Salary Workers Ages 25–34, by Educational Attainment: 1995–2009

Source: U.S. Department of Commerce, Census Bureau, Current Population Survey (CPS), March and Annual Social and Economic Supplement, 2010.

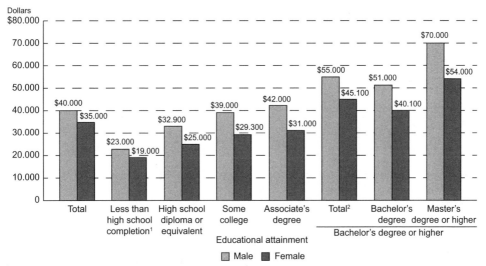

[1] Young adults in this category did not earn a high school diploma or receive alternative credentials, such as a General Educational Development (GED) certificate.

[2] Total represents median annual earnings of young adults with a bachelor's degree or higher. NOTE: *Full-year worker* refers to those who were employed 50 or more weeks during the previous year; *full-time worker* refers to those who were usually employed 35 or more hours per week.

Figure 5.5 Median Annual Earnings of Full-Time, Full-Year Wage and Salary Workers Ages 25–34, by Educational Attainment and Sex: 2009

Source: U.S. Department of Commerce, Census Bureau, Current Population Survey (CPS), March and Annual Social and Economic Supplement, 2010.

became economically successful. However, the odds are much better for individuals to become economically successful if they have more education rather than less.

Cost-Benefit Approach

At different school levels, the cash-value approach to measuring the economic desirability of obtaining an education does not give the entire picture. While the cash-value method is useful, it does not take into account the important element of costs, but focuses exclusively on the benefits. To take costs into consideration requires a more complex analysis of the value of education.

The cost-benefit approach is schematically represented in Figure 5.6. Here it shows negative cost to schooling that must be overcome by income in order for there to be a positive return at retirement age. This schematic is, of course, not drawn to scale. If it were, the costs would possibly show an even more dramatic difference because of foregone income. If we assume that the profile represents individual or private returns on educational investment, and we further assume that the education is taking place in a public school, then the costs to the individual at the elementary level are quite small. Foregone income is very little, since the annual earnings of illiterate or semiliterate children are indeed small. Additionally, the individual does not incur direct costs in attending a public school since the state pays for the education in its entirety. Thus, the benefits of elementary education to the individual can be expected to be very impressive since the costs are so low. On the other hand, if one is considering social benefits, the direct costs of schooling must be taken into account, thereby reducing the benefit-cost.

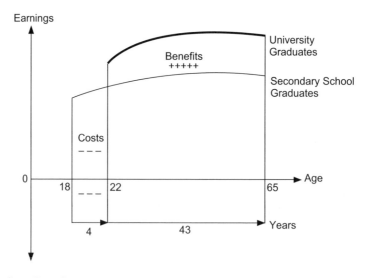

Figure 5.6 Cost-Benefit

Source: George Psacharopoulos, "The Value of Investment in Education: Theory, Evidence, and Policy," *Journal of Education Finance,* Vol. 32, No. 2 (Fall 2006), pp. 113–136. Reprinted by permission of the *Journal of Education Finance.*

With a public high school education, the costs are expected to be greater for the individual because of foregone income. The benefit-cost ratio will therefore be reduced somewhat even though income of the high school graduate is greater.

The individual costs to a college graduate are greater than to either the elementary school or high school graduate since the state does not pay the full costs of a higher education and the student must pay out of pocket for tuition, books, room and board, in addition to greater foregone earnings. Persons completing graduate-level degrees experience yet higher individual costs than individuals completing undergraduate study, and therefore must have a correspondingly higher income set to offset costs.

PRIVATE AND SOCIAL COSTS

Education has both private and social costs, which may be both direct and indirect. If the student is attending a private school, direct private costs are incurred for tuition, fees, books, and room and board. In a public school, the majority of these costs is subsumed by the public treasury, and thus become social costs. The indirect costs of education are embodied in the earnings which are foregone by all persons of working age; however, foregone earnings are also a cost to society, a reduction in the total productivity of the nation. This may be viewed in macroeconomic terms, but can also be measured in the amount of tax funds which a state foregoes when an individual is unemployed. Of course, the state here assumes, as does the individual, that earnings foregone for the sake of education at some early point in the person's career will yield greater returns later. This is the essence of the idea of investment in education. Table 5.1 shows the major types and categories of costs.

It is within the realm of costs that much of the disenchantment with cost-benefit studies has been generated. Schultz maintained that only about one-half of the total social costs for education should be considered as an investment. It must be acknowledged that all education is not undertaken as an investment. Much of the educational

Table 5.1 Types and Categories of Private and Social Educational Costs

Types of Costs	Private	Social
Direct Costs	Tuition and fees	Salaries of teachers, administrators, and nonprofessional personnel
	Books, supplies, and equipment (out-of-pocket expenditures)	Books, supplies, and equipment (total)
	Extra travel	Transportation (total)
	Room and board	Room and board (total)
		Scholarship and other subsidies to students
		Capital expenditures
Indirect Costs	Earnings foregone	Earnings foregone

experience of most persons is simply consumed and enjoyed with no thought to what the education will earn them in the future. Does the student make an economically rational choice to invest in education, as he or she would in stocks and bonds?

PRIVATE AND SOCIAL BENEFITS *of education*

Benefits from education may be either monetary or nonmonetary, and either private (individual) or social. Monetary returns are measurable and are therefore most commonly used in cost-benefit studies. The social externalities of education are difficult to quantify and are therefore seldom relied on for estimating returns to education. Presented in Table 5.2 is a categorization of both the private and social benefits of education.

Direct benefits to the individual are typically measured by increases in earning power after completion of the educational program. The natural ability of the individual, ambition, family connections, family social and economic status, inherited wealth, race, sex, and education of parents may all have a bearing on future earning potential, but cannot be accurately quantified.

Table 5.2 Private and Social Benefits of Education

Private (Individual) Benefits	Social Benefits
Direct Benefits	
Monetary	• Increase in taxes paid by the educated as a result of education
• Net increase in earnings after taxes	
• Additional fringe benefits	
Nonmonetary	
• Increased satisfaction derived from exposure to new knowledge and cultural opportunities for both students and parents	
Indirect Benefits	
Monetary	Increases in other income due to:
• Work options available at each educational level	• Increasing productivity of future generations as children become better educated (intergenerational effect)
• Increased consumption of goods and services due to extra income	• Previously unemployed workers taking jobs vacated by program participants (vacuum effect) (indirect income effect)
Nonmonetary	
• Intergenerational effect between parent and child	• Reduced tax burden (tax effect)
• Job satisfaction	• Incremental productivity and earnings of workers (indirect income effect)

Source: Adapted from table by Asefa Gabregiorgis, "Rate of Return on Secondary Education in the Bahamas." (Ph.D. dissertation, 1978, University of Alberta), p. 75.

For example, it has been estimated that anywhere from 5 to 35 percent of income differentials are attributable to differences in ability,[61] while some studies have estimated that the bias attributable to ability is only about 10 percent.[62] While estimates of the influence of native ability on economic returns vary widely, the variance in ability contributions does not appear to be a serious source of bias to determination of returns to investment in education.[63]

BOX 5.1

Social Internal Rate of Return

The social internal rate of return refers to the costs and benefits to society of investment in education, which includes the opportunity cost of having people not participating in the production of output and the full costs of the provision of education rather than only the cost borne by the individual. The social benefit includes the increased productivity associated with the investment in education and a host of possible non-economic (or nonmarket) benefits, such as lower crime, better health, more social cohesion and more informed and effective citizens.

Source: *Education at a Glance*, OECD, Paris, 2002, Glossary.

INTERNAL RATES OF RETURN TO EDUCATION INVESTMENT   *5a-charopodus*

The internal rate of return is the most commonly used approach in educational investment studies. Many such studies have been conducted with varying results, depending on the particular statistical technique employed by the researcher; but by and large they show that education is a good investment for both the individual and the state. This holds true internationally as well as within the United States. Psacharopoulos, in synthesizing the findings of 53 rates-of-return studies in 32 countries, found that both private and social internal rates of return (IROR) for education were generally higher than returns to investment in physical capital.[64] Psacharopoulos concluded that per capita income differences among countries "can be better explained by differences in the endowments of human rather than physical capital."[65] Averaging rates of return for the 53 studies, he found that private rates of return for primary school were 23.7 percent per year, while for high school and college they were 16.3 and 17.5 percent, respectively. For social rates of return, he found primary education to be 25.1 percent; secondary, 13.5 percent; and college, 11.3 percent (see Figure 5.7).[66] When averages for developed and underdeveloped countries were considered, it was found that overall the returns to investment in human capital were greater in underdeveloped countries. Subsequent analysis by Psacharopoulos of developing countries confirmed the magnitude of these rates of return.[67]

churches, philanthropic organizations and businesses

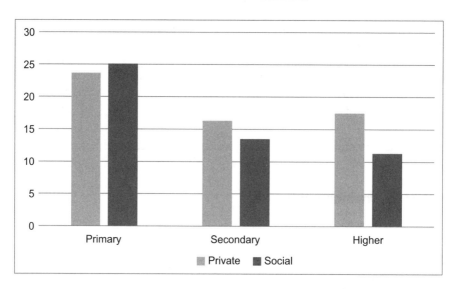

Figure 5.7 Returns to Investment in Education by Level, Latest Year

Source: George Psacharopoulos and Harry A. Patrinos, *Returns to Investment in Education: A Further Update* (September 2002). World Bank Policy Research Working Paper No. 2881. Copyright © 2002 World Bank. Reprinted by permission of World Bank Publications.

BOX 5.2

Private Internal Rate of Return

The private internal rate of return is equal to the discount rate that equalizes the real costs of education during the period of study to the real gains from education thereafter. For example, in higher education, in its most comprehensive form, the costs equal tuition and fees, foregone earnings net of taxes adjusted for the probability of being in employment minus the resources made available to students in the form of grants and loans.

Source: OECD Glossary.

EXTERNAL NONMARKET BENEFITS ESTIMATED BY McMAHON

Up to this point we have considered only a portion of the benefits to investment in education. The entire value of education must also be viewed in light of its total social possibilities and consequences. The monetary benefits considered in rates of return include only the value of increased earnings of the individual and the value of additional taxes collected by the state. However, these numbers do not include the nonmarket benefits. The best estimates of the value of these nonmarket benefits have been provided by Walter W. McMahon, an eminent scholar in the field of the economics of human capital. He explains that nonmarket benefits of education should be distinguished from market benefits and from social benefits, although some are duplicative of market benefits.[68] McMahon explains that "nonmarket" benefits of education are those that result from the use of "human capital during non-labor market hours."[69] Nonmarket benefits include the productive time spent at home and in the community and the nondirect economic benefits of education to individuals and society, such as, for example, better health, less smoking, less depression, lower infant mortality, civic participation, racial tolerance, parenting, lower crime, etc. George Psacharopoulos has identified several nonmarket benefits and their evidences, shown in Table 5.3.

These nonmarket benefits must be added to the economic benefits both private and social that are normally quantifiable in the various human capital studies. The questions are: If quantified, how much do they increase the returns normally attributable to investment in education? What is the actual value of these nonmarket benefits? For example, in studying developing countries, McMahon shows that provision of secondary education of females has a "significant negative relation to net population growth rates."[70] If one compares fertility rates and education levels of females in both developed and developing countries, the result shows striking negative net population growth rates and female gross secondary school enrollment rates.[71]

Table 5.3 Mainly Nonmarket and External Benefits of Education

Benefit	Evidence
Crime	Per capita police expenditure decreases by $170 for an additional year of schooling in community.
Nonwage remuneration	The better educated get higher fringe benefits and better working conditions.
Child education	Parental education affects child's education level and scholastic achievement.
Consumption efficiency	More schooling improves consumer choice.
Fertility, desired family size	Mother's education lowers daughter's birth rate. More schooling improves contraceptive efficiency.
Household health	More education increases life expectancy. Net family assets increase by $8,950 for an additional year of schooling.
Job search efficiency	More schooling reduces cost of search, increases mobility.
Charity	More schooling increases donations.
Technological change	Schooling helps R & D dissemination.
Social cohesion	Schooling increases voting and reduces alienation.
Income transfers	More schooling reduces dependence on transfers.
Savings	Savings rate increases with schooling.

Source: George Psacharopoulos, "The Value of Investment in Education: Theory, Evidence, and Policy," *Journal of Education Finance* 32(2) (Fall 2006), pp. 113–136. Adapted from Wolfe and Zuvekas (1997). Reprinted by permission of the *Journal of Education Finance*.

In an interesting and convincing statistical analysis, McMahon defines and measures the most obvious and important nonmarket benefits of education among which are political stability, overpopulation, climate change, poverty, life span, etc. Concerning those attributes of society that constitute a working definition of political stability or instability in OECD and developing countries, such as rule of law, racial and ethnic tensions, political terrorism, etc., he concludes that a country's contributions to education result not only in economic growth, but have a significant impact in the enhancement of democracy, human rights, and increased political and economic accord.[72]

Nearly all problems facing human beings are caused or exacerbated by overpopulation. The denial of access of women to secondary education in developing countries tends to keep fertility rates and population growth rates very high, the consequences of which have a dominant deleterious effect on the environment. Overpopulation causes destruction of the forests and the relentless rise of carbon dioxide along with air and water pollution. McMahon shows how these ill-effects on the environment are related to levels of education. He has concluded that higher education reduces fertility and population growth rates which, in turn, helps abate destruction of forests, wildlife, and positively affects air and water pollution. Higher incidences of secondary education in developing countries helps reduce rural poverty which therefrom enhances care of forests and reduces air and water pollution.[73]

Concerning crime curtailment, a general observation is that investment in public schools reaches lower income groups, reducing poverty, and correspondingly helps mitigate crime rates.[74] Also, McMahon notes that the mere fact that higher percentages of teenagers are under supervision of schools in and of itself reduces crime rates.[75]

If these and other nonmarket benefits are taken into account, McMahon concludes that "standard social rates of return can be seen to seriously underestimate the true return to education."[76] His conclusions, buttressed by studies of Wolfe and Haveman,[77] estimate the value of nonmarket benefits to be "equal to or a little more than the value of the market values." This means that in the United States where various studies have shown that the standard social rates of return for high school graduation are at least 10.4 percent, for a two-year associate's degree in community college are about 16 percent, and for a college bachelor's degree graduate are an average 15 percent, then the actual social returns would be at least twice those numbers, market and nonmarket benefits added together. McMahon's estimates are shown in Table 5.4.

Table 5.4 Social Rates of Return to Education in the United States, 2004: Market, Nonmarket, and Total Social Rate

	Market Benefit	*Nonmarket Benefit Total*	*Benefit of Education*
High school graduation	10.5% +	10.5% =	21%, in real terms
2-year Associate's degree	16% +	16% =	32%
Bachelor's degree	15% +	15% =	30%

Source: Adapted from Walter W. McMahon, "Education Finance Policy: Financing the Nonmarket and Social Benefits," *Journal of Education Finance*, Vol. 32, No. 2 (Fall 2006), pp. 264–284.

From all of this, McMahon concludes that such estimates of the benefit of education, 21 percent, 32 percent, and 30 percent, are about two times the normal benchmark, when nonmarket benefits are not included. Thus, one can logically conclude that with these types of potential returns there is currently an underinvestment in education.[78]

SUMMARY

The value of investment in education is discussed in this chapter. It is now recognized throughout the world that the wealth of nations is dependent more on human capital than physical capital. This chapter discusses how economists have estimated the value of education in human capital production.

The wealth of nations is highly dependent on the extensiveness of the knowledge of its people. The modern technological state is highly brain intensive as opposed to earlier labor-intensive societies. Various studies since World War II have shown that sustained economic growth is largely attributable to education.

Today, education reform is at the head of national priorities in virtually all countries, both developed and underdeveloped, in the Americas, Europe, and Asia. In these countries education is no longer treated as a consumer good but rather as a productive asset.

The classical economic view espoused by Adam Smith in 1776 did not capture the value of investment in knowledge and assumed that all economic growth resulted from the interaction of the markets. Modern economists have shown that the classical approach did not fully appreciate the catalyst nature of education and its causes for economic growth.

Investment in physical capital cannot be discounted, but it is now known that the quality of human capital is the active ingredient that enables the efficient use of physical capital.

Nations investing in education must gauge and balance their created systems of elementary, secondary, and higher education as well as give due cognizance to technical training.

The primacy of early or primary education is undisputed and to ignore this sector of education impairs the efficiency of investments in higher levels of education. A country that foregoes investment in early education in favor of higher education will undermine its own economic growth.

Returns to investment in education are usually greater to the individual than to society, but both show that investment in education is very lucrative.

Investments in early childhood and elementary education yield greater returns, on the average, than investments in secondary or higher education. On the whole, secondary education yields greater return than higher education.

Education increases worker productivity and is an indirect but real benefit to society. Higher levels of education produce an external benefit of increased opportunities and employment options. The better educated are more easily employed, are unemployed less, have more continuity and longevity in their jobs, produce a greater quantity and quality of goods and services, and are more satisfied with their employment.

Better-educated persons have less need for health services, commit fewer crimes, are less needful of welfare, have a greater social consciousness, conduct more efficient households, and transfer more beneficial knowledge to their children. Moreover, the better educated are less likely to overpopulate, while educated women are more active and productive in the labor force. At the same time, better-educated women have proven to be more adept and attentive mothers.

KEY TERMS

- Labor intensive
- Brain intensive
- World Bank
- Gender equality
- Human capital
- Absorption effect
- Skill acquisition
- Cash value
- Cost-benefit

- Annual earnings
- Private costs
- Social costs
- Private benefits
- Social benefits
- Internal rates of return
- Market benefits
- Nonmarket benefits

NOTES

1. Jeffrey D. Sachs, *The Price of Civilization: Reawakening American Virtue and Prosperity* (New York: Random House Trade Paperbacks, 2011), p. 19.
2. Ibid.
3. For an excellent discussion on the history of human capital see Elchanan Cohn and Terry G. Geske, *The Economics of Education*, 3rd edn. (Oxford: Pergamon Press, 1990), pp. 13–24.
4. Barbara W. Tuchman, *A Distant Mirror: The Calamitous 14th Century* (New York: Alfred A. Knopf, 1978), pp. 119–120.
5. Theodore W. Schultz, "Investment in Human Capital," *American Economic Review* 51 (March 1961), pp. 1–17.
6. World Bank, *World Development Report 1991, The Challenge of Development* (Oxford: The World Bank and Oxford University Press, 1991), p. 42.
7. "Where Tigers Breed, A Survey of Asia's Emerging Economies," *The Economist*, 321:7733 (November 16, 1991), pp. 4–5.
8. Ibid., p. 5.
9. Ibid.
10. Mark Blaug, *Economic Theory in Retrospect, 5th edition* (Cambridge: Cambridge University Press, 1996), p. 208.
11. Adam Smith, *The Wealth of Nations*, rev. edn. (New York: Modern Library, 1937), p. 265.
12. Adam Smith, *The Wealth of Nations, Books IV–V* (London: Penguin Books, first published in 1776, this edition 1999), p. 371.

13. Ibid.
14. R. Blandy, "Marshall on Human Capital: R Note," *Journal of Political Economy* 75 (December 1967), pp. 874–875.
15. Blaug, *op. cit.,* p. 401.
16. Ibid.
17. Alfred Marshall, *Principles of Economics*, 8th edn. (London: MacMillan, 1930), pp. 787–788.
18. John Stuart Mill, *Principles of Political Economy*, vol. 1, rev. edn. (London: Colonial Press, 1900), p. 9.
19. See: J. B. Schneewind, "Making Our Lives Our Own: An Introduction to John Stuart Mill," *The Basic Writings of John Stuart Mill* (New York: The Modern Library, 2002), p. 15.
20. John Stuart Mill, *On Liberty, in Utilitarianism, On Liberty, Essay on Bentham* (ed. Mary Warnock (New York: Meridian, Penguin Books, 1974), pp. 238–240.
21. John Stuart Mill, *The Basic Writings*, "The Subjection of Women," 1869, Chapter IV (New York: The Modern Library, 2002), p. 209.
22. Ibid., p. 211.
23. Blaug, *op. cit.,* p. 213.
24. Horace Mann, from the 12th Report (1848), one of twelve *Annual Reports* made by Mann to the State Board of Education, Massachusetts.
25. Ibid.
26. See E.A. Caswell, *The Money Value of Education* (Washington, DC: U.S. Government Printing Office, 1917).
27. Theodore W. Schultz, *Investment in Human Capital* (New York: Free Press, 1971), p. 22.
28. Ibid.
29. Ibid., pp. 1–17.
30. Frederick H. Harbison, *Human Resources as the Wealth of Nations* (New York: Oxford University Press, 1973), p. 3.
31. Ibid.
32. W. Arthur Lewis, *The Theory of Economic Growth* (London: George Allen & Unwin, 1977), pp. 183–184.
33. Mark Blaug, ed., *Economics of Education* (New York: Penguin Books, 1972).
34. Jee-Pang Tan and Alain Mingat, *Education in Asia, A Comparative Study of Costs and Financing* (Washington, DC: The World Bank, 1992), p. 78.
35. Ibid., p. 79.
36. Lewis, *op. cit.,* p. 183.
37. Eli Ginsberg, *The Human Economy* (New York: McGraw-Hill, 1976), p. 47.
38. Ibid., pp. 70–71.
39. Pitirim A. Sorokin, *Hunger as a Factor in Human Affairs* (Gainesville, FL: University Presses of Florida, 1975), pp. 156–157.
40. Burton A. Weisbrod, "Education and Investment in Human Capital," *Journal of Political Economy* 70, no. 5 (Pt. 2, 1962 Supp.), pp. 106–123.
41. H.R. Bowen, *Investment in Learning* (San Francisco: Jossey-Bass, 1977), pp. 159–160.
42. Jacob Mincer, "On-the-Job Training: Costs, Returns, and Some Implications," *Journal of Political Economy* 70 (October 1962 Supp.), pp. 50–79.
43. Richard Perlman, *The Economics of Education* (New York: McGraw-Hill, 1973), p. 32.
44. John D. Owen, *School Inequality and the Welfare State* (Baltimore: Johns Hopkins University Press, 1974), p. 91.
45. Ibid.
46. *The Economist*, "Education: Coming Top," *op. cit.,* p. 4.
47. Weisbrod, *op. cit.*

48. J. Ronnie Davis, "The Social and Economic Externalities of Education," *Economic Factors Affecting the Financing of Education,* vol. 2, eds. R.L. Johns and others (Gainesville, FL: National Educational Finance Project, 1970), p. 66.

49. Fritz Machlup, *Education and Economic Growth* (Lincoln, NE: University of Nebraska Press, 1970), pp. 7–8.

50. Weisbrod, *op. cit.*

51. W. G. Bowen, "Assessing the Economic Contribution of Education: An Appraisal of Alternative Approaches," *Higher Education. Report of the Committee under the Chairmanship of Lord Robbins, Report: 961–63* (London: HMSO, 1963), pp. 73–96.

52. Education Department, Chamber of Commerce of the United States, *Education: An Investment in the People* (Washington, DC: U.S. Government Printing Office, 1961), pp. 2–3.

53. *The Economist*, "Education: Coming Top," Nov. 21, 1992.

54. Ibid., pp. 4–23.

55. "Targets for Education in Europe" (Paper delivered at Washington conference of OECD, 1961), p. 75.

56. The simplest form of this production function is a linear model expressed as $y = F\,(KL)$, where physical capital is K and labor is L. For further information see George Psacharopoulos, "The Contribution of Education to Economic Growth: International Comparisons," *in International Productivity Comparisons and the Causes of the Slowdown*, ed. J. Kendrick (Cambridge, MA: Ballinger, 1984).

57. John W. Kendrick, *Productivity Trends in the United States* (Princeton, NJ: Princeton University Press, 1961), p. 79.

58. For an excellent explanation of the aggregate production function, see Elchanan Cohn and Terry G. Geske, *The Economics of Education*, 3rd Edn (Oxford: Pergamon Press, 1990), pp. 142–145.

59. Theodore W. Schultz, "Education and Economic Growth," in *Social Forces Influencing American Education*, ed. N.B. Henry (Chicago: University of Chicago Press, 1961), pp. 46–88.

60. George Psacharopoulos and Maureen Woodhall, *Education for Development, An Analysis of Investment Choices* (Oxford: Oxford University Press, 1985), pp. 17–19.

61. P. Taubman and Terence Wales, "Education as an Investment and a Screening Device," in *Education, Income and Human Behavior*, ed. F. Thomas Juster (New York: McGraw-Hill, 1975), pp. 95–121; P. Taubman "Personal Characteristics and the Distribution of Earnings," in *The Personal Distribution of Incomes*, ed. A.B. Atkinson (London: George Allen and Unwin, 1976), pp. 193–226.

62. Zwi Griliches and William M. Mason, "Education, Income and Ability," in *Investment in Education*, ed. T.W. Schultz (Chicago: University of Chicago Press, 1971), p. 87.

63. John C. Hause, "Earnings Profile: Ability and Schooling," in T.W. Schultz, ed., *op. cit.*, p. 131.

64. Psacharopoulos, *op. cit.*

65. Ibid., p. 17.

66. Ibid., p. 65.

67. George Psacharopoulos, "Returns to Education: An Updated International Comparison," *Comparative Education* 17, no. 3 (1981), pp. 321–324.

68. Walter W. McMahon, "Education Finance Policy: Financing the Nonmarket and Social Benefits," *Journal of Education Finance*, Vol. 32, No. 2 (Fall 2006), pp. 264–284.

69. Ibid.

70. Walter W. McMahon, *Education and Development: Measuring the Social Benefits* (Oxford: Oxford University Press, 1999), p. 76.

71. Ibid., pp. 87–90.

72. Ibid., pp. 92–109.

73. Ibid., pp. 127–140.
74. Ibid., p. 151.
75. Ibid.
76. McMahon, "Education Finance Policy", *op. cit.*, p. 93.
77. B. Wolfe and R. Haveman, "Social and Nonmarket Benefits from Education in an Advanced Economy," In Y. Kodrzycki (ed.), *Education in the 21st Century: Meeting the Challenges of a Changing World* (Boston: Federal Reserve Bank of Boston, 2003).
78. McMahon, "Education Finance Policy", *op. cit.*, p. 94.

CHAPTER 6

The Politics of School Finance

TOPICAL OUTLINE OF CHAPTER

- Politics and the Public Good
  - The Balance of the Commons
  - Schools for the Common Good
- Coloration of Politics
- Nature of Politics
- The Political Cycles
- Politics of Race
- Politics of Business Corporations
  - Corporations, Money, and Politics
- Politics of Stability
- Politics and Social Justice
- Political Reality
- Shaping of Attitudes
- Politics of Religion
- Urban-Suburban Politics
- Politics at the State Level
  - Educational Interest Groups
  - The State Legislature
  - Politics of Federal Aid

INTRODUCTION

Public schools are an integral part of the politics of the United States. The formation of public schools was originally a political consideration and its subsequent governance and financing are entirely political in nature. As a public democratic institution, the schools are conducted by political processes to obtain the ends assigned by society. The reliance on political considerations in the conduct of the schools is in keeping with the United States' tradition of republican government. Politics thus permeates all aspects of public school finance. By definition, politics has to do with public affairs, and education is at the heart of virtually all considerations of public policy. Every chapter in this book, in fact, encompasses some aspect of politics. Tocqueville in the 1830s observed that politics was "the only pleasure an American knows,"[1] and Bryce half a century later noted that political parties were "organized far more elaborately in the United States than anywhere else in the world."[2] Smith, the American historian, cites the watershed of the maturation of modern United States politics to be the election of Andrew Jackson, after which democratic politics and a kind of people's capitalism merged to form the basis of a *laissez-faire* economic individualism that still prevails.[3] It was about that time that the germination and growth of public schools began. This chapter deals with a few of the political issues that have affected the public schools.

BOX 6.1

Definition

Politics is the pursuit of ends. It is about what is to be done. It is, in other words, about policy – the making of socially directive decisions and the allocation of the resources and instruments necessary to carry them out.

Source: John Kane, *The Politics of Moral Capital* (Cambridge: Cambridge University Press, 2001), p. 12.

POLITICS AND THE PUBLIC GOOD

The heart of politics is to calibrate the power of the sovereign to the best advantage of the well-being and liberties of the individual. Essentially, politics is the process by which individuals decide that authority and power which is delegated to the commonwealth and that which is retained for them. As Thomas Hobbes explained, the common power of all protects the individual, "Where there is no common power, there is no law, no injustice,"[4] and, of course, no protection and justice. Without the commonwealth government there is no "common peace and safety."[5] In order to have liberty, the individual must "unite" with the "multitude" in a "commonwealth." The "commonwealth" is the sovereign, of whose Acts a Great Multitude, by mutuall Covenants one with another, have made themselves every one the Author, to the end he may use the strength and means of them all, as he shall think expedient, for their Peace and Common Defence.[6]

In the state of nature, man without a sovereign and the common laws by which all must abide, no one is safe, and there are no "public officers" to protect him.[7]

Locke built on Hobbes and is helpful to us in understanding some rudiments of the idea of politics.[8] Locke explains in his *Second Treatise* that when man enters into society, he gives up a certain amount of his "equality, liberty and executive power" and turns it over to society to be disposed by the legislature of the society to the extent that the "good of society" requires.[9] This relinquishment of the individual rights and interests "can never" or should never, "extend further than the *common good* " (emphasis added),[10] the end being "the peace, safety, and *public good.*"

The Balance of the Commons

It is, thus, the role of *politics* to set the boundaries that calibrate the *necessary balance* between the individual and the sovereign, between man and the state. Establishing that *balance* is the political process, democracy is thought to be the best means to do so. Implicit in this process, essential to the *necessary balance*, is the determination of the breadth and scope of the public or common good. Familiar issues and discord arise most frequently in two basic areas. Defining the span of *common* for which public fiscal resources should be committed is crucial. Is a turnpike *common* or should it be paid for through tolls by individuals who use it? Were the great western plains of America *common*, or could they be fenced and privatized, cattlemen versus sheep farmers? The land enclosures of England fashioned by the wealthy landlords and magnates were examples of a few who controlled the government to the detriment of the many. Are the ocean beaches of the coastal areas of the United States common grounds for all to use or are they subject to purchase and exclusivity of a few with wealth?

BOX 6.2

Defining Public Goods

Public goods are usually defined as goods with non-excludable benefits and non-rival consumption. Non-excludability means that it is technically, politically, or economically infeasible to exclude someone from consuming the good. Non-rivalry means that one person's consumption of the good does not detract from its availability to others. If a good is non-rival, it can be made available to additional users at zero – or close to zero – cost . . . Knowledge is an example.

Source: Inge Kaul, Pedro Conceicao, Katell LeGoulven, and Ronald V. Mendoza, "How to Improve the Provision of Global Public Goods," in *Providing Global Public Goods,* edited by the same authors above (Oxford: Oxford University Press, 2003), pp. 21–22.

The nature of public and common goods is critical to the balance between the public and private sectors. Today, the green and sustainability question, i.e., the ozone level and climate change, where there is no reasonable argument as to what are the *commons* and the deleterious consequences, is subject to intense political debate between those who would use the *commons* for their own gain and those who would preserve it. Other examples of contests over the public good versus private interest, such as rain forests, whales and fish in the sea, nuclear energy, fracking for gas, oil wells in the Gulf of Mexico, all have to do with the scope of the public or common good.

Schools for the Common Good

Public schools have historically been considered common schools, schools for the common good, because their benefits and positive externalities extend to society at large. The debate is over the role of government in regulating the vicissitudes of the *laissez-faire* capitalism, the marketplace, and the commons. What is the common interest and what is the private interest is at the heart of the matter.

BOX 6.3

Politics

The science of government; the art or practice of administering public affairs. Pertaining to, or incidental to, the exercise of the functions vested in those charged with the conduct of government; relating to the management of affairs of state; as political theories; of or pertaining to exercise of rights and privileges or the influence by which individuals of a state seek to determine or control its public policy.

Source: *Black's Law Dictionary*, 4th edn. (St. Paul, MN: West Publishing Company, 1968), p. 1319.

Frank, in his book *The Darwin Economy: Liberty, Competition and the Common Good*, writes that the invisible hand of the marketplace usually prevails in the United States' economy. In the balance between the public interest and the private interest, competition will not necessarily promote the common good.[11]

COLORATION OF POLITICS

Politics itself is value-free: it may be moral or immoral, beneficial or harmful. Politics as we know it has at its foundation the social obligations presumptive in a liberal democratic state. Politics taken out of a democratic or other ideological context is Plato's *techne*, merely an art or a craft similar to any other ordinary social interaction. It is technique, simply steering the ship of state while not deciding course or direction. In a democratic state, the course is supposedly set by ideological standards broadly enunciated in constitutional law. The politician, as helmsman, is to steer the ship in the constitutionally prescribed direction. In fact, the word *governor* derives from the Latin translation of the Greek for *helmsman*.[12]

For the public schools, the governors, legislators, and judges are the helmsmen who both steer and interpret direction set by the people through constitutions and political processes. The primary problems experienced in funding education derive from not knowing which ideological bent of politics should steer the public schools.

Politics may of course misguide so as to subvert the people's intent. When this happens democratic government may falter and its purposes become obscure. Lately, Americans have experienced disenchantment with politics to the extent that the term *politics* itself has taken on a broadly pejorative connotation. Thus, most criticisms of politics have little to do with politics *per se*, but rather are remonstrances against a particular ideological direction toward which politics is thought to lead. It is the coloration of politics that is objectionable to most persons and not politics itself.

NATURE OF POLITICS

"Politics," according to Raphael, "concerns the behavior of groups and individuals in matters that are likely to affect the course of government."[13] Politics in a democratic state is the means by which the sovereign power of the state is enforced.[14] Politics in a democracy is the peaceful process by which certain persons are acknowledged and authorized to exercise power and authority over others.[15] Subjugation by war or force cannot be construed to be *politics* because there is not acknowledgment of, or acquiescence to, authority without compulsion.[16]

Volition. According to Locke, "Politic societies all began from a voluntary union and the mutual agreement of men freely acting in the choice of their governors and forms of government,"[17] and "that the beginning of politic society depends upon the consent of individuals to join into and make one society."[18] Without consent and volition on the part of the governed, the system of government cannot acquire unity and hold together. As a part of this volitional arrangement in a democracy, the public schools are dependent upon the free will of the people to contribute in common through their taxation for the general educational benefits of all. When voters withhold their support of public schools at the local, state, or federal levels they are exercising their Lockean political prerogatives to withdraw their private consent from the whole. Of course, once the majority decides to tax itself for the provision of education, all, dissenters included, must join in payment of taxes regardless of whether or not they individually believe in the purposes of public schools.

Obligation. Republican politics authorizes some persons to act as the representatives of the people to protect, restrict, enable, or constrain for the common good of all. In public education, we vote for school board members and give them the authority to impose taxes on us and to expend our money for our public schools. By politics we elect legislators and governors to make and enforce laws that both enhance and restrict us. A democratic society cannot function as a viable institution without the means of authorizing power to be vested in a few persons for the conduct of government. Politics in a democratic state can only function if it is grounded in a political obligation of

those governed.[19] The citizen is obliged to obey the rules established by those individuals who by election are given the authority to act. Political authority implies (1) an
obligation to obey the commands issued by the person or body vested with authority;
and (2) implies the person or body (representative) has a right to issue the commands
and possesses a right to be obeyed.[20]

This means, of course, that in the conduct of public schools, failure to abide by
the laws and regulations of school authorities may result in the punishments that are
specified by society. Failure to pay properly levied taxes, refusal to abide by compulsory attendance laws, or failure to stop behind school buses all have consequences that
flow from the obligations implicit in the politics of public education in a democratic
society.

Moral Ends. Although politics itself is value-free, a reciprocal obligation between
the governors and the governed can only be justified in a democratic state if the
objectives are moral ones. The ends of politics must be moral to promote social justice
for the common good.[21] If an obligation is merely a legal one without moral underpinnings, no political obligation exists to acquiesce to the authority. Simply having
power without a moral foundation is insufficient.

BOX 6.4

Politics in America

America has given the world its most modern and efficient economic organizations. It has pioneered social benefits for the masses: mass production, mass
education, mass culture . . .

The distinctive American contributions to politics are in the organization of
popular participation. The one major political institution invented in America is, of
course, the political party. Americans created the caucus before the Revolution
and committees of correspondence during the revolutionary crisis. Upon these
beginnings at the end of the eighteenth century they organized the first political
parties.

Source: Samuel P. Huntington, *Political Order in Changing Societies* (New Haven and London:
Yale University Press, 1968), pp. 130–131.

The particular moral ends that support our democratic government are couched
in a basic belief in liberty and equality. "Liberty and equality are distinctive aims of
democracy,"[22] and the direction of United States politics properly prescribed will be
in keeping with these goals. According to Raphael, "Liberty and equality are what distinguish the democratic ideals from the other political ideals."[23]

Educated Voters. A well-educated and governmentally active citizenry is more
capable of governing itself than an educated one. As our founders observed,
it is difficult to constrain and deny liberty and equality to a well-educated and

Table 6.1 Education Level of Voters

Education Level	Total	Voted	Registered, No Vote	Not Registered	No Response
High school not complete	100.0	25.1	19.5	37.0	18.4
Completed high school	100.0	37.9	20.2	23.3	18.6
Some college	100.0	44.3	22.4	16.8	16.6
Associate's degree	100.0	50.7	21.3	13.0	14.9
Bachelor's degree	100.0	57.7	17.6	9.4	15.3
Advanced degree	100.0	67.1	13.9	6.3	12.7

Source: *Voting Hot Report*, U.S. Census Bureau, Current Population Survey, November 2010.

governmentally active electorate. Security of democracy is enhanced by education. The effect of education on voting behavior in Congressional elections, as shown in Table 6.1, indicates there is a strong positive relationship between voting and schooling. Voter participation increases with educational attainment. Only 25 percent of high school dropouts voted in 2010 as opposed to 57.7 percent for the college bachelor degree graduates, and advanced degree holders had still a higher voting rate of 67.1 percent.

THE POLITICAL CYCLES

Since the presidency of Andrew Jackson, politics in the United States has emerged as action and reaction, an ebb and flow of governmental policy as it is shaped and molded by the interplay between public and private interests. Periodically, throughout U.S. history, swings in public opinion between the conservative self-interest and the public common interest result in a divergence of governmental policies that produce a political pendulum effect. Schlesinger referred to these swings in public opinion as cycles of political history.[24] In documenting these cycles he comments:

> In short, the conservatism formed in the 1980s among intellectuals, religious zealots and the young does not necessarily prove a fundamental transformation in the national mood. It is exactly what the historian would expect during the private-interest swing of the political cycle.[25]

The emergence of any swing toward self-interest and away from common public interest finds its philosophical justification in Adam Smith's *Wealth of Nations* in which he states that as the individual promotes his own interests he effectively promotes the public interest as well. During the 1980s, this ethos of private self-interest was the dominant political philosophy.[26] The arc of the pendulum had banked in the 1980s to the opposite extreme from the "New Society" programs of the 1960s. The pendulum began to move back as voters expressed another political vision as reflected in the elections of presidents and the Congress of the United States. These political phenomena, of course, have a direct effect on policies of the public schools. The implicit reliance of public schools on political businesses makes equality of educational opportunity much more problematic in some eras than in others.

POLITICS OF RACE

> **BOX 6.5**
>
> ## Politics of Race
>
> When the official subject is presidential politics, taxes, welfare, crime, rights, or values . . . the real subject is *race*.
>
> Source: Thomas Byrne Edsall with Mary E. Edsall, "Race," *Atlantic Monthly* 267, no. 5 (May 1991), p. 53.

In America, racial discrimination is near to the base of almost every economic public question. The pendulum of which Schlesinger spoke remains on the conservative swing away from Fourteenth Amendment rights of individuals in legal precedents by judges who were appointed in recent years by conservative presidents. Most notably are the social and political consequences of racial discrimination. As Gary Orfield documented in his study, *Schools More Separate: Consequences of a Decade of Resegregation*,

> [I]n the South from 1988 to 1998, most of the progress of the previous two decades in increasing integration in the region was lost. The South is still more integrated than it was before the civil rights revolution, but it is moving backward, or toward segregation at an accelerating rate.[27]

After *Brown v. Board of Education* in 1954, the percentage of African-American students in the South attending majority-white schools increased from 2.3 percent in 1964 to 43.5 percent in 1988, but subsequently the percentage declined from 39.2 percent in 1991 to 32.7 percent in 1998, the latest year of Orfield's data. The Supreme Court rendered its decision in the *Seattle* and *Louisville* cases, 2007,[28] where it effectively countermanded the constitutional meanings of its earlier pro-integration decisions.[29] This decision dramatically changed school desegregation law by placing upon a public school board the burden of proof to show that its motive for assigning students was not to use race to effectuate racial balances in schools. Chemerinsky, a constitutional law scholar, points out that "color blindness" sounds noble, but there is every difference in the world between using race to discriminate and using race to desegregate.[30] Jeffrey Toobin, in his book *The Oath* (2013), asks the essential political question regarding school desegregation, "Was *Brown* essentially a libertarian decision which simply forbade all recognition of race by the government? Or, perhaps the political question of the age in America, did *Brown* mandate, or allow, government to take steps to foster integration"?[31]

Race as the transcendent issue, the "American Dilemma," that has pitted conservatives against liberals since 1787, is still very much on the table as the *Seattle* and *Louisville* cases verify. When the issue appears on the surface to be federalism, housing, unemployment, schooling, etc., the underlying issue is usually race. In 2013, the U.S. Supreme Court, made up of a majority of conservative appointees, held a key part of the Voting Rights Act of 1965, a touchstone of Congress' commitment to rectify racial discrimination throughout U.S. history, to be unconstitutional. In *Shelby County, Alabama v. Holder*,[32] the U.S. Attorney General, the Court ruled that Section 4 of the Voting Rights was unconstitutional. Section 4 was a central and necessary provision concerning the "coverage formula" that defined the "covered jurisdictions" which had a suspect record of human rights violations. In a *New York Times* front page article, August 25, 2013, Justice Ginsburg, one of the dissenting justices, labeled the decision "stunning in terms of activism" by "one of the most activist Supreme Courts in U.S. history."[33] The decision is one of a series of decisions that evidences the degree to which Schlesinger's political pendulum has swung far to the right.

Thus, politics in a democracy is not value-free but reflects those ideals that are value-laden in the conduct of a virtuous government. Authority is vested through politics, and the obligations of the governed will be assured so long as the democratic ends are maintained. However, if imbalances toward inequality or repression become too great, the government will either adjust or possibly even fall as individual obligations to sustain it become tenuous and subverted to group or self-interest which is detrimental to the whole of society.

POLITICS OF BUSINESS CORPORATIONS

Public school financing is, of course, almost totally dependent on the good graces of the public. The views of the taxpayers as perceived from not only personal experiences, but also, importantly, from media, have much to do with adequate financing of the public schools. The politics of school financing is, moreover, not only dependent upon the impressions of individual taxpayers, but also perhaps equally important are the political positions taken by the private sector, the corporations, and the big businesses of the nation.

In a *New York Times* editorial in 2013 titled "Justice for Big Business," Erwin Chemerinsky argued that the all too apparent mission of the majority members of the United States Supreme Court is to support big business.[34] According to Chemerinsky, the five conservative members of the court, Chief Justice Roberts and Associate Justices Alito, Kennedy, Scalia, and Thomas, have a clear record favoring the interests of big business over the interests of employees. A very important part of the majority's strategy to support big business capitalism is to set up a line of defense on the "standing" issue, meaning that persons injured by business corporations do not have a legal basis to sue big business. As examples, Chemerinsky cites restrictions on employee standing, under federal civil rights legislation (citing the Lily Ledbetter case discussed below), of injured persons to sue the large pharmaceutical companies,[35] cell phone contracts,[36] and other cases favoring management over the employees, such as *Vance v. Ball State University* decided on June 24, 2013, and *American Express v. Italian Colors Restaurant.*[37] In each of these cases, three of which were rendered in 2013, according to Chemerinsky,

> These cases evince a disquieting theme about the conservative majority of the Roberts Court. It obviously believes, and sometimes expressly says, that there is a need to protect big business from litigation. But in discrimination, product liability and arbitration, it has left injured employees, consumers, and small businesses without recourse.[38]

We should note, as Chemerinsky implies, that among corporations, the Supreme Court favors big businesses over the employees, big businesses over the small businesses, and private corporations over public corporations.

When we consider in totality the politics of the private sector, the most important aspect is the political power of those corporations to influence government and the individual citizen. Corporations as entities find their life and existence in state law; however, over the years the federal role has become more essential. Perhaps, perversely, corporations are considered to be "persons" and protected by the United States Constitution as though they were living, breathing individuals. Yet, they are even more than sentient beings; corporations do not die unless they so desire. The watershed case declaring corporations are "persons" was *Santa Clara County v. Southern Pacific Railroad*[39] (1886), where a post-Civil War Supreme Court that was notorious for denial of the rights of African-Americans, later made infamous for its *separate-but-equal* decision in *Plessy v. Ferguson*,[40] 1896, *in dictum* said that corporations were "persons" within the meaning of the *Equal Protection Clause* of the Fourteenth Amendment. Then from 1890 to 1937, in various rulings concerning *due process and freedom to contract*, corporations were given increasing constitutional interests and rights to the disadvantage of employees, "unions, consumers and state legislatures."[41]

A further strengthening of the corporation in law and society came in 1978 in the *First National Bank v. Bellotti decision*,[42] which expanded the corporations' First Amendment right of free speech. These decisions and a host of others have sanctified the corporation as the lynchpin of capitalism. "American capitalism . . . would be unthinkable without the giant, multistate business corporation . . ."[43] Until the Great Depression in 1929 and during the New Deal of Roosevelt, the corporations continued to gain Supreme Court approval of their powers and authority as opposed to federal regulations and/or individual worker rights. A leading case prior to the Depression was the Supreme Court decision in *Hammer v. Dagenhart,* 1918,[44] that held a federal child labor act unconstitutional because, according to the Court, the federal statute violated the Commerce Clause, Article I, § 8[3] of the Federal Constitution because Congress could not show that the child-labor law was necessary as interstate commerce. The pro-business and anti-labor makeup of the Supreme Court began to change post-1936, resulting from President Roosevelt's appointments, and became more liberal, pro-labor, and less adherent to capitalistic philosophy of government.

In more recent years with the Supreme Court dominated by appointments by conservative presidents, the Court had taken a marked turn toward a harder line pro-business capitalism. The politics of this has been clearly shown in ongoing decisions by the Court, the most notable being, perhaps, the taxpayer "standing" decision, *DaimlerChrysler v. Cuno,*[45] in which the Court ruled that taxpayers did not have standing to challenge in Toledo, Ohio, the local tax breaks provided to corporations. The pro-business disposition of the members of the current Supreme Court is vividly reflected in its decision in the *Lilly Ledbetter* case,[46] a decision that has important financial and wage implications for females as individuals against corporations whether the company employer is either private or public. This case involved the enforcement of the Equal Pay Act of 1963 and Title VII of the Civil Rights Act of 1964.

Plaintiff Lilly Ledbetter alleging discrimination under the Equal Pay Act and Title VII had 180 days to file a complaint with the Equal Employment Opportunity Commission (EEOC) and 300 days if there were a state agency which shares enforcement duties and responsibilities with the EEOC. The filing deadlines must be strictly followed; however, lower federal courts did not agree on the starting time of the filing clock. Some courts had held that the starting point occurred with the first paycheck and other courts determined that each paycheck tolled the starting bell anew.

The Supreme Court in *Ledbetter v. Goodyear Tire & Rubber Co.,*[47] in 2007, settled the matter ruling that the time clock for Equal Pay claims must run from a point when the company made the decision to pay women differently than men. In so ruling, the Supreme Court held against Lilly Ledbetter who was the only woman working as an area manager and whose salary was substantially lower than that of any male area manager. She made $3,727 per month, and the men doing the same job were paid between $4,286 and $5,236 per month. The Supreme Court's ruling was strikingly pro-business and highly discriminatory against women who did not learn of pay disparities until sometime after the 180-day deadline. The injustice of the matter was quickly sensed by Congress, which promulgated legislation establishing a more reasonable filing period. Two bills emerged, one named the Lilly Ledbetter Fair Pay Act[48] and the other named the Fair Pay Registration Act. In spite of Congress' concern and desire to change the law, President G.W. Bush let Congress know that he would veto the law and never sign such a law as long as he was president. Bush's second term ended in January 2009 and Congress quickly passed a renewed bill titled, "The Lilly Ledbetter Fair Pay Act." The bill was introduced in the Senate on January 9, 2009, and passed with a 61 to 36 vote. The house passed the bill five days later; the vote was 250 to 177. President Obama signed the bill on January 29, 2009. The new law now provides in pertinent part that an aggrieved party "may receive back pay for up to two years preceding the filing of the charge"[49] against the company.

Thus, the case of *Lilly Ledbetter* tells us that when the Supreme Court is left to its own philosophy in interpreting federal statutes of the U.S. Constitution, it is likely to give substantive priority to the corporation's prerogatives over rights of individuals. That is the situation *except* where the corporation is a labor union. The present members of the United States Supreme Court apparently have little regard for the corporate prerogatives of teacher labor unions. Importantly, the Supreme Court has in recent years whittled away at the treasuries of the teacher unions. This the Court has done by increasingly lessening teacher labor union rights when in contest against employees who do not want to be in a union or do not agree with their union's political decisions. A case in point is the progression of precedents subsequent to the Supreme Court's decision in *Chicago Teachers Union v. Hudson*.[50] The teacher union, as a corporation, has had its monies collected from union members' fees carefully circumscribed and parsed in such a way that the union's "political and ideological" views may be separated from the "political and ideological" views of the individual union members. This is called the *Hudson Rule* and requires unions to provide procedures that permit nonunion members the opportunity to challenge the use of the service fees that they are required to pay. Non-union workers are those that are to pay union fees, because not to do so would permit "free rider" employees to benefit from union collective bargaining without paying anything *Abood v. Detroit Board of Education*.[51] So the Court in 1986, becoming progressively more anti-union, permitted in *Hudson* the criterion requiring unions to identify and set aside monies that may have been spent for "political or ideological" reasons.[52] Later in *Lehnert*,[53] the Court established a general rule governing the parsing of union fees based on the "germaneness" of the collective bargaining to union as a whole, and that it would, however, violate nonmembers' First Amendment rights if their fees were used for "political" activities of unions. In 2007, in *Davenport*, Justice Scalia, one of the most ideologically business-oriented justices, further held that states were free to further limit union fiscal powers by requiring that nonmembers give affirmative authorization to allow unions to utilize their fees for political reasons.[54]

BOX 6.6

Politics of the U.S. Supreme Court

At its heart, *Citizens United* was a case about Republicans versus Democrats. Since the Progressive era, Republicans had been the party of moneyed interests in the United States. For more than a century, Republicans had fought virtually every limitation on corporate or individual participation in elections. Democrats supported these restrictions. It was a defining difference between the parties. So, as the chief justice chose how broadly to change the law in this area, the real question for him was how much he wanted to help the Republican Party. [Chief Justice] Roberts' choice was: a lot.

Source: Jeffrey Toobin, *The Oath: The Obama White House and the Supreme Court* (New York: Anchor Books: A Division of Random House, Inc., 2013), p. 181.

Finally, yet another restraint in a public union's ability to raise money was set forth by the Supreme Court, in *Ysursa v. Pocatello Education Association*, 2009,[55] wherein Chief Justice Roberts extended the anti-union theme of the Court by ruling that a union as a corporation did not have a First Amendment right to challenge a state's ban on union members' payroll deductions for political activities. This series of cases has systematically circumscribed and reduced the financial capabilities of teacher employee unions, as corporate entities, to raise funds to engage in lobbying or supporting candidates for public office. Thus, what unions do is politics, their strength and vitality is dependent on their ability to raise money to support their political endeavors, and the above-mentioned legal precedents restrict their financial viability.

Corporations, Money, and Politics

A critical macro-issue concerning federal, state, and local politics, and, perhaps, the strength of the democratic form of government, is the highly political ruling of the U.S. Supreme Court in the *Citizens United* case.[56] The highly partisan decision basically unleashes the power of the purse of big corporations to control elections at all levels of government; the Supreme Court held unconstitutional the McCain-Feingold law[57] and other federal statutory provisions that regulated funding of political campaigns. The case had started about a narrow issue regarding the partisan corporate funding of the movie *Hillary* that painted Hillary Clinton in a highly unattractive light and clearly indicated that she was unfit to hold public office. The decision held that corporations' speech rights were identical to individuals: they are both persons, and as such, that speech right can be exercised by unlimited contributions to political campaigns. According to Jeffrey Toobin, a Supreme Court scholar, *Citizens United* holds immense implications for American politics.[58] Among those implications are, of course, not only the adequacy and equity of the funding of public schools, but even the structure and viability of the public school concept. Whether large corporate contributions to political campaigns in races for state legislatures and governorships will be influenced in such a way as to affect taxation for schools and/or eventually alter the entire structure of tax-supported education in America is a distinct probability.

POLITICS OF STABILITY

Well-conceived political systems ensure stability of government preservation and maintenance of existing rights. This function has as its guiding objective the maintenance of the *status quo*. This was the dominant governmental theory of the seventeenth and eighteenth centuries that held that present rights were to be protected and that the role of government was to preserve the current privileges, rights, and liberties, and had no reason to upset the inertia of the status quo. The politics of stability, then, was calculated to prevent encroachments on already established privately determined social and economic conditions. This objective of politics, of course, has a deleterious effect on progress and positive reform. The reality though is that reactionary resistance to change is an important aspect of the human need for stability and certainty. It will therefore always be a potent force in the politics of education.

The Peacekeeper. This minimalist conservative view of politics, the *peacekeeper doctrine*, seeks to preserve rather than change and is thereby an important aspect of stability. As may be expected, this particular political philosophy is most favored by the affluent. The more advantaged "haves" usually strive to keep things as they are and the "have-nots" agitate for change. This minimalist function was the only aspect of politics with which Bentham's utilitarianism was concerned. To Bentham the role of politics was to preserve and reflect the objectives of the majority.[59] E. H. Carr best summarizes the politics of stability in this way:

> The political arena is the scene of a more or less constant struggle between conservatives who in a general way desire to maintain the existing legal situation, and radicals, who desire to change it in important respects; and conservatives, national and international, have the habit of posing as defenders of the law and of decrying the opponents as assailants of it. In democracies, this struggle between conservatives and radicals is carried on openly in accordance with legal rules. But these rules are themselves the product of a pre-legal political agreement. Every system of law presupposes an initial political decision, whether explicit or implied, whether achieved by voting or by bargaining or by force, as to the authority entitled to make and unmake law. Behind all law there is this necessary political background. The ultimate authority of law derives from politics.[60]

One can easily find many examples of this political conflict between stability and change in school finance. Those that have quality schools for their children seek to defend them and ensure their preferential status. The more affluent attempt, through political processes, to defend their local fiscal advantage of greater income and property wealth. Attempts to equalize educational opportunity by introducing more equalization into state school finance programs often meet with intense political lobbying on the part of the rich school districts that are seeking stability or maintenance of their present elevated position. Parents in property-poor school districts are typically advocates for changing funding schemes in the cause of greater equalization. Such changes tend to upset political stability and are therefore confronted with substantial opposition.

Political Equilibrium. Thus, the politics of public school finance commonly has been a two-tier struggle in destabilizing the political equilibrium. First, public school advocates have sought to acquire a shift of private fiscal resources to the public sector, and second, to rearrange the fiscal resources, once shifted to the public by way of taxation, in such a way as to equalize educational opportunities.

The former is sometimes called the adequacy issue whereby overall adequate funding is sought based on the educational needs of the children and the ability of the private sector of the state or nation to bear the tax burden. Elsewhere in this book this condition is documented showing how the politics of school financing has produced widely varying levels of expenditure and fiscal effort among localities, states, and nations.

Politics of Exclusion. Reich observes that in the United States there is a growing philosophy that reveres the politics of exclusion. He says that "generosity and solidarity end at the border of similarly valued properties."[61] The result, according to Reich, is that the more affluent congregate in enclaves of affluence and do not exercise their political strength for the betterment of the whole community, state, or nation beyond the narrow boundaries of their own advantaged neighborhoods.

He notes that the wealthy exercise political muscle to protect and defend their position resulting in a *secession* of the wealthy citizens who have effectively "withdrawn their dollars from the support of public spaces and institutions shared by all and dedicated the savings to their own private services."[62] This political phenomenon accurately describes the plight of urban public schools and their loss of political strength in garnering support for more local or state funding.

As a result of this secession phenomenon the public schools in certain areas of the various states are deprived of the political leadership that could ensure adequacy of funding. The status quo as established by private economic conditions is upheld. The secession phenomenon described by Reich also affects equalization of resources among school districts. The enclaves of political strength that have tended to cluster in the suburbs of large cities have sapped both core cities and rural areas of political and economic strength and have resulted in a skewing of influence in favor of the more affluent. William Schneider has said that "the third century of American history is shaping up as the suburban century," and the "word that best describes the political identity of the middle class is *taxpayers*."[63]

The taxpayers in suburban enclaves see their economic advantage of residing in an affluent, property-rich suburb as an existing right, and through political processes will resist redeployment of state and local school funds for the purpose of equalizing educational opportunities. State equalization programs are interpreted as an encroachment on the integrity of their favorable economic circumstance. The politics of affluent school districts, usually suburban, tends to be employed to preserve the existing wealth advantage to maintain stability and to resist change, because change can only reduce their relative advantages. In some instances, suburban school districts have similar resources as the inner city and have similar problems and characteristics. An excellent example of this phenomenon is St. Louis, Missouri School District and several of the twenty-five school districts that ring St. Louis.

POLITICS AND SOCIAL JUSTICE

An essential purpose of politics in society is the promotion of welfare and justice, and it tends to run counter to the politics of stability. This is a newer, largely nineteenth and twentieth century view of politics in the modern state. This philosophy asserts that a vital role of politics is to improve the condition and well-being of all members of society and is couched in the moral imperative of social justice. The social justice philosophy supports the use of taxation as a governmental mechanism for the redistribution of wealth and income, maintaining that government has a positive role in correcting income and wealth disparities caused by the interactions of the private marketplace. This same perspective led to the adoption of the Sixteenth Amendment to the U.S. Constitution in 1913 permitting Congress to enact a graduated individual income tax, one of the purposes of which was to redistribute wealth.

This positive role of politics reflects the philosophy of *The Enlightenment* that assigns to government the role of correcting the abuses of the economic marketplace. Found herein is the grand design of the United States, the essence of enlightened humanity, to implement a political system that elevates social and economic conditions through an enlightened intellect. It was thought that "if political rulers were men of merit and talent and governed only in the public interest, they would naturally command affection and respect of the people."[64] Wood has said, in reviewing the radical nature of the new political system established in early America, that "the first steps in constructing a new republican society were to enlighten the people and to change the nature of authority."[65]

The foundation of this political philosophy, as observed earlier in this book, is universal public education. Conversely, the stability or minimalist view of politics advanced by Bentham and Adam Smith supports private schools, asserting that those who are most capable and possess the economic wherewithal are entitled to education, and government has no definitive role in expanding educational opportunity to the less able. On the other hand, the social justice or changed view of politics calls for the governmental creation of public schools to advance the condition of individuals who are not able to finance their own education.

BOX 6.7

Politics and Education

The effect of education on political attitudes is complicated, but there are reasons for thinking it at least creates the conditions for democratic society. The self-professed aim to modern education is to "liberate" people from prejudices and traditional forms of authority. Educated people are said not to obey authority blindly, but rather learn to think for themselves. Even if this doesn't happen on a mass basis, people can be taught to see their own self-interest more clearly and over a longer time horizon. Education also makes people demand more of themselves and for themselves; in other words, they acquire a certain sense of dignity which they want to have respected by their fellow citizens and by the state.

Source: Francis Fukuyama, *The End of History and The Last Man* (New York: Avon Books, 1992), p. 116.

The latter view of politics supports initiatives to increase the relative level of public school funding and to increase the equitable allocation of school resources. Also, this political view moves a society to attempt to remediate educational disadvantages caused by natural, economic, or environmental conditions. The politics of social justice argues for governmental action to address differing educational needs as well as to mitigate the educational disadvantages of children in low-income and property-poor school districts.

POLITICAL REALITY

The adequacy of financing public schools is dependent on certain political realities. These realities bear strongly on the global question of the willingness of the private sector to release fiscal resources for the public enterprise of education. The extent of receptivity to taxation and funding of public schools has much to do with the economy, demography, and attitudes of society toward public education, all of which interplay in various ways to complicate the politics of public schools.

The condition of the national or state economy may have much to do with the level of tax effort devoted to public schools. In a period of high inflation and relatively low economic growth, expenditures for public schools tend to diminish. Or one may find that a slowdown in economic productivity restricts the revenues gained from taxation and a nation or state lacks the necessary resources to invest in education. As a result, the plight of public education is to contend with a reduction in revenues and experience a concomitant decline in quality. Of course, public attitudes and federal leadership have much to do with the level of education expenditure, and the economy is not the only issue, but the overall economic problems resulting from a federal budget deficit and debt are not an unimportant factor.

There is, of course, a very real danger that government in a time of economic downturn will make inappropriate political choices and will restrict its outlays for economically productive investments. Also, a danger exists that government will continue to expend money for governmental activities that have little or no continuing stimulus effect on the economy. This topic of economic stimulus versus austerity, the Great Recession of 2008, and the effects of the federal government's sequestration of funds for education is discussed in more detail in Chapter 9, "The Federal Role in Financing Education."

SHAPING OF ATTITUDES

The better educated are less predisposed to propaganda and political delusion. One of the most important attributes of a highly educated citizenry is that it is less susceptible to being propagandized and led in directions that are contrary to its own best interest. Barbara Tuchman in her bestseller, *The March of Folly,* marvels at how at times entire societies may be influenced to pursue directions that are opposed to their own interest.[66] She cites the Trojan horse, the Renaissance Pope's provocation of Protestant secession, Britain's political intransigence in the loss of her colonies, and the American debacle in Vietnam as persuasive cases in point. Societal attitudes, and sometimes deceptions, may emanate from some stimulus of government leadership, or at times may simply develop unaided as a cycle of political history. While the well-educated and highly literate are more fortified against deceptions and provocations of leadership, all are to some degree susceptible.

POLITICS OF RELIGION

The politics of religion is too obvious and too complex to discuss in any detail here, yet, we would be remiss not to mention its pervasive political force and its interconnection with the financing of public schools. The intensity of the issue and the historical strife resulting from organized religion caused Thomas Jefferson, James Madison, and other forefathers to attempt to separate the politics of the church from that of the state. With such a separation they sought to strengthen both church and state. Here they were paradoxically not at odds with the laissez-faire political economy of Adam Smith who voiced in *The Wealth of Nations* in 1776 a strong opposition to the use of public money for religious purposes. Adam Smith, the *paterfamilias* of the conservative politicians, said,

> It may be laid down as a certain maxim, that, all other things being supposed equal, the richer the church, the poorer must necessarily be, either the sovereign on the one hand, or the people on the other; and in all cases, the less able must the state be to defend itself.[67]

Smith gained his insights from observations of the religious conflicts that had transpired in Europe and their resulting negative economic effects on the state and the people.

Jefferson and Madison, contemporaries of Adam Smith, also viewed the same religious strife in Europe, and believed that separation of church and state would make religion more viable while at the same time strengthening the functioning of a democratic government. The result has been much as Jefferson and Madison had anticipated, not only has the U.S. government been strong and viable, but religion in the United States has thrived.

URBAN-SUBURBAN POLITICS

The politics of cities and suburbs is today one of the most potent forces affecting the financing of the public schools. The lure of the city has long been a reality of humankind and today, 2014, worldwide migration to cities is inexorable. Today over half the world population live in urban areas. By 2030 the number of people living in and around cities of the world will rise to nearly 5 billion.[68] This is a rural to urban phenomenon. In the United States, over 80 percent of the people live in urban areas, yet migration continues, but in the case of the United States, the migration is from urban to suburban urban.[69] The social nature of the human being in concert with prospects for better economic circumstances has inexorably drawn people into larger groups with more complex interactions.

The reasons for the movement of people to and within urban areas are exceedingly complex, but at least two phenomena are most noticeably basic. *First*, urban life often offers economic options that are not apparent in the rural areas. This is particularly true in countries where people are poorly educated and the fertility of the soil has been depleted or never existed. Mexico City, Cairo, and Istanbul provide excellent examples of ballooning movement to cities that has been caused by the poverty of rural areas and the search for perceived, but seldom delivered, prosperity in the urban areas. The *second* reason, related to the first, is that as more people are freed from the search for food directly from the soil, they are free to acquire food from secondary sources in urban areas.

The "lure of the city" as Arthur Schlesinger called it, has to do with social and psychological reasons as well as economic ones. As Degler has observed, the people, the noise, the lights, the gaiety, the cultural opportunities, and the variety and mystery of the cities generally prove compelling for humankind.[70] Degler, in surveying hundreds of novels concerned with the newcomer to the city, concluded that people come to cities for the eminently reasonable objective of finding "more favorable surroundings and enlarged opportunities."[71]

Thus, as agriculture has become more efficient and more persons have been released from the soil, more have moved to the cities. In 1945, eight urban families were fed by a single farm family, and by the decade of the 1980s this figure rose to 33 families being fed by one farm family.[72] Cities have therefore grown as the efficiency of food production has increased, and more persons have been released from the soil to move to urban areas to assume other lifestyles and means of sustaining themselves.

The urban reality in the United States today is a bifurcation between cities and suburbs. The core cities are growing less, even declining, and the suburbs are growing into cities. Urban decline has been accompanied by a massive "secession" of whites to enclaves in the suburbs. This emigration from cities to suburbs and suburbs to exurbia by whites has left the cities populated primarily by lower-income African-Americans and Hispanics. Moreover, within the boundaries of the cities themselves there exist large bands or sectors of segregated living.[73]

It may, of course, be argued that the plight of the cities, their poverty and economic importance, is a function of political decision. Unfortunately, many political decisions have been a factor in exacerbation rather than remediation of the problem. Welfare requirements by the federal government have actually given incentives to the neediest groups to remain isolated and segregated within the nation's central cities.[74] Also, the plight of cities was caused to a great extent by the racial discrimination and poverty of poor states, primarily in the South, from which the poor are left to seek better economic circumstances in the northern cities.

The resulting condition of the central city in 2013 is one of relatively lowering economic conditions relative to the rise of affluent suburbs. The problem is worsened by the fact that those who populate the cities have vastly greater educational needs emanating from deprivations caused primarily by poverty. Yet, while educational burdens are heavier and the costs of educational programs are greater, the cities have correspondingly fewer fiscal resources than do suburbs and other school districts with fewer educational problems.

Suburban Political Power. The political dilemma faced by cities is ironically made worse by the dilution of political power. As a result of *Baker v. Carr,*[75] the one-person, one-vote case, fundamental shifts in the political strength have occurred throughout the nation. One result has been that political power has flowed from central cities and rural areas to the suburbs that have generally gained in both population and wealth.

The net effect has been for suburbs to become economically insular, racially and economically segregated, and more politically powerful. For example, the area encompassing northern Virginia and the Maryland suburbs of Washington, DC has been referred to by the Greater Washington Board of Trade as the 51st state, or the "State of Potomac," an economic powerhouse.[76] This area has 16 central business districts, *edge cities*, as defined by Joel Garreau in his book *Edge City.*[77] These huge suburban or outer-urban core areas, such as Tyson's Corner in northern Virginia, which are twice as large as downtown Miami and San Diego in terms of office rental space and employment, are able to translate economic strength and population size into political power. This *edge city* phenomenon in the United States is having a direct effect on the way state legislatures view the allocations of state and local revenues among core cities, suburban communities, and rural areas.

In many states, suburban communities have banded together to resist more equal distribution of school funds. For example, strong suburban education lobbies now exist in Missouri, Ohio, New Jersey, New York, Massachusetts, and Michigan that seek to maintain the present state systems of school funding that have created substantial revenue disparities favorable to the suburbs.

Buying Your Government. The political reality of the suburb is accurately depicted to a substantial degree by Schneider when he wrote,

> A major reason people move out to the suburbs is simply to be able to buy their own government. These people resent it when politicians take their money and use it to solve other people's problems, especially when they don't believe that government can actually solve those problems.[78]

There is considerable resistance to state taxation for the purpose of equalizing educational opportunity through state-aid formulae, and it is strongest among suburban voters.[79] The urban poor, on the other hand, are cynical about the prospects for economic and educational change, as are the poorly educated.[80] Suburban voters are primarily property owners and are highly tax sensitive.[81]

Some commentators believe that the middle-class suburban voters will support public works expenditures like good schools, highways, and a clean environment, things that they directly benefit from, but will not support social-welfare type programs that may assist the poor in core cities or rural areas.[82]

The polls indicate that people of the suburbs want more to be done about public education, but generally object to improvements being made in other school districts if they must share their tax money. Such political orientation emanates from a belief in specified benefits as well as special purpose taxes. "Special purpose taxes are the suburban idea – not just private government but private taxes."[83] Such a mindset militates against state measures to alleviate the educational funding problems of core cities and poor rural school districts. To a great extent, this political situation has fueled the recent series of judicial actions challenging state school finance programs. Also, one cannot ignore the phenomenon of "gated communities" and charter schools sanctioned by the state and the federal government that have resulted in a dramatic return to racial and economic segregation.[84]

POLITICS AT THE STATE LEVEL

Whenever there is a shift in school support from local taxes to state taxes, it has been accompanied by political controversy. Wealthy areas of states often object to a policy that results in their contributing more in state taxes than they receive in state grants. State legislators from wealthy school districts have frequently opposed state equalization formulas that apportion state school aid in an inverse relationship to local taxpaying capacity. Such legislators in many states have either opposed increases in state support of the public schools or insisted that if state aid were provided, it should be apportioned on a flat grant basis without consideration of variations in local taxpaying capacity. An examination of methods used by the states for allocating state funds[85] shows that political compromises have been reached in many states by allocating part of state funds on a flat grant basis or by guaranteeing a minimum of state funds to wealthy school districts to secure passage of a state equalization appropriation.

Another political factor involved in increasing the percentage of school revenue from state sources is fear of the erosion of local control of education if state financing is increased. The virtues of local control are continually extolled by politicians seeking office. They also inveigh against the dangers of central controls despite the fact that public school education is a state responsibility. It has become folklore to believe that "he who pays the fiddler will call the tune." While there is some truth to this assumption, the state can constitutionally establish state controls over education without providing any state financing. It can also allocate state funds for the schools with few or no controls, or it can attach many controls. State and federal school legislation after 2002 greatly increased central control over localities without commensurate increases in funding. In fact, the innovations of this era that included a many-fold increase in student testing, increases in graduation requirements, and curriculum content changes were seldom accompanied by adequate funding.

The politics of school financing at the state level deals with many issues, but the principal one is the extent and adequacy of school funding. The principal actors in the politics of state school financing include teachers' organizations, parent-teacher associations, school administrators' organizations, school board organizations, the chief state school officers, state boards of education, governors, and legislators. Other groups such as Chambers of Commerce, the Farm Bureau, associations of industries, and anti-tax groups also participate in the politics of school financing from time to time, especially when issues of taxation arise.

Educational Interest Groups

The education power structure in most states is rather complex, involving many groups and individuals with special interests. Some years in the past, administrators' associations, school board associations, teachers' associations, parent-teacher associations, and state education agencies commonly worked together on state school financing proposals. This is no longer true. Teachers' associations for many years have insisted that administrators have had too much influence on educational policy. As discussed earlier, adversarial relationships have developed among teachers, school administrators, and boards of education in many states. Consequently, these different interest groups have frequently advocated conflicting fiscal policies. This conflict has no doubt retarded progress in school financing in a number of states. In some states, the primary legislative goal of school finance reform has not been to improve school financing, but rather to reform taxation. This conflict between the goals of state legislatures and the goals of education interest groups makes it all the more politically desirable that education interest groups compromise their differences and form coalitions that speak to the governors and the legislatures with one voice.

Governors, as well as state legislators, are influenced by education interest groups and other special-interest groups. In some states, education associations have become politically active in supporting or opposing candidates for the governorship or seats in the legislature. When they happen to support successful candidates, their influence is augmented, but if their candidates do not win, their influence is diminished.

In more recent years the National Governors Association and the Education Commission of the States have encouraged governors to exercise a more proactive role in education. This has been accomplished primarily through governors' budgeting prerogatives, which if exercised fully can give the chief executive almost limitless control over education. Such extensive control while viewed by some as highly desirable has been viewed with a cautious eye by others.

It is particularly important that the state education agencies and education interest groups work cooperatively with their governors in developing the fiscal program they present to their legislatures. Competing state services will certainly present their needs to the governor and the legislature. It is highly important that each governor have a full understanding of the fiscal needs of public education before presenting their proposed budget to the legislature.

The State Legislature

The legislature plays the most important role in determining state school fiscal policy. It first must pass a bill before the governor can either approve or veto it. The legislature deals with school fiscal matters through a committee structure. Usually there is an education committee in both houses of the legislature. There will also usually be a finance committee, a ways and means committee, or a committee on taxation, as well as an appropriations committee in one or both houses. Those interested in educational finance, if they are to be politically effective, must lobby all of these committees as well as individual legislators. The term *lobby* should not be considered derogatory. It is the constitutional right of all groups and individuals to present their needs and interests to the legislature. In order for the democratic process to be successful, it is essential that lobbyists be ethical in their activities. If all lobbying were prohibited by law, the legislature would have insufficient information with which to make intelligent decisions.

BOX 6.8

Politics Is Not a Game

It exists to resolve the largest questions of the society – the agreed-upon terms by which everyone can live peaceably with one another. At its best, politics creates and sustains social relationships – the human conversation and engagement that draw people together and allow them to discover their mutuality. Democracy promises to do this through an inclusive process of conflict and deliberation, debate and compromise. Not every citizen expects to speak personally in the governing dialogue, but every citizen is entitled to feel authentically represented.

Source: William Greider, *Who Will Tell the People* (New York: Simon and Schuster, 1992), pp. 13–14.

Politics of Federal Aid

Federal control of education is opposed by practically everyone. However, the appropriation of federal funds through categorical grants is a powerful federal control. Furthermore, court decisions and certain federal laws establish federal controls that affect school financing.[86] As a matter of fact, establishment of a federal requirement sometimes results in political pressure being brought on Congress to provide additional federal funds to meet the new requirement. Examples are court-ordered busing, resulting in emergency school aid appropriations to assist in racial integration, and federal requirements with respect to the education of the disabled, resulting in large federal and state increases in appropriations for the disabled.

Increasing the amount of federal aid for the public schools is opposed by many lay interest groups and political conservatives. Such powerful organizations as the National Association of Manufacturers, the U.S. Chamber of Commerce, and the Farm Bureau Federation have generally opposed federal aid for the public schools. Certain religious sects also oppose federal aid for education unless they can share in it.

SUMMARY

In this chapter we attempted to define the nature of politics as it affects school finance. We observed the historical cyclical movement of attitudes between the liberal and conservative philosophies of government. Importantly, the overall purposes of politics are for the "public good," and are as such related to public school finance. Four potent areas of political concern – the economy, religion, the urban-suburban cleavage, and the problems of race relations – were discussed specifically. The following main points were emphasized.

Public schools are by nature an integral part of the politics of the United States. Public schools are creatures of the political system of a liberal democracy and are in fact a foundational element of liberal democracy.

The public schools are reflective of the historical interest that Americans have for politics. Public schools have contributed to the strength of the nation, and both the nation and public schools have benefitted from the political involvement of the citizenry. Political populism and equality merge with the ideals of capitalism and laissez-faire economics to form the unique brand of U.S. politics.

The political fortune of public schools is dependent on the interplay between public and private interests and the acquisition of fiscal resources. When conservative political forces unnecessarily restrain the distribution of the wealth of a state or nation by way of taxation for education, public schools are diminished.

Politics in and of itself is value-free, and it is only its application that creates desirable or objectionable results. U.S. democracy sets a positive direction for politics through fundamental, constitutional laws that basically call for liberty and equality. Departure from these ends misshapes politics and deters human advancement.

The political system of a republic requires a political reciprocity between the governed and the governors, while each has an obligation. The citizen must obey reasonable laws, and the representatives of the people must make reasonable laws, carrying out the general will of the people.

Educated voters are more capable of governing themselves than uneducated voters. The better educated tend to vote in higher percentages and their preferences are usually more in keeping with the moral objectives of a liberal democracy. Today there is some worrisome evidence that the center may not hold and that various political interest groups will tend to "disunite" America.

The theoretical purposes of politics may be seen as falling into two main categories: stability and change. The stability of government is premised on the quality and adequacy of its educational system. Yet, stability that freezes in inequality may be detrimental, maintaining differences in class that are created by the economic environment of the private sector. Change, if equitably implemented, would result in governmental action to compensate for the vagaries and disparities created by the marketplace. An educated citizenry is more inclined to stimulate equitable change than an uneducated one. Equitable change in school finance would result in more adequate and equal funding of public schools. More advanced societies put forth greater fiscal effort to fund education than do underdeveloped societies. Equality of funding is also an indicator of a better educated and more enlightened citizenry.

Political reality warns that the adequacy and equity of educational funding may be affected by the economic conditions of a state or nation as well as by other conditions that may create political discord. The recent federal budget deficit has undoubtedly had an adverse effect on public school financing. Not all deterrent effects though emanate from economic conditions, but may emerge from social or group differences. For example, negative attitudes toward public school financing may be fostered by a government that has philosophical beliefs that are contrarily predisposed. Various ideologies may assert strong political energies to use public resources to fund alternatives to public schools such as parochial or religious schools, private preparatory schools, home schools, race- or ethnic-oriented schools, or for-profit schools. Political philosophies supporting these alternatives call for reduced funding of public schools and increased funding for alternative types of education.

The politics of religion tends to become a powerful force in shaping governmental education policy. During the past decade the political importance of the religious school lobby has increased substantially. Under the rubric of choice and liberty, church school groups have influenced educational funding at both federal and state levels. Moreover, these groups have attempted to convey negative images of public schools in an attempt to enhance the attractiveness of their respective educational interests.

The demography and the urban nature of U.S. society have had a profound effect on the way schools are funded. The decline of the central city and the corresponding rise of suburban communities have important implications on the equity of educational financing. Also, racial overtones attendant upon political decisions permeate the governments at both state and federal levels. The new urban reality in combination with problems of race cast a daunting shadow over the politics of school finance in the country at large, and in virtually all the large populous states of the United States.

Reason for optimism is to be found in the strength of the philosophical conceptualization of public common schools and the viability of that concept as a cornerstone of a liberal democracy.

KEY TERMS

- Politics
- Decline of middle class
- Cycle of history
- Politics of security
- Lure of the city
- Political pendulum
- Politics of stability
- New urban reality
- Coloration of politics
- Politics of change
- Edge city
- Volition in political society
- Peacekeeper doctrine
- Politics of race

- Obligation of the governed
- Political equilibrium
- Political alliances
- Moral ends of politics
- Politics of exclusion
- Suburban flight
- Issue politics
- Politics of secession
- Power structures
- Crisis of regime
- Self-interest
- Interest groups
- Disuniting of America
- Politics of religion

NOTES

1. Alexis de Tocqueville, *Democracy in America*, I, Ch. XIV (New York: Colonial Press, 1899).
2. James Bryce, *The American Commonwealth* (New York: Macmillan, 1888), p. 506.
3. Page Smith, *The Rise of Industrial America*, vol. 6 (New York: McGraw-Hill, 1984), p. 455.
4. Thomas Hobbes of Malmesbury, "Of Man," *Leviathan*, 1651 (London: Penguin Books – Great Ideas, 2005), p. 52.
5. Ibid., p. 57.
6. Ibid., p. 58.
7. Ibid., p. 50.
8. John Locke, *Second Treatise of Government, 1690*, edited by C.B. Macpherson (Indianapolis and Cambridge: Hackett Publishing Company, Inc., 1980), pp. 66–69.
9. Ibid.
10. Ibid.
11. Robert H. Frank, *The Darwin Economy: Liberty, Competition and the Common Good* (Princeton: Princeton University Press, 2011), p. 30.
12. Michael Walzer, *Spheres of Justice* (New York: Basic Books, 1983), p. 286.
13. D. D. Raphael, *Problems of Political Philosophy* (Houndsmills, England: Macmillan, 1976), p. 27.
14. Ibid., p. 55.
15. Ibid., p. 69.
16. Hobbes would disagree that acquiescence of the governed by force is not politically legitimate. He maintains that choice of governments is based on fear. Hobbes says that fear is the basis on which political society is formed; each person seeks protection and is willing to concede certain rights and liberties to acquire the protection of common, concerted power of an absolute monarchy, democracy, or any other form of government. Thomas Hobbes, *Leviathan*, first published in 1651 (New York: Macmillan, 1962), p. 151.

17. John Locke, *Second Treatise of Government*, originally published in 1690 (Indianapolis: Hackett Publishing Company, 1980), p. 55.
18. Ibid., p. 56.
19. Ibid., p. 108.
20. Ibid., p. 81.
21. Ibid.
22. Ibid., p. 142.
23. Raphael, *op cit.*
24. Arthur M. Schlesinger, Jr., *The Cycles of American History* (Boston: Houghton Mifflin, 1986), p. 40.
25. Ibid.
26. Adam Smith, *The Wealth of Nations*, published in 1776 (New York: Modern Library, 1937), p. 41.
27. Gary Orfield, *Schools More Separate: Consequences of a Decade of Resegregation* (Cambridge, MA: Harvard University Press, 2001), p. 39.
28. *Parents Involved in Community Schools v. Seattle School District No. 1* and *Meredith v. Jefferson County Board of Education (Louisville)*, 551 U.S. 701, 127 S. Ct. 2737 (2007).
29. *Swann v. Charlotte-Mecklenburg Board of Education*, 402 U.S. 1, 91 S. Ct. 1267 (1971).
30. Erwin Chemerinsky, *The Conservative Assault on the Constitution* (New York: Simon and Schuster Paperbacks, 2010), pp. 60–61.
31. Jeffrey Toobin, *The Oath: The Obama White House and the Supreme Court* (New York: Anchor Books, 2013), p. 89.
32. *Shelby County, Alabama v. Holder*, 679 F.3d 848 (2012), 570 U.S. __ (2013), 133 S. Ct. 2612 (2013).
33. Adam Liptak, "Court Is 'One of Most Activist,' But Ginsburg Vows to Remain," *The New York Times*, August 25, 2013.
34. Erwin Chemerinsky, "Justice for Big Business," Op-Ed, *The New York Times*, Tuesday, July 2, 2013.
35. *Mutual Pharmaceutical Company v. Bartlett*, No. 12–142, June 24, 2013.
36. *AT&T Mobility v. Concepcion*, 131 S. Ct. 1740, 563 U.S. 321 (2011).
37. *Vance v. Ball State University*, 570 U.S. ____, (2013), 133 S. Ct. 2434 (2013); *American Express v. Italian Colors Restaurant*, 570 U.S. ____, (2013), 133 S. Ct. 2304 (2013).
38. Chemerinsky, *op cit.*
39. *Santa Clara County v. Southern Pacific Railroad*, 118 U.S. 394 (1886).
40. *Plessy v. Ferguson*, 163 U.S. 537 (1896).
41. *The Oxford Companion to the Supreme Court of the United States*, edited by Kermit L. Hall, "Corporations" (Oxford: Oxford University Press, 1992), pp. 198–199.
42. *First National Bank v. Bellotti*, 435 U.S. 765 (1978).
43. *The Oxford Companion to the Supreme Court of the United States*, *op cit.*, p. 118.
44. *Hammer v. Dagenhart*, 247 U.S. 251 (1918).
45. *DaimlerChrysler Corp. v. Cuno*, 547 U.S. 332 (2006).
46. *Lilly Ledbetter v. Goodyear Tire & Rubber Co.*, 550 U.S. 618 (2007).
47. We rely and quote explaining the *Lilly Ledbetter* case, on Kern Alexander and M. David Alexander, *American Public School Law*, 8th Edition (Belmont, CA: Wadsworth/Cengage, 2012), p. 947.
48. Public Law, 111–2 · Stat. 123 Stat. 5 (2009).
49. Klinton W. Alexander and Kern Alexander, *Higher Education Law: Policy and Perspective* (London: Routledge, 2011), p. 373; "The Lilly Ledbetter Fair Pay Act," signed by President Obama on January 29, 2009; *Ledbetter v. Goodyear Tire & Rubber Co.*, 550 U.S. 618, 127 S. Ct. 2162 (2007).
50. *Chicago Teachers Union, Local No. 1 v. Hudson*, 475 U.S. 292, 106 S. Ct. 1066 (1986).

51. *Abood v. Detroit Board of Education*, 431 U.S. 209, 97 S. Ct. 1781 (1997).
52. *Chicago Teachers Union Local 1 v. Hudson*, 475 U.S. 292, 106 S. Ct. 1066 (1986).
53. *Lehnert v. Ferris Faculty Association*, 500 U.S. 507, 111 S. Ct. 1950 (1991).
54. *Davenport v. Washington Educational Association*, 551 U.S. 177, 127 S. Ct. 2372 (2007).
55. *Ysursa v. Pocatello Education Association*, 555 U.S. 353, 129 S. Ct. 1093 (2009).
56. *Citizens United v. Federal Election Commission*, 558 U.S. 50, 130 S. Ct. 876 (2010).
57. Public Law 107–155.
58. Toobin, *op cit.*, p. 185.
59. John Stuart Mill, *Utilitarianism on Liberty: Essay on Bentham*, ed. Mary Warnock (New York: Meridian/Penguin Books, 1974), pp. 115–116.
60. E. H. Carr, *The Twenty Years' Crisis 1919–1939* (New York: Harper Torchbooks, 1939), pp. 180–181.
61. Robert B. Reich, "Succession of the Successful," *New York Times Magazine* (January 20, 1991), Section 6, p. 42.
62. Ibid.
63. William Schneider, "The Suburban Century Begins," *Atlantic Monthly* 270, no. 1 (July 1992), p. 33.
64. Gordon S. Wood, *The Radicalism of the American Revolution* (New York: Alfred A. Knopf, 1992), p. 189.
65. Ibid.
66. Barbara W. Tuchman, *The March of Folly, From Troy to Vietnam* (New York: Alfred A. Knopf, 1984).
67. Adam Smith, *The Wealth of Nations*, published in 1776 (New York: Modern Library, 1937), p. 765.
68. United Nations, UNFPA Report, "Linking Population, Poverty and Development," *State of World Population 2007: Unleashing the Potential of Urban Growth Report*. See: Fred Pearce, *The Guardian*, Friday, September 17, 2010.
69. U.S. Census Bureau, 2000 Census of Population and Housing, www.census.gov/prod/cen/2000index.
70. Carl N. Degler, *Out of Our Past, Third Edition* (New York: Harper Torchbooks, 1984), p. 334.
71. Ibid.
72. Ibid., p. 333.
73. Paul E. Peterson, *The New Urban Reality* (Washington, DC: The Brookings Institution, 1985), p. 15.
74. Ibid., p. 25.
75. *Baker v. Carr*, 369 U.S. 186, 82 S. Ct. 691 (1962).
76. Stephen Soltis, "A Power Plant on the Potomac," *Washington Flyer Magazine* (March/April, 1993), p. 16.
77. Joel Garreau, *Edge City* (New York: Doubleday, 1991).
78. Schneider, *op. cit.*, p. 37.
79. Ibid.
80. Ibid.
81. Ibid.
82. Ibid., p. 38.
83. Ibid.
84. See: Arizona, Florida, and Indiana as examples.
85. *Public School Finance Programs* periodically compiled by the Department of Education, U.S. Office of Education (Washington, DC: U.S. Government Printing Office).
86. Kern Alexander and M. David Alexander, *American Public School Law*, 3rd edn. (St. Paul, MN: West Publishing Company, 1992).

CHAPTER 7

Fiscal Capacity and Tax Effort in the Funding of Public Schools

---

TOPICAL OUTLINE OF CHAPTER

- Fiscal Capacity
  - Fiscal Capacity of Nations
  - A World View
- Measurement of State Fiscal Capacity
  - Gross Domestic Product (GDP)
  - Personal Income
  - Fiscal Capacity Comparisons among States
- Local Fiscal Capacity
  - Measurement of Local Fiscal Capacity
  - Equalized Assessment of Property Valuation
- Tax Effort to Support Public Schools
  - Fractionalization and Tax Effort
  - Racial or Ethnic Fractionalization
  - Tax Effort of States
  - Local Tax Effort of School Districts

INTRODUCTION

As observed elsewhere in this book, those nations and states that have made investments in human resources have been rewarded with economic growth and higher standards of living. We know that the wealth of a nation lies in the proper mix of physical and human capital and both require cultivation and investment. If funding for human capital is inadequate, malapportioned, and unequal, then the nation or state suffers and underdevelopment is the result. The waste of human capital becomes a major source of economic inefficiency.

Governments bear the responsibility of overcoming such inefficiencies and for helping to reduce fiscal disparities that deny equality of educational opportunity. This is accomplished by more equitable and uniform distribution of fiscal resources. In a nation the size of the United States, with over 14,000 school districts scattered throughout 50 states, all with different physical and human characteristics, the task of maximizing human capital productivity as well as attending to the moral and ethical responsibility of providing equality of education is not an insignificant undertaking.

FISCAL CAPACITY

At first glance it appears to be a relatively simple matter to use resources from a central government level to even out incapacities at the state local levels and to use tax resources to equalize the revenues of schools. The problem is, however, more complex because there is little agreement as to how fiscal capacity is to be measured and how much is needed for educational services. The matter is further complicated by the myriad social and economic conditions which lead some nations, states, or localities to put forth greater financial effort than others to support their educational programs.

This chapter will first provide some insight into the fiscal capacity of the United States relative to that of other nations and then discuss the differences in capacity of states and school districts within the United States. The discussion will then turn to fiscal effort to support education at the national, state, and local levels.

BOX 7.1

Definitions

Fiscal Capacity. The tax base of a governmental entity measured in terms of income, wealth, or other fiscal measures of economic productivity.

Fiscal Position. Sometimes distinguished from fiscal capacity because capacity alone has nothing to do with need for services. Fiscal position has to do with the ability of a jurisdiction to perform its fiscal tasks taking into account both its capacity relative to the requirements of need for the particular public service. Two school districts may have the same fiscal capacity but have a much different fiscal position (ability) because the incidence of educational need in one is much greater than in the other.

Source: Richard A. Musgrave and Peggy B. Musgrave, *Public Finance in Theory and Practice* (New York: McGraw-Hill, 1980), pp. 545–546.

Although the primary focus of this book is on the funding of public schools in the United States, it is helpful to gain some perspective by briefly viewing the world situation that bears so directly on every aspect of education as a major element in a world economy.

Fiscal Capacity of Nations

The amalgam of physical and human resources producing the economic capacity of a nation, state, or community may be described in terms of various fiscal measures. For nations, relative fiscal capacity may be measured in terms of *gross national product, gross domestic product, gross national income,* or *net national income*, and a host of other measures that seek to determine relative economic stata of countries through analyses of their monetary holdings, manufacturing activities, foreign trade amounts, balance of payments, external debt, and so on.[1]

We have seen in recent years that some countries (e.g., Saudi Arabia and the United Arab Emirates) may become economically powerful in the short range by merely selling off and depleting their natural resources, but long-term sustained economic growth is predicated on educated citizenry. Japan is, of course, the prime example of a country without physical resources, but rich in human resources, and currently, along with the United States, possesses one of the most powerful and viable economies in the world. The United States has historically been an economic power because it is rich in both human and physical resources. It is a phenomenon of modern technological development that the balance between human and physical resources required to make a rich and prosperous nation is becoming increasingly dependent on human resources. The importance of physical resources to the wealth of nations will become even less important as we move further into the new information age.

Reich observes this trend in his book *The Work of Nations*. He foresees a postnational economic system in which we are rapidly progressing to a stage in which the physical resources of a country will become less and less necessary for economic growth. The communication technology on which the advanced nations now prosper has significant implications for the future. The new internationalism will be a non-oil-based industrialization that requires little in the way of physical assets, but great human intellectual power. Reich says that,

> We are living through a transformation that will rearrange the politics and economics of the coming century. There will be no national products or technologies, no national corporations, no national industries . . . All that will remain rooted within national borders are the people who comprise a nation. Each nation's primary assets will be its citizens' skills and insights.[2]

The United States is a great and powerful nation with a population of over 320 million people, third only to China and India. It possesses vast fiscal resources that in totality dwarf other individual national economies of the world; consequently, no other country today approaches the United States in total economic strength when intellectual, physical power, and wealth are taken into account. The United States is a rich country regardless of the fiscal measure. Using the measure Gross National Income per capita,

---

BOX 7.2

Definitions

Gross National Product (GNP). The total value at current market prices of all goods and services produced by the economy of a nation during a year.

Gross Domestic Product (GDP). The total output produced within a country during a year. GDP is different from GNP in that GDP measures the total output produced by all factors owned by the country (private and public) regardless of where the production takes place.

Gross National Income (GNI). The total of the incomes of all individuals in a nation earned in the forms of wages, interest, rents, and profits. It is calculated before deductions are taken for income taxes and excludes transfer payments.

Net National Income (NNI). NNI is equal to GNI net of depreciation.

Sources: Richard A. Musgrave and Peggy B. Musgrave, *Public Finance in Theory and Practice* (New York: McGraw-Hill, 1980), pp. 545–546; *OECD Factbook: Economic, Environmental and Social Statistics*, 2013, p. 60.

---

for OECD countries, the United States with $47,195 per capita ranks behind only Luxembourg ($61,346), Norway ($57,945), and Switzerland ($51,537).[3] At the bottom of the OECD countries we find Indonesia ($4,221), South Africa ($10,743), Mexico ($14,982), Chile ($14,221), and Russia ($18,278).[4] See Figure 7.1.

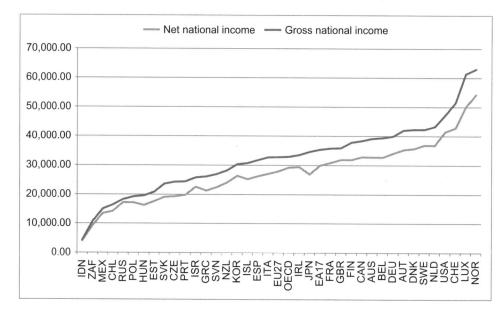

Figure 7.1 Gross and Net National Income Per Capita
US dollars, current prices and PPPs, 2011 or latest available year

Source: Based on OECD Factbook 2013. http:dx.doi.org/10.1787/888932706907.

Bear in mind that OECD countries, except for a few at the bottom of the list, are the countries with the highest standards of living in the world. These are largely the countries that have a culture and ethnicity that value knowledge and progress. As to why some countries are rich and others are poor is a subject of some limited discussion in Chapter 3. Shown in Figure 7.2, there is a longitudinal aspect that has been rather consistent for nearly 1,000 years, 1000 to 1998. Figure 7.2 shows a pattern of countries in the various regions of the world retaining their advantages over many

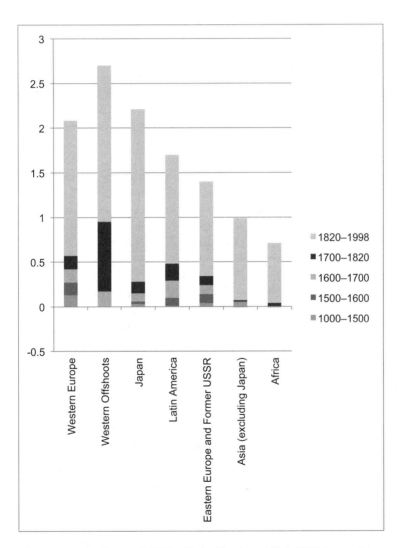

Figure 7.2 Growth of Per Capita GDP by Major Region, 1000–1998 (annual average compound growth rate)

Source: Based on Angus Maddison, "The World Economy: A Millennial Perspective," in *Development and Underdevelopment: The Political Economy of Global Inequality, 4th edition* (Boulder/London: Lynne Rienner Publishers, 2008), p. 77.

centuries as measured by growth of the per capita GDP by major region. The difference is definitive.

A World View

Maddison does not hazard a guess as to why the differences exist, but he cites what Landes believes.[5] The essence of current thinking about development is captured in the book *Why Nations Fail: The Origins of Power, Prosperity and Poverty*, by Daron Acemoglu and James A. Robinson (also discussed in Chapter 3 of this book). They see two very different national economies, the "extractive" and the "inclusive." The "extractive" economic and political institutions exploit the people over vast regions of the planet,[6] while "inclusive" institutions foster and promote prosperity, technology, and education that by their nature sustain economic growth.[7]

Lawrence Harrison maintains that prosperity happens where there is a world view that includes, *a priori*, a belief in human improvement coupled with a society that encourages human creative capacity.[8] Such a society does so in seven basic ways:

1. Through creation of an environment in which people expect and receive fair treatment.
2. Through an effective and accessible education system: one that provides basic intellectual and vocational tools; nurtures inquisitiveness, critical faculties, dissent, and creativity; and equips people to solve problems.
3. Through a health system that protects people from diseases that debilitate and kill.
4. Through creation of an environment that encourages experimentation and criticism (which is often at the root of experimentation).
5. Through creation of an environment that helps people both discover their talents and interests and mesh them with the right jobs.
6. Through a system of incentives that rewards merit and achievement (and, conversely, discourages nepotism and "pull").
7. Through creation of the stability and continuity that make it possible to plan ahead with confidence. Progress is made enormously more difficult by instability and discontinuity.[9]

The differences among nations in fiscal capacity worldwide are marked by great disparity and vast deprivation. Paul Kennedy writes that the prospects for elevating the poorer countries appear to be bleak if nations are unable to magnify the role of education, control population by decreasing fertility rates, and enhance the quality of political leadership among all the nations.[10]

The danger is all too apparent. As a nation becomes less capable economically it may err by investing less in education, thereby increasing its downward spiral. As data presented in this chapter show, such a trend is discernible now to some degree in the United States as we lose relative economic strength and invest less in education. Although this country remains the world's most powerful in total productivity, economic strength, and military might, there has been certain decline from its earlier position of uncontested preeminence.

BOX 7.3

A World View of Capacity to Know

If the society's world view encourages the belief that humans have the capacity to know and understand the world around them, that the universe operates according to a largely decipherable pattern of laws and the scientific method can unlock many secrets of the unknown, it is clearly imparting a set of attitudes tightly linked to the ideas of progress and change. If the world view explains worldly phenomena by supernatural forces, often in the form of numerous capricious gods and goddesses who demand obeisance from humans, there is little room for reason, education, planning, or progress.

Source: Lawrence E. Harrison, *Underdevelopment Is a State of Mind: The Latin American Case* (Lanham, MD: Madison, 1985) p. 6.

MEASUREMENT OF STATE FISCAL CAPACITY

Fiscal capacity is the ability of state and local school systems to obtain revenues from their own sources through taxation.[11] It may be broadly defined as a quantitative measure of economic resources within a governmental unit which can be used to support public functions. Relative fiscal capacity among states or localities is determined by dividing the measure of capacity by a standard unit such as population or pupils.

Traditionally, policymakers have relied on personal income and tax revenues as economic indicators of fiscal capacity. Personal income is most commonly used among states because the data are kept current by the United States Department of Commerce, Bureau of Economic Analysis.[12] Data for tax revenues also are collected annually by various departments of the federal government and by several independent agencies.

Gross Domestic Product (GDP)

The GDP per capita for each state is probably a more comprehensive measure of a state's fiscal capacity than is Personal Income (PI). The Bureau of Economic Analysis defines:

> Gross Domestic Product (GDP) is calculated as the sum of what consumers, businesses and government spend on final goods and services, plus investment and net foreign trade. In theory, incomes earned should equal what is spent, but due to different data sources, income earned, usually referred to as gross domestic income (GDI), does not always equal what is spent (GDP).[13]

In 2012, the real GDP per capita by state ranged from a high of $61,183 in Delaware to a low of $28,944 in Mississippi. The per capita GDP for the United States was $42,784. The real GDP by state is an inflation-adjusted measure of each state's production based on a weighted average of national prices for those products produced within each state.

Personal Income

When the income of the people of each state is known, it is possible to determine the per capita income, the income per child of school age (ages 5–17 are generally used), or the income per pupil in average daily membership or average daily attendance. The ratio of children to total population varies considerably among states, depending upon which pupil measure is used. The personal income per average daily attendance or average daily membership rather than either population or children of school age population are superior measures for determining the state fiscal capacity to support the public schools. The use of school-age population broadens the measure by including children in nonpublic schools, thus inflating the divisor; the relative fiscal capacity of states with large nonpublic school enrollment would be substantially reduced. Similarly, the use of population as the divisor does not relate consistently to the numbers of children served by the public schools.

Personal income is the amount of current income received from all sources, including transfer payments from government and business but excluding transfer payments from other sources. The major part of personal income is derived from labor income, proprietors' income, rental income, dividends, interest, and transfer payments.

Personal income, however, does not reflect the total fiscal capacity of the state for two basic reasons: *First,* personal income represents a measure of the flow of capital and does not capture the stock of wealth that a state might possess. Personal and real property are not included. Income is not wealth; wealth constitutes the total value of the stock of all assets, physical and financial, held at a particular time.[14] *Second*, resident personal income does not capture the potential capacity which a state may have from its ability to export its tax burden to other states, such as Florida and Nevada that possess the ability to tax tourists through sales, hotel, and amusement taxes, or the ability of Alaska, Louisiana, West Virginia, Texas, New Mexico, and Wyoming to levy severance taxes on exported oil and mineral deposits.

Fiscal Capacity Comparisons among States

The quality of education in the United States to a great extent is dependent on the financial capacity of the states, but there exist substantial differences in capacity that impede efforts to provide equality of educational opportunity nationwide. Over the years, comparisons of fiscal capacity show that there is a slight ebb and flow of state fiscal fortune, just as there is among countries; nevertheless, by and large, the rich remain relatively affluent and the poor tend to cluster near the lower extremes of incapacity.

As shown in Table 7.1, in 2012 Connecticut was ranked first among the states with $58,908 in per capita personal income while Mississippi was in last place with $33,073,

Table 7.1 Per Capita Personal Income by State, 2012 Ten Richest and Ten Poorest

State	Dollars	Rank
Connecticut	59,687	1
Massachusetts	55,976	2
New Jersey	54,987	3
North Dakota	54,871	4
Maryland	53,816	5
New York	53,241	6
Wyoming	50,567	7
Alaska	49,436	8
New Hampshire	49,129	9
Virginia	48,377	10
Arizona	36,243	41
Alabama	35,926	42
New Mexico	35,682	43
Kentucky	35,643	44
Arkansas	35,437	45
Utah	35,430	46
West Virginia	35,082	47
South Carolina	35,056	48
Idaho	34,481	49
Mississippi	33,657	50

Source: Bureau of Business and Economic Research (2012, Sept. 30). Reprinted by permission.

possessing 56 percent of the capacity shown by Connecticut. Twenty years earlier in 1992, Connecticut was ranked first, registering $28,287 per capita personal income, and Mississippi was last with a per capita personal income of $14,651.

The relative fiscal capacity of states may vary depending on whether the capacity measures are divided by the total state population (capita) or by the number of pupils in the public schools. Which is more accurate: a per capita or a per-pupil measure of capacity? Some argue that relative fiscal capacity is best measured if one takes into account the entire population because the tax system must support governmental services for all the people. It is correctly maintained that the income and wealth of all the people constitute the total fiscal capacity of a state. On the other hand, it may be reasonably argued that for education purposes, capacity should be measured in terms of the number of children to be educated. States have varying demographics, and a retirement state like Florida has fewer children aged 5–17, compared to the total state population, than other states. Also, some states have much higher percentages of private school pupils resulting in differing public school financial burdens. Thus, the denominator for calculating fiscal capacity may be either population (capita) or numbers of pupils. As noted previously, the number of pupils attending public schools is preferred. If the number of students is used, it is usually expressed in terms of enrollment, average daily membership, or average daily attendance. See Table 7.2.

Table 7.2 Personal Income per Student in Average Daily Attendance, 2010 ($) Top and Bottom 10 States

Rank	State	$
1	Massachusetts	371,971
2	Vermont	355,153
3	Rhode Island	354,041
4	Maryland	353,586
5	Connecticut	347,307
6	Hawaii	341,074
7	Wyoming	317,213
8	North Dakota	315,021
9	New Hampshire	314,825
10	New Jersey	313,013
41	New Mexico	216,568
42	Arkansas	216,113
43	Texas	215,172
44	Nevada	213,652
45	West Virginia	211,794
46	Arizona	210,435
47	Georgia	209,479
48	Utah	200,865
49	Mississippi	199,012
50	Idaho	188,281

Source: Data from *Rankings & Estimates: Rankings of the States 2012 and Estimates of School Statistics 2013,* December 2012, www.nea.org/assets/img/content/NEA_Rankings_And_Estimates-2013_(2).pdf, Table D-8. Used with permission of the National Education Association. Copyright © 2013. All rights reserved.

LOCAL FISCAL CAPACITY

Each state has its own methods and idiosyncrasies in determining local fiscal capacity; no two are identical. However, the choices made by each state in determining local fiscal capacity have important effects on the extent and effectiveness of the state equalization program. Weighting some local capacity factors more than others will inevitably result in substantial shifts in state equalization funds among local school districts.

Disparities in the fiscal capacity of school districts are generally much greater than the variation in capacity among the states. The variation of fiscal capacity among districts in states where districts have been reorganized is much less than in states with many small districts. This is inevitably the case because when several small districts with wide differences in wealth per pupil are combined to form one district, differences are eliminated within the combined area.

Even when all school districts are of reasonably adequate size, considerable difference remains among the districts in their ability to finance educational programs. If no state aid were provided in states, the low fiscal capacity districts would have to make many times the fiscal effort their high capacity peers do to finance an adequate program of educational opportunity. The situation in the states that maintain large numbers of very small school districts is, of course, much more serious with the range often exceeding 100 to 1.

School finance litigation in many states gives testimony to great disparities; for example, in Texas, the evidence presented in the *Edgewood* litigation, 1989, showed that the highest-capacity school district had over $14,000,000 of property wealth per pupil while the poorest district had about $20,000, a wealth disparity ratio of approximately 700 to 1.[15]

In the famous *Serrano I* case, 1969–1970, legislative reports in California were cited that showed a range of assessed valuation per pupil between the highest- and lowest-capacity elementary school districts to be $952,156 to only $103 per pupil, while the high school districts exhibited a range of $349,093 to $11,959 per pupil.[16] When the Supreme Court of Oregon rejected plaintiffs' pleas for greater equalization funding in the case of *Olsen v. State*,[17] (1976), the wealth differential in True Cash Value (TCV) of property between the wealthiest and poorest unified districts in Oregon ranged from $203,000 to $19,300 per pupil, a 10.5 to 1 disparity ratio.

Thus, the fiscal capacities among school districts in some states have such great variance to be almost incomprehensible while in others the ranges are of more modest proportions. Regardless of magnitude, however, it is easy to understand why local systems of taxation are unable to provide for equality of educational opportunity. Moreover, it is obvious that the current battle to reduce or eliminate the disparities of educational services that exist among school districts in most states will continue as long as states rely extensively upon local non-neutralized tax resources.

In no state can the least fiscally able districts finance a reasonably satisfactory program of education from local funds without an inequitable tax effort. In many districts, the tax effort required would be prohibitive, unless the state neutralizes the variance in fiscal capacity that exists among districts. The differences in wealth in small district states are so great that no program involving state and local support is likely to solve all the financial equality problems until further reorganization occurs. Until further progress is made in district organization in many states pursuant to the financing of schools, inequalities in educational opportunity are certain to continue. Substantial numbers of students in many states cannot expect to have even reasonably adequate educational opportunities under present conditions.

Measurement of Local Fiscal Capacity

Equalization of educational opportunity hinges on the appropriate and accurate measurement of local fiscal capacity. The need to equalize the disparities in local fiscal capacity through allocation of state aid has long been recognized, and all states have taken some steps to ameliorate this situation. In 1906, Cubberley observed that "any attempt at the equalization of opportunities for education, much less any attempt at equalizing burdens, is clearly impossible under a system of exclusively local taxation."[18] The state must take action to overcome the disparities inherent in the diverse economic conditions which characterize different local school districts. This issue has persisted as one of the most complex questions facing states in their attempts to meet the educational needs of all children regardless of where they attend school.

Early analysis showed that fiscal equalization could not be accomplished without the states assuming greater responsibility for financing the schools. A recognized function of state government was to provide for a uniform educational program among all local school districts. This can be accomplished utilizing equalization formulae that allocate state funds in inverse relationship to local fiscal capacity. (See details on the types of state aid formulae discussed elsewhere in this book.) The basic dilemma is to determine how best to measure local fiscal capacity in order to bring about optimal equalization. This subject has been much debated in school finance circles in recent years. Three basic approaches have been used to address the problem: (1) tax base, (2) tax-base surrogate, and (3) economic indicator.

First. The *tax-base approach* simply determines taxpaying ability by using the available tax base(s). For example, if real property is the school tax base, then equalized valuation of property is used as the measure of fiscal capacity. If a sales tax or other nonproperty source also is used as a portion of the tax base then it is included also in the measure of fiscal capacity.

The *second* approach, the *tax-base surrogate*, was used in several states in an earlier era when property tax assessments were too unevenly administered to be either a reliable or valid measure of fiscal capacity. This method, sometimes called an index of taxpaying ability, utilized selected variables which were predictive of equalized valuation of property at some point in time. The problem, of course, in order to set up a predictive equation, was to find a time in which property values were reasonably well assessed. This approach served as an interim measure while property tax administration was in the process of being developed and improved.

Third. The *economic-indicator approach* is a theoretical determination of fiscal capacity utilizing measures of income, wealth, and consumption regardless of whether they are accessible through local taxation. It is not a proxy or surrogate measure for equalized assessed valuation of property. It departs materially from the other two measures in that it presumes that determination of fiscal capacity does not need to be tied to an accessible local tax base. This approach suggests that since all taxes must be paid out of income and/or accumulated wealth, it does not matter which particular tax base is used locally to actually collect the revenues.

Opponents of this approach maintain that local taxing units only have taxpaying capacity relative to their accessibility to legislatively designated tax bases. If inequality of local resources exists, it is created by variation in the capacity of taxpayers to pay the particular available tax. Equalization of funding must therefore be directed toward erasing disparities created by the revenues from legally levied taxes. If full equalization is to be attained, fiscal capacity must be determined by each and every one of the locally available tax bases.

The tax-based approach addresses this issue by determining the actual ability to pay the schools rather than using a theoretical measure of fiscal capacity such as economic indicators. Burrup observed that economic indicators are inappropriate for comparing fiscal capacities of localities unable to tap major wealth bases.[19] Other authorities agree, maintaining that the fiscal capacity of a community is its access to legally permissible taxes.[20]

The quest for better measurement of local fiscal capacity is not new; in 1923, George Strayer and Robert Haig suggested that economic indicators could be used as an alternative to property valuations for purposes of school fund equalization. They recommended that local fiscal capacity be determined in New York by summing taxable income with one-tenth of the full value of real estate, then dividing the result by two. Reasoning that this measure was more comprehensive, since the relative position of localities was much different with each measure, they suggested that the combination would give a more accurate picture of overall economic resources.[21]

Ten years later, Paul Mort criticized economic indicators recommended by Strayer and Haig, observing that they defined theoretical taxing capacity under an ideal system of taxation, not the actual situation. Mort noted that the power to tax rests with state legislatures, not the local taxing units. He said,

> The true criterion of the relative ability of local units to pay for education is the ability-to-pay under the taxing system established by the state rather than the ability-to-pay under an ideal taxing system . . .

> Since we must deal with communities which have no power over their tax systems except through state action, we cannot consider their ability as it would be under an ideal tax system. To build our system of state aid on such a foundation would throw excessive burdens upon actual taxpayers in some communities, simply because there happened to be wealth in those communities that was not taxable under the existing system of taxation.[22]

The theoretical measure of fiscal capacity advocated by Mort continues to be the prevailing view today. Most states use only those measures of ability which relate directly to taxable sources. These states have implicitly followed the philosophy which maintains that local taxpaying capacity should, appropriately, be a measure of accessibility to local tax revenue. The Mort position was reinforced by the National Educational Finance Project several years ago:

> The local taxpaying ability of school districts in reality is not their theoretical taxpaying ability, but rather a measure of their accessibility to local tax revenue. If a district only has the authority to levy property taxes, then its local taxpaying ability (or effort to support schools) should be measured only in terms of the equalized value of the taxable property of that district. However, if a district has the power to levy local non-property taxes, such as payroll taxes, sales taxes, utility taxes, etc., then the yield of such local non-property taxes can justly be incorporated in the measure of the taxpaying ability of that district.[23]

Note that school finance authorities do not distinguish fiscal capacity from taxpaying ability, but rather use the terms interchangeably.

Equalized Assessment of Property Valuation

The aforementioned tax-based approach largely pertains to taxation of real property, since the major portion of local revenues for schools is derived from this source.

Because real property is the major resource of local public school funds, the state aid formulae of most states use equalized assessed valuation of property as the sole criterion for equalization of state funds. As noted earlier, difficulty with property tax administration is a traditional problem that continues to be inextricably linked to public school financing.

If all property in every state were assessed at 100 percent of Fair Market Value (FMV), i.e., Full Value, True Value, or even at a uniform percentage of Full Value, the problem of determining local fiscal capacity would be much simpler than it is under present conditions. However, the assessment practices in most states traditionally have been far from uniform. Studies of assessment ratios within states show a range of from less than 2 to 1 percent of value to more than 8 to 1. Such variance results in many complications, not only in attempts to determine local taxpaying ability, but also in efforts to devise equitable and satisfactory state plans for financing schools.

One difficulty arises from the wide differences of opinion about the method that should be used to determine the full value of property. It cannot be the original cost because in many areas purchase price or the original cost of construction represents only a small percentage of current value. It cannot in all instances be the sales price, because there may be sales, among relatives or under enforced conditions, at a price far below that for which similar properties are being sold.

The goal in every state undoubtedly should be to attain uniform assessment procedures, but thus far, only a few states have made satisfactory progress in that direction. Existing assessed valuations in most states, therefore, do not provide a full satisfactory basis either for determining local fiscal capacity or for prescribing local uniform effort.

TAX EFFORT TO SUPPORT PUBLIC SCHOOLS

The fiscal effort to support education is influenced by many factors: the people's interest in and attitude toward public education, the proportion of pupils in nonpublic schools, the people's "feeling" about government and taxes, the tax structure, the amount of taxes they pay for purposes other than public schools, whether they have children or grandchildren in school, their reaction to the programs offered by the schools, and probably their reaction to the political party in power and to the governmental leadership. No one has been able to determine, up to this time, the effects of any one factor, or any combination of factors such as these, upon the fiscal effort made by any state to support its public schools.

BOX 7.4

Definition

Fiscal Effort is the ratio of revenue (or expenditures) to the tax base.
Effort = Revenue (or Expenditure) ÷ Tax Base.

Fiscal or tax effort is defined as the extent to which a government utilizes its fiscal or tax capacity to support the public schools and has frequently been characterized as the level of taxpayer exertion made to fund a specific governmental service. Computation of expenditures or revenues per pupil of a nation, state, or locality is insufficient to indicate tax effort accurately. With either of these measures, a richer nation, state, or local district putting forth the same effort as a poorer counterpart will always appear to be making a great effort. Thus, fiscal effort must be expressed in terms of a percentage relationship between expenditures (from state and local sources), or revenues, and the overall fiscal capacity.

International Comparisons. Although international comparisons of fiscal efforts to support elementary and secondary schools are relatively imprecise, and many caveats must be extended, certain impressions may be obtained.[24] Rasell and Mishel have pointed out that, "The claim that the United States spends more than other nations on education is misleading. By most comparisons, the United States devotes a smaller share of its resources to pre-primary, primary, and secondary education than do most industrialized countries."[25]

It is important to remember that expenditures or revenues per pupil do not alone measure fiscal effort to support education. Fiscal effort is a ratio of expenditures or revenues to the measure of fiscal capacity. A poor country or state with moderate expenditures per pupil may be putting forth high effort while the same level of expenditures per pupil made by a rich country or state would indicate only moderate or even low effort. Thus, because the United States, a rich country, has a high expenditure per pupil, it does not necessarily mean that it has a correspondingly high fiscal effort.

Fractionalization and Tax Effort

Fractionalization is a quantifiable measure of diversity for a specified variable in a population.[26] Why do some nations and states put forth high tax effort for education and other social transfers while others do not? In recent years, several economists and political scientists have turned their attention to this question, and after considerable analysis have advanced some plausible explanations. One hypothesis that has much to recommend it is that countries that have more centralized governmental systems tend to devote relatively more fiscal commitment to social redistribution because there is more competition and diverse vying for fiscal resources from broader interest groups at a central or national level. It is argued that more localized and geographically diverse systems will result in more local "pork-barrel" distribution, where more centralized systems will tend to fund broader and more universal transfer programs to larger more generic groups such as education, pensions, health care, and other programs for the poor. This explanation is, of course, difficult to accept when one considers the tarnished image of influence peddling by big money interests in Washington. Yet, it can be argued that the more decentralized systems may tend to create more multiform considerations that limit the continuity of effect of the centralized universal measures. A good example of such a phenomenon transpired in the recent Great Recession as the central United States government sought to return to normalcy of employment by economic stimulus while the state governments, stripped of revenues, laid off thousands of state and local employees. Alesina and Glaeser[27] have pointed out that one of the main arguments advanced by more centralized European governments is that favorable social redistribution is enhanced by less decentralization. Also, Persson and Tabellini likewise argue that "Universalistic spending is more redistributive than geographically targeted spending."[28]

Concerning the United States, *per se*, Alesina and Glaeser maintain that the system of separation of powers at the central federal level and at the state level militates against positive social welfare policies. Moreover, they observe that the court system in the United States, an important separate branch of government at both federal and state levels, on balance, has served as a buttress against social transfers, as was the case on the New Deal conflict with President Franklin Roosevelt,[29] and more directly with education in stifling the efforts of plaintiffs in *San Antonio v. Rodriguez*[30] in which the U.S. Supreme Court froze the redistributive effects of the Equal Protection Clause.

BOX 7.5

Fractionalization and Social Welfare Spending

At the state level . . . welfare payments are less generous in American states that have a higher proportion of minorities. At the country level . . .[there is] a pervasive connection between fractionalization and the degree of social welfare spending – countries with greater racial division spend less on welfare.

Source: Alberto Alesina and Edward L. Glaeser, *Fighting Poverty in the U.S. and Europe: A World of Difference* (Oxford: Oxford University Press, 2004).

With regard to decentralized governmental structure as a deterrent to tax effort for social transfer programs, a reasonably strong argument was advanced by Tiebout,[31] an economist, who argued that individuals, particularly wealthy ones, will move to local districts with lower taxes and more amenities consistent with their values, an altogether rather obvious theory, that results in the more affluent moving to the suburbs where the taxes are lower and the living conditions are higher. As Richard and Peggy Musgrave have cogently summarized, the Tiebout theory explains, "the tendency for the wealthy to flee the poor and for the poor to follow the wealthy . . . [a] reason for segregating and using zoning devices to keep out the poor."[32] Thus, governmental structures that are more decentralized may have inclinations toward lower tax effort to support public schools where centralized federal and state governmental structures may be disposed toward greater tax effort with redistributive features. However, the main thrust of Alesina and Glaeser's theory is that tax effort for education and other social purposes has much to do with the fragmentation or heterogeneity of society.

Alesina and Glaeser further argue that the degree of racial, ethnic, linguistic, and religious fractionalization has a negative effect on taxpayer effort for public education and other social services. It is their thesis that a fractionated nation or state will put forth less effort for the common or the public good. As the most race conscious country among the developed nations of the world, tax effort to support public schools in the United

States may be affected by racial overtones. Robert Kagan points out in his bestseller *Dangerous Nation*, a foremost consideration for progress of the United States has much to do with mitigation of the influence of racial overtones on governmental policy.[33] Alesina and Glaeser cite a wealth of literature that shows that racial or ethnic prejudice materially affects people to not have empathy for those who are different from themselves.[34] Racial or ethnic differences, therefore, may have much to do with high and low tax effort to support social programs such as public schools. They say that "[r]acial, religious, and ethnic divisions distract . . . and reduce the ability to forge a common class-based identity."[35] Alesina and Glaeser estimate that 50 percent of the gap in welfare spending between the United States and Europe countries is due to racial fractionalization.

Alesina and LaFerrara developed an index to quantify fractionalization in states or nations.[36] The calculation is the same as the percentage equalization index utilized by some states' school funding formulae to distribute funds to local school districts.

Racial or Ethnic Fractionalization

$$\Sigma = \text{races or ethnicities} = 1 - \Sigma \left(\frac{\text{Population in Race or Ethnicity}}{\text{Total Population}} \right)^2$$

This calculation can be applied to not only racial and ethnic differences but to linguistic and religious differences as well. Thus, as shown in Figure 7.3, the people of the United States are much more diverse and fractionated than the populations of European countries. With regard to race, specifically, the United States is clearly much more diverse than the European countries, and concerning ethnicity the United States' diversity is only exceeded by Belgium and Switzerland.

Linguistic fractionalization is greater than the United States in Belgium, Netherlands, Spain, and Switzerland. Interestingly, the linguistic mix to some degree reflects the degree of private school funding in these countries. Finally, as displayed in Figure 7.3, the religious fractionalization is much greater in the United States than in any European countries.

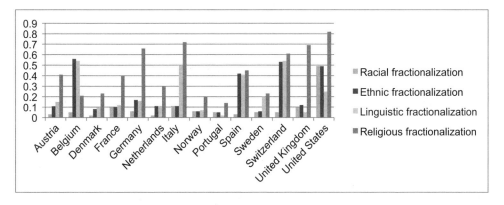

Figure 7.3 Fractionalization Indices

Source: Based on Alberto Alesina and Edward L. Glaeser, *Fighting Poverty in Europe: A World of Difference* (Oxford: Oxford University Press, 2004), p. 139.

Other researchers have shown that degree of income equalization is related to the heterogeneity of the racial make-up of the nation; racism and xenophobia lead to lower levels of social solidarity and consequently lower the willingness of a majority group to tax itself for the benefits of the minority.[37] Equalization declines as the degree of racism increases.[38] As white Americans see poverty in racial terms, the African-Americans are stereotyped as the poor and lazy. The white American majority are predisposed to put forth less tax effort to support the public schools in geographical areas where most minority children are educated.[39]

The same situation prevails with linguistic differences, and the responses by those who speak the majority language may be even more pronounced when making decisions regarding the school funding of programs for a linguistic minority. A tangible example is the renowned case of *Lau v. Nichols* in which instance the several thousand children of Chinese ancestry who did not speak English were denied language transition programs until the United States Supreme Court held such denial violated the Civil Rights Act of 1964.[40] Another good example involving both language, ethnicity, and race was the denial of funds on behalf of all Latino children of alien parents for a public school education by the State of Texas. Such prevailed until the denial was found to be unconstitutional in 1982.[41] Justice Brennan in this case captured the essence of the issue of denying benefits and tax effort to help those who are different when he declared that alien children are "persons" under the U.S. Constitution and that children of a "disfavored group" cannot be denied an education regardless of how the majority class decides to discriminate.

Religiosity also plays a role in tax effort for social spending. Scheve and Stasavage maintain that the nature of religion is to the spiritual and not the temporal, to serve as a "psychic" escape from the economic problems and social travails of earthly matters, thus, substituting religious belief for social programs, public schools, and such civic matters.[42] Benabou and Tirole maintain that religious beliefs in the spiritual rather than the earthly, more or less, the "Protestant ethic" that ties heavenly rewards to industriousness while on earth, militate against support for redistribution; rewards are in heaven.[43] Thus, possibly, a negative effect on tax effort to support the public schools is a belief that secular public education is godless and is destructive to parental and clerical beliefs and, therefore, deleterious to the propagation of ecclesiastical dogma and is thereby unworthy of public fiscal provision. This phenomenon is pervasive as the histories of public school development have shown in most of the developed world.[44]

As the above discussion indicates, the factors affecting governmental fiscal support for investment in education and redistribution relating to other social services are very complex and, thus, extremely difficult to address with any degree of certainty. Clearly, however, the extant studies reveal group dynamics reflecting an amalgam of interests related to race, ethnicity, language, religion, and presumably a host of other factors and factions that lend themselves to a near inscrutable and probably fluid array of social and economic conditions. One can only conclude the measurement of fractionalization is a developing area of political and social science.

Tax Effort of States

Fiscal effort may be measured at the state level for any or all governmental services for which revenue or expenditure data are available. The fiscal effort of states may be determined for all governmental services or for subparts such as health, welfare, transportation, corrections, and so forth. State fiscal effort for education is reasonably accurate for policy purposes and can provide information about how a state prioritizes its fiscal resources across programs and services. Such information can be helpful in evaluating in an analytical way the results of non-empirical decisions that are made in the state political processes.

An analysis of state effort to support the public schools should not include federal funds in either revenue or expenditure calculations. To include federal revenues or expenditures when conducting an analysis of state effort falsely inflates state fiscal effort and contaminates precise estimates of a state's actual fiscal commitment. Thus, interstate comparisons of fiscal effort should be calculated as the ratio of state and local revenues or expenditures to the fiscal capacity measure with federal funds excluded. The only arguable exception to this general rule would be where federal revenues are in lieu of tax payments provided to the state to offset the loss of real property taken off the tax rolls for federal purposes. Such an example is provided by Federal Impact Aid that provides federal funds to local school districts "impacted" by federal installations.[45]

Arrayed in Table 7.3 is the fiscal effort put forth by states to support their public schools. Tax effort in this table is defined as state and local public school revenues per $1,000 of personal income in the named state. As is indicated, Alaska is ranked first in effort with $63 per $1,000 personal income and Florida is at the bottom. Wyoming and Vermont are near the top with $62 and $61, respectively, while Tennessee with $32 and North Dakota with $31 per $1,000 of personal income are near the bottom. Note that fiscal effort does not necessarily equate to individual tax effort. In the case of Alaska and Wyoming, the preponderance of state revenues is obtained from petroleum taxes while the taxes on individuals are modest indeed.

Table 7.3 State and Local Revenue for Public Schools in 2009–2010 Per $1,000 of Personal Income in 2010 ($)

Rank	State	Revenue
1	Alaska	63
2	Wyoming	62
3	Vermont	61
4	Rhode Island	53
5	New Jersey	52
6	Delaware	51
7	Maine	50
8	Pennsylvania	50
9	West Virginia	49
10	Georgia	46
11	Indiana	46
12	New York	46
13	Wisconsin	46

(Continued)

Table 7.3 (Continued)

Rank	State	Revenue
14	New Hampshire	45
15	South Carolina	45
16	Arkansas	44
17	Maryland	44
18	Texas	44
19	Utah	44
20	Connecticut	43
21	Idaho	43
22	Kansas	43
23	Massachusetts	43
24	Missouri	43
25	New Mexico	43
26	Arizona	42
27	Kentucky	42
28	Hawaii	41
29	Minnesota	41
30	Ohio	41
31	Illinois	40
32	Iowa	40
33	Oregon	40
34	Louisiana	39
35	Colorado	38
36	Michigan	38
37	Montana	38
38	Nebraska	38
39	Virginia	38
40	Alabama	37
41	Mississippi	37
42	California	36
43	Washington	36
44	Oklahoma	35
45	Nevada	33
46	North Carolina	32
47	South Dakota	32
48	Tennessee	32
49	North Dakota	31
50	Florida	30

Source: Data from Rankings & Estimates: Rankings of the States 2012 and Estimates of School Statistics 2013, December 2012, www.nea.org/assets/img/content/NEA_Rankings_And_Estimates-2013_(2).pdf, Table F-6. Used with permission of the National Education Association. Copyright © 2013. All rights reserved.

Local Tax Effort of School Districts

There are several possible measures of local fiscal effort. Expenditures may constitute a very rough indication of effort but are inaccurate because a school district with high capacity may be able, with little effort, to expend a larger amount of funds than a district with low capacity could expend with much higher effort. Expenditures, therefore, give some indication of the investment in education, but not necessarily of the fiscal effort being made to support the schools.

Local tax levies likewise are often considered an indication of the effort made by a school district. However, a relatively high levy in a district having a low ratio between assessed and full valuation may constitute less fiscal effort than a much lower levy in a district with a relatively high assessment ratio.

Due to variations in assessment practices, relative levels of local effort are difficult if not impossible to determine in many states. A high tax levy in a district may or may not represent high effort, depending upon the assessment ratio in the district as compared with that in other parts of the state. In some states, laws limiting the levy for school purposes may mean that the people in a number of districts are levying far less than they would be willing to make available if the laws permitted.

Despite such factors, it is not uncommon to find school districts in a state that are levying from two to four or even six times as much for support of schools as other districts. Undoubtedly, in many cases this represents a major difference in fiscal effort. In addition, districts in states where the laws permit may be receiving funds from other local tax sources, such as payroll or sales taxes. In some cases, however, these other sources of revenue are used in lieu of levies that otherwise would be made on real property. Consequently, property taxes are lower in those districts than in districts which are not permitted or do not choose to use nonproperty taxes as a source of revenue.

If local support is to be utilized, equality of opportunity might theoretically be attained in either of two ways:

1. Limit the effort that may be made by school districts, and perhaps remove and distribute to other districts some of the state funds now received by districts with sufficient revenue to provide a reasonably adequate program.
2. Provide sufficient funds from state sources to enable all districts to have as large an amount available per pupil as is now available in the more favored districts.

The possibility of limiting local fiscal effort or capturing funds from some of the higher-capacity districts might appeal to some people who are concerned about high taxes and believe that too much money is now being devoted to public education. People usually want to effect improvements where they are needed instead of limiting opportunities that are now available in the more favored districts and states, although even those people who favor equitable distribution of educational funds might change their opinion if they lived in some of the more favored districts. In states that do not neutralize fiscal capacity and permit unrestrained local effort, the high-capacity districts will always have more local funds available per pupil or per classroom unit than low-capacity districts. Thus, unless limitations are imposed on these high-capacity districts, there will continue to be some inequality in educational opportunity.

Why fiscal effort varies among school districts is a question of great interest to educators and economists alike and has been discussed above in a macro-sense. Why some populations have higher aspirations for education and are willing to exert greater fiscal effort is a more complex issue than was suggested earlier with the argument that variation in income is the determinant.

School districts with less property wealth often put forth greater fiscal effort than their wealthier counterparts. One may assume that people in poor school districts would naturally put forth less effort for education for two very good reasons. *First,* the poor have less disposable income and the marginal dollar is more valuable to them because they must devote each additional dollar to the immediate needs of food, shelter, and clothing. On the other hand, the more affluent, having their basic needs fulfilled, may look to nonmaterial goods such as education to satisfy their wants and desires. *Second,* because the affluent are better educated, one could naturally expect them to place more value on education and to want more and better education for their own children. Both of these reasons are quite valid from both an economic and a psychological point of view, yet, in fact, the more affluent do not always put forth greater effort.

In the Texas school finance case *Edgewood v. Kirby,*[46] the Supreme Court of Texas noted that: "the lower expenditures in the property-poor districts are not the result of lack of tax effort. Generally, the property-rich districts can tax low and spend high while the property-poor districts must tax high merely to spend low."[47] In Texas, the court found that the 100 poorest school districts had an average tax rate of 74.5 cents and spent only $2,975 per pupil, while the rich districts had an average tax rate of 47 cents and spent an average of $7,233 per pupil.

Other factors, however, can play an important role in a community's level of tax effort to support public schools. McLoone, in an early study, found that areas with good schools and high taxes tended to have a relatively rapid turnover of young families with children in public schools.[48] Voters over age 50 are less likely to vote for higher tax rates, and professional and white-collar workers are more likely to approve increased school taxes than blue-collar workers and retirees.[49] Also, cyclical economic effects, beyond mere income levels, may affect taxpayers' willingness to pay taxes. In times of rapid inflation, resistance to additional taxes intensifies.[50]

Willingness to provide tax support for public schools is also influenced by the politics and power structure of the community. Districts with competitive power structures tend to make higher local fiscal effort in proportion to their capacity than do districts with noncompetitive or monopolistic power structures. Education appears to benefit from a pluralism of competing power structures, that is, where various power groups are forced to seek allies in order to be politically effective. Educational advocates in such a setting have been found to be effective political allies. Where a school district is dominated by a monolithic, noncompetitive power structure influenced largely by economics, the political effectiveness of educational interests is substantially reduced.[51]

Thus, the nature of local fiscal effort is quite complex, with factors as diverse as the political, educational, social, and economic conditions of each community. Undoubtedly, the wealth and income of the people is an important element, but this alone does not explain why two school districts of the same relative economic level will have greatly different school fiscal efforts. The answer can only be found in the myriad pluralistic conditions of our democratic system of government.

SUMMARY

This chapter provided a discussion of fiscal capacity and fiscal effort of nations, states, and local school districts. In various ways this chapter shows how a nation, state, or local school district can measure its fiscal capacity and then gives comparisons of the efforts that these entities actually make for purposes of public education. The following main points were emphasized.

Fiscal capacity varies greatly among governmental entities creating widely disparate conditions of educational opportunity.

Both physical and human resources combine to produce the economic capacity of a government.

Internationally, measures of gross national product, gross domestic product, and gross national income are commonly utilized to measure fiscal capacity.

Human resources will continue to become increasingly more instrumental in the wealth of nations than physical capacity.

The total economic power of the United States dwarfs all other nations, but in terms of per capita capacity it falls below several other developed countries. Moreover, the relative position of the United States has declined in recent years and may well decline still further in the near future.

Worldwide, there is a great chasm between the developed and underdeveloped nations. Although the United States cannot lay claim to being the absolute richest country per capita, both its total and per capita incomes are virtually incomprehensible when compared to the third world countries.

Slippage in economic strength calls for greater attention to education as both an investment and a deterrent to exacerbation of inequalities.

Fiscal capacities of states in the United States vary substantially although there has been a trend toward narrowing of the gap between the richest and the poorest states over the past half-century. Unfortunately, during the most recent ten years we have seen the trend reversed, as poorer states have seen their fiscal capacities deteriorate still further.

Fractionalization, as defined by Alesina and Glaeser, is a concept that seeks to explain the phenomenon of the variance in tax effort among nations, states, and even school districts. Their theory is one that is very promising and presents fertile ground for further research.

The quality of education among the states is largely dependent on the selective fiscal capacity of the states. States with substantial wealth and income usually have higher expenditures per pupil for public elementary and secondary education.

Per capita comparisons of fiscal capacity may give a slightly different picture of a state's relative position in financing education than do per-pupil comparisons. Some states educate much higher percentages of children in public schools as compared to the overall population.

Variations in local fiscal capacity create wide differences in financial capability that must be overcome by state governments if equality of educational opportunity is to be achieved.

Local fiscal capacity is commonly measured by three approaches, or combinations thereof: tax base, tax-base surrogate, and/or economic indicator. The most common method is the tax-base use of the equalized assessed valuation of real property.

Economic indicators, using both property valuation and personal income, are coming into more common usage, but most argue against the inclusion of income unless income is made available as a local optional tax.

Property valuation as a measure of fiscal capacity is often subject to criticism for several reasons, but most often it is related to problems of administration and the tax-payers' perennial aversion to property taxation.

The extent of fiscal effort that citizens are willing to put forth to support their schools is subject to many factors including demographics, education attainment of adults, percentage of children attending private schools, income level, and the political leadership of the state or community.

Fiscal effort for education is not always a manifestation of the affluence of the community. In many instances low-capacity states and school districts exert a greater fiscal effort to support the public schools than their higher-capacity counterparts.

Although international comparisons of national fiscal effort to support education must be used with considerable caution, available data indicate that the fiscal effort of the United States is not high relative to other developed industrialized nations. Fiscal effort for public education may not always be reflective of a state's effort to support all governmental services. Some states have high fiscal effort for public education and low tax effort for general governmental services. This pattern will be reversed in other states.

The fiscal effort of school districts tends to have important effects on local revenues, but fiscal capacity is far more determinative of equality of fiscal resources. In many instances low-capacity school districts put forth substantially more fiscal effort than do more affluent school districts, but low-capacity districts' fiscal effort cannot come near to offsetting their fiscal incapacities.

KEY TERMS

- Fiscal capacity
- Personal income
- Economic indicator
- Fiscal position
- Tax revenues
- Multiple deductions
- Gross national product
- Representative tax system (RTS)
- Equalized assessed valuation of property

- Gross domestic product
- Tax base
- Gross national income
- Tax-base surrogate
- Fiscal effort
- Per capita
- Sales ratio
- Fractionalization

NOTES

1. World Bank, *World Tables 1992* (Baltimore: Johns Hopkins University Press, 1992), for an array of national economic measures.
2. Robert B. Reich, *The Work of Nations* (New York: Alfred A. Knopf, 1991), p. 3.
3. OECD Factbook 2013 @ OECD 2013.

4. The latest number for the Russian Federation is for 2009.

5. D. S. Landes, *The Unbound Prometheus* (Cambridge: Cambridge University Press, 1969).

6. Daron Acemoglu and James A. Robinson, *Why Nations Fail: The Origins of Power, Prosperity and Poverty* (London: Profile Books, 2012), pp. 73–78.

7. Ibid.

8. Lawrence E. Harrison, *Underdevelopment Is a State of Mind: The Latin American Case* (Cambridge, MA: The Center for International Affairs, Harvard University, 1985), pp. 1–9, by President and Fellows of Harvard College.

9. Ibid., p. 230.

10. Paul Kennedy, *Preparing for the Twenty-First Century* (New York: Random House, 1993), p. 339.

11. Advisory Commission on Intergovernmental Relations, *Measures of State and Local Fiscal Capacity and Tax Effort of State and Local Areas* (Washington, DC: U.S. Government Printing Office, 1962), p. 3.

12. U.S. Department of Commerce, Bureau of the Census, *Finances of Public School Systems in 1978–79* (Washington, DC: U.S. Government Printing Office, 1980), p. 9.

13. Ibid.

14. C. T. Sandford, J .R. M. Willis, and D. J. Ironside, *An Annual Wealth Tax* (New York: Holmes & Meier Publishers, 1975), p. 3.

15. *Edgewood Independent School District v. Kirby*, 777 S.W.2d 391 (1989).

16. *Serrano v. Priest*, 135 Cal. Rptr. 345, 557 P.2d 929 (1976).

17. *Olsen v. State*, 276 Or. 9, 554 P.2d 139 (1976).

18. Ellwood P. Cubberley, *School Funds and Their Apportionment* (New York: Teachers College Press, Columbia University, 1906).

19. Percy E. Burrup, *Financing Education in a Climate of Change* (Boston: Allyn and Bacon, 1974).

20. Roe L. Johns and Edgar L. Morphet, *The Economics and Financing of Education: A Systems Approach*, 3rd edn. (Englewood Cliffs, NJ: Prentice-Hall, 1975).

21. George D. Strayer and Robert Murray Haig, *The Financing of Education in the State of New York* (New York: MacMillan, 1923).

22. Paul R. Mort, *State Support for the Public Schools* (New York: Teachers College Press, Columbia University, 1926), p. 16.

23. Roe L. Johns, "The Development of State Support for Public Schools, in *Financing Education: Fiscal and Legal Alternatives*, eds. Roe L. Johns, Kern Alexander, and K. Forbis Jordan (Columbus, OH: Charles E. Merrill, 1972). See also James A. Hale, "Measuring School Districts Fiscal Capacity," in *Texas Tech Journal of Education* 7, No. 3 (Fall 1980).

24. Stephen M. Barro, *International Comparisons of Education Spending: Some Conceptual and Methodological Issues* (Washington, DC: SMB Economic Research, 1990), and Deborah Verstegen, *International Comparisons of Education Spending: A Review and Analysis of Reports* (Washington, DC: National Governors' Association, 1992).

25. Edith M. Rasell and Lawrence Mishel, "Short-changing Education: How U.S. Spending on Grades K-12 Lags Behind Other Industrial Nations" (Washington, DC: Economic Policy Institute Briefing Paper, January 1990).

26. Douglas Moeller, "Fractionalization and Tax Effort to Fund Illinois Public Schools: An Equity Analysis," Ph.D. dissertation, University of Illinois at Urbana-Champaign, 2012.

27. Alberto Alesina and Edward L. Glaeser, *Fighting Poverty in the U.S. and Europe: A World of Difference* (Oxford: Oxford University Press, 2005), p. 78.

28. Torsten Persson and Guido Tabellini, *Political Economics: Explaining Economic Policy* (Cambridge, MA: MIT Press, 2000). Cited in Nolan McCarty and Jonas Pontusson, "The Political Economy of Inequality and Redistribution," in Wiemer Salverda, Brian Nolan, and Timothy M. Smeeding, editors, *The Oxford Handbook of Economic Inequality* (Oxford: Oxford University Press, 2009), p. 677.

29. Jean Edward Smith, *FDR* (New York: Random House Trade paperbacks, 2007), pp. 377–389.
30. *San Antonio Independent School District v. Rodriguez*, 411 U.S. 1, 93 S. Ct. 1278 (1973).
31. Charles M. Tiebout, "A Pure Theory of Local Government Expenditures," *Journal of Political Economy*, October 1956.
32. Richard A. Musgrave and Peggy B. Musgrave, *Public Finance in Theory and Practice* (New York: McGraw-Hill Book Co., 1980), pp. 520–521.
33. Robert Kagan, *Dangerous Nation* (New York: Alfred A. Knopf, 2006), pp. 270–283.
34. Alesina and Glaeser, *op. cit.*, p. 134.
35. Ibid.
36. Alberto Alesina and E. LaFerrara, "Participation in Heterogeneous Communities," *Quarterly Journal of Economics*, 115 (2000), pp. 847–904.
37. Nolan McCarty and Jonas Pontusson, "The Political Economy of Inequality and Redistribution," in *The Oxford Handbook of Economic Inequality*, editors, Brian Nolan, Wiemer Salverda, and Timothy M. Smeeding (Oxford: Oxford University Press, 2011), p. 683.
38. Ibid.
39. Martin Gilens, *Why Americans Hate Welfare* (Chicago: University of Chicago Press, 1999). See: McCarty and Pontusson, *op. cit.*, p. 684.
40. *Lau v. Nichols*, 414 U.S. 563, 94 S. Ct. 786 (1974).
41. *Plyler v. Doe*, 457 U.S. 202, 102 S. Ct. 2382 (1982).
42. Kenneth Scheve and David Stasavage, "Religion and Preferences for Social Insurance," *Quarterly Journal of Political Science*, 1 (2006), pp. 255–286. See also: McCarty and Pontusson, *op. cit.*, pp. 682–683.
43. Roland Benabou and Jean Tirole, "Belief in a Just World and Redistributive Politics," *Quarterly Journal of Economics*, 121(2) (2006), pp. 699–746.
44. Owen Chadwick, *The Secularization of the European Mind in the 19th Century* (Cambridge: Cambridge University Press, 1975); Karl A. Schleunes, *Schooling and Society: The Politics of Education in Prussia and Bavaria, 1750–1900* (Oxford: Berg, 1989); Marjorie Lamberti, *State, Society & The Elementary School in Imperial Germany* (Oxford: Oxford University Press, 1989); Isser Woloch, *The New Regime: Transformation of the French Civic Order, 1789–1820s* (New York: W. W. Norton & Company, 1994); Denis Mack Smith, *Mazzini* (New Haven: Yale University Press, 1994); and John T. McGreevy, *Catholicism and American Freedom* (New York: W. W. Norton & Company, 2003).
45. Title VIII of the Elementary and Secondary Education Act of 1965 (ESEA).
46. *Edgewood v. Kirby*, 777 S.W. 2d 391 (1989).
47. Ibid.
48. Alfred Victor Meyers, "The Financial Crisis in Urbana Schools: Patterns of Support and Nonsupport Among Organized Groups in an Urban Community" (Ed.D. dissertation, Wayne State University, 1964); Eugene McLoone, *Background Paper on State and Local Taxation* (Albany: New York Educational Conference Board, July 1969).
49. Irving M. Witt and Frank C. Pearce, *A Study of Voter Reaction to a Combination Bond-Tax Election* (San Mateo, CA: San Mateo College, 1968).
50. James M. Buchanan, "Taxpayer Constraints on Financing Education," *Economic Factors Affecting the Financing of Education*, eds. Roe L. Johns, Irving Goffman, Kern Alexander, and Dewey Stollar (Gainesville, FL: University of Florida, 1970), pp. 278–282.
51. Ralph B. Kimbrough and Roe L. Johns, *The Relationship of Socioeconomic Community Power Structure to Local Fiscal Policy, Final Report,* Office of Education, Cooperative Research Project #1234 (Gainesville, FL: University of Florida, 1968), pp. 187–190.

CHAPTER 8

Taxation for Public Schools

TOPICAL OUTLINE OF CHAPTER

- Adam Smith's Tax Maxims
- Taxes Are Low in the United States
- State Taxes in the United States Are Regressive
- Types of Taxes
- Power to Tax
- Taxing at State Level
    - Sacrifice and Benefit Theories
    - State Delegation of Taxing Power
- The Levy of Taxes
- Property Taxes
- Property as a Regressive Tax
- Consumption Taxes
    - Regressive Nature of Sales Tax
- Individual Income Taxes
- Corporation Income Taxes
- Other Taxes
- Possible New Taxes
    - Wealth Tax
    - Value-Added Tax
    - Expenditure Tax
- Property Tax Control Points
    - Homestead Exemptions and Circuit Breakers
    - Assessment Reform
    - Property Tax Classification
    - Site-Value Taxation

- Tax Exemptions or Tax Expenditures
  - Income Tax Exemptions
  - Sales Tax Exemptions
  - Exemptions to Attract Industry
  - Exemptions for Favored Groups
  - Exemptions for Nonprofit Institutions
  - Exemptions for Religion and Charities

INTRODUCTION

The beliefs and attitudes of the people about public schools and taxation are usually incorporated, in general terms, into federal and state constitutions and statutes. The legislature of each state has what is commonly called *plenary power* over taxation and education; that is, it may pass any laws it considers desirable, and these laws must be observed unless they are later found to be inconsistent with provisions of the state constitution or in conflict with federal constitutional provisions. Recent school finance cases have addressed the inviolate nature of the legislative prerogative and have rendered legislative power less plenary as it affects taxation and school funding.

Laws constitute an expression of state policy. If in any state a serious attempt has been made to agree upon long-range policies, and if the policies relating to taxation and education have been wisely and carefully developed, the laws are likely to be much more defensible than those in a state in which such foresight and vision have not been exercised. Ideas for laws come from many sources; therefore, public school finance involves issues concerning taxation, distribution, or the appropriate management of public funds. Legal questions of taxation bear on equity and justice to taxpayers with regard to the state or school district's discretion to tax, procedures for the levying of taxes, and the nature of the burden the taxpayer must sustain.

ADAM SMITH'S TAX MAXIMS

Adam Smith in Book V of his great work, *The Wealth of Nations*, set forth his four maxims (or objectives) on taxation.

First, "Subjects of every state ought to contribute towards the support of the government, as nearly as possible, in proportion to their respective abilities . . . In the observation or neglect of this maxim consists what is called the equality or inequality of taxation."

Second, "The tax which each individual is bound to pay ought to be certain, and not arbitrary. The time of payment, the manner of payment, the quantity to be paid, ought all to be clear and plain to the contributor, and to every other person."

Third, "Every tax ought to be levied at the time, or in the manner, in which it is most likely to be convenient for the contributor to pay it."

Fourth, "Every tax ought to be so contrived as both to take out and to keep out of the pockets of the people as little as possible or and above what it brings to the public treasury of the state."[1]

Adam Smith's maxims of taxation have been a standard for public finance experts, economists, and legislators since 1776. Whether they have adhered to the maxims is another question. Each maxim states a desirable principle that if followed will help make taxation as palatable as possible.

A little different twist on taxation is prescribed by Stiglitz, the Nobel Prize winner for economics 2002, in his textbook, *Economics of the Public Sector,*[2] where he advances five desirable principles for a *good* tax system.

1. Economic efficiency: the tax system should not interfere with the efficient allocation of resources;
2. Administrative simplicity: the tax system ought to be easy and relatively inexpensive to administer;
3. Flexibility: the tax system ought to be able to respond easily (in some cases automatically) to changed economic circumstances;
4. Political responsibility: the tax system should be designed so that individuals can
   ascertain what they are paying and evaluate how accurately the system reflects
   their preferences; and
5. Fairness: the tax system ought to be fair in its relative treatment of different
   individuals.[3]

A brief word about each principle will help to explain some aspects of each that directly touch education and economic growth. With regard to the first, *economic efficiency,* Stiglitz notes that taxation has behavioral effects on individuals, such as decisions to enter and stay in the workforce, become educated, send children to college, save money, buy a home, get married or divorced, as well as myriad effects on institutions and corporations. Ease of *administration* and costs of collection has to do with simplicity, the complexity of government machinery to account for col- lections, and the acceptability of the taxes for political consumption. To explain this particular principle, Stiglitz cites Jean-Baptiste Colbert, finance minister to Louis XIV, who famously said, "The art of taxation consists in so plucking the goose as to obtain the largest amount of feathers with the least possible amount of hiss- ing."[4] Possibly the most important administrative development in taxation was the U.S. system of withholding taxes from wages and earnings before the money ever reached the taxpayer. Withholding made the income tax easier for government to collect, but, importantly, it reduced to a large degree the *hissing* of taxpayers. *Flex- ibility* has much to do with the effectiveness of taxation as it affects the economy. As economic conditions change, such as the 2008 recession, it may become desirable to leave more money in the hands of the taxpayers in order to stimulate spending. In this regard, an income tax is much more flexible and more responsive to economic change than a property tax that not only is encumbered by rate inflexibility but also lags in response to variations in the tax base. Regarding *political responsibility,* the heart of the matter rests with the idea of transparency – that the nature of the tax burden should be clear to the taxpayer; the effects and incidence of the tax should be translucent to a person of reasonable intelligence. Finally, the *fairness* of the tax should be an *a priori* consideration by the legislature of any state or nation. The general principles of horizontal equity (equal treatment of equals) and vertical equity (unequal treatment of unequals) should be foundational aspects of all tax systems. Persons with greater taxpaying ability should be taxed at a higher rate than taxpayers of lesser ability.[5] The *fairness* of a tax is determined by three broad classifications, *progressive*, *regressive*, and *proportional*.

BOX 8.1

Stiglitz's Principles of Taxation

Economic efficiency – the tax system should not be distortionary; if possible, it should be used to enhance economic efficiency.

Administrative simplicity – the tax system should have low costs of administration and compliance.

Flexibility – the tax system should allow easy adaptation to changed circumstances.

Political responsibility – the tax system should be transparent.

Fairness – the tax system should be seen to be fair, treating those in similar circumstances similarly and imposing higher taxes on those who can better bear the burden of taxation.

Source: Joseph E. Stiglitz, *Economics of the Public Sector,* Third Edition (New York: W.W. Norton & Company, 2000), pp. 456–458.

As is shown later in this chapter and the following chapter, the adherence to the fairness principle in taxation by the federal government has been much better than those legislated by state governments. The progressive nature of the federal income tax, while not ideal, nevertheless tends to tax the rich at a higher percentage of income level than it does the poor. Figure 8.1 shows how a progressive tax system obliges the upper income families to pay taxes at a higher rate than the poor and middle income families.

TAXES ARE LOW IN THE UNITED STATES

Americans are among the least taxed of any of the developed countries of the world. In 2010, the United States was third from the bottom of the 34 OECD countries in the overall tax effort to support governmental services, federal, state, and local. Tax effort for the nation is measured by collected taxes as percentage of the Gross Domestic Product (GDP). As shown in Figure 8.2, the United States ranked only

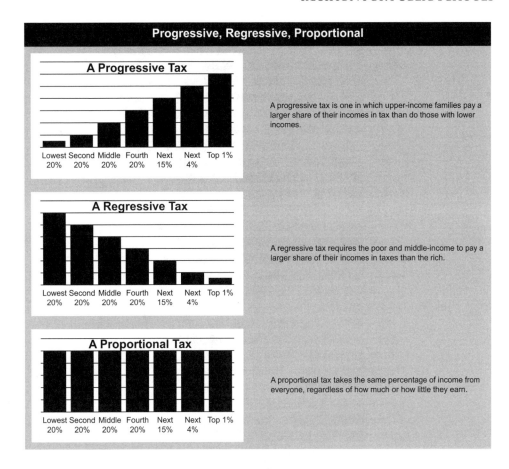

Figure 8.1 Progressive, Regressive, Proportional

Source: Institute on Taxation & Economic Policy, *Who Pays? A Distributional Analysis of the Tax Systems in All 50 States,* 4th Edition (Washington, DC: January 2013), p. 7. Reprinted by permission of The Institute on Taxation & Economic Policy.

above the lowest ranked countries, Chile and Mexico. The tax effort of the citizenry and corporations of the United States has fallen from a rank of 16th in 1979.[6]

STATE TAXES IN THE UNITED STATES ARE REGRESSIVE

When all the total state and local taxes in the United States are averaged, the result is a large regressive tax system. As displayed in Figure 8.3, the persons in the lowest income group, the 20th percentile, are taxed at 11.1 percent of their income, the second 20th percentile at 10.0 percent, middle 20th percentile at 9.4 percent, and the fourth 20th percentile at 8.7 percent. Within the top 20th percent, taxation percentages continue to fall to the lowest in the top 1 percent who pay only 5.6 percent of their income.[7]

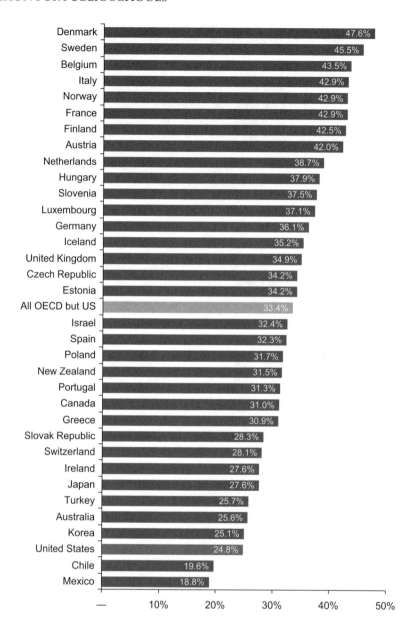

Figure 8.2 OECD Countries' 2010 Taxes as % of GDP

Source: Citizens for Tax Justice, "The U.S. Continues to Be One of the Least Taxed of the Developed Countries," April 8, 2013, http://ctj.org/pdf/oecd2013.pdf. Reprinted by permission.

Based on 2010 tax data, the 2013 study from The Institute on Taxation & Economic Policy identified the states with the most regressive and the most progressive tax systems. The principal funding of the state and local tax structures is simply that "virtually every state's tax system is fundamentally unfair, taking a much greater share of income from middle and low income families than from wealthy families."[8]

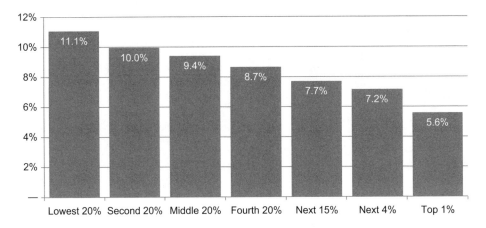

Figure 8.3 Averages for All States

Source: Institute on Taxation & Economic Policy, *Who Pays? A Distributional Analysis of the Tax Systems in All 50 States,* 4th Edition (Washington, DC, January 2013), p. 3. Reprinted by permission of The Institute on Taxation & Economic Policy.

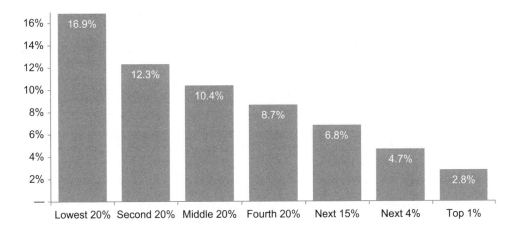

Figure 8.4 Washington State and Local Taxes

Source: Institute on Taxation & Economic Policy, *Who Pays? A Distributional Analysis of the Tax Systems in All 50 States,* 4th Edition (Washington, DC, January 2013), p. 119. Reprinted by permission of The Institute on Taxation & Economic Policy.

However, some states are far less fair than others. The worst, the *Terrible Ten*, the most regressive, as the Institute brands them, are Washington State, followed by Florida, South Dakota, Illinois, Texas, Tennessee, Arizona, Pennsylvania, Indiana, and Alabama.[9] Washington State taxes the poor at 16.9 percent of their income and the rich, top 1 percent, at 2.8 percent. See Figure 8.4.

There are two main reasons for the unfairness in these states; five of the ten *terrible* derive about two-thirds of their tax revenue from sales and excise taxes, and five of the ten do not levy broad-based personal income taxes. Of the three main categories

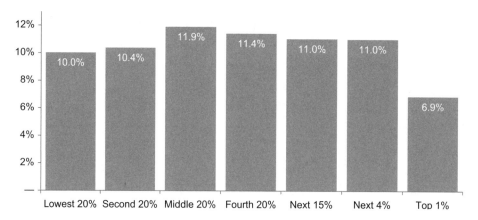

Figure 8.5 New York State and Local Taxes

Source: Institute on Taxation & Economic Policy, *Who Pays? A Distributional Analysis of the Tax Systems in All 50 States,* 4th Edition (Washington, DC, January 2013), p. 89. Reprinted by permission of The Institute on Taxation & Economic Policy.

of taxes – income, property, and consumption – only the income tax has progressive features that enhance the fairness of the state tax structures.[10]

The states that have the least regressive tax systems are Delaware, New York, Oregon, and Vermont. Washington, DC also joins this group.[11] New York (see Figure 8.5) and Washington, DC have tax systems that tend toward a flat system of taxation mainly due to features in their tax codes that levy relatively high rates upon persons with high incomes and are not as generous in bestowing tax exemptions upon favored citizens, institutions, and corporations. Delaware, Oregon, and Vermont are least unfair because of their substantial reliance on progressive income taxes, and they have low or no sales and consumption taxes.[12]

TYPES OF TAXES

Taxes may be categorized into two groups:

1. those levied on the *flow* of production derived from purchases and sales; and
2. those on a *stock* or wealth.

Taxes on the monetary flow in the production process include the major taxes: individual income, corporate income, and retail sales taxes. Property taxes, which are the mainstay of tax revenue for public schools, are taxes on stocks or a portion of the wealth. Taxes within the cycle of monetary flow are those derived from individual or corporate income coming from market activity producing wages, dividends, payrolls, and profits. Household consumption or expenditures of the firm may be taxed through a sales tax on the purchase of consumer or market goods.[13] The second broad type of tax, on wealth, is typified by the property tax but also includes those taxes which are imposed on the transfer of wealth by inheritance or gift.

Another classification of taxes, *in rem* and *in personam*, is commonly used. Taxes *in rem* are levied on *things*; taxes *in personam*, on the person. Property taxes are classified as *in rem* rather than *in personam* because as a *thing* the property has a distinct location, can be assessed, and can be held as security for payment of taxes. The *in rem* tax makes no provision for taxing the equity of the property, only the value of the property itself. It makes no difference that the owner's equity usually is only a small percentage of the full value, and a mortgage holds the major value. On the other hand, *in personam* taxes assume the *situs* of the individual being taxed, rather than his possessions, as in the case of income or poll taxes.[14]

Taxes can also be divided into two other basic categories, *direct* taxes and *indirect* taxes. *Direct* taxes are on individuals and corporations and *indirect* taxes range over several taxes on goods and services.[15] The Federal government relies on three primary direct taxes:

1.   the individual income tax, the payroll tax, which is a percentage of wages used to finance social security;
2.   the corporate income tax; and
3.   the estate and gift taxes.

The main indirect taxes at the federal level are customs duties on imports and excise taxes on such as luxuries, airplane travel, and telephone service.

BOX 8.2

Definition

Direct Taxes. Those taxes levied directly on individuals or firms, including taxes on income, labor earnings and profits. Direct taxes contrast with *indirect taxes*, which are those levied on goods and services and, thus, only indirectly on people, and which include sales taxes and taxes on property, alcohol imports, and gasoline.

Source: Paul A. Samuelson and William D. Nordhaus, *Economics*, 14th edn. (New York: McGraw-Hill, 1992), p. 724.

Main sources of revenues for the states are obtained from sales taxes, personal income, and corporate income taxes. Nine states do not levy personal income taxes: Alaska, Florida, Nevada, New Hampshire, South Dakota, Tennessee, Texas, Washington, and Wyoming. Seven of these nine states have no tax at all on income, while New Hampshire and Tennessee have a restricted tax on income or interest and dividends from stocks and bonds. At the local level property is the primary base for taxation.

Five states do not have statewide sales taxes: Alaska, Delaware, Montana, New Hampshire, and Oregon. The five states with the highest average combined state and local sales taxes are Tennessee (9.44 percent); Arizona (9.16 percent); Louisiana (8.87 percent); Washington (8.86 percent); and Oklahoma (8.67 percent). The five states with the lowest average combined state and local sales taxes are Alaska (1.69 percent); Hawaii (4.35 percent); Maine (5 percent); Virginia (5.25 percent); and Wyoming (5.34 percent).[16]

With regard to property taxes, *The Tax Foundation* analyzed data for 2,922 counties in the fifty states from The Census Bureau for five years, 2005–2009, and found that New Jersey and New York had the highest median property taxes paid on homes and Louisiana and Alaska had the lowest.[17]

POWER TO TAX

The power to tax is vested in the federal government via the General Welfare Clause, Article I, Section 8, of the United States Constitution. Amendment XVI of the United States Constitution specifically gives Congress the power to levy "taxes on incomes." State governments have sovereign powers to tax. The United States Supreme Court has explained the general taxing authority of the states in the following way:

> In our system of government the states have general dominion, and, saving as restricted by particular provisions of the Federal Constitution, complete dominion over all persons, property, and business transactions within their borders; they assume and perform the duty of preserving and protecting all such persons, property, and business, and in consequence, have the power normally pertaining to governments to resort to all reasonable forms of taxation in order to defray the governmental expenses.[18]

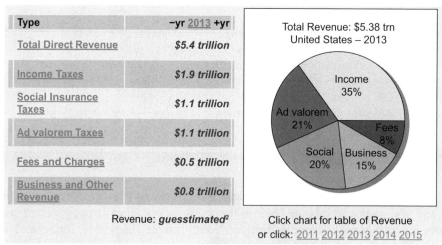

Type	−yr 2013 +yr
Total Direct Revenue	$5.4 trillion
Income Taxes	$1.9 trillion
Social Insurance Taxes	$1.1 trillion
Ad valorem Taxes	$1.1 trillion
Fees and Charges	$0.5 trillion
Business and Other Revenue	$0.8 trillion

Revenue: *guesstimated*[2]

Total Revenue: $5.38 trn
United States – 2013

Income 35%
Ad valorem 21%
Fees 8%
Social 20%
Business 15%

Click chart for table of Revenue or click: 2011 2012 2013 2014 2015

Note:
1. Federal revenue after 2012 is budgeted.
2. State revenue after 2011 and local revenue after 2010 are "guesstimated" by projecting the latest change in reported revenue forward to future years

Data Sources:
GDP: Fed. Budget: Hist. Table 10.1
Federal: Fed. Budget: Hist. Tables 2.1, 2.4, 2.5, 7.1
State and Local: State and Local Gov. Finances
"Guesstimated" by projecting the latest change in reported revenue forward to future years

Figure 8.6 Total 2013 Taxes by Type

Source: Federal State Local Government Revenue in United States for 2013. www.usgovernmentrevenue.com/total_revenue_2013USrn.

At the state level, the power of taxation is exercised through legislative acts and is limited only by state and federal constitutions. The United States Supreme Court has said, "Unless restrained by provisions of the Federal Constitution, the power of the state as to the mode, form, and extent of taxation is unlimited, where the subjects to which it applies are within her jurisdiction."[19] The Federal Constitution restrains state taxation only when it is imposed in such a way as to deny an individual right or freedom. Figure 8.6 indicates the total revenues collected by means of the various types of taxes.

TAXING AT STATE LEVEL

Taxing authority at the state level must be derived from state constitutions or state statutes and is not considered to be inherent in local school districts. School taxes are state taxes although they may be levied at the local level, and the decision to levy is vested in local district education authorities. When public schools were first organized, the state legislatures usually authorized localities to tax for education by levying rates on the assessed valuation of property. This led to a presumption on the part of many that school taxes were local taxes. This is not the case, however, and the state legislature may, in the exercise of its legitimate discretion, arrange to support the schools by taxes levied at the state or local level, or by a combination of the two. In nearly all states legislatures have used a combination of state and local revenues, but regardless of where the tax is levied, public school taxes are considered by law to be state taxes. State constitutions may be general or quite specific with regard to state taxation, and some constitutions specifically prohibit certain types of taxes. For example, Florida's constitution prohibits legislature to tax personal income. Generally, the state legislative taxing prerogative is quite broad and has been described by some courts as plenary in nature.[20]

Sacrifice and Benefit Theories

Taxation philosophy has become a judicial consideration in those cases in which the courts have adopted the *sacrifice* theory rather than the *benefit* theory as a justification for taxation. Controversy has existed for centuries over whether a tax should be justified merely on the *quid pro quo* rationale – that the taxpayer should receive a benefit commensurate with the value of the tax. The courts have rejected this benefit theory of taxation with regard to public schools.

> It is no defense to the collection of a tax for school or other purposes that the person or property taxed is not actually benefitted by the expenditure of the proceeds of the tax nor as much benefitted as others. Accordingly, a childless nonresident or corporate owner of property may be taxed for school purposes.[21]

In the same vein, other courts have said that the taxes do not need to bear a relationship to the benefits received. One court observed that the benefits may be "intangible and incapable of pecuniary ascertainment,"[22] thus, no direct benefits can be determined, especially in the area of public education.

State Delegation of Taxing Power

As a general rule, state legislatures cannot delegate their legislative authority; however, with proper authorization specifying what is to be taxed and how, the legislature can delegate the power to levy a tax to local school districts. Not only can the legislature delegate the power to tax at the local level, but it can also compel local school districts to levy particular rates.[23] Legislation which is permissive, however, will not be upheld by the courts as a proper legislative delegation of taxing authority. The power to tax must be either expressly granted or derived from necessary implication of powers which have been expressly granted.[24] Courts look on the power to tax with particular circumspection and will not easily grant taxing power on mere implication. The power to tax goes to the heart of the governmental process; where taxes are concerned, the courts are careful not to interpret implied powers too broadly. The Supreme Court of Kansas has said:

> The authority to levy taxes is an extraordinary one. It is never left to implication unless it is a necessary implication. Its warrant must be clearly found in the act of the legislature. Any other rules might lead to great wrong and oppression, and when there is a reasonable doubt as to its existence the right must be denied. Therefore, to say that the right is in doubt is to deny its existence.[25]

Thus, a school district cannot levy a tax unless the power is conferred by statute. The precise limits of implication are not easy to define. In one of the historic cases in education, the *Kalamazoo* decision, the Supreme Court of Michigan drew very broad implications from a statute allowing taxation for secondary grades when the statute only explicitly conferred authority to tax for primary education.[26] The court reasoned that the grades and branches of knowledge should not be limited if the voters consented to raise taxes for an expansion of educational services.

THE LEVY OF TAXES

Whether a tax may be levied for school purposes depends on the individual state constitution and statutes. Although states have traditionally relied on local property taxes for the basic support of public schools, there is no reason that a state cannot also provide for the levy of local sales, income, or other taxes. Some states have used poll taxes, bank share taxes, liquor license taxes, occupational taxes, and business taxes at the local level. The imposition of a tax on the wages of residents and on the net profits of businesses and professions by school districts in Pennsylvania has been upheld. Pennsylvania, though, has a relatively unique situation by virtue of the legislature's so-called *Tax Anything Act*, which by its nature allows local taxing prerogatives not typical in most other states.

The importance of the property tax as a local source of school revenue is evidenced by the substantial amount of litigation which has arisen about it over the years. The general rule is that the governmental unit in which the property is located has the prerogative of levying the tax. *Situs* of real property is determined by the place where it is located or personal property of the owner's domicile. Real estate may be taxed only in the state or school district in which it is located. Thus, if a piece of real property lies in two school districts, each district can tax only the portion that lies within its geographical boundary.

Tangible personal property, because it can be easily moved, creates problems of taxation not present with real estate. Such property may be taxed at either the domicile of the owner or at the place of its location, but not at both. The United States Supreme Court held in 1905 that if tangible personal property has acquired taxable *situs* in one state, it cannot be taxed at the domicile of the owner in another state without violating the *due process clause* of the Fourteenth Amendment.[27] Within one state, the legislature may establish the taxable *situs* of personal property, whether tangible or intangible, at either the *situs* of the property or the domicile of the owner.

Sales and use taxes have in recent years come into the forefront of school financing, having been levied at both state and local levels. A Washington State use tax of 2 percent, placed on the privilege of using products from neighboring states, was upheld by the United States Supreme Court in 1937.[28] The tax was levied generally, except on property which had already been subjected to an equal or greater sale or use tax in Washington or any other state. This exception, the Supreme Court observed, was within the standard of equality required by the *Interstate Commerce clause*[29] in that the tax did not impose greater burdens on the stranger than on the dweller within the state; therefore, in-state and out-of-state products were treated in the same way.

Sales of goods brought in from other states are subject to nondiscriminatory taxation by the recipient state. Thus, a tax confined to the sale of goods manufactured outside of the state and not applied to the same products manufactured within the state was set aside as unconstitutional.[30] According to Justice Reed, "The Commerce Clause forbids discrimination, whether forthright or ingenious."[31]

Besides property taxes, sales taxes, and use taxes, the states rely on both personal and corporate income taxes for educational financing. A state has the authority to tax the income from the property owned by a person who is a resident of another state. Similarly, the income from a business conducted or located in a state can be taxed regardless of where the person who owns the business resides. The United States Supreme Court has said

> That the State from whose laws property, business and industry derive the protection and security, without which production and gainful occupation would be impossible, is debarred from exacting a share of those gains in the form of income taxes for the support of the government, is a proposition so wholly inconsistent with fundamental principles as to be refuted by its mere statement. That it may tax the land but not the crop, the tree but not the fruit, the mine or well but not the product, the business but not the profit derived from it, is wholly inadmissible.[32]

The cardinal rule, though, is that a state cannot impede trade and the normal flow of commerce beyond state boundaries. Overall, when the sovereign power of taxation is viewed in its broadest context, the state has great legal latitude for deriving revenues to support public schools.

PROPERTY TAXES

The property tax has always been the mainstay of public school financing in this country. Although general usage of the term *property tax* may refer to tangible personal, intangible personal, or real property, the primary source of revenue for public schools derives from the tax on real property. This tax is sometimes called an *ad valorem* tax, meaning a tax levied as a percentage of the value of the property. *Ad valorem* taxes are different from taxes levied earlier in western states and called *specific acreage taxes* – constituting a set amount per acre regardless of the value of the land.[33]

The tax levied on property may be expressed in terms of mills or as a percentage of a value. A mill is a unit of monetary value amounting to 0.001 of a dollar, one-tenth of a cent, or one part per thousand. The term "mill" is from the root word "mill," which means "thousand." If a homeowner has a house and lot with a taxable value of $100,000, and the tax rate is 5 mills, she will pay $500 in property taxes. The formula for determining the exact rate would be:

$$\frac{\text{Amount of tax revenue to be raised}}{\textit{Tax base (value of property)}} = \text{Rate}$$

$$\frac{\$125,000}{\$25,000,000} = 0.5 \text{ percent or 5 mills}$$

The property tax has been roundly criticized for many years and reforms have not come easily. Comments about the inequity of the property tax today are not unlike those of Adam Smith in 1776 in his *Wealth of Nations*:

> A land tax . . . necessarily becomes unequal in process of time according to the unequal degrees of improvement or neglect in the cultivation of the different parts of the country. In England the valuation according to which the different countries and parishes were assessed to the land-tax by the 4th William and Mary was very unequal, even at its first establishment.[34]

Taxpayer opposition to property taxes is largely engendered by the fact that property taxes are highly visible with most taxing jurisdictions simply billing taxpayers with one tax notice each year. The property tax thus seems to be psychologically more onerous than other taxes simply because of the method of payment and the timing of the tax bill. Sales and income taxes are more easily digested by the taxpayer because the bites taken are smaller.

The reasons for the unpopularity of the property tax are given by Shannon:

1. No other major tax in our public finance system bears down so harshly on low-income households, or is so capriciously related to the flow of cash into the household;
2. When compared to the preferential treatment accorded outlays for shelter under both the income and sales taxes, the property tax stands out clearly as an anti-housing levy. Moreover, as the tax increases steadily, it is viewed by a growing number of families as a threat to homeownership;

3. Unlike income and sales taxes, the property tax imposes a levy on unrealized capital gains . . . (Homeowners, unlike economists, are inclined to view such gains as mere "paper profit" and beyond the purview of taxation until converted to income.);
4. The administration of the property tax is far more difficult than in the case of either the income or sales tax. At best, the property tax assessment is based on an informed estimate of the market value of property . . .
5. The dramatic increase in taxes (and resultant taxpayer shock) that often follows in the wake of an infrequent mass reappraisal has no parallel in the administration of the income or sales tax. As inflation pushes property values up, the assessment hikes become more pronounced and the taxpayer shocks become more severe; and
6. The property tax is more painful to pay than the "pay as you go" income and sales taxes. This is especially true for those property taxpayers who are not in a position to pay the tax on a monthly installment basis.[35]

Although all of these criticisms of the property tax are valid, some contribute more to taxpayer resentment than others. Two of them, harshness on low-income households and general administrative problems, bear further consideration.

PROPERTY AS A REGRESSIVE TAX

It is often said that the property tax is a regressive tax and, therefore, government should be encouraged to move toward more progressive or proportional revenue sources. There are differing schools of thought on this issue, each based on a different theory of property tax incidence. One school, the traditional, maintains that the property tax is regressive, particularly in the case of owner-occupied homes where the owner is unable to shift the burden. It is assumed that renters bear the burden of the tax through higher rent payments. Under this theory, the property tax is assumed to be an excise tax on users of commodities and services produced by the taxable real property.[36] Several studies have shown that the lower the income, the higher the percentage of property taxes paid.

The opposing view maintains that the property tax is primarily levied on capital and is shared by all owners of capital in proportion to their holdings.[37] Where the owner's effective tax rate is above the national average, it is assumed that the excess burden is distributed among landowners, workers, or consumers in the particular community. This theory asserts that property tax incidence is split between an average national property tax rate of between 1.5 and 2 percent and a second component of incidence, which is the amount that a particular jurisdiction varies from the average. This *new view* argues that owners of capital cannot avoid the average or uniform tax, since the tax is uniform on all capital. If the property is in a school district with higher than average tax, then the owner must bear the excess burden. This theory assumes that reactions of taxpayers will have differing effects in the long run, since in the short run taxpayers may not be able to shift the incidence of a higher than average tax. If this theory is correct, the property tax should be classified as a progressive tax or at least a proportional one. If one assumes that assessment procedures are relatively uniform and capital market conditions are perfect, then a 2 percent tax levied on the valuation of property may be translated into an income tax on the income derived from that piece of property.

Whether the property tax can be classified as regressive or progressive must hinge on assumptions regarding the nature of the market, uniformity of property tax assessments, and, most important, on whether tax burdens are distributed among all owners of capital. All in all, the prevailing view still appears to be that the property tax is regressive and at best proportional. However, with the new view becoming more acceptable among public finance theoreticians, the reputation of the property tax may be enhanced in the future.

The second major issue regarding the property tax has to do with its administration. It is probably the most difficult of all the important taxes to administer equitably and has less justification for use as a major tax on the basis of many of the accepted principles of taxation than any other important tax. Nevertheless, it continues to be a major source of revenue for the local support of schools (and other local governmental agencies) in most states. Inequities and injustices in the procedures utilized to assess property and collect property taxes still exist, although significant improvements have been made in many states during the past few decades.

The concept of tying expenditure for any single government service (especially a service as extensive as education) to a single source of taxation has been challenged by political scientists and authorities in public administration. A strong case can be made, however, for revenue sources such as gasoline and similar taxes being used primarily for the benefit of those who operate automobiles and utilize the highways. Such a distinction does not exist in relation to education and the property tax. Many persons who benefit from schools do not pay property taxes in the community, and many who pay property taxes receive little direct or easily identifiable benefit from existing public school systems. Moreover, the mobility of the population has given rise to another inequity with reference to the use of the property tax as a major base for the support of education. Many youths educated in one locality may become taxpaying citizens in a locality far removed from the one that contributed to their economic status.[38]

Within the *system* of property tax administration – determining fair property values, carrying out equitable assessment procedures, establishing rates of taxation, and collecting taxes – there are many variations and anomalies throughout the nation. For some years authorities have been concerned about the defects in existing policies and practices relating to property taxation.

In both theory and law in most states, property is to be assessed at a uniform percentage of full market value. In many localities, local assessors (who in most states are elected officials) determine the value of property. In many states, these officials have no required training for or background in arriving at fair and just property values. Another significant disparity often results from the time span between reappraisals or reassessment years, causing property values to increase or decrease significantly.

The fragmentation of governmental units impairs the equity of the property tax. Many local governmental units are too small to employ full-time, well-trained assessors or to utilize modern assessing techniques. Moreover, dividing the state into a large number of school districts results in great disparities in taxable wealth and extreme variations among different districts in terms of the tax burdens they bear.

The variation among the fifty states regarding property valuation per pupil and its direct influence on educational expenditures per pupil has been well documented by countless studies. Compounding the problem of the effects of wealth on the quality of educational services focuses on the inefficient governance structures maintained by several states. Those states that have continued to operate inordinately large numbers of local school districts generally suffer from both diseconomies of scale and a much greater range in the wealth per pupil among its school districts. Thus, problems relating to financing public schools are made more difficult and complex by the existence of many school districts. Especially difficult is the problem of equalizing educational resources across wide-ranging variations in local wealth as measured by assessed valuation per pupil.

In the process of establishing property tax rates, the usual procedure is that officials of the local governmental body (authorized by state law to establish the rate of taxation) obtain the records giving the aggregate assessed value of properties and the level or amount of expenditures required to meet the anticipated budget for the services needed. The tax rate necessary to meet the budget request is calculated following the aggregation of assessed valuation of property. Unfortunately, this kind of public action gives rise to a very uneven and non-uniform practice of establishing property tax rates from locality to locality and from year to year within the same locality. Although this brief explanation is an oversimplification of the fiscal operations of local units of government, it should serve to indicate how major disparities and inequities creep into property tax administration procedure.

Problems also arise in equal application of the property tax to all classifications of property and commensurate classifications of families according to age and income. The fact that taxes on residential property (with the exception of farms) are usually shifted to the consumer or renter creates added burdens. The question arises: Given these and other difficulties, should the local property tax be replaced with other forms of local taxation, or should we turn to policies that seek to cope with the major difficulties in property tax administration and bring about reforms? The answer to this question appears to be overwhelmingly the latter course of action. This is partly due to the fact that the property tax plays such a key role in financing the services of local governments, among which public education is of the greatest order of magnitude by far.

CONSUMPTION TAXES

Consumption taxes are levies on commodities and transactions, the incidence of which falls upon the consumer through prices paid for goods and services.[39] Consumption taxes are levied on expenditures for consumption and may be classified into seven major categories: customs, excise, sales, use, transfer, gasoline, and tobacco. Of these, the most familiar, as a major revenue producer for general state funds, is the sales tax.

Consumption taxes are justified on the basis that they

1. provide an adequate and immediate flow of revenue;
2. are easily controlled;

3.   provide a relatively stable source of revenue;
4.   promote tax consciousness; and
5.   are economical to collect and convenient to pay.[40]

The most glaring deficiency of consumption taxes is their regressive nature.

During the past few decades, the use of sales taxes has increased dramatically as states have sought new revenue sources to offset rising costs of government and to reduce their dependency on the property tax. Sales taxes used by the states are both selective and general. Selective sales taxes are justified on the grounds of the benefit theory. For example, a selective sales tax on motor fuel can be justified as a *quid pro quo* for use of public highways, to which the taxes are usually designated. If the tax were not levied, the cost of the public highway would be borne not by the user but by the entire community through general taxes. The selective sales tax may also be a consumption tax levied to reduce consumption of certain items. For example, selective sales taxes are levied on liquor, tobacco, and pari-mutuels. Such taxes, though, traditionally have not been high enough to significantly diminish consumption.

Early state adoption of the general retail sales tax was retarded somewhat by the success of selective sales taxes and by the fear that the levy of such a tax would violate United States Supreme Court prohibitions against taxing interstate commerce. This legal interpretation was relaxed during the Great Depression, which saw the dismal response of income taxes and the collapse of property taxes in many jurisdictions. Also, Congress in 1931–1932 indicated that a sales tax at the federal level was unacceptable.[41] Mississippi adopted a general sales tax in 1932, followed by thirteen other states in 1933, and by the end of 1938, nine more states had followed suit. By 1944, the general retail sales tax had become the most important state revenue producer and has been so ever since.

The retail sales tax is a single-stage tax which excludes sales to industrial customers either through the ingredient test or the client-use test. The ingredient test removes from the tax base property which is an ingredient in the product to be sold. The direct-use test excludes from the tax base sale of property which is used directly in the production of goods.[42]

In most instances, services are excluded from the retail sales tax. The Tax Foundation has estimated that "discretionary exemptions (i.e., goods and services considered suitable for taxation but exempt in most states) amount to one-half the volume of total taxable sales."[43]

Five states have no retail sales taxes: Alaska, Delaware, Montana, New Hampshire, and Oregon. Thirty-seven states have local sales taxes. When state plus the average local sales taxes are combined, the states with the highest sales taxes are Tennessee, Arizona, Louisiana, Washington, and Oklahoma. Of those states with retail sales taxes, the five lowest are Alaska, Hawaii, Maine, Virginia and Wyoming. Shown in Table 8.1 are retail sales tax rates as published by The Tax Foundation for 2013 for the state tax rate and the average local city, county, and municipal rates. The average local rates are computed by weighting the population figures.

Table 8.1 State and Average Local Retail Sales Taxes

	State %	Average Local %	Combined %
Highest			
Tennessee	7.0	2.44	9.44
Arizona	6.6	2.56	9.16
Louisiana	4.0	4.87	8.87
Washington	6.5	2.36	8.86
Oklahoma	4.5	4.17	8.67
Lowest			
Alaska	None	1.69	1.69
Hawaii	4.0	0.35	4.35
Maine	5.0	None	5.00
Virginia	5.0	None	5.00
Wyoming	4.0	1.34	5.34

Source: Adapted from Scott Drenkard, *State and Local Sales Tax Rates in 2013,* The Tax Foundation, Fiscal Fact No. 357, February 11, 2013. http://taxfoundation.org/article/state-and-local-sales-tax-rates-2013. Reprinted by permission of The Tax Foundation.

Regressive Nature of Sales Tax

The most important objection to the sales tax is its inequity. As a tax on consumption, the sales tax absorbs a higher percentage of the income of the poor than of the wealthy. If equity is measured in terms of a tax to income ratio, then the sales tax is regressive, since the sales tax paid by the poor is a higher percentage of their income than that paid by the rich. The burden on the poorer families becomes much greater in states that rely on sales and excise taxes for a high percentage of their governmental revenues. Middle-income families may pay 6 percent or more of their income in sales and excise taxes in states that rely heavily on sales taxes. Sales taxes generally violate the principle of vertical equity (unequal treatment of unequals), and as for horizontal equity (equal treatment of equals), the tax may be even more inequitable. In the absence of definitive studies of this question, one may conclude that horizontal inequity is substantial since the tax does not account for family characteristics and needs.

John Kenneth Galbraith, in his classic work *The Affluent Society*, minimized the importance of conventional wisdom which opposed extension of the sales tax. He maintained that in the affluent society the spending of most persons is so far above the subsistence level that the regressive nature of the sales tax is of little importance.[44]

Seligman probably best characterized the use of the sales tax, after a survey of the tax system of several countries, when he said,

> The conclusion to be drawn from this historical survey is that the general sales tax constitutes the last resort of countries which find themselves in such fiscal difficulty that they must subordinate all other principles of taxation to that of adequacy.[45]

A state sales tax may be made less regressive by relieving low-income persons of the excessive burden of the tax. John Due recommended that this be accomplished by providing a credit against the state income tax representing sales tax paid on a minimum necessary level of expenditures, with a cash refund to those having no income tax liability.[46] A number of states have attempted to reduce the regressive effect of the sales tax by exempting food and medicine. However, this policy does not reduce the regressive effect of the sales tax nearly as much as the approach recommended by Due. Excise taxes, including state gasoline taxes and cigarette taxes, are even more regressive than general state sales taxes. State gasoline taxes impose 16 times as great a burden, measured as percentage of income, on the poor than on the rich, and cigarette taxes are even worse, consuming 27 times as great a percentage of the income of the poor as the rich.[47]

INDIVIDUAL INCOME TAXES

State individual income taxes find their precedence in the faculty taxes of the colonial days. The faculty taxes were a crude form of taxation which combined specific property taxes with income taxes. In the financial panic of 1836, several states adopted state income taxes, but only Virginia was able to administer the tax efficiently enough to produce income taxes imposed on salaries and specific kinds of personal incomes. These taxes were generally undesirable because they were levied at a flat rate and were based on *estimated* income as measured by a person's *trade* or *calling* rather than actual income. Administration continued to be weak, and eventually most states abandoned such taxes.[48]

A great advance for state income taxes came in 1911 when Wisconsin first imposed an entirely new type of income tax. It introduced a tax on net income at progressive rates which was placed under the control of a powerful state tax commission. The actual administration was conducted by trained civil service employees assigned to districts in the state. The revenues from this tax were so substantial that other states adopted variations of the Wisconsin program.

The federal experience with the income tax had its origins with the financial exigency of the Civil War. From 1789 to 1909 the federal government relied almost exclusively on excise and customs taxes for its revenues. The Civil War income tax was in effect from 1862 through 1871, at which time it lapsed. At its peak, in 1866, it accounted for almost 25 percent of federal internal revenues.[49] After its expiration, the income tax was not revived until 1894 during the wave of enthusiasm for trust and monopoly reform. The tax applied to both personal and corporate income and levied a low flat 2 percent. This tax was almost immediately challenged under the constitutional restraint that no *direct tax* shall be levied except in proportion to population.[50] In a five-to-four decision, the United States Supreme Court held that the income came *from property* and that the tax was tantamount to a direct tax on property itself, and was thus unconstitutional.[51] The effect of this ruling was that no federal income tax could be levied until the Constitution was amended. This was not accomplished until 1913, when the Sixteenth Amendment removed the constitutional barrier. The amendment provided:

The Congress shall have power to lay and collect taxes on incomes, from whatever source derived, without apportionment among the several states, and without regard to any census of enumeration.

Only seven months after this amendment was adopted a new income tax was imposed on both personal and corporate incomes. This rather low but modestly graduated income tax was upheld as constitutional by the United States Supreme Court in 1916.[52]

The income tax has become the major source of revenue for the federal government. Today, the personal income tax produces approximately one-half of the receipts at the federal level.

Despite the apparent virtual preemption of the individual income tax by the federal government, the majority of states have found the income tax to be a lucrative source of revenue. Most states have adopted the federal tax base, with some modifications, a move which helps both the state and their taxpayers to determine the tax liability.

State individual income taxes are graduated, but to a more modest degree than the federal income tax. All states except Alaska, Florida, Nevada, South Dakota, Texas, Washington, and Wyoming utilize the personal income tax. New Hampshire and Tennessee have narrowly restricted income taxes, limited to dividend and interest income.[53] Figure 8.7 shows the nine states that have no or narrowly restricted personal income taxes.

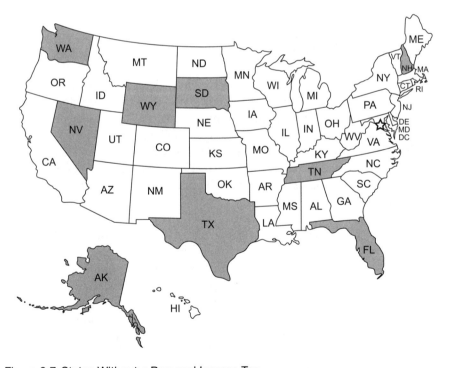

Figure 8.7 States Without a Personal Income Tax

Source: Institute on Taxation & Economic Policy, *Who Pays? A Distributional Analysis of the Tax Systems of All 50 States*, Fourth Edition (Washington, DC, 2013), p. 126. Reprinted by permission of The Institute on Taxation & Economic Policy.

State income taxes usually have certain general characteristics that include some form of withholding procedure, and they most often use the income determination of the federal income tax as the tax base. Some states simply apply a state tax percentage to the federal income tax liability; this approach assumes for the state the federal income definition.

State personal income taxes are the most progressive of major state taxes, and by their use, most states mitigate the regressive effects of other taxes. Importantly, too, beyond their progressive nature, state personal income taxes are a flexible source of revenue readily generating increased revenue flows as the economy of the state grows.

The fairness of state income taxes has increased in recent years by removing poor families, in the lower fifth of family incomes, from the tax rolls completely. The states that do not now levy personal income taxes on the poor are Arizona, Colorado, Kansas, Louisiana, Maine, Maryland, Minnesota, Mississippi, Nebraska, New Mexico, North Carolina, Rhode Island, South Carolina, Vermont, and Wisconsin. Although the trends toward increased tax equity deriving from more progressive use of the income tax are encouraging, the movement is not unanimous. Three states, Alabama, Indiana, and Oregon, have actually increased the income taxes on the poor since 1985. Overall, though, the state's personal income tax is the most equitable of state taxes and generally has been considered a very positive development.[54]

CORPORATION INCOME TAXES

The corporation income tax has been used at the federal level since 1909 when, to avoid a constitutional confrontation, Congress levied the tax as an excise on the privilege of doing business as a corporation.[55] Before 1941, this tax was the most effective revenue producer at the federal level, yielding the most revenue in 17 of the 28 years immediately prior to World War II. After 1941 it was the second major revenue producer until it was overtaken by payroll taxes in 1968.[56] The corporation income tax at the state level finds its origins, as did the individual income tax, in the Wisconsin tax of 1911.

The basic method for determining taxable income under this tax is to ascertain the net income by subtracting the costs of doing business from the gross income. One of the major criticisms of the corporation income tax is that it may tend toward *double taxation* of distributed corporate profits. It is argued that since the corporation is a separate legal entity with its own income it should be taxed as an independent being. The double taxation argument loses much of its rationale when one considers that *pass-through* entities are taxed and only under the personal income tax and not under the corporate income tax. Moreover, the effective tax rates on non-pass-through corporations are very low with many avoiding corporate income taxes altogether. Corporations in Fiscal Year 2011 paid an *effective* federal corporate tax rate of only 12.1 percent, not the 35 percent official corporate income tax rate.[57] Regardless of views, the governments of the various states have found the tax to be an important source of revenue which should be continued. An attractive feature of the corporate income tax is its progressivity. McIntyre and others found that the corporate income tax was the most progressive of all major taxes "taking six times as large a share of income from the richest families as from the middle- and low-income people."[58]

A major issue surrounding the state corporation income tax is its apportionment among states so as not to impede interstate commerce. Presently, states use different methods for the division of a net income base for tax purposes. This assumes that business activities can be split into separate pieces based on geography, when in fact most are unitary.[59] Congress has only acted to prohibit state taxation if the corporation only solicits business in the state and does not operate therein.[60] The basic issues of taxation of interstate commerce have not been resolved, and the result has been discrimination against certain businesses and excessive costs of administration.

As noted above, the federal statutory corporate income tax rate of 35 percent is high compared to most other advanced nations; however, the *effective* corporate tax rate, which corporations actually pay as a percentage of their profits, is far lower due to the many loopholes that allow United States corporations to avoid corporate taxes by a broad range of deductions and credits and international mechanisms that take advantage of differing tax provisions between and among countries.[61] The big international corporate tax news in 2013 was that tax avoidance strategies, all legal, of Apple, Google, Starbucks, Amazon, Vodafone, and others cost the United States government billions of dollars. A United States Senate investigation showed that Apple had paid only 2 percent tax on income of $74 billion due to adroit tax planning and exploitation of loopholes, all legal. United States Senator Carl Levin, Chairman of the United States Senate Permanent Subcommittee on Investigations, summarized the international tax loophole situation; he said, "Apple wasn't satisfied with shifting its profits to a low-tax offshore tax haven. Apple successfully sought the holy grail of tax avoidance. It has created offshore entities holding tens of billions of dollars while claiming to be tax resident nowhere."[62] Such corporate tax avoidance is said to be costing the United States and European countries an estimated $100 billion per year in lost tax revenue. A company can be incorporated in Ireland, controlled in California, and not pay taxes anywhere.[63]

A study by Citizens for Tax Justice found that 280 profitable Fortune 500 companies "collectively received $233 billion in tax breaks due to loopholes, and 31 of these companies collectively paid effective negative tax rates."[64]

OTHER TAXES

Aside from the major taxes discussed above, the state and federal governments levy a wide variety of taxes including estate, death, gift, and use taxes. Of particular importance to this discussion though are the payroll taxes which were first introduced at the federal level in 1935 by the Social Security Act.

In 1935, the original programs provided for two social insurance programs: federal old-age benefits, more commonly known as *social security*, and a federal-state system of unemployment compensation. The original programs have undergone substantial change, including the addition in 1966 of hospital and medical benefits for persons age 65 and older. The federal unemployment compensation tax rate has increased significantly since its inception. As the benefits rise, the rates of this earmarked tax rise, producing revenues which are a higher percentage of the gross national product each year.

Forms of estate, death, and gift taxes are among the oldest forms of taxation. In fact, the trust as we know it today was developed as a device to subvert the government's efforts in England to tax or take property by death transfer as early as the thirteenth century.[65] Taxes at death were also avoided by making direct transfers of property by gifts *inter vivos* (between living persons). The federal and some state governments have thus tied estate, inheritance, death, and gift taxes together to prevent avoidance by various means. State governments impose inheritance taxes on the privilege of receiving property from the dead, while the federal government imposes an estate tax on the privilege of transfer on the one who dies. Bequests and gifts increase the recipients' ability to pay and could conceivably be taxed as income; however, it would be somewhat unfair to tax a one-time transfer at the fully graduated rates of the personal income tax. The rates of gift taxes are therefore set at lower levels.

Before 1977, estate and gift taxes were separate taxes at the federal level, but were unified in that year. The tax base for the estate tax consists of the gross value of all property at the time of death, including stocks, bonds, real estate, mortgages, and any other quantifiable property. The gross estate encompasses gifts made within three years prior to death, insurance, and the value of any revocable trust. The gift tax is determined by the additional property acquired during the taxable year.

Estate and gift taxes are levied on only a small portion of the privately owned wealth in the United States.[66] Generous exemptions, especially since 1987 when larger exemptions were authorized, prevent encroachment of the tax on the estates of most middle-income taxpayers. For deaths after 1986, an estate tax base of $600,000 has a credit of $192,800.

POSSIBLE NEW TAXES

Three new major taxes have been proposed by various sources in recent years: wealth tax, value-added tax, and expenditure tax.

Wealth Tax

The wealth tax is a tax on assessed wealth. Wealth is synonymous with capital or *net worth*. Its base is determined by the value of the stock of all physical and financial assets, less those liabilities held at a particular time.[67] It differs from the *real property tax*, which is a tax on the gross value of only one type of property. The wealth tax is used principally in Europe – Denmark, Germany, The Netherlands, Norway, and Sweden, for instance. Tax rates are usually about 1 percent of the annual net worth of an individual: Denmark has a progressive rate; Germany proportional; The Netherlands proportional; Norway progressive; and Sweden progressive.

Advocates of the wealth tax maintain that it increases horizontal equity because it captures the entire ability to pay of each family, whereas an income tax only identifies one element. This view has been illustrated by the comparable positions of the beggar who has neither income nor property and the Maharajah who has no income but keeps the whole of his wealth in jewels and gold. They both would pay the same income tax, but a much different wealth tax.[68] Another advantage observed by Due is that a wealth tax, "while not taxing increases in capital values as such, does reach the higher values as they accrue,"[69] whereas a capital gains tax only reaches those values when they are realized. A third argument for the wealth tax is that it is very effective in the redistribution of wealth. Finally, it is argued that such a tax is direct and cannot be readily shifted to the consumer or to lower economic groups.

Those opposing the wealth tax maintain that it poses very difficult administrative problems and that it can have adverse overall economic consequences. Concerning the latter, it almost certainly would reduce the incentive to save which has been the bulwark of personal economic objectives since the founding of this country. Importantly, some maintain the wealth tax is not needed because the diverse system of taxation of both state and federal governments in this country covers those bases – real, personal, and intangible personal property – and is nearly as pervasive as the wealth tax anyway.

Value-Added Tax

The value-added tax (VAT) is a consumer tax on goods and services. The value-added tax, unlike the wealth tax, has been seriously advocated in this country at the federal level. The value-added tax base is the value that a business firm adds in the course of its operations to the goods and services it has previously purchased from other firms.[70] That amount added at each level of production can be measured as the difference between the dollar amounts of the firm's purchases and its sales. The amount of purchases would include costs for merchandise and supplies, advertising, freight, utilities, and so on. The tax is most commonly determined by the *credit-invoice* method where all sales by businesses are taxable, but firms at lower levels of the chain of production are able to claim credits for all taxes they have paid on purchases from other businesses.[71]

In analyzing the value-added tax (VAT) in other countries, the United States Government Accountability Office (GAO), 2008, found that the administration and enforcement of a VAT is quite complex and requires a substantial cost for enforcement.[72] In studying the VATs of Australia, Canada, France, New Zealand, and the United Kingdom, the GAO concluded that the compliance burden on business, bookkeeping, and reporting requirements would make transition to such a system in the United States extremely difficult. If such a tax were imposed at the state level in the United States, the yield would be sufficient to make all residential property tax exempt, with a very substantial surplus.[73]

Proponents of the VAT observe that it is economically neutral; it would not distort economic decisions among "products and methods of production or between present and future consumption,"[74] and it would not favor labor-intensive industries over those that are capital intensive. On the other hand, it is a consumption tax and as such is regressive in nature. The tendency would be for business to forward shift the tax to the consumer who is least likely to have the ability to pay.[75] The regressive feature of the VAT could, to some extent, be ameliorated by exemptions or tax credits, but the burden is likely to remain on the poorer segment of society. Further, other critics of a federal VAT say that it would upset the uneasy balance in fiscal federalism by allowing the federal government to encroach on the consumption revenues now largely dominated by the state sales tax. It is, though, maintained by some that the tax would be particularly desirable as a state tax. At the federal level, a VAT has two intergovernmental strikes against it:

1. it is viewed as an intrusion on the state-level use of the sales tax; and
2. it cannot be readily coordinated with the retail sales tax of states and localities.[76]

This, coupled with its lack of equity, greatly diminishes its attractiveness as a major new tax.

Expenditure Tax

A tax which has gained considerable attention of late is the personal expenditure tax. Some experts now believe that this tax is a better alternative than trying to reform the federal individual income tax.[77] Proponents of progressive taxation advance this tax as superior to the value-added tax. The expenditure tax has the theoretical attractiveness of being neither a tax *in personam*, like the income tax, nor an *in rem* tax, like the consumption tax, but constitutes a combination of the two.[78] Unlike the other taxes now in use, the expenditure tax would use consumption as an index of taxpaying ability. The taxpayer would determine his or her consumption for the year, subtract out exemptions and deductions, and apply a progressive tax rate to the residual amount. Musgrave and Musgrave suggest that the most feasible approach to determining taxable expenditure would be to,

1. determine bank balance at the beginning of the year,
2. include all receipts,
3. add net borrowing (borrowing minus debt repayment or lending),
4. subtract net investment (costs of assets purchased minus proceeds from assets sold), and
5. minus the bank balance at the end of the year.[79]

Proponents of the expenditure tax maintain that it is superior to the income tax because it encourages saving and offers incentive for capital formation. Those who oppose the tax claim that it would not be as progressive as the present federal income tax and that it would lead to excessive accumulation of wealth. The opposition further points out that it would be much more difficult to administer than the present federal income tax. On the other hand, advocates of the expenditure tax say the federal income tax has now become so unwieldy that a completely new tax is the only answer. On balance, the expenditure tax appears to be well worth extensive examination, particularly in an era when the nation's economy is in need of policy to encourage the formation of capital.

PROPERTY TAX CONTROL POINTS

State policymakers can control property taxes and local school expenditures by imposing restrictions on rates, levies, assessments, and revenues of expenditures. A common method is to *limit the local school property tax rate*. Maximum rates, expressed in dollars or mills, may be set for governmental policy boards and levied without the vote of the people. Maximum rates may also be established beyond which the local electorate cannot exceed. This method of control does not limit school-tax revenue if assessed valuation of property continues to grow, as inflation, property improvements, economic growth, or reassessment of property will cause it to do.[80]

Controls may also be placed on the rate of assessment increases, as was done in California under *Proposition 13*.[81] *Assessment-ratio controls* may also be used to limit the taxable value to a small percentage of the full market value of the property.

A *revenue freeze* can also be used to control increases in property taxes. Here the amount of revenue may be restricted to the level of the previous year or may be allowed to increase at a given percentage per year, e.g., 6 percent per annum. Since property values will increase as a result of economic growth or inflation, this type of control will probably result in local school districts having to reduce property tax rates.

Another device used to control local use of the property tax is the *full disclosure law* by which the existing political processes are brought more directly into play. Under this method, usually if a local school board wants to increase its tax rate, or possibly revenues, from the previous year, it must advertise and hold public hearings, and only then can the rate be set. This, it is theorized, will bring about greater public accountability on the part of school boards to more fully justify expenditures.

Homestead Exemptions and Circuit Breakers

The regressive features of the property tax have been corrected in two major ways. The *first* of these is *homestead exemptions*. Exemptions are provisions enacted by the state that exclude a portion of the assessed value of a single-family home from its total assessed value before applying the exiting tax rate. Such action helps taxpayers whose income is modest and/or who live in low-valued residences. Under this method, for example, the first $5,000, or some other set amount of assessed valuation on property, is not considered in determining the tax for the resident owner. In a number of states, additional levels of exemption are allowed for senior citizens and veterans.

The *second* reform which constitutes a more complex way of achieving some relief from regressive difficulties is called a *circuit breaker*. This relief is based on the assumption that an excessive tax burden is borne by householders at the low end of the income scale, particularly the elderly. An effort is therefore made to ensure that the property tax bears a reasonable relationship to the flow of cash income into a household. The circuit breaker (the administration of which requires the collection of considerably more information than that of the homestead exemption) may be efficiently administered by a state agency which rebates to the taxpayer the calculated relief in accordance with provisions of the program. Individual income tax returns and information from property tax administration can usually be used to determine the amount of rebate the state will pay to individuals who qualify.

Two types of circuit breakers are most common: a threshold type and a percentage-of-tax-liability type.[82] The *threshold circuit breaker* establishes an acceptable amount of tax which a homeowner or a renter in a certain income category should pay. The state will rebate to the taxpayer the amount of money paid for property taxes above the limit. The threshold rate may be held constant (fixed) over the various income groups, or it may vary, increasing as income increases.

The *percentage-of-tax-liability formula* rebates a part of the actual tax liability, returning higher percentages as the amount of income declines. This approach is demonstrated by the Indiana law which provides that 75 percent of property tax paid be rebated for the $0 to $500 household income category; 70 percent for the $500 to $1,000 category; 50 percent for the $1,000 to $1,500 category; and so on down to 10 percent for the $4,000 to $5,000 household income category.[83]

Assessment Reform

One of the more serious problems in property tax programs is that of ensuring fairness and equality in the process of assessing properties. To some extent this may be overcome by requiring property assessors to be professionally trained and to maintain and update their competencies to value properties accurately. It also may mean that assessors should become civil service employees of the state government rather than partisan elected officials. Uniform and standardized procedures for guaranteeing fairness in the assessment process are more easily achieved by state regulation than by attempting to ensure uniform action across many entities of local government. Some states are beginning to implement such measures.

Nearly all states now have some form of property tax equalization strategy at the state level, including state assessment of utilities and major corporations. The efficiency and effectiveness of these strategies vary considerably from state to state. The ultimate outcome of property tax reform measures targeted at assessment and commensurate administrative difficulties is to make the property tax a state-administered tax. Most states have made considerable progress toward achieving this end.

Property Tax Classification

Through the utilization of state-mandated programs of property classification it is possible to shift the property tax burden from one class of property to another. For example, if state policymakers believe that residential homeowners are overburdened through a particular classification scheme, they could shift a major portion of the property tax burden from residential homeowners to business properties. Some of the classification schemes are rather complicated. The usual plan, however, is a much simpler one in which property is divided into roughly four classes; transportation and communication property, utility property, commercial and industrial property, and residential and farm properties.

Site-Value Taxation

One of the newest forms of property tax improvements suggested by theorists is *site-value taxation*. The concept of site-value taxation is old; the possibility of using it is much more modern. Essentially, site-value taxation provides for a tax on land; it varies in accordance with the value of land and excludes improvements in existence on such land. Those who advocate this reform counter that site-value taxation would remove the financial deterrent to rehabilitation, especially of slum properties in the major cities. Opponents of site-value taxation point out that the existing property tax program takes into account the actual value as the tax base and, if fairly administered, would bring about abrupt and dramatic changes in the incidence of the property tax burden. Though this theory is particularly appealing to many who seek to overcome the economic difficulties confronting large cities, the likelihood of its adoption appears remote.

TAX EXEMPTIONS OR TAX EXPENDITURES

Tax exemptions substantially affect the amount of both state and local revenue available for support of the public schools as well as other governmental services. The four principal types of tax exemptions are:

1. Exemptions granted for the purpose of adjusting tax liability to taxpaying ability;
2. Exemptions granted to attract business and industry;
3. Exemptions granted to give preference to certain groups in the population; and
4. Exemptions granted to governmental, religious, charitable, educational, and other nonprofit institutions.

Income Tax Exemptions

The exemption for dependents allowed by the federal income tax law is a good example of exemptions granted for the purpose of adjusting tax liability to taxpaying ability. This exemption is actually a part of the progressive rate structure and, therefore, is fully justified if one accepts that the progressive income tax is an equitable tax.

Sales Tax Exemptions

The general sales tax laws enacted by the states vary considerably in the number of items exempted. Some states exempt a great many items, usually on the theory that those items are *necessities*. However, what may be necessities for one person may not be for another. The purpose behind this type of exemption is laudable if it is to make tax liability contingent on ability to pay. However, it is an awkward method of accomplishing this purpose. The regressive feature of the sales tax can much more readily be reduced by the methods recommended by Due, already discussed earlier in this chapter. Exemptions from the sales tax also contribute to tax avoidance. It is much easier for a retail establishment to conceal its tax liability when it sells both exempted and non-exempted articles than when all its sales are subject to tax.

Exemptions to Attract Industry

Exemptions granted to attract industry have been particularly troublesome. Conditions for maximizing the economic progress of the nation are unfavorably affected when artificial barriers or subsidies cause industry to locate at points other than those most favorable for efficient production and distribution.

Despite this fact, states and political subdivisions within states frequently give industry (especially new industry) favored tax treatment. States can do this simply by not having a state corporation income tax or by having very low rates. States also have exempted new industries from property taxes for a given number of years.

The competition for new industries is particularly keen among the political subdivisions of a state. Tax favors usually are granted to industries by entirely exempting them from property taxes for a given number of years or by assessing their properties at a very low rate. Some units of local government have given permanent property tax exemptions to certain industries by actually constructing industrial plants and leasing them to private corporations. Ownership of the property is retained by the local government, and it is completely tax exempt. These types of property tax exemptions seriously affect school financing in many school districts. New industries often bring many additional pupils, but the tax base remains the same. Thus, the school district has less taxable wealth per pupil for school support after the new industry is brought to the district than before. Experts on public finance and economics generally agree that if an industry cannot operate in a particular locality without a tax subsidy, the community is better off without it. Furthermore, it is also believed that the influence of tax exemptions or of low tax rates on the location of industries is greatly exaggerated in public thinking. Such factors as access to necessary raw materials, access to markets, quality of the public schools, and availability of labor, water, power, and community services far more powerfully affect the location of industry than do tax exemptions or low tax rates.

Exemptions for Favored Groups

As discussed earlier in this chapter, tax exemptions are sometimes given to certain groups, such as veterans or homeowners. Exemptions to veterans seem to have little or no justification. This practice certainly cannot be defended by any generally accepted principle or theory of taxation. Its purpose seems to be to establish a group with special privileges, but that practice finds no defense in the principles of American democracy.

The practice of granting exemptions to homeowners emerged during the depression in the 1930s. It had great emotional appeal during those times because many financially distressed persons were in danger of losing their homes. While homestead exemption has a laudable purpose, it is difficult to defend from the standpoint of fiscal policy. The circuit-breaker approach discussed before is a far more preferable policy for increasing the equity of the property tax.

Exemptions for Nonprofit Institutions

It is practically a universal practice in the United States to exempt from property taxes all property used for governmental, religious, charitable, educational, and philanthropic purposes. Some have questioned the wisdom of this policy, but it has become so firmly established that it is unlikely to be changed.

Property taxes are levied principally on the enterprises where people work and on the homes in which they live. If the principal enterprises at which people work in a school district are exempted from taxes, then the tax base is greatly reduced. Tax-exempt enterprises bring pupils to a community as do other enterprises, and this adds not only to school costs, but also to the costs of other local governmental services. The federal government has ameliorated this condition in communities receiving a heavy impact from federal activities by providing special grants-in-aid for schools. The Federal Impact Aid Program[84] is designed to directly compensate local school districts for:

1. local revenue lost due to the presence of federally owned, and therefore tax-exempt, property; and
2. costs incurred due to "federally connected" students, such as the children of armed services personnel working at a nearby military base. Unlike most other forms of educational assistance, Impact Aid disburses roughly $1.2 billion annually in unrestricted federal funds directly to local school districts rather than through state agencies.

Established in 1950, the Impact Aid Program was a major general aid source for 1,192 school districts nationwide in 2011, or approximately 9 percent of all districts. For some school districts, Impact Aid supplies as much as 75 percent of the local education operating budget. The federal government also makes payments in lieu of taxes where large areas of national forests are located.

But there are many tax-exempt institutions other than federal properties. For example, state institutions and private colleges may be concentrated at certain locations. States that use the equalization method of apportioning state school funds have taken a step toward solving this problem insofar as school financing is concerned.

Exemptions for Religion and Charities

A large sector of nonprofits is made up of religious and charitable organizations. Since Constantine, 300 A.D., when the Christian religion gained state power, Christian churches and their appendages (hospitals, parochial schools, parsonages, diocese residences, offices, etc.) have enjoyed tax exempt status in most of the western world. Church exemptions from the property tax alone are so vast that reliable estimates are impossible to ascertain. In the United States, alone, much less than other nations that give such preferential treatment to churches, the value of church property would be in the trillions, and lost revenue therefrom would, of course, amount to billions of lost dollars for the public schools; as a result, taxpayers have higher property tax rates to partially accommodate the failure of religious organizations to pay taxes.[85]

Adam Smith, in his great treatise, 1776, warned of the dire effects of the state foregoing income and enriching ecclesiastical foundations. Smith admonished that the "revenue of every established church diverts general revenue from the state to the church."[86] Smith wrote,

> The rent of land (is) the principle fund from which . . . all great monarchies . . . must be supplied. The more of this fund that is given to the church, the less, it is evident, can be spared to the state. It may be laid down as a certain maxim that, all other things being supposed equal, the richer the church, the poorer must necessarily be, either the sovereign on the one hand, or the people on the other; and in all cases, the less able must the state be . . .[87]

Tax exemptions for churches and charities apply to taxes, other than those on property, at both the state and federal levels. Everyone is familiar with the huge numbers of 501(c)3 tax exempt organizations throughout the United States. To this is added the 501(c)4 organizations that have become so popular as to cause a flood of applications with IRS that have incurred United States House and Senate investigations of 2013. The magnitude of the tax dollars foregone due to such loopholes in United States tax policy is beyond estimate.

These loopholes are termed *tax expenditures* in IRS parlance and define immense amounts of income lost to federal and state governments. The Pew Trust has attempted to establish a database to help capture the scope and dimensions of these tax expenditures in the United States. Pew calls this effort *Subsidyscope*,[88] the first such database to determine federal income tax expenditure estimates from the United States Department of the Treasury and the Joint Committee on Taxation of Congress. Tax Expenditures are defined by Pew as revenue losses, to wit:

> Tax expenditures are a measure of the government revenue losses resulting from provisions in the tax code that allow people or businesses to reduce their tax burden by taking certain deductions, exemptions, exclusions, preferential rates, deferrals or credits. By reducing the revenue that would otherwise have been collected by the government, tax expenditures are similar to government spending.[89]

Tax expenditures at the federal level extend beyond religion, charitable, and educational organizations to include the expensing of business costs, employer contributions for medical insurance, mortgage interest deductions, and the list goes on and on.

At the state and local level, the Illinois Supreme Court held in 2010 that Provena Covenant Medical Center,[90] Urbana, Illinois, was not entitled to charitable property tax exemption because it did not treat the requisite percentage of low-income patients to qualify for exemption under Illinois state statute. The Illinois legislature promptly, in 2011, changed the state statute to reinstate the Provena charitable exemption. The exemptions cost the Urbana, Illinois school district, and other school districts in the close vicinity over $6 million in property tax revenues.

The Lincoln Institute of Land Policy has pointed out that the tax exemptions for non-profits registered with the IRS grew by 65 percent from 1995 to 2010 while the nation's economy grew only 38 percent during the same period.[91] Such growth in tax exemptions for the nonprofit sector imposes increasing fiscal hardships on public schools and other public agencies, especially in the cities where such nonprofits are located in huge numbers. The Lincoln Institute observed the reality that: "For cities heavily reliant on the property tax, the exemption of nonprofits from property taxation means that homeowners and businesses must bear a greater share of the property tax burden."[92]

Beyond the shifting of the property tax burden to place it more heavily on those that pay their property taxes, the nonprofits, churches, et al., add costs to public services like police protection, fire protection, street maintenance, etc.[93]

SUMMARY

This chapter discusses the major types of taxes that are used to fund education and other governmental services. Property taxes receive particular attention because of their attachment and importance to local school districts. The primary points of the chapter are summarized below.

There are two general classifications of taxes: *in rem*, on things, and *in personam*, on the person. Property taxes are taxes on things. Property taxes are sometimes called *ad valorem* taxes.

Tax rates may be expressed in dollars, cents, or mills. A mill is one-tenth of a cent or one-thousandth of a dollar.

Most experts consider property taxes to be regressive, to fall more heavily on the poor than on the rich. Some, though, contend that the property tax is not as regressive as it appears because property owners are unable to readily shift the incidence of the tax to the poor.

The methods of administering the property tax usually make the tax more objectionable. Assessment practices and lump sum billing procedures make the tax both controversial and difficult to pay.

Consumption taxes are levies on commodities and transactions which fall on the consumer. Such taxes include levies on sales, excise, use, transfer, customs, and gasoline. Sales taxes are relatively popular taxes by policymakers, being more palatable because of their ease of payment. Despite popularity of the sales tax, it imposes a heavier burden on the poor than on the rich. The regressive effect of the tax, however, can be mitigated by exemption of necessities such as food and medicine. Excise taxes are more regressive than sales taxes.

Individual income taxes are usually calibrated to be progressive and are the mainstay of the federal tax system. Nearly all states employ the personal income tax with Florida, Texas, and Washington being the largest states to reject the tax.

Other taxes that have been discussed for possible use in the United States include the wealth tax, the value-added tax, and the expenditure tax. The wealth tax and the value-added tax (VAT) have been commonly used in other countries. The expenditure tax has been proposed in the United States by academics, but has never been seriously considered by Congress or state legislatures.

KEY TERMS

- Taxes *in rem*
- Property tax
- Direct taxes
- Taxes *in personam*
- Real property
- Wealth tax
- Tax base
- Personal property

- Value-added tax
- Tax rate
- Consumption taxes
- Expenditure tax
- Assessed valuation of property
- Excise taxes
- Tax expenditures

NOTES

1. Adam Smith, *The Wealth of Nations*, Books IV–V, first published 1776 (London: Penguin Books, 1999), pp. 415–417.
2. Joseph E. Stiglitz, *Economics of the Public Sector,* Third Edition (New York: W.W. Norton & Company, 2000), pp. 457–458.
3. Ibid.
4. Ibid., p. 467. Colbert cited in *Newsweek*, April 16, 1984, p. 69.
5. Ibid., pp. 456–469.
6. Institute on Taxation & Economic Policy, *Who Pays? A Distributional Analysis of the Tax Systems in All 50 States*, 4th Edition (Washington, DC: January 2013), www.itep.org.
7. Ibid.
8. Ibid., p. 1
9. Ibid.
10. Ibid.
11. Ibid.
12. Ibid.
13. Richard A. Musgrave and Peggy B. Musgrave, *Public Finance in Theory and Practice*, 2nd edn. (New York: McGraw-Hill, 1976), pp. 224–225.
14. William H. Anderson, *Taxation and the American Economy* (Englewood Cliffs, NJ: Prentice-Hall, 1951), p. 120.
15. Stiglitz, *op. cit.,* p. 453.
16. Scott Drenkard, *The Tax Foundation*, February 11, 2013, www.taxfoundation.org.
17. Nick Kasprak, "New York, New Jersey Lead Nation in Property Tax Burden," *The Tax Foundation*, Data Source U.S. Census Bureau, May 17, 2011, www.taxfoundation.org.
18. *Shaffer v. Carter*, 252 U.S. 37 (1970).
19. Ibid.
20. *Miller v. Childers*, 107 Okla. 57, 238 P. 204 (1924).
21. *Dickman v. Porter*, 35 N.S. 2d 66 (Iowa 1948).
22. *Morton Salt Co. v. City of South Hutchinson*, 177 F.2d 889 (10th Cir. 1949).
23. *State v. Board of Commissioners of Elk County*, 58 P. 959 (Kan. 1899).

24. Leroy J. Peterson, Richard A. Rossmiller, and Marlin M. Volz, *The Law and Public School Operation* (New York: Harper & Row, 1978), p. 150.
25. *Marion & McPherson Railway Co. v. Alexander*, 64 P. 978 (Kan. 1901).
26. *Stuart v. School District No. 1 of Village of Kalamazoo*, 30 Mich. 69 (1874).
27. *Union Refrigerator Transit Co. v. Kentucky*, 199 U.S. 194 (1905).
28. *Henneford v. Silas Mason Co.,* 300 U.S. 577 (1937).
29. Article I, §8, clause 3.
30. *Welton v. Missouri*, 91 U.S. 275 (1876).
31. *Best & Co. v. Maxwell,* 311 U.S. 454 (1940).
32. *Shaffer v. Carter, op. cit.*
33. Ibid., p. 122.
34. Adam Smith, *The Wealth of Nations* (London: Chiswick Press, 1912), p. 394.
35. John Shannon, "The Property Tax: Reform or Relief?" *Property Tax Reform*, ed. George E. Peterson (Washington, DC: Urban Institute, 1973), pp. 26–27.
36. Abt Associates, Inc., *Property Tax Relief Programs for the Elderly, Final Report* (Washington, DC: U.S. Department of Housing and Urban Development, 1975), p. 38.
37. Henry Aaron, *Who Pays the Property Tax? A New View* (Washington, DC: Brookings Institution, 1975), p. 59.
38. This section was prepared with the collaboration of Harry L. Phillips, formerly of the Office of Legislation, U.S. Department of Education, and formerly executive director, Maryland Commission on the Structure of Governance of Education.
39. Anderson, *op. cit.*, p. 394.
40. Ibid., p. 397.
41. James A. Maxwell and Richard Aronson, *Financing State and Local Governments*, 3rd edn. (Washington, DC: Brookings Institution, 1977), p. 102.
42. Ibid., p. 104.
43. *State and Local Sales Taxes* (New York: Tax Foundation, 1970), p. 63.
44. John Kenneth Galbraith, *The Affluent Society* (New York: New American Library, 1958), p. 246.
45. Edwin R.A. Selilgman, *Studies in Public Finance* (New York: MacMillian, 1925), pp. 131–138.
46. John F. Due, "Alternative Tax Sources for Education," *Economic Factors Affecting the Financing of Education*, eds. Roe L. Johns and others, vol. 2 (Gainesville, FL: University of Florida, 1970), p. 310.
47. Robert S. McIntyre, Douglas P. Kelly, Michael P. Ettlinger, and Elizabeth A. Fray, *A Far Cry from Fair, CTJ's Guide to State Tax Reform* (Washington, DC: Citizens for Tax Justice, 1991), p. 12
48. Anderson, *op. cit.*, pp. 177–178.
49. Joseph A. Peckman, *Federal Tax Policy*, 3rd edn. (Washington, DC: Brookings Institution, 1977), pp. 288–289.
50. Art. I, Sec. 9, C1.4
51. *Pollock v. Farmers' Loan and Trust Co.*, 157 U.S. 429 and 158 U.S. 601 (1895).
52. *Brushhaber v. Union Pacific R.R. Co.*, 240 U.S. 1 (1916).
53. William H. Hoffman, Jr., Eugene Willis, and James E. Smith, eds., *West's Federal Taxation: Individual Income Taxes* (St. Paul, MN: West Publishing Company, 1990), pp. 1–14.
54. McIntyre et al., *op. cit.*, pp. 9–11.
55. Peckman, *Federal Tax Policy*, 5th edn., Brookings Institute, 1987, p. 123.
56. Ibid.
57. Damian Paletta, "With Tax Break, Corporate Rate is Lowest in Decades," *The Wall Street Journal*, February 3, 2012.
58. McIntyre et al., *op. cit.*, pp. 14–15.
59. Maxwell and Aronson, *op. cit.*

60. Public Law 86–272, Sept. 14, 1959.
61. Citizens for Tax Justice, *Apple Holds Billions of Dollars in Foreign Tax Havens*, May 20, 2013.
62. See: Dominic Rushe, *The Guardian*, Monday, May 20, 2013, and Jesse Drucker, *Bloomberg Businessweek*, May 21, 2013.
63. Ibid.
64. Blair Bowie, Dan Smith, Richard Phillips, and Steve Wamhoff, Citizens for Tax Justice and U.S. PIRG Education Fund, *Loopholes for Sale: Campaign Contributions by Corporate Tax Dodgers*, March 2012, pp. 1–3.
65. Alexander and Erwin S. Solomon, *College and University Law* (Charlottesville, VA: Michie Company, 1972), p. 266.
66. Peckman, *op. cit., Federal Tax Policy*, p. 225.
67. C.T. Sandford, J.R.M. Willis, and D.J. Ironside, *An Annual Wealth Tax* (New York: Holmes and Meier Publishers, 1975), p. 3.
68. N. Kaldor, *Indian Tax Reform* (New Delhi: Ministry of Finance, Government of India, 1956), p. 20.
69. John F. Due, "Net Worth Taxation," *Public Finance,* vol. XV (1960), p. 316.
70. Advisory Commission on Intergovernmental Relations, *The Value-added Tax and Alternative Sources of Federal Revenue* (Washington, DC: ACIR, 1973), p. 18.
71. Tax Policy Center, Urban Institute and Brookings Institution, "Value-Added Tax (VAT)," www.taxpolicycenter.org.
72. Government Accountability Office, GAO-08-566, April 2008.
73. Kern Alexander, "The Wealth Tax as an Alternative Revenue Source for Public Schools," *Journal of Education Finance*, 2:4 (Spring 1977), pp. 451–480.
74. Ibid.
75. Alan A. Tait, *Value-Added Tax* (Maidenhead, England: McGraw-Hill (UK), 1972), pp. 92–93.
76. Ibid., p. 12.
77. Joseph A. Peckman, ed., *What Should Be Taxed: Income or Expenditure?* (Washington, DC: Brookings Institution, 1980), p. 336.
78. Musgrave and Musgrave, *op. cit.*, p. 333.
79. Ibid., p. 334.
80. Stephen E. Lile, Don Soule, and James Wead, "Limiting State Taxes and Expenditures," *State Government* (Autumn 1975) (Lexington, KY: Council of State Governments), p. 205.
81. Article 13A of the Constitution of the State of California.
82. Abt Associates, *op. cit.*, p. 47.
83. Ibid., p. 171.
84. Title VIII of the Elementary and Secondary Education Act of 1965 (ESEA).
85. Martin A. Larson and C. Stanley Lowell, *Praise the Lord for Tax Exemption* (Washington, DC: Robert B. Luce, Inc., 1969).
86. Adam Smith, *op cit.*, pp. 402–403.
87. Ibid.
88. *Subsidyscope: Pew's Tax Expenditure Database*, http://subsidyscope.org/tax_expenditures.
89. Ibid.
90. *Provena Covenant Medical Center et al., v. The Department of Revenue*, Opinion filed March 18, 2010, Docket No. 107328.
91. Daphne A. Kenyon and Adam H. Langley, *The Property Tax Exemption for Nonprofits and Revenue Implications for Cities* (Boston: The Lincoln Institute of Land Policy and The Urban Institute, 2011), p. 2.
92. Ibid.
93. Molly F. Sherlock and Jane G. Gravelle, *An Overview of the Nonpublic and Charitable Sector* (Washington, DC: Congressional Research Service).

CHAPTER 9

The Federal Role in Financing Education

TOPICAL OUTLINE OF CHAPTER

- Federal Role in Education
- General Welfare and Education
- Federal Public School Revenue Relative to States
- The Federal Budget Generally
- Tax Breaks
- Federal Deficits and Debt
- Sequestration of Federal Funds: Stimulus or Austerity
  - Sequestration
- The Federal Income Tax
- Limitations on the State
- Historical Development of Federal Aid
  - Early Land Grants
  - The Morrill Act
  - The Smith–Lever Act
  - The Smith–Hughes Act
  - Vocational Education
- ESEA and IDEA
  - Elementary and Secondary Education Act (ESEA)
  - Unfunded Mandates
  - Individuals with Disabilities Education Act
  - Federal Budget Glossary

INTRODUCTION

The role of the federal government in the financing of American education has historically been a subject of considerable controversy. Many believe that the federal government has a special responsibility for education that emanates from a national interest in the general welfare, and that this responsibility requires substantial federal financial commitment. Others maintain that the nature of American federalism places little financial reasonability for education on the central government. Still others are of the opinion that the federal government should provide funding only as a stimulus for change and innovation or to deal with educational needs that are of particular national interest. The issue of federal aid is further complicated by strong lobbies representing other interests that traditionally have had difficulty in accepting the political philosophy that supports public schools. To this state of affairs can be added the marketplace enthusiasts who believe that most good in society derives from competition and that it is not necessary for the federal government to fund public elementary and secondary education at any appreciable magnitude so long as the federal government creates schemes of organization and finance that enhance competition among schools, parents, and students. Any consideration of federal aid to public elementary and secondary schools must recognize and fashion political accommodations for these varied interests. Further discussion of the various interests and views toward public schools is contained in Chapter 6, the politics chapter of this book.

FEDERAL ROLE IN EDUCATION

Rather than being the primary governmental player in funding public elementary and secondary education, the United States Department of Education sees its role as serving as a source to provide funding in the interstices of educational needs throughout the country, a kind of an "emergency response system, a means of filling gaps in state and local support for education when critical national needs arise."[1] As such, the department policy accepts and reinforces the importance of education control as a state and local function.[2] The mission of the federal government in education as propounded by the United States Department of Education is "to promote student achievement and preparation for global competitiveness by fostering educational excellence and ensuring equal access."[3] To this end the cabinet post of Secretary of Education and the Department over which she/he resides attempt to fulfill the appointed mission thus:

> *First,* the Secretary and the Department play a leadership role in the ongoing national dialogue over how to improve the results of our education system for all students. This involves such activities as raising national and community awareness of the education challenges confronting the Nation, disseminating the latest discoveries on what works in teaching and learning, and helping communities work out solutions to difficult educational issues.
>
> *Second,* the Department pursues its twin goals of access and excellence through the administration of programs that cover every area of education and range from preschool education through postdoctoral research.[4]

This generalized mission adheres to the Congressional Act activated in 1980 that renamed the old United States Office of Education. The Congress, by this Act, gave education a new enhanced status by elevating the old post of Commissioner of Education to the more grandiose level of Secretary in the President's Cabinet and administered education departmental status as well. In this Act (Public Law 96–88, October 1979), Congress set forth a mission statement for the new department, to wit:

> Strengthen the Federal commitment to assuring access to equal educational opportunity for every individual;

> Supplement and complement the efforts of states, the local school systems and other instrumentalities of the states, the private sector, public and private non-profit educational research institutions, community-based organizations, parents and students to improve the quality of education;

> Encourage the increased involvement of the public, parents, and students in Federal education programs;

> Promote improvements in the quality and usefulness of education through federally supported research, evaluation, and sharing of information;

> Improve the coordination of Federal education programs;

> Improve the management of Federal education activities; and

> Increase the accountability of Federal education programs to the President, the Congress, and the public.[5]

The missions as enunciated by the two branches of the federal government – Executive (United States Department of Education) and Legislative (Congress) – are, of course, limited by the third branch, the Judiciary, and its interpretations of the strictures of the United States Constitution. The United States Supreme Court's own view of the mission and control of education at the federal level is set out in its conceptualism of American federalism. To explain, we quote, in part, from *American Public School Law, Eighth Edition*,[6]

> The United States Supreme Court has enunciated a very strong opinion and, indeed, a constitutional philosophy that emphasizes the sovereignty of states in the design of our federal system. The Supreme Court reminds us that states do not derive their powers from the United States Constitution, but, rather, are possessed of inherent and sovereign powers of independent governmental entities, some of which were ceded or delegated to the central government by the United States Constitution. The present balance between the States and the Federal government reflects the opinion of five justices of the United States Supreme Court who are generally viewed as the conservative majority of the Court. This current Court has said that the founding document [the United States Constitution] "specifically recognizes the States as sovereign entities,"[7] and by so concluding, implicitly expands the concept of state sovereignty from the more limited quasi-sovereigns.

> The Tenth Amendment seals the delineation of federal versus powers, and clearly reserves education to the states respectively or to the people. Since education is

not mentioned or delegated to the central government in the structure of the United States Constitution, it is reserved as a state function. Thus, the Supreme Court makes it clear that: (1) states retain inherent sovereign powers that were not ceded or given up to the federal government in the Constitution; (2) the federal government has only those powers delegated; and (3) the Tenth Amendment is a positive expression that verifies the existence of the inherent state sovereignty, as well as a formal declaration of the preservation of the rights of the people.[8]

Accordingly, it is the position of the current Supreme Court that the inherent sovereign powers of the states are to be found and preserved in the design of the "federative"[9] system in the Constitution where "[t]he Federal Government, by contrast, 'can claim no powers which are not granted to it by the Constitution, and the powers actually granted must be such as are expressly given, or given by necessary implication."[10]

GENERAL WELFARE AND EDUCATION

Federal power with regard to education emanates principally from the Spending Clause, also known as the General Welfare Clause of Article I, Section 8, which provides, "The Congress shall have Power To lay and collect Taxes, Duties, Imposts and Excises, to pay the Debts and provide for the common Defence and general welfare of the United States . . ."[11] Alexander Hamilton maintained that this article conferred upon the Congress a general substantive power to tax and spend for purposes that would provide for the general welfare of the United States.[12] Hamilton's position prevailed, however not without stipulation. The Spending Clause does not give Congress unrestrained authority in the matter of education, but rather a "qualified" authority. The combination of the Spending Clause and the Tenth Amendment prescribe to Congress the power to spend for education, but it cannot extract from states involuntary submission to federal regulations without the consent of the state. Constitutionally, the states can be induced into compliance to obtain federal funds and attendant regulation, but they cannot be compelled to do so. Under the General Welfare Clause, a state must be provided volition, it must have the option of electing to participate in the federal program.[13]

In the field of education, the state-federal relationship must be in the nature of an "unambiguous" contract.[14] In *Rowley*, a special education case, the Supreme Court said that Congressional "Legislation enacted pursuant to the spending power is much in the nature of a contract,"[15] and, therefore, for a state to be bound "by federally imposed conditions, the recipients of the federal funds must accept them voluntarily and knowingly."[16] The Supreme Court reiterated this view in *Arlington*, another special education case rendered in 2006.[17] The United States Court of Appeals, Fourth Circuit, has best summarized the nature of federalism governing the distribution of federal tax dollars for education in accord with the Spending Clause, to wit:

1. The exercise of the spending power must be for the general welfare,
2. The conditions must be stated unambiguously,
3. The conditions must bear some relationship to the purpose of federal spending,
4. The conditions for the expenditures must not violate some other constitutional command, and

5. The financial inducement offered by Congress must not be so coercive as to pass
    the point at which pressure becomes compulsion.[18]

FEDERAL PUBLIC SCHOOL REVENUE RELATIVE TO STATES

The federal government's share of the fiscal load for public schools is relatively low
compared to the revenues provided by state and local governments. As Figure 9.1
shows, the federal contribution has hovered at about the 10 percent level for the last
ten years. Due to the federal stimulus, the average percentage for the federal government rose to a bit over 10 percent but has retreated since, and will retreat even further
as a result of the federal sequestration. The federal percentage of 11.7 was the total of
federal, state, and local revenue in 2010–2011, falling to an estimated 10.5 percent in
2011–2012.[19] The percentage of federal revenue for public schools, of course, varies
among the states, ranging from only 3.1 percent in New Jersey up to 18.3 percent in
Oklahoma. The percentages vary primarily because of the incidence of disadvantaged
children by state that are funded by the large ESEA, Title I program. Nevertheless,
even though the percentage of the school revenue from federal sources has been about
10 percent in the past decade, the federal on-budget for elementary and secondary
schools has increased 385 percent from $13.7 billion in FY 1965 to $88.8 billion in FY
2010. "On-budget" means federal discretionary appropriations.
    As Figure 9.2 shows, after adjustment for inflation, the federal on-budget fund-
ing actually decreased from 1980 to 1985, rose a bit in 1990, but did not return to the
1980 level until 1995 when it reached $48.1 billion.

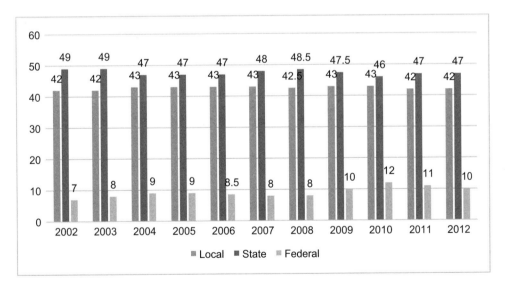

Figure 9.1 Percent of Annual School Revenue by Source, 2002–2012

Source: *Rankings & Estimates: Rankings of the States 2012 and Estimates of School Statistics 2013,*
December 2012, www.nea.org/assets/img/content/NEA_Rankings_And_Estimates-2013_(2).pdf, Figure F. Used with permission of the National Education Association. Copyright © 2013. All rights reserved.

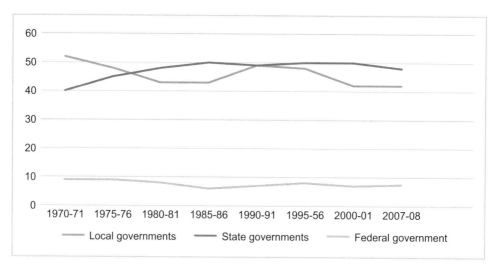

Figure 9.2 Percentage of Revenue for Public Elementary and Secondary Schools, by Source of Funds: 1970–1971 through 2007–2008

Source: United States Department of Education, National Center for Education Statistics, Revenues and Expenditures for Public Elementary and Secondary Education, 1970–71 through 1986–1987; and Common Core of Data (CCD), "National Public Education Financial Survey," 1987–1988 through 2007–2008.

Table 9.1 Federal On-Budget Funding for Education, by Category: Selected Fiscal Years, 1965–2010

Year	Total	Elementary/ Secondary	Post- Secondary	Other Education	Research at Educational Institutions
1965	$37.6	$13.7	$8.4	$2.6	$12.8
1975	$92.1	42.0	30.2	6.4	13.5
1980	$91.3	42.4	29.4	4.1	15.4
1985	$76.0	32.9	21.8	4.1	17.2
1990	$86.3	36.7	22.8	5.7	21.1
1995	$102.4	48.1	25.2	6.7	22.4
2000	$112.0	57.1	19.6	7.1	28.2
2005	$167.1	78.8	44.1	7.9	36.3
2010	$182.4	88.8	50.9	9.5	33.3

Note: Detail may not sum to totals because of rounding.

Source: United States Department of Education, Budget Service and National Center for Education Statistics, unpublished tabulations. United States Office of Management and Budget, *Budget of the United States. Government, Appendix,* various FYs. National Science Foundation, *Federal Funds for Research and Development,* various FYs.

    As shown in Table 9.1, between FY 1990 and FY 2000 elementary and secondary funding increased from $36.7 billion to $57.1 billion. After 2000 the appropriations increased more rapidly from $57.1 billion to $88.8 billion between 2000 and 2010.[20]

THE FEDERAL BUDGET GENERALLY

During the 2014 fiscal year, it is estimated that the federal government will expend for all purposes about $3.8 trillion. This huge amount of money, about 22 percent of the Gross Domestic Product (GDP), has a significant effect on the economic condition and productivity of the nation. The overall budget is divided by the United States Treasury Department into three basic parts: mandatory spending, discretionary spending, and interest on federal debt. Mandatory spending is primarily constituted of earned-benefit or entitlement programs such as Social Security, Medicare, Medicaid, and the Supplemental Nutrition Assistance Program (SNAP), known as the food stamp program. For these programs the expenditure amount is determined based on criteria for eligibility and is not dependent on the appropriations process.[21] This mandatory part amounts to about two-thirds of the total federal expenditures. Social Security is the largest of the mandatory expenditures, amounting to about a third of the entire mandatory category. Discretionary spending refers to that part of the budget that is set by the annual appropriations process. The level of appropriations for all programs is voted upon and passed by Congress.

The federal debt, a source of much controversy, is owed to all the creditors and is held by the American public. Debt amounts to about 6 percent of all expenditures. Figure 9.3 shows the estimated mandatory, discretionary, and debt spending for 2014.

Education as a percentage of the federal spending, if President Obama's 2014 Budget request comes to fruition, will be about 2 percent of the total discretionary

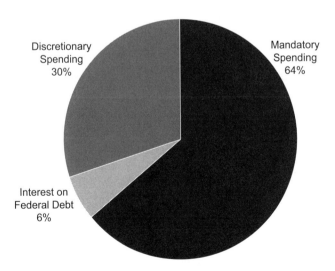

Figure 9.3 Projected Mandatory and Discretionary Spending and Interest on Fiscal Debt (Fiscal Year 2014)

Source: National Priorities Project, "Federal Spending: Where Does the Money Go," http://national priorities.org/budget-basics/federal-budget-101/spending. Reprinted by permission of the National Priorities Project (nationalpriorities.org).

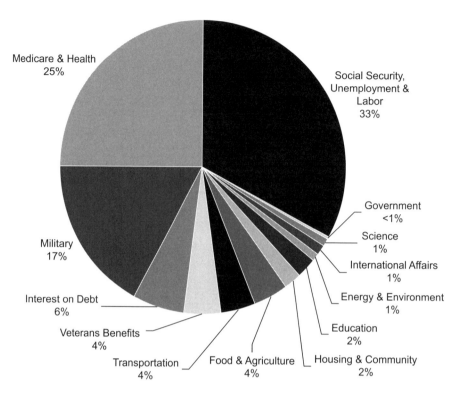

Figure 9.4 President's Proposed Total Spending (Fiscal Year 2014)

Source: National Priorities Project, "Federal Spending: Where Does the Money Go," http://national priorities.org/budget-basics/federal-budget-101/spending. Reprinted by permission of the National Priorities Project (nationalpriorities.org).

and mandatory spending. As illustrated in Figure 9.4, the military at current levels will consume about 57 percent of the 17 percent of the total spending, mandatory and discretionary combined. The amount shown for education includes all programs, early education through higher education. Thus, the entire total expenditure of the federal budget, including spending that is mandatory, discretionary, and interest on debt, as displayed in Figure 9.4, shows education in 2014 will probably amount to only about 2 percent of the total estimated for 2014, if Congress accepts President Obama's budget proposals.

TAX BREAKS

Tax breaks, also called *tax expenditures*, are yet another large part of the federal expenditure picture. With federal expenditures, mandatory, discretionary, and interest on debt, the federal government writes checks to the recipients, but tax breaks, or tax expenditures, are a major additional part of the federal fiscal picture that tends to slide by unnoticed. Tax expenditures are tax breaks that must be subtracted from the federal revenue pool: these are monies in circulation that are not collected and are kept in private hands to do with them largely as the private sector wishes. For example, these tax expenditures deprive the federal treasury of funds and are written into the federal tax code by lawmakers usually responding to special interest lobbies. Such tax breaks are in reality a type of government spending. Some, such as deductions for home mortgage interest, are designed to stimulate the economy and to encourage family saving, while other tax breaks such as capital gains are much more problematic in favoring the rich over the poor in society. The list of tax breaks is legion, including nonprofit foundations, by which wealthy individuals keep their wealth away for taxation to expend as they see fit for their own special interests.[22] Importantly, these foundations can have a profound effect on public policy and the overall direction that government takes on major decisions. Many of the tax breaks provide tax exempt nonprofit organizations substantial war chests that may advance causes that have deleterious effects in contradiction to the common good.

Figure 9.5 shows that the estimated tax breaks for 2014 will exceed the total federal discretionary spending. In the realm of education, such tax breaks include tax deductions and tax credits for parents to send their children to private schools, and tax credits and deductions for the private schools themselves. Such tax expenditures are also provided by state and local governments in the nature of tax credits and deductions for baseball stadiums in core cities, as well as for churches, charities, etc. There is no reliable source of information to determine the extent of such tax breaks that reduce the public treasuries of all levels of government. But as Figure 9.5 shows, a good estimate at the federal level alone is $1.18 trillion, which is more than the $1.15 trillion for all federal government discretionary spending.

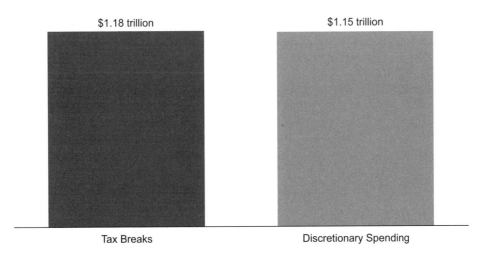

$1.18 trillion $1.15 trillion

Tax Breaks   Discretionary Spending

Figure 9.5 Tax Breaks Are as Large as All Discretionary Spending (Fiscal Year 2014)

Source: National Priorities Project, "Federal Spending: Where Does the Money Go," http://national priorities.org/budget-basics/federal-budget-101/spending. Reprinted by permission of the National Priorities Project (nationalpriorities.org).

FEDERAL DEFICITS AND DEBT

In order to stimulate the economy the federal government must be allowed to incur debt. The idea is, as explained by John Maynard Keynes, to prime the economic pump by putting more money into circulation. The problem is to know how much debt should be incurred.

Debt is different from a deficit. A deficit occurs when annual expenditures exceed annual revenues. If revenues exceed expenditures then there is a surplus. Figure 9.6 shows the deficits and surpluses in the annual budgets of the United States government during the years from 1973 through 2013. The period of surpluses was in the later years of the Clinton administration. When there is a deficit the government must borrow money to pay its bills, and as deficits reoccur the debt rises. In a period of economic recession or slow growth, less money is collected from taxation, and if expenditures are not reduced then, obviously, deficits will be the result.

In order to finance the debt the United States Treasury sells bonds and other securities and these can be bought directly from the Treasury or from banks or security brokers.[23] Treasury bonds and securities are loans to the United States Government. In addition, the federal government borrows from itself. For example, the federal government has a Social Security trust fund that protects Social Security funds, and these trust funds can be borrowed by the Treasury and later paid back to the trust fund plus interest. United States Treasury bonds can be bought not only by individuals and domestic institutions, but by foreign individuals, corporations, and governments as well. As of 2010, foreign governments held large amounts of United States bonds

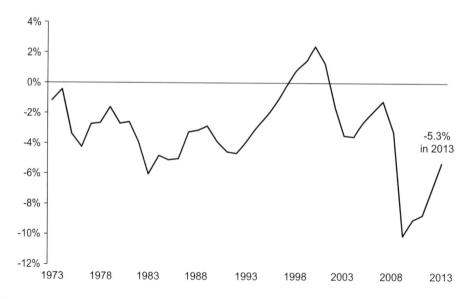

Figure 9.6 Annual Budget Deficits or Surpluses (as percentage of GDP)

Source: National Priorities Project, "Borrowing and the Federal Debt," http://nationalpriorities.org/en/budget-basics/federal-budget-101/borrowing-and-federal-debt. Reprinted by permission of the National Priorities Project (nationalpriorities.org).

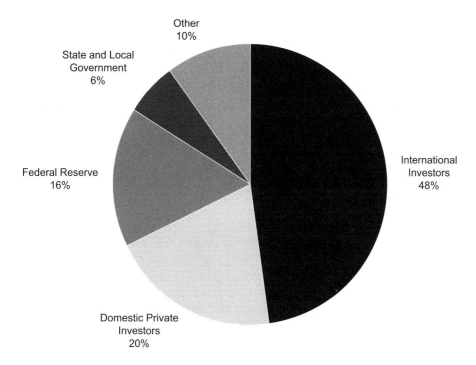

Figure 9.7 Federal Debt Held by the Public (as of June 2012)

Source: National Priorities Project, "Borrowing and the Federal Debt," http://nationalpriorities.org/en/ budget-basics/federal-budget-101/borrowing-and-federal-debt. Reprinted by permission of the National Priorities Project (nationalpriorities.org).

and other securities: China $1.1 trillion, Japan $800 billion, Middle Eastern countries $173 billion, Russia $168 billion, Brazil $164 billion, and Taiwan $152 billion.[24] Figure 9.7 shows the extent of federal government debt as of June 2012 that is held by the public. Notice the high percentage of the debt that is held by international investors.

SEQUESTRATION OF FEDERAL FUNDS: STIMULUS OR AUSTERITY

The Great Recession of 2008 from which the country has only gradually recovered dramatically revived one of the favorite battleground issues of economists, *stimulus versus austerity*. Liberal economists, following the philosophy of John Maynard Keynes, espoused in his most famous treatises, *The Economic Consequences of Peace*, 1919; *A Treatise on Money*, 1930; and *The General Theory of Employment, Interest and Money*, 1936, advanced the idea of the "quantity" of money theory – that the best medicine to emerge from a recession or a depression is to stabilize prices by vigorous government action, pumping more money into the economy, and lowering interest rates.[25] This is the basic approach utilized by the Obama administration, Congress, and the United States Federal Reserve System headed, until 2013, by Ben Bernanke, in reviving the United States' economy after the *Great Recession of 2008*. Janet Yellen succeeded Bernanke in 2014.

The opposing school of thought, austerity, credited primarily to Frederick Hayek, an Austrian economist who ended up at the University of Chicago, author of the famous work, *The Road to Serfdom*, 1944, argued for a very limited role of government, non-intervention, extreme economy of government.[26] This approach of *austerity*, also named *the shock doctrine* by Naomi Klein in her best seller *The Shock Doctrine: The Rise of Disaster Capitalism,*[27] documents many examples of the ill consequences of privatization and the exit of rational government policies. The *shock doctrine* encompassed the mostly failed ideas of Milton Friedman of the Chicago school of economics. These two schools of thought have been the focus of measures taken by nations in their efforts to return to economic normalcy and end the Great Recession of 2008. In response to the recession, some countries' remedies were weighted more toward stimulus and "quantitative easing," increasing the supply of money in the economy, while others weighted their recovery strategies toward austerity, that is, their governments spent less and sought to balance their budgets and were very parsimonious with the supply of money. At the time of this book going to press, 2015, the answer appeared to be quite definitive, that Keynesian "stimulus" prevailed over Hayekian "austerity." The United States early, 2010, took the Keynesian approach with greater stimulus while the European Union countries leaned heavily toward austerity as a remedy. In consequence, the United Kingdom and Germany have lagged under the austerity regime, and some of the European countries, in particular Spain and Italy, have found austerity to result in exceedingly high unemployment and a stagnant recovery.

In order to help extricate the economy from the Great Recession of 2008, President Obama proposed and Congress passed, in February 2009, the American Recovery and Reinvestment Act of 2009 (ARRA).[28] The law, called the *Stimulus Act*, was designed to jumpstart the economy along Keynesian lines, providing $787 billion dollars to be spent over ten years, composed of $288 billion in tax cuts, $224 billion in education, health care, and unemployment benefits, and $275 billion for job-creating using "shovel ready" federal contracts, grants, and loans.[29] The package was front-loaded to gain maximum impact by pushing forward $720 billion, or 91.5 percent of the money to the first three years. By July 31, 2013, $800.8 billion had been spent within which $256.6 billion had been expended on contracts, grants, or loans, a portion of which was for education.[30]

The stimulus plan, supplemented by the Federal Reserve's issuance of monthly bond sales to put more money into circulation, has been successful compared to European countries that opted for austerity; however, Paul Krugman, the Nobel Laureate in Economics, has argued that the ARRA could have been more effective in raising the nation from the recession if it had contained far larger quantities of money.[31] However, even with the lower level of funding, the Stimulus Act appears to have been a success. Before the stimulus, in March 2009, the GDP fell by 5.4 percent and the Dow Jones market dropped to 6,594. By 2009, the GDP was up 3.9 percent, the Dow was 10,428, and by late 2013 the Dow was over 16,000.

Sequestration

In the United States, those conservative members of Congress who adhere to austerity, small government, and pro-privatization theory, were able to impose late in the recovery,

2013, the *sequestration* of federal funding, an anti-Keynesian approach similar to that of the European Union austerity measures.[32] *Sequestration*, the terminology describing the imposition of holding expenditure of funds already appropriated, would best combat a recession according to the conservative sector of Congress. The short-term, immediate effect of such an austerity move was to draw down money in state and local education programs and to cause unemployment and result in lower salaries of teachers and other instructional employees. The long-range effects are probably even more damaging to the United States' investment in that the human capital will be negatively affected for decades. See the human capital chapter of this book, Chapter 5.

Sequestration is the holding back of money by the United States Department of the Treasury that has been appropriated in separate spending bills that exceeds the cap set by the Budget Resolution by Congress for that year. The amount is sequestered by the Treasury, thus denying funds to the various governmental departments that distribute and administer federal funds. The Budget Control Act of 2011 established a Joint Select Committee on Deficit Reduction ("super committee") that was charged with reducing the deficit by $1.2 to $1.5 trillion over a period of ten years. The committee failed to reach an agreement on November 21, 2011; however, in the case that the committee's recommendations were not accepted, the Budget Control Act of 2011 included a provision that required an automatic sequestration of $1.2 trillion over a period of nine years which went into effect on March 1, 2013. The reductions apply to "discretionary" spending by the federal government agencies and are divided into two major categories: $500 billion for defense budgets and $700 billion for nondefense budgets. The budget cuts are across-the-board and cannot be modified by the Executive Branch. The sequestration resulted in a reduction in all federal discretionary funds for all federal agencies of $85.3 billion and funds for education of $4.1 billion in 2013.

Thus, sequestration, austerity, and cutting of government spending in the unstable economy in the process of recovering from the Great Recession of 2008 will, according to Keynesian economics, tend to act against the federal stimulus measures instituted by the United States Federal Reserve System. This type of European austerity will almost certainly produce a continuing drag effect on the long awaited recovery.

THE FEDERAL INCOME TAX

Various constitutional provisions are specifications of limitations on Congressional or state power. Foremost among such limitations are the provisions in the Bill of Rights, but there are others.

Article I, Section 9 of the Constitution sets forth certain powers denied to Congress. Two of its subsections have some relationship to financing education. Subsection 4 reads as follows: "No Capitation, or other direct, Tax shall be laid, unless in Proportion to the Census or Enumeration herein before directed to be taken." This provision of the Constitution has effectively prevented Congress from levying a property tax.[33] It is obviously impracticable to levy a property tax in proportion to the census. The last time Congress attempted to levy such a tax was during the Civil War. Had it not been for this provision of the constitution, Congress probably would have levied property taxes very early in our history.

As mentioned in Chapter 8, this subsection also prevented Congress from levying income taxes until it was removed by the Sixteenth Amendment, ratified in 1913. It reads: "The Congress shall have power to lay and collect taxes on income, from whatever sources derived, without apportionment among the several States, and without regards to any census or enumeration." This amendment greatly increased the taxing powers of Congress.

The federal government obtains far greater tax revenues from the income tax than any other tax source. This broadening of the taxing powers of Congress has made it possible for the federal government to greatly extend federal services and to increase equity through the redistribution of wealth and income among the people.

Subsection 5 prohibits Congress from laying taxes or duties on articles exported from any state. This provision and the provisions of Subsection 4 as amended by the Sixteenth Amendment are the only specific limitations upon the taxing powers of Congress, except for the provision of Article I, Section 8, Clause 1, requiring that "all Duties, Imposts and Excises shall be uniform throughout the United States." Therefore, the Constitution vests Congress with very broad taxing powers. The enormous amount of revenue collected annually by the federal government is evidence of that fact.

The federal government has another important advantage in obtaining revenues. When taxes are levied nationwide, the difficulties of competition among states and local governments are avoided. The federal income tax, both personal and corporate, is levied nationwide. A person or corporation cannot escape the federal income tax by moving to another political jurisdiction within the nation. But the income taxes and certain other taxes of state and local governments can be avoided by moving into jurisdictions not levying the tax. Tax competition therefore limits the potential tax revenues of state and local governments.

LIMITATIONS ON THE STATE

Article I, Section 10 of the United States Constitution sets forth the powers denied the states. There are only a few provisions of this section that are related to the financing of education. Subsection 1 includes the provision that no state shall pass any law impairing the obligation of contracts. Subsection 2 provides:

> No State shall, without the Consent of the Congress, lay any Imposts or Duties on Imports or Exports, except what may be absolutely necessary for executing its inspection Laws; and the net Produce of all Duties and imposts, laid by any State on Imports or Exports, shall be for the Use of the Treasury of the United States; and all such Laws shall be subject to the Revision and Control of the Congress.

Subsection 3 provides: "No State shall, without consent of Congress, lay any Duty of Tonnage. . ." These are the only limitations placed upon the taxing powers of the states by the Constitution. They are relatively minor and therefore place no serious restrictions on the states with respect to levying and collecting taxes.

But it should not be assumed that Article I, Section 10 of the Constitution contains the only federal limitations upon the states in the operation of systems of public education. The Constitution as interpreted by the United States Supreme Court is the supreme law of the land. Any law of any state on any matter including education which is in conflict with any provision of the Constitution is null and void if so declared by the United States Supreme Court. People who argue that the federal government should have no control whatsoever over public education seem to have overlooked this fact. It would be impossible to have a federal government of the United States if the states could nullify the Constitution. Therefore, some measure of federal control of public education is inescapable.

HISTORICAL DEVELOPMENT OF FEDERAL AID

There is no complete record of all the federal funds that are, or have been, expended for education. Actually, no office or agency of the federal government can give an accurate statement of federal funds being expended directly or indirectly for education. Even objective investigators working independently cannot arrive at the same total of federal funds expended for education during any given fiscal year. Therefore, it would not be possible to present an accurate history of federal aid even if space permitted. However, it is possible to present certain examples that cast some light on its development.

Early Land Grants

A national interest in education was revealed even before the adoption of the Constitution. It all started when the Congress, operating under the Articles of Confederation, set aside lands from the national domain for public schools in each new state upon entry into the Union. The Ordinance of 1785 provided the manner in which western territory would be surveyed and further specified a portion of each section for creation of public schools.[34] The Ordinance of 1785, however, did not actually carry out the transfer and sale of the lands, postponing such procedures to later legislation, in the Ordinance of 1787. Titled "An Ordinance for the Government of the Territory of the United States, North West of the River Ohio," this ordinance, also referred to as the Northwest Ordinance, was adopted on July 13, 1787. The document itself made no stipulation for the reservation of lands for public schools even though the Ordinance of 1785 had specified land for that purpose. The only reference in the Ordinance of 1787 to public education was found in the third article, the oft-quoted section that enunciated the belief that education was necessary for good government and the happiness of the people. Thirteen days after the passing of the second ordinance, a third ordinance was passed on July 27, 1787 for the sale of over 5 million acres to the Ohio Company. This geographical area encompassed what became in 1803 the state of Ohio. These were the origins of the federal government's involvement in the financing of public schools in the United States.[35]

Two characteristics of these early land grants were of great significance. First, the grants were for general public school purposes. Second, the federal government exercised no control over education as a condition for receiving the grants. Despite this early precedent establishing a pattern of nondirective federal aid, practically all federal grants-in-aid to the public schools after 1862 have been special-purpose, i.e., categorical grants.

National Domain. One may ask, however, how the central government acquired land to grant to the states in the first place? What were land grants and where did the land originate that was being granted? The answer is that these were lands that were known as the "national domain," and was constituted of the western territory beyond the agreed upon boundaries of the original 13 colonies. Harvey explains that seven of the colonies, Massachusetts, Connecticut, New York, Virginia, North Carolina, South Carolina, and Georgia, had laid claim to all the westward territory to the Mississippi River,[36] but the boundaries had yet to be surveyed and were indefinite. The six remaining colonies also feared that probable annexation of these lands would make the other seven colonies too powerful. A compromise was struck in the Articles of Confederation by which the seven colonies claiming dominion over these territories would cede their claims to the central government. These promises were fulfilled between 1781 and 1802 thus placing these lands in the national domain under the control of Congress. Cubberley clarifies:

> While the treaty of 1783 had recognized the boundary of the new Nation as extending westward to the Mississippi, there were many conflicting claims to the land west of the Alleghenies. By way of settling the matter, the Continental Congress, in 1780, proposed that the different States cede their claims to the National Government and thus create a national domain. New York, in 1781, was the first to do so, followed by Virginia (1784), Massachusetts (1785), Connecticut (1786), South Carolina (1787), North Carolina (1790), and Georgia (1802). The "common estate" thus created served as a real bond of union between the States during the critical period in the life of the new Nation.[38]

Illustrated in Figure 9.8 is a map showing dates of the cessions of the western lands.

Ordinance of 1785 (First Ordinance). Beginning in August 1776, Congress, operating under the Articles of Confederation, had promised lands to Revolutionary War soldiers ranging from 500 acres for a colonel to 100 acres for each noncommissioned officer.[38] In 1780, additional grants were made of 1,100 acres to a major general and 850 acres to a brigadier general. The granting of western lands also was stimulated by Congress' need for money to pay other war debts. The selling of western lands was the most immediate solution to the problem. The western lands were therefore considered valuable currency for the new government. Before sales could be consummated, however, the land had to be surveyed.[39] In response to a petition by 200 Revolutionary War officers in 1783 who sought to claim their lands, Congress appointed a committee headed by Thomas Jefferson to ascertain a method of locating and disposing of public lands.[40] This committee recommended an ordinance requiring lands to be divided into "hundreds" or townships of ten geographical miles square, and these hundreds were to be divided into "lots" of one mile square (640 acres) and numbered from 1 to 100. "These numbers were to commence in the northwestern corner, continue from west to east, and then from east to west."[41]

The recommendation of the Jefferson committee was carried over to the Continental Congress of 1785 where it was referred to a new committee and debated. It was argued that practicality required smaller tracts of less than the recommended ten square miles. Ultimately the Continental Congress decided that a township should be

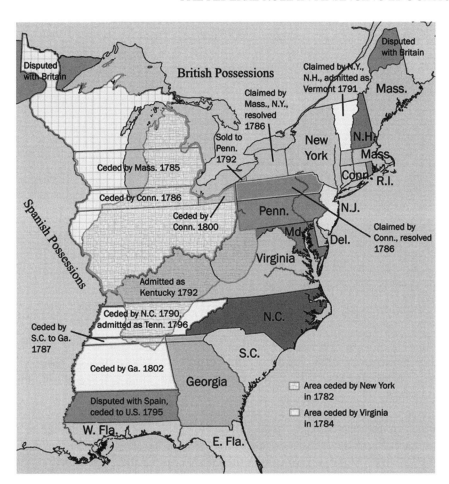

Figure 9.8 State Land Claims and Cessions to the Federal Government, 1782–1802

Source: Karl Musser, Wikimedia Commons, http://en.wikipedia.org/wiki/File:United_States_land_claims_and_cessions_1782-1802.png.

six miles square and the Ordinance of 1785 was finally passed on May 20.[42] The idea of "Congressional townships," illustrated in Figure 9.9, was maintained, as were the basic dimensions of one square mile or 640 acres.[43]

The ordinance, officially entitled "An ordinance for ascertaining the mode of disposing of lands in the Western Territory," established the method for the survey and sale of the land of the Northwest Territory.[44] The pertinent provision for public schools in the Ordinance of 1785 was as follows:

> The surveyors . . . shall proceed to divide the said territory into townships of six miles square, by lines running due north and south, and others crossing these at right angles, as near as may be . . .

> The plots of the townships respectively, shall be marked by subdivisions into lots of one mile square, or 640 acres, in the same direction as the external lines and numbered from 1 to 36.

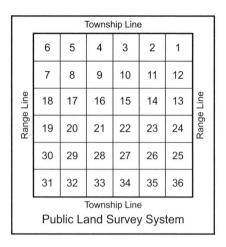

Figure 9.9 Public Land Survey System

Source: Kansas Society of Land Surveyors, www.ksls.com/about_surveys.htm.

There shall be reserved for the United States out of every township, the four lots being numbered 8, 11, 16, 19 . . . for future sale. There shall be reserved a lot No. 16, of every township, for the maintenance of public schools, within the said township . . .[45]

This was the origin of the sixteenth-section land grant for public schools that was carried throughout the subsequent Congressional legislation admitting new states into the Union.[46] Swift points out that the ideas behind public land policy ultimately benefitting public schools emanated from several sources including the following: (1) Connecticut, Massachusetts, and other colonies had reserved sections for schools in newly surveyed townships; (2) an abiding interest in education by enlightened legislators (not the least of whom was Thomas Jefferson who had chaired the committee in 1784); (3) the urgent need for revenues and the inability of the Continental Congress to raise funds from other sources; and (4) the desire to make westward expansion attractive.[47]

Ordinance of 1787 (Second Ordinance). As indicated earlier, the Ordinance of 1787, passed on July 13, 1787, did not actually reserve or convey lands for education, but the Continental Congress, meeting in New York in July 1787, simultaneously with the Constitutional Convention meeting in Philadelphia, forged the often quoted statement of education's value to a new nation, to wit: "Religion, morality and knowledge, being necessary to good government and the happiness of mankind, schools and the means of education shall forever be encouraged."[48] However, there was no specification as to how these lands would be used to advance education. This was to come later in a third ordinance and ultimately with the enabling act that admitted Ohio as the first state of the Northwest Territory in 1803.

The Land Rush. As may have been expected, the ordinances had been accompanied by intense lobbying by land speculators who saw a huge profit from real estate transactions in the new territories. Land speculation was a well-regarded profession of the day with impressive and respectable British forerunners such as Parliament's creation of the Muscovy Company (1553), the Levant Company (1592), the East India Company (1600), and the Hudson Bay Company (1669). All had been highly successful ventures for both economic development and commerce. Reputable speculators in the new colonies included George Washington who had been a principal promoter of the Mississippi Company in 1763 and had lobbied vigorously for his Continental Army officers to obtain land grants as payment for their services.[49]

Following the precedents of the British Parliament, Congress sitting in New York established the Ohio Company and conveyed 1.5 million acres of choice land at nine cents per acre at the juncture of the Ohio and Muskingum rivers[50] to Manassah Cutler, founder of the Ohio Company. The remaining 3.5 million acres were reserved for private speculation. A quorum of only eight states was present in New York when the ordinance was passed, and it was widely known that the United States' biggest contract was vividly marked by widespread corruption and graft as congressmen, speculators, and squatters reaped huge profits.[51] Cutler himself jubilantly wrote,

> We obtained the grant of near five million acres . . . one million and a half of the Ohio Company and the remainder for a private speculation, in which many of the principal characters of America are concerned. Without connecting this speculation, similar terms and advantages could not have been obtained for the Ohio Company.[52]

It was these "principal characters of America," including congressmen, who were the beneficiaries of the speculation.[53] Although self-interest, laissez-faire capitalism, and avarice were principal motivations of those persons in power, the common person did eventually become a beneficiary of the transaction through the education policy enunciations of 1785 and 1787 and the ultimate westward expansion and economic development. However, it remained for a fourth stage of the land grant policy to more clearly determine how the land could be used for the educational benefit of the people.

Ohio and the Land Grant. Clarification and implementation of the educational intent of the Ordinances of 1785 and 1787 were not achieved until negotiations began between the new state of Ohio and the United States Congress of 1802. Ohio agreed not to tax the public lands of the United States if the United States would in turn give to the new state of Ohio the sixteenth section of land in every township for the maintenance of schools within the township.[54] The enabling act for the admission of Ohio as a state thus became the precedent that formally reserved the sixteenth-section lands for public schools and other designated lands for public use.[55] The Enabling Act of 1802 stated in part:

> *First.* That the section numbered sixteen in every township, and where such section has been sold, granted, or disposed of, other lands equivalent thereto, and most contiguous to the same shall be granted to the inhabitants of the township for the use of schools.[56]

The Enabling Act fashioned for Ohio was used by all new states except Texas, which owned its own land, and West Virginia and Maine, which were carved from original states.[57] With the admission of California in 1850, and for new states thereafter, the grant was increased to two sections in each township, the sixteenth and thirtysixth sections. Later when Utah (1896), Arizona (1912), and New Mexico (1912) were admitted due to sparsity and the low value of land, an additional two sections, totaling four, were set aside for public schools. For all the 48 contiguous states the federal government granted for schools and other public purposes approximately 145 million acres or about 226,562 square miles of public lands.[58] This constituted an area larger than France and nearly four times the size of New England.[59] Figure 9.10 shows the section land allocations from the national domain that were set aside for public schools upon entry of the states to the Union.

Alaska and Hawaii came into the Union in 1959 under the two-section provision that designated sections 16 and 36 for the benefit of public schools. In Hawaii the enabling act of admission did not designate a section (or sections) of land for public schools, but rather stated,

> The lands granted to the State of Hawaii (by the United States) . . . shall be held by said State (Hawaii) as a public trust for the support of the public schools and other public educational institutions . . . The schools and other educational institutions

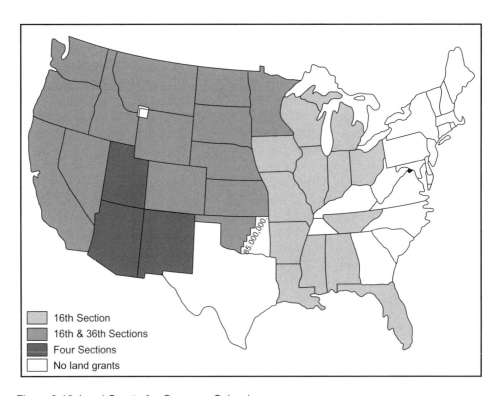

16th Section

16th & 36th Sections

Four Sections

No land grants

Figure 9.10 Land Grants for Common Schools

Source: Land Grants Map, *Public Education in the United States, A Study and Interpretation of American Educational History*, Ellwood P. Cubberley, The Riverside Press, Cambridge, MA (1934), p. 93.

supported, in whole or in part, out of such public trust shall forever remain under the exclusive control of the State; and no part of the proceeds or income from the lands granted under this Act shall be used for the support of any sectarian or denominational school, college, or university.[60]

Although Hawaii's admission did not designate specific surveyed sections of land, it did set aside public lands in trust for the support of public schools.

Thus, it may be concluded that the federal government, through its land-grant policy emanating from 1785, was a substantial force in the creation of public schools in the United States. It cannot be maintained that the policy was the sole motivating force for public schools, or the motivation at all in some of the states, the 13 original colonies, as well as Vermont, Kentucky, West Virginia, Maine, and Texas, established their systems without the land-grant impetus. The federal land-grant policy neverthe-less must certainly be counted as one of the most potent forces in the establishment and financing of public schools in the United States.

The Morrill Act

The first Morrill Act was passed by Congress in 1862 providing for a grant of 30,000 acres to each state for each representative and senator then in Congress. This same grant of land was made available to states thereafter admitted to the Union. The act provided for the giving of scrip to the states in which the public lands were insufficient to make up the allotment. It was provided that the land be sold and the proceeds used for the

> endowment, maintenance and support of at least one college where the leading object shall be, without excluding other scientific and classical studies and includ-ing military tactics, to teach such branches of learning as are related to agriculture and the mechanic arts in such manner as the legislatures of the state may respec-tively prescribe.

Another stated purpose of the act was "to promote the liberal and practical education of the industrial classes in the several pursuits and professions of life."[61]

This original Morrill Act is the first instance of the federal government provid-ing a grant for specific educational purposes. It should be noted that federal require-ments were limited to specifying that agriculture, mechanic arts, and military tactics be taught in those institutions. No limitation was placed on other subjects that might be taught. Also, the act specifically placed the determination of the educational poli-cies of the land-grant institutions in the hands of the respective state legislatures.

This act is of great significance because it again demonstrated the national interest in education and it also showed that, when existing educational institutions did not provide adequately for the general welfare, the federal government could and would take action.

At the time the Morrill Act was passed, the institutions of higher learning were largely classical and academic in character. They catered primarily to the select few. The land-grant colleges have been called *people's colleges*. Their curricula included subjects that were not "academically respectable" in 1862, but their educational programs grew in popularity. The influence of these land-grant colleges has been so great that they have contributed substantially to liberalizing the educational programs of many nonland-grant colleges. But more importantly the land-grant universities have served as models of practical research throughout the world and have been in the forefront of technological and agricultural advancement. In 32 states, a land-grant college is also the principal state university.

The Smith–Lever Act

The Smith–Lever Act was approved by Congress in 1914. It provided for extension services by county agricultural and home demonstration agents, 4-H leaders, and specialists in agriculture and homemaking, and for the professional training of teachers in those subjects. This act was far more specific in detailing the purposes for which the grant funds could be spent than was the Morrill Act. Actually, the services provided under the Smith–Lever Act were practically nonexistent prior to its passage. This act is additional evidence that Congress, when it deems it desirable to do so, will provide or stimulate the creation of educational services that are not being furnished by the educational organizations. The extension services provided under the Smith–Lever Act are not an integral part of the system of public schools. The service at the local level is usually allocated to the control of the county governing body. The extension services effectively brought the *people's colleges*, principally the land-grant universities, to the local community.

The Smith–Hughes Act

Between 1862 and 1917 the federal government seemed to be concerned primarily with inadequacies in the programs of institutions of higher learning. No new federal act of any major significance to the public schools was passed by Congress during that period. In 1917 Congress passed the Smith–Hughes Act, which provided funds for vocational education below the college level. Appropriation was provided for vocational education in agriculture, trades and industry, and homemaking. The Smith–Hughes Act provided the first special-purpose grants to the public schools by Congress.

Grants-in-aid for vocational education have been criticized on the grounds that such grants tend to turn the educational programs in the direction of the subsidized purpose. The more generously financed programs often become the centerpiece of the several programs regardless of whether they meet the needs of the students or the community. This was no doubt true in the years immediately following 1917, but that was probably one of the purposes of the Smith–Hughes Act. Any special-purpose grant influences the direction of the educational program. Therefore, a special-purpose grant of any kind, state or federal, contains an element of control.

Defense-Related Educational Programs. A long-term federal program that was designed primarily to assist states and local communities support defense-related activities was enacted in 1941. This law, known as the Lanham Act, or federal impact aid, provided for the construction, maintenance, and operation of community facilities in areas where defense and war activities created unusual burdens for local governments. Schools received considerable federal aid for building construction and for current expenses under the provisions of this act. The Lanham Act was superseded in 1950 by Public Laws 815 and 874, which continued approximately the same types of benefits.

The year 1958 marked a turning point in the relationship of the federal government to education. The launching by the Russians of the first satellite in 1957 caused great alarm in the United States. It was a popular myth that the Russians could not possibly develop advanced science and produce high-tech goods under their socialist system. When pundits are found to be wrong, they seldom admit error, but blame others. Therefore, the first reaction of many people to the success of the Russians was to blame the public schools for alleged inefficiency. Fortunately this state of public opinion did not last very long and, beginning in 1958, successive sessions of Congress enacted a long series of laws designed to improve education in the United States, extending from the preschool training through college and university education and continuing throughout adult life. The National Defense Education Act of 1958, Public Law 85-864, authorized the expenditure of substantial sums for the defense-related education in schools and universities.

Vocational Education

A major federal initiative for vocational education took place when Congress enacted the Vocational Education Act of 1963 – Public Law 88-210. This act more than quadrupled federal appropriations for vocational education, and it greatly broadened the purposes of the original Smith–Hughes Act. The major purpose of the act of 1963 was to provide occupational training for persons of all ages and achievement levels in any occupational field that does not require a baccalaureate degree, and to provide for related services that will help to ensure programs of quality. It also provided financial assistance for the construction of area vocational facilities, work-study programs, and residential schools.

Another major step forward for federal funding of vocational education transpired with the reauthorization of the Carl D. Perkins Career and Technical Education Act of 2006.[62] It was signed into law by the president on August 12, 2006. This Act provides for an increased focus on academic achievement in career and technical education and to enhance the connections between secondary and post-secondary education.[63]

ESEA AND IDEA

Of the aforementioned federal education acts for all states and school districts, the two most fiscally potent are the Elementary and Secondary Education Act of 1965 (ESEA) and the Education for All Handicapped Children Act of 1975 (Public Law (PL) 94-142), later renamed in 1990 the Individuals with Disabilities Education Act (IDEA). With the possible exception of vocational education laws, these two laws constitute the weightiest federal assistance to elementary and secondary education, both in terms of money and regulation. For this reason we will discuss the main provisions of both acts. ESEA's primary purpose is to help states provide meaningful instruction for educationally deprived children.

Elementary and Secondary Education Act (ESEA)

The concern over the proliferation of the number of federal categorical programs and the burden of extensive reporting requirements that had fallen on states and localities had created a desire to consolidate funding sources and the attendant procedures and processes. As a result of this perceived problem, Congress passed the Education Consolidation and Improvement Act (ECIA) which became effective in July 1982. Under the reauthorization of ESEA, the old Elementary and Secondary Education Act was replaced by block grants that eliminated several categorical programs. The enunciated intent of the new legislation was to allow state education agencies to administer the funds "with a minimum of paperwork."[64] This block grant consolidation was emblematic of the evolving nature of ESEA which has continued into the era of ESEA as NCLB.

Upon the 2001 reauthorization of the Elementary and Secondary Education Act of 1965 (ESEA), the law was given the new cumbersome sobriquet of No Child Left Behind (NCLB) by the Bush administration. NCLB was proposed by George W. Bush on January 23, 2001, passed the United States House of Representatives on May 20, 2001, passed the Senate on June 14, 2001, and was signed into law by Bush on January 8, 2002. Features of the law called for states to institute standards-based reform, high student achievement standards with measurable goals for students that could be assessed and evaluated.

The overall objective of Title I of ESEA/NCLB is set forth in its heading, Section 101 of the Act, *Improving the Academic Achievement of the Disadvantaged.*[65] The Statement of Purpose of the Act is outlined as follows:

1. Ensuring high-quality academic assessment, accountability, and teacher preparation and training,
2. Meeting educational needs of low-achieving children in highest poverty schools,
3. Closing the achievement gap between high- and low-performing children,
4. Holding schools, local educational agencies, and states accountable,
5. Distributing and targeting resources sufficiently to make a difference,
6. Improving and strengthening accountability, teaching, and learning by using state assessment systems,
7. Providing greater discretion and flexibility to schools in exchange for greater student performance,
8. Providing children an enriched and accelerated educational program,
9. Promoting and ensuring that children will have scientifically based instructional strategies,
10. Elevating the quality of instruction by providing staff with professional opportunities,
11. Coordinating services under this title,
12 Affording parents meaningful opportunities to participate in the education of their children.[66]

After the enactment of ESEA/NCLB, the complexion of federal funding for elementary and secondary education changed dramatically. It became a highly prescriptive

Table 9.2 No Child Left Behind Major Programs

Program	FY 2006	FY 2007	FY 2008	FY 2009*	FY 2010	FY 2011	FY 2012	FY 2013
Title I Grants to Local Educational Agencies	12,713	12,838	13,899	14,492	14,492	14,442	14,516	13,760
Improving Teacher Quality State Grants	2,887	2,887	2,935	2,948	2,948	2,465	2,467	2,338
Impact Aid	1,228	1,228	1,241	1,265	1,138	1,274	1,291	1,224
21st Century Community Learning Centers	981	1,081	1,131	1,131	1,166	1,154	1,152	1,092
English Language Acquisition	669	669	700	730	750	734	732	694
Safe and Drug-Free Schools and Communities, State Grants	569	577	513	295	—	—	—	—
School Improvement Grants	—	125	491	546	546	535	534	506
State Assessments	408	408	409	411	411	390	389	369
Reading First State Grants	1,029	1,029	393	—	—	—	—	—
Education Technology State Grants	272	272	267	270	100	—	—	—
Math and Science Partnerships	182	182	179	179	180	175	150	142
Teacher Incentive Fund	99	200	97	97	400	399	299	284

* Excludes economic stimulus funding under the American Recovery and Reinvestment Act.

Source: U.S. Department of Education, www2.ed.gov/about/overview/budget/tables.html.

umbrella of a host of categorical funding requirements. Indicated in Table 9.2 are some of the major programs that were included under the generalized heading of NCLB. Shown in this table are funding levels from FY 2006 through FY 2013.

Perhaps the most important new elements of the law were the penalties to be imposed on public schools if students failed to meet the requisite Adequate Yearly Progress (AYP) standards. As the Bush administration originally proposed, the law would have taken significant strides toward privatization of education by permitting students from the alleged failed public schools to take public financial resources, vouchers, and enroll in private schools. In the Senate, Senators Edward Kennedy and Christopher Dodd stemmed the Bush initiative for vouchers amending the effort by substituting remediation measures. The resultant legislation provided that schools that failed to make AYP for a second consecutive year were publicly labeled as being "in need of improvement" and were required to establish a two-year improvement plan for the subject matter in which the school had underperformed.

Also, students were given the option to transfer to a better public school within the school district if such schools existed. If the school missed AYP for a third year, the school must offer remediation services, such as tutoring and other supplemental services for underperforming students. A fourth consecutive year of a school's failure to achieve the AYP target required the school to be designated as requiring "corrective action," which could result in removal of teachers and staff, designing a new curriculum, or extending the time that students were in class. A failure by the school to achieve AYP in the fifth year required a complete restructuring to be implemented in the sixth year, which could include closing the school, resorting to a charter school, or having the school run directly by the state education agency. States were required to assess AYP each year via test scores. The Act did not provide for a national achievement standard; rather, each individual state was required to set its own standards. The law exhibited unprecedented federal control over education policy, tying funding to extraordinary federal goals and requirements. Thus, under NCLB, the federal role in education was greatly expanded in various ways through annual testing, annual academic progress, report cards, teacher qualification requirements, and alterations in funding methods.

Unfunded Mandates

After 2002, the complexion of ESEA/NCLB changed in that it became a complex for a host of categorical federal programs with attendant administrative costs for each. See Table 9.2 indicating some of the major programs and their funding levels from FY 2006 to FY 2013.

States have been concerned that NCLB has imposed unfunded mandates on states. Administrative costs for reforms related to test administration, data collection, and school improvement have been significant with the states bearing most of the burden.[67] State legislators and governors have complained about the lack of federal funding of these mandates.[68]

In 2003, the United States Government Accounting Office (GAO) conducted a study that revealed administrative costs to states would be largely dependent on the types of tests administered by the states; multiple choice and essay costs are considerably higher than multiple choice alone.[69] Displayed in Figure 9.11 are the state expenditures for the different types of tests estimated for years 2002–2008. Some states conducted their own studies; for example, an Ohio study estimated that it would cost that state over a billion dollars each year to meet NCLB requirements,[70] with at least one state, Connecticut, unsuccessfully suing the federal government in the United States Court of Appeals, Second Circuit.[71] A three-judge panel of the Court of Appeals ruled against Connecticut holding that the issue was not "ripe" for review. "Ripeness" means that the legal dispute before the court had not had time to build a more developed administrative record to buttress the claim alleged by Connecticut. The appeals court modified the district court's decision of the suit without prejudice, meaning that the state could refile the suit when the evidence of administrative costs was such that the issue was "ripe" for a decision.[72] There has been no Connecticut action since then; however, the court left the door open.

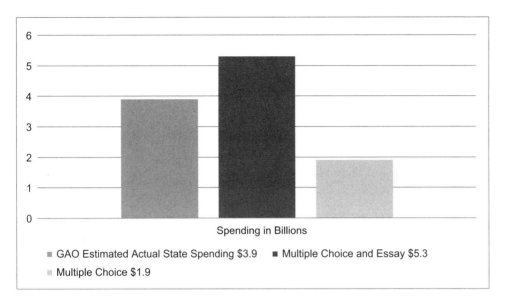

Figure 9.11 Administrative Costs of NCLB Testing

Source: United States General Accounting Office, "Characteristics of Tests Will Influence Expenses; Information Sharing May Help States Realize Efficiencies" (May 2003), www.gao.gov/new.items/d03389.pdf.

In further litigation regarding unfunded mandates, the United States Court of Appeals for the Sixth Circuit split on the question with an 8 to 8 vote of the judges, letting stand a federal district court decision that held that the "unfunded mandates" did not violate a provision of NCLB, 20 U.S.C. § 7907(a), that prohibited federal officials from imposing mandates not paid for by NCLB. In this case, as in the aforementioned Connecticut case, the issue pertained to federal regulations requiring the NCLB testing regimen.[73] The federal law in question that appeared to prohibit unfunded mandates states:

> Nothing in this Act shall be construed to authorize an officer or employee of the Federal Government to mandate, direct, or control a State, local educational agency, or school's curriculum, program of instruction, or allocation of State or local resources, or mandate a State or any subdivision thereof to spend any funds or incur any costs not paid for under this Act. 20 USC § 7907(a).

The United States Supreme Court declined to review the decision;[74] thus, unfunded mandates, to date, do not offend federal law.

In a nutshell, the overarching purpose of ESEA, now NCLB, is "to raise achievement and to close achievement gaps."[75] In 2013 reauthorization hearings were held in the United States Senate and the United States House of Representatives.[76] Federal Title I funding has increased $5.0 billion, or 56 percent, since 2001.[77]

The distribution for Title I ESEA (NCLB) funds, the flagship program, is now separated into four formulas: Basic Grant, Concentration Grant, Targeted Assistance Grant, and the Education Finance Incentive Grant funding formulae. School districts have some limited discretion in deployment of Title I funds. The law now requires that priority be given highest concentration to poverty schools. Figure 9.12 shows the percentages for each of the four Title I Grants.

Basic Grants. The Basic Grant formula distributes money to school districts based on the number of local income children served. All school districts with at least 10 poverty children or 2 percent of its students in poverty receive funding under the Basic Grant. In fiscal year 2013, $6.2 billion, 45 percent of all Title I funding,[78] was distributed through this formula.

Concentration Grants. The formula for Concentration Grants provides that these funds flow to school districts having 15 percent of the children in poverty or 6,500 poor children, whichever is less. These two allocation criteria serve as "cliffs" less than which the school districts receive zero Concentration Grant funding.[79] Concentration Grants are in addition to funds received by school districts under the Basic Grant. In Fiscal Year 2013, $1.3 billion or 9 percent of Title I funds were distributed under this Concentration Grant formula.[80]

Targeted Formula. This part of Title I, Targeted Assistant Grant, is distributed based upon a sliding scale providing more money to school districts as the rate of poverty children in a school district rises. In other words, high-poverty school districts receive more money per poverty child than do districts with lower percentages of poverty children. Each additional child in poverty above 38 percent is allocated four times as much money up to 16 percent of children in poverty.[81] Target grants also provide cost weightings for students in large, primarily big city, school districts. The program provides each additional child in poverty above 35,135 in the school district three times as much Title I funding as the district's first 691 children in poverty. In FY

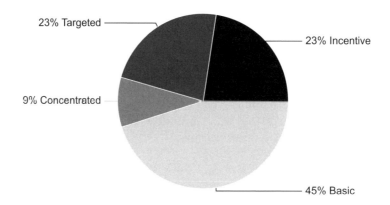

Figure 9.12 Share of Title I Appropriations by Formula Grant Type, Fiscal Year 2013

Source: Federal Education Budget Project, "No Child Left Behind Act – Title I Distribution Formulas" (2013, July 10), http://febp.newamerica.net/background-analysis/no-child-left-behind-act-title-i-distribution-formulas. Reprinted by permission of The New America Foundation.

Table 9.3 Targeted Title I Formula Poverty Weights

School Districts % of Children In Poverty	Per Child Weight In Funding Formula
0–15.6	1
15.6–22.1	1.75
22.1–30.2	2.5
30.2–38.2	3.25
>38.2	4
School Districts # of Children In Poverty	Per Child Weight In Funding Formula
0–691	1
692–2,262	1.5
2,263–7,851	2
7,852–35,514	2.5
>35,515	3

Source: Based on data from Elementary and Secondary Education Act, www2.ed.gov/legislation/ESEA/sec1125.html.

2011, $3.1 billion or 23 percent of Title I funding was distributed via this Targeted Assistance Grant formula.[82] The pupil weights for the Targeted formula are shown in Table 9.3.

Education Finance Incentive Grant. This part of the Title I grant provides additional funding for states that have more equitable state financing programs. It seeks to reward states for high fiscal effort (percentage of per capita income devoted to education) and for the extent of equity in state and local financing. Money is distributed in a way similar to the "Targeted Assistance Grant, except that in 'bad school finance' states, the weights for each child in poverty are doubled."[83] In the FY 2012, $3.1 billion or 23 percent of federal Title I funding was distributed through this formula.[84]

Individuals with Disabilities Education Act

The second most important federal initiative after ESEA is federal assistance for the education of disabled children. This is the successor law to the Education for All Handicapped Children Act of 1975 (EAHCA), Public Law 94-142 enacted November 29, 1975 and amended several times, 1978, 1932, 1986, 1990, 1997, and 2004, becoming IDEA in 1990. The purpose of this act is to assure that all children with disabilities have available to them a "free appropriate public education" which emphasizes special education and related services designed to meet the children's unique needs.

Public concern for the education of disabled students was activated in 1971 by a Pennsylvania case, *Pennsylvania Association of Retarded Children*, in which a federal district court held that a disabled child was entitled to a "free, public program of education and training appropriate to the child's capacity" and that such a child had a right to "placement in a special public school class." Closely following the Pennsylvania case, a federal district court in Washington, DC rendered a high profile decision that attracted nationwide attention, the *Mills* case.[85] The Mills' court held that to deny a child a "free and suitable" education violated the child's constitutional right to an education.[86] The court said "denying plaintiffs and their class not just an equal publicly supported education but all publicly supported education while providing such education to other children is violative of the Due Process Clause,"[87] of the Fifth Amendment of the United States Constitution.

Significantly, the Federal court in Washington, DC ruled that the lack of money could not be an excuse for not providing such public education. The court said,

> If sufficient funds are not available to finance all of the services and programs that are needed and desirable in the system, then the available funds must be expanded equitably in such a manner that no child is entirely excluded from a publicly supported education consistent with his needs and ability to benefit therefrom . . . The inadequacies of the District of Columbia Public School System whether occasional by insufficient funding or administrative inefficiency certainly cannot be permitted to bear more heavily on the "exceptional" or handicapped child than on the normal child . . .[88]

The *Mills* court then set forth requirements for the due process to be extended to each disabled child ascertaining the type of educational program needed for every disabled child. The requirements enunciated by the court became the heart of the 1975 law for "free appropriate public education (FAPE)" to be applied to all the states.

IDEA – Funding Distribution. Federal special education funds in FY 2013 were distributed via three main grant programs and several competitive categorical or discretionary programs.[89] The main, and the largest, program is *Part B* of the authorization providing funds to state and local agencies to offset the *excess costs* of educating disabled children. In FY 2013, IDEA was funded at $11.98 billion. However, the sequestration withholding reduced the amount to about $10.98 billion. Part B funding in FY 2013 has two basic parts. *First* there is a provision that guarantees that base funding will not be less than the amount appropriated during the 1999 fiscal year.[90] A *second* provision provides that funds above the 1999 level will be distributed at a level above the previous year with 85 percent allocated to states as determined by the state's relative portion of children in the IDEA age range, and 15 percent is allocated based on the state's share of children within the law's age range that are living in poverty. The relevant age range for IDEA is 3 to 21 years. Part B also provides for state administrative costs of up to 10 percent of the grant for "other state-level activities, such as monitoring, professional development, and establishing risk pools."[91] The law provides for a maximum of $800,000 or the state's set-aside for administration of the FY 2004 base year.

Part B can be divided into formula funding, Section 611, that covers a pupil count for children ages 3 to 21 years of age, and Section 619 that targets funding for children ages 3 to 5. Of the total of $11.98 billion funding for IDEA in 2013, the lion's share of $10.97 was funded through Section 611.[92] However, as noted above,

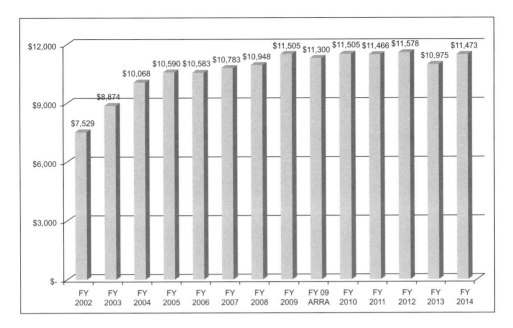

Figure 9.13 Special Education State Grants (IDEA Part B–Sec. 611)

Source: IDEA Money Watch, Balance Sheet, http://ideamoneywatch.com/balancesheet/?p=648. Reprinted by permission of The Advocacy Institute.

the sequestration requirement took a bite out of this amount for 2013. Figure 9.13 shows the Part B–Section 611 funding for each year, from 2002 to the estimated amount for 2014.

Excess Costs. When IDEA was enacted, the excess costs, or marginal costs, for education of special education children, calculated by Rossmiller, University of Wisconsin,[93] for the National Educational Finance Project in 1971, had to have a wide range of costs depending on the nature of the child's disability, ranging from a low excess cost for speech disability to a high excess cost for disability due to certain physical conditions.[94] For all disabled children the excess costs exceeded a two to one ratio. The IDEA law followed Rossmiller's guidance estimating excess costs for educational programs for disabled children on average to be about twice that of regular classroom programs.

In a 2004 study, the Center for Special Education Finance estimated that schools spent about 1.9 times more in total expenditures and 2.08 times more in current operating expenditures for students with disabilities.[95] The two to one ratio has been used to estimate the total fiscal need for special educational services in the country. Congress took this estimate into consideration, setting the maximum amount to be federally funded at 40 percent. The federal appropriations for IDEA have never come close to the 40 percent; in fact, federal appropriations have never reached 20 percent. Shown in Figure 9.14, the federal appropriation percentage of excess costs since 1995 amounted to only 16 percent in 2012.

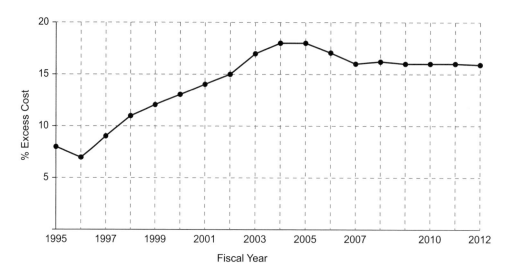

Figure 9.14 Federal IDEA Contribution to Excess Cost of Educating Children with Disabilities

Source: Based on data from United States Department of Education, www2.ed.gov/about/overview/ budget/tables.html, http://nces.ed.gov/programs/digest/d08/tables/dt08_052.asp, http://nces.ed.gov/ programs/projections/projections2018/xls/table_34.xls.

SUMMARY

With regard to the federal role in stimulating equity, Alexander[96] in testimony before the United States House Education and Labor Committee said that a federal initiative for elementary and secondary education should recognize and take into account several factors:

1. A federal plan should acknowledge the importance of investment in education in "nation building" and confirm that adequate funding of elementary and secondary schools is in the national interest and is a national priority. Such a plan should advance the value of elementary and secondary education as a public investment and call for the fashioning of investment strategies in keeping with that objective.
2. A federal plan should provide incentives for states to create and fund more uniform and equitable state systems of education. Attention should be explicitly given to the problems of fiscal disparities among school districts and to the effects of unequal education on the lower economic and working classes of Americans. Measures should be taken to accelerate efforts taken by state courts and legislatures to reduce these problems of disparate and inadequate funding.
3. The plan should be funded by the federal government at a level sufficient to maintain a competitive standard of federal fiscal effort and to provide an incentive and impetus for states to more adequately and equitably fund their elementary and secondary schools.
4. The plan should, importantly, take into account the fluid and changing mix of educational needs of children and the corresponding educational burdens confronting state school systems.

While these guidelines may generally apply to nearly all federal programs for education, they are particularly appropriate for federal plans that would promote equity in state school funding formulae.

In this chapter we saw how the federal role in the financing of education evolved from the original system of land grants to the specific categorical financial grants of today. An historical, political, and constitutional perspective was presented, all of which had important implications for the forming of the present structure of federal and state relations in education.

United States federalism is the foundational concept on which the federal role is premised. Education is primarily a function reserved to the states by the United States Constitution. The federal role is indirect, but may be pervasive depending on the nature of the federal interest.

Criteria for federal aid are set out as having been formed by both law and convention. These criteria call for an appropriate federal role, administrative arrangements conducive to sound federal-state relationships, adequacy of provision of education, and the fostering of equality of educational opportunity.

Political realities have fashioned federal involvement in education. Both Democratic and Republican positions toward federal aid have changed over the years.

Fear of control, fiscal conservatism, religious opposition, and racial segregation have all played important parts in the extent of federal activity in education.

The General Welfare Clause and the Commerce Clause have been the constitutional vehicles that empower the Congress to provide funding for education.

State governments are also constitutionally limited by the federal Bill of Rights, as well as the Fourteenth Amendment in the governance and control of education.

The federal impetus for the founding of the public school system was grounded in the early ordinances and land grants of the late eighteenth century. The Congressional requirements for the conversion from national domain to statehood compelled new states to make provisions for public schools. Beyond the 13 original colonies, enabling legislation for the entry of new states into the Union was fashioned to form and encourage public instruction.

The Morrill Act of 1862 continued the land-grant stimulus of forming comprehensive education systems by originating the great land-grant universities of the United States.

Through other acts of the early twentieth century, including the Smith–Lever Act of 1914 and the Smith–Hughes Act of 1917, the federal government began to provide grants in the form of money rather than land. From that point on, Congressional appropriations resulted in a more obvious and aggressive federal role in education.

The Elementary and Secondary Education Act of 1965 was a watershed event in federal aid to education. At this point the federal government recognized that greater federal funding was in the national interest. Nearly a half century later this act remains the main vehicle for federal aid to elementary and secondary schools.

The ESEA is primarily supplemented and complemented by IDEA, the education of disabled children. This legislation has continued and received renewed support over the years. The authorization goal of federal funding, 40 percent of the cost, has never been achieved by federal appropriations. Today the level is far less.

The federal formulae in totality, especially those of the ESEA, tend to equalize funds among local school districts. Because the funds flow to children from poor families, those districts with more poor children tend to get a greater proportion of financial aid.

The future of federal funding will, of course, hinge on the economic condition of the country, the extent of the continuing federal deficit, and the prevailing political philosophy. The philosophy of the federal administration will also have much to do with the future strength and viability of the public schools.

KEY TERMS

- Division of power
- Sixteenth section
- Individuals with Disabilities Education Act (IDEA)
- General Welfare Clause
- Morrill Act
- Commerce Clause
- Smith–Lever Act
- Vouchers and tuition tax credits

- Land grants
- Smith–Hughes Act
- Ordinance of 1785
- Ordinances of 1787
- Defense-related federal acts
- Elementary and Secondary Education Act (ESEA)
- National domain
- Congressional township

FEDERAL BUDGET GLOSSARY

Appropriations Bill. This bill allocates the funds approved by an authorization bill to individual federal agencies. It specifies how much money can be spent on a given program, and grants the government authority to enter into legal obligations that are later paid in outlays. Reviewed by the corresponding subcommittees of the Appropriations committees in both the House and Senate, appropriations bills must also be approved by the full House and Senate before being signed by the president.

Authorization Bill. This bill gives a government agency the legal authority to fund and operate its programs, sets maximum funding levels, and includes policy guidelines. The bill must be adopted by the full House and Senate before being signed by the president. Government programs can be authorized on an annual, multi-year, or permanent basis. Specific amounts authorized are ceilings on the amounts that subsequently may be appropriated in an appropriations bill, but not as minimums; either the House or Senate may recommend appropriating lower amounts or nothing at all.

Debt. Accumulated total of annual deficits and surpluses over the years.

Debt Ceiling. The legal (statutory) limit set by Congress on the amount of total debt that the federal government can assume. If the debt amount exceeds the debt ceiling limit, the government is unable to borrow additional funds to support continued operations, triggering a government shutdown and default on existing loans. Congress has the legal authority to raise the debt ceiling limit as needed.

Deficit. When spending exceeds revenues in a given year.

Direct Spending. Also referred to as mandatory or entitlement spending. Direct spending is directly controlled through eligibility requirements and benefit payments mandated in laws other than appropriations bills. Unlike discretionary spending, direct spending can occur without the annual approval of Congress and the White House. Examples include Social Security and the Food Stamp Program.

Discretionary Spending. Spending that is newly appropriated each year through Congress' annual appropriations process. This spending makes up roughly one-third of the federal budget.

Entitlement Programs. Programs such as Social Security and the Special Nutrition Assistance Program (SNAP) that pay benefits to anyone who applies for benefits and meets the eligibility requirements for that specific program.

Mandatory Spending. Spending that is essentially automatic and therefore bypasses the annual appropriations process. It includes entitlement programs like Social Security, Medicare, and the Supplemental Nutrition Assistance Program (SNAP) – formerly the Food Stamp Program – where benefits are received by those who meet specific eligibility requirements (e.g., if you're over 65 you can collect Social Security). Spending levels can fluctuate up or down depending on the number of people eligible for payment under these programs. Mandatory spending accounts for roughly two-thirds of the federal budget.

Multiplier Effect. When an increase in spending leads to an even larger increase in economic activity.

Sequestration. A series of automatic federal spending cuts that occur when the government fails to achieve a set of predetermined goals. In the current context, sequestration refers to the set of automatic across-the-board cuts mandated by the Budget Control Act of 2011 that are legislated if Congress fails to enact $1.2 trillion in deficit reduction initiatives.

Social Insurance. Payments made by the government for programs such as Social Security and Medicare.

Trust Funds. Pots of money that are earmarked for specific purposes and which generally have a dedicated revenue source. There are over 200 trust funds, the largest of which is Social Security and including Medicare and railroad retirees' pensions.

NOTES

1. U.S. Department of Education, *Overview: The Federal Role in Education*, ED.gov, www/2.ed.gov/about/overview/fed/role.html.
2. Ibid.
3. Ibid., Mission.
4. Ibid.
5. Ibid., ED.gov.
6. Kern Alexander and M. David Alexander, *American Public School Law*, Eighth Edition (Belmont, CA: Wadsworth/Cengage Publishers, 2012), pp. 82–87.

7. *Seminole Tribe of Florida v. Florida*, 517 U.S. 44, 116 S. Ct. 1114 (1996).

8. Jack N. Rakove, *Original Meanings: Politics and Ideas in the Making of the Constitution* (New York: Vintage Books, 1997), pp. 324–325.

9. John Locke used the term *federative power* in describing aspects of a government concerned with relations among several states. See Rakove, *op. cit.*, p. 167.

10. *Alden v. Maine*, 527 U.S. 706, 119 S. Ct. 2240 (1999). See *Martin v. Hunter's Lessee*, 1 Wheat 304 (1816); *City of Boerne v. Flores*, 521 U.S. 507, 117 S. Ct. 2157 (1997); *United States v. Lopez*, 514 U.S. 549, 115 S. Ct. 1624 (1995).

11. Article I, § 8, cl. 1.

12. See Alexander and Alexander, *op. cit.*, p. 83–85.

13. Ibid., p. 85.

14. *Pennhurst State School and Hospital v. Halderman*, 451 U.S. 1, 101 S. Ct. 1531 (1981).

15. *Board of Education of Hendrick Hudson, Central School District v. Rowley*, 458 U.S. 176, 102 S. Ct. 3034 (1982).

16. Ibid.

17. *Arlington Central School District v. Murphy*, 548 U.S. 291, 126 S. Ct. 2455 (2006).

18. *Constantine v. Rectors and Visitors of George Mason University*, 411 F.3d 474 (4th Cir. 2005).

19. *Rankings & Estimates: Rankings of the States 2012 and Estimates of School Statistics 2013*, NEA Research, December 2012, National Education Association, p. 38, nea.org

20. U.S. Department of Education, Digest of Education Statistics, 2011, Chapter 4, Federal Programs for Education and Related Activities, p. 543.

21. See: *National Priorities Project: Democratizing the Federal Budget*, "Federal Budget 101: Where Does the Money Go?," OMB, National Priorities Project, www.nationalpriorities.org/budget-basics/federal-budget-101/spending.

22. *Citizens United v. Federal Election Commission*, 558 U.S. 50, 130 S. Ct. 876 (2010).

23. See: *National Priorities Project, op. cit.*

24. Ibid.

25. Robert Skidelsky, *Keynes: The Return of the Master* (U.K.: Allen Lane, 2009).

26. Nicholas Wapshott, *Keynes and Hayek: The Clash that Defined Modern Economics* (New York: W.W. Norton & Company, 2011).

27. Naomi Klein, *The Shock Doctrine: The Rise of Disaster Capitalism* (New York: Henry Holt and Company, 2007).

28. Pub. L. No. 111-5, 123 Stat. 115, 516 (Feb. 19, 2009).

29. www.useconomy.about.com/od/candidatesandtheeconomy/a/Obama-stimulus.htm.

30. Ibid.

31. Kimberly Amadeo, "Was the Stimulus Package a Success? Obama's First Major Act to Stimulate the Economy," About.com. U.S. Economy, www.useconomy.about.com/od/candidatesandtheeconomy/a/Obama-stimulus.htm.

32. *Financial Times*, Wednesday, September 4, 2013, September 7 and 8, 2013.

33. John E. Novak, Ronald D. Rotunda, and J. Nelson Young, *Constitutional Law*, 3rd edn. (St. Paul, MN: West Publishing Company, 1980), p. 181.

34. Ira Harvey, *A History of Educational Finance in Alabama, 1819–1986* (Auburn, AL: The Truman Pierce Institute for Advancement of Teacher Education, Auburn University, 1989), p. 11.

35. Ibid., p. 12, citing *Journals of the American Congress, From 1774–1788, Vol. IV* (Washington, DC: Way and Gideon, 1823).

36. Ibid.

37. Ellwood P. Cubberley, *Public Education in the United States* (Boston: Houghton Mifflin, 1934), p. 91.

38. Ibid.

39. Benjamin Horace Hibbard, *A History of the Public Land Policies* (New York: Macmillan, 1924, pp. 32–33.

40. Harvey, *op. cit.*

41. J. M. Faircloth, "Land Surveying in Alabama" (Montgomery, AL: The Board of Registration for Professional Engineers and Land Surveyors, 1916).

42. Ibid.

43. Harvey, *op. cit., p.* 12.

44. Ibid.

45. United States Congress, *Journals of the American Congress Vol. IV, op. cit.*, p. 217.

46. Willis G. Clark, *History of Education in Alabama* (Washington, DC: U.S. Government Printing Office, 1889), p. 217.

47. Fletcher Harper Swift, *A History of Public Permanent Common School Funds in the United States, 1785–1905* (New York: Henry Holt, 1911), p. 217.

48. See Harvey, *op. cit.,* p. 12, citing *Journals of the American Congress, From 1774–1788, Vol. IV* (Washington, DC: Way and Gideon, 1823), p. 753.

49. Catherine Drinker Bowen, *Miracle at Philadelphia* (Boston: Little, Brown, 1966), p. 172.

50. Ibid., p. 173.

51. Harvey, *op. cit.*, p. 13.

52. Bowen, *op. cit.*, p. 173.

53. Ibid.

54. Cubberley, *op. cit.*, p. 92.

55. Harvey, *op. cit.*, p. 13.

56. Ibid., p. 13, citing *Land Laws of the United States*, vol. I, p. 88.

57. Cubberley, *op. cit.*, p. 92.

58. Ibid., p. 93.

59. Ibid.

60. *Hawaii – Admission Into Union*, Public Law 86-3; 73 Stat. 4, March 18, 1959, Laws of 86th Congress – 1st Session, Sec. 5(f).

61. U.S.C.A. Title 20, Education 81 to 1686.

62. U.S. Department of Education, ED.gov. http://www2.ed.gov/policy/sectech/leg/perkins/index.html.

63. Ibid.

64. Federal Register 47, no. 22 (November 19, 1982), *Rules and Regulations* (Washington, DC: U.S. Government Printing Office, 1982), p. 1.

65. U.S. Department of Education, ED.gov, http://www2.ed.gov/policy/elsec/leg/esea02/pg1.html.

66. Ibid.

67. *Federal Education Budget Project*, "Background and Analysis," http://febp.newamerica.net/background-analysis/no-child-left-behind-funding.

68. Ibid.

69. Ibid.

70. Ibid.

71. *Connecticut v. Duncan*, No. 08-2437 (2nd Cir. July 13, 2010).

72. Ibid.

73. *School District of Pontiac v. Duncan* (09-0852), *cert. denied*, U.S. Supreme Court. See: Kent Talbert, Court Cases: *Education Law Review: Elementary and Secondary School Legislation, Unfunded Mandate*, www.educationlawreview.com/KI-12-education/courtcases.

74. Ibid.

75. No Child Left Behind Act (NCLB/ESEA), National Education Association (NEA), http://www.nea.org/home/NoChildLeftBehindAct.html.

76. Ibid.

77. *Federal Education Budget Project*, http://febp.newamerica.net/background-analysis/no-child-left-behind-act-title-1-distribution-formulas.

78. Federal Education Budget Project, Background and Analysis, *No Child Left Behind Act – Title I Distribution Formulas*, http://febp.newamerica.net/background-analysis/no-child-left-behind-act-title-i-distribution-formulas.
79. Ibid.
80. Ibid.
81. Ibid.
82. Ibid.
83. Ibid.
84. Ibid.
85. *Mills v. Board of Education of District of Columbia*, 348 F. Supp. 279 (E.D. Pa. 1972).
86. Ibid.
87. See: Kern Alexander and M. David Alexander, *American Public School Law, Eighth Edition* (Belmont, CA: Wadsworth/Cengage Learning, 2012), pp. 563–566.
88. *Mills*, op. cit.
89. *Federal Education Budget Project, Background & Analysis, Individuals with Disabilities Education Act-Funding Distribution*. http://febp.newamerica.net/background-analysis/individuals-disabilities-education-act-funding-distribution.
90. Ibid.
91. Ibid.
92. Ibid.
93. Richard Rossmiller, "Resource Configurations and Costs in Educational Programs for Exceptional Children," *Planning to Finance Education*, Volume 3, edited by R. L. Johns, Kern Alexander, and K. Forbis Jordan (Gainesville, FL: National Educational Finance Project, 1971), p. 59.
94. Ibid.
95. Jay G. Chambers, Thomas Parrish, and Jennifer Harr, *What Are We Spending on Special Education Services, 1999–2000* (Center for Special Education Finance, 2004).
96. Kern Alexander, "Financing the Public Schools of the United States: A Perspective on Effort, Need, and Equity," *Journal of Education Finance* 17:3 (Winter 1992), pp. 142–143.

CHAPTER 10

Teacher Compensation

TOPICAL OUTLINE OF CHAPTER

- Policies Relating to Personnel and Finance
- Classroom Teachers' Salaries
- Teachers' Salaries International
- Purchasing Power Parity
- Economic Costs of Being a Teacher
- Teacher Organizations and Unions
- Collective Bargaining
- Teacher Pension Funds
  - Types of Teacher Pension Plans
  - State Remedies for Pension Deficits
- Supply and Demand
- Economic Effects of Teachers
- Teacher Effectiveness
  - Value-Added Teacher Productivity
  - Merit Pay
- State Methods of Allocating Teacher Salaries
- Determination of Local School District Salary Policy
- Salaries of Administrative and Supervisory Staff
- Salary Adjustments Based on a Cost-of-Living Index

INTRODUCTION

As noted in an earlier chapter of this book, it was countries in Europe and North America that were most directly influenced by *The Enlightenment* and its ideals of world progress, knowledge, science, and public instruction. At its base, as Padgen writes, was the idea of "modern liberal democracy – the kind of political system"[1] from whence the concept of *citizenship* emerged. At the root of this citizenship was the condition precedent of a knowledgeable people. Throughout the more advanced world that knowledge would be conveyed inter-generationally via the means of publicly employed teachers. It was not until the late eighteenth century after Rousseau had penned his great book *Emile, or On Education,* 1762, that Pestalozzi, the great Swiss teacher, was prompted to examine the nuances of the "art of teaching."[2] Kant, the philosopher, reinforced the belief that progress requires the "rational study of nature"[3] to be developed through education of the public, and government had the responsibility to ensure learning and rationality by the means of public instruction.

An adequate education requires teachers to employ methods to develop the child's "natural, emotional, intellectual, and social potentialities" and must "equip students with the technical skills and self-discipline they need to learn."[4] In order to achieve this end, Kant believed that the public school would be the best type of education because it "would attract the most competent teachers,"[5] that is, teachers who have been taught how to teach. Kant went into great detail in defining desirable methods of teaching. One such method, he explained, is for the teacher to act as a "midwife for students to reason, using questions and cases to initiate dialogue with the students to help them clarify their thinking."[6] Thus, essential to the education process was that teachers not only have knowledge of subject matter, but they also must "know how to teach": thus, the necessity for a teaching profession, normal schools, and teacher certification by the state.

The state's essential role in ensuring the public that teachers, in fact, know how to teach, trained in teaching methods, is a condition precedent to universal education, and that teaching has a methodological basis that emanates from documented authority. Implicitly, this means that the state should not spend taxpayers' money for instructors who are untrained in pedagogy. It further means that the mere possession of a college diploma does not *ipso facto* qualify a person to be paid from the public purse to teach unless that person is able to show public verification and certification of pedagogical training and capability to teach. Thus, you cannot, in building a universal system of common schools, place a basic reliance on those who are untrained in pedagogy, are not professionals, and are merely sojourning in teaching while en route to other careers.

Sufficient funds must be made available to provide adequate and appropriate compensation for all members of the teaching and managerial staff of public schools. Expenditures for personnel (certified and noncertified) in school systems currently constitute about 80 percent of the funds expended for the current operation of the schools. Policies relating to provisions for personnel and the expenditure of funds significantly influence the quality of education in a school system. It is important, therefore, that school boards and legislators of the citizenry make every effort to ensure that fiscal conditions are favorable and conducive to providing a high-quality program of education.

POLICIES RELATING TO PERSONNEL AND FINANCE

The development of appropriate personnel policies is of crucial importance in every state and local school district. In fact, policy planning is a major aspect of comprehensive long-range planning, which is essential for the continuous improvement of education in any school system. These plans and policies should include careful consideration of the following:

1. Aims (the establishment and maintenance of instructional and instructional-support programs);
2. Organizational structure (concerned especially with positions generated by the aims structure); and
3. Personnel processes (those designed to attract, develop, and retain personnel needed to maintain and improve the system generated by the aims structure).

Each of these important personnel processes must be, of course, further subdivided into sequential tasks that are essential to achieving the purposes and goals of the system.[7] All of the major policies established through this process have important implications for the financial support that is essential if the system is to function effectively.

Policies relating to personnel may be stated in law, in state and local school board regulations, and administrative directives, or they may be unwritten and consequently somewhat intangible. Both written and unwritten policies are important in every community. Written policies and fiscal procedures serve as guidance and are expected to be observed until they are repealed or revised. Unwritten policies are often the most difficult to successfully manage and monitor. They are expressed through the attitude of the people of the community, the local school board, and the administrative staff toward teachers and other employees. This attitude determines the climate or conditions under which school personnel provide educational services. If the attitude is favorable to schools and to school personnel, working conditions are likely to be better and morale much higher than where attitude is one of distrust, suspicion, and criticism. In fact, the attitude of the people of a state or community may determine whether the funds provided for salaries of teachers are adequate or inadequate, and it may even have a decided effect on whether funds are used wisely or unwisely in terms of the personnel services provided.

Personnel administration in education has moved from a somewhat peripheral and largely managerial position to one more concerned with the human condition as well as organizational goals. Studies by psychologists, sociologists, economists, and the resulting modifications in management theory, have contributed significantly to this development, which has had a considerable influence in industry as well as in education. Modern concern both for employees and for students has directly contributed to the maximum development and utilization of the potential of individuals and to efforts to encourage greater self-direction and responsibility.

Many factors today interplay with modern management theory, having important implications for the financing of school personnel. Problems associated with urbanization as well as the unique problems of the large cities have been and continue to be of paramount importance. Demographic trends, the ebb and flow of teacher supply and demand, and unemployment and salary considerations in the collective bargaining context also have resulted in strong effects upon management personnel policies.

CLASSROOM TEACHERS' SALARIES

The average classroom teacher's salary in the United States in 2012–2013 was estimated by the National Education Association to be $56,383.[8] This amounted to a 1.7 percent increase over the previous year calculated in current dollars which does not take inflation into account. However, as shown in Figure 10.1, for the 20-year period from 1993 to 2013, the average teacher's salary remained about the same, about $45,000 in *deflated* dollars.

In 2012–2013, the estimated *current* teacher salary, not inflation adjusted, for the United States, ranged from lows of $38,804 in South Dakota and $41,646 in Mississippi to highs of $73,398 in New York and $71,721 in Massachusetts.

In way of perspective, if a school teacher is the sole source of income for a family of four in South Dakota or Mississippi, her/his child would qualify for federal reduced-price meals as a student in school. See Table 10.1. The level of qualifications for a school reduced-price meal in 2012–13 was $42,643. Thus, the teacher compensated at the average level or below in either of these two states falls below this particular measure of relative poverty. The borderline poverty pay for a public school teacher in some states may also be illustrated when compared to the federal Earned Income Tax Credit (EITC) which is designed to specifically help elevate low and moderately low income families out of poverty. It does serve as an unfortunate commentary on the

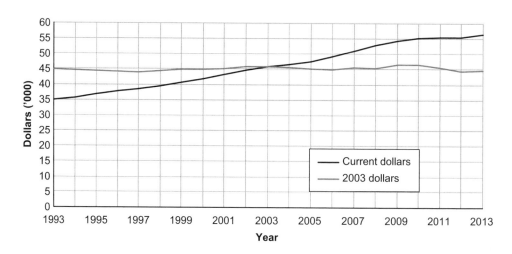

Figure 10.1 Average Classroom Teacher Salary, 1993–2013

Table 10.1 Five Highest and Five Lowest States for Teachers' Salaries 2011–2012

State	Average Salary
New York	$73,398
Massachusetts	$71,721
Connecticut	$69,465
California	$68,531
New Jersey	$67,078
U.S. Average	$55,418
New Mexico	$45,622
West Virginia	$45,320
Oklahoma	$44,391
Mississippi	$41,646
South Dakota	$38,804
Federal Reduced Priced Meal (Family of Four)	$42,643
Poor Tax Relief (EITC) (Family of Four)	$43,038

Sources: *Rankings of the States 2012 and Estimates of School Statistics 2013*, NEA Research, December 2012. National School Lunch Program, United States Department of Agriculture, *Income Eligibility Guidelines*, 2012–2013. IRS, 2013 EITC Income Limits, *Tax Law Updates*.

relative value that the citizenry places on the teaching profession for a married teacher with two children, filing jointly with a spouse, with income less than $43,038, qualifies for the federal relief of a tax credit.

TEACHERS' SALARIES INTERNATIONAL

The more that states and nations can pay for teachers' salaries in the employment marketplace, the more competitive public schools are in the competition for quality teachers. While the marketplace for teachers is primarily intra-state and certainly intra-country, there is, nevertheless, vigorous movement of good teachers toward more desirable teaching conditions and higher pay.

The relative pay of teachers compared to the general economic condition of a country is perhaps more important to consider than the absolute wages received. A teacher receiving what would be an average or lower salary on an international scale may be well paid compared to other workers in an underdeveloped or low-income country. Undoubtedly, a teacher at the lowest of the pay scales in the United States would be relatively well paid if he or she made the same salary in an underdeveloped country. On the other hand, a teacher of average pay on an international scale may be considered to be poorly paid if employed in a high-income nation such as the United States, Sweden, or Switzerland.

The quality of the teaching force is materially affected by such relative wage conditions. When teacher salaries are in a relatively low ratio to the per capita personal income of a nation, or are low relative to some other measures of national fiscal capability such as gross domestic product per capita or private consumption per capita, less able people will enter the teaching profession. Prospective teachers will, all other things being equal, choose alternative white-collar employment that requires comparable education and training.

PURCHASING POWER PARITY

Purchasing power parity theorizes that the exchange rates between or among countries will adjust to reflect the differences in price levels.[9] Paul Samuelson defines purchasing power parity as *what incomes will buy*.[10] Any currency may be used for a comparative basis, but by general practice, for purposes of international economics, the United States dollar is used. An interesting explanation of purchasing power statistics is furnished by *The Economist*, in terms of a purchasing power parity based on the cost of McDonald's *Big Mac Hamburger*, which is now sold throughout the world.

Normally, however, purchasing power parity is calculated by means of a market basket broader than a Big Mac (although the Big Mac may be a good proxy) typified by methodology and by the Organization for Economic Cooperation and Development (OECD) in Paris.[11] By applying the OECD method to salaries, a more accurate picture of the relative value of teachers' salaries can be determined.

BOX 10.1

Salaries in Constant Dollars

Constant dollars differ from current dollars in that constant dollars have been corrected for inflation over time. The correction is usually made using the **Consumer Price Index (CPI),** a statistical measure of the changes in prices of goods and services purchased by a typical urban household. It indicates pricing patterns that have a direct bearing on the cost of living.

Source: U.S. Department of Commerce, *Statistical Abstract of the United States* (Washington, DC: U.S. Government Printing Office, 1991).

From this analysis one can draw two basic conclusions. First, the relative economic position of United States teachers within the nation's economy is lower than provided teachers in other countries relative to their own economic system. That is, salaries of teachers in the United States are less competitive compared to the per capita national income. Put another way, teachers in the United States are not as well off relative to incomes earned by teachers in other countries.

Of late, much has been said about international achievement test scores and the rankings of United States students that are lower than what most Americans would desire. After inspecting relative PISA[12] average national test scores for reading, math, and science, it is natural to compare the international rankings of test scores to the rankings of teachers' salaries. Determining teachers' salaries among countries requires that the money of different countries, first, be converted to purchasing power parity (PPP) and then, secondly, ascertain what level of schooling and teacher experience levels are being compared. Such is shown for Teachers' Salaries, Figure 10.2, adjustments made for purchasing power parity to comparable United States dollars for teachers with fifteen years' experience at the upper secondary level for selected OECD countries.

Displayed in Table 10.2 are 2011 OECD data for teacher salary costs per student converted to United States dollars, for parity of purchasing power. The OECD

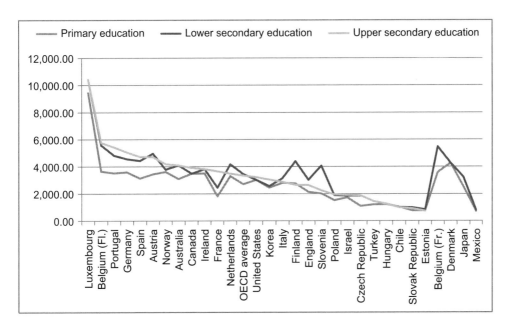

Figure 10.2 Salary Costs of Teachers (in U.S. Dollars) per Student, by Level of Education (2011)

Source: Based on OECD, *Education at a Glance* (2013), Chart B7.1, p. 240.

Table 10.2 2011 Teachers' Salary Costs Per Student, Lower or Upper Secondary, in Equivalent United States Dollar (USD) Converted to Purchasing Power Parity

Country	Amount
Austria	$ 4,703
Belgium (Flanders)	$ 5,760
Czech Republic	$ 1,856
Denmark	$ 4,265*
Finland	$ 4,396*
France	$ 3,647
Germany	$ 5,063

(*Continued*)

Table 10.2 (Continued)

Country	Amount
Greece	—
Ireland	$ 3,816
Italy	$ 3,135*
Japan	$ 3,220*
Korea	$ 3,045
Luxembourg	$10,409
Netherlands	$ 4,172
Norway	$ 4,181
Poland	$ 1,942
Portugal	$ 5,421
Spain	$ 4,729
Sweden	—
Switzerland	—
United Kingdom	$ 3,033**
United States	$ 3,235
OECD mean	$ 3,344

* Salaries are for lower secondary education
** Does not include Scotland
— No data

Source: Equivalent USD converted using PPP, OECD, Table B7.1, "Financial and Human Resources Invested in Education," Teachers' Salaries – Education: Key Tables from OECD Library Annual Statutory Salaries in Public Institutions, 15 years' experience, upper/lower secondary education.

average is $3,344 and the United States average salary is $3,235. Luxembourg has, by far, the highest salaries per student, the Czech Republic provides the lowest, and the United States resides in the middle of the pack. We see that of the major international economic competitors, contrasted to the United States, Japan is comparable, Germany spends considerably more, France more, and Korea less.

Even more revealing, arrayed in Table 10.3 the United States is compared to selected OECD countries relative to cost per student as a percent of the GDP per capita. This table is most valuable for comparisons in that it reflects not only salary costs per student, but adds the element of the economic capability of the respective countries. This measure shows that the fiscal effort of the United States for per-pupil costs is quite low. The OECD average percentage is 9.9 and the United States, at only 6.7 percent, is considerably lower. In fact, the fiscal effort of the United States, for teachers' salaries, taking into account both the number of students and the country's economic ability, is the lowest of any of the major OECD countries.

Another striking number having important fiscal implications is shown in Table 10.4, and contains a display of the ratio of students to teaching staff. Low ratios, obviously, are much more costly. Of the 21 OECD countries for which data were available, with the exceptions of Korea and the Netherlands, the United States had the

Table 10.3 Teachers' Salaries Costs Per Student, Lower or Upper, as Percent of GDP Per Capita, 2011 Selected OECD Countries

Country	Amount
Austria	11.4
Belgium (Flanders)	15.6
Czech Republic	7.8
Denmark	11.5*
Finland	12.6*
France	10.7
Germany	13.5
Greece	—
Ireland	10.3
Italy	10.2*
Japan	10.6*
Korea	11.2
Luxembourg	12.7
Netherlands	8.5
Norway	7.4
Poland	9.8
Portugal	24.0
Spain	16.2
Sweden	—
Switzerland	—
United Kingdom	7.7*
United States	6.7
OECD mean	9.9

* Salaries are for lower secondary
** Does not include Scotland
— No data

Source: Equivalent USD converted using PPP, OECD, Table B7.1, "Financial and Human Resources Invested in Education," Teachers' Salaries – Education: Key Tables from OECD Library Annual Statutory Salaries in Public Institutions, 15 years' experience, upper/lower secondary education.

Table 10.4 Ratio of Students to Teaching Staff. Selected OECD Countries, 2011

Country	Ratio
Austria	9.1
Belgium (Flanders)	8.1
Czech Republic	11.1
Denmark	11.8
Finland	9.3
France	14.8

(Continued)

Table 10.4 (Continued)

Country	Ratio
Germany	14.2
Greece	7.9*
Ireland	14.4
Italy	11.5
Japan	14.2
Korea	18.8
Luxembourg	9.6
Netherlands	15.3
Norway	10.0
Poland	10.0
Portugal	8.2
Spain	10.3
Sweden	11.3
Switzerland	—
United Kingdom	14.6
United States	15.2
OECD (EU21)	13.2

*2010 Data
— No data

Source: Equivalent USD converted using PPP, OECD, Table B7.2b, "Financial and Human Resources Invested in Education," Teachers' Salaries – Education: Key Tables from OECD Library Annual Statutory Salaries in Public Institutions, 15 years' experience, upper/lower secondary education.

highest ratio. These numbers clearly indicate why, as the above tables also show, the United States has relatively low costs per student based on its capacity to fund public schools.

All of these international numbers suggest that the United States conducts a relatively low-cost elementary and secondary education system. Such salary and teacher staffing data would suggest that the recent disappointing international achievement PISA test data are not necessarily caused by inefficiencies or failure of teacher productivity, but rather emanate from, or are at least related to, the simple lack of fiscal resources. Shown in Table 10.5 of 21 selected OECD countries, United States teachers' salaries rank number 8.

These salary comparisons are corrected for purchasing power parity for teachers with fifteen years' experience at the upper secondary level, but do not take into account the *relative economic condition* of teachers' salaries within the country in which they are employed. This is accomplished in Table 10.6 by displaying the rank of United States teachers' salaries as a ratio of national income per capita for each selected OECD country.

This more accurate picture of relative teachers' salaries among countries shows a rather poor United States average salary, ranking 17th among the OECD countries.

Table 10.5 Teachers' Salaries Selected OECD Countries, 2011

Country	Salary	Rank
Austria	$ 46,317	11
Belgium (Flanders)	$ 58,399	5
Czech Republic	$ 21,733	20
Denmark	$ 58,347	6
Finland	$ 43,302	14
France	$ 36,398	18
Germany	$ 69,715	3
Greece	$ 28,184	19
Ireland	$ 54,954	7
Italy	$ 36,926	17
Japan	$ 45,741	12
Korea	$ 48,146	9
Luxembourg	$100,013	1
Netherlands	$ 63,695	4
Poland	$ 21,518	21
Portugal	$ 39,424	15
Spain	$ 46,479	10
Sweden	$ 37,584	16
Switzerland	$ 77,500	2
United Kingdom	$ 44,269	13
United States	$ 49,414	8

Source: Equivalent USD converted using PPP, OECD, "Financial and Human Resources Invested in Education," Teachers' Salaries – Education: Key Tables from OECD Library Annual Statutory Salaries in Public Institutions, 15 years' experience, upper/lower secondary education.

Table 10.6 Relative National Effort for Teachers' Salaries. Ratio of Teachers' Salaries to National Income Per Capita: Rank Order

Country	Rank
Austria	15
Belgium (Flanders)	7
Czech Republic	20
Denmark	10
Finland	13
France	18
Germany	1
Greece	19
Ireland	3
Italy	14
Japan	11
Korea	2

(Continued)

Table 10.6 (Continued)

Country	Rank
Luxembourg	4
Netherlands	6
Poland	16
Portugal	5
Spain	9
Sweden	21
Switzerland	8
United Kingdom	12
United States	17

Source: Calculated Ratio of National Income Per Capita PPP to OECD Average Teachers' Salaries for teachers with 15 years' experience at upper secondary level, PPP OECD Factbook, 2013, Economic, Environmental and Social Statistics.

In other words, taxpayer effort to fund teachers' salaries in the United States aligns near the PISA test scores for United States students. Low pay generally accompanies low test scores.

ECONOMIC COSTS OF BEING A TEACHER[13]

Myriad economic and social constraints affect the adequacy of compensation of public school teachers in America today. One predominant and underlying factor is the citizenry's general view of the importance of the public school system. At the heart of that system is, of course, the quality of the teaching staff, the single most important element in determining the level of learning. Because they are dependent on government tax support for their well-being, however, teachers receive only marginal compensation, i.e., marginal in that most public schools are so precariously fiscally balanced that a slight shift in funding can deprive students of an efficient level of teaching knowledge and expertise.

The quality of the teaching force is largely determined by the pay that teachers receive. Whereas employment in other sectors of society can yield a net gain in income over a lifetime, teachers must consider the costs of *alternatives forgone* when deciding whether to enter and/or remain in the public schools. The problem of determining the level and adequacies of pay, endemic to the issue of public school finance, is not new. In 1927, Ellwood Cubberley wrote that "it has always been easier to secure adequate pay for policemen, firemen, city hall clerks, and general municipal employees than for teachers."[14] He noted that during the post-World War I era, the nation's economy developed in such a way that wages of carpenters, plumbers, painters, bricklayers, and other private-sector employees rose steadily, without a corresponding increase in wages for teachers. Cubberley concluded that the increased cost of education, while real, was actually being absorbed by lowering the teachers' standard of living:

In the purchase of what we eat and wear and in the rent, we pay the increased cost, but not for education, as the teachers there help pay the increased cost of producing an output – teaching – which the public enjoys at a lower relative cost than it does almost any other thing it buys.[15]

Cubberley's point is obvious, and remains so today, motivating us to think not only about the economic status of teachers, but also about improvement in the quality of the public schools, generally. Importantly, it compels us to consider how much should be paid and who should pay it. In recent years, several states have launched drives to improve the effectiveness of the public schools through a host of legislative requirements. The majority of the legislated requirements have been punitive sanctions under the banner of greater accountability. Some legislatures have increased funding, but many have done little to raise the general level of support. On one hand, they modify the system to give the public better schools yet, on the other hand, they fail to provide a corollary or commensurate increase in funding. Thus, the public schools, as an entity, may absorb the increased costs by making internal organizational adjustments or, alternatively, the school teachers themselves absorb the added costs. Effectively, then, to some undefined extent, *public school teachers personally subsidize the improvements in education* from which the taxpayers benefit but do not choose to ameliorate through increased taxes.

There is always a high degree of receptivity to distributing the costs of public operations among various segments of our society. Sometimes these costs are shifted to the *workers*, as in the case of teachers. At other times, the costs may be shifted to the *users* of the public service, for example, through increasing public college tuition or charging fees for the use of school laboratories and textbooks. In other instances, shifts occur as costs of government are channeled from one economic class of citizens to another class through legislated changes in the tax structure. Musgrave observed, "It must be recognized that in the end, the entire tax burden must be borne by individuals."[16] Seldom does altruism overcome the innate propensity of individuals to push the burden off to someone else in society. Because increases in public school costs require greater outlays of public funds, and sometimes tax increases, there is a strong tendency for taxpayers to shift the burden away from themselves to either the users (students) or the workers (teachers). In higher education the shift is to student tuition and fees. In the case of public schools, when taxpayers fail to respond, the teachers absorb the costs or schools engage in fee charging. This type of cost shifting has occurred in many states where the legislatures have attempted to lengthen the school day without providing a corresponding increase in funding.

Annually, legislators and school boards require students (or parents) to pay fees for laboratories, student transportation, use of library, textbooks, and other services and materials. Attempting to shift costs to students in this fashion shows the failure to understand and value education as a public good. Some lawmakers and school boards believe that the student as user or consumer should bear a large portion of the costs of public education. To correct this erroneous belief requires that the citizenry have a general conviction that the *externalities* or *social spillovers* from education are sufficient to justify the financing of public schools from tax sources.

A reluctance to provide teachers with higher pay may also occur as a result of shifting the tax burden from the more affluent and better educated to the poorer, less educated segment of the population. If government does actually redress the needs of the lower class, the tendency is for the upper classes to structure a tax system in which the lower and middle classes pay for their services.

Nearly all state tax structures are regressive, and much of public school revenue is dependent upon the regressive property tax. See Taxation for Public Schools, Chapter 8. Moreover, the middle and lower classes often reject funding for public schools that would go toward providing reasonable compensation for teachers. For so long as teachers' pay is closely linked to regressive tax structures, which generally make the most demands of the poorly educated, low-income segment of the population, little change is likely to come about in the overall economic status of teachers.

Teachers' subsidization of public education is largely passive. When educational costs rise, either through inflation or additional services, and teachers do not receive a corresponding increase in wages or benefits, then their subsidization of the public schools automatically rises. To shift increased costs of public education to the taxpayers, local school boards or legislatures must levy taxes that will address the rising costs. Legislative or constitutional provisions requiring referenda at the state or local levels further increase the difficulty of public assumption of costs.

Whether the citizenry is willing to subsidize its appropriate share of educational costs is speculative and dependent upon one's philosophical view of public education in the economy. The definition of *appropriate* may vary greatly on a broad spectrum between the liberal and conservative views of education. The more liberal viewpoint, as enunciated by John Kenneth Galbraith, early argued that the affluent society has been undermined by a calculated starvation of the public sector. He observed that Americans have viewed some of the most trivial commodities "with pride," while conversely viewing "some of the most significant and civilizing services," such as education, as a "burden to be discharged or paid for with regret."[17] Galbraith condemned the "failure to keep public services in minimal relation to private production" and maintained that there is a necessity to create a "social balance" between the two.[18]

BOX 10.2

Teachers Bear Public Burden

In the purchase of what we eat and wear and in rent we pay the increased cost, but not for education, as the teachers there help pay the increased cost of producing an output – teaching – which the public enjoys at lower relative cost than it does almost any other thing it buys. This is not because our people believe that the social worth of the teacher is less than that of the plumber or painter, but because teaching has always been on a competitive basis, since the tax rate is always concerned, and because we have . . . no proper standards for computing what teachers' salaries should be.

Source: Ellwood P. Cubberley, *State School Administration* (Boston: Houghton Mifflin, 1927), p. 652.

Whether schooling takes place in public or private schools, though, teachers subsidize the educational program. Actually, the teacher may be not only a producer of educational services but a financier of them as well. The extent of the individual subsidy varies depending upon the teacher's potential for alternative employment, personal costs incurred in academic preparation to become a teacher, and attendant costs related to experience or internships required in becoming a teacher.

Public school teachers are required by the state to attend universities and to participate in internships in order to be certified so as to assure the public of a minimal level of qualification. This certification process is usually quite costly, particularly for a public school teacher who holds a bachelor's or master's degree, as required for certification, and the education is acquired while the prospective teacher is unemployed. Foregone earnings add measurably to the teacher's education costs. In short, the cost of a teacher's personal investment of time and money in becoming a teacher tends to increase the personal subsidy that teacher will give to the public. Public school teachers' subsidies go to the general public benefit, to all children in common, and to the public enterprise or commonwealth, generally.

It is probably impossible to establish the exact economic balance at which teacher compensation could minimize the required subsidy. Historically, teachers have been paid wages lower than those given to artisans and even day laborers. Dan Lortie observed that "economists may argue that teachers have been paid the 'going rate,' but many in our society have considered teacher incomes as somehow inappropriate given the importance of education."[19] To some, this suggests that a *just wage* would provide teachers with greater income. In this regard, it could be maintained that the difference between the going rate and a just wage is the amount by which the teacher personally subsidizes the public enterprise.

The monetary value of a teacher subsidy to the state is mitigated by trade-offs such as job security, a predictable and steady income, relative autonomy, and intellectual stimulation. Where these factors are sufficient to offset the net subsidy loss of the teacher, a balance is reached that will keep the teacher from seeking an alternative employment. But from a purely economic viewpoint, the teacher's subsidy contributed to the public school may be most nearly assessed by the traditional benefit-cost ratio or rate-of-return approach to determine whether the costs incurred to become a teacher are offset by lifetime earnings.

Edlow Barker found that the benefit-cost ratio and the internal rate of return for a teacher who studied full time for a master's degree are both negative. In other words, the costs of earning a master's degree on a full-time basis exceeded earnings. For example, he shows that on the average a person will lose .745 percent a year on the educational investment of a full-time master's degree. The benefit-cost ratio was found to be .6565, or less than a one-to-one ratio, indicating that earning a master's degree by full-time study is not economically feasible for a teacher.[20]

Such negative result indicates that the teacher who returns to the university full time to study for a master's degree will incur a net loss in economic returns upon reentering the teaching ranks. It may be concluded that the extent of this net loss is the extent to which the teacher with the master's degree (earned full time) subsidizes the public school program. A benefit-cost ratio at a breakeven one-to-one ratio would indicate that the teacher does not fiscally subsidize the public school operation but receives no benefits either. To the extent that teachers are willing to absorb the uncompensated costs of their own training, which improves the overall quality of education, they subsidize the public while taxpayers enjoy a public school program at a cost substantially below its actual monetary value.

If state proposals for the improvement of education are to have a practical and lasting effect on the quality of education, policymakers must necessarily regard each in relation to its economic impact on the teacher's economic condition. Programs that shift the burden of costs toward greater teacher subsidization will likely, and should, fail.

TEACHER ORGANIZATIONS AND UNIONS

Teacher organizations have contributed much to the public school system of the United States. Female teacher associations were the backbone of early public schools. In 1829, Catherine Beecher wrote that "it is to mothers and to teachers that the world is to look for the character which is stamped on each succeeding generation."[21] When the first public normal schools were organized in Massachusetts in 1839–1840, Horace Mann observed that such special training required requisite preparation and females to be qualified as teachers.[22] School reformers, the new education of that era, saw the development of universal public education to be dependent upon a combination of teacher associations, teacher institutes, and normal schools as the principal sources for academic training and professionalization. According to Cremin, it was these organizations that "nurtured a form of professional consciousness, a culture of professionalism oriented to knowledge, technical skill, efficient organization, peer evaluation, and public service" that were to similarly develop in medicine, dentistry, pharmacy, and law.[23] The teacher associations arose in tandem and in support of the establishment of public schools not only in the United States, but in other countries as well. France preceded the United States in realizing that democracy could never exist without public instructors, teacher training, and the advancement of the *art of teaching*.[24]

The advancement of the reality of public schools was a basic political plank of working class trade unions in the United States at least as far back as the 1830s. Kaestle writes that "Antebellum workingmen's groups enthusiastically endorsed tax-supported public education in the 1830s . . ."[25] A most notable teacher association called the American Institute of Instruction was organized in Boston in 1830.[26] Later, beginning in 1845, state associations of teachers formed, holding meetings for the advancement of public schools and publishing journals to that end.[27] By 1857 various teacher and school administration organizations had progressed to the stage of a national consolidated effort "to elevate the character and advance the interests of the profession of teaching, and to promote the cause of popular education in the United States."[28] Regular annual meetings after 1857 were held by the National Teachers' Association (NTA). In 1906, the NTA was incorporated by an Act of Congress and changed its name to the National Education Association (NEA). By 1930, the NEA had 220,000 members and today numbers about 3.2 million. The American Federation of Teachers (AFT) dates back to the early twentieth century and became a major force in teacher collective bargaining in 1964. Today the AFT has about 1.1 million members.

In the 1830s the importance of pedagogy, teaching methodology, and the teaching profession gained a foothold in Europe as well as the United States.[29] Trade unions in France became common after the 1848 revolution, but teacher organizations did not fully develop to any important degree until after 1907, when France declared separation of church and state.[30] Interestingly, and understandably, mass public education is credited with the abatement of revolution and decline of overthrow of governments in France, particularly the uprisings of the poor in 1830, 1848, and 1871. As public instruction and secular teaching became more common, government became less repressive of the common people and of workers' rights, and political confrontations became more socially responsible, less frequent, and less necessary.[31]

BOX 10.3

Correlation between Teacher Unions and Student Test Scores

There is much talk in the United States about the need to reduce the power of the unions over our schools . . . But when we look at the experience of the top-performing countries, we see that some are home to some of the strongest teachers unions in the world.

Source: Marc Tucker, *Governing American Education* (Washington, DC: Center for American Progress, 2013), p. 24, www.americanprogress.org.

Similarly, in Germany the teacher organizations were, at least, as fundamental to the creation of a public school system as in France. Elementary school teachers in Prussia were required to pass examinations and be certified as early as 1826.[32] By the 1840s, the younger teachers "vented their grievances and called for the emancipation of the school from the church."[33] By 1840, teachers' associations had sprung up in opposition to unlivable wages.[34] It was said that "The poor schoolteacher in Bavaria had no right to a home until he reaches his grave."[35] In March 1848, the All German Teachers' Association organized and became active in political action and sought reform of schools and the removal of conservative Protestant and Catholic control of the educational system.[36] The Prussian Teachers' Association led the struggle to wrest education from the clutches of the clergy. By 1904, the Prussian Teachers' Association had 62,000 members.[37] In other major economically developed countries, teacher unions also rose and were instrumental in advancing the establishment of public secular schools.

Concerning the United States, *per se,* Marc Tucker, a leading education thinker in the United States maintained, in a publication titled *Governing American Education,*

that teacher unions, strong economics, and high student test scores are highly correlated. Tucker refers to the rising political conservatism in America that is anti-union
and anti-public schools and cites specifically recent state conflicts where some governors and legislators have enacted legislation to reduce the fiscal capabilities and
political strength of teacher unions and of other organizations of public employees.[38]
Michigan, Wisconsin, Indiana, Ohio, and North Carolina are major examples.[39] Conservative politicians are well aware of the complementary nature of public school
funding and the strength of teacher organizations. Tucker points out that if teacher
unions

> were a major enemy of student achievement at high levels, we would expect to
> see the highest student performance where we find the weakest unions, and the
> weakest student performance in the states with the strongest unions. But that is
> the opposite of what we actually see.[40]

If one examines the evidence pursuant to Tucker's statement (see Box 10.3) it
is obvious that his point is well taken. Student achievement test scores in Finland,
Netherlands, Belgium, Norway, Estonia, Switzerland, Germany, Canada, Singapore,
etc., find little relationship with the extent and degree of unionization of teachers. If a
pattern could be discerned it would show that countries with more liberal and democratic regimes with stronger unions tend to have higher test scores. Also, importantly,
Mahler, Jesuit, and Paradowski have recently shown in countries of Europe, including
the United States, that there is a positive relationship between union density, elec-
toral votes turnout, and more equalizing redistribution effects in a nation's economic
system.[41]

In the United States, only about 11.3 percent of the total working population report
that they belong to a union. Sixty percent of the working population in Denmark and
Sweden, high student achievement test score countries, belong to unions. Furthermore,
union density is also positively related to overall higher living standards of countries.[42]

COLLECTIVE BARGAINING

The right of public school teachers to engage in collective bargaining entails important
fiscal and legal issues, such as the employees' right to organize, the authority of the
school board to bargain, the right to strike, and the authority of the school board
to submit to compulsory arbitration. Whether a public school district or any other
agency of a state has collective bargaining is governed by state statute.[43] The scope and
boundaries of collective bargaining are, therefore, dependent on state legislation. Public
employees have a right to associate and join unions, but whether their associations
or unions can actually engage in collective bargaining is a matter of state law. However, public employees do have a constitutional right to join a labor organization, but
whether the organization can negotiate or bargain collectively or strike is not a constitutional right and is subject to state law.[44] Statutes prohibiting public employees' right
to strike do not violate the state or federal constitutional mandates of equal protection.

In 34 states, plus the District of Columbia, school districts can be required by teacher organizations to engage in collective bargaining.[45] Eleven states have statutes that permit collective bargaining by local school boards and other public institutions and five right-to-work states prohibit public collective bargaining.

Most public collective bargaining laws generally follow the private sector's requirements under the Taft-Hartley Act[46] to bargain wages, hours, and other terms and conditions of employment. The overall scope of the area of bargaining, though, is difficult to define and is always fluctuating. Wages, we know, cover regular pay, over-time, and cost of living, while conditions of employment may include fringe benefits, holidays, vacations, sick leave, pregnancy leave, and so forth.

Labor union membership in the United States has declined by about 30 percent in the last fifty years. As discussed above, currently only about 11.3 percent of the labor force belongs to unions.[47] The 11.3 percent is a 97-year low for private and public union membership in the United States.[48] According to the Bureau of Labor Statistics, the public sector workers in education, training, library occupations, and protective service occupations had a unionization rate of about 35 percent, considerably higher than the private sector. In 2012, 7.3 million employees in the public sector belonged to unions and 7.0 million in the private sector. In 2012, employees in education, train-ing, and library professions who were represented by unions had weekly earnings of $1,028 while non-union employees earned $814 per week, or $214 less per week than the union employees.[49]

Public sector unions, most notably teacher unions, have recently come under a barrage of attacks in states that have elected anti-union governors and a majority of like-minded legislators in the last few years; Wisconsin is the most highly publicized example. As pointed out above, of these remonstrations against public sector unions have been based on a reluctance to sustain public employee pension benefits. Com-parisons have been drawn between compensation of public and private sector workers, as private sector unionization has fallen into decline.[50] The conservative view contra public sector unions has, it is argued, fueled the rise of public funding of "charter schools, vouchers and education tax credits," as methods to bypass unions.

BOX 10.4

Teacher Unions

The unions have become a convenient scapegoat in urban areas because they divert attention from the real ills of urban poverty. Moreover, busting the unions seems on the surface to promise lower costs and higher quality. This is just one more magic bullet that distracts us from the hard, consistent work that we need to do to raise the quality of education for all children, and especially poor children.

Source: Jeffrey D. Sachs, *The Price of Civilization* (New York: Random House Trade Paperback, 2012), p. 196.

The precise impact of collective bargaining upon the financing of public schools is not fully understood. Whether it leads ultimately to an improved quality of education or to better wages and working conditions for teachers is a subject of much needed objective research. A few studies, that cannot be considered conclusive, found that salaries increased in bargaining districts over non-bargaining districts from about 0 to 4 percent for the year in which the studies were conducted.[51] Yet other studies have found either no effect at all or even an adverse effect of collective bargaining on the salaries of teachers. In an interstate study, Kasper showed that "there is no statistically significant positive effect of teacher organizations on salaries once other variables such as income and urbanization are taken into account."[52] In another study, Balfour found a negative association between salaries and collective negotiations. Similarly, Zuelke and Frohreich found that collective bargaining had a significant negative effect on teacher salaries in small- and intermediate-sized districts in Wisconsin.[53] It is important to note that this latter study was conducted in school districts in which collective bargaining had been in effect for many years. Several studies that did show increased salaries as a result of collective bargaining measured only the short-term positive effects of bargaining.

In recent years, teacher unions have been challenged to prove their social worth to education by documenting that their existence is justified as measured by student achievement test scores. Lindy, writing in *The Yale Law Journal*, after an extensive review of extant literature concerning the effects of teacher unions on student achievement, concluded that

> it is troubling that there is remarkably little empirical evidence of the true impact of teacher bargaining on student achievement . . . the existing empirical literature on teacher bargaining suffers from a series of methodological flaws, and as a result it has produced inconsistent evidence.[54]

Lindy, in conducting his research on the matter, concluded that where teachers organize and bargain under a mandatory collective bargaining law, the empirical result is that SAT scores tend to increase. Further, he concluded that high school graduation rates may decline. He speculates that this happens because teachers are under pressure to raise achievement test scores and, to some degree, the teachers will be diverted from tending to the educational needs of disadvantaged students who often do not complete high school or take SAT exams to attend college.[55] Thus, this and other attempts to connect teacher unionization with student achievement have not produced compelling evidence that unions affect, either positively or negatively, student achievement. The financial consequence of such attempts to show that teacher unions affect student achievement, at least to a degree, is a suspect criterion for any reliable conclusions concerning school improvement.

This line of research, therefore, suggests a high degree of uncertainty and inconclusiveness. The research does not measure the other effects that bargaining may have on teacher working conditions or the general quality of education. Even more difficult to measure is the psychological effect of bargaining on teachers and their communities. Presumably, the quality of the educational program is positively affected by greater teacher morale in that bargaining provides teachers with a formal structure through which their voices can be heard at policy levels. Therefore, of course, little evidence exists to show that long-range improvements are achieved in this manner.

Some maintain, to the contrary, that the adversarial roles implicit in collective bargaining may have an overall detrimental effect.

The educational efficacy of collective bargaining cannot be reduced to a mathematical formula. We must conclude that teachers generally feel that the benefits to the teaching profession and to education outweigh the detriments, as evidenced by collective bargaining activity in education.

TEACHER PENSION FUNDS

The total financial benefits in the public pension systems (including teachers) in the United States are low compared to the average of OECD countries. Citing Frick and Grabka, 2009,[56] the average wealth of pensions in the OECD countries is about 300,000 U.S.D. (United States Dollars) while pension wealth in the United States on average is only about $173,000, 58 per cent of the OECD average. The United Kingdom is $224,000, or 74 percent of the OECD average, while Germany and France are higher than the OECD mean with $342,000 and $330,000, respectively.[57]

Underfunded state teacher pension funds in the United States present a daunting fiscal problem for many states. A comprehensive study in 2012 estimated that underfunded teacher pension liabilities amounted to about $325 billion.[58] The overall public employee state pension fund gap, between what the state employees and the states have actually appropriated into the systems, is estimated to be in excess of $1 trillion.[59] Figure 10.3 shows the ten states with the largest teachers' pension liabilities.

States with largest teachers' pension liability, in billions

California	$57.1
Illinois	43.5
Ohio	40.7
Texas	24.1
Pennsylvania	19.7
Michigan	17.6
New Jersey	16.3
Colorado	12.7
Indiana	11.1
Kentucky	11.1

Note: For systems that include members other than teachers, the total reported unfunded liability was adjusted to reflect the percentage of teachers in the system

Figure 10.3 Delayed Retirement

Source: Stephanie Banchero, "States Faulted Over Teacher Pension Shortfall," *The Wall Street Journal* (2012, Dec. 13). Reprinted with permission of *The Wall Street Journal*, Copyright © 2012 Dow Jones & Company, Inc. All Rights Reserved Worldwide. License number 3327760743963.

On average, state teacher pensions were funded at about 73 percent of the required level in 2012.[60]

The underfunding of teacher pension funds now being experienced by some states is made even worse when teacher retiree health benefits are added to the equation. The Pew Center on the States estimated that state obligations for retirement health care benefits for all state employees require about $51 billion to pay for estimated health care commitments; but as of 2010, only $17 billion of that amount had been allocated. Pew's estimates of state health care obligations include all public employees, including teachers.[61]

BOX 10.5

Teacher Pension Funds Underfunded

Most teacher pension systems across the nation are underfunded, many severely so. State and local governments have knowingly contributed less than their required portion to fund promised benefits, and lower than expected investment returns have exacerbated those actions.

Source: Kathryn M. Doherty, Sandi Jacobs, and Trisha M. Madden, *No One Benefits: How Teacher Pension Systems are Failing Both Teachers and Taxpayers* (Washington, DC: National Council on Teacher Quality, 2013), p. 12.

Displayed in Table 10.7, there is a great range of teacher pension fund liabilities among the states. The top ten states, with New York first, have stayed current with their matching obligations while, at the other extreme, Indiana and Illinois are marked by extremely poor management of their contractual responsibilities to their public school teachers.

Types of Teacher Pension Plans

Doherty et al., in a comprehensive study, identified four types of teacher pension plans: (1) defined benefit pension plan; (2) defined contribution pension plan; (3) cash-balance pension plan; and (4) hybrid pension plan. Briefly, the *defined benefit plan* obligates the state to pay a specified amount per month for life to each teacher who retires after serving a requisite number of years or after attaining a predetermined age. Thirty-seven states have this plan. The *defined contribution plan* establishes a fixed level of contributions for both the teacher and the state, and permits selection of investment options such as stocks or bonds, etc. Only Alaska has this plan. The third type, the *cash-balance plan*, allows teachers to set up individual retirement investment accounts; in this the teachers' investments are protected by a state minimum guaranteed amount, and, thus, are not entirely subject to the vagaries of the marketplace.

Table 10.7 Teacher Pension Systems: States with Highest and Lowest Percentages of Funding

Highest States	*Percentage*
New York	100.3
Wisconsin	99.9
South Dakota	96.4
North Carolina	95.4
Tennessee	94.7
Delaware	94.0
Idaho	90.2
Oregon	86.9
Georgia	85.7
Lowest States	*Percentage*
Rhode Island	59.4
Hawaii	59.4
Ohio	58.8
New Hampshire	57.4
Kentucky	57.1
Oklahoma	56.7
Louisiana	55.1
West Virginia	46.5
Illinois	46.5
Indiana	44.3

Source: Based on Kathryn M. Doherty, Sandi Jacobs, and Trisha M. Madden, *No One Benefits: How Teacher Pension Systems are Failing Both Teachers and Taxpayers* (Washington, DC: National Council on Teacher Quality, 2013).

Kansas has such a plan and Louisiana intends to implement a similar plan. The fourth type, the *hybrid plan,* has features of both a defined benefit plan and a defined contribution plan. The hybrid plan is used in several states including Indiana, Michigan, Oregon, Rhode Island, and Virginia.[62] A few states provide for teachers to choose among all four of the above plans.[63]

Concerning Social Security, the U.S. Department of Labor estimated that 73 percent of public school teachers are covered by Social Security.[64] In 35 states, teachers participate in Social Security, in three states local school districts provide such participation for teachers. Thirteen states do not participate in Social Security. Doherty et al., make the very important observation that the *state pension fund crisis* has a debilitating effect on teachers' salaries, and indeed, on the salaries of all state employees. Poorly funded pension systems obviously depress annual increases in teacher pay.

State Remedies for Pension Deficits

Because of the failure of states to annually provide actuarially defensible appropriations to state employee and teacher pension funds, several of the aforementioned states find themselves in a severe bind to catch up with and backfill for past years.

In order for states to address the fiscal problems presented by pension fund deficits, these states have a few alternatives, all of which have important policy, political, and fiscal implications. *First*, states could embark on a long recovery mode by ever-increasing state appropriations which would be feasible only when accompanied with tax increases. *Second,* states could help their fiscal situation by lowering their annual cost-of-living adjustments. Twenty-two states have done so. *Third*, states could increase the age at which teachers can retire. Some 25 states have taken this approach. *Fourth,* states could lengthen the number of years used to establish a base for calculating the final average compensation.[65] That is, for example, if a state now uses the average salary of the last three years of employment for the base, it could decrease the base by using the last five years instead. This would effectively reduce the teacher retirement system's monthly payments to retiring teachers. Twenty states have followed this avenue. *Fifth,* states could change the multipliers as a way to reduce benefits to the teachers. The benefit multiplier balances the age of the retiree against the number of years that the benefit will be received. Based on the age of the retiree, the younger the teacher the smaller the monthly benefit, thus reducing the state's fiscal commitment. If the multiplier is based on years of service, rather than age, young retirees will gain an advantage because they would draw payments over a longer period of years. Thirteen states have adjusted their multipliers.[66] *Sixth,* states could increase teacher contributions for their pensions. This is a simple approach that has been resorted to in 27 states. *Seventh,* states could attack the fiscal problem by the most obvious way, reducing benefits while increasing the teacher's contributions. Some 21 states have taken this direct approach.[67]

SUPPLY AND DEMAND

Teachers who complain that their salaries are too low may take some solace in the fact that their situation has not changed significantly in over 200 years. In 1776, Adam Smith attributed the low compensation of teachers in England and Scotland to oversupply, which was caused by the education of vast numbers of clergy, who, unable to find positions in churches, overflowed into the teaching profession. The education of these clergy was paid at *public expense*. Smith observed:

> The usual reward of the eminent teachers bears no proportion to that of the lawyer or physician; because the trade of one (the teacher) is crowded with indigent people who have been brought up to it at public expense; whereas those of the other two [professions] (lawyers and physicians) are encumbered with very few who have not been educated at their own expense.[68]

The parallels between the world of Smith and today are tenuous at best, but his supply-and-demand analogy, with other professions, may well be appropriate for the twenty-first century. During the Smith era, greater numbers of people went into the clergy and into teaching because they could not afford to pay for the more expensive education required to become lawyers or physicians. Thus, the numbers of teachers swelled and, according to Smith, as their supply increased their wages declined. The law of supply and demand explains why prices rise and fall in a free market economy and naturally affect teachers. Predating Smith, the theory of supply and demand was explained by John Locke as he sought to describe the natural operation of the market:

> All things that are bought and sold raise and fall their price in proportion as there are more buyers or sellers. Where there are a great many sellers to a few buyers, they use what art you will, the thing to be sold will be cheap. On the other side, turn the tables, and raise up a great many buyers for a few sellers, and the same things will immediately grow dear.[69]

Whether teachers are held dear depends to a degree on their supply. Teachers' salaries may then be at least partially determined by the student population as representative of demand and the quantity of teachers as indicative of supply.

It is safe to say that markets in their natural unregulated state are neither rational nor moral. Justin Fox in his fine work, *The Myth of the Rational Market*, argues that markets cannot be rational because "[P]rices cannot perfectly reflect the information which is available"[70] to the consumer. Importantly, all people cannot be depended upon to be uniformly *selfish* and able to *optimize* their own self-interested wants,[71] and have the same information to satisfy their greed and covetousness. Some people are good and altruistic, a condition that confounds the economic marketplace. Individual motivations may be different, a problem that in market terms produces irrational choices, or at least, do not fit the mold of market theory. So, normal unregulated market assumptions may not apply to the actual supply and demand of the teaching profession. Rational market theory would predict that teachers would seek employment with the highest wages and lowest credentialing costs; however, the behavioral predilections of each prospective teacher are not identical and, therefore, their market response to employment will differ dramatically.[72] Also, in their native state, unregulated markets cannot by their nature be moral and just. Justness must emanate from a source external to the workings of the market itself.[73] Where the market is applied to teacher supply and demand without regulation applied to teacher qualifications, certifications, standards, and the like, any and all incompetent individuals could hold themselves out to the public as teachers, and the consequences would be a society rife with ignorance fed by an oversupply of uneducated low-paid persons holding themselves out to the public as teachers. Such is not a defensible moral condition for either the student or the teacher. Thus, the market must be regulated by the state.

In its simplest form, the supply and demand principle may be applied to teacher salary determination as depicted in Figure 10.4. Demand, D_T, represents both the private demand for public education and the spillover demand of society in general. Private demand is the want of families with school-age children who desire education for individual benefit. At the same time, there are social or spillover benefits to society so that everyone gains from having an educated citizenry. The curve indicates that at very high salaries, fewer persons will buy education and fewer teachers will be demanded. The supply curve, S_T, suggests that as teacher salaries rise, assuming other salaries remain constant, more persons will enter the teaching profession.

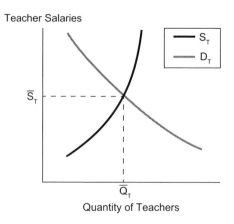

Figure 10.4 Supply of and Demand for Teachers

Source: James A. Richardson and J. Trent Williams, "Determining an Appropriate Teacher Salary," paper delivered at American Education Finance Association Conference, New Orleans, 1981.

On the other hand, as Adam Smith observed, as the supply of teachers dramatically increases, salaries will fall.

The simplicity of the marketplace model, however, may be deceiving where public school teachers are concerned. The demand for teachers is, of course, affected by the numbers of students to be educated, but beyond this, as Richardson and Williams have observed, the value and significance that the public places on education must be taken into account if one is to relate salaries to demand.[74] In other words, the level of salaries or price may not relate directly to demand in public education as it does in the marketplace of Adam Smith. In public education, salary levels are largely controlled by the legislature, particularly in states where various types of caps and limitations have been placed on local school districts to enhance overall statewide equalization. Also, the state legislature establishes certification standards and, regardless of the numbers of students, can effectively regulate the supply of teachers by raising or lowering the requirements necessary for entering the teaching profession. Minimum accreditation standards for schools are also governed by the state, which may greatly influence the demand for teachers. Many other factors contribute to the state's influence on both the supply of teachers and the demand for their services. For example, the state may choose to expand services to certain types of students, such as the disabled, and thereby create a substantial new demand for teachers trained in that area.

Therefore, public school teachers' salaries are not established in the conventional sense of the marketplace. Hale suggested that the economic pattern has aspects of both an oligopoly and an oligopsony.[75] An oligopoly is a market structure in which a small number of firms control a major portion of an industry's output. In education, the state legislature is in a position to control both the certification of teachers and the accreditation of schools, both of which can significantly affect supply. An oligopsony is a market structure in which there are relatively few buyers with a high degree of concentration or interdependence.[76] When a state greatly influences the demand for teachers through the creation or deletion of programs, alteration of required pupil-teacher ratios, or other policy determinations, the result is a *kinked demand curve*, deviating substantially from the expected curve under unregulated market conditions.[77] States with greater numbers of local school districts and lower levels of state regulation could be expected to evidence greater adherence to the supply-and-demand characteristics of the marketplace than states with few school districts and more centralized control.

Regardless of how one classifies the teacher market, it is certain that it does not function and probably should not function in the traditional sense of the *laissez-faire* market. No one will deny, however, that the forces of the marketplace are present and undoubtedly influence the salaries of teachers. As to whether these forces actually control teachers' salaries remains highly debatable.

ECONOMIC EFFECTS OF TEACHERS

We have always understood that students receive real consumption and economic benefits passed on to them by their teachers. Having knowledge is largely an immeasurable value to the individual and, at least at the beginning, the conveyance of knowledge must be formalized in schools taught by teachers. The overall individual and social benefits of education are discussed in another chapter; however, here we briefly discuss the question of the effects of teachers that may be long term having both consumption and monetary value as the result of being exposed to knowledge provided by a teacher.

In recent years much of the school reform efforts have implicitly assumed that much of the student achievement lag of the United States compared to other post-industrial countries is largely attributable to the poor quality of teaching in United States public schools. As a caveat in this regard, Richard Rothstein makes a very cogent point.[78] He observes that back as far as 1966 and the Coleman Report,[79] federal and state governments tended to minimize the importance of the adequacy of funding for low-income and African-American students and instead emphasized a presumption that poor quality teaching is the principal culprit for disparity in achievement. He writes that "School reformers claim today that improving teacher quality will equalize achievement, in the absence of addressing poverty of many black children,"[80] structural poverty is the foundational issue. Rothstein further reasons that "the fear of education reformers today, the discussion of social and economic impediments to learning, will only lead to 'making excuses' for poor teaching and will undermine support for federal aid to education."[81] Thus, there is one school of thought that believes that greater concentration of funding for low-income children, in addition to a more aggressive system of family social transfers, is the remedy, and yet another view that hypothesizes the problem of low achievement can principally rest at the doorstep of the teachers whose poor quality teaching is the cause of lower levels of student achievement.

Rothstein suggests that the federal and state governments should have a more pronounced objective: reduce the systemic, adverse socioeconomic effects on poverty children and their families "to prepare them to take advantage of good instruction."[82] Most importantly, Rothstein writes that

> It is incontrovertible . . . that steady improvement in black students' performance is inconsistent with the conventional claims of reformers that teachers of

disadvantaged students are poorly trained, have low expectations, and fail to exert their best efforts. Data cannot disprove this story, but they do not support it either.[83]

A primary premise, however, of a major portion of the reform agenda is that funding is now adequate, and the primary route to improvement of student achievement is by stimulating greater efficiency and effectiveness of teachers.

TEACHER EFFECTIVENESS

Basing teacher pay, promotion, tenure, and retention on teacher effectiveness criteria is currently highly problematic. As in all aspects of human endeavor, there exist spans in the quality of performance, and teaching children is not an exception. Teachers are no different than physicians, lawyers, architects, engineers, etc. The trick, in the realm of education, is to reduce or remove teachers with lesser capacities at the lower ranges of the quality curve. There is some evidence, indeed, common knowledge, to support the assertion that many teacher training institutions convey an inferior quality of pedagogy. Yet, there is little reliable extant research to verify that training in the United States is of lesser quality than in other advanced countries of the world. However, parenthetically, we should note, as shown earlier, that teachers in the United States work longer hours and are paid at a lower rate per student than teachers in the majority of other post-industrialized countries. Moreover, significantly, as discussed in Chapter 3, equality indicates that teachers in the United States' public schools deal daily with greater percentages of children in relative poverty than is confronted by teachers in other nations with advanced economics. Be that as it may, however, the need for improved methods of teacher evaluation should be on the agenda of all state education systems, in concert with appropriate priority to the adequacy of teacher compensation.

The state-of-the-art in the measurement of teacher quality is rather primitive, but as greater data are gathered concerning student achievement and teacher quality, more reliable studies may emerge. For example, a widely reported study by Chetty, Friedman, and Rockoff[84] has shown that students of high quality teachers have a significantly higher rate of students attending college than do students of teachers of lesser quality and, importantly, students who have been taught by higher *value-added teachers* have greater life-time earnings. Moreover, exposure to higher value-added teaching has other important social side effects such as reduction in the probability of teen births of female students.[85] Although the statistical interpretations of this study have been challenged, the logic of the conclusions offered by the study is not unreasonable, i.e., that good teaching has long-term positive effects on students in their adulthood. Baker,[86] a leading school finance expert, in critiquing the Chetty et al. study, points out that the study does not really solve the statistical problem of isolating the value added by a high quality teacher from the *classroom effect* of types, capabilities, and synergies of other students in the classroom or the nature and quality of the school environment. Further, Baker questions the Chetty et al. conclusions regarding the high rate of economic returns to the students in adulthood.

In essence, the Chetty et al. study makes a good case, but probably not a compelling case based on a remarkable synthesis of data, to draw the following conclusions: *First*, that teachers' own *value-added* quality scores are in some measure predictive of future students in adulthood growth and economic benefit and, *second*, that a student's experiences in the classroom with a teacher of high quality have statistically significant effects on the student's economic livelihood in adulthood.[87]

Value-Added Teacher Productivity

A developing field of research commonly known as Value-Added Modeling (VAM) is now getting considerable attention in some economic and education research circles. The basic purpose of these studies is to identify teacher capabilities or incapacities that have some causality relationship with student achievement. In other words, these studies seek to anatomize, assess teacher quality in definitive aspects that can be shown to relate to student test scores.

Probably most prominent among these efforts is the project funded by the Bill and Melinda Gates Foundation and titled, *Measures of Effective Teaching* (MET); its purpose is "to improve the quality of information about teaching effectiveness."[88] The heart of the project is to estimate the causal effects in a laboratory-type setting in which over 3,000 teachers are rated by students over time according to several dimensions of teaching, such as control of classroom, care for students, etc.[89] The study has two basic premises: (1) teacher evaluations should depend to a significant degree on student achievement gains and, (2) classroom observations of teachers validly foretell student achievement gains.[90] A major first report of the MET Project[91] listed four essential findings:

1. In every grade and subject, a teacher's past track record of value added is among the strongest predictors of their students' achievement gains in other classes and academic years;
2. Teachers with high value added on state tests tend to promote deeper conceptual understanding as well;
3. Teachers have larger effects on math achievement than on achievement in reading or English Language Arts, at least as measured on state assessments; and
4. Student perceptions of a given teacher's strengths and weaknesses are consistent across the different groups of students they teach. Students seem to know effective teaching when they experience it.[92]

These conclusions have been only marginally accepted by researchers and have been roundly panned by some, especially Jesse Rothstein, a prominent economist from the University of California at Berkeley, who, citing MET research procedures, pointed out that the principal conclusion of the study, to wit, "a teacher's past track record of value-added is among the strongest predictors of students' achievement gains in other classes and academic years . . . is not supported by the underlying analysis."[93] The MET study, Rothstein says, "examines only student perception surveys and few would expect these to be among the strongest measures of teacher effectiveness."[94] The totality of Rothstein's comprehensive critique is well-reasoned and learned casting much doubt upon the MET study design, findings, and conclusions. Yet, though MET is probably flawed, the pursuit of measures of teacher effectiveness by such studies does contribute to the store of research literature in the improvement of teaching in the public schools. However, use of such value-added studies as a basis for live evaluations of teachers utilized for teacher pay purposes, promotions, tenure, and, even, dismissals would be highly questionable knowing the state-of-the-art.

Merit Pay

Merit pay may become more defensible as teacher evaluation or value-added systems become more sophisticated and reliable. Many citizens contend that salaries for teachers should be related in some way to their competency. Whenever salary increases are proposed, there are those who indicate that they would support higher salaries for the most competent teachers, but they are opposed to salary increases for all teachers. They insist that industry has had merit pay plans for a number of years and has used them successfully, and that these plans could readily be adapted for use by the public schools.

Many teachers, administrators, and teacher organizations have opposed merit pay. They call attention to the difficulty of establishing an objective and effective plan for determining merit and point to the danger that subjective factors cause in any merit rating plan.

Proponents of merit pay, on the other hand, argue that the disrepute of merit pay plans is contrived by teacher unions who feel that their ranks are weakened when teachers are forced to compete for salary increases. Proponents further maintain that rewards or incentives for teachers would elicit desirable competitive responses as are found in other occupations where money is the incentive for greater productivity. Merit pay proposals are, therefore, most often justified on two basic assumptions.

1. Teachers are motivated primarily by monetary incentives; and
2. The opportunity for extra compensation can be effectively used to motivate teacher behavior throughout their teaching careers.[95]

There is an argument that these two assumptions are not necessarily valid. Regarding money as the primary motivator, some research has shown that the monetary incentive lacks uniformity among teachers. For example, money is more important to young teachers while working conditions and an agreeable teaching atmosphere are of greater importance to more experienced teachers. For example, Greenberg and McCall[96] found that career teachers are more likely to seek transfer or reassignment to schools in higher socioeconomic neighborhoods not so much for pay increases but for non-pecuniary rewards. Sewell[97] found similar propensities in experienced teachers who were willing to remain in inner-city schools if their class sizes were reduced, they were given paraprofessional support, and their working conditions were generally improved.

Thus, merit pay alone may well fail to fully provide the motivation and incentive suggested by its proponents. At the very least, research suggests that what drives some teachers to greater performance may not produce the same effects on others. In this regard Johnson notes,

> While teachers unquestionably deserve higher salaries and will not remain in teaching without financial security . . . incentive strategies for keeping our best teachers in schools should center on the workplace rather than on the pay envelope.[98]

STATE METHODS OF ALLOCATING TEACHER SALARIES

As previously discussed, state laws and regulations may directly affect salary provisions in the local school districts. If only limited funds for schools are provided from state sources, the salary level in each school system will be determined chiefly by the willingness and the ability of the citizens in the district to provide funds for schools. When state funds are meager, salaries in the least wealthy districts generally may be expected to be much lower than salaries in the most wealthy. However, when an adequate and realistic state funding program has been established, all districts, regardless of their wealth, should be placed in a satisfactory position to provide the necessary funding for teacher salaries.

Many states, because of concern about this problem, have taken one step or another relating directly to salaries. Several have established state minimum salary schedules. West Virginia apparently established the first state minimum salary law in 1882. By 1937, 20 states had some kind of minimum salary legislation.[99] There are three major types of state minimum salary laws relating to teachers:

1. Those that provide a state minimum salary schedule recognizing both training and experience;
2. Those that fix a minimum salary on the basis of two or more flat rates but with no recognition of experience; and
3. Those that fix a minimum salary as a single flat amount.

The interest of states in minimum salary schedules first developed largely because salaries paid in some districts were obviously inadequate. Those who were concerned with the problem apparently assumed that if a state minimum salary schedule could be established by law, the problem would be solved. With the early salary schedules, however, the modern ones still have difficulty in establishing salaries that are scientifically based. Those states that have utilized salary schedules have generally identified teacher training and experience as the primary criteria for salary schedule differentials. Other considerations such as teacher locale, teaching results, and merit factors have been used, but only infrequently.

Principles that should ideally be used to create salary schedules have been occasionally borrowed from collective bargaining agreements and other education and teacher welfare guidelines. A partial list of these principles includes:

1. The *comparability principle*. Teachers should have a wage comparable to other white-collar employment;
2. The *education and training principle*. The schedule should provide incentive for higher levels of knowledge and pedagogical expertise;
3. The *improvement principle*. Teachers should be given incentive to refurbish their knowledge of their particular field of learning;
4. The *experience principle*. Experience is preferable to inexperience and retention of professional teachers is desirable;[100]
5. The *teaching load principle*. Some measure of work load should be considered (e.g., number of pupils per teacher); and

6. The *efficiency principle*. The schedule should be designed so as not to encourage the retention of poorer quality teachers. In this regard some form of merit factor accompanied by periodic evaluations of professional growth should be included.[101]

It is safe to say that no state to date has successfully merged all or even a majority of these principles in a state salary schedule.

One of the problems with state salary schedules is uneven fiscal capacity of local school districts. Many poor districts cannot maintain desirable pupil–teacher ratios, provide a satisfactory length employment, or conform to the minimum salaries required for all teachers. Since state laws in many cases require a certain minimum length of term, the only alternatives for these districts have often been to maintain the minimum school term, increase the number of pupils per teacher, employ only teachers with minimal training and experience, and/or to levy onerous local taxes. Thus, the state salary schedule must be fiscally equalized if it is to work effectively, compensating for the fiscal incapacities of poorer school districts.

Most states in recent years have attempted to develop an adequate and realistic plan for financing schools from state and local revenues. Progress in this direction facilitates provisions for reasonably adequate salaries, rather than emphasizing minimum salaries as the basic salary policy.

DETERMINATION OF LOCAL SCHOOL DISTRICT SALARY POLICY

Salary policies constitute one important aspect of general personnel policies. There has been a decided tendency during the past quarter of a century for school districts to develop written statements relating to salary policy. These are usually developed with the cooperation of the staff or through the joint efforts of representatives from the staff and citizens of the community. These groups, however, can only recommend salary policy, since the local school boards may or may not approve their recommendations. However, when committees have done a good job of developing sound policies, the recommendations usually have been approved by the boards without major altercation. The purposes of salary policies are to give assurance to the community that sound procedures will be observed in compensating employees, to give assurance to the staff that recognized policies rather than haphazard procedures will be followed, and to provide guidance to administrators and their staff in developing satisfactory procedures for obtaining and retaining the services of competent personnel.

Suggestions for salary policies or schedules have been recommended by a number of studies. The following suggestions may serve as a guide for policy considerations.

1. Meet reasonable competition for good beginning teachers without attempting to offer the highest starting salary;
2. Assure dignified living standards for maturing personnel;
3. Contribute an uplifting influence to the dignity and prestige of teaching in the United States;
4. Help to attract and hold teachers and principals of the highest quality;
5. Stimulate increased substantive graduate study through the master's degree;

6. Encourage study, research, and travel beyond the master's degree;
7. Provide markedly distinguished salaries for teachers who, in the tradition of the community, make substantial and measurable contributions to education in the school district;
8. Provide a relatively long period of salary improvement before reaching maximum, with safeguards against automatic advancement if a teacher's work is unsatisfactory;
9. Provide an opportunity for teachers to achieve professional distinction and corresponding salary recognition without having to forfeit their teaching position for administrative or supervisory positions;
10. Recognize special economic factors in the community; and
11. Serve the long-term needs of the district, the board of education, and the faculty, and not be merely a temporizing, stopgap measure.[102]

It is also desirable for policies to include adequate leaves for study, conferences, travel, and generous fringe benefits for all personnel. The importance of adequate provisions for in-service education is likewise necessary board policy in addition to the salary policies proposed.

SALARIES OF ADMINISTRATIVE AND SUPERVISORY STAFF

In some school systems, administrators and supervisors are considered to be paid for their administrative competence and leadership qualities and their salaries have no relationship to the salaries of teachers. Many hold that there should be some defensible relationship between the salaries of teachers and those of administrators and supervisors. On the assumption that some relationship should exist, attempts have been made to devise a formula that can be used in developing a schedule for salaries of administrators and supervisors. Should the salaries of administrators and supervisors be based on a ratio to teachers' salaries and automatically increased as teachers' salaries are increased? Should administrators represent the board of education in collective bargaining with teachers if their salaries are tied to the teacher salary schedule? Should school administrators represent the board in the collective bargaining process?

For some time, many school systems that provide summer or extended-year programs for some students and teachers have recognized that a time factor should be utilized to determine the additional compensation for teachers who serve beyond the regular school term. Thus, one-ninth, as in most universities, or some other specified salary supplement would be added to the salary of a teacher who served for a month beyond the regular term of nine months. This factor is also utilized for administrators and supervisors who serve beyond the customary term.

The other factor commonly utilized in the index is a responsibility ratio that can be utilized for all professional personnel who have assignments requiring special competencies and extra responsibilities. For example, if the responsibility ratio for a regular teacher is 1.0, the ratio for the head of a teaching team might be 1.15, and for a principal of a larger school the ratio might be 1.75 to 2.00. Such ratios need to be developed on the basis of detailed studies and analyses made with the concurrence of the entire professional staff.

A narrowing of the differential between salaries of teachers and administrators is desirable. Factors to be considered are:

1. a greater public concern for quality instruction; and
2. a growing public concern that too few financial resources of the school districts are actually directed to the classroom.

Whatever the reason, the movement toward higher relative pay for teachers would appear to be desirable. Measures taken to make classroom teaching positions more attractive to prospective teachers would undoubtedly serve to enhance the quality of the public schools by attracting and retaining better qualified teachers.

SALARY ADJUSTMENTS BASED ON A COST-OF-LIVING INDEX

Cost-of-living escalators have become commonplace in collective bargaining agreements in the private sector in recent years and have been increasingly built into government wages and programs.[103] Many school systems have related salaries to the Consumer Price Index. The idea has been proposed in several other school systems and has even been considered by some states as a basis for determining the amount of the apportionment for salaries appropriated through the state-aid program.

Some of the arguments in favor of using a cost-of-living index to adjust amounts in a salary schedule are:

1. Many discussions and controversies regarding salary adjustments could be avoided;
2. The use of an index would provide an automatic plan for adjustments and would eliminate subjective factors; and
3. Salaries would automatically increase or decrease as the cost of living increased or decreased.

The primary objective to a cost-of-living index is that it constitutes a political assumption that inflation is inevitable and has to be accommodated. Unfortunately, cost-of-living factors help to drive inflation and reduce the effectiveness of government in dealing with inflation. One must ask if indexing is an appropriate policy of government, for if teachers are allowed to index, then shouldn't everyone else in all parts of the economy do the same? On the other hand, teachers will not want to be excluded from the indexing game if everyone else is participating. Thurow characterizes the dilemma in this way: "Each of us organizes to avoid being subject to falling prices. But if we all succeed, we have an economy where inflation is endemic. To stop inflation, someone's income must go down."[104] The question is: Should teachers make the personal sacrifice for the national economy? This is an issue which has not been resolved for any other working group in either the public or private sector.

Another valid objection to such an index, from the teacher's perspective, is that salaries for teachers and other school employees are much less than the salaries paid to many other kinds of workers. Consequently, if cost-of-living index were tied to present salaries, it would merely result in an adjustment upward or downward of salaries that are already inadequate and would not provide for desirable improvements. Many teachers believe that before there is any attempt to use a cost-of-living index to adjust salaries, there should be more realistic and comprehensive studies of standards of living and of budget requirements for various standards of living.

SUMMARY

This chapter gives selected attention to certain personnel policies that bear on school financing and provides specific detail and discussion of teachers' salaries. Of concern is the relative financial condition of teachers in the United States' economy.

Personnel policies that address both the needs of the children and the welfare of the teachers are necessary for a productive educational system. Such personnel policies are affected by the supply of a quality teaching force as well as by the economic and demographic conditions of the school district.

Collective bargaining plays an important role in the welfare of teachers in over half of the states; but, the evidence is inconclusive as to whether, over the long term, teachers' salaries are higher in states and school districts where collective bargaining is practiced.

Teachers have historically been subjected to low levels of compensation. As early as 1776, Adam Smith attributed the low wages of teachers to the plentiful supply. The fact that public school teaching is not subject to conventional market forces with regard to both supply and demand prevents teachers' salaries from being competitive with other white-collar employments. Rather than having the characteristics of an open marketplace the public school teaching profession exists as an oligopoly wherein the state legislature can, if it so chooses, control supply and demand.

The measurement of both the supply and demand of teachers is extremely complex. The supply is generally dependent on the number of teachers continuing in the profession and the number of new entrants. Both variables are dependent on factors such as age of teachers, retention power of the profession, opportunities for other employment, and the like. Further complication is added by the length and number of career breaks and the gender of teachers.

Investment in public schools and the economic conditions of teachers is influenced by the general condition of the economy. In periods of revenue shortfalls, teachers tend to personally absorb or cushion the effects of the economy.

An objective measurement of how much teachers should be paid to provide a quality education is not likely to be found; but, by comparative statistics, the condition of the teaching profession can be broadly determined. If teachers' salaries exceed the rise of inflation it is thought to be good. Also, if teachers' salaries in the United States are relatively better than in other countries, there may be reason to assume some relative elevation of teaching status in the economic system.

Today, teachers' salaries fall short of most other white-collar professions in the United States, but appear to provide greater purchasing power for United States teachers than teachers' salaries in other advanced nations.

State school finance programs may or may not contain salary schedules that force local school districts to pay specified minimums. State salary schedules are, however, frequently employed to assure that state funds flow to teachers or that local school districts will not be permitted to pay below a specified level.

At the local level, teacher salary schedules should be calibrated to attract and retain the highest quality teaching staff available. Considerations that should come into play when fashioning local salary schedules include: comparability to other professions, education level and training desired, incentive for improvement, reward for experience, workload measures, and an efficiency criterion that seeks to attract highly competent teachers and free the school districts of less productive teachers.

Administrators and supervisory staff should be paid in a measured relationship with teachers. Time factors and responsibility ratios may be legitimately employed to provide administrative personnel wages beyond that of teachers. The gap between superintendents' and teachers' salaries today is less than it was in prior decades indicating that teachers' status has improved somewhat. This may be attributable to greater public concern for quality instruction or to a decline in the status of administrators in the eyes of the public in a period of fiscal parsimony.

Merit pay has been employed in some states and/or school districts with the purpose of giving an incentive to teachers to be more productive. Merit pay has a long and controversial history and has been generally opposed by teacher organizations. Critics of merit pay maintain that such selective incentive devices are merely gadgets with no proof of success and, in fact, are a detriment to overall school productivity. Merit pay schemes may be more notable for their failures than for their successes. Such failures have been largely attributed to a lack of clear and measurable performance standards. Yet, most agree that teachers need and desire some incentives to be more productive and rewards for those who are more effective.

Cost-of-living escalators have been included in many salary arrangements, in particular many of those that have been negotiated in a bargaining process. Such indices have been used in other public and private employment. Yet, legislatures and school boards remain reluctant to tie their fiscal fortunes to such provisions.

KEY TERMS

- Certified personnel
- National income
- Noncertified personnel
- National effort for teachers' salaries
- Deflated dollars
- Value-added teacher productivity
- Constant dollars
- Merit pay
- Consumer price index
- Salary index
- Purchasing power parity
- Cost-of-living index

NOTES

1. Anthony Padgen, *The Enlightenment and Why It Still Matters* (Oxford: Oxford University Press, 2013), p. 348.
2. Karl A. Schleunes, *Schooling and Society: The Politics of Education in Prussia and Bavaria, 1750-1900* (Oxford: Berg, St. Martin's Press, 1989), pp. 14, 287–290.

3. Roger J. Sullivan, *Immanuel Kant's Moral Theory* (Cambridge: Cambridge University Press, 1989), p. 8.
4. Ibid., p. 287–288.
5. Ibid.
6. Ibid., p. 299.
7. For a more extensive discussion of this important area see Edgar L. Morphet, Roe L. Johns, and Theodore L. Reller, *Educational Organization and Administration: Concepts, Practices and Issues*, 4th edn. (Englewood Cliffs, NJ: Prentice-Hall, 1982), Ch. 18 and references.
8. *Rankings of the States 2012 and Estimates of School Statistics 2013*, National Education Association, NEA Research, 2012, p. 76.
9. William J. Baumol and Alan S. Blinder, *Economics, Principles and Policies,* 4th edn. (San Diego and New York: Harcourt Brace Jovanovich, 1988), p. 411.
10. Paul A. Samuelson and William D. Nordhaus, *Economics,* 14th edn. (New York: McGraw-Hill, 1992), p. 693.
11. Organization for Economic Cooperation and Development, *Educational Expenditure, Costs and Financing: An Analysis on Trends: 1970–1988* (Paris: OECD, 1992).
12. PISA 2009 Results, Executive Summary. *What Students Know and Can Do: Student Performance in Reading, Mathematics and Science,* OECD, Database.
13. This section is taken primarily from a chapter by Kern Alexander, "Observations on Teacher's Economic Subsidies," in a book titled *Attracting and Compensating America's Teachers,* edited by Kern Alexander and David H. Monk (Cambridge, MA: Harper & Row, Publishers, Inc., 1987).
14. Ellwood P. Cubberley, *State School Administration* (Boston: Houghton Mifflin Company, 1927), pp. 651–652.
15. Ibid., p. 652.
16. Richard A. Musgrave and Peggy B. Musgrave, *Public Finance in Theory and Practice* (New York: McGraw-Hill Book Company, 1980), p. 259.
17. John Kenneth Galbraith, *The Affluent Society* (New York: Houghton Mifflin Company, 1958), pp. 127–128.
18. Ibid.
19. Dan C. Lortie, *School Teachers, A Sociological Study* (Chicago: The University of Chicago Press, 1975), p. 7.
20. Edlow Garrett Barker, "A Cost-Benefit Analysis of Investment in Graduate Education by Virginia Public School Teachers" (Ph.D. dissertation, Virginia Tech University, 1987).
21. Lawrence A. Cremin, *American Education: The National Experience, 1783–1876* (New York: Harper & Row Publishers, 1980), p. 144.
22. Ibid., pp. 146–147.
23. Ibid., p. 364. See also: Willard Elsbree, *The American Teacher: Evolution of a Profession in a Democracy* (New York: American Book Company, 1939).
24. Isser Woloch, *The New Regime: Transformations of the French Civic Order, 1789–1820* (New York: W.W. Norton & Company, 1994), pp. 188–189.
25. Carl F. Kaestle, *Pillars of the Republic: Common Schools and American Society, 1780-1860* (New York: Hill and Wang, 1983), p. 146.
26. Ellwood P. Cubberley, *Public Education in the United States* (Boston: Houghton Mifflin Co., 1934), p. 704.
27. Ibid., pp. 708–709.
28. Ibid., p. 709.
29. Roger Price, *A Social History of Nineteenth Century France* (London: Hutchinson, 1987), p. 327.
30. Ibid., pp. 240–258.

31. Ibid., p. 258.
32. Marjorie Lamberti, *State, Society, and the Elementary School in Imperial Germany* (Oxford: Oxford University Press, 1989), p. 27.
33. Ibid.
34. Karl A. Schleunes, *School and Society: The Politics of Education in Prussia and Bavaria*, 1750-1900 (Oxford: Berg, 1989), p. 108.
35. Ibid.
36. Lamberti, *op. cit.*
37. Ibid., p. 197.
38. Marc Tucker, *Governing American Education* (Washington, DC: Center for American Progress, 2013).
39. Sean Cavanagh, "Another GOP vs. Teachers' Union Battle Emerges in Michigan," *Education Week*, October 2011. See http://blogs.edweek.
40. Tucker, *op cit.*, p. 25.
41. Vincent A. Mahler, David K. Jesuit, and Piotr R. Paradowski, "Political Sources of Government Redistribution in High Income Countries," in Janet C. Gornick and Markus Jäntti, *Income Inequality: Economic Disparities and the Middle Class in Affluent Countries* (Stanford, CA: Stanford University Press, 2013), pp. 157–158.
42. Ibid., pp. 145-172. See also Istvan György Toth and Tamás Keller, "Income Redistribution Inequality Perceptions, and Redistributive Preferences in European Countries," in Janet C. Gornick and Markus Jäntti, *op. cit.*, pp. 173–206.
43. Kern Alexander and M. David Alexander, *American Public School Law*, 8th edn. (Belmont, CA: Wadsworth/Cengage Learning, 2012), pp. 968–969.
44. Ibid.
45. Benjamin A. Lindy, "The Impact of Teacher Collective Bargaining Laws on Student Achievement: Evidence from a New Mexico Natural Experiment," *The Yale Law Journal*, March 2011, Issue 5, Vol 120:1130. See also Emily Cohen, Kate Walsh, RiShawn Biddle, National Council on Teacher Quality, "Invisible Ink in Collective Bargaining," pp. 16–24 (2008), http://www.nctq.org/p/publications/docs/nctq_invisible_ink.pdf.
46. 80 H.R. 3020, Pub.L. 80–101, 61 Stat. 136, enacted June 23, 1947
47. Bureau of Labor Statistics, U.S. Department of Labor, *Union Members, 2012*, January 23, 2013. See also W. Craig Riddell, "Unionization in Canada and the United States: A Tale of Two Countries," ICTWSS Database, cited Kris Warner, Bloomberg, *Dispatches from Economic History*, January 23, 2013.
48. Steven Greenhouse, *New York Times*, January 23, 2013.
49. Bureau of Labor Statistics, Economic News Release, Table 4, "Medium Weekly Earnings of Full-Time Wage and Salary Workers by Union Affiliation, Occupation, and Industry," January 23, 2013.
50. Chris Edwards, "Public Sector Unions and the Rising Costs of Employee Compensation," *Cato Journal*, Vol. 30, No. 1 (Winter 2010).
51. National Education Association, *Estimates of School Statistics 1979–1980* (Washington, DC: NEA, 1980), p. 16.
52. H. Kasper, "The Effects of Collective Bargaining on Public School Teachers' Salaries," *Industrial and Labor Relations Review*, vol. 24 (October 1970), pp. 57–72.
53. Robert Thornton, "The Effects of Collective Negotiations on Teachers' Salaries," *Quarterly Review of Economics and Business* 2 (Winter 1971), pp. 37-46; Robert N. Baird and John H. Landon, "The Effects of Collective Bargaining on Public School Teachers' Salaries: Comment," *Industrial and Labor Relations Review*, vol. 27 (October 1973), pp. 18–35; W. Clayton Hall and Norman E. Carroll, "The Effects of Teachers' Organizations on Salaries and Class Size," *Industrial and Labor Relations Review*, vol. 26 (January 1973), pp.

834–841; David Lipsky and John Drotning, "The Influence of Collective Bargaining on Teachers' Salaries in New York State," *Industrial and Labor Relations Review* 27 (October 1973), pp. 18-35; Donald E. Frey, "Wage Determination in Public Schools and the Effects of Unionization," Working Paper 42E, Princeton University, Industrial Relations Section, 1973; A. G. Balfour, "More Evidence That Unions Do Not Achieve Higher Salaries for Teachers," *Journal of Collective Negotiations in the Public Sector* 3 (Fall 1974), pp. 289–303; and D.C. Zuelke and L.E. Frohreich, "The Impact of Comprehensive Collective Negotiations on Teachers' Salaries: Some Evidence from Wisconsin," *Journal of Collective Negotiations* 6, no. 1 (1977), pp. 81–88.

54. Benjamin A. Lindy, *op. cit.*, pp. 1134–1135.
55. Ibid.
56. Joachim R. Frick and Markus M. Grabka, "Public Pension Entitlements and the Distributions of Wealth," in Gornick and Jänthi, *op. cit.*, p. 364.
57. Ibid.
58. Kathryn M. Doherty, Sandi Jacobs, and Trisha M. Madden, *No One Benefits* (Washington, DC, National Council on Teacher Quality, 2013), pp. i–ii.
59. Stephanie Banchero, "States Faulted Over Teacher Pension Shortfall" (New York: *The Wall Street Journal*, December 13, 2012).
60. Ibid.
61. Robert Clark, "Retiree Health Plans for Public School Teachers after SASB 43 and 45," *Education Finance and Policy*, Fall 2010, pp. 438–462.
62. Doherty et al., *op. cit.*
63. Ibid.
64. The U.S. Department of Labor, Social Security, cited in Doherty et al., *op. cit.*, p., 11.
65. Ibid.
66. Ibid.
67. Ibid.
68. Adam Smith, *The Wealth of Nations*, rev. edn. (New York: Modern Library, 1937).
69. Locke, who lived from 1632 to 1704, was best known for his famous philosophical and political investigations, but he also wrote in pure economics. The quotation comes from his book *Some Considerations of the Consequences of the Lowering of Interest and Raising the Value of Money* (1691), published as *Essay on Interest and Value of Money* (London: Alex Murray & Son, 1870), p. 245.
70. Justin Fox, *The Myth of the Rational Market* (New York: Harper Business, 2009), p. 182.
71. Ibid., p. 178.
72. Ibid., pp. 200–202.
73. Paul J. Zak, Editor, *Moral Markets: The Critical Role of Values in the Economy* (Princeton: Princeton University Press, 2008), pp. 248–249.
74. James A. Richardson and J. Trent Williams, "Determining an Appropriate Teacher Salary," *Journal of Education Finance* 7: 2 (Fall 1981), pp. 193–194.
75. James A. Hale, "The Supply and Demand for Public Elementary and Secondary School Teachers," *Educational Need in the Public Economy*, eds. Kern Alexander and K. Forbis Jordan (Gainesville, FL: University Presses of Florida, 1976), pp. 125–126.
76. Douglas Greenwald and Associates, *Dictionary of Modern Economics* (New York: McGraw-Hill, 1973), p. 409.
77. Hale, *op. cit.*, p. 126.
78. Richard Rothstein, *For Public Schools, Segregation Then, Segregation Since: Education and the Unfinished March* (Education Policy Institute Report, August 27, 2013).
79. James Coleman et al., *Equality of Educational Opportunity* (Washington, DC: Office of Education, United States Department of Health, Education, and Welfare, 1969).

80. Ibid.

81. Ibid.

82. Ibid.

83. Ibid.

84. R. Chetty, J.N. Friedman, and J.E. Rockoff, "Teacher Value-Added and Student Outcomes in Adulthood," *National Bureau of Economic Research*, Working Paper, No. 17699, December 2011, Revised, January 2012.

85. Ibid.

86. See Baker Blog, *School Finance 101*, http://schoolfinance101.wordpress.com/2012/01/07/fire-first-ask-questions-later-comments-on-recent-teacher-effectiveness-studies/.

87. Henry Braun, "Earning from Recent Advances in Measuring Teacher Effectiveness," Brief, *Institute of Education Sciences,* Washington, DC, August 9, 2012.

88. Jesse Rothstein, "Review of Learning About Teaching: Initial Findings from Measures of Effective Teaching Project" (2011), Boulder, CO: National Education Policy Center.

89. Ibid.

90. Ibid.

91. See MET Report, "Learning about Teaching: Initial Findings from the Measures of Effective Teaching Project," Bill and Melinda Gates Foundation, December 10, 2010.

92. Ibid., p. 9.

93. Rothstein, *op. cit.*

94. Ibid.

95. Stephen L. Jacobson, "Merit Pay and Teaching as a Career," *Attracting and Compensating America's Teachers,* eds. Kern Alexander and David H. Monk (Cambridge: Ballinger, Harper & Row, 1988), p. 162.

96. David Greenberg and J. McCall, "Teacher Mobility and Allocation," *Journal of Human Resources* 9 (Fall), pp. 480–502.

97. O. Sewell, "Incentives for Inner City School Teachers," *Phi Delta Kappen* (October), p. 129.

98. Suzan Moore Johnson, "Merit Pay for Teachers: A Poor Prescription for Reform," *Harvard Educational Review* 54 (May), pp. 175–185.

99. National Education Association, Research Division, *State Minimum Salary Laws for Teachers, 1950–51* (Washington, DC: NEA, 1950).

100. "Musical Chairs," *The Economist,* July 17–23, 1993, p. 67. *The Economist* reports that among the advanced industrial nations Japan has the least labor market turnover for all employment with workers having an average of 10.9 years of tenure, Germany is second with 10.4 years, and France is third with 10.1 years. The United States has the greatest rate of labor market turnover, next to Holland with average job tenure of only 6.7 years. Moreover, *The Economist* observes that only 10 percent of young recruits into the U.S. labor force have any type of formal training from their employer, while in both Japan and Germany employer training of young recruits is about 70 percent.

101. Cubberley, *op.cit.*, 1927, p. 656.

102. *Report of the Winnetka Citizens Advisory Committee on Teacher Salaries* (Winnetka, IL: The Committee, 1958), pp. 12–13.

103. Lester C. Thurow, *The Zero-Sum Society* (New York: Penguin Books, 1980), p. 59.

104. Ibid., p. 61.

CHAPTER 11

Public Funding of Private Schools: Charter Schools and Vouchers*

* This chapter was written by Kern Alexander.

INTRODUCTION

Taxpayer funding of private sector interests and enterprises is an issue endemic to the conduct of all governments. The boundaries between the public good and private interests are nearly always indistinct and subject to partisanship and degrees of self-interests. Political parties to a large extent function as adherents and advocates to an array of economic, social, cultural, and religious ideologies that may exhibit considerable strength in gaining taxpayer funding. Active forces advocating privatization of education have increasingly gained political indulgence and support resulting in a major financial restructuring of American education at the higher education and primary and secondary education levels. In higher education it came as a result of the federal government largely abandoning institutional-based financing and redirecting its method of financing to the student, "student choice," via the route of government vouchers (Pell grants)[1] and student loans. A similar fiscal rationale has lately been applied to public elementary and secondary funding for privatized schooling through the mechanisms of charter schools and vouchers. This chapter provides an overview of public funding of *parental choice* in support of charter schools and vouchers for the support of clerical schools.

The creation of charter schools and the public funding of vouchers represent the most fundamental structural changes in American education since the establishment of the public common schools in the 1830s.[2]

Forty-two states and the District of Columbia have charter school laws. Only eight states, Alabama, Kentucky, Montana, Nebraska, North Dakota, South Dakota, Vermont, and West Virginia, do not have laws allowing charter schools. Charter schools have been promoted by both sides of the political aisle.[3] A charter school is a "school established under a contract between public authorities and a private organization or a group of private individuals."[4] Voucher schools are primarily Roman Catholic and conservative Protestant with a small sprinkling of schools for other religious groups and a few that are not sectarian.

CHARTER SCHOOLS

Charter schools are private corporations, the funding for which is provided by state legislatures. Procedures for their creation and funding are a matter of specific state statutory provision. A substantial amount of litigation has ensued as a result of denials of applications for state or local licenses for charter schools.[5] The first charter school in the United States was established in St. Paul, Minnesota, in 1992, and today there are over 5,000 such schools in 42 states, the most active of which are in Arizona, California, Florida, Indiana, Louisiana, Michigan, New Jersey, New York, Pennsylvania, and Texas. An increasing number of virtual charter schools that reach into several states add to this list.

The idea of the charter school found its modern origins in the United Kingdom with school reform legislation introduced by Margaret Thatcher[6] in 1988. Thatcher, the Tory conservative prime minister, invented the idea as a mechanism to bypass Labor-controlled local education authorities. The law enacted by Parliament encouraged local schools, teachers, administrators, and parents to "opt out" from under the local authorities and to obtain direct funding from Parliament. These so-called "opt-out" schools were by statute named "Grant-Maintained Schools" and were designed to be incorporated as privatized business models with *laissez-faire* competitive and entrepreneurial freedom from state regulatory and labor union constraints. Each school was controlled by its own independent board. The effectiveness of these schools has been much debated, and later governments have substantially modified the approach to fashion a more viable structure.

The charter school in the United States, in its most favorable light, seeks to increase the choice of educational programs without fueling private self-interests that separate and segregate children of the community. It places great store in the importance of competition to improve the quality of schools. As Minow observes, charter schools are "anchored in faith in consumer sovereignty and confidence in market-style mechanisms,"[7] and that by such means of competition, the freedom of an educational marketplace will make schools more efficient and productive.

The *charter school* was first proposed in the United States as a definitional alternative to traditional public and private schools, redefining the term *public* to include private schools of a wide range of shapes and structures. The approach as it originated was to permit all private schools to become chartered in their respective states by meeting minimal state-established criteria. These minimal criteria, "roughly corresponding to the criteria many states now employed in accrediting private schools,"[8] would then allow a private school to be "chartered as a public school and granted the right to accept students and receive public money."[9] By this means, any and all private participating schools would *ipso facto* become "public schools" as defined by the new system.[10] Such newly defined "public schools" would retain their independence while avoiding constitutional restrictions that normally apply to the public sector. This "definitional reshuffling," as Henig called it, was proposed earlier by Jencks, who advocated the use of charter schools as a means to achieve the intent of public funding of private schools without actually resorting to tuition vouchers or tuition tax credits. Jencks said that, "a lot of our thinking about the voucher system is based on an attempt to rethink the question of where the line between the public and private should be drawn."[11]

The idea to redefine public schools was advanced by President H.W. Bush in 1992 when he explained that, "[w]hether a school is organized by privately financed educators or town councils or religious orders or denominations, any school that serves the public and is held accountable by public authority provides public education."[12] Henig points out that such an indiscriminate stretch of the label *public* to "cover largely deregulated, market-based systems of educational choice is possible only because the term *public* has been so devalued."[13] In its ungarnished primitive form, the *charter school* is designed to remain private, *sans* public control and accountability. As described by Minow, "These independent schools are intended to operate with public funds, but outside the regulations of the public system."[14]

The early thrust of the charter school concept changed dramatically when President Clinton advocated school choice that could be exercised only in public schools and not in private or parochial schools. As charter schools have developed, however, they have taken on various permutations in state legislation. Moving away from the base form of a private sectarian institution, in keeping with the Clinton definition, the charter school has evolved in most states as a form of quasi-public nonsectarian corporation that must diversify and not discriminate based on race. Federal charter school legislation[15] passed in 1994 and, bearing President Clinton's imprint, defines such schools as having the following features: They are exempted from state and local regulations that inhibit flexible management, yet they are operated under general public supervision and direction, designed with specific educational objectives as their purpose; they are nonsectarian in their programs, admissions, policies, and employment practices and are not affiliated with a sectarian school or religious institution; they are free of tuition and fees; they must be in compliance with federal civil rights legislation; they must provide for admission of students by lottery; they must comply with federal and state financial audit requirements as do other public elementary and secondary schools; they must meet required federal, state, and local health and safety requirements; and they are required to operate in accordance with state law.[16] This law makes it clear that the concept of the *charter school* adopted by the federal government is a school operating under public auspices and control. It is not a private school defined as public. Yet, these requirements apply only if a state desires to receive federal funding for the planning, design, and implementation of charter schools.

President Obama has made the public charter school one of the central aspects in his educational reform initiative. Taking a page from Margaret Thatcher's "opt-out" schools competitive business model, the United States Department of Education emphasizes, "the need for additional effective education entrepreneurs to join the work of reforming America's lowest performing schools."[17] To stimulate states to place emphasis upon the development of more charter schools, the Obama government has monetarily incentivized states to make charter schools an integral part of a larger reform initiative named the "Race to the Top" program.[18]

Charter School Structure

Whether a charter school is for-profit introduces an important feature relevant to the grant of federal funds. The United States Court of Appeals, Ninth Circuit, has held that for-profit charter schools are ineligible to receive federal funds under both the Elementary and Secondary Education Act (ESEA) and the Individuals with Disabilities Education Act (IDEA).[19] The for-profit issue was the focus of a suit that arose from a United States Department of Education (USDOE) audit revealing that the State of Arizona had distributed over $1 million to 11 private for-profit organizations that operated 75 charter schools. Federal law, the court observed, limited, by definition, the authorized recipients of federal funds to public schools and "non-profit institutional day and residential schools."[20] Neither ESEA nor IDEA permits federal funds to flow to for-profit schools or organizations. The court observed that although both of these major federal subventions have been amended and refined, Congress has not modified its express intent to make for-profit schools eligible to receive funding.[21]

Thus, the state laws for charter schools vary widely, indicating the diversity of social, economic, religious, and political forces that define state education policy. Some state laws permit wide private discretion and little state or local control. For-profit schools may receive state funds and local funds. Also, state laws differ in that some may limit the number of charter schools or the number of students permitted to enroll in such schools. Others designate various agencies that can sponsor charter schools, such as state boards of education, local school boards, boards of community colleges, boards of public university, state boards of regents, or special state charter boards. In some states, charters may be granted to schools that were previously public schools or schools that were previously private. The exact legal status of charter schools may also vary among states. Charter schools may be independent entities, corporate entities, or nonprofit organizations, or may remain an organizational component of the local school district. A range of conditions may govern employment of personnel, including independent employment with the charter school as the employer or as public employees remaining within the personnel system of the local school district. In a few states, charter schools are subject to public collective-bargaining laws, and in other states the statutes are silent on the subject, and, if they are considered private, are subject to National Labor Relations Board (NLRB) regulations. Therefore, state charter school legislation ranges from sincere attempts to improve the public schools, by providing greater parental choice and involvement in the educational process, to the obvious efforts of simply diverting public funds for private gain.

Charter School Litigation

In a relatively short time, charter school litigation has become a cottage industry. In Pennsylvania alone over two dozen appellate court cases have been launched. The most important legal issues involve the effect of the charter school concept in changing the structure of public schools. The essence of charter school legislation among the states is that it shifts the control and conduct of the school from public school boards, made up of elected local citizenry, to private boards, removed from direct public influence, governed by board members who are not elected by the public. The contractual arrangement between state boards of education and/or local boards and the charter school corporate entity is, thus, a major structural change in how the public common schools of the United States have historically functioned as organs of the polity.

Cases that probably best describe the basic structural change in public education are increasingly better defined by ongoing litigation. Importantly, it should be noted that, by and large charter schools avoid public school teacher unions and administrative "inconveniences" such as tenure for teachers and much of the attendant complications emanating therefrom that vest teachers with constitutional property and liberty interests. Yet, the charter schools themselves may have governmental protections from liability for tort claims,[22] and/or have immunity from state laws that specify conditions and procedures for private contracts with public bodies.

Private School Rationale

Proponents of privatization of public elementary and secondary education, i.e., charter schools and voucher schools, argue that public tax funds should be diverted from public school instruction to private and parochial school instruction. Their rationale for such redeployment directly to charter schools and via vouchers to clerical schools is threefold. First, that *efficiency* of public expenditure will be enhanced if public schools engage in *competition* with private schools for public funds. Second, a large segment of opinion has existed since the founding of public schools that a portion of tax funds for education should be placed under clerical control. Third, that *competition* is the best means to enhance the schooling of youth, a mantra of conservative economists led in the United States by Milton Friedman, now deceased, a former economist at the University of Chicago. The latter position of clerical control has been the stance of the Roman Catholic Church and conservative Protestant sects, as well as that of Islamic countries in support of Madrasses, for hundreds of years.

The idea of the economic worthiness of *competition* and *laissez-faire* capitalism has been tirelessly advanced in recent years by private school proponents, Hoxby, Hanushek, Rivkin, Peterson, et al.[23] Hoxby enunciates a strong endorsement of Catholic school education and the economic virtues of choice, competition, and generally the reduction of government enterprises.[24] All of her research seeks to buttress her belief in the viability and efficiency of the unfettered economic marketplace and the advantages of ecclesiastical instruction. Hoxby argues that public policy, generally, and education policy, in particular, is best devised by economists who, by means of the economic marketplace, have a better understanding of educational policy than do "education policymakers whose eyes glaze over at the thought of learning more about taxes than they need to know in order to avoid being audited."[25] Hoxby obviously has little regard for education policymakers who by training are not professional economists. She unalterably maintains that school choice by parents is the key to better and more efficient education. In that light, she observes that the "school choice debate is . . . plagued by confusion about *supply* of schools of choice,"[26] and that if "we wish to understand what the supply of schools would look like under choice, it is . . . useful to know the preferences of parents who are most bound by the constraints" of school choice programs.[27] Hoxby is much concerned that Roman Catholic schools were largely denied funding until June 28, 2002, when the United States Supreme Court in *Zelman v. Simmons-Harris*[28] upheld the Cleveland, Ohio, voucher program, the funds for which primarily went to fund parochial schools. She exclaims that, "For a long time, I have thought that the church-state issue in school choice debates was a red herring,"[29] but the belief that a full scale voucher program "would lead to a great many more students to attend religious schools . . . is simply incorrect."[30] She, thus, concludes that "in urban areas where school choice could be an active force, very few voucher recipients would choose a religious private school if a full blown voucher program were in effect."[31]

Most importantly, Hoxby asserts that the "threat of competition" is actually what matters in school productivity and fiscal efficiency. In keeping with the competition theory, Hoxby argues that the mere threat of competition will benefit not only private schools, but also the public schools, due to public funding of private schools.[32] She uses as examples of the benefits of competition the United States health care system, before the Affordable Care Act, Health Insurance Reform, Healthcare Reform (PPACA, ACA),[33] and the trucking and parcel services industries.[34]

In support of for-profit charter schools, she maintains that "managers of for-profit schooling companies believe that there are *economies of scale* in schooling because the firm can pay lower prices for its inputs if it pools purchasing, curricular research and development, and information processing across multiple schools."[35] Hoxby, in her research, has never found contradictions to the theory that competition, parental choice, and funding private schools will not enhance educational productivity so long as the public funding of the private schools is of such magnitude as to induce competition.[36] She concludes that, "If all schools in the United States experienced high levels of the traditional forms of choice, school productivity might be as much as 28 percent higher than it is today."[37]

Hanushek, of The Hoover Institution, a conservative think tank, like Hoxby, has written extensively to the effect that privatization of education is preferable to the current system of public schools in that public funding of private schools by means of direct funding of charter schools and church schools will excite a competitive fervor of market forces and make all schools more efficient and effective. Hanushek cites, approvingly, research that supports the assertion that Roman Catholic schools generally, "on average, outperform public schools."[38] He, further, cites his own "regression results that suggest competition improves school quality in larger areas with substantial numbers of school and district choices."[39] In that vein he argues that "more competition tends to increase teacher quality."[40]

Peterson, of Harvard University, a strong and persistent leader in opposition to public schools, cites the effects of vouchers in certain urban settings to have a positive effect on African-American students, but not for students of other ethnic backgrounds.[41] From surveys of parents who used publicly funded vouchers to enroll their children in private schools, he and colleagues theorize that positive achievement gains were due to more homework, closer communication with families, and smaller classes.[42] Without evidence, he implies that public schools do not have such attributes.

Questioning Charter School Effectiveness

Most studies of charter schools and voucher schools have not been as sanguine about privatization's educational productivity and efficiency as have the aforementioned researchers. For example, Bifulco and Bulkey,[43] in a review of the effects of charter schools have found the following:

1. Charter schools tend to hire younger less experienced teachers and more uncertified teachers than typical public schools. Thus, in order to turn a profit, "charter schools must maintain relatively high rates" of teacher turnover. Less experienced teachers "undermine instructional cohesiveness."[44]
2. Qualitative rather than quantitative studies indicate that testing is more the regimen in charter schools than in public schools.
3. Research on parental involvement in charter schools versus public schools is inconclusive; however, various studies show that it is the involved parents who choose to send their children to charter schools in the first place.
4. Charter schools typically enroll a higher percentage of white students than the nearest traditional public school. Bifulco and Ladd, using longitudinal data, found that white charter school students transfer from public schools that have higher percentages of black students to charter schools that have lower percentages of

black students, "suggesting that charter schools exacerbate racial isolation for both groups."[45]

5. More college-educated parents choose to transfer their children to charter schools than non-college-educated parents.[46] Thus, where and if charter schools are found to be more productive it is largely because of parental knowledge, home and family factors, and not attributes of the charter schools.

6. Asymmetric preferences, that is, parental choices of schools that don't necessarily relate to quality of instruction, suggest that "racial composition" influences parents' choices of charter schools.[47] Race is a "powerful predictor of the schools [that] parents choose."[48] The several studies on the issue of race as an important factor in parental choice "suggest that differences in preferences related to the racial composition of schools are playing a role in generating student segregation in charter schools."[49]

Segregation by choice is a transcending issue to charter and voucher schools. The issue regarding charters is elaborated upon by Carnoy, Jacobsen, Michel, and Rothstein in a book titled *The Charter School Dust-Up*.[50] They point out that parental choice generally results in African-American families choosing schools that have more black students while white families choose charter schools that have fewer black students.[51] These researchers conclude that: "The possibility of increased segregation is one of the costs policymakers should consider in evaluating charter schools' impact . . . charter schools could be causing harm even if their achievement were neither better nor worse than that of regular public schools."[52]

The Center for Research on Education Outcomes (CREDO) at Stanford University has conducted two large sample studies in 2009 and 2013 involving charter school data collected from 16 and 27 states, respectively.[53] The studies present an array of information and conclusions that neither fully supports the concept of charter schools nor rejects it. The study does make at least three structural observations regarding confounding variables of charter schools.

1. The study points out the problem of asymmetric parental choice in that parents will tend to enroll their children in charter schools for reasons other than quality instruction. The study implicitly questions the typical parent's "access to information and ability to discern academic quality from other attributes" that are unrelated to quality instruction.[54]

2. The CREDO study also points out that low-performing charter schools generally inflate the statistics of overall charter school quality when the poorer quality charters close their doors and the children are forced to return to public schools, or the charter schools may reincorporate under a different name and recruit a new crop of students.[55] The dropout rate of low-performing charter schools tends to lead to uncertainty regarding charter schools when they are compared to traditional public schools.

3. The CREDO study interestingly observes that comparisons between charter schools and traditional public schools are skewed because in instances too difficult to quantify, low-performing charter schools "are not being shut quickly enough and some low-performing charter schools are being permitted to replicate."[56]

Table 11.1 Performance of Charter Schools Compared to Their Local Markets of Traditional
Public Schools (TPS) in 27 States

Subject	Worse Growth than TPS	Growth No Different than TTP	Better Growth than TPS
Reading	19%	56%	25%
Math	31%	40%	29%

Source: Center for Research on Education Outcomes, "National Charter School Study," 2013, http://credo.
stanford.edu/ documents/NCSS%202013%20Final%20Draft.pdf, Table 20, p. 86.

To simplify, thus, in comparing a complexity of data, CREDO indicates that charter schools and traditional public schools reveal mixed results. Table 11.1 gives a brief and reasonably intelligible summation of the CREDO analysis.

As shown in Table 11.1, in the 27-state CREDO study, charter schools' performance compared to local markets of traditional public schools, their mutual student markets for reading were worse than traditional public schools in 19 percent of the instances, about the same in 56 percent, and better in 25 percent of the cases, indicating overall that for reading, charters were marginally better. The opposite was true for math where the charter schools were worse than the traditional public schools in 31 percent of the cases, about the same in 40 percent, and better in 29 percent of the instances. Such numbers, while interesting, are certainly not supportive of a privatization overhaul of the school system of the United States, particularly in view of the risk of increasing racial and ethnic segregation of education and the implicit potential for rising fractionalization of society.

Another large scale analysis that draws into question the alleged superiority of charter schools over traditional public schools was reported by two highly regarded researchers, Christopher A. Lubienski and Sarah T. Lubienski, in a book titled *The Public School Advantage: Why Public Schools Outperform Private Schools,* published in 2014.[57] The charter school part of this study, that drew conclusions regarding charter school effectiveness, utilized the huge NAEP (National Assessment of Educational Progress) 2013 database of 190,147 fourth graders and 153,189 eighth graders from a sampling of public and private schools, among which there were 7,485 schools at fourth grade level and 6,092 schools at the eighth grade level. The Lubienski study revealed that *charter school students'* average mathematics achievement scores were lower than the scores for students in traditional public schools.[58] Based on their statistical analyses, these researchers directly challenge the faith in "marketism" that is so fervently advanced by proponents of charter schools. The idea that public funding of private corporations to run schools in competition with traditional public schools is severely impugned by the Lubienski study. They show that "*marketism* may actually be hindering or even diverting schools in the independent sector from higher achievement as they use their freedom (*from state control and standards*) in embracing stagnant, less effective curricular practices"[emphasis added].[59]

Negative Market Effects of Charter School Competition

A negative effect of charter school competition that has not been widely considered or researched has been highlighted by a report by Moody's Investors Service,[60] 2013, and Standard & Poor's in 2012. Moody's, Standard & Poor's, and Fitch are major bond rating houses that determine the risk of indebtedness of school districts, state governments, and the federal government. Investors utilize these ratings to adjudge the relative risk that they may incur in the purchase of bonds. These bond rating services fell under great criticism for not properly analyzing and foreseeing the bank mortgage crisis and the derivative fiasco that was instrumental in causing the Great Recession of 2008. These three major bond rating houses have vast resources and employ huge stables of fiscal analysts who rate bond issues with letter grades from Aaa down to D (see Chapter 16 for further discussion of bond rating services). As the rating declines the interest rates demanded by buyers will rise until a bond sale will fail because the agency (in our case public school districts) selling the bonds cannot afford the higher interest rates.

In August 2013, Standard & Poor's Ratings Services issued an advisory noting that the charter school enrollment will continue to grow at about 13 percent per year. Despite this rapid growth rate, state per pupil funding, for both charter schools and traditional public schools, is expected to have difficult funding problems. Standard & Poor's points out that new IRS rules could prohibit charter school companies from participating in state retirement plans, which may affect 95,000 charter school employees. In spite of this warning and uncertainty, Standard & Poor's concluded that states will probably lift charter school enrollment caps and increase charter school state funding, making it easier for charters to acquire facilities.[61]

Moody's, however, is not as optimistic about the future of bond ratings for either charter school companies or traditional public schools.[62] It is Moody's view that the competition, the marketplace for bonds, may have a detrimental effect on both school sectors. In particular, according to Moody's analysts, the competition for students and state funding may likely, particularly in economically weak urban areas, exacerbate an underlying economic and demographic stress that is already visited upon urban public school districts. Moody's cites the reality of charter school competition that materially harms the traditional public schools by pulling enrollment away from them and, thereby, reducing their state funding. In most instances the revenues would decline more rapidly than the school districts could reduce expenditures by cutting programs and services.[63] Particular fiscal damage will befall older core cities such as Cleveland, Detroit, Kansas City, St. Louis, and Washington, DC where one-fifth of enrollments have already moved to the private charter school companies.

Moody's cites four major risk factors that probably will create debt problems for school districts. *First* is the demographics of declining public school enrollments. *Second*, as mentioned above, is the limited ability to quickly cut expenditures by reducing the numbers of employees, services, and operators. *Third*, the traditional public schools are weighted down by state regulations and fiscal approval processes. The state, on the other hand, permits relatively liberal capital approval procedures for the new charter corporations with few limits, generous funding, and few or no limits on growth. *Lastly*, school districts that are not fiscally integrated into community, city, or state government, that permit them to benefit from overall fiscal strength of a collaborative public approach to capital financing, will suffer most.[64]

At the present time Moody's median rating for traditional public schools is at A3, considerably higher than charter schools, which have a median rating of only Baa. This rating evidences the unreliability of charter school corporations, significant risks for investors, due to "volatility of charter school enrollments, limited capital funds, little revenue raising flexibility,"[65] and uncertain business practices. These problems of the charter schools are not generally conditions that exist in public school districts that have public scrutiny and reliable accounting systems.[66] The lack of fiscal reliability of charter schools is exhibited by the fact that their average credit quality Moody rating falls below private independent and clerical schools.[67]

Charter School Funding

Charter school companies are funded with public tax dollars that follow students enrolled in such schools. Charter schools, as noted above, are private school companies, either for-profit or not-for-profit, incorporated in a state. These private corporations are given by law much more budgetary autonomy than traditional public schools. In order to fund charter schools, states usually deploy public school district dollars directly to the charter schools without measurably increasing state appropriations for all elementary and secondary education.

State laws fund charter schools on a per-student-enrolled basis. Shen and Berger of the National Conference of State Legislatures[68] divide the technical aspects of state charter school funding into three types. The first type that is used in eight states provides charter schools with revenue on a per-pupil basis equal to that of the public school district from which the students are recruited. This is done by the state requiring the local public school district to pass on to the charter school the state and local revenues that the public school district receives.

The second type of formula described by Shen and Berger is based on "per-pupil revenue of the authorizer."[69] In most instances the *authorizer* is the traditional public school district that permits the establishment of the charter school and allows deployment of its students to the charter school. This funding approach is utilized in 29 states. Some states may allow the authorizer to retain a small percentage of the revenues for administrative costs. In some of these states, the legislation permits the traditional school district to raise additional local funds by permitting an *override* above the regular property tax limit, in which case the revenue from the override is not shared with the charter school.[70]

A third type of formula is to provide charter school funding from a state-wide per-pupil appropriation. Five states and the District of Columbia employ this method of allocation. Such funding schemes seek to provide charter schools with funds comparable to traditional public schools.

The consequences of these funding approaches may have implicit incentives, including the obvious strategy for charter school operators to recruit students from school districts that have higher levels of revenues per pupil. Overall, charter schools may receive marginally less per-pupil funding from state and local sources than do traditional public school districts. Reasons for some charter schools to receive less taxpayer funding than the public school district may be quite reasonable and attribut-able to the following:[71]

(a) Traditional public schools have greater fixed per-pupil costs such as facilities in that the public school district has the same building maintenance costs even after charter schools have siphoned off their students and current operating funds;
(b) Students in the public schools may have differing educational needs, some more costly than others. For example, charter schools typically have fewer students with disabilities than do school districts that require greater current operation expenditures;
(c) Charter schools in most instances do not have the additional costs for pupil trans-portation, health care, and school food services that may be required of public schools but are not fully funded by either state or federal funds; and
(d) Charter schools in most cases, as noted above, have high turnover of inexperi-enced, uncertified teachers who are not salaried on the same basis as better quali-fied traditional public school teachers.[72]

BOX 11.1

Academic Results: Charter Schools vs. Traditional Public Schools

Advocates of charter schools claim they produce better academic results than traditional public schools and cost less because of lower overhead. Neither of these promises have been fulfilled. The academic results of charter schools are inconsistent because the sector itself is so variable . . . Most studies consistently conclude that on average the academic results of charters are no better than those of traditional public schools serving the same sorts of students.

Source: Diane Ravitch, *Reign of Error* (New York: Alfred A. Knopf, 2013), p. 167. See: Matthew Di Carlo, "The Evidence on Charter Schools and Test Scores," Albert Shanker Institute, December 2011.

Charter School Inefficiency

One measure of school efficiency is to determine precisely the funds that filter down to the student for classroom instruction. As the above discussion indicates, charter schools nationwide, on average, have not been shown to be more produc-tive or efficient than traditional public schools. One main budgetary marker of effi-ciency has been traditionally the costs of administration relative to the total school budget or to the total school budget for instruction. A 2012 study by David Arsen and Yongmei Ni[73] found that charter schools in Michigan "spend more on admin-istration and less on instruction than traditional public schools."[74] Michigan public schools spend 60.5 percent of their current operating budgets on instruction while charters spend only 47.4 percent. In Michigan, for-profit charter schools constitute about 80 percent of all charter schools.[75] As to causes for high administrative costs and low instruction costs for both not-for-profit and for-profit charter schools, a sample inspection of the budgets of both types indicates that administrative costs are high in for-profits because that is where the profit can be identified, and for non-profits it is the administration function where administrative salaries are reported. The cost of instruction is low because most charter schools employ young uncertified teachers who are poorly compensated and have no contracts of employment or simply work at the pleasure of the employer. In contrast, all traditional public school teachers must be certified and hold written contracts of at least one year or have continuing employment.

Table 11.2 contains descriptions for major budgetary functions such as administration, instruction, pupil support, building expenditure, and staff support for the traditional public schools and charter schools in the State of Ohio.

Ohio is a large state that has privatized education extensively through the vehicle of charter schools. In 2011 there were 326 operating charter schools with about 95,000 students of the total of 1.8 million students in the state. Ohio, too, had a very large number of school districts numbering 610 in 2011. In analyzing the relative expenditures for the aforementioned five budgetary functions of both public schools and charter schools in Ohio for fiscal years 2006 through 2011, William Phillis and Mike Fuller, school finance experts, found that charter schools are highly inefficient and

Table 11.2 Descriptions for Major Budgetary Functions in the State of Ohio

1) Administration Expenditure per Pupil covers all expenditures associated with the day to day operation of the school buildings and the central offices as far as the administrative personnel and functions are concerned. Items of expenditure in this category include salaries and benefits provided to all administrative staff as well as other associated administrative costs.

2) Instructional Expenditure per Pupil includes all the costs associated with the actual service of instructional delivery to the students. These items strictly apply to the school buildings and do not include costs associated with the central office. They include the salaries and benefits of the teaching personnel and the other instructional expenses.

3) Pupil Support Expenditure per Pupil includes the expenses associated with the provision of services other than instructional that tend to enhance the developmental processes of the students. These cover a range of activities such as student counseling, psychological services, health services, social work services, etc.

4) Building Operation Expenditure per Pupil covers all items of expenditure relating to the operation of the school buildings and the central offices. These include the costs of utilities and the maintenance and the upkeep of physical buildings.

5) Staff Support Expenditure per Pupil includes all the costs associated with the provision of support services to school districts' staff. These include in-service programs, instructional improvement services, meetings, payments for additional trainings and courses to improve staff effectiveness and productivity.

6) Total Expenditure per Pupil is the combination of all of the components of expenditure listed above.

Source: Ohio Department of Education, FY 2011 District Profile Report, http://education.ohio.gov/GD/Templates/Pages/ODE/ODEDetail.aspx?page=3&TopicRelationID=1441&ContentID=122224.

expend on average a much larger proportion of their budgets on administration than on classroom and instructional services. Shown in Figure 11.1, *administrative expenditure* as a percentage of total budget for charter schools was about double that of public schools.[76]

In 2011 the percentage of the budget for public schools that was devoted to the *administrative* function for public schools was 12.96 percent of total budget, while the charter schools recorded a very high 26.20 percent.

Instruction is the largest function of school budgets, and as Figure 11.2 shows, public schools consistently expended a higher percentage of their total budgets for instruction than did charter schools.

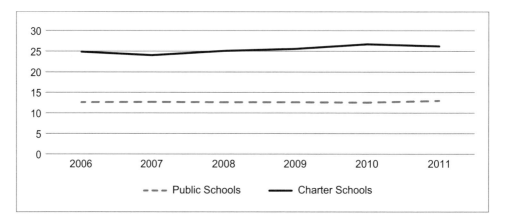

Figure 11.1 Ohio Public School and Charter School Average Administrative Expenditure as a Percentage of Total Budget, 2006–2011

Source: Based on data generated by William Phillis and Mike Fuller.

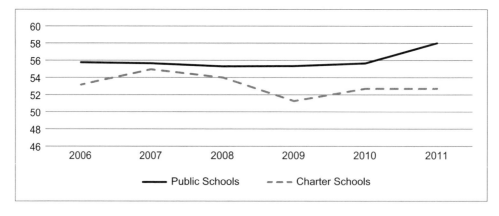

Figure 11.2 Ohio Public School and Charter School Average Instructional Expenditure as a Percentage of Total Budget, 2006–2011

Pupil support expenditure, illustrated in Figure 11.3, is another measure of how much of the school budget finds its way down to the students. By this measure, the public schools' percentage in 2011 more than doubled the percentage provided by charter schools, or 9.99 percent compared to 4.00 percent.

Building operation expenditure is a relatively large part of a school budget that quantifies how much of the budget is centered on the operation of school facilities as compared to the total school district budget. By this measure, the public school average expenditure was again much higher than charter schools, indicating relatively greater expenditure devoted to the operation of the school buildings, as shown in Figure 11.4. In 2011, the Ohio public schools expended 20.18 percent for building operation while charter schools expended 11.69 percent.

Staff support, a very small percentage of the total school budget, along with administrative expenditures, were the two functions for which expenditure percentages were higher for the charter schools. With regard to *staff support*, a small part of the budget, the percentage was 5.42 in charter schools compared to 2.64 in public schools. The higher percentage of expenditure for staff support in charter schools probably reflects the costs of a high turnover rate of tending staff in charter schools.

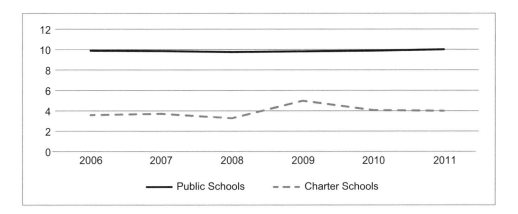

Figure 11.3 Ohio Public School and Charter School Average Pupil Support Expenditure as a Percentage of Total Budget, 2006–2011

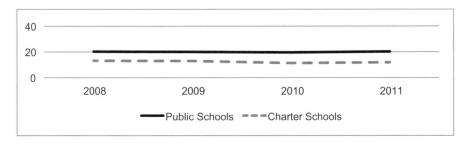

Figure 11.4 Ohio Public School and Charter School Average Building Expenditure as a Percentage of Total Budget, 2006–2011

Charter schools typically do not provide teachers with tenure and in many cases no annual contracts; thus, job security for teachers is tenuous and uncertain and teacher turnover is high, requiring an ongoing concentration of funding for inexperienced new teachers.

The most revealing comparison of percentages, however, is the very high cost of administration that is incurred by charter schools. The Phillis and Fuller study did not seek to determine why *administration* costs in charter school budgets are so very high. Regardless, their study reveals that a much higher percentage of public school expenditures ultimately rests in student instruction rather than in administrative overhead as in charter schools.

VOUCHERS FOR CHURCH SCHOOLS[77]

A voucher is a coupon valued at a predetermined amount of public money that is conveyed to a private or parochial school by the parent when their child is enrolled, whereupon the school and parent endorse the voucher and the school claims the public money from the state or local school district. As noted previously, vouchers that provide public funds for Roman Catholic or other clerical schools have been ruled by the United States Supreme Court to not violate the Establishment Clause of the First Amendment.[78]

Milton and Rose Friedman, in their book *Free to Choose,* proposed and defended vouchers as a method of funding education. The Friedmans, as arch *laissez-faire* economists, viewed public common schools as a socialistic holdover from another age. The Friedmans, however, expressed a major caveat regarding vouchers in that they believed that government vouchers for parental choice of schooling was desirable for a wealthier society that had achieved a reasonably high level of equality. According to the Friedmans, parents in a nation with high conditions of wealth and equal distribution of income could afford to pay larger shares of the cost of education than parents in a poorer nation with disparate incomes among the people. They said, "[I]t would appear that the wealthier a society and the more evenly distributed is income within it, the less reason there is for government to finance schooling."[79] According to these criteria of wealth and income equality, the United States, as evidenced in other chapters of this book, is a badly disparate nation ranking near the bottom of the OECD countries. Thus, presumably a voucher scheme would not be well suited for the United States. It is this theory of diverting the cost of education onto the users, via tuition and fees, many of whom cannot afford it, that has produced the higher education financing debacle in the United States where student debt is now at $1.3 trillion and rapidly increasing, more than the total credit card debt of all Americans for all purposes.

Carl, in his book, *Freedom of Choice: Vouchers in American Education,*[80] 2011, reviews the state and federal voucher initiatives in the United States since the 1950s and has concluded that there have been four distinct political groups that have advanced vouchers for privatization of education: (1) whites in the South who sixty years after the 1954 *Brown* decision still seek segregated schools by means of private school choice, (2) parochial school supporters in the North, (3) racial and ethnic minorities in the nation's big cities who desire a privatization by means of parental choice, and (4) political and religious conservatives who do not agree with the concept of public common schools.[81]

Voucher History

Vouchers or similar devices are not new; they have been used as a conduit to move public funds to the private sector, not only for education, but also for various health, welfare, and other functions of government as well. Yet, vouchers are most closely understood in the public's mind as devices to funnel money from general taxation to church schools. The voucher's connection with the struggle between religious schools and public schools goes back, at least, to the French Revolution where, in 1793, the Catholic Church thwarted the French government's efforts to create a system of public schools, and in its place, initiated a system whereby parents were given vouchers for cash to employ teachers and form schools that best suited them. The voucher committed the state to pay the tuition (*rétribution scolaire*) for each student at a standard rate.[82]

BOX 11.2

Struggle between Religion and Public Schools

In predominately Catholic countries, notably France and Italy, and later, almost every country in Latin America, Catholics and anticlerical liberals engaged in protracted struggles over matters of public education. [I]n the English-speaking Protestant North Atlantic, the German and Irish Catholic diaspora of the 1840s thrust the religious problem into center stage . . . As one American Catholic writer put it in 1850, the battle over religion and education is "the fierce contest in Ireland; the same in France; the same in Belgium; the same in Prussia and the petty states of Germany; the same in Bavaria; the same in Austria; the same in Piedmont . . ." The education issue became especially volatile in the United States.

Source: John T. McGreevy, Professor of History, University of Notre Dame, *Catholicism and American Freedom: A History* (New York: W.W. Norton & Company, 2003), pp. 37–38.

Vouchers were again proposed in France after the Franco-Prussian War when Bismarck and the Prussian armed forces besieged Paris and soundly defeated France. Many French citizens in looking for scapegoats blamed the emerging public schools for the disaster of the War. Their mantra was that "the Prussian teacher won the war."[83] A proposal for vouchers to improve education was proposed to a French parliamentary commission in 1872 by providing money for religious school vouchers, similar to the religious school vouchers in Indiana in 2011. The French people, having experienced decades of church and state struggles over the control of education, rejected the voucher funding scheme[84] and followed, as Furet has written,[85] with a public school system. The French public school was finally advanced and achieved by Jules Ferry in his great manifesto of April 10, 1870, in which he called for public school instruction to provide "education in its full sense. The idea of the secularization of the state and of non-clerical, free and compulsory education formed [with] the cement of republic ideology."[86]

Vouchers and Racial Segregation

In the modern era, the use of tuition vouchers for private schools in the United States did not arise in any significant degree until the public schools were racially desegregated after 1954 and tuition vouchers were used in the South to circumvent the Equal Protection Clause of the Fourteenth Amendment. Most notably, in an attempt to nullify the effects of *Brown v. Board of Education,*[87] the Virginia legislature enacted a tuition voucher law in 1956, and an amended one in 1959, that permitted the closing of public schools and the opening of private, segregated academies.[88] Per the Virginia legislation, a private group formed a school for white children only, and the Board of Supervisors of Prince Edward County awarded the parents tuition vouchers and tax credits to attend. In the case of *County School Board of Prince Edward County v. Griffin,*[89] the Virginia Supreme Court upheld the validity of the law. On appeal of the question to the United States Supreme Court, the public school closing and the tuition voucher and tax credit scheme was held to be in violation of the Equal Protection Clause of the Fourteenth Amendment.[90] Thus, the tuition voucher as a means for conveying public funding to private schools in circumvention of constitutional protections established a lamentable legal precedent in race relations.

Church and State: Federal Funding

Without reviewing the entire compendium of disharmony regarding the philosophical and ideological differences regarding public schools, religion, civil rights, and parental self-interests, suffice it to say that a combination of forces, to a great extent, finding a watershed in the Civil Rights Act of 1964 and the Elementary and Secondary Education Act (ESEA) over a long range of evolution, created a political condition that resulted in today's parental choice and voucher movement. The Great Society had two important effects. *First*, in aiding desegregation and human rights it activated Southern voters' opposition to civil rights. *Second*, the ESEA statutorily sanctified the idea of government funding of religious schools. The public funding of clerical schools came about as a political compromise in order to acquire the needed parochial school vote in the Congress that had always opposed federal aid for education because at that time public funds could not constitutionally flow to Roman Catholic Schools. In order to gain the clerical school vote in Congress, the Johnson Administration seized on the "child benefit theory" as a compromise solution; government money going to parochial schools was for the "benefit of the child" and not for the benefit of the church. Augustus F. Hawkins who for many years served on the House Committee on Education and Labor gave President Johnson credit for "resolving the two great barriers to federal aid."[91] *First*, Johnson resolved the fear of federal funds relative to racial desegregation by establishing that the federal government, by means of the Civil Rights Act of 1964, was going to be involved in desegregation "whether federal funds flowed to schools or not."[92]

Secondly, according to Hawkins, President Johnson mitigated the parochial school vote in Congress, about 100 strong, by taking on the "separation of church and state" issue by resorting to the "child-benefit" idea, the theory having gained traction in an earlier Louisiana case involving the state's loan of textbooks to parochial schools. Fraser writes that, "Hawkins noted that Catholics had opposed previous aid bills because they did not benefit parochial schools."[93] He pointed out that Johnson, through ESEA language, "changed the terms."[94] ESEA, said Hawkins, was "crafted on the basis that the aid was not to the school but to the individual student, [t]his removed . . . a lot of the opposition."[95] Johnson's team reviewed over three decades of constitutional law to arrive at this solution.[96] The loan arrangement for parochial schools was the heart of Title II of ESEA. With regard to Title I of ESEA, Johnson seized upon the fine line drawn in another Supreme Court case that permitted the release of students from the public school campus to attend religious services elsewhere.[97] This "release time" logic morphed into the "dual enrollment" that permitted Roman Catholic school students to have access to Title I funds for instruction.

The Johnson government also enacted the Higher Education Act of 1965 which incorporated the idea of student grants and loans rather than institutional grants. The benefit to student rather than institution circumvented the problem of church and state in higher education, a key issue, in that the vast majority of institutions of higher education were and are denominational, and the issue of providing taxpayer money to such institutions was not resolved until the 1971 United States Supreme Court case of *Tilton v. Richardson*[98] which held that grants to sectarian colleges under the Higher Education Facilities Act of 1963 did not violate the Establishment Clause of the First Amendment.[99] Aid to students versus aid to institutions is "one of the oldest issues"[100] in education. From the GI Bill to the Johnson Great Society, and the Higher Education Act of 1965 to President Johnson's "child benefit" compromise under ESEA, the idea of student voucher grants, as opposed to institutional grants, gained much credibility by the mid 1960s and early 1970s.

The school voucher is, thus, of long lineage and has to do with public propagation of ecclesiastical institutions. Vouchers, as explained above, are basically a method of appropriation of public funds to church schools through the conduit of parental choice. By inserting the parent between the state and the church, the legislature circumvents constitutional restraints that possibly may be forbidden under the Establishment Clause of the United States Constitution or compel support of religion prohibitions of state constitutions. This voucher approach to aiding religious schools was sanctified by the United States Supreme Court in its rejection of the separation of church and state doctrine as set forth by James Madison in his *Memorial and Remonstrance against Religious Assessments,* 1785, and Thomas Jefferson's *Act for Establishing Religious Freedom,* 1779, in a series of recent United States Supreme Court cases.

The separation of church and state standard that had been clearly enunciated by the Supreme Court in *Everson v. Board of Education* in 1947[101] was overturned and effectively abrogated by the present Supreme Court in two decisions, *Agostini v. Felton*[102] (1997) and *Zelman v. Simmons-Harris*[103] (2002). In *Agostini*, Justice O'Connor, writing for the majority of the Supreme Court, said,

> The doctrine of *stare decisis* (precedent) does not preclude us from recognizing the change in our law . . . As we have often noted, "*stare decisis* is not an inexorable command," but instead reflects a policy judgment . . . Our Establishment Clause jurisprudence has changed significantly . . . We therefore overrule . . . those decisions . . . inconsistent with our current understanding of the Establishment Clause . . . [104]

That new jurisprudence of the Establishment Clause is the legal basis on which the Cleveland, Ohio, voucher program was upheld in *Zelman*. The *Zelman* case legitimated the idea that the parent, not the state, makes the decision to give taxpayer's money to the clerical school and church.

BOX 11.3

Public Money for Religion: The New Jurisprudence

. . . there is no doubt that the State could, consistent with the Federal Constitution, permit [a public voucher program for students] to pursue a degree in devotional theology . . . [a State can provide public funds for] students to attend pervasively religious schools so long as they are accredited.

Chief Justice Rehnquist, *Locke v. Davey*

Federal Voucher Policy

The strength of the voucher, privatization, and aid to religion has permeated not only the federal government's recent faith-based domestic policy, but its foreign policy as well, influencing the World Bank and the International Monetary Fund to require tuition voucher systems in developing countries.[105] Domestically, economic and social forces have combined to establish a national political agenda that aggressively advances privatization of education. In response, President George W. Bush announced a voucher plan for the FY 2004 budget for the District of Columbia, the only school system operated directly by the federal government.[106] Earlier, in July 2002, a presidential commission under the Bush Administration recommended empowering parents to exercise choice for students served by the Individuals with Disabilities Education Act (IDEA).[107] Also, the statute, *No Child Left Behind* (NCLB), in its original form, was designed to permit students to opt out of failing public schools and, with vouchers, attend church-related and private schools. Before NCLB was amended in the United States Senate, under the leadership of Senators Edward Kennedy and Christopher Dodd, NCLB would have followed the Florida voucher plan that provided incentive for students to leave public schools that had failed to achieve statewide assessment benchmarks and to obtain vouchers for enrollment in other public schools or private religious schools. This is the approach to funding clerical schools via vouchers that was used in Ohio, Indiana, Louisiana, and other states.

Recent State Voucher Initiatives

An early tuition voucher program established for Milwaukee, Wisconsin, in 1990 and expanded in 1995 was designed to provide vouchers to students from low-income families to attend private or religious schools. On review of the Milwaukee voucher plan, the Wisconsin Supreme Court held that it did not offend the First Amendment, nor did it violate Article I, Section 8 of the Wisconsin Constitution which prohibits money to "be drawn from the treasury for the benefit of religious societies, or religious or theological seminaries."[108] The Wisconsin court disagreed with the plaintiff's contention that the voucher aid benefitted the church. The court concluded that the "primary effect" of such funds was not to the benefit of the religious school if the state funds were washed through a third party. The Wisconsin court said, "Public funds may be placed at the disposal of third parties so long as the program on its face is neutral between sectarian and nonsectarian alternatives and the transmission of funds is guided by the independent decision of third parties."[109] The legal contest over this voucher plan ended when the United States Supreme Court denied *certiorari*,[110] and the Wisconsin court's ruling prevailed.

In 1995, the Ohio legislature enacted the Cleveland voucher program which provided funds for tuition at private and parochial schools. In upholding the Cleveland voucher program in the aforementioned case of *Zelman v. Simmons-Harris*,[111] the United States Supreme Court established the long sought-after precedent by church groups that expounded a constitutional justification for voucher aid to church-related schools. Chief Justice Rehnquist, writing for the majority, relied on a neutrality or non-preference rationale, saying that the "program permits the participation of *all* schools within the district, religious or nonreligious . . . Program benefits are available to participating families on neutral terms, with no preference to religion."[112] According to the Court, the fact that "46 of the 56 private schools . . . participating in the program are religious schools does not condemn it as a violation of the Establishment Clause."[113] *Zelman* is the definitive legal statement regarding vouchers and church-state relationships in America. Under this decision, it would be difficult to envisage any type of government aid program, vouchers or otherwise, to church schools that could be so overtly religious that the present Supreme Court would strike it as a violation of the Establishment Clause of the First Amendment.

Voucher School Fiscal Accountability and Performance

Most of the public tax money for vouchers goes to the Catholic Church that owns and operates the largest private school system in the United States, indeed in the world. At least two essential issues arise with regard to the allocation of tax money to this large school system: (1) *fiscal accountability* and (2) *educational effectiveness* and *performance*.

First, concerning *fiscal accountability*, the Catholic school system has a corporate structure governed by canon law. Regulations for public fiscal accountability and transparency are always subject to the world of centuries' old Roman Catholic Church practices, both spiritual and temporal. Thus, the limits of public fiscal accountability as they intersect Church policy are uncertain at best. Fiscal accountability depends on the beneficiary as seen by both church canon law and state law. As a technical matter, state voucher school revenues conveyed to the Catholic Church are held by the beneficiary, for Church purposes, the *juridic* person.[114] A *juridical person* is described by canon law, thusly, "Juridical persons have the status of a moral person by divine disposition."[115] Under "divine disposition," the parish is the corporation, the juridical person, with one physical person in charge, the diocesan bishop. Therefore, the bishop, so vested by Church law, is the individual with ultimate parish control over the school voucher money and the conduct of the parochial school. The actual fiscal boundary between the state and the church is uncertain.

Second is *effectiveness*. The issue of school performance or effectiveness in comparing public schools to voucher schools is of particular importance. Do students in such private schools actually, academically, outperform students in traditional public schools? As mentioned above in reference to *marketism* and charter schools, one of the most definitive studies to date measuring school effectiveness was conducted by Christopher A. Lubienski and Sarah Theule Lubienski in their aforementioned book titled, *The Public School Advantage: Why Public Schools Outperform Private Schools*.[116] With regard to *voucher schools*, Roman Catholic and conservative Christian schools, the researchers found that when measuring school outputs based on a cross-sectional analysis of NAEP (National Assessment of Educational Progress) for 131,497 students from 5,377 schools, in mathematics achievement, Grade 8, and controlling for both student and school demographic differences, test score means of public school children "are significantly higher than those of Catholic and conservative Christian schools and statistically equal to means for Lutheran and other private schools." This study shows that "when compared [to] public schools, the mean mathematics achievement of schools with similar demographics/location is a statistically significant 3.8 points lower for Catholic schools and a significant 10.6 points lower for conservative Christian schools."[117] Overall, with the same statistical methodology applied to mathematics NAEP achievement scores for the Fourth Grade and the Eighth Grade, the results indicated that school factors accounted for very little of the differences among types of schools.[118]

In a second analysis of *voucher schools*, another set of data, Early Childhood Longitudinal Study, Kindergarten Class of 1998–1999 (ECLS-K), were utilized to measure gain or value added while students were in elementary school. The database for the study included 9,791 students in 1,531 public and private schools, 1,273 in public and 258 in private. The racial make-up for those two groups showed that public schools had 13.0 percent African-American students, Roman Catholic schools had 4.0 percent, and other private schools had 6.0 percent.[119] The public schools had substantially higher proportions of low-income and minority students and higher numbers of students with disabilities. After accounting for the student background factors, the Lubienski analysis showed that over the range of the data, Kindergarten to the end of Fifth Grade, measuring from initial mathematics achievement test scores, the academic gains for the period of five years were nearly identical for public school and Catholic school children.[120] In the most revealing part of the analysis, see Figure 11.5, the Lubienski study showed, using the ECLS-K to Fifth Grade mathematic achievement scores, that public school student gains exceeded student gains in both Roman Catholic and other private schools. In other words, value added by public schools in those elementary school years was greater than for either Catholic schools or other private schools. The Lubienskis concluded as follows,

> After controlling for demographic background issues in order to isolate school effects, students in public schools start out scoring the lowest of all groups when they enter kindergarten, but they learn at least as much as "other private" school students during elementary school, and their gains substantially outpace those of Catholic school students.[121]

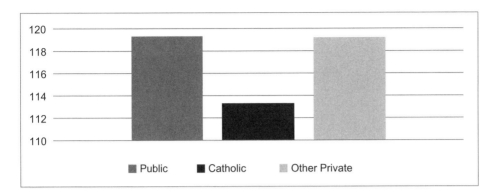

Figure 11.5 ECLS-K Fifth Grade Mathematics Achievement after Adjusting for Demographics and Kindergarten Scores.

Source: Christopher A. Lubienski and Sarah Theule Lubienski, *The Public School Advantage: Why Public Schools Outperform Private Schools* (Chicago: University of Chicago Press, 2014), p. 91. Copyright © 2014 by The University of Chicago. All rights reserved. Reprinted by permission of University of Chicago Press.

Therefore, the actual motivation for states to create state-funded voucher programs for Roman Catholic and other private schools must be for reasons other than school efficiency and productivity.

These data do not support the notion that parental choice and the competitive educational marketplace is a panacea for the alleged ills of public elementary and secondary education in the United States. Such is particularly troubling when one considers that fiscal accountability in the private sector cannot and will not approach the level of transparency due to the inherent nature and constructs of religious and private corporations. Moreover, the Lubienski study calls into question the parental choice and marketplace theory that undergirds the public funding of both charter schools and clerical voucher schools.

Methods by which States Fund Church Schools

States fund clerical and other private schools by a combination of statutory provisions for vouchers, tax credits, tax deductions, property tax exemptions, and pupil transportation. For example, Indiana and Ohio all have such provisions. The state voucher funding of clerical and private schools is, itself, fluid with expanding eligibility requirements and increases of funding. The eligibility and funding criteria are as follows.[122]

States with No Cap on Vouchers:

- Arizona: Students with disabilities and students attending public schools with D or F in state grading system are eligible. The amount funded is 90 percent of the amount the school district would have received in state funding for each student.
- Florida: Disabled students with Individual Education Plans (IEPs) are eligible. The amount funded is the same as the public school would receive for each student.

- Georgia: All students with household incomes up to 150 percent of the free and reduced price lunch level are eligible. The amount funded is the same as the amount the public school would receive minus federal funds.
- Louisiana: All K–12 students with household incomes up to 250 percent of federal poverty guideline and K–8 students with disabilities and IEPs are eligible. The amount funded is the same as the state per-pupil allocation. Special education students receive up to 50 percent of the state per-pupil allocation.
- Maine: Students residing in territories with no public schools are eligible. The amount funded is the same as statewide average per-pupil allocation.
- Mississippi: Special education children diagnosed with dyslexia are eligible. The amount funded is the same as the state's base per-pupil funding plus federal.
- Ohio: Has programs based on income (funded at about $5,000 per student), a program for students from low-performing schools (funded at about $5,000 per student), a Cleveland Tutoring Voucher Program (funded at about $6,500 per student), scholarships for children with disabilities (funded at about $20,000 per student), and scholarships for children with autism (funded at about $20,000 per student).
- Oklahoma: Students with disabilities and IEPs are eligible. Annual funding is set by appropriation.
- Utah: Students with disabilities and IEPs are eligible. The amount funded is determined by the state formula for disabled children.
- Vermont: Children in territories with no public schools are eligible. The amount funded is the same as the amount set for nonresident tuition average for public schools.
- Washington, DC: Students from households with incomes up to 150 percent of federal poverty guideline are eligible. The amount funded is $8,136 for grades K–8 and $12,205 for grades 9–12.

States with a Cap on Vouchers:

- Indiana: All students with household incomes up to 150 percent of the free and reduced price lunch and siblings of children already receiving vouchers, and all students in F schools as determined by state rating system, are eligible. The amount funded is 90 percent of state per-pupil funding appropriation amount on a sliding scale related to income.
- Wisconsin: There is no cap in Milwaukee, but a cap of 500 in Racine. Students from families with household incomes up to 300 percent of federal poverty guideline are eligible. The amount funded is the same as public school funding.

PARENTAL CHOICE COMPETITION AND ASYMMETRIC INFORMATION[123]

Charter schools are creatures of the spirit of capitalism,[124] and it is theorized that public funding of them will increase competition, making all schools more efficient and academically better, especially public schools. Vouchers are basically of another genre, the age-old pressure of established religious organizations to obtain public money for the inculcation of particular religious beliefs. For the economic "spirit of capitalism" theory to work, it is hypothesized that parents as "rational people will make choices as to the education of their children in perfect markets."[125] In the realm of economics, this reasoning is called the "rational expectations hypothesis" or the "efficient markets hypothesis."[126]

The "efficient markets" idea applied to schools via parental choice means that parents will, in their wisdom, utilize public money to send their children to private schools, and that *ipso facto* the education level of the nation rises commensurate with the level and intensity of competition among parents in choosing private, clerical, and/ or corporate charter schools. For the education level to rise requires, of course, that parents make rational decisions relative to quality education. Essential to the concept is that parents have the knowledge necessary to make informed educational choices. In a perfect market, information is presumed to "flow like water – faster than water,"[127] and it is necessary that those things irrelevant to quality education, or even detrimental to it, are not present in parental decision making. If parental choice is not based on quality education and instead the school choices are rooted in race, religion, wealth, ethnicity, or some other non-educational value, then you will have "imperfect competition." There is considerable research that shows that parents, in selecting charter schools, tend to move their children toward those schools that match their own race, thus increasing racial segregation.[128] The same is obviously true of religion, as parochial schools testify,[129] and migration to persons with like wealth and income requires no citation. The issue of ethnicity segregation and charter schools has been a source of considerable litigation.[130] Imperfect competition would result in the overall decline in the quality of education.

Rational Expectations

In the economic marketplace, "rational expectations" serve as the engine to improve the economy. At bottom, these expectations of individuals and corporations foster efficiency, production costs fall, and profits increase. Improvement of educational quality via a scheme of parental choice, however, is much more complex. If the state seeks to drive its economic progress by means of the wisdom of parental choice, it must be sure that the parental choices add to some worthwhile store of knowledge for the next generation. That education in which public money is invested must be calibrated to the end of producing productive knowledge, the "training of intellect" is designed to "stimulate the mind of the individual to improve his present condition, and [that it] aids him in devising ways and means to do so."[131]

Thus, the basic competition school theory is that the nation will improve its standard of living by having parents use public tax money to make choices of schools based on their own information, knowledge, and perceptions of educational reality. The theory assumes that parents know what constitutes quality education, and that they have rational expectations as to the quality of science programs, mathematics, reading, political thought, literature, and all the liberal arts.

However, unfortunately, experience indicates that parental choices are ensnared by the parents' own limited experiences, level of learning, ignorance, biases, and mythology on which they depend to make educational choices for their children and are, thus, in many cases, quite suspect.[132] Such problems with rational choices are recognized by a school of economics known as "behavioral economics" that attempts to enter into the economic equation the actual motivations of individuals in the marketplace.

Parental choice is drawn into question by behavioral economic thought that reveals that standard economic theory relies on the misconception that individuals have well-informed rational preferences in exercising choices. Yet, in fact, preferences may not be rational nor reasonable but, rather, may be based on prior beliefs that influence the processing of the information on which choices rely. Information that is consistent with parental prior beliefs is deemed by them to be relevant to their choices, and the information that is inconsistent with their prior beliefs is ignored, disregarded, discounted, or forgotten. Such fictions weigh heavily in skewing choices away from rationality.

Behaviorists also argue that the summation of individual choices, in totality, cannot be relied upon to ensure the progress of mankind and the enhancement of the public good. The aggregate does not necessarily produce rationality; rather, it is more likely to result in inefficiency and inequality.[133] The behaviorists maintain that forces, riding the rationale of the grail of competition, tend to warp the public good causing both inefficiency and inequality. Put simply, the public good is more than the sum of individual preferences and choices. It is a great misunderstanding to believe that people acting in their own self-interest can achieve the public good.[134] We have known this since it was explained to us by Rousseau in 1758, as a cornerstone of democratic thought, that "personal interest is always in inverse ratio" to the common interest.[135] Thus, a system where parents take public money and indulge their self-interests is highly problematic for the education policy of a state or nation.

Stiglitz and Asymmetric Information

Joseph E. Stiglitz helps clarify why the "rational markets" theory is not likely to work efficiently in the marketplace of educational choice. Stiglitz was co-recipient of the Nobel Prize for Economic Science, 2001; formerly Chief Economist at the World Bank; Chairman of President Clinton's Council of Economic Advisors; and Professor of Finance and Economics at Columbia University. Stiglitz documents, in *The Price of Inequality*, 2012,[136] how the theory of rational markets has produced an unequal and inefficient condition that is pervasive in the United States and cannot be easily remedied. He maintains that external political influences on government tend to cause ever increasing economic inefficiency and inequality. In the realm of education, inefficiency and inequality are exacerbated by government-stimulated exertion of self-interests via such devices as charter schools and vouchers.

Stiglitz, in keeping with the reasoning of Muhammad Yunus, another Nobel Prize Laureate, avers that most inequality is not an unguided phenomenon; rather, Yunus says that "American inequality didn't just happen. It was created."[137] Further, Stiglitz argues that while market forces help contribute to inequality, it is actually anti-egalitarian government policies that shape those *market forces*. Much of the inequality that exists today is a result of government policy that has accommodated private factions and self-interest.

Stiglitz's primary contribution to economics was explaining why unregulated markets cannot be trusted to advance the economic and social interests of peoples and nations. His thesis is that regulation by governments is necessary because of *market imperfections* created by *asymmetric information*. As expressed in his writings, it is a truism that markets are neither rational nor moral and are, in their freestanding state, economic manifestations of the selfish gene, exhibit a Hobbesian self-interest, and are, in the end, engines of predatory selection.

Stiglitz's theory of *asymmetric information* and its effects on competition has pierced, with very large holes, the prevailing economic assumptions of Friedrich Hayek, the conservative Austrian political philosopher, author of the conservative manifesto, *The Road to Serfdom* (1944), and, of course, Milton Friedman. With regard to Friedman, Stiglitz renders Friedman's parental choice rudderless because parents are generally poorly informed about the quality of schools and, worse, parents normally exercise school choice based on information that has little or nothing to do with quality schooling. Thus, parental information is generally, by nature, imperfect and asymmetric. In his textbook, *Economics of the Public Sector*,[138] Stiglitz provides detail as to how *imperfect information* affects and, in many instances, negates the perceived benefits of competition in the marketplace. He indicates that this is particularly true in medical services and education. Asymmetrics of information are obvious in medicine where the patients are largely in the dark when they buy a "doctor's knowledge and/or information."[139] Patients cannot "effectively assess and evaluate a doctor's advice."[140] Because of such consumer uncertainty, governments require doctors to be licensed and drugs to be regulated. These constraints in medicine are required of medical doctors whether they practice with public or private hospitals.

Similar problems of quality and consumer protection exist in education. In education, as in medicine, imperfect information decreases and distorts the "effective degree of competition."[141] With education, the conditions of the marketplace do not exist. Parents are all, to a greater or lesser degree, ill-informed about the qualifications of teachers, their expertise, certifications, and are usually poorly informed about the subject matter conveyed and the teaching techniques required. That is why states require public school teachers to follow strict and complex educational processes to be certified. Such, however, is not normally required for teachers and administrators employed by private voucher schools or charter schools.[142] Therefore, parental choice and market competition in the realm of education, as in medicine, is uniquely suspect, and in the case of tuition vouchers and charter schools, is normally reduced to a condition of state-subsidized legal segregation.

Concerning Friedman and his choice argument, Stiglitz recalls that he tried to explain in long discussions with Friedman the importance of the externalities of "asymmetric information," the doubts that it cast upon rational choice, and how it mitigates Friedman's beloved and unregulated free market theory. Stiglitz remembers that "Friedman couldn't or wouldn't grasp" the concept. He says that Friedman, of course, "couldn't refute them – [rather he] simply *knew*" that the economic research on "information imperfections" had to be wrong.[143]

In spite of Stiglitz's decimation of Friedman's choice theory, conservative politicians, parental choice advocates, and for-profit charter school investors advance the quest for public funding under the guise of free market dogma, competition, and choice in order to advance their own largely unrelated special interests. Stiglitz clearly exposes a principal sophism in such parental choice fabrications in that parental choice contributes to the wide disparities in wealth and income in the United States and to some degree leads to degradation of the social fabric and contributes to economic inefficiencies that will eventually lower the standard of living of the nation.

Parental Choice and *A Priori* Biases

Therefore, parental choice, in most instances, may have nothing to do with education, but rather merely reflects educationally irrelevant beliefs causing educational market distortion. Such beliefs are usually *a priori* biases based on race, gender, ethnicity, wealth, social status, and, of course, religion. Mead and Green[144] point out that parental choice and charter schools as vehicles for racial segregation is of more than trivial social consequence (see above in this chapter). They cite a UCLA Civil Rights Project report,[145] titled in part, "Choice without Equity: Charter School Segregation," that documented that 70 percent of black charter school students attend schools that are highly segregated, i.e., comprising 90–100 percent racial minorities. This percentage is particularly concerning in view of the fact that it is double the percentage of black students who are enrolled in intensely segregated traditional public schools. Moreover, 43 percent of black charter school students attended charter schools that were 99 percent minority. This percentage was "nearly three times as high as Black students in traditional public schools,"[146] and it is particularly troubling since charter school laws in several states are only "hortatory" as to restraints on charter school racial segregation, such as California, Florida, Hawaii, Ohio, and Wisconsin. And, importantly, as observed above, the United States Supreme Court decision in 2007 in the *Seattle* and *Louisville*[147] school desegregation decisions essentially extracted the teeth from the Equal Protection Clause of the Fourteenth Amendment, at least as far as school desegregation is concerned. Further reason for concern regarding charter schools as havens of racial segregation, via the vehicle of parental choice, was effected when in 2010 the United States Court of Appeals, Ninth Circuit, ruled in an Arizona case that a charter school operator, a private nonprofit corporation, was not a state agency subject to the Fourteenth Amendment Due Process Clause.[148]

Privatization of education is supposed to work because Friedman and other conservative economists assume that parents are, in fact, "selfish, rational people interacting in a perfect" educational market.[149] Yet, parents are not necessarily rational in that they have no substantive idea as to what constitutes a good school. Parents' choices are dominated by what Fox calls *noise*. Justin Fox, in his book, *The Myth of the Rational Market*,[150] explains that *noise* in information muddles and misshapes the choices of consumers. Without government intervention, markets are not rational; rather, they are to a great degree irrational or at least imperfect. This is true for both the microeconomic and macroeconomic senses of the entire marketplace.

With regard to parental choice this obscures rational preferences by parents in their choices of schools. That *noise* in parental choice is misapprehended information based on or influenced mostly by non-educational impulses. The main *noise* in the educational marketplace, as Walzer says, is the "guarantee that children go to school with other children whose parents . . . were very much like their own."[151] The choice of like-minded parents with similar ideologies and biases is far distant from parents who make school choices based on curriculum content, school environment, and teacher quality.

Government funding of vouchers and charter schools will, if it continues to spread, contribute to social disunity and inequality. The Wall Street desire to make significant privatization incursions into the areas of public goods, human needs, health, education, and welfare, and to correspondingly avoid government regulation is a strong *laissez-faire* profit motivation. To deregulate these traditional governmental functions leaves Wall Street in the enviable position of near total discretion in raising "transaction costs" that assure profit maximization. Stiglitz observes how Enron is the banner child for such unbridled deregulation. CNBC's "Squawk Box" each morning trumpets that government regulation is bad for business. Stiglitz points out that the private business sector even believes that, "Regulations that prevent child labor are bad for business."[152] Stiglitz, in emphasizing his point, is on target. Historically, as we saw in the mid nineteenth century, the principal opposition to child labor laws and compulsory school attendance was led by businesses, prelates, and parents.

Vouchers and an Unregulated Market

Stiglitz further views the consequences of vouchers by pointing to the federal and state higher education funding dilemma. One of his central thrusts has to do with the everlasting problem of the wealthy private sector controlling government and using regulations and deregulation to its economic advantage. The phenomenon is natural in that the Hobbesian self-interest applies to primary and secondary education and to the higher education student loan debacle. As pointed out above, the federal government in 1971, in attempting to enhance the college going rate and at the same time aid private religious institutions, moved to provide federal aid via a tuition voucher system named after Claiborne Pell, a Senator from Rhode Island.[153] The voucher system placed few meaningful regulatory limits on institutions that received the money. However, private institutions voraciously consumed the Pell voucher money and correspondingly and methodically raised tuition with the result that Pell vouchers actually stimulated increases in tuition. As tuitions rose, students continued to suffer a financial burden gap. Later, the federal government then, at the behest of the banks who are always desirous of loaning money when there is no risk, lobbied Congress and achieved two crucial regulatory concessions. The federal government subsidized the interest on the loans and, importantly, by law, assured the banks that students who were unable to repay their loans could not escape their debt obligation to the banks by means of personal bankruptcy.

The result is that in this non-regulated United States higher education voucher/loan system, the students and taxpayers are misused, deluded, and beguiled while the private sector, private and private for-profit institutions in concert with banks and the Wall Street investors, reaps huge fiscal rewards. Today, institutions of higher education, public and private, remain largely segregated by race, religion, and economic conditions. Predominantly white colleges and universities remain white, black institutions remain primarily black, and denominational institutions remain even more religiously identifiable. Such segregation is sanctified with massive appropriations of federal and state funds in the forms of tuition vouchers, tax credits, and government-subsidized loans. The Obama administration has been largely foreclosed from remedying the situation for fear of offending powerful political forces representing the investors and private institutions. The higher education voucher/loan dilemma portends a probable scenario for the future of tuition vouchers and charter schools at the primary and secondary levels.

Self-Interest Understood

Stiglitz quotes Alexis de Tocqueville who said that the main element of the "peculiar genius of American society" is "self-interest properly understood."[154] The last two words, "properly understood," are the key, says Stiglitz. According to Stiglitz, everyone possesses self-interest in the "narrow sense." This *narrow sense,* with regard to educational choice, is usually exercised for reasons other than educational quality, the chief reasons being race, religion, economic and social status, and similarity with persons with comparable information, biases, and prejudices. But Stiglitz interprets Tocqueville's "properly understood" to mean a much broader and more desirable and moral objective: that of *appreciating* and paying attention to everyone else's self-interest. In other words, the common welfare is, in fact, "a precondition for one's own ultimate well-being."[155] Such commonality in the advancement of the public good is lost by the narrow self-interest. School tuition vouchers and charter schools are the operational models for implementation of the "narrow self-interest." It is easy to recognize, but difficult to justify.

SUMMARY

In recent years, a major restructuring of public education has occurred in the United States. At the higher education level, the federal government has deployed funds by mechanisms that flow directly to students rather than to institutions. The federal funding programs by and large have been by the fiscal mechanisms of vouchers and subsidized student loans. Such funds flow to private not-for-profit, private for-profit, and public institutions. An unintended result has been a huge increase in student debt as private institutions have greatly increased tuition and fees to absorb the federal largesse. State funding effort for higher education has declined and student loan debt has skyrocketed, exceeding the aggregate of credit card debt in the United States.

The elementary and secondary levels are tending to follow the same pattern, at least at the state level where 42 states have set up charter school programs that parallel and compete with public schools. The charter schools are private corporations that are given the statutory sobriquet of *public schools*, even though they are private corporations and are, in fact, privately controlled by for-profit and not-for-profit companies operating under several varieties of generalized state education statutes that contain certain authorizing provisions that connect the charter corporations to either state agencies or to the local school districts. The connections may be quite loose or may have some potentially effective contractual control provisions.

Research as to the efficiency and effectiveness of charter schools in privatizing education is not at all conclusive. Research concerning charter schools is inconclusive and by and large is biased toward the ideology of the individual researchers. A prevailing lack of objectivity, largely in the camp of proponents of privatization, is a rather far-reaching detriment to effective public policy decision making. The research that appears to be reliable suggests that the charter school, on average, is less effective than public schools in learner gains, when all demographic factors are taken into account. However, the wide variety of charter schools form a generic type that tends to defy objective and reliable research.

There are at least three conclusions that can be drawn with some degree of reliability. First, the belief that the "competition" of charters will improve public schools has not been proven. It is a theory unsubstantiated by dependable research. Rather, there is considerable evidence that the presence of charter schools has little economic effect apart from reducing the amount of taxpayer funds that were formerly allocated to traditional public schools. There is objective evidence that the bond ratings of public schools by major credit agencies will decline as students and state funding are diverted from public school districts to private charter schools. Concerning educational productivity, charter schools appear to be no more effective than public schools. Concerning deployment of public funds to voucher schools, largely Roman Catholic schools, the effort appears to be driven, almost solely, for the propagation of religion with public tax funds appropriated to strengthen church schools and churches. The voucher, aside from vouchers specifically designated for disabled children, appear to be for the primary purpose of bolstering the financial condition of Roman Catholic schools that have suffered from a decline of pupil enrollments in recent years, due in part to the devastating demise of the core city and other fiscal dilemmas of recent years.

With regard to educational value added, comparing public school elementary student gains to Roman Catholic school children, a most recent study of a very large sample of both sectors suggests that public schools are probably statistically more effective. However, with regard to vouchers for clerical schools, the issue that is most relevant to the public policy issue is not whether the religious schools are more educationally effective than public schools, but rather whether the people of a state collectively desire to provide public tax dollars to financially enhance churches and church schools.

Finally, we should note that the field of behavioral economics suggests that *parental choice* is an inappropriate way to make educational funding decisions. The sum of parental choices does not and probably cannot result in rational public policy decisions. Individual parental interests tend to obscure rational preferences as to school choices. Rational parental choices pursuant to the quality of schooling are indistinct and affected by *noise:* asymmetric considerations, biases, or prejudices that are unrelated to education quality.

We can observe today the forces of economic determinism and sectarian interests that are endemic to most societies, more severe at certain times than at others, and such is apparent in the United States today as the public school ideal is engaged in a contest with ideologies of pluralism and private school choice. Pluralism is, of course, integral to a free society. The right to remain distinctive and different in ethnic origin, religion, or culture in a nation or society is desirable and, indeed, a basic consideration to a free people. Yet one can easily confuse individual liberty with the inequity of group pluralism to the detriment of the community interest and commonality of purpose of a democratic state. Many of today's arguments for pluralism are masked attempts to preserve some economic or social advantage or to use public funds to advance special economic or sectarian interests. John Dunn in his memorable work *Western Political Theory in the Face of the Future* observed, "Most recent pluralist political theory rests fairly banally at the level of vulgar politics and offers no intellectually coherent conception of human value at all."[156] Clearly, special interest groups in the United States appeal to pluralism in order to preserve educational privilege in enclaves of wealth in suburbs, or to cloak religious fundamentalist quests for the use of public funds for sectarian purposes. Such constitutes intolerance masquerading as virtue.

As with pluralism, choice is invoked as a justification to support various methods of distributing public funds to support private exclusive schools. We should always be mindful of a Rousseau aphorism wherein he drew the vital connections among liberty, virtue, and citizenship through education. He said, "There can be no patriotism without liberty, no liberty without virtue, no virtue without citizens: create citizens (by means of education), and you have everything you need."[157] Yet the right to be individual and distinctive must have some boundaries. To exercise individualism may move a long way toward disregarding the interests of others or destroying community interests that are beneficial to all. Being individualistic, exercising various liberties, and asserting the right of choice must be subject to some definition. Choice exercised in self-interest can easily veer toward a negative and immoral end. Choice as a manifestation of liberty holds the imprimatur of morality and cannot be directly contradicted; however, when choice becomes a safe haven for those who desire to practice the politics of exclusion by capturing public resources and turning them to their direct advantage, then the end can quickly become immoral. Reinhold Niebuhr effectively identified the real purposes of individual choice when he pointed out that, "The moral attitudes of privileged groups are characterized by universal self-deception and hypocrisy."[158] They seek to clothe economic inequality and sectarian interests in the respectable coat of morality. Those who try to capture public funds for their own special and exclusive purposes invent "specious proofs for the theory that universal values spring from," and they maintain and attempt to convince others that the general interests of society are best served by affording such special privileges. Those special privileges may be for economic advantage, educational hegemony, or for racial, religious, ethnic, or cultural separatism. The public common school stands as a bulwark against such incursions and is therefore subject to attack by those groups that seek special privilege at public expense.

Allowing special interests to capture public resources for their own private purposes works to erode the liberties of the majority who are relegated to a position of relative disadvantage by the reduction in the residual resources available for public common interests. There is, therefore, good logic to support those who contend that if public funds are siphoned off by the private schools, the remaining public school children will be denied not only equal opportunity but also those liberties that are dependent on such opportunities. Thus, the cant about pluralism and choice serves most efficiently as a cover for the conversion of public school resources to private advantage, clearly inhibiting liberty rather than enhancing it. An understanding of public school finance presupposes an ability to detect the true purposes and intentions for diversions of the public's financial resources.

KEY TERMS

- Charter schools
- Opt-out schools
- *Laissez-faire* capitalism
- Parental choice
- Marketism
- Bond ratings

- Budget formations
- Voucher schools
- Asymmetric information
- Rational markets
- Behavioral economics

NOTES

1. Higher Education Act of 1965 (HEA), Title IV, Part A, Subpart 1; 20 U.S.C. 1070a.
2. Kern Alexander, *State and Federal Restructuring of American Education* (Oxford: The Oxford Education Society, Department of Education, University of Oxford, June 17, 2013). www.oxes.org.UK/about-us/news/.
3. Rick Perlstein, "Chicago Rising: Teachers, Parents and Activists Fight Rahm Emanuel's Austerity Agenda," *The Nation*, July 22–29, 2013, Mayor Emanuel closed 49 public schools and created new charter schools in Chicago in 2013.
4. Robin Cheryl Miller, 78 A.L.R. 5th 533 (originally published in 2000, updated in 2010).
5. *Comprehensive Community Solutions v. Rockford School District, No. 205*, 216 Ill. 2d 455, 837 N.E.2d 1 (Ill. 2005); *School Board of Osceola County v. UPC of Central Florida*, 905 So.2d 909 (Fla. Dist. Ct. App. 2005); *Central Dauphin School District v. Founding Coalition of Infinity Charter School*, 847 A.2d 195 (Pa.Commw. Ct. 2004).
6. Margaret Thatcher served as Prime Minister of the United Kingdom from 1979 to 1990.
7. Martha Minow, "Reforming School Reform," 68 *Fordham L. Rev.* 257 (1999).
8. John E. Chubb and Terry M. Moe, *Politics, Markets and America's Schools* (Washington, DC: Brookings Institution, 1989), p. 219.
9. Ibid.
10. Ibid.
11. Jencks, cited in James A. Mecklenburger and Richard W. Hostrop, *Education Vouchers: From Theory to Alum Rock* (Homewood, IL: ETC Publishers, 1972), pp. 112–113.
12. Jeffery R. Henig, *Rethinking School Choice, Limits of the Market Metaphor* (Princeton, NJ: Princeton University Press, 1994), p. 94.
13. Ibid.
14. Minow, *op. cit.*
15. 20 U.S.C.A. § 8061 to § 8066.
16. Ibid.
17. "Race to the Top," ED.gov., United States Department of Education, http://www2.ed.gov/news/pressreleases/2009/06/06082009.html.
18. Ibid.

19. *Arizona State Board of Charter Schools v. U.S. Department of Education*, 464 F.3d 1003 (9th Cir. 2006).
20. Ibid.
21. Ibid.
22. *Warner ex rel. Warner v. Lawrence*, 900 A.2d 980, 210 *Ed. Law Rep.* (Pa. Commw. Ct. 2006).
23. See generally a full presentation of this position in *The Economics of School Choice*, edited by Caroline M. Hoxby (Chicago: The University of Chicago Press, 2003).
24. Ibid., pp. 1–22.
25. Ibid., p. 5.
26. Ibid., p. 10.
27. Ibid., p. 11.
28. *Zelman v. Simmons-Harris*, 536 U.S. 639, 122 S. Ct. 2460 (2002).
29. Hoxby, *op. cit.*, p. xi.
30. Ibid.
31. Ibid.
32. Ibid., pp. 11–12.
33. Public Law 111–148, Stat.124 Stat. 119 through 124 Stat. 1025.
34. Hoxby, *op. cit.*, pp. 294–295.
35. Ibid., p. 297. *Note:* Hoxby appears to be unaware that such pooling has been utilized among hundreds of school districts nationwide for many years.
36. Ibid., p. 339.
37. Ibid.
38. Eric A. Hanushek and Steven G. Rivkin, "Does Public School Competition Affect Teacher Quality?," in *The Economics of School Choice*, edited by Caroline M. Hoxby (Chicago: University of Chicago Press, 2003), pp. 23–47.
39. Ibid., p. 35.
40. Ibid., p. 45.
41. Paul E. Peterson, William G. Howell, Patrick J. Wolf, and David E. Campbell, "School Vouchers: Results from Randomized Experiments," in *The Economics of School Choice, op. cit.*
42. Ibid.
43. Robert Bifulco and Katrina Bulkey, "Charter Schools," in *Handbook of Research in Education Finance and Policy*, edited by Helen F. Ladd and Edward B. Fiske (New York and London: Routledge, 2008), pp. 425–446.
44. Ibid.
45. Ribert Bifulco and Helen F. Ladd, "School Choice, Racial Segregations and Test Score Gaps: Evidence from North Carolina's Charter School Program," *Journal of Policy Analysis and Management*, Volume 26, Issue 1, Winter 2007, pp. 31–56.
46. Ladd and Fiske*, op. cit.*, p. 431.
47. Bifulco and Ladd, *op. cit.*; See also: J. R. Henig, "The Local Dynamics of Choice: Ethnic Preferences and Institutional Responses," in *Who Chooses? Who Loses? Culture, Institutions and The Unequal Effects of School Choice*, B. Fuller and R. Elmore editors (New York: Teachers College Press, 1996), pp. 95–117.
48. Bifulco and Bulkey, *op. cit.,* p. 433.
49. Ibid.
50. Martin Carnoy, Rebecca Jacobsen, Lawrence Michel, and Richard Rothstein, *The Charter School Dust-Up: Examining the Evidence on Enrollment and Achievement* (New York: Economic Policy Institute, Teachers College Press, 2005), pp. 97–98.
51. Ibid.
52. Ibid.

53. *National Charter School Study, 2013* (Stanford, CA: Center for Research on Education Outcomes), http://www.credo.stanford.edu.
54. Ibid., p. 83.
55. Ibid.
56. Ibid., p. 83.
57. Christopher A. Lubienski and Sarah Theule Lubienski, *The Public School Advantage: Why Public Schools Outperform Private Schools* (Chicago: The University of Chicago Press, 2014), pp. 64–65.
58. Ibid., pp. 65–70.
59. Ibid., p. 127.
60. Moody's Investors Service announcement titled "Moody's: Charter Schools Pose Greatest Credit Challenge to School Districts in Economically Weak Urban Areas," New York: October 15, 2013. http://www.moodys.com/research/Moodys- charter-schools-pose-greatest-credit-challenge-to-school-districts--PR_284505.
61. Standard & Poor's Ratings Services, *Ratings Direct*: "Despite Funding and Regulatory Hurdles, the U.S. Charter School Sector Continues to Grow," August 26, 2012, www.standardandpoors.com/RatingsDirect.
62. Moody's, *op. cit.*, p. 1.
63. Ibid.
64. Ibid.
65. Ibid., p. 2.
66. Ibid., p. 2.
67. Ibid., p. 3.
68. Yilan Shen and Alexander Berger, "Charter School Finance" (National Conference of State Legislatures (2011). www.ncsl.org/documents/educ/charterschoolfinance.pdf.
69. Ibid.
70. Ibid. See Colorado Charter School Law.
71. Ibid.
72. Ibid.
73. David Arsen and Yongmei Ni, "Resource Allocation in Charter and Traditional Public Schools: Is Administration Leaner in Charter Schools?," *National Center for the Study of Privatization in Education*, March 2012, http://www.ncspe.org/publications_files.
74. Diane Ravitch, *Reign of Error: The Hoax of the Privatization Movement and the Danger to America's Public Schools* (New York: Alfred A. Knopf, 2013), p. 167.
75. Ibid., p. 168.
76. William Phillis and Michael Fuller, "Ohio Charter School Budgets: 12 Years of Expenditure Data" (Columbus, Ohio: Ohio Coalition for Equity and Adequacy of School Funding, 2013).
77. With permission, this part is taken largely from Kern Alexander and M. David Alexander, *American Public School Law, Eighth Edition* (Belmont, CA: Wadsworth/Cengage, 2012), pp. 219–220.
78. *Zelman, op. cit.*
79. Milton Friedman and Rose Friedman, *Free to Choose* (Orlando: Harcourt, Inc., 1979), pp. 161–162.
80. Jim Carl, *Freedom of Choice: Vouchers in American Education* (Santa Barbara, CA: Proeger, 2011).
81. Ibid.
82. Isser Woloch, *The New Regime, Transformations of the French Civic Order, 1789–1820s* (New York: W. W. Norton & Co., 1994), p. 180. The Bougier Law was adopted by the Convention on December 19, 1793.

83. Alex Molnar, The Center for Educational Research, Analysis, and Innovation (CERAI), *Educational Vouchers: A Review of the Research,* http://nepc.colorado.edu/publication/educational-vouchers-a-review-research. See also: Pierre Birnbaum, *The Idea of France* (New York: Hill and Wang, 2001), pp. 106–108.

84. Ibid.

85. Francois Furet, *Revolutionary France, 1770–1880* (Oxford, UK: Blackwell Publishers, 1999), p. 527.

86. Ibid.

87. *Brown v. Board of Education*, 347 U.S. 483, 74 S. Ct. 686 (1954).

88. *Griffin v. County School Board of Prince Edward County*, 377 U.S. 218, 84 S. Ct. 1226 (1964), rev'g *County School Board of Prince Edward County v. Griffin,* 204 Va. 650, 133 S. E. 2d 565 (1963).

89. *County School Board of Prince Edward County v. Griffin*, 204 Va. 650, 133 S. E.2d 565 (1963), rev'd sub.nom., *Griffin v. County School Board of Prince Edward County*, 377 U.S. 218, 84 S. Ct. 1226 (1964).

90. *Griffin v. County School Board of Prince Edward County, op. cit., rev'g County School Board of Prince Edward County v. Griffin, op. cit.*

91. James W. Fraser, *Between Church and State: Religion & Public Education in a Multicultural America* (New York: St. Martin's Griffin, 2000), p. 152.

92. Ibid.

93. Ibid.

94. Ibid.

95. Barbara C. Jordan and Elizabeth D. Rostow, *The Great Society: A Twenty Year Critique* (Austin, TX: 1986), p. 106.

96. *Cochran v. Louisiana State Board of Education*, 281 U.S. 370, 50 S. Ct. 335 (1930).

97. *Zorach v. Clauson*, 343 U.S. 306, 72 S. Ct. 679 (1952).

98. *Tilton v. Richardson*, 403 U.S. 672, 91 S. Ct. 2091 (1971).

99. Roger E. Bolton, "The Economics and Public Financing of Higher Education: An Overview," in *The Economics and Financing of Higher Education in the United States, A Compendium of Papers,* Joint Economic Committee, Congress of the United States, 91st Congress, 1st Session (1969), United States Government Printing Office, p. 69.

100. Ibid.

101. *Everson v. Board of Education*, 330 U.S. 1, 67 S. Ct. 504 (1947).

102. *Agostini v. Felton*, 521 U.S. 203, 117 S. Ct. 1997 (1997).

103. *Zelman, op. cit.*

104. *Agostini, op. cit.*

105. Joseph E. Stiglitz, *Whither Socialism?* (Cambridge, MA: The MIT Press, 1996), pp. 173–178, 262. See also Joseph E. Stiglitz, *Globalization and Its Discontents* (New York: W.W. Norton & Co., 2003), p. 76.

106. Craig Timbert, "Williams Sheds Light on Vouchers' Stance," *Washington Post*, May 3, 2003, p. B1.

107. United States Department of Education, "A New Era: Revitalizing Special Education for Children and Families," Presidential Commission on Excellence in Special Education, July 2002.

108. *Jackson v. Benson*, 578 N.W.2d 602 (Wis. 1998), *cert. denied*, 537 U.S. 1106, 123 S. Ct. 851 (2003).

109. Ibid.

110. Ibid.

111. *Zelman, op. cit.*

112. Ibid.

113. Ibid.
114. See: Jason Berry, *Render Unto Rome: The Secret Life of Money in the Catholic Church* (New York: Crown Publishers 2011), pp. 274–275.
115. Canon Law, Chapter II, Canon 42§1
116. Lubienski and Lubienski, *op. cit.*, pp. 74–77.
117. Ibid., p. 77.
118. Ibid., p. 74.
119. Ibid.
120. Ibid.
121. Ibid., p. 92.
122. National Committee of State Legislatures, "School Voucher Laws," www.ncsl.org/research/education/voucher-law-comparison.aspx
123. This discussion of parental choice and asymmetric information is taken from Kern Alexander, "Asymmetric Information, Parental Choice, Vouchers, Charter Schools, and Stiglitz," *Journal of Education Finance,* Vol. 28, No. 2, Fall 2012.
124. Liah Greenfeld, *The Spirit of Capitalism: Nationalism and Economic Growth* (Cambridge, MA: Harvard University Press, 2001).
125. Justin Fox, *The Myth of the Rational Market: A History of Risk, Reward, and Delusion on Wall Street* (New York: Harper Business, 2001), p. 178.
126. Ibid.
127. Ibid., p. 182
128. Carnoy et al., *op. cit.*
129. John T. McGreevy, *Catholicism and American Freedom: A History* (New York: W.W. Norton & Company, 2003), and Jason Berry, *Render Unto Rome: The Secret Life of Money in the Catholic Church* (New York: Crown Publishers, 2011).
130. *Villanueva v. Carere*, 85 F.3d 481 (10th Cir. 1996).
131. See: Greenfeld, *op. cit.*, p. 355, quoting W.H. Campbell, Rutgers University.
132. See: Kern Alexander and M. David Alexander, *American Public School Law, 8th Edition* (Belmont, Calif.: Wadsworth/Cengage, 2012), pp. 284–327 and pp. 337–394.
133. Fox, *op cit*, pp. 191–196.
134. Joseph E. Stiglitz, *Whither Socialism* (Cambridge, MA: MIT Press, 1996), p. 179.
135. Jean-Jacques Rousseau, *A Discourse on Political Economy (1758),* in *The Social Contract and Discourses*, translation by G.D.H. Cole (London: J.M. Dent & Sons, 1973), p. 133.
136. Joseph E. Stiglitz, *The Price of Inequality* (New York, NY: W.W. Norton & Company, 2012)
137. Muhammed Yunus, *The New York Times*, Sunday, December 8, 2006, p. 34.
138. Joseph E. Stiglitz, *Economics of the Public Sector, Third Edition* (New York: W.W. Norton & Company, 2000).
139. Ibid., p. 309.
140. Ibid.
141. Ibid., p. 434.
142. Ibid., p. 435.
143. Ibid.
144. Julie F. Mead and Preston C. Green, III, "Chartering Equity: Using Charter School Legislation and Policy to Advance Equal Educational Opportunity" (Boulder, CO: National Education Policy Center, 2012), p. 6.
145. E. Frankenberger, G. Siegel-Hawley, and J. Wang, "Choice Without Equity: Charter School Segregation and the Need for Civil Rights Standards," 37 (Los Angeles, CA: The Civil Rights Project, UCLA, 2010). See www.civilrightsproject.ucla.edu.
146. Ibid. Also see Mead and Green, *op. cit.*

147. *Parents Involved in Community Schools v. Seattle School District No. 1., et al.*, and *Meredith v. Jefferson County Public Schools (Louisville), et al.,* 127 S. Ct. 2738, 551 U.S. 701 (2007).
148. *Caviness v. Horizon Community Learning Center, Inc.,* January 4, 2010. See: Diane Ravitch, *Reign of Error: The Hoax of the Privatization Movement and the Danger to America's Public Schools* (New York: Alfred A. Knopf, 2013), p. 163.
149. Fox, *op. cit.*
150. Fox, *op. cit.*, pp. 200–201.
151. Michael Walzer, *Spheres of Justice* (New York: Basic Books, 1983), p. 218.
152. Stiglitz, *The Price of Inequality, op. cit.*, p. 178.
153. See also: *The Economics and Financing of Higher Education in the United States,* Joint Economic Committee, Congress of the United States, 91st Congress, 1st Session, 1969.
154. Stiglitz, *The Price of Inequality, op. cit.*, p. 288.
155. Ibid.
156. John Dunn, *Western Political Theory in the Face of the Future* (Cambridge: Cambridge University Press, 1990), p. 51.
157. Jean-Jacques Rousseau, *A Discourse on Political Economy*, as cited in N.J.H. Dent, *A Rousseau Dictionary* (Hoboken: John Wiley & Sons, 1992), p. 69.
158. Reinhold Niebuhr, *Moral Man and Immoral Society* (New York: Charles Scribner's Sons, 1932), p. 117.

CHAPTER 12

Education Production Functions: Whether Money Matters*

TOPICAL OUTLINE OF CHAPTER

- The Background
- Implications for School Finance Policy
- The Concept of Production Functions
  - The Industrial Model
  - The Education Model
  - Comparison of the Models
  - Returns to Scale
  - Substitutability
- The Cost Side of the Equation
  - Human Variables
  - Time as a Cumulative Variable
  - Teacher Differences
- Attenuated Data
- Sequence of Inputs
- Threshold Effect
- Variations in Variables
- Statistical Procedures and Problems
- Experimental Conditions
- Model Specifications
- The *Coleman Report*'s Flawed Data and Analysis
- Other Production-Function Studies
- Improvement of Production-Function Studies

*This chapter was adapted from Aubrey Price, *Education Production Functions in Policy Making: A Critical Analysis* (Doctoral dissertation, Virginia Tech, 1994).

INTRODUCTION

Much has been said about the limits of investment in education. Many governmental leaders at both the federal and state levels have vigorously argued that more money for education is simply throwing *good money after bad*. The supporting rationale for this position has emanated largely from several studies that have attempted to relate inputs of dollars to outputs as measured by pupil achievement test scores. The majority of these studies have shown that there is no consistent relationship. These analyses, called production-function studies, have been widely misinterpreted to argue that such a lack of co-linearity is good evidence to support either reductions in public school funding or no further increases.

Proponents of this position maintain that until public schools can show that there exists a systematic relationship between money inputs and achievement outputs no additional funds should be forthcoming. Moreover, this argument has been widely used by states to defend inequities in fiscal distributions to local school districts. The argument goes this way: if additional resources do not result in measurable additional cognitive learning, then there is no justification to expend more money on public schools. The discussion in this chapter is largely dependent on the research and writing of Aubrey Price.[1]

THE BACKGROUND

Recently the education and economic journals have been filled with hundreds of production-function studies that have sought to prove or disprove the efficacy of public schools and the appropriate measures that should be taken for reform and the restructuring of the American education system. Employing a vast array of independent and dependent variables, these studies have basically been used to support a particular ideology in which the researchers dogmatically and faithfully believe and are active adherents. The research results, unfortunately, nearly always support the ideology of the researchers. Lately, the regressions have proliferated in a war between adherents of traditional public schools versus the forces of those who advocate privatization of schooling in the United States.

BOX 12.1

Productivity in Education

The concept of productivity in education has various meanings but is fundamentally concerned with the quantity and quality of educational outcomes that result from a given investment of resources.

Source: Jennifer King Rice and Amy Ellen Schwartz, "Toward an Understanding of Productivity in Education," in *Handbook of Research in Education Finance and Policy*, edited by Helen F. Ladd and Edward B. Fiske (New York: Routledge, 2008), p. 132.

About these studies, Brian Barry,[2] one of the most highly regarded American political philosophers of the last half of the twentieth century, explains the *system*, a daunting and complicated dilemma placed on formal schooling by society in its attempts to remediate the economic, social, and cultural ills that affect each succeeding generation of American children. Barry explained that this system is described and discussed by Muhammed Yunus and is presented in more detail earlier in this book:

> [I]n practice there is probably no country that has completely equalized the quality of schooling, measured in terms of the physical facilities and the quality of the instructors, but some have got close enough to make it apparent that educational attainment would not be equalized by equalizing the quality of the schooling. Nor, after all, is this surprising since children spend only a fraction of their time in school and are already highly differentiated in relevant ways by the time they start attending school. Moreover, at a cost of some millions of dollars, sociologists discovered the rather obvious fact that a large part of the educational environment of a child consists of the other children in the school. Given the tendency of people in a neighborhood within any city to have similar education and cultural backgrounds, this entails that (at any rate in urban areas) the effects of individual parents on their children's prospects will be multiplied by the likelihood that the other children will have similar parents. Nothing short of scattering children at random over an entire metropolitan area could avoid this.[3]

Production-function studies in education have a five-decade history. The production-function or input-output analysis is a model of relationships based on the economic theory of United States industry. It requires the measurement of precise increments of resource inputs that yield specific increments of production outputs. The model is a valuable tool for planning industrial production. The unity of theoretical design, empirical analysis, and practical result has been basic to the development of the production-function model. In education, however, wide variations in the use of the model in empirical studies under very diverse conditions have resulted in confusing and contradictory results. Unfortunately, premature claims about the efficacy of this analytical tool for policymaking can result in counterproductive decisions that reduce the efficiency and productiveness of schools.[4] Yet, policymakers cannot ignore the opportunity to develop a more precise understanding of the links between resource investment and achievement in education.

Education production-function analysis began with the *Equality of Educational Opportunity*, a report often cited as the *Coleman Report* for its principal author.[5] The project, funded by Section 402 of the Civil Rights Act of 1964, represented a major comprehensive effort to collect and analyze data on a national scale. The researchers sought to determine the extent to which differing expenditures affected the quality of education with a particular focus on school segregation. The four major questions examined by the study were:

1. The extent to which racial groups were segregated in the public schools;
2. The presence of equal educational opportunities by criteria regarded as indicators of quality: tangible characteristics of schools in physical facilities; curriculum areas

such as high school tracking; characteristics of teachers including salary, verbal ability, experience, and attitudes; student body characteristics including self-attitudes and academic goals, socioeconomic status (SES), and parent education levels;

3. How much students learn as measured by standardized tests; and
4. The relationship between what students learn and the kinds of schools they attend.

These objectives covered most of the areas investigated by the education production-function analysis. Since many readers interpreted the *Coleman Report* to indicate that schools had little influence on student achievement independent of family background and general social context, it provided great impetus for further research.[6] This report and the debate it initiated have been the catalysts for much of the research into education cost-quality issues that have employed production-function analyses.[7]

BOX 12.2

Definition

Product Function indicates the maximum amount of product that can be obtained from any specified combination of inputs, given the current state of knowledge. That is, it shows the largest quantity of goods that any particular collection of inputs is capable of producing.

Source: William J. Baumol and Alan S. Blinder, *Economics: Principles and Policies* (San Diego: Harcourt Brace Jovanovich, 1988), p. 515.

The questions about the influence of financial resources on the achievement of students that emerged from the *Coleman Report* lie at the heart of two dramas now playing on state education stages: one is the national reform effort that began with *A Nation at Risk*; the other is the wave of state litigation that seeks to reshape education finance and distribute resources more equally among all students.[8] In both dramas in education, the use of production-function analysis has provided information to justify the perspectives and decisions of policymakers. Equity suits have involved the litigants in arguments about the importance of financial resources based on education production-function analyses.[9] These examples testify to a role that such studies have played, and continue to play, in federal and state education finance policies.

IMPLICATIONS FOR SCHOOL FINANCE POLICY

The *Coleman Report* and its genre tend to perpetuate misconceptions about public education, providing ammunition to those who oppose investment in public education on philosophical grounds. The formulation of policy on the basis of a half-formed conceptual methodology can result in faulty policy decisions and undermine support for social science research. Using the findings from education production-function studies to determine important policy issues merely multiplies the errors. More importantly, though, such research has been used to launch anti-public school attacks that have been deleterious to the adequate funding of education, generally. Premature advocacy of production-function conclusions that are based on poorly specified research models can lead to diversions as expressed by Christopher Edley, Jr.:[10]

> However imperialistic lawyers can be in offering their services and habits of mind in the solution of all problems, economists are even more dangerous with implicit claims that their grossly simplified models should displace the instincts and experiences of professionals, such as educators, who have worked for decades to understand the ingredients of progress. Crucial research must focus not on the empirical analysis of aggregated input-output models, but on the more conventional, less tidy, applied problem of program evaluation and replication. That is how social science can best serve struggling educators and advocates who ought not to be diverted to rebutting and perfecting flawed economic models.[11]

THE CONCEPT OF PRODUCTION FUNCTIONS

The concept of the production-function model was developed and applied first to industry where it achieved reasonable success. When later applied to education, the production-function model has proven to be both flawed and controversial.

The Industrial Model

The production-function or input-out analysis is a model of the economic relationship between the maximum amount of output that can be produced and the inputs required to make that output. The model is defined for given technological levels that are subject to change differentially. When linked with cost analyses, the production-function model can be used to measure increments of resource inputs that yield specific increments of production outputs at precise cost estimates. The model is a valuable tool for efficiently planning industrial production based upon least cost input estimates. "There are thousands of different production functions in the American economy; at least one for each firm and product."[12]

In the early development of the production-function model, Cobb and Douglas tried to measure changes in the amount of labor and capital used to create a given amount of goods and to determine the relationships between the product, labor, and capital.[13] They quantified the components for a given time and estimated the relationship between factors using regression analysis. Although data collection in the late nineteenth and early twentieth century was imperfect, Cobb and Douglas compared the results of their analytical model to information provided from federal government sources, thereby enabling the concept to be validated. Today, of course, cost and quantity data are abundant for measuring the physical factors in production.

The Education Model

The goal of the education model is to explain the relationships between inputs and outputs that would permit the maximization of student achievement from a given combination of input factors. This approach employs the use of regression analysis for explanatory purposes. Such a use of regression analysis requires the specification of a conceptual model from which the data can be meaningfully interpreted.[14] Variables in the education equation may include some measures of the individual's ability, family, peer, financial, and school inputs to a measure of student achievement as the output factor.

Put simply, education production functions seek to determine whether an increase in the input of resources will result in a commensurate rise in output as measured by a particular measure of educational gain. For example, will graduation rates or achievement test scores rise with a specified increase in funding? Another formulation is whether an increase in efficiency can produce increased outcomes without an increase in funding. As Rice and Schwartz explain "can we increase performance by eliminating waste or improving efficiency?"[15] Yet, another specification of a production function model may be whether a particular amount of school expenditure will produce a commensurate increase in measurable outcome.[16] Rice and Schwartz,[17] citing Levin,[18] clearly set forth in Box 12.3 the mathematics of the education production function.[19]

BOX 12.3

The Mathematics of the Education Production Function

An education production function typically takes the following general form:

$A_{it} = g(F_{it}, S_{it}, P_{it}, O_{it}, I_{it})$, where
A_{it} = a vector of educational outcomes for the $_i$th student at time t;
F_{it} = a vector of family background characteristics relevant to the $_i$th student at time t;
S_{it} = a vector of school inputs relevant to the $_i$th student at time t;
P_{it} = a vector of peer or fellow-student characteristics relevant to the $_i$th student at time t;
O_{it} = a vector of other external influences (e.g., community) relevant to the $_i$th student at time t;
I_{it} = a vector of characteristics of the $_i$th student relevant at time t.

Where $g(.)$ is the transformation that captures the technology linking them.

Since precise measures for the inputs do not exist, proxies developed and collected for other purposes must be entered into the regression equation. Proxies are measurable variables that are assumed to correlate highly with a latent, immeasurable variable identified in the model. The true variables cannot be identified from proxies, only estimated. The qualities and interactions considered in the true variables are not normally purchased in the marketplace.[20] The marginal products identified in the conceptual model refer to the true variables – those which yield output changes when altered, not to proxy variables. Therefore, a true education production function is not available and under present circumstances cannot be known. Any policy decision based on an estimated production function is clearly speculative.

The proxies for each variable in most education models represent a broad range of demographic and economic data.

1. *Family background.* "Income level, SES, parents' education, number of people in the family, the family structure, languages spoken in the home, size of home, indices of parent interest in education, and so forth."[21]
2. *Peer influence.* "Appropriately aggregated vectors of the attitudes, backgrounds, and performances of other students and children which the individual comes into contact with. Empirically this implies using aggregates of proxy measures of home environment."[22]
3. *Initial endowments.* "In empirical work, no measure of initial endowments is available."[23]
4. *School factors.* "Teacher characteristics and attitudes, physical characteristics of the school, curriculum, etc. . . . School inputs to the individual should be analyzed."[24]
5. *Achievement measures.* Mean verbal and mathematics scores on standardized tests were used for separate analyses.

Comparison of the Models

Several features of the industrial model deserve attention because of differences from the education model. Foremost among the differences is the measurement of the marginal product. The marginal product of an input is the additional output produced by a unit of that input when all other inputs are held constant. It is a function of the law of diminishing returns. "The law of diminishing returns holds that the marginal product of each unit of input will decline as the amount of that input increases, holding all other inputs constant."[25] Monk says that the dependency on teachers (hired inputs) epitomizes a reliance on one factor of production that economists would find alarming.[26] Without alternative instructional inputs being available, the theoretical probability is that the marginal product will decline. The education model, however, assumes a linear relationship between inputs and outputs in which there is a constant and unchanging marginal product. In the industrial economic analysis model, the marginal product displays a curvilinear relationship to the input. It is important to identify these fundamental differences between the industrial and the education models so that policymakers do not assume a false equality between them.[27]

Returns to Scale

Another problem in relating the two models lies in the economic concept of *returns to scale*. *Returns to scale* refers to the "responsiveness of total product when *all* the inputs are increased *proportionately*."[28] Economists usually seek to identify increasing, decreasing, or constant returns to scale. Constant returns to scale are assumed to be attainable in most production activities.[29]

One method of addressing returns to scale in education has been through the consolidation of smaller districts into larger ones.[30] The research suggests that larger districts produce lower achievement than smaller districts.[31] The per-pupil expenditures in large cities, however, must address dysfunctional socioeconomic conditions that smaller localities may not have. This comparison of larger and smaller school districts, therefore, may too often ignore conditions within the districts that work against achievement. For example, the Fairfax County system in Virginia is the largest in the state and produces an enviable record of achievement.[32] Socioeconomic factors in the Fairfax district strongly favor high investment in education and equally high student achievement. Throughout the country, however, per-student costs in the range of district size from 500 to 5000 students tend to differ very little.[33] These results suggest that constant or increasing returns to scale are not the norm in education and illustrate yet another area in which the industrial and the education production-function models diverge in substantive ways.

BOX 12.4

Definition

Returns to Scale. The amount that output will expand if all inputs are increased simultaneously by the same percentage. Returns to scale can be contrasted with returns to a single input which is the amount that the output will expand with the increase of just one input, holding all other input quantities unchanged.

Source: William J. Baumol and Alan S. Blinder, *Economics: Principles and Policy*, 4th edn. (San Diego: Harcourt Brace Jovanovich, 1988), p. 521.

Substitutability

The substitutability of elements (input substitution) in the production-function model is a rationale for its use in manufacturing and industry. If the price of one factor falls while other factor prices remain the same, substituting the lower-priced input for another could allow for a reduction in costs without any loss of quantity or quality.[34] To do this, it is necessary to identify inputs that contribute to outcomes, determine how much difference each input makes and its costs, and substitute effective resources for less effective ones.[35] The opportunity to evaluate the substitution of elements in the education model is severely limited. Children require human supervision and guidance, restricting the possibilities of the substitution of capital for labor. Beyond this condition, however, it is a consequence of the limitations imposed on experimental research within the school setting. From another perspective, it represents the inflexibility of the education model. If classroom level analyses were developed to the point that teacher effects could be assessed, then alternative classroom level inputs might be evaluated.

Moreover, problems with substitutability among education inputs are a consequence of the interpretation of analytical results.

> If we find that two variables – an input and an outcome – are unrelated statistically, it may be because (a) the data are accurate and in fact the two variables are unrelated; (b) the variables are related but one (or both) of the measures is insensitive (not detecting variance that actually exists) or is producing random values; or (c) the variables are unrelated as the data show but we have failed to measure a relevant outcome that the input does contribute to in some significant manner.[36]

Teachers remain the most important schooling input. The addition of electronic teaching aids, such as computers, has not reduced the need for professional instruction. The use of paraprofessionals to replace teachers is as close to the concept of substitutability as education has come. The substitution of longer hours in the school day or the extension of the school year into the summer to more efficiently use facilities represent efforts to substitute resources – traditional downtime for building use substituted for the cost of additional facility construction. Unfortunately, the inability to provide information on resource arrangements within the educational model limits the value of the production-function study to meet the needs of decision makers.

BOX 12.5

Definition

Input Substitution or Substitutability. As any one input becomes more costly relative to other competing units, the firm is likely to substitute one input for another; that is, to reduce its use of the input that has become more expensive and to increase its use of competing inputs.

Source: William J. Baumol and Alan S. Blinder, *Economics: Principles and Policy*, 4th edn. (San Diego; Harcourt Brace Jovanovich, 1988), p. 518.

Technological change is the "invention of new products, improvements in old products, or changes in the processes for producing goods and services."[37] In education, technology encompasses the methodology of instruction (processes) as well as the hardware of computers and other media. Education has remained labor intensive as other industries have replaced people with machines. The inability to substitute capital for labor in education makes teacher training a primary means to transform the process. Teacher behaviors, however, lie outside the ability of the production-function analysis to evaluate. Therefore, crucial policy information that could transform the education system also lies outside the purview of the production-function study.[38]

Since the education model lacks direct measures of the variables identified in the conceptual design, and proxies must be selected from available data to serve as substitutes in a regression equation, there is no opportunity to validate the model against data supplied from other sources. A comparison of the estimated production-function model cannot be made with the true inputs since only proxy data are available. Using this kind of comparison with true data enabled Cobb and Douglas to validate and refine the industrial model.[39] The education model, however it may be defined, remains unverified by any objective methodology.

THE COST SIDE OF THE EQUATION

Costing-out variables is a relatively simple task for calculations using the industrial model. The costing-out of variables for the education model remains in a primitive condition, partially because inputs and outputs are not exclusively physical. Efforts such as those of Rossmiller and Ferguson[40] remain promising but are relatively unmatched examples of the possibilities of costing-out variables for U.S. schools.

Human Variables

Human variables play a significantly different role in the industrial and education models. Cobb and Douglas recognized that neither the quality of labor nor the intensity of work could be measured quantitatively in their initial application of the industrial model. This is a reasonable certainty for the education model as well. Nevertheless, labor inputs in the industrial model could be quantified and held as a measurable factor to determine the relative input value since other factors were easily quantifiable. Teacher and student inputs remain less easy to quantify. The student is both an input and an output factor. In the industrial model the output commodity is inert and is not an active participant on the input side. The child in school is both an active input and the output commodity in the education model. This dual role of the student in the model adds a confounding characteristic to education production. If one could assume along with the economists that student acquisitiveness was maximized (for knowledge, in the education model, as the equivalent to wealth in the economic model), the problem of student behavior would be less of a conundrum. Such an assumption is difficult to sustain for production functions in the K–12 school environment.

Time as a Cumulative Variable

The use of time in the industrial model is recognized as a continuum on which certain measurable material conditions exist.[41] It is not an independent factor in production. Time affects the definition of an input as fixed or variable (changeable) based on the length of the production planning period.[42] In education, time is a contributor to the product of student achievement. "Time inputs are important determinants of cognitive achievement."[43] Quantitative proxies for specific time inputs may be determined, but the estimate of cumulative effect is unspecified for the short time period or cross-section of time analyzed by most education studies.

The relationship of initial student abilities to achievement in an academic year, for example, can be measured, and this may offer a means to evade the problem of cumulative effect. Yet since important time factors remain in the control of students (homework time for specific subjects and television time), reliable measures remain elusive. Unfortunately, measures of initial endowments are often excluded from equations. IQ may be challenged as a baseline because it is demonstrably a changeable measure and time may have a significant unmeasured cumulative effect upon it.[44] Thus, the dynamism and the evolving nature of the human intellectual condition present a variable that remains unspecified to a degree of reliability.

Teacher Differences

The inability to measure skill differences between teachers who share similar quantifiable attributes such as level of education, years of experience, or certification credentials is a deficiency in education research and, thus, in production-function analysis. Differences in teaching styles, strategies, attitudes, and behavior of teachers are likely to be important factors in student achievement. Significantly different amounts of learning do occur in different classrooms in the same school and among different schools. Clearly, teachers and schools can have significant effects on student achievement. Production-function studies are simply unable to capture the behaviors that produce achievement.[45]

Murnane and Nelson argue against the use of production-function analysis in education because of teacher differences.[46] Production-function analysis is based on a standardized process derived from fully articulated and detailed production inputs and techniques that allow very little variation. Teaching is characterized by techniques that are essentially situation specific and idiosyncratic. Teachers are constantly making production decisions in the classroom about methods, procedures, and materials. This produces considerable variation in the teaching process. Teaching inherently involves constant experimentation to identify those techniques that will increase student performance in the classroom. Education inputs and techniques gradually evolve as teachers reshape and modify instruction. Research is normally conducted away from the setting of schools and does not capture the realities of the process of constant adjustment and modification necessary to meet the needs of individuals and classroom groups. The problems contained herein are thus obvious, and their solutions for production-function model specification are extremely cloudy.

ATTENUATED DATA

Production-function analyses have not generally addressed several other critical problems.[47] While outputs of individuals vary widely, school inputs (i.e., expenditures per pupil) often may not vary greatly at all. When there are small input differences, the effect of the input may not be statistically significant because of the attenuation of variance in the measurement of samples. An example provided by the measurement of the effects of facilities illustrates this point. Hanushek[48] found statistically significant effects of facilities on student achievement in a study of Brazilian education, but he found no such relationship in his earlier studies in the United States. The differences in the resources available in the two settings provide statistical evidence that money does matter in facilities investment when there is a significant variance in the measures compared. When the variance in facilities is reduced (attenuated) by limited measurable differences between the samples, no statistical significance is found. Production-function analyses have rarely addressed attenuated variance, although it is normally present in district-level analyses within states that provide moderate equalization in funding, especially among expenditures per pupil that cluster closer to the mean. Pass/fail measurements of student achievement are particularly vulnerable to the problem of attenuated variance.[49]

BOX 12.6

Methodological Problems

Since the United States' *Coleman Report*, a large number of studies have addressed this issue in both developed and developing countries. The results of these "educational production functions" vary widely and are fraught with methodological problems, not least of which are that it is unclear what unit of production to use (individual pupil, classroom, school, school district) and whether the relevant unit of production is maximizing academic achievement or some other output. Neither do any of the studies specify an underlying theory of learning that would define the nature of the school inputs – academic achievement relationship: they all assume that teacher inputs can be measured by teacher characteristics (education, experience, and aptitude), ignoring the way or the degree to which those characteristics are engaged in the teaching-learning process.

Source: Wadi D. Haddad, Martin Carnoy, Rosemary Rinaldi, and Omporn Regel, *Education and Development, Evidence for New Priorities* (Washington, DC: The World Bank, 1990), p. 50.

SEQUENCE OF INPUTS

The interaction between inputs can have an effect on output measures. Bronfenbrenner demonstrated that preschool intervention involving parents and schools can have measurable effects on IQ scores, but interventions that did not involve parents failed to produce measurable effects.[50]

According to Piaget, the sequence of inputs can be important in the acquisition of knowledge. Attempts to teach reading before the child is *ready* will fail. Accordingly, failure to provide learning experiences at the suitable time can limit a child's development. Ethologists and psychologists provide evidence that suggests *windows of opportunity, readiness, and critical periods* in the development of individuals. Production-function studies have been much too limited in scope to examine such issues. The results of a production-function analysis can fail to assess the presence or absence of important time-related learning inputs that have significant effects on achievement.

THRESHOLD EFFECT

The need for the application of a certain amount of an input before it produces measurable results is called the threshold effect.[51] The analogy to the *take-off* period in Walt Rostow's *The Stages of Economic Growth*[52] is a useful comparable construct. Certain material preconditions must develop before a society can move into a sustained growth economy. Before these conditions are met, a ceiling exists on the attainable output.[53] Earlier analyses by Fortune[54] suggest that a threshold of $600 to $700 per pupil may be linked to measurable achievement differences in otherwise homogenous school districts in several states where average expenditures per pupil for the state are in the range of $3,500 to $4,500. The threshold would, of course, change with the average level of expenditure for the state. While Fortune is careful to explain that such findings are frequently lost in the analysis of very diverse systems, and the amount of money is likely to vary from state to state, the evidence of a threshold effect that relates student achievement to financial resources is a new and interesting perspective.

VARIATIONS IN VARIABLES

Most education production-function analyses select from a common set of variables. Studies include some or all of the following on the input side of the model formula: characteristics of the home or family, the community, peers, individual students, and the school or district. Such examples indicate the current dilemma in selecting appropriate measures that effect student achievement. Variable selection contributes to the discrepancies that exist in the results of empirical studies, although it is by no means the sole explanatory element.

Selecting variables for a production-function model is a decision complicated by the need to measure the variables. No one simple, direct, and complete measurement exists for family characteristics or any of the other variables. Consequently, a variety of existing measures or proxies are used to operationalize the constructs. The following list taken primarily from Lau[55] is reasonably thorough.

Home background (family characteristics) may include: IQ, age, education, income, occupation, race, religion, attitudes, expectations, preferences, or values of either or both parents; the structure and stability of the family; the number of siblings; and locational stability. Indicators of the home learning environment may include: possession of books, radios, and televisions; frequency of travel; and knowledge of foreign languages. Direct home inputs to the learning process could include the time that either or both parents, an older sibling, or even a tutor devoted to the instruction of the students being assessed.

School characteristics include the type of school (public, parochial, private), type of curriculum, level (K–12), size, ethnic composition of enrollment, class size, per-pupil expenditure, or method of instruction. Direct inputs may include facilities or specific features such as science laboratories or libraries; administrators – quantity, quality (degree, experience, or other accomplishments), attitudes, and other attributes (including IQ or verbal ability, knowledge of subject, ability to communicate, responsiveness to questions); and teacher time inputs to preparation, lecturing, student consultation, and grading. Instructional methodology emphasized in the school must be measured and may include: traditional forms, instructional televisions, computer-assisted instruction, virtual classrooms, or variations and combinations of these or other technical processes.

Community characteristics are intended to measure the degree of support for education: type of neighborhood, size of the city, degree of community interest, attitudes, average age, education, income, socioeconomic status (SES) (described by some measure of community wealth) of the community, and property value are among the measures selected. In some studies the peer group variable is incorporated into community characteristics.

Student characteristics include: measures of ability (IQ), age, aptitudes, race, sex, birth order, number of siblings, and previous educational achievements on standardized tests. Measures of subjective conditions that may affect achievement such as attitudes, interests, motivation, self-concept, self-expectations, and values have been used. Student time inputs to homework, class attendance, laboratory work, or self-study have been used.

Peer group characteristics are selected from the proxies for student and community characteristics. The influence of peers is included because of the effect on individual student achievement. These characteristics also influence teacher classroom behavior. These proxies may shift from one category to another in different studies. SES is determined by another measure such as personal income or percent of students qualifying for free and reduced price lunches depending on whether the SES of the student body (peers) or the community is the variable. Without belaboring the obvious, studies on the proxies selected for variables may produce results that are significantly influenced by the proxies selected rather than the actual variables.

STATISTICAL PROCEDURES AND PROBLEMS

Nearly all education production-function studies use a variation of regression analysis.[56] Linear model equations (ordinary least squares) have been the predominant tools of analysis. Stepwise regression, variance-partitioning, commonality analysis, and path analysis have also been used. Simultaneous equations (two-stage least squares) procedures have been employed with greater frequency recently. Ferguson[57] used this procedure in his analysis of data drawn from Texas. Thompson and Correa[58] tested for significant differences between groups before utilizing regression procedures.

Regression analysis, as observed above, may be used for prediction or explanation. Hanushek depended on various regression analyses studies to draw conclusions that "money doesn't matter."[59] The Hanushek procedures and conclusions have, of course, been roundly criticized and refuted by Krueger.[60] In education, the purpose has been to explain the variation in student achievement on the basis of the inputs selected for the model. The ultimate goal is to be able to predict the effect of inputs, to calculate the cost of changes to these inputs, and to maximize student achievement for the lowest cost. The percent of the variance in the dependent variable, explained by the regression model, and the amount of change in the dependent variable (student achievement) for a unit change in each independent variable, however, do not represent causal relationships in education.[61] The researcher is forced to recognize the speculative and uncertain nature of the findings from such an analysis.

EXPERIMENTAL CONDITIONS

Aside from the lack of hard data from measurable material relationships, education research is plagued by a basic problem: lack of experimental conditions. Experimental conditions allow the researcher to randomly select treatment and control groups to test hypotheses. A random sample is one that is selected by chance from a larger population. When this principle is followed, the assumption can be made that the presence of any characteristic or subgroup will be as large or small in the sample as it is in the population at large. This principle is the foundation for any conclusions the research can form about the larger population from the sample selected and analyzed.[62] The education researcher must work with students, classrooms, schools, or school districts that cannot be altered to meet the needs of the researcher. Even a project as huge as that conducted for the *Coleman Report* could not avoid the claim of systematic bias in the final result.[63] Without the opportunity to randomize the samples with which a research study is conducted, the findings are diminished in power and reliability.[64]

MODEL SPECIFICATIONS

The general term for the description of the variables and the model is *model specification* . . . The true model is the starting point in all of our developments and the frame of reference by which to judge results. But the exact and correct formulation is not always known. The theories of the social scientist are usually not developed to the point of giving a complete model specification . . . Nor can one always expect to have the required data . . . Both of these situations, incomplete theories and incomplete data, can lead to specification errors.[65]

Specifically, an important variable may be left out of the model, or it may be included in the model, but no satisfactory measure may exist for it. In his study, Coleman did not include a measure of the innate ability of students. He thus conducted his empirical analysis without an important variable. Therefore, a specification bias exists in the estimated regression coefficients for this analysis. Such a specification error will tend to bias the results.

THE *COLEMAN REPORT*'S FLAWED DATA AND ANALYSIS

The *Coleman Report* has been a major influence on governmental policy. The influence of this study, however, goes beyond its effect on policy. The report has had a pervasive influence on production-function studies as a data source. Because the report was interpreted to mean that schools have little or no independent effect on the education of children beyond the influence of family and peers, it has been subjected to considerable analysis.

Hanushek and Kain[66] provided a substantive critique of the *Coleman Report* in which they described problems that undermined the reliability of the report's data and analytical procedures. While the plan for data collection was enormous, many difficulties plagued the project. The student sample size of 900,000 was reduced by nonresponse to 569,000. The failure to link students to specific schools limited the accuracy of the analysis. Further, reductions in usable data resulted in stratification by grade, race, region, and rural/urban divisions. Systematic nonresponse was a major problem since 41 percent of 1,170 schools were not included in the study, so the conclusions may be misleading. Since many sensitive questions were not answered, many questionnaire items relating to qualitative conditions were unusable. Cross-checking showed many miscoded responses. The frequency of such errors raises doubt about the reliability of the Coleman survey data in general.[67] Other concerns involved the failure to ask questions about the quality of facilities, to collect information on per-pupil expenditures, and to collect data on school organization.

The Coleman researchers employed analysis of variance (ANOVA) as the statistical methodology, a useful analytical procedure if no relationship exists between independent variables, and if they are indisputably independent without any correlations between them. Unfortunately, when the variables have high correlations, as they do in social research, multi co-linearity makes interpretations of an ANOVA exceedingly difficult. Frequently, interaction terms become the most significant source of variance between samples and must be explained if the research is to provide meaningful information. The method of analysis of interaction variables was highly questionable in the *Coleman Report,* however. The order of variable entries in the equation was a major factor in the results since interaction variance was added to the first term entered into the equation, weighing its explanatory power unjustifiably and inaccurately. Family background was entered first and school inputs last. Thus, family background consumed explanatory powers that may have belonged to schooling. The temporal order by which a student experiences the variables may not have a necessary relationship to the way interaction terms are distributed. Indeed, the main issue is how interaction effects should be partitioned among explanatory variables. In fact, since interaction effects could not be partitioned, the *Coleman Report* assigned all the interactions to family background. They could as easily have been assigned to school inputs. Hanushek and Kain[68] also found that there were not enough independent variations in the school factors, which resulted in attenuated variance. The absence of any measure of student ability undermined the conclusions. Since within-school variance is much greater than between-school variance, school inputs may vary more significantly within schools than between them. The authors of the report suggested this possibility, but the issue was not researched.

Teachers were not considered a school input in the report. Systematic departures of variables actually used in the analysis from those in the conceptual design were greatest for school inputs. For example, a 12th-grade student is likely to have attended several schools and experienced wide differences in educational experiences to a much greater extent than in peer and family experiences. The heterogeneity of student experiences in schools represented by vocational and college preparatory tracking obscures the variability of school experiences as reflected in mean standardized test results and school-level input aggregations.

According to Hanushek and Kain, the finding by Coleman of little school effect is a result of the method of analysis and not the *underlying behavioral reality*. Such a conclusion is *dangerous and destructive* as policy.

> The extent to which minority groups are systematically discriminated against in the provision of educational inputs is still unknown. This is a serious matter since the correction of input inequalities is a logical necessary first step in insuring equality of opportunity for minorities.[69]

In summary, the sample size of the study was reduced by a 41 percent nonresponse rate. Systematic nonresponse appeared to occur, particularly on sensitive issues. Many responses were miscoded and the frequency of such errors raised doubt about the reliability of the data in general. Information was collected about per-pupil expenditures, school organization, and the quality of facilities. In fact, the report found little difference between schools that were predominantly black or white. The data did not provide information on students by school, so the value of a large sample was significantly reduced. Finally, the researchers stated no theoretical model with which to interpret the data.

OTHER PRODUCTION-FUNCTION STUDIES

Burkhead compared small-community high school achievement to that of Chicago and Atlanta.[70] He described the education formula as an exploration, not a true production function. Unlike the industrial model, he recommended changing factor combinations to find the best configuration for increasing education output. This study included a value-added approach in the Chicago and Atlanta studies. He described three levels of resource use: acceleration, perpetuation, and amelioration. Acceleration referred to the practice in Atlanta in the early 1960s of investing more money in wealthier, higher-achieving white schools. The perpetuation design involved equal expenditure across all students. This maintained the existing condition in achievement reflected in the Chicago schools of the period. Amelioration required greater investment in schools for lower-income and lower-achieving students. His study demonstrated the importance of family income in student achievement. To improve student performance, he found it necessary to break the linkage of educational inputs to community income levels. If family income could not be changed, improvement in school outputs required dramatic increases in inputs or significant changes in resource combinations. This proposition could lead to the assumption of an unidentified threshold effect for breaking the link between family income and student success, as well as leading to experimentation with resource combinations in educational production.

Hanushek[71] emphasized the importance of production-function studies in policy decisions. His central concern was the education of minorities and the ability of education to cure the conditions of minorities in income, jobs, and life expectancy. Hanushek was careful to identify the problematic nature of conclusions from his analyses.

Because of the complexity of high school production functions and the difficulty of assessing cumulative factors in student performance, Hanushek examined elementary schools. He collected data at the individual school level in one of his three analyses. The other two studies were based on data from the *Coleman Report*.

Hanushek assumed that a public institution is inefficient because it does not operate in an openly competitive market. Incentives do not exist for the efficient maximization of resource use or educator performance. The production-function study could identify, with greater precision than existing methods, where efficiencies could be achieved. Hanushek defined efficiency as consisting of two elements: knowledge of the relationship between inputs of the educational process, and a research decision that connects costs of various inputs of the educational process to their educational outputs. Armed with this knowledge, policymakers could mix resources in ways that would be efficient and productive for student achievement. He conducted three studies that suggested areas of inefficiency in the purchase of teacher experience and additional education. Schools were incapable of curing the condition of minorities without changing the pattern of expenditures.

Rossmiller[72] evaluated public elementary school classrooms in relation to equity and efficiency. Analyzing data at the classroom level enabled Rossmiller to examine the achievement of students who directly received specific resources at precise costs. Time utilization, school expenditures, home environment, and teacher characteristics and attitudes were all carefully studied. Money and time correlated negatively with achievement because of the greater application of these resources to assist lower-achieving students. This suggested a trade-off between economic efficiency and efforts to ameliorate student achievement deficits. Thompson and Correa[73] researched a specific cohort of students in a private elementary school setting. They rated the cumulative effect (over three years) of certain input variables on student achievement. Using Glasman and Biniaminov as a reference, they found differential effects of these variables on private and public school students. As in public school analyses, teacher and school variables played a minor role in the prediction of variance in student achievement. Student academic ability was more important than school inputs. Teacher fluency, academic degree, and annual salary correlated with higher math achievement in contrast with achievements of public school students in both reading and math. Class and school size correlated negatively with private school achievement, but positively in some public school studies. The authors concluded that "caution should be used when applying the results of effective school research conducted in the public school directly to the private schools."[74] The results of this private school study, where there is a competitive market, did not differ in any significant way from the results of public school analyses.

BOX 12.7

Indefensible Use

In my view, it is simply indefensible to use the results of quantitative studies of the relationship between school resources and student achievement as a basis for concluding that additional funds cannot help public school districts.

Source: Richard J. Murnane, "Interpreting the Evidence on 'Does Money Matter'?," *Harvard Journal on Legislation* 28, No. 2 (Summer 1991), p. 457.

Ferguson[75] used an unusually large and complete data set from 900 districts in Texas that provided information on a student population five times that of the *Coleman Report*. Using a district-level analysis, Ferguson examined the determinants of student test scores, factors that influence which districts attract the most effective teachers, and how and why money matters in student achievement.

According to Ferguson, money is important in producing higher student test scores when it purchases teachers with strong literacy skills, reduces class size to 18 students per teacher, retains experienced teachers, and increases the number of teachers with advanced degrees. In addition to equalizing funding per pupil, ameliorative programs for low SES districts could include state-subsidized higher pay for teachers in lower SES districts. Good teachers are attracted to higher SES districts and the salaries they pay. Offering salary subsidies is a market decision that would encourage higher quality teachers to accept the challenge of teaching in difficult conditions. Possibly this could begin to break the link Burkhead found between family income and student achievement. This study uses other recent research to undermine the basic conclusions of the *Coleman Report* and the findings of less data-rich studies about the impact of teacher quality on student achievement.

IMPROVEMENT OF PRODUCTION-FUNCTION STUDIES

At the very least, an education production-function model requires that variables can be manipulated and are predictable. The questionable validity of the model remains the overriding concern for the usefulness of the production-function analysis in education. A method must be found to fashion a valid model before production-function studies can be taken seriously as policy instruments. Subsequently, a particular model must be designed for each specified educational setting. There may be a different production function for every individual, school, or school district.[76] Quality variations in inputs refer in part to differences of type. Some inputs are fixed for long periods of time, such as basic facilities and type of school (elementary, middle, or high, and public or private); some are variable in the long run but fixed in the short run, such as teacher characteristics; some are variable in the short run, such as teacher and student time. No one manager controls all these inputs, yet every actor influences their effect on the production-function. For production-function studies to be of any value for policy purposes a means must be found to validate the model in a given setting. To do so requires greater attention to overcoming difficulties in the identification and quantification of inputs.

The findings of empirical studies have been challenged for mixing levels of analysis between district, school, classroom, and student. Model adequacy requires uniformity of level. The important question to address, however, is the appropriate level for an accurate, policy-useful model. Some researchers have concluded that "there probably aren't many policy manipulable predictors of academic achievement much above the level of the individual classroom."[77] Since this is the focus of direct school inputs to each student's education, it is not a surprising conclusion. It would, however, render most research in the area invalid for policy purposes.

The collection of data at the classroom level is the direction research activities must take in order to develop a useable production-function model. That is not to say that other levels of analysis cannot be valid. It only appears that the sequence of development is best pursued inductively.

Determining the contribution of school factors to student achievement became an important research objective in the wake of the *Coleman Report*. The recognition of the need for a measure of ability or achievement as a pretest score is also a vital concern in the development of an adequate model of education production. Lau[78] and others have acknowledged the *uninformative* nature of cross-sectional studies that lack such measures. Bowles described achievement scores as measures of gross output. The goal was "to estimate the relationship between school inputs and net output, or value added."[79] Measures that allow the assessment of value-added performance are generally regarded as important components of an adequate model. The lack of such data seriously impairs the usefulness of empirical studies.

The development of an adequate model requires the purposeful collection of data that have a direct relevance to a conceptual production-function design. A national testing program could provide the impetus for such a collection process. Yet, a strong movement among educators challenges the adequacy of quantitative measures of student achievement. The development of a broad-based qualitative methodology for student evaluation through portfolio building has begun to spread across the country. This approach is partially based on dissatisfaction with purely statistical appraisals. For this reason alone, any effort to collect national data for production-function analyses would probably face vigorous political opposition.

SUMMARY

In this chapter we sought to present the concept of production functions and to identify some of the shortcomings of such studies in their application to education. The discussion explained how poorly conceived model specifications and research design have led to baseless conclusions about both adequacy and equity of funding for public schools. The production function's use in industry as compared to education helps to clarify some of the problems of directly applying a rather simple industrial concept to a complex social phenomenon like education. The production-function model is an industrial model, and its application to education requires a specification and precision of measurement that is difficult to quantify.

The use of poorly specified production-function analyses in education has led some researchers to erroneously conclude that money has little bearing on the quality of education.

Foremost among the production-function studies was the famous *Coleman Report* that was widely quoted as evidence that more funds for *education would not increase the educational achievement of students.* While the *Coleman Report* was often misquoted, it was nevertheless a poorly designed and carelessly analyzed project that has very little continuing educational research value.

The education production-function process is of such a complex nature that it is safe to say that no production-function study has yet been designed to accurately capture the value of increments of fiscal inputs. The elusiveness of both inputs and outputs in education prevents the researcher from measuring direct inputs and outputs. Instead, the researcher is forced to use proxy variables that introduce varying degrees of invalidity.

Education productivity does not track the industrial model in several ways, but two of the most troublesome areas are the failure of measurement for returns to scale and the issue of substitutability. Neither applies as readily to education as to the industrial situation.

A primary difficulty in most education production-function studies is the inability to relate costs directly to the educational process. Most studies have aggregated data by school district or school rather than by classroom. Also, such cost data have often included expenditures for aspects of education, e.g., student transportation, school facilities, debt service, etc., that are not applicable to the particular educational function being analyzed. Such studies have also been unable to capture the changes over time. Most have constituted mere cross-sectional views of the educational process.

One major shortcoming of production functions when applied to education is the inability to capture the essence of the teacher process itself. So little is known about what constitutes effectiveness in teaching that measurement is problematic at best.

The characteristics of the home backgrounds, the students themselves, the schools, and the community all bear on the educational process, but their relative magnitude and importance is virtually impossible to discern.

Production-function studies in education could be useful if models of measurement were so specified as to reveal reliable and valid results. To date, however, such studies have major flaws that greatly limit their value. Unfortunately, these studies, regardless of their accuracy, have been misconstrued and sometimes misappropriated in an attempt to influence public policy choices in education. Having poorly conceived models accepted as the basis for important educational investment decisions or as a deterrent to school finance reform are the chief dangers presented by the present crop of production-function studies.

KEY TERMS

- Production function
- Initial endowments
- Industrial model
- Returns to scale
- Education model
- Substitutability

- *Coleman Report*
- Human variables
- Family background
- Attenuated data
- Peer influence
- Threshold effect

NOTES

1. Aubrey Price, *Education Production Functions in Policy Making: A Critical Analysis* (Doctoral Dissertation, Virginia Tech, 1994).
2. Brian Barry, *Culture and Equality* (Oxford: Polity Press, Blackwell Publishers, Inc., 2001).
3. Brian Barry, *Theories of Justice* (Berkeley: University of California Press, 1989), pp. 220–221.
4. D. H. Monk, *Educational Finance: An Economic Approach* (New York: McGraw-Hill, 1990); D.C. Berliner, "Educational Reform in an Era of Disinformation," *Education Policy Archives: An Electronic Journal*, vol. 1, no. 2 (1993).

5. J. S. Coleman, Ernest Campbell, Carol Hobson, James McPactland, Alexander Good, Frederick Weinfeld, and Robert York, *Equality of Educational Opportunity* (Washington, DC: Government Printing Office, 1966).

6. E. A. Hanushek and J. F. Kain, "On the Value of Equality of Educational Opportunity as a Guide to Public Policy," in F. Mosteller and D. P. Moyniham, eds., *On Equality of Educational Opportunity* (New York: Vintage Books, 1972).

7. J. Coons, W. Clune, and S. Sugarman, *Private Wealth and Public Education* (Cambridge, MA: Howard Belknap, 1972); and E. A. Hanushek, *Education and Race: An Analysis of the Education Production Process* (Lexington, MA: D.C. Heath, 1972), pp. 423–456.

8. National Commission on Excellence in Education, *A Nation at Risk* (Washington, DC: U.S. Government Printing Office, 1983); Educational Testing Service, *The State of Inequality* (Princeton, NJ: ETS, Policy Information Center, 1991).

9. Testimony of H.J. Walberg, "In the Matter of *Raymond A. Abbott, et al. vs. Fred G. Burke, et al.,* 100 N.J. 269, 499 A.2d 376," State of New Jersey Office of Administrative Law, EDU-5581-85 (Roseland, NJ: Essex-Union Reporting Services, April 27, 1987); J.C. Fortune, *Rebuttal to the Deposition of Eric A. Hanushek*, unpublished document (Blacksburg, VA: Virginia Tech, 1992).

10. C. F. Edley, Jr., "Lawyers and Education Reform," *Harvard Journal on Legislation* 28, no. 2 (Summer 1991), pp. 293–305.

11. Ibid., p. 296.

12. P. A. Samuelson and W. D. Nordhaus, *Economics,* 13th edn. (New York: McGraw-Hill, 1989), p. 499.

13. C. W. Cobb and P. H. Douglas, "A Theory of Production," *American Economic Review Supplement* (1928), pp. 139–165.

14. E. J. Pedhazur, *Multiple Regression in Behavioral Research: Explanation and Prediction*, 2nd edn. (New York: CBS College Publishing, 1982).

15. Jennifer King Rice and Amy Ellen Schwartz, "Toward an Understanding of Productivity in Education," in Helen F. Ladde and Edward B. Fiske (eds), *Handbook of Research in Education Finance and Policy* (New York: Routledge, 2008), p. 135.

16. Ibid.

17. Ibid., p. 139.

18. H. M. Levin, "Concepts of Economic Efficiency and Educational Production," in J. T. FroomKin, D. T. Jamison, and R. Radner (eds.), *Education as an Industry* (Cambridge, MA: Ballinger Books).

19. Rice and Schwartz, *op. cit.,* p. 139.

20. Hanushek, *op. cit.*

21. Ibid., p. 27.

22. Ibid.

23. Ibid., p. 30.

24. Ibid., p. 31.

25. Samuelson and Nordhaus, *op. cit.,* p. 501.

26. Monk, *op. cit.*

27. S. Bowles, "Towards an Educational Production Function," in W. L. Hansen, ed., *Education, Income, and Human Capital* (New York: National Bureau of Economic Research, 1970); G. R. Bridge, C. M. Judd, and P. R. Moock, *The Determinants of Educational Outcomes: The Impact of Families, Peers, Teachers, and Schools* (Cambridge, MA: Ballinger, 1979).

28. Samuelson and Nordhaus, *op. cit.*, p. 503.

29. Ibid.

30. D. A. Verstegen, "Efficiency and Economies-of-Scale Revisited: Implications for Financing Rural School Districts," *Journal of Education Finance* vol. 16, no. 2 (Fall 1990), pp. 159–179;

H. J. Walberg and W. J. Fowler, Jr., "Expenditure and Size Efficiencies of Public School Districts," *Educational Research* vol.16, no. 7 (1987), pp. 5–13.

31. Ibid.

32. *Outcome Accountability Project: 1992 Virginia Summary Report* (Richmond, VA: Virginia Department of Education).

33. H. J. Walberg, "The Knowledge Base of Educational Productivity," *International Journal of Educational Reform 1*, No. 1 (January 1992), pp. 5–15.

34. Samuelson and Nordhaus, *op. cit.*

35. Bridge et al., *op. cit.*

36. Ibid.

37. Samuelson and Nordhaus, *op. cit.,* p. 506.

38. Walberg, *op. cit.*

39. Cobb and Douglas, *op. cit.*

40. R. Rossmiller*, Resource Utilization in Schools and Classrooms: Final Report* (Madison, WI: Wisconsin Center for Educational Research, University of Wisconsin) (ERIC Document Reproduction Service No. ED 272 490), 1986.

41. Cobb and Douglas, *op. cit.*

42. J.M. Henderson and R.E. Quandt, *Microeconomic Theory: A Mathematical Approach* (New York: McGraw-Hill, 1971).

43. L.J. Lau, "Educational Production Functions," in *Economic Dimensions of Education* (Washington, DC: The National Academy of Education, 1979), p. 42.

44. Berliner, *op. cit.*

45. Hanushek, *op. cit.;* R. J. Murnane, *The Impact of School Resources on the Learning of Inner City Children* (Cambridge, MA: Ballinger, 1975). See: Caroline M. Hoxby, ed., *The Economics of School Choice* (Chicago: University of Chicago Press, 2003).

46. R. J. Murnane and R. R. Nelson, "Production and Innovation When Techniques are Tacit," *Journal of Economic Behavior and Organization* 5 (1984), pp. 353–373.

47. Bridge et al., *op. cit.*

48. Hanushek, *Education and Race, op. cit.*

49. J. C. Fortune, D. C. Strickland, and A. H. Price, "Methodological Differences in the Use of Educational Productivity Function Analyses," in *Proceedings of the 11th Annual Conference of the Association of Management 11*, no. 1 (1939), pp. 53–58; A. H. Price, D. C. Strickland, and J. C. Fortune, "A Critical Review of Walberg and Hanushek's Contribution to School Equity Issues," in *Proceedings of the 11th Annual Conference of the Association of Management 11,* no. 1 (1993), pp. 80–85.

50. Urie Bronfenbrenner, *Ecology of Human Development: Experiments by Nature and Design* (Cambridge, MA: Harvard University Press, 1979).

51. Bridge et al., *op. cit.*

52. Walt Rostow, *The Stages of Economic Growth* (Cambridge, MA: Cambridge University Press, 1971).

53. Bridge et al., *op. cit.*

54. Fortune et al., *op. cit.*

55. Lau, *op. cit.* See also: Rice and Schwartz, *op. cit.,* 2008.

56. J. A. Thompson and L. H. Correa, "A Study of School and Teacher Inputs on Student Achievement Outputs," *Journal of Education Finance* 14 (Winter 1989), pp. 390–406; F. MacPhail-Wilcox and R. A. King, "Production-Functions in the Context of Educational Reform," *Journal of Education Finance* 12 (Fall 1986), pp. 191–222; F. MacPhail-Wilcox and R. A. King, "Resource Allocation Students: Implications for School Improvement and School Finance Research," *Journal of Education Finance* 11 (Spring 1986), pp. 416–432; N. S. Glasman and I. Biniaminov, "Input-Output Analyses of Schools," *Review of Educational Research* 51, no. 4 (Winter 1981), pp. 509–539; Bridge et al., *op. cit.*

57. Ferguson, *op. cit.*

58. Thompson and Correa, *op. cit.*

59. Eric Hanushek, "Assessing the Effects of School Resources on Student Performance: An Update," *Educational Evaluation and Policy Analysis*, 19, No. 2 (summer), pp. 141–164 (1997).

60. James J. Heckman and Alan B. Krueger, *Inequality in America* (Cambridge, MA: The MIT Press, 2003), pp. 33–37.

61. Pedhazur, *op. cit.*; L. J. Cronbach, G. C. Gleser, H. Nanda, and N. Rajaratnam, *The Dependability of Behavioral Measurements: Theory of Generalizability for Scores and Profiles* (New York: John Wiley & Sons, 1972).

62. D.C. Howell, *Statistical Methods for Psychology*, 2nd edn. (Boston: PWS-Kent, 1987).

63. Hanushek and Kain, *op. cit.*

64. Howell, *op. cit.*; Pedhazur, *op. cit.*

65. E. A. Hanushek and J. E. Jackson, *Statistical Methods for Social Scientists* (New York: Academic Press, 1977).

66. Hanushek and Kain, *op. cit.*

67. Ibid., p. 121.

68. Ibid.

69. Ibid., p. 131.

70. J. Burkhead, *Input and Output in Large-City High Schools* (Syracuse: Syracuse University Press, 1967).

71. Hanushek, *Education and Race*, *op. cit.*

72. Rossmiller, *op. cit.*

73. Thompson and Correa, *op. cit.*

74. Ibid., p. 406.

75. Ferguson, *op. cit.*

76. Monk, *op. cit.*

77. K. T. Hereford and T. Z. Keith, *Effects of Local Financial Effort on School District Achievement* (Blacksburg, VA: Virginia Tech, 1991), p. 27.

78. Lau, *op. cit.*

79. Bowles, *op. cit.*, p. 26.

CHAPTER 13

Analyzing Equity and Adequacy of State School Finance

INTRODUCTION

This chapter has three parts. *First*, it sets forth a rationale for defining equity from various philosophical viewpoints. For clarity we explain that *equity* is in fact *justice*. They are synonymous. We apply equity in allocative theory to state school fund distribution. This part of the chapter breaks equity or justice theory into four state school finance levels or categories of an "allocative hierarchy" that has four aspects: (1) *commutative allocation*, the lowest level; (2) *alimentative allocation*, which means nourishment of fiscal condition; (3) *restorative allocation* which redresses differences in fiscal or tax effort among school districts in a state; and (4) *ameliorative allocation,* which may be described as accommodation of natural needs beneficence, the equivalent of moral or right conduct.

Second, this chapter explains in considerable detail the standard statistical methods for measuring fiscal equalization or horizontal equity.

Third, the last section of the chapter addresses the various ways that school finance experts seek to determine the *adequacy* of school funding in a state. In short, how, in the political climate on which school financing is fully dependent, can a rational and defensible case be made to establish a reasonable dollar level for state school financing?

PART I: CONCEPTS OF EQUITY IN SCHOOL FINANCING[1]

A primary goal of all public school finance systems should be to ensure equitable treatment for all school children. Yet, the goal of *equity* does not lend itself to easy definition.[2] Basically, *equity is fairness or justice*. "In its broadest and most general signification, the term denotes the spirit and the habit of fairness, justness, and right dealing."[3] It is an ethical obligation of persons to each other. It was defined by Justinian, "to live honestly, to harm nobody, to render to every man his due."[4] Rousseau probably best defined equity in the context of the common interest: "in which each person necessarily submits to the conditions he imposes upon others, and this admirable agreement between interest and justice gives to the common deliberation an equitable characteristic."[5]

The view of educational opportunity as having an intrinsic requirement of fairness and equitability beyond mathematical quantification is not foreign to the thinking of many concerning educational opportunity. Much has been written about equality of education, and in much of the literature a standard of equity emerges which exceeds mere mathematical nicety. Tumin explains that equal education does not mean the same education, but it does mean equal concern, "that each child shall become the most and the best that he (she) can become."[6]

The measure of equality should be that every child is learning and that the conditions for learning are equal among all the children. Accordingly, every child must be able to perceive the opportunity and advance according to his ability.[7] In the same vein, it may be argued that the school should be held responsible for providing differential educational experiences designed for the special abilities that the child brings to the educational setting.[8]

That the state should provide for an adequate level of education and compensate for background variance for each student suggests not only equal treatment but also a supplementary standard based on individual needs. This accommodation of educational needs departing from a strict adherence to mathematical equality is the nature and essence of educational equity. In legal philosophy, sometimes the grossest discrimination can lie in treating things that are different exactly alike. At this point strict adherence to mathematical equality is insufficient, since equity and justice cannot be obtained through equal treatment of unequals.

This is precisely the issue which has perplexed educators and lawyers alike since the early 1970s when educational finance litigation began in earnest. Throughout the litigation, three major issues have prevailed: *First,* how and to what extent can school district fiscal capacity be equalized? *Second*, how can educational needs be measured, and should such measures be used to allocate funds to local school districts? *Third*, should the tax effort among school districts be mandated at a uniform level? These issues circumscribe reasonably well three basic issues that involve school finance equity and adequacy that characterize all litigation and state school finance studies.

Horizontal and Vertical Equity. School finance specialists have typically explained *equity* as having two aspects, horizontal and vertical.[9] Horizontal equity is defined as "equal treatment of equals," simple *equality*, best understood as Berlin's "Cakes and Shares," cited earlier in Chapter 4. However, equal treatment of equals does not necessarily do justice or provide equity for those who, for no reason attributable to their own fault, have greater needs. Vertical equity, on the other hand, is "unequal treatment of unequals," which in the nomenclature of school finance means that differences in the educational needs of children are taken into account in funding formulae that recognize differences by providing measurably more funds to those children who are disadvantaged. Vertical equity, according to Rawls' "difference principle," calls for society acting via the state to provide greater levels of assistance for the least advantaged.[10] Vertical equity may also be helpfully defined as fairness and justice.

Equity Generally. Equity in its broadest sense encompasses justice, equality, dignity, humanity, morality, and right. To address the term *equity* requires substantial explication, for what is equitable depends to a great extent upon the orientation of both the dispensers and receivers of equity. Equitable treatment may find its basis in natural law. In the context of today's governments it is difficult to reduce the grand design of natural law to an operational definition. Provision for the common wealth may create conditions which are favorable to a few but harmful to many.

But, as explained above, *equity is more than equality.* Like justice, it is abstract and not readily susceptible to definition. Equality, as a general standard, conveys an element of prescription and measurability. While justice may be commonly defined as giving everyone his due, the term *equality* more specifically refers to division, partition, distribution, Berlin's "cakes and shares."

Equity and Right. Kant relates equity to right, saying that "equity is founded not on any principle of beneficence, benevolence, or charity, but upon right."[11] His *right* was both natural and positive, the former being based upon pure rationality while the latter emanated from the will of the legislator. To him an innate right is vested in every person at birth, a birthright, while acquired rights are founded upon juridical acts. For Kant, this innate right is the obligation which equity must address.

As observed above, equity and justice may be viewed as attributes of each other and as virtually interchangeable. In the eyes of the jurist, equity is an essential element of the broader concept of justice, while the economist will usually view equity as *a priori* condition of which justice is a basic part. Regardless of this semantic relativity, though, justice and equity entail the virtue of attributing to everyone his right and in accordance with his needs. Jean Dabin, one of the most notable twentieth century legal philosophers of Europe, wrote in 1944 that a primary and inherent problem in quantifying justice is that it must be defined by *aequalitas* rather than by the *aequum*. He says, "The virtue that renders to everyone his right or his dignity deserves to be defined, in a strict sense, not merely by the loose idea of equity (*aequum et bonum*) but by the mathematical idea of equality (*aequalitas*)."[12] Regardless, relative to problems of measurement, most agree that equity and justice have broader qualities than those which are measurable in terms of simple equality.

ALLOCATIVE THEORY

In their philosophical context, equity and justice have the same attributes of right and humanity of purpose. In the very broad and unrestricted context, equity may be coextensive with the wide moral expanse of natural law and the western ideals of charity and fairness. In this regard, then, social and economic philosophy of school fund distribution may be interpreted as having four degrees of symmetrical progressive transfers of money. Each degree depends to some extent upon the conditions which are extant in society generally and government in particular. Allocative justice in education finance, therefore, can be viewed in light of four concepts or types of allocation: (1) commutative allocation, (2) alimentative allocation, (3) restorative allocation, and (4) ameliorative allocation.

Allocative Hierarchy

Although philosophical equity, justice, and the reality of school finance are not easily reconciled, commonalities can be found. As shown in Figure 13.1, a hierarchy, or staircase, of allocative justice can be fashioned, progressing from the lowest level of *commutative allocation* upward to the highest level of *ameliorative or beneficent*. The steps in the hierarchy, when related to a school finance legal theory, produce a pattern of supplementary progressive attributes, which, if combined, produce funding of natural ideal or justice. *Any of the first three steps taken alone would be defective and fall short of the ideal.*

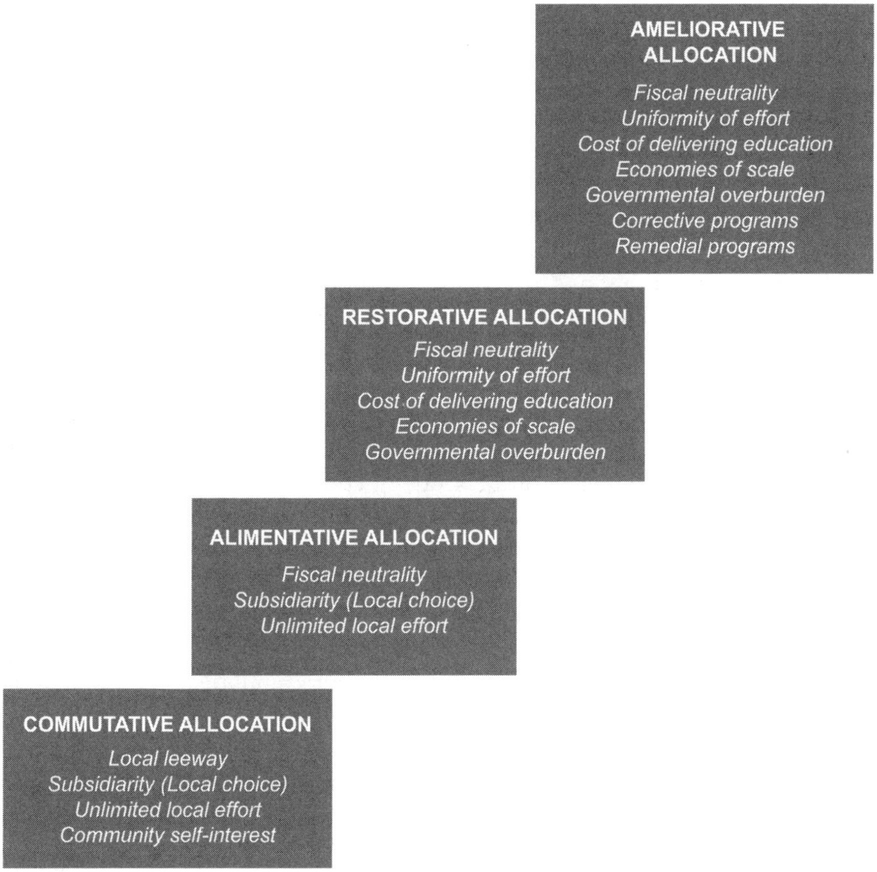

Figure 13.1 Staircase of Allocative Equity (or Justice)

Commutative Allocation

Commutative allocation of social resources entitles a person to something simply because it is his, he now holds it in his possession, and it leaves the partitioning produced by the market place unaltered. It, in fact, has little if any features of equity, aside from a narrow band of local *quid pro quo*. It is libertarian in its orientation and concept. Here someone owns something by virtue of a private and individual relationship.[13] It constitutes neither *horizontal* nor *vertical* equity. This particular aspect of allocation includes what is commonly known in other countries as private law, the inviolability of property, freedom to contract, and duty to compensate another for damages. It maintains that the order in which certain operations are performed, and hence presumptive endowments, does not matter. On a staircase of allocation, beginning at the lowest level, a *commutative* allocation would simply be an exchange of resources which are indifferent to considerations of equality, educational need, initial endowments, etc. Shifting taxation to the local level tends to produce this result, and most state school funding systems permit the individual school district to retain their own resources regardless of need or fiscal capability. Assets are retained and no redistribution takes place. In this sense local tax prerogative and choice maintain economic homogeneity, but only within local boundaries. In the sense of school finance, *communitarianism* is a narrow idea of fiscal localism, nesting in a community without concerns for the larger more comprehensive view of statewide duty and responsibility, less concern for the whole.[14] This is the habituate of thought that sees the public good in a narrow band where the public or common good is a constricted concept. It advances the notion of political restraint, neutrality, and a distrust of central government authority. Raz says that it is "anti-perfectionism,"[15] conservatism, that any departure from the *status quo* requires that government bear a burden of proof of necessity.

As Pagden recently wrote in his highly regarded work, *The Enlightenment*, "communitarians" see no duty beyond their own culture, religion, school district, parish, or village, and do not recognize an "Enlightenment cosmopolitanism."[16] They, in essence, have a constrained view of the scope of common humanity and do not recognize an expansive duty beyond their local considerations.[17] Pagden says that *communitarianism* narrows the field of "common humanity" as far as to "imply that 'others' should [probably not] be eligible for the same political rights as 'us.'"[18] There is no obligation to "share" advantages or favorable conditions with anyone "beyond our immediate social environment."[19] It is this communitarianism that rears its head in states where there is great disparity between affluent school districts in the suburbs and the less fiscally able school districts in core cities and rural areas, and in its more extreme sense is a principal basis for private schools. *Commutative* allocation cannot accommodate the broader ideals of equity in their normal sense. It suggests a system of *laissez-faire* self-interest which is not unlike the result of a governmental allocation system, the proceeds of which flow to the private sector benefiting only those who already have the financial resources.

With commutation, government does not redistribute resources. Instead, it is assumed either that there is no action, or that the state action manifestly produces no disparate or unjust results upon any segment of the population. In such a state of affairs, no further government action is necessary, and individualism, libertarianism, and the effects of the market prevail. Thus, *commutative* allocation provides for no corrective or remedial state action to redress disparate conditions created in the private sector. It is conservative, unchanging, *status quo*.

Alimentative Allocation

Alimentative allocation, on the other hand, encompasses conditions created by various kinds of social conditions which every society is called upon to respond. It is here that the issues of equality in public school finance generally arise.[20] The redistribution of the resources of society to the individual is one side of the equation, while the debt of the individual (what is owed by society) is the other. These interact to circumscribe a degree of equality which should be maintained in the educational system.

This second step of the allocative staircase seeks to nourish a more progressive distribution under the presumption that the educational system is an obligation of the state and that in its implementation, the state treats all children in local school districts in a *fiscally neutral* manner; all should have access to the same amount of money per pupil. The alimentation rule posits that allocations of funds will correct and redress natural tendencies of the marketplace that skew resources toward inequality and unfairness. A structure of such distribution assumes a given degree of fairness from taxation to allocation for viability and stability of the public school system. The state here is not primarily concerned with uniformity of services, efficiency of operation, or thoroughness of the educational program; rather, it endeavours to equalize the fiscal base for all school districts regardless of where they are located, and it is a local prerogative to decide entirely upon what level of educational program is desired. The determination of the level of tax effort *is, thus, a local prerogative*. At this level, educational equity is defined as full fiscal neutrality, the only prescribed standard. The school finance formula most closely associated with this level of equity would be district power equalization or guaranteed tax yield/base. In its most primitive form, district power equalization would fully fiscally equalize, but due to subsidiarity gaps in tax effort and, therefore, educational opportunity, would be permitted to continue to exist.

Restorative Allocation

Restorative allocation, as a concept of equity, recognizes that unjust distribution of advantage in society may be exacerbated by undesirable state action, and it seeks to compensate for the impact. With full knowledge that providing justice to one party may create injustice for another, the state government institutes redistributive tax and expenditure policies to correct for inadvertent or inappropriate antecedent inequitable governmental actions.

This third level is classified as *restorative* because it requires that the state recompense and requite local school districts for problems created by state or privately created economic or social conditions. *It is a return, a rectification or reparation, a making good.* Here the state responds to local conditions which cause educational opportunities to vary from some established norm. Implicit in this level of allocation is an established desirable level of educational opportunity. Requiting, as this third level, is only provided for those structural issues of the system, whether social or economic, and is not related to the child's personal educational needs.

Restorative allocation requires the state to mitigate fiscal inequities created by diseconomies of scale in schools or school districts, cost variations in delivering comparable educational services, and adjustments for local tax effort disparities among school districts. Most important to this level of allocation is that it *equalizes tax effort. Here the state must equalize and level the fiscal effort among school districts.* This can be accomplished by high levels of required local effort or charge-backs, i.e., local required effort, in foundation programs. Traditional, unembellished percentage-equalization formulae do not normally have the capability to correct for low tax effort. Restitution for the vagaries of differing tax efforts constitutes a high level of equity when combined with full fiscal equalization or fiscal neutrality. Restoration conveys the philosophy that education is a state function and, as such, the state has not only the responsibility but also the obligation to rectify and indemnify fiscal shortcomings at the local school district level.

Ameliorative Allocation

Ameliorative allocation is the essence of that which is considered to be beneficent, just, right, and fair. At the highest level of equity, as shown in Figure 13.1, fiscal equity demands that the unique and high-cost programs which are designed to meet individual *needs* of children be fully financed. It is positivist in the context of government policy, a moral intervention. This is *Rawlsian Equity*, which justifies intervention if it is designed to help the *least advantaged*. In the realm of education, types of needs include corrective programs for those children with natural deficiencies which can be moderated by effective education processes. Programs for children with disabilities fall into this category. Herein, also, is justified a kind of fiscal affirmative action whereby those who suffer disadvantages because of economic, social, or cultural conditions are provided the benefits via specially designed and financed remedial educational programs.

Equity of educational finance encompasses a complexity of issues related to equal educational opportunity. It is important to be mindful that, from both the philosophical and legal viewpoints, equity is much broader than the simple fiscal equalization. Fiscal equalization alone, while it is probably the most important building block in an equitable system, is insufficient. Its deficiencies may be related to overall fiscal inadequacy, a lack of uniformity in fiscal effort, failure to identify and accommodate appropriate costs, and the lack of recognition of educational needs.

A concept of equity, *natural justice* requires that government act affirmatively to correct inherent or innate natural disadvantages and disparities among individuals. Such may issue from a basic right or from a moral and humanitarian necessity to alleviate conditions which have befallen a segment of the population through no fault of the individuals or the state. Under this theory anyone who is disadvantaged, even by nature or misadventure, has a right to have the condition ameliorated by state action. *Natural equity or justice* is premised upon a moral obligation to assist those who are disadvantaged, although their inferior position is not the result of governmental action. Kant supports this in his argument for a duty of beneficence, and Rawls justifies it with his principle of benefit to the "least advantaged."

Each of these concepts of equity, or justice, may be applied to educational finance in establishing a framework through which educational opportunity may be viewed.

PART II: MEASURING EQUITY OF STATE SCHOOL FUNDING

The concept of fiscal equalization of educational opportunity has been earlier discussed, and the subconcepts of vertical and horizontal equity of state systems of school finance have been introduced. Further, taxpayer equity was discussed in Chapter 8. Collectively, these concepts and subconcepts provide the philosophical basis for the measurement of equity that may be applied to the 50 state systems of school finance.

The several types of intergovernmental revenue transfer systems, or grants that are used by states to allocate state resources to local school districts, were presented elsewhere in this text. The primary objective of state grants, through shared local and state funds, is to fiscally equalize educational resources and to provide adequate financing of local school districts. The measurement of equity provided by state systems of school finance is quite complicated and has required the development of sensitive and sophisticated statistical measures. The measurements of both horizontal equality and taxpayer equity pursuant to state systems of school finance lends itself to statistical treatment of fiscal data. As suggested by Berne and Stiefel in their definitions, the measurement of vertical equity is dependent, at least partially, upon the values and educational priorities of those who conduct equity analyses. Following the discussion of horizontal and taxpayer equity measurement, recommendations concerning the measurement of vertical equity are provided. Prior to the statistical measurement of equity, it is necessary to establish and refine the state database, a process that requires several key research decisions. The following recommendations for preparation of the state database, while not universally accepted, are based upon best practice.

Preparation of State Database

Ideally, the application of the several equity statistics to a state database would be conducted precisely the same by all school finance researchers. The data from the 50 states would be configured identically, including similarity of school district organization, fiscal capacity measure, accounting terminology, fund structure, pupil unit, and other factors. Unfortunately, while some commonality does exist among states, significant differences exist and will continue to exist for the foreseeable future. While adherence to the following nine procedural steps for preparation of the state databases will not completely satisfy the problems created by the dissimilarity of state systems of school finance, such adherence should make interstate comparisons of fiscal equity analyses more reliable.

1. While either revenue or current expenditure may be used as the input cost measure, *current expenditure per pupil (adjusted by deducting federal revenue) is likely the more reliable measure*. There is an argument to use state and local revenue since it is a measure of total fiscal resources available to local school districts. However, the revenue input reported by states often contains nonrevenue for capital outlay, making revenue a volatile input measure.[21]

2. The *unit of analysis* should be based upon pupils and not the local school district. Some researchers inappropriately use local school districts as the unit of analysis, thus disregarding the differences in numbers of pupils served by local school districts. To achieve horizontal equity analysis, the focus should be upon pupils served throughout the state and not on the administrative structure that serves only as a vehicle for delivery of educational services. In the case of Virginia, by treating school districts as the unit of analysis, Highland County Public Schools, serving approximately 350 pupils, would exert an identical statistical influence as Fairfax County, serving approximately 135,000 pupils. While current school accounting does not provide individual per-pupil revenue or expenditure data, an acceptable alternative is to assume a common per-pupil expenditure for a single school district and weight the school district proportionally to the number of pupils served.

3. Local school districts should be *segregated according to district type* before the application of equity statistics. It is inappropriate to statistically treat elementary,

secondary, and K–12 school districts together. Even if identical educational programs were being provided among all local school districts, the differences in per-pupil revenue or expenditure that inherently exist among elementary, secondary, and K–12 districts would likely distort horizontal equity analyses.

4. *Specially configured local school districts should be excluded* from the equity analysis. Intermediate, cooperative, and regional districts, as well as special education service centers, vocational area districts, and other specially configured districts (schools) are often funded uniquely and complicate the interpretation of equity analyses. While the exclusion of specially configured districts is necessary prior to statistical analysis, their services and concurrent costs to local school districts need to be assigned only to benefitted local school districts.

5. *Local school districts that are structural anomalies should be excluded* from the equity analysis. Due to geographical constraints, states occasionally experience exceptionally high per-pupil costs to provide educational services for limited numbers of pupils.

6. *Federal funds should be excluded* from the equity analysis. Federal grants contain provisions that require that states not supplant federal funds.[22] The non-supplanting provisions make a powerful argument for excluding all federal funds, with the possible exception of federal impact aid. Federal impact aid specifically authorizes states to *take into consideration* a portion of federal impact aid allocated to their local school districts if the state can meet certain equity requirements.[23]

7. *Categorical funds, whether contained within the basic state grant or separately funded, should be included* in the equity analysis. This procedure does not enjoy universal acceptance among school finance researchers. Some researchers argue that horizontal and vertical equity analyses should be conducted separately; and as a consequence, they argue that the horizontal equity criteria should be applied only to client groups where equality can be agreed upon.

    Those opposed to the exclusion of categorical funds from the equity analysis suggest that high-capacity school districts often are able to compete more effectively for competitive grants than other districts. Further, due to a lack of accounting uniformity and grant structures among states, interstate comparison of equity statistics is complicated by attempting to exclude categorical from equity analyses. Finally, if differences among client groups, school district characteristics, and educational programs are accommodated properly prior to the application of the several equity statistics, the evaluation of horizontal and vertical equity can be conducted simultaneously. Further discussion of this procedure is presented later in this chapter.

8. The differences that exist among school districts due to client needs, school district characteristics, and educational programs should be identified and per-unit weights should be applied, resulting in a weighted pupil count for each school district included in the equity analyses.

9. In longitudinal studies, either appropriate inflators or deflators should be applied to current expenditures in order to convert to constant dollars. While most equity statistics are unaffected by constant-dollar adjustments, the range, restricted range, and measures of central tendency are subject to distortion due to inflationary pressures and should be converted to constant dollars for cross-time comparisons.

Measurement of Horizontal and Vertical Equity

Contained in Box 13.1 are two terms that provide the boundaries for the measurement of fiscal equalization. Precisely defined is the ultimate goal of fiscal equalization as well as a definition of an acceptable level of fiscal equalization that may be achieved politically.

BOX 13.1

Absolute Fiscal Equalization

- Variance in fiscal capacity among local school districts has been neutralized;
- Variance in fiscal effort among local school districts has been eliminated; and
- Variance in educational needs of students has been accommodated.

Acceptable Fiscal Equalization

- Variance in fiscal capacity among local school districts has been neutralized;
- Constrained variance in fiscal effort among local school districts is permitted; and
- Variance in educational needs of students has been accommodated.

As defined earlier, horizontal equity requires that equal resources are provided to pupils who have similar needs. If all pupils required identical educational services, the measurement of horizontal equity could be achieved by simply applying a series of dispersion statistics to a properly prepared state database. Unfortunately, each state, local school district, school, and classroom serve diverse clients who require varying amounts and forms of educational services. As a consequence, the different amounts and forms of educational services result in considerable variance in per-pupil costs. If the objective is to measure horizontal equity without consideration of vertical equity, one could exclude all pupils who require unequal services and their concomitant costs from the data, that is, categorical funds and eligible pupils. Application of dispersion statistics to the remaining pupils and costs would provide an analysis of horizontal equity. While the nine-step procedure will effectively measure horizontal equity, it does not yield an analysis of vertical equity, and does, in fact, greatly complicate such an analysis. Due to limitations of fiscal accounting practices employed by most public schools, precise identification and assignment of the full costs required to provide services for unequal pupils has proven extremely difficult.

According to Berne and Stiefel, the measurement of vertical equity is value-laden, certainly an understatement for researchers who have struggled with this difficult problem. While most school finance authorities agree that unequal pupils require unequal treatment, there is little agreement regarding either client identification or the costs required to provide educational services to identified clients. Even among client programs universally accepted as requiring unequal or extraordinary costs, such as for children with disabilities, there is little agreement regarding what constitutes either appropriate educational services or their respective costs. Each of the 50 states has established unique systems for providing and funding educational services to a varied array of student groups. How then should the level of vertical equity by a state system of school finance be measured?

Perhaps the most defensible procedure is to conduct the analysis of horizontal and vertical equity simultaneously as suggested by procedural step 7. In order to conduct a simultaneous evaluation of horizontal and vertical equity, all current costs, excluding federal funds, should remain in the analysis. A series of state-specific pupil weights should be developed based upon a cost-accounting analysis of statewide historical data.[24] These state-specific weights should be developed relative to pupils who are not eligible for unequal costs. For example, a cost-accounting analysis might show that children with disabilities identified as *learning disabled* who receive educational services through self-contained classrooms require twice the per-pupil expenditure than normal children, resulting in a weight of 2:1. The weights thus developed would be applied to the identified clients for each local school district, yielding a weighted pupil count. Current costs, excluding federal funds, for each school district would be divided by its respective weighted pupil count, resulting in costs per weighted pupil for all local school districts in the state database.

Following is a series of dispersion statistics commonly used to measure horizontal and vertical equity, each including its definition, strengths, weaknesses, and interpretation. Since this book is not intended to be used as a statistical manual, it does not include discussions of formula derivation and their theoretical bases.

Range

Among local school districts that are ranked from high to low per-pupil inputs, either revenue or expenditure, within a state, the range is the difference between the highest and lowest per-pupil inputs within a state.

Strengths and Weaknesses. The range is calculated simply and easily explained; however, its utility is limited since it focuses exclusively upon extremes rather than the entire distribution. For example, due to circumstances unique to a particular state, high per-pupil inputs for very small, isolated school districts may be necessary and are justified. Reliance solely upon the range as a measure of horizontal and vertical equity may suggest erroneously that considerable disparities exist although the vast majority of pupils are provided equitable educational services.

Interpretation. As the range increases, the levels of horizontal and vertical equity decrease.

Restricted Range

Among local school districts that are ranked from high to low per-pupil inputs within a state, the restricted range is the difference between the per-pupil inputs at selected percentiles, that is, the 95th and 5th percentiles. The per-pupil inputs for local school districts in which the 95th and 5th percentiles of all pupils in the state fell are used as proxies for the per-pupil inputs for the 95th and 5th percentiles of pupils.

Strengths and Weaknesses. Conceptually, the restricted range ignores the upper and lower ends of the continuum, thus correcting some of the weaknesses of the range measure. The restricted range is calculated simply and is easily explained, but it provides little information concerning the entire distribution of per-pupil inputs.

Interpretation. As the restricted range increases, the levels of horizontal and vertical equity decrease.

Restricted Range Ratio

The restricted range ratio is calculated by dividing the per-pupil inputs at the 5th percentile by the per-pupil inputs at the 95th percentile.

Strengths and Weaknesses. Again, calculation of the restricted range ratio, like the range and restricted range, is calculated simply and is easily explained. The use of a ratio, rather than actual dollars, provides a statistic that can be used, albeit roughly, for longitudinal and interstate comparisons. However, identical to the range and restricted range statistics, the restricted range ratio focuses on the extremes and provides little information concerning the entire distribution of per-pupil inputs.

Interpretation. As the restricted range ratio increases, the levels of horizontal and vertical equity decrease.

Federal Range Ratio

The federal range ratio is a statistic used by the federal government to determine eligibility for states to *take into consideration* federal impact aid payments to local school districts.[25] The federal range ratio is calculated by subtracting the per-pupil inputs at the 5th percentile from the per-pupil inputs at the 95th percentile and dividing the result by the per-pupil inputs at the 5th percentile.

Strengths and Weaknesses. The federal range ratio is mathematically equivalent to the restricted range ratio and possesses identical strengths and weaknesses. However, since it is a standard codified into federal law that establishes a specific equity standard, the federal range ratio enjoys a certain amount of governmental prestige.

Interpretation. As the federal range ratio increases, the levels of horizontal and vertical equity decrease.

Coefficient of Variation (CV)

The coefficient of variation is the standard deviation of a distribution of per-pupil inputs divided by the mean, expressed as a percentage.

Strengths and Weaknesses. The coefficient of variation is designed to measure the variability of the distribution of per-pupil inputs relative to the mean. The CV is easily calculated and can be explained simply to those who have a basic understanding of elementary statistics. Further, the CV utilizes the entire distribution of per-pupil inputs to measure the dispersion of per-pupil inputs.

Interpretation. As the coefficient of variation increases, the levels of horizontal and vertical equity decrease.

Lorenz Curve and Gini Coefficient

The Lorenz Curve is developed by plotting data for cumulative proportions of pupils and cumulative proportions of per-pupil inputs on coordinate axes. Local school districts are sorted by ascending order of per-pupil inputs (i.e., revenues or expenditures). The cumulative proportions of pupils are represented by the horizontal axis and the cumulative proportions of total inputs accounted for by these districts are represented by the vertical axis. The curve thus plotted would be a 45-degree straight line if the per-pupil inputs were identical for all school districts. The Gini Coefficient is defined as the area between the plotted curve and the 45-degree line, expressed as a fraction of the total area below the 45-degree line. A graphic portrayal of the Lorenz Curve is presented in Figure 13.2. Thus, the measure of inequality as defined by the Gini Coefficient (G) is given by the formula in Figure 13.2.

Strengths and Weaknesses. The Lorenz Curve provides a visual measure of the level of horizontal and vertical equity provided by a state system of school finance and can be explained simply. However, calculation of the Gini Coefficient is more difficult to explain, and interstate comparisons are somewhat problematic.

Interpretation. As suggested, if the plotted curve conforms precisely to the 45-degree straight line, per-pupil inputs would be identical for all school districts, representing

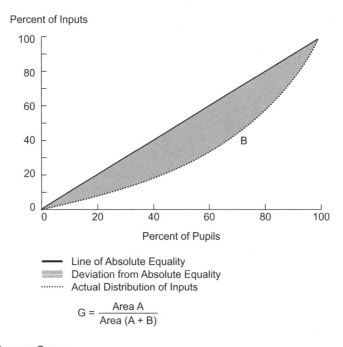

$$G = \frac{\text{Area A}}{\text{Area (A + B)}}$$

Figure 13.2 Lorenz Curve

absolute equalization. The further the plotted curve falls, or sags, below the 45-degree line, the more inequitable is the state system of school finance. In regard to the Gini Coefficient, the coefficient may vary from 0.0 to 1.0; when the coefficient falls to 0.0, absolute equalization is presumed to exist, and as the coefficient increases, the levels of horizontal and vertical equity decrease.

McLoone Index

The McLoone Index is the ratio of the actual inputs for all pupils below the median per-pupil inputs relative to the total inputs these pupils would receive if they were posited at the median per-pupil input level for the entire distribution.

Strengths and Weaknesses. It is calculated simply and is easily explained to those with a basic understanding of statistics. The primary weakness of the McLoone Index is that it measures equity provided pupils located below the median per-pupil inputs for the state, thus ignoring pupils served above the median. Implicit in the conceptual base of the McLoone Index is the assumption that horizontal and vertical equity is necessary only up to the median per-pupil inputs.

Interpretation. The McLoone Index ranges from 0.0 to 1.0, and as the McLoone Index increases, the levels of horizontal and vertical equity also increase.

Theil Index

The Theil Index, an equity measure based on information theory, was originally designed to measure the inequality of income distribution. In place of income, per-pupil inputs are used to assess the horizontal and vertical equity of state systems of school finance. Additionally, the Theil Index can be used to gain insight into the subsets of the distribution.[26]

Strengths and Weaknesses. The Theil Index is a powerful econometric measure designed to measure the dispersion of income within societies and has been adapted to measure the level of horizontal and vertical equity provided by state systems of school finance. Unfortunately, while calculation of the Theil Index is not particularly difficult, explanation of its conceptual and theoretical base has proved problematic.

Interpretation. The Theil Index ranges from 0.0 to 1.0, and as the Theil Index increases, the levels of horizontal and vertical equity decrease.

Atkinson Index

The Atkinson Index is based upon a function that converts a distribution of per-pupil inputs into a single number that theoretically measures the social welfare (desirability) of the distribution. The welfare function simultaneously considers the magnitude of per-pupil inputs and the horizontal and vertical equity provided pupils. Parameters, referred to as E, can vary from 0.0 to ∞ and are incorporated into the welfare function, The larger value assigned to the parameter, the more concern provided the lower end of the distribution, as measured by per-pupil inputs.

Strengths and Weaknesses. Similar to the Theil Index, the Atkinson Index is a powerful econometric measure, adapted for application to the measurement of horizontal and vertical equity. Also, similar to the Theil Index, explanation of its conceptual base and theoretical base has proved problematic.

Interpretation. The Atkinson Index ranges from 0.0 to 1.0, and as the Atkinson Index increases, the levels of horizontal and vertical equity also increase.

Verstegen Index

The Verstegen Index calculates the ratio of the total amount of resources above the median and the amount that would be available to the same number of observations at the median per student revenue or expenditures. The Verstegen Index is used to measure the degree of concentration of resources in the top half of the distribution.

Strengths and Weaknesses. Similar to the McLoone Index, the Verstegen Index is designed to measure the level of equity for one-half of the population of a state; however, instead of focusing upon the lower half, the Verstegen Index measures the equity for the upper half of the population. Application of the Verstegen Index compensates for the weakness noted for the McLoone Index.

Interpretation. The Verstegen Index ranges from ≤ 1.0 to $1.0 \geq$ with a target score of 1.0.

Measurement of Fiscal Neutrality (Taxpayer Equity)

Several commonly used statistics have been used to measure the relationship of the fiscal capacities of local school districts to their respective per-pupil inputs. That is, statistics are employed to assess the strength of the relationship that exists between fiscal capacity and the quality of education provided by a state system of school finance. Following are definitions, strengths, weaknesses, and interpretations for several commonly used statistics: correlations, regressions, slopes, and elasticities.

Correlation

The Pearson Product-Moment Correlation is commonly used to measure the relationship between per-pupil inputs of local school districts and their respective fiscal capacities.

Strengths and Weaknesses. The correlation statistic has been used widely by researchers of all professions. It is calculated simply and is easily explained to those with a basic understanding of statistics. The often-cited weakness of the correlation statistic is that it fails to show causality and measures only the strength of a relationship between variables. Further, the correlation statistic by itself does not measure the magnitude of the variance of per-pupil inputs among local school districts. Finally, and most serious, the conduct of a simple correlation does not control for the variance in per-pupil inputs created by varying levels of fiscal effort.

Interpretation. The correlation coefficient may vary from 0.0 to ≥ 1.0. A correlation coefficient of 0.0 would indicate that there was no relationship between fiscal capacities of local school districts and their per-pupil inputs, and as the correlation coefficient increases, the level of fiscal neutrality decreases.

Regression

The square of the simple correlation is the fraction of variation in the dependent variable that is explained by the regression line.

Strengths and Weaknesses. Instead of discussing a coefficient of correlation, the relationship between variables is explained on the basis of a fraction, or percentage of the variance. Since the regression statistic is a function of the simple correlation, it possesses similar qualities.

Interpretation. The regression percentage may vary from 0.0 to 100.0. A regression equation that explains 0.0 percent would indicate that there was no relationship between fiscal capacities of the local school districts and their per-pupil inputs, and as the percentage of variance explained increases, the level of fiscal neutrality decreases.

Slope

The *slope* shows the size of the change in the dependent variable (per-pupil inputs) associated with a one-unit change in the independent variable (fiscal capacities of the local school districts) in absolute terms.

Strengths and Weaknesses. Unlike the correlation and regression statistics, the slope measures the magnitude rather than the strength of the relationship that exists between fiscal capacity and per-pupil inputs. It is calculated simply and is easily explained to those with a basic understanding of statistics. However, similar to the correlation and regression statistics, the slope neither shows causality nor does it control for other factors, including varying levels of fiscal effort generated by local school districts. Due to its dependence on absolute values, interstate and longitudinal comparisons of slope values are problematic.

Interpretation. The slope may vary from ≥0.0 to any amount. A slope of 0.0 would indicate that there was no relationship between fiscal capacity and per-pupil inputs, and as the slope increases, the level of fiscal neutrality decreases.

Elasticity

The *elasticity,* identical to the slope, measures the magnitude of the relationship that exists between fiscal capacity and per-pupil inputs. Unlike the slope, elasticity is reported in terms of percentage changes rather than absolute values.

Strengths and Weaknesses. Elasticities are derived from the same equations that yield correlations, regressions, and slopes and have similar deficiencies regarding their inability to show causality or control for other factors. Elasticities are calculated simply and are easily explained to those with a basic understanding of statistics. Since elasticities are reported as percentage changes rather than absolute values for slopes, some of the problems of interstate and longitudinal comparisons are eliminated.

Interpretation. The elasticities may vary from ≥0.0. An elasticity of 0.0 would indicate that there was not a relationship between fiscal capacity and per-pupil inputs, and as the elasticity increases, the level of fiscal neutrality decreases.

It is interesting to note that regardless of the equity score, there does not appear to be a discernible pattern relating to whether litigation has occurred. Even states that rank relatively high have not been exempt from fiscal equalization lawsuits. The evidence suggests that absolute fiscal equalization has rarely occurred, and even acceptable fiscal equalization has remained an elusive goal.

PART III: DETERMINING AN ADEQUATE BASE COST OF EDUCATION

This section of the book utilizes quotes and adapts the Deborah Verstegen approach for determining the costs for an adequate education. It is a procedure, a process, which Verstegen employed in a comprehensive cost analysis that she designed and employed in Massachusetts. The explanation given here, utilizing what Verstegen calls the *Multi-Method Approach*, was described in detail in an article published in the *Journal of Education Finance*.[27]

What is the cost of an adequate education in a state under a curriculum framework? How do costs vary for special needs students and school districts? Does the state provide funding levels necessary to support an adequate education? The state must determine the funding levels necessary for different school districts to meet state standards, laws, regulations, and objectives that define an adequate education. Cost studies provide a rational basis for determining the amount of funding necessary for all children to have a meaningful opportunity for an adequate education. They raise the level of discussion and are a vast improvement over the political decision making and residual budgeting practices of the past that based the amount of resources devoted to education on the amount of money that was available. In many states, legislatures and courts have relied on cost studies to formulate their education funding decisions.[28]

The Four Basic Methods

Scholars have identified a variety of methods for calculating the cost of education.[29] The principal methods include: (1) *resource cost method*, also called the *professional judgment approach*, based on judgments of experienced educators and relevant research; (2) *empirical approaches,* such as deductive inference from exemplary school districts and their schools, also referred to as the *successful school approach*, (3) *econometric modeling*, also called a *cost function approach*; and (4) *costing comprehensive school reform programs,* recently revised and termed the *evidence-based approach*. Each of these methods provides an average base cost of education for a general education student that is further adjusted for special students and district characteristics.[30] Recently, states have begun to rely on these methods to determine the cost of an adequate education or use the multi-method approach.

Professional Judgment Method. Using the professional judgment approach for determining costs, resources or "ingredients" deemed necessary to meet state laws, objectives, and standards are identified by service providers, and then prices are attached and summed. The result is the estimation of an average base cost of a defined set of resources in the average school district needed to achieve particular state standards and objectives that define adequacy. Resources that are priced include personnel, class size, materials, supplies, technology, and equipment. This approach aligns resources with state laws and standards but does not determine how funding is distributed or how funds should be used in the districts or schools. The advantages of the approach are that it is easy to understand and is transparent. It is not reliant on current state spending because it is a bottom-up approach to the determination of costs. In addition, it is not limited by state performance data. It can determine the cost of a broad array of state laws, requirements, and standards in addition to areas that are not easily measured, such as citizenship and art. The disadvantages are that it may be based on current practice and, therefore, should be supplemented (not supplanted) by research to ensure that resource configurations and strategies are able to produce the desired results. This method has been implemented using various approaches, with some studies more rigorous and reliable than others.

Successful School Method. The successful school approach for defining costs of an adequate level of funding identifies schools or school districts where student performance meets desired targets and determines the *level* of resources expended by such schools or school districts to estimate costs. It can include controls for non-school factors that may affect student achievement and costs related to special student or district needs.[31]

Some scholars have noted that this approach of inferring costs from *exemplary districts* is intuitively appealing and understandable. However, how success is defined varies, resulting in different costs, and may be based upon limited state performance data. The approach as implemented usually eliminates outlier school districts, adding or using questionable efficiency screens, leading to the possibility of recommendations that underfund education. Exemplary districts generally are affluent districts with few high-need students, so adjustments must be made for school districts with greater diversity. Also, if the funding system is inadequate for all districts in the state, rich and poor alike, as was the case in the Commonwealth of Kentucky under the Kentucky Supreme Court *Rose* decision, then correlating current spending in select districts to student outcomes will not capture the actual cost of an adequate education. This is a difficulty with both this method and the following econometric modeling method.

Econometric Modeling Method. In econometric modeling, costs are derived by associating total district spending with predetermined pupil performance levels or proficiencies, such as student achievement test scores. The statistical technique is the least squares analysis. In essence, this approach statistically isolates factors contributing to school costs independent of other related factors and adjusts them by the cost factors to achieve an overall cost figure; controls may be used for student characteristics and non-school factors contributing to these costs. Thus, the calculation summarizes all the information about costs into a single number, which indicates how much each school district must spend to achieve a given level of educational output, such as the current average level of student performance in a state.

The strength of this approach is that it appears scientific and uses state data to produce costs. However, the approach requires a well-developed state database. The often widely varying costs of education produced through econometric modeling weaken confidence in the findings. Moreover, the assumptions undergirding the models are not obvious. These and other problems can raise questions about the defensibility of the findings emerging from the studies.

Comprehensive Cost Method. Another approach for developing an adequacy target is based upon determination of the cost of comprehensive, whole school reform models that link educational strategies to resources.[32] The approach is a variant of the original resource cost model: Resources needed to implement a comprehensive school reform model are identified, priced, and summed. These model costs are then added to a base cost of education or substituted for resources currently used in schools to arrive at a cost estimate that can be adjusted for the special needs of students and districts.

A new iteration of the whole school reform approach has been called the *evidence-based approach*. This approach uses research to isolate proven, effective strategies, attaches costs to each, and then sums them. A difficulty is that not all elements costed have a research base, such as central office costs. Finally, this approach assumes that the whole is a sum of its parts, but that is not always the case.

Although cost studies have raised the level of discussion and increased the scrutiny and debate over the amount of funding needed to support an adequate education, there is increasing interest in the contributions each of the major methods provide in determining the cost of an adequate education. As a result, cost studies are becoming more rigorous and hybrid approaches or multiple methods are being used across the states.

A Multi-Method Approach

The *professional judgment method* augmented by the *evidence-based approach* focuses on a zero-based budgeting, bottom-up approach. School resources needed under the state's curriculum frameworks in the context of state laws, objectives, and standards are identified and prices are affixed, which, when applied across all resource components and summed, produce a cost estimate.[33] Costs for elementary, middle, and high schools are combined with district level costs to produce an overall average base cost of education. The average cost of education produced is then adjusted to include the excess costs necessary to educate students with special needs and for districts with exceptional circumstances or uncontrollable high costs.

Using panels of highly qualified education professionals and the professional judgment method for determining costs, augmented by research, the resource needs of prototype elementary, middle, and high schools may be determined. School resource needs may be based upon current characteristics and demographics of the school districts in the state. Multiple panels are feasibly constructed to represent the diversity that exists across the state and focuses on districts of different sizes. Different panels may be used for sets of districts and each cost level (school, district, and state). Several school level panels can work exclusively on estimating the resource needs of school sites. Several district level panels can review the work of the school level panels and estimate district level resource needs. An expert panel can also be employed to bring consistency across divergent state resource elements identified by the previous panels and therefrom make decisions about prices.

These panels must consider the variety of laws, rules, and regulations to which local school districts are held accountable, including input and output measures. For example, there are input measures that define state requirements for specific resource inputs, such as the minimum number of days and hours that school must be in session, graduation requirements, maximum class sizes, personnel requirements, and curriculum standards. The second type of measure is based upon outputs that include indicators of student performance levels, dropout and attendance rates, average yearly progress on tests, and gaps between disaggregated demographic student groups.

Curriculum frameworks may be used to ascertain the curriculum content that will be assessed for accountability and high school graduation. The state specifies the minimum length of the school year (180 days) and the total hours of instruction (900 hours for elementary school and 990 hours for high school). The state's key output indicator – such as the State Comprehensive Assessment System – may be used to assess student capabilities in reading, English language arts, mathematics, science and technology, and history and social sciences. Student outcomes are then classified as *warning/failing*, *needs improvement*, *proficient*, or *advanced*. A level of *needs improvement* in English language arts and mathematics (on the 10th-grade test) is required of all students to graduate from high school; a level of "proficient" under the federal No Child Left Behind Act is required of all students, and important output measures may be used.[34]

How are the aforementioned *panels* determined? Panels may be created to determine the amount of funding needed to provide all students meaningful opportunities to obtain an adequate education. Of these, a few may be directed to school sites to identify the resource ingredients needed to deliver an adequate education to students under the curriculum frameworks in the context of state laws and standards. The professional judgment panels may consist of experienced, well-qualified professional educators, including teachers, curriculum personnel, special educators, librarians, and site administrators employed in the state public schools. Each locality determines the characteristics of the type of professionals needed for the school site meetings and secures the people working on the panels, i.e., principals, teachers, specialists, and categorical program personnel.

The school site panels work together to create prototype elementary, middle, and high schools, including defining prototypical school sizes, the number and size of classes, curriculum, and the required numbers and types of personnel, supplies, equipment, technology, student activities, and any opportunities that would be available outside the school day, such as extended days, summer school, and before- and after-school programs and services. Panels may provide enhancements and resource additions as needed for students with disabilities, economic disadvantages, and gifted and talented students. The work of the panels is entered into computer records and summarized for review by the prototype school district panels.

For the school district level, additional panels may be created. The district panels may review the work of the school site panels, modify resource configurations, if needed, review approaches for determining district level costs, and make relevant judgments. After the work of the district panels is completed, choices are entered into computer records and comparisons are made for review by an expert panel. The expert panel considers the recommendation and reviews variations in resource configurations across all panels as related to state level issues, such as the length of the school year, and make decisions. The panel sets prices and suggests recommendations for different resource elements that would be used to estimate costs for the prototypes. Subsequently, prices are added to resource components, summed, and compared. The ability to replica costs is confirmed for the work of the panels operating independently and under similar conditions.

Resource Prices. Efforts to attach prices to the resource enhancements or resource elements should focus on personnel costs, including salary and benefits, and how costs and expenditures might differ. Panel members should review available data related to salaries in the state for the relevant year. Teacher salaries can be set based on nationally published estimates of average teacher salaries in the state provided by the United States Department of Education or the National Education Association. The same salary schedule may be used for other certified positions such as guidance counselors, librarians, technology specialists, nurses, and social workers. Costs for classified positions may be calculated on hourly rates and the number of days employed.

To compare salary costs to expenditures, the price of teachers in the same labor market for personnel should be compared with those of the surrounding states. With adjustments to ensure comparability for cost of living, teacher education, and experience, average state teacher salaries should be roughly comparable to the average salary for surrounding states.

Central office costs are calculated separately and included for expenditures for school district administration, including business services and other support personnel. Also included are costs for plant maintenance and operations, student transportation, and *other* (i.e., school support services). Normally, central office costs per pupil fall as district size increased.

Finally, determining the adequacy of facilities should be considered. Average expenditures for debt service are reported by the state.

School-level costs that result from applying the prices to the resources specified in the study should be summarized across categories of elementary, middle, and high school. The per-pupil figures are then computed for general education students and special needs students by combining all resources and dividing by the number of students, respectively. The first category, base spending, includes core costs (personnel salaries and benefits, substitute costs, materials, supplies, equipment, and other costs), professional development, and technology (excluding infrastructure). Other programs included in base spending, such as library and textbook costs, are also computed. The second category includes costs for special needs students; prices were based upon funding averages. Obtained from available and relevant research, the panels may adopt statewide funding weights for special education.

Central district costs for central office and administration, plant maintenance and operations, transportation, and *other* should be summed. Then, base school district and school costs are to be summed to produce a total base cost per pupil by district type. Then the costs for special needs students, student transportation, and preschool are added. Costs across all categories are summed, which gives the average total costs per student.

Additional key resource needs identified by professional judgment panels include voluntary preschool for children beginning at age 3, full-service centers in low-income communities, differentiated pay in hard-to-staff schools, and adequate professional development funding. This may suggest that significant new funding is needed over time if the state is to provide an adequate education of high quality for all children and youth.

Thus, this multi-method, professional judgment approach, although time-consuming, has the virtue of intensive collaboration and involvement of several sectors of personnel who are well-educated in the ways and needs related to the good conduct of schools.

SUMMARY

This chapter has three parts. *First,* it gives a general discussion of equity and justice in their philosophical sense. Equity is justice in both the contexts of philosophy and in law. With regard to the specific area of state school financing of education, equity and justice are described as the fourth and highest level in a staircase of public school finance. This top level is defined as natural or perfect equity or justice. This highest level achieves justice by taking into account, in the allocation of resources, local fiscal capacity, local tax effort, and the diversity of educational needs of children. *Second,* the chapter defines the various statistical procedures for calculating equality, equity, and justice. These are reflected in the many short statements in this summation. *Third,* the chapter utilizes the *Verstegen synthesis* and explanation of the various methods for determining realistic costs in the provision of state school financing.

Equity and justice require:

1. Adequate funding of basic *developmental educational programs* in such a way as to establish thorough, efficient, and uniform educational opportunity throughout the state.
2. A basic formula adjustment which will fully *fiscally equalize* among all school districts in the state. This is probably the most important single element in the determination of equity, but it cannot stand alone if true equity is to be achieved. The term *fiscal neutrality* will suffice as a reasonably definitive standard.
3. A level of *fiscal effort uniformity* at such a high level as to prevent a child's education from being a function of low educational aspiration of the community, or to prevent external local political influences, unresponsive to or unconcerned with public education, from denying appropriate educational opportunity. Local tax leeway, unlimited local choice, or subsidiaries are all earmarks of an inequitable system.
4. Financing for *corrective educational programs* designed to meet particular and individual needs of children which are due to ill-luck or circumstances of nature deficiencies adversely affecting educational achievement. Such programs must not establish unreasonable or legally irrational classifications of children.
5. Financing for *remedial educational programs* designed to provide measures to offset educational disadvantage caused by social or economic distortions. Such financing may be justified as offsetting individual deficiencies of the least advantaged.
6. Financing for diseconomies *of scale* created by geographic and demographic conditions.

7. Financing for *governmental overburdens* which tend to drain local tax resources on which the local school district must rely.
8. Financing which is designed to correct for differences in the *cost of delivering comparable educational services* throughout a state. Such a factor goes beyond a simple adjustment for cost of living as determined by an economic market basket; instead, its purpose is to correct for disparities in the power of school districts to purchase educational services.

True educational justice is only obtainable through a complexity of financial considerations, not one of which can accommodate the desired standard. Fiscal equalization among school districts is probably the most important single component in an equitable system, but it is insufficient in and of itself. The concept of equity in provision of education has been central to discussions of state school finance.

Fiscal neutrality is a limited concept. It merely postulates that a child's education should not be a function of the wealth of the local community. It only applies to measurement of the degree of equalization of taxpaying capacity among local school districts; and it does not attempt to measure a more pervasive standard of educational equity. Despite its limitations, it is an attractive concept from an economist's perspective primarily because it suggests a quantifiable definition of fiscal equalization, equal treatment of equals.

The fiscal neutrality standard requires that the variance in revenue per student unit not be systematically related to variance in local fiscal capacity. Justice requires more than simple fiscal neutrality or fiscal equalization. The complexity of the educational enterprise creates financing problems which transcend mere mathematical equalization of local taxpaying capacity.

A technical discussion of the statistical measurement of horizontal equity, vertical equity, and fiscal neutrality was presented. Contained within the discussion, a step-by-step procedure for the preparation of a state database prior to the application of equity statistics was outlined.

A series of horizontal equity, vertical equity, and fiscal neutrality statistics were reviewed. The review included definitions, strengths, weaknesses, and interpretations for each statistic.

The last part of this chapter also sets forth methods that may be utilized to establish the cost of an adequate education. The basic types are:

(a) Resource cost method, also called the *professional judgment* approach,
(b) Empirical methods, also referred to as the *successful school* approach,
(c) Economic modeling, alternatively termed the *cost function* approach, and
(d) Costing of comprehensive school reform programs, more widely known as the *evidence-based* approach.

Each methodology is designed to determine the average basic cost of a regular education program in a state. As the discussion in the chapter indicates, these methods can be combined to form a multi-method approach. The essence of this last approach is the use of professional judgment panels in concert with the more empirical methodologies.

KEY TERMS

- Horizontal equity
- Theil Index
- Federal range ratio
- Fiscal neutrality
- Correlation
- Lorenz Curve
- Range
- Slope
- McLoone Index
- Restricted range ratio

- Vertical equity
- Atkinson Index
- Coefficient of variation
- Unit of analysis
- Verstegen Index
- Regression
- Gini Coefficient
- Restricted range
- Elasticity

NOTES

1. Updated and adapted from: Kern Alexander, "Concepts of Equity," in *Financing Education: Overcoming Inefficiencies and Inequity*, edited by Walter M. McMahon and Terry G. Geske (Urbana, IL: University of Illinois Press, 1982), pp. 193–214.
2. See excellent discussion of equity in Bruce D. Baker, Preston Green, and Craig E. Richards, *Financing Education Systems* (New Jersey: Pearson/Merrill Prentice Hall, 2008), pp. 98–99.
3. *Black's Law Dictionary*, Revised Fourth Edition (St. Paul, MN: West Publishing Company, 1968), p. 634.
4. Ibid.
5. Jean-Jacques Rousseau, "The Social Contract," 1762, in *The Social Contract and Discourses*, translated by G.D.H. Cole (London: J.M. Dent & Sons, Ltd., Everyman's Library, 1988), p. 206.
6. Melvin Tumin, "The Meaning of Equality in Education." Paper presented at the Third Annual Conference of the National Committee for Support of Public Schools, Washington, DC, in 1965.
7. Ralph Tyler penned personal correspondence dated October 9, 1967, cited in *On Equality of Educational Opportunity*, ed. Frederick Mosteller and Daniel P. Moynihan (New York: Random House, 1972), p. 428.
8. Roe L. Johns, K. Alexander, and R. Rossmiller, *Dimensions of Educational Need* (Gainesville: National Educational Finance Project, 1969).
9. For a particularly good explanation see Baker, Green, and Richards, *op. cit.*, p. 98.
10. John Rawls, "Distributive Justice," in *Collected Papers John Rawls*, edited by Samuel Freeman (Cambridge, MA: Harvard University Press, 1999), p. 165.
11. Clarence Morris, *The Great Legal Philosophers* (Philadelphia: University of Pennsylvania Press, 1971), p. 243.
12. Ibid., p. 490.
13. Freidrich A. Hayek, *Law, Legislation and Liberty, II* (Chicago: University of Chicago Press, 1976), p. 31.
14. Anthony Pagden, *The Enlightenment and Why It Still Matters* (Oxford: Oxford University Press, 2013), pp. 334–335.
15. Joseph Raz, *The Morality of Freedom* (Oxford: Clarendon Paperbacks, 1989), p. 113.
16. Pagden, *op. cit.*, pp. 334–335.

17. Ibid.

18. Ibid.

19. Ibid.

20. Hayek, *op. cit.*, p. 86.

21. See explanation of why revenues usually exceed expenditures in National Education Association, *Estimates of School Statistics, 1991-92* (Washington, DC: NEA, 1992), p. 26.

22. 45 C.F.R. Subsection 116.17(h) (1974) as cited in *Bennett v. Kentucky*, 470 U.S. 656, 105 S. Ct. 1544 (1985).

23. 34 C.F.R. Ch. 11 (11-1-89 Edition) Section 222.61(a).

24. A case could be made to develop a set of national weights required to service the traditional client groups. If national rather than state-specific weights were used, interstate equity analyses would become more reliable and meaningful. See Robert Berne and Leanna Stiefel, "Equity Standards for State School Finance Programs: Philosophies and Standards Relevant to Section 5(d)(2) of the Federal Impact Aid Program," *Journal of Education Finance* Vol. 18, No. 1 (Summer 1992), pp. 89–112.

25. 34 C.F.R. Ch. 11 (11-1-89 Edition) Section 222.61(a).

26. Berne and Stiefel, *op. cit.*, p. 21.

27. Deborah A. Verstegen, "Has Adequacy Been Achieved? A Study of Finances and Costs a Decade after Court-Ordered Reform," *Journal of Education Finance*, Vol. 32, No. 3 (Winter 2007), pp. 304–327. Deborah Verstegen is Professor of Finance, Policy, and Leadership at the University of Nevada, Reno. The essence of the article is presented here with copyright permission from the *Journal of Education Finance*.

28. M. A. Rebell, "Educational Adequacy, Democracy and the Courts," in *Achieving High Standards for All*, ed. T. Ready, C. Edley, and C. Snows (Washington, DC: National Academy Press, 2002).

29. D. A. Verstegen, "Financing the New Adequacy," American Education Research Association Annual Meeting, San Francisco, CA, April 2006; J. W. Guthrie and R. Rothstein, "Enabling *Adequacy* to Achieve Realty: Translating Adequacy into State School Finance Distribution Arrangements," in *Equity and Adequacy in Education Finance*, ed. H. F. Ladd, R. Chalk, and J. S. Hansen (Washington, DC: National Academy Press, 1999), pp. 209–250; and J. Myers and J. Silverstein, "Calculation of the Cost of a Suitable Education in Montana in 2001–2001, Using the Professional Judgment Approach," mimeo August 2002.

30. Verstegen, "Financing the New Adequacy", *op. cit.,* and M.F. Addonizio, "Toward a New Adequacy in Public School Finance: Analytical and Political Issues," *Educational Considerations* 32(1) (Fall 2004), pp. 55–61, available at http://coe.k-state.edu/annex/edconsiderations/.

31. In the northeastern state being examined here, a study using this approach, "Projected Costs Associated with Implementing the English Language Arts and Math Curriculum Frameworks in the State," was conducted. Costs were analyzed for 75 districts meeting Cycle II School Performance Ratings of "high" or "very high," based on English language arts and mathematics MCAS test scores. (Data were not available on the other subject areas of the curriculum frameworks.) A base student cost and total cost per pupil were calculated, which excluded capital, transportation, and food service but included adjustments for high-cost students, such as children with disabilities. See Augenblick & Myers, Inc., *Projected Costs Associated with Implementing the English Language Arts and Math Curriculum Frameworks,* mimeo (Denver, CO: Augenblick & Myers, April 2003).

32. See A. Odden and C. Busch, *Financing Schools for High Performance* (San Francisco: Jossey-Bass, 1998).

33. Prices are different from expenditures and therefore can vary.

34. See *McDuffy v. Secretary of the Executive Office of Education*, 415 Mass. 545, 615 N.E.2d 516 (1993).

CHAPTER 14

State School Funding Methods

INTRODUCTION

The legal authority for the maintenance and operation of public schools has rested with the fifty state governments since the ratification of the Bill of Rights of the United States Constitution in 1791. Nonetheless, in most states, local communities initially assumed responsibility for financing and managing public schools. During the early years, the United States was primarily an agrarian nation composed of many small communities, most of which established rudimentary public schools during the *common schools movement* of the nineteenth century. The federal government did not provide revenue for the support of the newly formed common schools; however, as the number of states increased from the original 13 which declared their independence from England in 1776, each new state was required to ratify a state constitution containing a clause that mandated the establishment of a system of public schools.[1] For administrative purposes, pursuant to the constitutional required systems of public schools, states arranged its public schools into geographical areas, usually referred to as *school districts*. Often, the boundaries of local governmental agencies, i.e., counties, cities, and townships, were made coterminous with the boundaries of the newly formed school districts. However, in some instances, particularly in the Midwest, school district boundaries crossed the boundaries of other local governmental agencies, a structure that has continued to the present. As recently as 1929–1930, nationally, there were approximately 120,000 public school districts that enrolled nearly 26 million students. By 2010–2011, the number of public school districts had fallen to 13,588 while the number of students enrolled had increased to approximately 49.6 million.[2] Thus, over eight decades, the mean number of enrolled students per school district increased from 217 to 3,606. The reduction in the number of school districts and the concurrent increase in the number of students enrolled per school district were caused by several factors, most prominently due to demographic changes and the increased pressure for greater cost efficiency.

In 1929–1930, for the nation as a whole, state governments provided a modest 16.9 percent of revenue for public schools, and local governments provided 82.7 percent. The federal government provided only 0.4 percent of public school revenue.[3] By 2012–2013, the pattern of fiscal support had changed significantly. The National Education Association estimated that state governments provided the largest percentage of public school revenue, 45.8 percent, followed closely by local governments which provided 44.2 percent. The federal government had increased its percentage of support for public schools to 10.1 percent. Among the fifty states, there is considerable variance in the percentage of revenue provided by the three levels of government.[4] At one end of the continuum, for 2012–2013, Hawaii provided 87.6 percent of revenue for public schools from state sources and only 2.2 percent from local sources.[5] The federal government provided Hawaii 10.3 percent of its public school revenue. Hawaii has a unique administrative structure and administers public schools as a single school district, which explains the very high percentage of state fiscal support for public schools. At the other end of the continuum, for 2012–2013, Illinois provided 20.5 percent of public school revenue from state sources and 65.9 percent from local sources. The remaining 13.6 percent of Illinois public school revenue was provided by the federal government.[6]

GRANTS-IN-AID

The fiscal support of public schools evolved from an institution funded nearly exclusively from local resources to complex tripartite fiscal systems with revenue provided by the three governmental agencies, i.e., federal, state, and local governments. Each of the states and the federal government developed intergovernmental revenue transfer programs, i.e., grants-in-aid, to support the operation of public schools by the localities. Undergirding the early development and implementation of state systems for the transfer of revenue to local communities was the recognition by state policymakers that if excessive dependence were placed on local communities to fund its public schools, disparate school systems usually occurred, a result that has been validated repeatedly over the years. From a national perspective, federal policymakers also have recognized that considerable variance in the quality of state public schools occurs among the fifty states, so they have implemented federal grants containing equalization devices for the allocation of revenue to the several states and territories.[7]

In order to insure the provision of a rudimentary education throughout their respective constitutional boundaries, most state governments during the early decades of the twentieth century began to design and implement a series of financial grants to local communities. These grants were dedicated for the support of public schools, normally referred to as common schools. Usually, the state allocations for public schools were allocated through use of flat grants that did not take into consideration the fiscal capacities of the localities. The state allocations were based entirely upon some uniform measure of educational need, such as the number of resident population ages 5–17, number of students served, etc. Nevertheless, since the states relied upon the taxable resources contained within each state as a whole, the flat grants did result in some redistribution of fiscal resources from high fiscal capacity areas to areas of low fiscal capacity. In essence, the early state grants were not designed to address specifically the public schools' disparities caused by variance in fiscal capacities of local communities; but commencing in the 1930s, states began to design and implement funding formulae that directly addressed the disparity issue. Most often, these later grants were referred to as *Minimum Foundation Programs*.[8]

The federal government, commencing in the 1950s, also developed and implemented a series of grants that were designed to address national priorities for public elementary and secondary education. To a limited extent, federal grants began to address the disparity issue both among the fifty states and within each state.

Presented graphically in Figure 14.1 is a model of a typical state school finance system.[9] Note that the local school districts are sorted by their fiscal capacities (wealth), which illustrates the disparity inherent in a system that relies extensively upon local resources, shown by the sections respectively entitled, *local required effort* and *local leeway funds*. The section entitled *state equalization aid* relies upon a combination of state and local funds to guarantee a certain state-prescribed level of fiscal support. The section labeled *state categorical grants*, provides an illustration of the effect created by the implementation of typical flat grants often used to distribute categorical aid, which raises the funding level for all school districts, those with high and low fiscal capacities. Usually, a series of flat grants is designated for specific educational programs, e.g., special education, vocational education, etc., and is considered *categorical aid*,[10] in contrast to *general aid*.[11] The far right section labeled *local leeway finds* shows the fiscal effect of local leeway funds which increase the likelihood of a disparate system of public schools. As the amount of local leeway funds increases, the funding disparities inevitably increase as well.

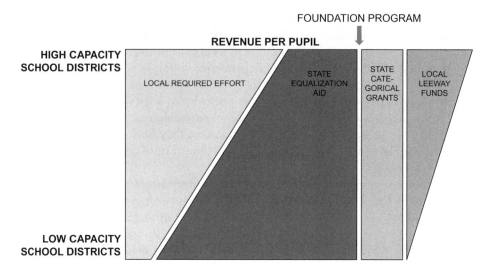

Figure 14.1 A Typical Model of a State System of School Finance

Presented below are descriptions and examples of the several grants employed by states for the intergovernmental transfer of revenue to local school districts. Currently, almost all states use a combination of state grants to fund their public schools, selecting from an array of flat grants, matching grants, foundation programs, power-equalization formulae, and guaranteed tax yield programs. Each grant is presented and discussed below.

Flat Grant Formula

$$S_i = P_i F$$

Where: S_i = State flat grant to $_i$th district
$\quad\quad P_i$ = Units of the $_i$th district
$\quad\quad\quad\quad$ (pupils, teachers, other measures of educational need)
$\quad\quad F$ = Flat grant unit value

Example:

If: F = $5,000 per ADM and
$\quad$ Pi = 1,000 ADM, then
$\quad$ Si = ($5,000 x 1,000) or
$\quad\quad\quad$ $5,000,000 State Aid

Although relatively few states employ flat grants as their primary state-aid allocation system, North Carolina provides an excellent example of a state that does so. The
flat grant used by North Carolina is a sophisticated system that employs an elaborate
instructional unit (positions) weighting system.[12] The *positions* funded by the state
include administrators, classroom teachers, teachers who teach disabled children,
teachers who teach disadvantaged students, etc., dollar allotments, and categorical
allotments.[13] In addition, North Carolina employs a fiscal equalization grant entitled
Low Wealth Counties Supplemental Funding that allocates state aid inversely based upon
the local fiscal capacity for each locality. The state uses local property valuation and
per capita income to calculate the fiscal capacities of its localities.[14] For FY 2013, it is
estimated that North Carolina provided 56.0 percent of public school revenue from
state resources; 32.8 percent were allocated by local agencies; and 11.2 percent were
furnished by the federal government.[15]

Displayed in Figure 14.2 is a typical state system of school finance that relies
exclusively on a series of flat grants and is not illustrative of the North Carolina system. Historically, North Carolina partially overcame the dis-equalizing effect of the
flat grant by allocating from state sources a relatively high percentage of its total current expenditures, thus providing a relatively high level of fiscal equalization among
its school districts. In recent years, however, the previous high regard the public held
for North Carolina Public Schools has fallen precipitously. Partially due to a dramatic
decline in state appropriations for public schools coupled with large public appropriations to private charter schools, North Carolina, and several other states, have seen
their state capitols captured by far right ideologues who apparently intend to destroy
the institution of public common schools.

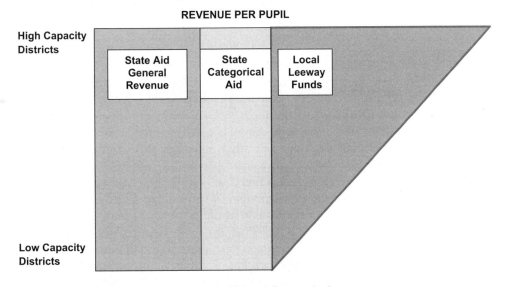

Figure 14.2 Flat Grant Program – Basic Aid and Categorical

Matching Grant Formula

$$S_i = P_i(F - U_i)$$

Where: S_i = State matching grant to $_i$th district

P_i = Units of the $_i$th district

(pupils, teachers, other measures of educational need)

F = Matching grant unit value

U_i = Local matching requirement (LMR), e.g., 20% match

Example:

If: F = $5,000 per ADM,

P_i = 1,000 ADM,

U_i = (.2 x $5,000) or $1,000, then

S_i = [($5,000 x 1,000) – (.2 x ($5,000 x 1,000)] or

= ($5,000,000 – $1,000,000) or

$4,000,000 State Aid and

$1,000,000 LMR

Summary:

State	$4,000,000
Local (LMR)	1,000,000
Total	$5,000,000

Once popular, matching grants have lost favor by most states due to their tendency to increase funding disparities among local school districts. High fiscal capacity localities have the ability to raise the required match of revenue from local resources to qualify for the grant allocation, while the low capacity localities often lack this ability. Whenever a matching grant is used by either a state or the federal government, the matching grant typically is relatively small and often requires the local school districts to match only a small percentage of the total grant.[16] One such example is provided by Virginia, which uses a *percentage-matching grant* to allocate state aid designated for the improvement of technology. The Virginia grant is entitled *VPSA*[17] *Technology*[18] and requires that the localities provide 20 percent of the calculated value of the grant.[19] The *VPSA Technology* is a small categorical grant and contributes only 1 percent of the total state appropriations. For FY 2012, it is estimated that Virginia provided 38.0 percent of public school revenue from state resources; 55.6 percent were allocated by local agencies; and 6.4 percent were furnished by the federal government.[20]

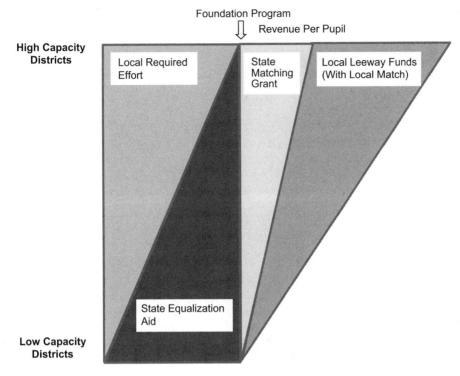

Figure 14.3 Foundation Program with Matching Grant

Displayed in Figure 14.3 is a model of a foundation program, explained below, with matching grant for allocation of categorical aid that illustrates its tendency to dis-equalize the resources among school districts. The higher capacity school districts have the resources to match the state allocations, while the less fiscally able school districts lack the ability and often the will to exert the additional fiscal effort to qualify for the state appropriations. The inevitable result is the preponderance of the state appropriations flow to the higher capacity school districts.

Fiscal Equalization Grants: Foundation Program

$$S_i = P_iF_i - UV_i$$

Where: S_i = State equalization grant to $_i$th district
P_i = Units of the $_i$th district
  (pupils, teachers, other measures of educational need)
F_i = Foundation program per unit value
  (determined by the state)
U = Uniform required local effort (RLE)
V_i = Local fiscal capacity
O_i = Local leeway (local tax levy × local tax base)

Example:

If: F_i = \$5,000 per ADM and

   P_i = 1,000 ADM and

   U = 10 mills and

   V_i = \$100,000,000, then

   S_i = [(\$5,000 x 1,000) – (\$100,000,000 x \$0.01)] or

      = \$5,000,000 – \$1,000,000

      = \$4,000,000

Plus: O_i = 2 mills x \$100,000,000, then

         = \$100,000,000 x \$0.002, or

         = \$200,000

Summary:

State	**\$4,000,000**
Local RLE	**\$1,000,000**
Local Leeway	**\$ 200,000**
Total	**\$5,200,000**

Approximately 80 percent of the states utilize various forms of the foundation program to allocate state equalization aid to their localities. The foundation program formula was implemented extensively during the 1920s and 1930s by two researchers, George Strayer and Robert Haig, at Teachers College, Columbia University, who referred to their concept as a *Minimum Foundation Program (MFP)*.[21] Following Strayer and Haig, several school finance researchers, including Roe L. Johns, Edgar Morphet, and Paul Mort, refined the MFP and assisted state legislatures and state executives to implement adaptations of the MFP in their respective states. The MFP was not intended to achieve absolute fiscal equality among school districts; instead, it was designed to guarantee a base, i.e., minimum educational program throughout a state. Proponents of the MFP indicated that one of its important features was to allow local communities to implement superior and inevitably more expensive educational programs, thereby becoming *Lighthouse Districts*. It was assumed that the *Lighthouse Districts* would influence other districts to follow their examples. Unfortunately, the combination of meager resources and an absence of fiscal effort by many school districts stymied the assumed influence of the *Lighthouse Districts*.

Normally, the local school districts were required by their respective state governments to provide funds based upon a uniform local tax effort and were permitted to provide additional local funds if they elected to do so. The additional local funds, those funds in excess of the required local effort, are referred to technically as local leeway funds.

Over the years, the *Minimum (M)* gradually was omitted from *Minimum Foundation Program* and is now popularly referred to as a *Foundation Program.* The employment of foundation programs throughout the United States substantially equalized educational services among school districts within states. One of the primary characteristics of Foundation Program formula that made it popular among policymakers is that with limited state resources, coupled with a local required tax effort, a specific level of funding is insured throughout the state. An example of a traditional foundation program is provided by Alabama, which employs instructional units that are comprised of teachers, principals, counselors, librarians, etc. The instructional units are based upon the number of students per various instructional personnel, and the costs are determined by multiplying the number of instructional units by a series of state-prescribed salaries. Other categorical costs are added to the Alabama Foundation Program from which a uniform local required fiscal effort (10 mills × property valuation) is deducted. For FY 2013, it is estimated that Alabama provided 56.1 percent of public school revenue from state resources; 32.0 percent were allocated by local agencies; and 11.9 percent were furnished by the federal government. Displayed in Figure 14.4 is a model of a typical foundation program formula including a series of categorical flat grants. Note that in this example some school districts did not generate revenue for local leeway funds.

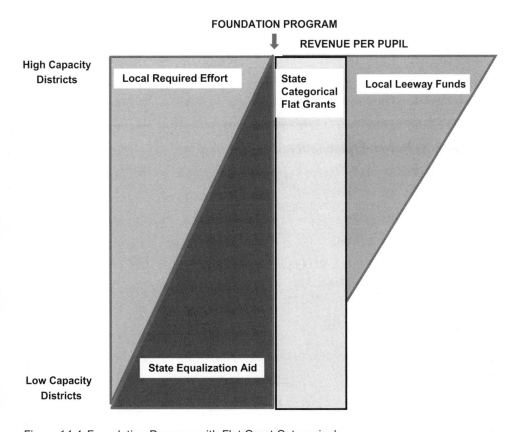

Figure 14.4 Foundation Program with Flat Grant Categoricals

Fiscal Equalization Grants: Power-Equalization Program

$$S_i = P_i F_i \times T_i$$

Where: S_i = State equalization grant to ith district
  P_i = Units of the ith district
    (pupils, teachers, other measures of educational need)
  F_i = Power-equalization program per unit value
    (determined by the local school district)
  T_i = State Aid Ratio (SAR) and is calculated as follows:
  $T_i = [1 - (V_i / G) \times k)]$ and the Required Local Effort or
RLE = 1 – SAR

Where: V_i = Local Fiscal Capacity per ADM
  G = State Fiscal Capacity per ADM
  k = Constant set by the state

If local leeway funds are permitted, an optional program such as the following may be employed:

$$O_i = R_i B_i$$

Where: O_i = Yield from optional local tax
  R_i = Local tax rate
  B_i = Local tax base

Example: Power-Equalization Program

If: P_i = 1,000 ADM and
  F_i = $5,000 per ADM and
  $T_i = [(1 - (\$1,000,000/\$2,500,000) \times .5000)]$ or
    = 0.8000, or the SAR and
RLE = (1 – .8000) or .2000

Then: State Aid = $[(1,000 \times \$5,000) \times .8000]$ or
        $4,000,000 and
RLE = $[(1,000 \times \$5,000) \times .2000]$ or
    $1,000,000

Local Leeway Funds
Where: O_i = Yield from optional local tax
    R_i = 2 mills
    B_i = $100,000,000 and
    O_i = 2 mills x $100,000,000, then
      = $100,000,000 x $0.002, or
      = $200,000

Summary:	
State	$4,000,000
Local RLE	$1,000,000
Local Leeway	$ 200,000
Total	$5,200,000

A unique fiscal equalization program also was introduced during the 1920s and 1930s by Harlan Updegraff, who termed his program *percentage-equalization* that later became known as a *power-equalization program.* While the foundation program was designed initially to retain absolute funding control by state governments, the power-equalization program transfers some fiscal authority to local school districts. As is evident from an examination of the above formula, unlike the foundation program, the power-equalization formula permits the local school districts to specify their per-unit values, and the state is obligated to share a funding responsibility that is based on the combination of the fiscal capacity and district-specific fiscal effort of the local school district. The above example uses the power-equalization formula to allocate the primary fiscal support provided by the state; however, the power-equalization formula is more often used to supplement state aid. It is typically superimposed over a foundation program allocation and is then referred to as a *Tier Program* shown in Figure 4.5.

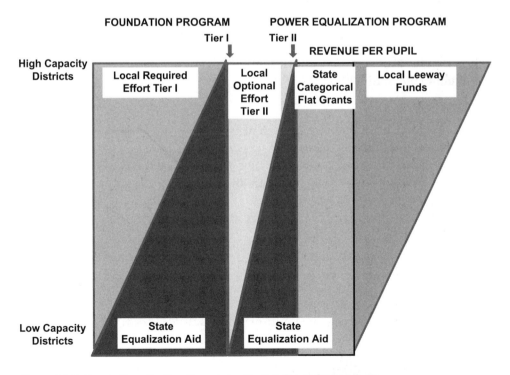

Figure 14.5 Power Equalization Program with Flat Grant Categoricals

The foundation program and percentage-equalization (power-equalization) program can be made mathematically equivalent. The power-equalization formulae have not been widely adopted; although Vermont serves as an example of a state that has adopted a variant of this system to distribute funds from its primary grant. Vermont titled its school finance system as *Full State Funding*, although technically, it meets the definition of a *power-equalization program*. Prior to the current power-equalization formula used by Vermont, its local school districts generated local revenue from application of locally determined property taxes. Vermont elected to cease use of local property taxes and installed a state-administered property tax. The revenue generated by the state property tax flows into a state fund from which the state allocates revenue to the local school districts pursuant to each district's approved budget expenditures. The *Vermont General Education Funding System* as explained by the Vermont Department of Education states,

> The state now pays each district the amount needed to fund the district's locally adopted budget through an education fund. This amount equals the total voter approved expenditure budget less any amounts for expenditures that have specific funding.[22]

For FY 2013, it is estimated that Vermont provided an estimated 87.6 percent of public school revenue from state resources; 4.6 percent were allocated by local agencies; and 7.8 percent were furnished by the federal government.[23] Arrayed in Figure 14.5 is a two-tier power-equalization program, but it should not be confused with the one-tier power-equalization program employed by Vermont.

Fiscal Equalization Grants: Guaranteed Tax Yield Program (Two Tiers)

First Tier: $S_i = P_iF - UV_i$

Where: S_i = State equalization grant to ith district
P_i = Units of the ith district
(pupils, teachers, other measures of educational need)
F_i = Foundation program per unit value
(determined by the state)
U = Required local effort
V_i = Total local fiscal capacity

Second Tier: $S_i = P_iX_i - O_iV_i$

Where: S_i = State equalization grant to ith district
P_i = Units of the ith district
(pupils, teachers, other measures of educational need)
X_i = Guaranteed yield per ADM per mill
O_i = Local leeway (number mills levied)
V_i = Total local fiscal capacity

First Tier Example:

If: F_i = $5,000 per ADM and
P_i = 1,000 ADM and
U = 10 mills and
V_i = $100,000,000, then
S_i = [($5,000 x 1,000) − ($100,000,000 x $0.01)] or
= $5,000,000 − $1,000,000
= $4,000,000

Second Tier Example:

Where: S_i = State equalization grant to the $_i$th district
P_i = Unit (ADM) of the $_i$th district
X_i = Guaranteed yield per ADM per mill
O_i = Local Leeway (Number mills levied)
M_i = Local fiscal capacity
V_i = Local fiscal capacity per ADM
And: $S_i = ((P_i X_i − M_i P_i) \times O_i$ or $((P_i X_i − V_i) \times O_i$
P_i = 1,000 ADM
X_i = $500 per ADM per mill
O_i = 2 mills
M_i = $100,000,000
V_i = ($100,000,000/1,000) or $100,000
Then: $S_i = ((1,000 \times $500) − ($100,000,000/1,000)) \times 2$
= ($500,000 − $100,000) × 2
= $400,000 × 2
= $800,000

Summary:

State (First Tier)	**$4,000,000**
State (Second Tier)	**800,000**
Local	**1,200,000**
Total	**$6,000,000**

Another version of the power-equalization concept that transfers a portion of state fiscal authority to local school districts is the guaranteed tax yield program displayed in Figure 14.6. Rather than providing locally-approved expenditures from the application of statewide property tax (heretofore a local property tax) as illustrated by the Vermont example, Utah guarantees a state-specified per-pupil unit yield per unit of local tax effort that is superimposed over a traditional foundation program formula. The Utah state aid formula also could be defined as a *Two-Tier Funding Program*. The Utah foundation program is entitled *Minimum School Program*[24] and its guaranteed tax yield program is referred

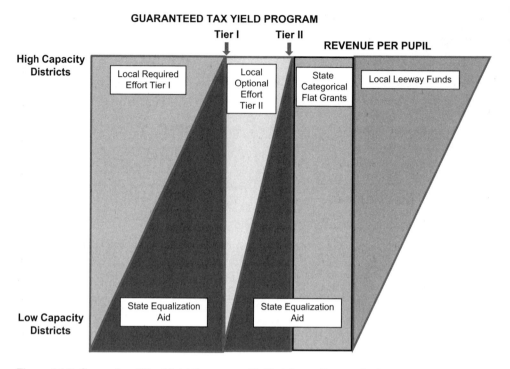

Figure 14.6 Guaranteed Tax Yield Program with Flat Grant Categoricals

to as the *State-Supported Voted Leeway Program*.[25] For FY 2013, it is estimated that Utah provided 51.2 percent of public school revenue from state resources; 38.2 percent were allocated by local agencies; and 10.6 percent were furnished by the federal government.[26]

An interesting feature available for both power-equalization programs and similar guaranteed tax yield programs is the employment of *Recapture Provisions*, although as may be expected, few states have opted to incorporate them into their systems of school finance. A *Recapture Provision*, by definition, requires that high fiscal capacity school districts submit to the state for redistribution, those local required revenues in excess of a specified amount per student. The Utah *Minimum School Program* does contain an example of a recapture component within Tier I.

Technical Observations of Fiscal Equalization Programs

1. Fiscal equalization among school districts can be achieved by any of the programs discussed above, excluding Matching Grants. A state can achieve a high level of fiscal equalization, even through use of a Flat Grant, if the state provides a high percentage of total revenue appropriated to the local school districts;
2. If a state constrains the generation of local leeway funds, as legislated by Florida, the level of fiscal equalization among school districts will be enhanced;
3. An efficient procedure available for states to achieve high levels of fiscal equalization while simultaneously improving adequacy among local school districts is to increase the Required Local Effort (RLE) of the local school districts while concurrently raising the foundation level (or guaranteed tax yield program);

4. Fiscal equalization among local school districts can be achieved more easily by states that have been organized into cost-efficient entities such as county units; and

5. The achievement of a high level of fiscal equalization among local school districts **does not** insure that adequate resources have been provided.

Full State-Funded Program

Several states, including Delaware, Hawaii, Idaho, Michigan, Minnesota, New Mexico, and Vermont, have either implemented or moved significantly toward *full state-funded programs* for public elementary and secondary education. However, only Hawaii has chosen to use a single administrative agency to oversee and manage its system of public schools. The other states continue to administer their public schools through the traditional local school district model. The state funds are distributed through a series of state grants to the local school districts, and the local school boards, usually elected, are charged with the responsibility to administer their schools pursuant to state legislation. The primary reason that the six states moved toward full state-funded programs, excluding Hawaii which transited from a monarchy to a state, was to reduce funding disparities that existed among their local school districts.

Despite the implementation of equalization programs, there are vast funding disparities among states and even greater disparities among school districts within states.[27] More disturbing is that funding disparities among local school districts appear to be increasing, likely exacerbated by the prolonged recession.[28] In contrast, Canada addressed the disparity issue within each of its ten provinces and three territories by centralizing fiscal responsibilities and virtually eliminating funding disparities.[29] For example, the provincial government of British Columbia and its sixty elected Boards of Education co-manage the education system. The province establishes the amount of the grant funding for public education annually and uses a sophisticated funding formula to allocate funds to the local school boards. Consistently, the Canadian system of education is ranked highly internationally.[30]

Most western and industrialized nations finance their public schools through systems of national taxation. For example, England has implemented a state-funded elementary and secondary system of schools where approximately 93 percent of pupils, ages 3–18 years, attend school. However, it is the local communities that provide most of the fiscal resources allocated to the state-funded schools. As a result, in 2011, the variance in per-pupil expenditures ranged from £4,300 to £8,500 among geographical regions,[31] thereby rivaling the per-pupil disparities in the United States. While the state-funded schools are permitted to charge fees for certain activities, e.g., extracurricular events, they still have to provide these services for those pupils who cannot afford to participate. A small percent of pupils, ranging from 7 to 18 percent, attend independent, or private schools, which are financed from pupil fees.

MEASUREMENT OF FISCAL CAPACITY AND FISCAL EFFORT[32]

Whenever states or the federal government[33] implement equalization grant programs, they have to measure the fiscal capacities of their localities. In addition, most equalization grants require that the localities exert minimum levels of fiscal effort (tax effort) in order to qualify for state or federal allocations. In order to determine the fiscal capacities of their local school districts, most states use property valuation, a measure of wealth which has been equalized in order to take into consideration the variance in property assessment practices among the various localities.[34]

Usually, the equalization of property values is accomplished through use of sales-ratio studies conducted by the states. Sales-ratio studies are designed mathematically to compare the selling values of property for each locality during a tax year to their respective assessed values recorded by the localities and then adjust the total value of property of the individual school districts accordingly. For example, if a locality reports that the value of all property sold during a specified tax year was double its recorded or local assessed value, the state assumes that the locality is undervaluing property by 50 percent. The state then adjusts the total value of property of the locality by doubling its reported value, thus equalizing property assessment practices. Various terms are used to label property so equalized, including Fair Market Value (FMV), Fair Cash Value (FCV), Equalized Value (EV), True Value (TV), etc. The State of Georgia serves as an example. Assessment of property is performed by the 159 counties, and two departments of state government where each conducts tests of assessment digests (tax rolls) through use of annual sales-ratio studies. The Sales Ratio Division of the Audit Department conducts its test using annual ratio studies solely for the purpose of equalizing the distribution of state aid to schools. The Property Tax Division of the Department of Revenue uses a sales-ratio study to evaluate whether each county's digest is maintained at the statutory limit of 40 percent of True Market Value (TMV) and simultaneously tests for uniformity among parcels' assessments as well as equalization among counties.[35]

If the federal government legislates that the fiscal capacities of the states are to be taken into consideration, it normally uses per capita personal income, a measure of economic activity which is calculated for each state by the Bureau of Economic Analysis, United States Department of Commerce.[36] A related measure based upon the number and percent of children who qualify for *reduced price and free lunches*[37] also is used to allocate federal aid through *No Child Left Behind Act (NCLB) – Title I*.[38] Contained within the Act, four related formulae are used to distribute federal Title I funds, including the Basic Grant, Concentration Grant, Targeted Formula, and Education Finance Incentive Grant. Collectively, the four grants allocate larger per-pupil amounts to lower fiscal capacity schools and school districts than to their higher capacity peers.[39]

Some states use a combination of wealth and economic indicators, including per capita personal income, adjusted gross income, consumption (sales and excise) taxes, and other local and state taxes and/or revenue. If, from the calculated state share of revenue designated for local public schools, certain local revenue is deducted, in effect, the state has incorporated these revenue sources into its measure of fiscal capacity.[40] In some instances, states, including Pennsylvania and Virginia, have opted to merge mathematically several wealth and economic indicators into indices of fiscal, or taxpaying, ability. Pennsylvania employs an index of fiscal capacity entitled Market Value of Property and Personal Income Aid Ratio (MV/PI AR) that mathematically contrasts property and personal income data for each school district to identical data for the state as a whole.[41] Virginia employs three measures of fiscal capacity, True Valuation of Real and Public Service Corporations, Adjusted Gross Income, and Taxable Retail Sales Receipts, to form an index entitled *Local Composite Index*.[42] Oklahoma serves as an example where local school district proceeds from the yield of specified millage applied to Net Adjusted Valuation of real and personal property, plus revenue from School Land, Gross Production, Motor Vehicle, and R.E.A accounts, are deducted from the districts' Foundation Program, thereby broadening the Oklahoma measure of fiscal capacity.

In order to determine the required fiscal effort for each locality, states usually require their localities to apply minimum tax rates to their Equalized Tax Bases (EV), e.g., mills times the equalized value (EV), dollars per $100 EV, dollars per $1,000 EV, etc.[43] An alternate method used to determine local required fiscal effort is employed by several states. States that employ the alternate method set local percentages that are applied respectively to total calculated amounts mandated in order for the localities to receive state grants. The application of the percentages to the total cost of the state grants determines the localities' revenue or expenditure amounts. The local school districts then set their local tax rates, which are applied to their reported, or assessed, values of their respective tax bases.

RECOGNITION OF THE VARIANCE IN EDUCATIONAL NEEDS

Local school districts serve students who have unique needs, and they face a variance of costs due to the size of their student population, dispersion of students, geographical barriers, and other factors. In response to the variance of costs among school districts, states have responded by developing formulae that are designed to reduce the fiscal burden confronting local school districts. The formulae developed by states generally fall into two categories: *weighted pupil units* and *weighted instructional units*. Each formula and respective examples are presented below.

Weighted Pupil Unit

Weighted pupil units usually are determined through application of cost differentials that apply additional weights to the number of students served pursuant to various pupil accounting units, e.g., enrollment, membership, attendance, etc. For example, if a state decides to take into consideration the variance in the incidence of disabled children, disadvantaged students, vocational students, etc., it can develop cost differentials, as illustrated by Florida. Several examples of cost differentials established by the *Florida Education Finance Program (FEFP)* include: 4.935:1.0 for disabled children (Support level 5), 1.147:1.0 for students who attend *English for Speakers of Other Languages*, and 1.035:1.0 for students who attend career (vocational) education classes. Each cost differential (higher ratio) is multiplied by the number of students identified in the respective categories, which yields weighted pupil units.

Program Cost Factors and Weighted FTE

Program cost factors are intended to assure that each program receives an equitable share of funds in relation to its relative cost per student. Through the annual program cost report, districts report expenditures for each FEFP program. The cost per Full-Time Equivalent (FTE)[44] student of each program cost factor of the FEFP is used to produce an index of relative costs per FTE for Basic Programs, Grades 4–8, established

Table 14.1 Florida Education Finance Program 2013–2014

Cost Program	Program Cost Factors (Weights)
1. Basic Programs	
A. Basic Education Grades K–3	1.125
B. Basic Education Grades 4–8	1.000
C. Basic Education Grades 9–12	1.011
2. English for Speakers of Other Languages	1.145
3. Special Programs for Exceptional Students (ESE)	
A. Support Level IV	3.558
B. Support Level V	5.089
4. Special Programs for Career Education (9–12)	1.011

as the 1.000 base. Florida uses Average Daily Membership (ADM) as its pupil accounting unit prior to the determination of FTE by the type of educational service provided each student. In order to protect districts from extreme fluctuation of the program cost factors, the Florida Legislature typically uses three-year averages to stabilize cost factors. When a school district's FTE students for a program are multiplied by the appropriate cost factor, the result is a weighted FTE.[45] The Florida program cost factors established for use in 2013–2014 are shown in Table 14.1.

ESE students in Levels 4 and 5 are reported with the appropriate cost factor (weight) for their respective levels. ESE students who are not classified in Level 4 or 5 are reported in the applicable Basic Program with *ESE services*. Additional funding for these students is provided by the ESE Guaranteed Allocation component of the FEFP formula. In addition to the above cost differentials, Florida takes into consideration a number of other cost factors, including density of population, pupil transportation, cost-of-living, etc.[46]

Weighted Instructional Unit

In contrast to the weighted pupil unit calculation used by most states to account for cost variance in educational needs, the weighted instructional unit method generates several components, including classroom teacher units, administrative units, support units, etc., through use of various ratios of pupil units. Idaho provides an example of a state that employs instructional units to determine the foundation program allocations to their local school districts. Initially, Idaho calculates a total number of support positions and then applies several ratios to determine the number of instructional units allowed, i.e., numbers of classroom teachers, administrative positions, and classified staff positions. The previous units are then multiplied by a series of state-determined salaries respective to each position classification and then aggregated in order to determine the cost of its foundation program. For example, Idaho set FY 2013 salaries for instructional units, administrative units, and classified units at $23,123, $31,833, and $19,041, respectively. Additional units were provided for special education, remedial education, limited English proficiency, etc.[47] The salaries specified above were then multiplied by indices shown in Table 14.2, then aggregated, and became the total school personnel salaries for each local school district.[48]

Table 14.2 The Idaho State Teachers Salary Scale, FY 2013, Experience and Education

Years	BA	BA+12	BA+24	MA BA+36	MA+12 BA+48	MA+24 BA+60	MA+36 ES/DR
0	1.0000	1.0375	1.0764	1.1168	1.1587	1.2022	1.2473
1	1.0375	1.0764	1.1168	1.1587	1.2022	1.2473	1.2941
2	1.0764	1.1168	1.1587	1.2022	1.2473	1.2941	1.3426
3	1.1168	1.1587	1.2022	1.2473	1.2941	1.3426	1.3929
4	1.1587	1.2022	1.2473	1.2941	1.3426	1.3929	1.4451
5	1.2022	1.2473	1.2941	1.3426	1.3929	1.4451	1.4993
6	1.2473	1.2941	1.3426	1.3929	1.4451	1.4993	1.5555
7	1.2941	1.3426	1.3929	1.4451	1.4993	1.5555	1.6138
8	1.3426	1.3929	1.4451	1.4993	1.5555	1.6138	1.6743
9	1.3929	1.4451	1.4993	1.5555	1.6138	1.6743	1.7371
10	1.3929	1.4993	1.5555	1.6138	1.6743	1.7371	1.8022
11	1.3929	1.4993	1.5555	1.6138	1.7371	1.8022	1.8698
12	1.3929	1.4993	1.5555	1.6138	1.7371	1.8698	1.9399
13 or more	1.3929	1.4993	1.5555	1.6138	1.7371	1.8698	2.0126

SUMMARY AND CONCLUSION

In this chapter, the historical development of programs designed to fund public schools was discussed briefly, followed by a categorical presentation of various intergovernmental revenue transfer formulae currently used by several of the 50 states. Commonly used state-aid formulae presented included flat grants, matching grants, and equalization grants (foundation program, power-equalization grants, and guaranteed tax yield systems). Example states included Alabama, Florida, Idaho, North Carolina, Texas, Utah, and Vermont. The primary purpose of the majority of funding formulae was to equalize the resources among the various states' local school districts.

Following the discussion regarding equalization mechanisms, two methods, weighted student units and weighted instructional units, commonly used to determine the costs required to provide an adequate level of costs to be shared by the three governmental levels, i.e., state, local, and federal, were discussed and examples presented. Both methods used to determine costs can be made mathematically identical, although each method has advantages and disadvantages. The use of weighted students has the advantage of ease of explanation, while a weighted instructional unit has the advantage of determining units through student brackets. For example, the state may set a bracket of students, e.g., 1–20, thus generating an instructional unit, so that a school with 25 students in a certain grade would generate 2 instructional units, rather than 25 student units.

The measurement of fiscal capacity, an indispensable component of equalization grants, contained a discussion of the most common measure, equalized property value, plus the method, sales-ratio technique, used by most states to equalize assessment practices among their local school districts. In addition, multiple measures used by states to calculate fiscal capacity, including indices of fiscal capacity, were presented. State examples of fiscal capacity measures also were presented.

KEY TERMS

- Minimum foundation program
- Power-equalization grant
- Guaranteed tax yield/base program
- Flat grant
- Tier program
- Full state funded
- Matching grant
- General aid

- Categorical aid
- Leeway funds
- Local required effort (LRE)
- Lighthouse school districts
- Weighted pupils (students)
- Weighted instructional units
- Fiscal capacity
- Fiscal effort

NOTES

1. The *Land Ordinances of 1785* and *1787* provided land grants to states and set aside the 16th section of each township, later expanded to include additional sections, for the establishment and support of common schools.
2. National Center for Education Statistics, *Digest of Education Statistics, 2012* (Washington, DC: U.S. Government Printing Office, 2012). Retrieved from: http://nces.ed.gov/programs/digest/d12/tables/dt12_098.asp
3. Ibid.
4. National Education Association, *Rankings and Estimates of School Statistics* (Washington, DC: NEA, 2013). Retrieved from: http://www.nea.org/assets/img/content/NEA_Rankings_And_Estimates-2013_%282%29.pdf
5. Vermont also reported 87.6 percent from state resources, although its local share was higher, 4.6 percent, than the percent of local revenue, 2.2, provided by Hawaii. Additionally, Hawaii, due to the large federal presence in the state, received a larger percent of federal revenue, 10.3 percent, than the 7.8 percent received by Vermont. Thus, due to the very small percent of revenue provided from local resources, Hawaii rather than Vermont best meets the definition of *full state-funded,* a topic discussed more fully later.
6. National Education Association, *op. cit.*
7. See for example: *Vocational Education Act.* Title 20. Chapter 44, Subchapter I, Part A. §2321(a)(2)D(c).
8. Presentation of the Minimum Foundation Program origin and features will be discussed more fully later in this chapter.
9. See also: Ownings, William, and Leslie Kaplan, *American Public School Finance*, 2nd ed. (Stamford, CT: Cengage Learning, 2013).
10. Categorical grants are designated for a specific category of pupils or programs.
11. General Aid grants can be disbursed for any function or legal purpose.
12. A discussion of weighting systems commonly employed by the several states is presented later (See: Recognition of the variance in educational needs).

13. North Carolina Department of Education, *State Allotment Formula* (Raleigh, North Carolina: NCDOE, 2013). Retrieved from: http://www.dpi.state.nc.us/docs/fbs/resources/data/highlights/2013highlights.pdf

14. Ibid., *Low Wealth Supplemental Funding*. See: www.ncpublicschools.org/docs/fbs/allotments/.../lowwealthformula.xls

15. National Education Association, *op. cit.*

16. Matching grants remain popular among private foundations and commercial enterprises that desire to assist public schools meet their goals and objectives.

17. The acronym *VPSA* represents Virginia Public School Authority, the mechanism used to market state general obligation bonds for the purpose of funding technology and other purposes.

18. Virginia Department of Education, *Calculation Template, FYs 2013–2014:* (Richmond, Virginia: VDOE, 2013). Retrieved from: http://www.doe.virginia.gov/school_finance/budget/calc_tools/index.shtml

19. For FY 2014, the Virginia *VPSA Technology Grant* accounted for only 1.7 percent of the total state aid to local school districts.

20. National Education Association, *op. cit.*

21. George Strayer and Robert Haig, *The Financing of Education in the State of New York.* Report of the Educational Finance Inquiry Commission (New York: The Macmillan Company, 1923), p. 173.

22. Vermont Department of Education, *Overview of General Education Funding System* (Montpelier, Vermont: VDOE, 2013). Retrieved from: http://education.vermont.gov/documents/EDU-Finance_Education_Funding_System_2011.pdf

23. National Education Association, *op. cit.*

24. Utah State Office of Education, *School Finance* (Salt Lake City, Utah: USOE, 2013). See: http://www.schools.utah.gov/finance/Property-Tax/Tax-References/BasicGuarantee.aspx

25. Ibid. Retrieved from: http://www.schools.utah.gov/finance/Property-Tax/Tax-References/VotedGuarantee.aspx

26. National Education Association, *op. cit.*

27. David G. Sciarra and Bruce Baker, *Is School Funding Fair? A National Report Card* (Newark, NJ: Education Law Center, Rutgers University, 2012). Retrieved from: http://www.schoolfundingfairness.org/

28. The Great Recession (also referred to as the Lesser Depression, the Long Recession, or the Global Recession of 2009) was a marked global economic decline that began in December 2007 and took a particularly sharp downward turn in September 2008. According to the United States National Bureau of Economic Research, the recession commenced June 2007 and ended December 2009.

29. There is variance in per-pupil expenditures among the provinces and territories; however, most of the per-pupil expenditure variance can be attributed to geographical isolation and dispersion of population.

30. Organization for Economic Cooperation and Development, *Education at a Glance 2012, OECD Indicators* (Paris, France: OECD Publishing, December, 2012).

31. *The Guardian*, "George Osborne Promises National Funding Formula for Schools" (London: *The Guardian*, June 26, 2013). Retrieved from: http://www.guardian.co.uk/education/2013/jun/26/george-osborne-funding-formula-schools.

32. An in-depth discussion of fiscal capacity and fiscal effort may be found in Chapter 7.

33. Most federal grants are allocated to the several states for distribution to their localities; if the federal government intends to equalize funding among states, it also has to measure the fiscal capacities of the states.

34. See for example: Virginia Department of Taxation, *Assessment Sales-Ratio Studies* (Richmond, Virginia: VDOT, 2013). Retrieved from: http://www.tax.virginia.gov/Documents/2011SalesRatiov2.pdf.

35. Sales Ratio Division, Audit Department, *Annual Sales-Ratio Studies* (Atlanta, Georgia: Georgia Department of Taxation, 2012).

36. Retrieved from: http://www.bea.gov/newsreleases/relsarchivespi.htm

37. See: *Healthy Hunger-Free Kids Act of 2010.* Pub. L. §§111-296, 111th Congress, December 2010.

38. United States Congress, *No Child Left Behind Act – Title I* (Washington, DC: United States Department of Education, 2013) at Pub.L. §§107–110, 115 Stat. 1425, enacted January 8, 2002.

39. New America Foundation, *Federal Education Budget Project – NCLB – Title I* (Washington, DC: New America Foundation, 2012). Retrieved from: http://febp.newamerica.net/background-analysis/no-child-left-behind-act-title-i-distribution-formulas.

40. Oklahoma Department of Education, *Annual Report, State Aid Formula Used to Calculate Foundation and Salary Incentive Aid, 2011–2012* (Oklahoma City, Oklahoma: ODE, 2013). Retrieved from: http://ok.gov/sde/sites/ok.gov.sde/files/documents/files/2012_Annual2_%20Report_0.pdf.

41. Pennsylvania Department of Education, *Financial Data Elements, Aid Ratio, 2012–13* (Philadelphia, Pennsylvania: PDOE, 2013). Retrieved from: http://www.education.state.pa.us/portal/server.pt/community/financial_data_elements/7672.

42. See for example: *The Local Composite Index (LCI)* employed by the Commonwealth of Virginia. The Virginia LCI uses property valuation, adjusted gross income, and taxable retail sales to construct its measure of fiscal capacity. Retrieved from: http://www.doe.virginia.gov/school_finance/budget/compositeindex_local_abilitypay/index.shtml.

43. See for example: *Georgia Quality Basic Education (QBE)*, http://app.doe.k12.ga.us/ows-bin/owa/qbe_reports.public_menu?p_fy=2000.

44. Students are assigned percentages of the school day that they receive various educational services, e.g., general education, exceptional education, vocational education, etc. For example, a student may attend general education 50 percent of the school day, receive 30 percent exceptional education services, and attend career education the remaining 20 percent. The various forms of educational services are then multiplied by their respective cost differentials, yielding a weighted FTE.

45. The full description of the weighted student unit is Weighted Average Daily Membership in Full-time Equivalent, or WADMFTE.

46. Florida Department of Education, *Funding for Florida School Districts, 2013–2014* (Tallahassee, Florida: FDOE, 2013), Retrieved from: http://www.fldoe.org/fefp/pdf/20-13Firstcalc.pdf.

47. Idaho Department of Education, *Public Schools Budget, 2013:* (Boise, Idaho: IDOE, 2013). See: www.sde.idaho.gov/site/finance_tech/

48. While this explanation provides an overview of the Idaho Foundation Program, the methodology used to calculate the costs to be shared between the state and local school districts is more complex.

CHAPTER 15

Financial Accounting

TOPICAL OUTLINE OF CHAPTER

- Objectives of Financial Accounting
- Basic School Financial Accounts and Records
  - Fund Accounting
  - Control Accounts
- Accounting (Bookkeeping) Process
- Activity Funds
- Financial Auditing

INTRODUCTION

No institution of any size, public or private, can operate effectively without adequate accounting services, and the educational enterprise is one of the major activities of government. According to the National Education Association in Fiscal Year 2010, state and local expenditures for public elementary and secondary education accounted for 33.7 percent of total expenditures and was the single largest governmental expenditure.[1] Usually, public schools represent the largest enterprise of local communities, both in terms of the volume of financial transactions and in terms of the importance of the services provided.

School accounting can be classified into two broad categories: statistical and financial. Statistical accounting includes all quantitative information on the educational enterprise except financial data. Examples of statistical accounting are pupil accounting, personnel accounting, inventories, e.g., textbooks, library books, laptop computers, I-pads, supplies and equipment, and similar items. While statistical accounting is necessary for effective use of financial accounting, this chapter is focused exclusively on financial accounting. Financial accounting only records financial transactions; however, the financial procedures utilized directly affect the administration of the educational programs of the school district. While most school administrators are not accountants and have only limited training in accounting, they should have knowledge regarding the function and operation of the system of accounting employed by their district. School administrators must possess this competency in order to provide leadership for the business administration of their schools. Chapman et. al. stated that there were five principles of administration: planning, organizing, directing, coordinating, and controlling.[2] Financial accounting directly or indirectly affects all five principles of administration.

As observed by Ray, Candoli, and Hack, financial accounting has been broadened from budgetary control, i.e., assurance that all funds were used as appropriated, to include the concept of accountability,

> accounting, auditing, and reporting are used to provide necessary data and interpretation to determine costs and benefits within the financial foundations of educational institutions . . . to describe (1) the nature, sources, and amounts of revenue inputs; (2) the appropriation of revenues to various programs (or funds and accounts); and (3) the actual expenditures in these programs. These data are then related to program outputs or educational outcomes, so that citizens can understand the financial implications of program decisions and the program implications of financial decisions . . . the schools are accountable to the public, and the public has information on which it can exercise its decision-making power in areas of financial policy.[3]

The governmental structure adopted by states directly affects, fiscal accounting practices of school districts, no one more significant than the authority and control responsibilities between state governments and the localities. Displayed in Box 15.1 are definitions for fiscal independency and fiscal dependency that are key terms pursuant to the fiscal relationship between state and local education agencies.[4] The Education Commission of the States reported that over 80 percent of the nation's school districts are fiscally independent.[5] The advantages and disadvantages of fiscal independency and dependency have been debated for many years. Those who favor a fiscal dependency structure argue that a central local government can assess the financial needs for all local governmental requirements and apportion local revenue receipts according to need and priority. However, the weight of debate appears to reside with those who argue for fiscal independency. Public education is a constitutional requirement on state legislatures, and local school boards are components of state government.[6] School board members are considered officers of the state, and in some states, local school superintendents also are considered state officers.[7]

BOX 15.1

Definitions for Fiscal Independency and Fiscal Dependency of Local School Districts

- Fiscally independent school districts: School districts are granted legal authority by the state legislature to set the tax rate on real property, within state constitutional and legislative limits; to levy and collect taxes for the support of local schools; and to approve the expenditure of the funds collected. States require local school boards to prepare budgets of proposed expenditures. In fiscally independent school districts, local school boards of education have a relatively free hand in determining how and where expenditures are to be made, subject to limitations on the total amount by the state's constitution or statute.

- Fiscally dependent school districts: School districts are required by either the state constitution or statute to submit their budgets to an intervening local governing agency, i.e., county or municipality, for approval. The local school district prepares and adopts a budget specifying the anticipated expenditures and projected revenue needs. Then a different county or municipal government may reduce the total budget or eliminate items not required by state law and apportion the school taxes.

To have a local county or municipality *second-guess* and refuse to fund adequately the proposed budgets of local school boards would appear irrational and inappropriate.

OBJECTIVES OF FINANCIAL ACCOUNTING

Financial accounting is broader than bookkeeping. While budgeting, accounting, and reporting are different components of fiscal administration, they are interrelated and must be planned and integrated with other components. The primary purpose of financial accounting is to enable the business administration arm of the school district to provide maximum service to the educational program of the district. Specifically, the following objectives should be pursued:

- *Annual preparation of budgets.* The information furnished from accounting records is essential for budget development and administration.
- *Financial relationships between the school districts and other agencies and institutions.* Examples of other agencies and institutions include federal and state departments of education, banks, insurance companies, judicial systems, law enforcement,

retirement systems, other local governmental agencies, treasurers, vendors, etc. Financial records are essential for the orderly conduct of business with all these parties.

- *Authorization of expenditures.* The approved and appropriated budget provides general authorization of expenditures; however, budget control is necessary through designation of signatures for specified personnel. Clearance for expenditure of funds cannot be made without the necessary financial accounting records.

- *Purchasing and contractual procedures.* Purchases include a wide array of supplies, equipment, services, materials, real estate, and other items. Contracts are let by the school district for personnel services, building construction and repairs, insurance, loans, and other transactions. A system of authorized procedures must be developed and followed for all financial transactions.

- *Payment of obligations.* A procedural system that identifies outstanding obligations must be developed and implemented. Invoices must be verified confirming items received are in good order and the payment prices are accurate. Wage employee hours are checked pursuant to dates and times reported and compensation owed contract employees is determined. Capital facilities under construction contracts are inspected and the proportionate share of the contract due at a specified date is determined.

- *Payments recorded systematically.* As a minimum, payment records must indicate to whom payments are made, when made, and for what purpose.

- *Procurement of revenue.* The school district, through local taxation or appropriations, state and federal appropriations, student tuition (parent and other school districts), and non-revenue payments must acquire sufficient fiscal resources to meet its obligations. These revenue receipts must be recorded systematically by source and by fund and/or purpose for which they will be used. Special fund accounts must be maintained pursuant to law to discharge trust agreements. In general, revenue receipts are procured for current purposes, capital facilities, debt service, or for trust and agency obligations.

- *Individual school activity funds.* Activities conducted by individual schools may be funded by both public and private revenues. Regardless of the source of the revenues received by the individual schools, they are treated as public funds and under control of the school district.

- *Safeguarding of funds.* All school funds must be safeguarded, and the school board and school district employees must be able to prove that the funds have been faithfully accounted and have not been stolen, lost, or misused. All school funds are audited,[8] usually on an annual basis; as such, the financial accounting system has to provide information necessary for a comprehensive audit.

- *Public report to the public.* School districts, through leadership provided by their school superintendents, usually present to the public an annual report. The annual reports are normally prepared in a consistent format with the fiscal data provided through the system of financial accounting.

- *Official reports to state and federal agencies.* Much of the data submitted to the U.S. Department of Education (USDOE) are first submitted by school districts to their State Departments of Education (SDOE), submitted then in aggregate form by SDOEs to USDOE in conformance to a specified accounting format.[9] The school districts also submit reports for grants received to their state and federal sponsors, again, relying on the system of financial accounting to provide the fiscal data.

- *Evaluation of financial and educational policies.* Both financial and educational programs require evaluation through the conduct of cost analyses. Due partially to the extensive accountability requirements that have been placed on local school districts over the past several years, financial accounting systems have been designed to provide fiscal data that can be matched to the array of educational programs and projects that have been implemented.

BASIC SCHOOL FINANCIAL ACCOUNTS AND RECORDS

Fund Accounting

Unlike private sector accounting where the primary purpose of accounting is to maximize profit and increase equity for the enterprise, the primary purpose of public sector accounting is to expend and safeguard appropriated resources efficiently for their intended objectives. Public agencies, including public schools, manage the flow of revenue receipts and expenditure of resources through a series of funds. A fund is a separate fiscal and accounting entity with a self-balancing set of accounts recording cash and other financial resources, together with all related liabilities and residual equities or balances, or changes therein. Current fund classifications[10] are displayed in Box 15.2.

BOX 15.2

Classification of Accounting Funds Used by Public School Districts

Governmental Fund Types

General Fund: This fund is the chief operating fund of the school district. It is used to account for all financial resources of the school district except for those required to be accounted for in another fund. A district may have only one general fund.

Special Revenue Funds: These funds account for the proceeds of specific revenue sources (other than trusts or major capital projects) that are legally restricted to expenditure for specified purposes. Examples of special revenue funds are restricted state or federal grants-in-aid; expendable trusts that benefit or support the governmental entity; and restricted tax levies.

Capital Projects Funds: These funds account for financial resources to be used to acquire or construct major capital facilities (other than those of proprietary funds and trust funds). The most common source of capital projects funding is the sale of bonds or other capital financing instruments. A separate fund may be used for each capital project or one fund may be used, supplemented by the classification project/reporting code.

Debt Service Funds: These funds account for the accumulation of resources for, and the payment of, general long-term debt principal and interest.

Permanent Funds: These funds account for resources that are legally restricted to the extent that only earnings, and not principal, may be used for purposes that support the school district's programs.

Proprietary Fund Types

Enterprise Funds: These funds account for any activity for which a fee is charged to external users for goods or services. Examples of enterprise funds are activities such as the food service program, bookstore operation, athletic stadium, or the community swimming pool.

Internal Service Funds: These funds account for any activity within the school district that provides goods or services to other funds, school district departments, component units, or other governments on a cost-reimbursement basis. Examples of internal service funds are such activities as central warehousing and purchasing, central data-processing, and central printing and duplicating.

Fiduciary Fund Types

Trust Funds: These funds account for assets held by a school district in a trustee capacity for others (e.g., members and beneficiaries of pension plans and other postemployment benefit [OPEB] plans, external investment pools, or private-purpose trust arrangements) and that, therefore, cannot be used to support the school district's own programs. Examples of trust funds are:

- *Pension Trust Funds*. These funds account for resources that are required to be held in trust for members and beneficiaries of defined benefit pension plans, defined contribution plans, OPEB plans, or other benefit plans.
- *Investment Trust Funds*. These funds account for the external portion (i.e., the portion that does not belong to the school district) of investment pools operated by the school district.
- *Private-Purpose Trust Funds*. These funds account for other trust arrangements under which the principal and income benefit individuals, private organizations, or other governmental agencies.

Agency Funds: These funds account for funds that are held in a custodial capacity by a school district for individuals, private organizations, or other governments. Agency funds may include those used to account for student activities or taxes collected for another governmental agency.

There are three methods used to record revenue and expenditure transactions. Historically, school districts relied on the cash method of accounting until the more modern methods, accrual and modified accrual, recommended by the Governmental Accounting Standards Board (GASB) became the accepted accounting methods employed by school districts. The GASB is recognized as the official source of generally accepted accounting principles (GAAP) for state and local governments. Definitions of the three accounting methods are presented below:

- *The cash method.* The cash method is still employed by many of the nation's school districts, particularly small districts. Under the cash method, revenues are not recorded until they are actually received, either by check or electronic deposit, and expenditures are not recorded until they are actually made.
- *The accrual method.* Under the accrual method, transactions are recorded when the obligations are made and revenues when they become available and measurable, regardless of when the revenues for them (receivables) are actually received.[11]
- *The modified accrual method.* An accounting method commonly used by school districts that combines the accrual method with cash method of accounting. Modified accrual accounting recognizes revenues when they become available and measurable and, with a few exceptions, recognizes expenditures when obligations are incurred. The most common exception is the cost anticipated for personnel.

Prior to modern data processing, financial transactions were hand-recorded into two principal documents, a journal that was used to first record each transaction chronologically and later posted to a ledger by fund and function. School districts still use the structure of journalizing financial transactions and posting them into the general ledger; however, modern data processing provides simultaneous entries of the transactions into the journal and ledger. And, the ledger entries are much more detailed, permitting each revenue transaction to be posted by source, revenue or non-revenue, and fund as defined in Box 15.3. Expenditure transactions are recorded by fund, function, object, project, and level of instruction, as defined in Box 15.4.

BOX 15.3

Revenue Classifications as Promulgated by the Institute for Education Sciences

Fund: A fund is a separate fiscal and accounting entity with a self-balancing set of accounts recording cash and other financial resources, together with all related liabilities and residual equities or balances, or changes therein.

Revenue Receipts: Increases to assets which do not incur a liability or represent exchanges of property for cash.

Non-Revenue Receipts: Amounts received that do not increase assets, i.e., do incur a liability, are insurance adjustments, or are exchanges of property for cash.

Sources:
- Revenue from Local Agencies
- Revenue from Intermediate Agencies
- Revenue from State Agencies
- Revenue from Federal Agencies
- Revenue from Other Sources

Control Accounts

Control accounts, also known as general accounts or books of original entry, are necessary (1) for reconciling the records of the school board with the records of other officials, institutions, agencies, and persons with whom the board does business, (2) for reconciliation with revenue receipts and expenditures ledgers, and (3) for property control. Examples of control accounts include treasurer's accounts, depository accounts, revenue receipts accounts, check registers for payrolls, check registers for vouchers, and periodical summaries of cash. A control account is a summary account in the general ledger. The details that support the balance in the summary account are contained in a subsidiary ledger – a ledger that is external and ancillary to the general ledger. The purpose of control accounts is to keep the general ledger free of details, yet have the correct balance for the financial statements. For example, the revenue receipts account in the general ledger should be a control account, and its entries would be recorded in aggregate amounts with the details entered into the subsidiary ledger. Debt records should include accounts payable and records of long- and short-term obligations. Records for capital assets should be maintained for stores, furniture, equipment, real estate, and facilities. While the types of control accounts and accounting records vary among states and often among school districts within states, the superintendent and central office administrators should review frequently the control accounts of the district.

BOX 15.4

Expenditure Classifications as Promulgated by the Institute of Education Sciences

Fund: A fund is a separate fiscal and accounting entity with a self-balancing set of accounts recording cash and other financial resources, together with all related liabilities and residual equities or balances, or changes therein.

Function: The function describes the activity for which a service or material object is acquired. The functions of a school district are classified into five broad areas: instruction, support services, operation of non-instructional services, facilities acquisition and construction, and debt service.

Object: This classification is used to describe the service or commodity obtained as the result of a specific expenditure. Examples include Personal Services-Salaries, Official/Administrative Services, Student Transportation, etc.

Project: The project/reporting code permits school districts to accumulate expenditures to meet a variety of specialized reporting requirements at local, state, and federal levels. The project can be identified by funding source, authority, purpose, and fiscal year of the appropriation.

Instruction Level: This classification permits expenditures to be segregated by instructional level. Many state departments of education differentiate elementary, secondary, and postsecondary costs so they can calculate interdistrict tuition rates, compute general state aid, or both.

ACCOUNTING (BOOKKEEPING) PROCESS

It is necessary for both private sector managers and school district administrators to know the financial status of the district at a moment's notice. In essence, they need to determine what is owned versus what is owed, and the basic accounting equation used by the private sector can be stated as:

Owned minus Owed = Equity or Net Worth.

For public schools, private sector terminology is replaced as follows:

Assets are things owned;
Liabilities are things owed; and
Fund Balance replaces Equity or Net Worth.

The accounting equation, with an example, then becomes:

Assets – Liabilities = Fund Balance
If assets = $1,000,000 and liabilities = $100,000, the fund balance would = $900,000.

While some school districts, usually very small districts, employ a *single-entry system* of bookkeeping, the vast majority of districts rely on the more sophisticated and venerable *double-entry system.*[12] The financial status of the school district changes each time there is a financial transaction; and as discussed previously, the transaction is first entered into a journal and then posted to a ledger account.[13] "T" accounts are established for assets, liabilities, and fund balances, where each financial transaction is recorded by making two entries, a *debit* and *credit*. Those unfamiliar with accounting terminology often confuse *debits* and *credits* as meaning *decreases* and *increases,* respectively. The confusion results from equating a check register, where a debit does decrease and a credit does increase the checking account, to the "T" accounts for assets in the accounting equation. **However, it is important to understand that the term *debit* only means a left-hand entry and the term *credit* only a right-hand entry.** Displayed in Box 15.5 are debits and credits and their financial effects, i.e., increases or decreases, on the three components of the accounting equation.

BOX 15.5

Accounting Equation

Assets	−	Liabilities	=	Fund Balance

Debit	Credit	Debit	Credit	Debit	Credit
Increase	Decrease	Decrease	Increase	Decrease	Increase

As an example, assume that one of the T accounts under assets, *cash reserves*, is used to pay a vendor. You would credit assets, a right-hand entry, and debit fund balance, a left-hand entry. The credit under assets would decrease cash reserves while a simultaneous debit also would result in a decreased fund balance. For each financial transaction, multiple debits and credits may occur; regardless, an equal number of debits and credits are required. This is the signature of *double-entry accounting (bookkeeping).* The primary advantage of double-entry accounting has been explained by Thompson et al.,

> double entry is a tool that creates *a self-balancing set of books,* so that the assets of the district are not inflated. If this were not done, assets and liabilities would not balance, falsifying the actual cash position of the fund because appropriate additions and subtractions would not cross-balance revenue and expenditure activity – an error in financial position that would worsen if subsequent decisions were made on the basis of bad information.[14]

A more expansive presentation of the advantages of double-entry accounting (adapted from the private sector to advantages for public schools by authors) has been provided by Figurate, Ltd.,

* Provides a specific means to open and close fund balances;
* Provides an arithmetic check on bookkeeping since the total amount of debit and credit entries must balance;

- Provides immediate assessment of financial status of the school district; and
- Provides a means to detect and correct accounting errors.[15]

ACTIVITY FUNDS

As defined by the Institute of Education Sciences, school building *Activity Funds* are,

> established to direct and account for monies used to support co-curricular and extracurricular student activities. As a general rule, co-curricular activities are any kinds of school-related activities outside the regular classroom that directly add value to the formal or stated curriculum. Co-curricular activities involve a wide range of student clubs and organizations. Extracurricular activities encompass an extensive array of other district-directed activities, typified by organized sports and other nonacademic interscholastic competitions . . . Activity funds are unique to school districts. Two classifications are commonly recognized: *student activity funds*, which belong to the students and are used to support student organizations and clubs; and *district activity funds*,[16] which belong to the school district and are used to support [school] district programs.[17] [Italics added]

The major distinction between student and district activity funds centers on ownership of the assets of the activity funds. If the assets have been accumulated by and for students from nonpublic sources, e.g., sale of magazine subscriptions, private contributions, receipts from class plays, club membership fees, etc., the assets are owned and controlled by the students. Students not only assist in the acquisition of revenue receipts, but are involved in management and disbursement of funds acquired by their organizations. However, approval for disbursement of student activity funds normally requires authorization by the sponsor of the students' organization and the building principal or designee. In contrast, district activity funds usually are provided from public sources, e.g., local school board appropriations, grants, student fees,[18] etc., and are used to support school district purposes. While building principals manage district activity funds, disbursement of funds requires school board authorization and approval.[19]

For states where some of their local school districts are categorized as fiscally independent, unexpended and unencumbered district activity funds can be *balance-forwarded* to the subsequent fiscal year. States where some or all their districts are fiscally dependent normally require unexpended and unencumbered district activity funds to be returned to the central administration and perhaps to the local governing agency. In contrast, unexpended and unencumbered student activity funds usually can be *balance-forwarded* by both fiscally independent and fiscally dependent school districts.

Misuse and embezzlement of school activity funds are all too common and have resulted in career-ending scandals and, in some instances, incarceration of administrators, teachers, and support personnel.[20] Multiple employees interact with school activity funds, a small minority who break the public trust by mismanagement; and in some instances, they commit actual larceny or embezzlement. Activity funds are particularly susceptible to schemes that defraud and/or misappropriate resources since tangible cash receipts are collected from the sale of goods, athletic gate receipts, collection of student fees, gifts, etc. In some instances, school districts, usually large urban or suburban districts, have centralized all or some of their activity fund accounts. Often, centralization of activity funds has followed incidents of mismanagement or embezzlement of funds. In other cases, the inability to appropriately fund interscholastic athletic programs in some schools, while athletic programs in other schools flourished, motivated school boards to centralize and redistribute their athletic accounts. The primary advantage of centralized activity funds is that during economic periods when high yields from investments can be realized, the centralized and pooled activity funds can generate significant investment earnings. Such earnings should be returned to the schools and accounts through a *pro rata* system of distribution, excluding the athletic accounts.

FINANCIAL AUDITING

Most public schools are required by state statutes[21] to have financial audits conducted annually on all funds, including the activity funds managed by principals of individual school buildings. The Auditor General of British Columbia provides a definition of an audit:

> Financial audits are performed to obtain assurance as to whether an organization's financial statements are free of material misstatements. During a financial audit, an auditor reviews financial statements to provide a formal auditor's opinion. This opinion is attached to the front of the organization's financial statements to provide assurance that they are fairly presented – in other words, that they meet generally accepted accounting principles and have been scrutinized by an independent auditor.

> Absolute assurance cannot be attained because of:

- factors such as the use of judgment and the use of testing of the data underlying the financial statement;
- inherent limitations of internal control; and
- audit evidence available to the auditor is persuasive rather than conclusive in nature.[22]

Audits are usually required annually, although they can be requested and conducted at any time. Two types of audits are conducted:

- *Internal audits*: Internal auditors are employees of the audited agency. Internal auditing is commonly conducted as pre-audits before action is taken or just prior to an external audit. As described by the municipality of Anchorage, Alaska, "Emphasis is on providing the Municipal Assembly and the Mayor with objective information to determine whether the required high degree of public accountability is maintained, and to assist management in improving the efficiency and effectiveness of government operations and activities."[23]

- *External audits*: External auditors are not employees of the audited agency. External auditing usually is performed as post-audits pursuant to mandated schedules (i.e., annually, biennially, etc.) According to the municipality of Anchorage, their emphasis is on "the fairness of financial representations."[24] Displayed in Box 15.6 is a listing of records that should be furnished for analysis by both internal and external auditors. Also contained in this box are the required components of the completed audits.

BOX 15.6

Required Records for Analysis during Internal and External Audits

- School board minutes;
- School district or school budgets;
- Original documents relating to the authorization of expenditures;
- Original documents relating to the making of payments;
- Ledgers, registers, journals, and other accounting books;
- Internal accounts of individual schools;
- Tax collections and delinquencies;
- Revenue and non-revenue receipts records;
- Bank accounts;
- Investment records;
- Sinking funds, bond funds, capital accounts, trust funds, and all other special funds;
- Deeds to property and property inventories, including stores inventories;
- Insurance policies;
- Cash not deposited in banks; and
- Surety bonds.

Components of Completed Audits

- Letter of transmittal;
- Scope and limitations of audit;
- Summary of findings;
- Recommendations for improving financial accounting;
- Recommendations for improving business administration procedures;
- Necessary financial statements and schedules; and
- Statistical information within the scope of the audit.

Members of the public often are surprised that neither internal nor external auditors are required to report criminal activity found during an audit, e.g., fraud, embezzlement, etc., to law enforcement authorities. To the contrary, auditors are required to convey their findings *only* to their clients, e.g., local school superintendent, chair of the local school board, etc., and are bound to maintain confidentiality pursuant to Rule 301 of the American Institute of Certified Public Accountants' (AICPA) Code of Professional Conduct (Confidential Client Information): *A member in public practice shall not disclose any confidential client information without the specific consent of the client.*[25] If, for some reason, the client decides not to divulge the criminal violations to law enforcement authorities, with some exceptions, the auditors are required to abide by Rule 301.

SUMMARY AND CONCLUSION

Two broad categories of school accounting are presented: statistical and financial. This chapter focused on financial accounting at both the school district and school building levels. The governmental structures used by states, i.e., fiscal independency and fiscal dependency, were discussed regarding their effects upon financial accounting. In addition, the accountability movement and its role in expanding how financial transactions are recorded were also addressed. The objectives of financial accounting were operationally defined and the structures used by the various states and school districts identified. School districts normally use a series of funds to administer state, local, and federal educational objectives and record fiscal transactions through an elaborate system of revenue and expenditure classifications provided by state and federal education agencies. Revenue transactions are identified by source, i.e., local, intermediate, state, federal, and other agencies, while expenditures are recorded by fund, function, object, project, and instructional level. The accounting equation, as adopted by public school districts, basic terminology, and examples were provided. Most school districts use modern data processing to record their financial transactions, although the venerable double-entry bookkeeping process relies on the time-tested journals and ledgers to manage their budgets. Most state and local education agencies have adopted modified accrual as a means of budgetary control. The management of school activity funds was discussed and its career-ending potential was presented. The role of financial auditing and terminology was also provided.

KEY TERMS

- Fiscal Independency and dependency
- Cash accounting
- Accrual accounting
- Modified accrual accounting
- Control accounts
- Encumbrance
- Expenditure classification

- Revenue
- Non-revenue
- Single- and double-entry bookkeeping
- Debit
- Credit
- Fund accounting
- Activity fund

NOTES

1. National Education Association, *Rankings of the States (2012) and Estimates of School Statistics (2013)* (Washington, DC: NEA, 2013).

2. Brian Chapman, Frederick C. Mosher, and Edward C. Page, *Public Administration* (United Kingdom: Encyclopedia Britannia, 2013).

3. John R. Ray, I. Carl Candoli, and Walter G. Hack, *School Administration: A Planning Approach* (New York: Pearson Education, Inc., 2005).

4. Drawn primarily from Fred C. Lunenburg and Beverly J. Irby, *The Principalship: Vision to Action* (Belmont, California: Thomson Wadsworth, Inc., 2006).

5. Education Commission of the States, *Finance: Fiscally Dependent/Independent School Districts* (Denver, Colorado: ECS Information Clearinghouse, 1997).

6. All states, excluding Iowa, have provisions that mandate systems of *common schools.*

7. See for example: Commonwealth of Virginia, *Code of Virginia,* §22.1–64. Oath of superintendent.

8. See for example, *Code of Virginia,* §15.2–2511. Audit of local government records, etc.; Auditor of Public Accounts; audit of shortages.

9. Institute of Education Sciences, *Financial Accounting for Local and State School Systems: 2009 Edition* (Washington, DC: National Center for Education Statistics, 2009).

10. Abbreviated from a more detailed discussion provided by the Institute of Education Sciences, *Financial Accounting for Local and State School Systems: 2009 Edition* (Washington, DC: National Center for Education Statistics, 2009).

11. Both accrual and modified accrual accounting *encumber* obligations; by definition *encumbrance* is a contingent liability, contract, purchase order, payroll commitment, or legal penalty that is chargeable to an account. It ceases to be an encumbrance when paid-out or when the actual liability amount is determined and recorded as expenditure.

12. Frater Luca Bartolomes Pacioli devoted a chapter to the double-entry system in his treatise, *Divina Proportione*, in 1497, and is usually given credit for its invention. However, Pacioli credited Benedetto Cotrugli who wrote *Delia Mercatura et del Mercante Perfetto*, which included a brief chapter that described many of the features of double-entry bookkeeping.

13. Actually, modern accounting software records journal and ledger entries simultaneously.

14. David C. Thompson, Faith E. Crampton, and R. Craig Wood, *Money and Schools*. 5th Edn. (Larchmont, New York: Eye on Education, 2012).

15. Figurate, Ltd., *Advantages of Double-Entry Bookkeeping* (United Kingdom: Figurate, Ltd., 2007).

16. *District Activity Funds* are referred by various titles, including *Instruction Funds,* used by Virginia school districts, and *General Funds*, by other states.

17. Institute of Education Sciences, *op. cit.*

18. Some states prohibit assessment of most student fees. See for example: *Cardiff v. Bismarck Public School District*, 263 N.W.2d 105 (N.D. 1978) and *Granger v. Cascade County School District No. 1*, 499 P.2d 780 (Mont. 1972).

19. For recommended guidelines for management of activity funds, see: Charles E. Cuzzetto, *Student Activity Funds: Procedures and Controls* (Reston, Virginia: Association of School Business Officials, International, 2007).

20. See: *Code of Virginia*, §15.2–2511. Audit of local government records, etc.; Auditor of Public Accounts; audit of shortages, and *Vermont Statutes Annotated*, Title 24, Chapter 51, Subchapter 5, §§1681 et. seq., Auditors and audits.

21. See: *Central School District No. 3 v. Insurance Company of North America*, 55 A.D. 2d 1021, 391 N.Y.S. 2d 492 (1977).

22. Auditor General of British Columbia, *What is a Financial Audit?* (Victoria, British Columbia, Canada: Office of the Auditor General of British Columbia, 2013). Retrieved from: http://www.bcauditor.com/reach.
23. Municipality of Anchorage, *Internal Audit*. Retrieved from www.muni.org/departments/internal_audit/pages/default.aspx
24. Ibid.
25. American Institute of Certified Public Accountants. *Confidential Client Information, ET Section 301 – Confidential Client Information* (Washington, DC: AICPA, 1993).

CHAPTER 16

Financing School Facilities

TOPICAL OUTLINE OF CHAPTER

- Unmet Capital Facility Needs
- Financing Capital Facilities: Local Options
  - Current Revenues
  - School Building Reserve Funds
  - General Obligation Bonds
  - Private-Public Partnerships
  - Sale/Leaseback Agreements
  - Tax Increment Financing (TIF)
  - Qualified Zone Academy Bond (QZAB)
- Financing Capital Facilities: State Options
  - Full State-Funded
  - Grants: Flat
  - Grants: Equalization
  - Grants: Percentage-Matching
- Loans
  - Building Authorities and Bond Banks
  - Reimbursements
- Persistent Fiscal Problems in Financing Capital Facilities
- Characteristics of an Equitable Capital-Outlay Program

INTRODUCTION

Traditionally, most states have placed most, if not all, of the fiscal responsibility to purchase public school capital facilities and to retire any debt incurred for acquisition of facilities onto the local school districts. The costs incurred to purchase school facilities are not insignificant and place a financial burden on many school districts, particularly those districts with meager fiscal capacities. Nationally, from 1990 to 2012, capital outlay increased from $19.5 billion to $36.6 billion and capital outlay per pupil increased from $481 to $773. Concurrently, interest on school debt increased from $5.3 billion to $16.1 billion and interest on debt per pupil increased from $131 to $339. The aggregate expenditures for capital facilities and interest on debt increased from $24.8 billion in 1990 to $52.7 billion in 2012. As a percent of total expenditures, capital outlay and interest expenditures combined increased from 8.3 to 11.0 percent.[1] Displayed below in Box 16.1 are definitions for capital outlay and debt service.[2]

BOX 16.1

Definitions for Capital Outlay and Debt Service

Capital Outlay: An expenditure that results in the acquisition of fixed assets or additions to fixed assets which are presumed to have benefits for more than one year. It is an expenditure for land or existing buildings, improvements of grounds, construction of buildings, additions to buildings, remodeling of buildings, or initial, additional, and replacement equipment.

Debt Service: An expenditure for the purpose of retirement of debt and includes bond or loan principal, interest, and service charges. In order to analyze overtime the costs of school facilities and to avoid double-counting, it is necessary to remove bond or loan principal from the analysis. Most agencies, including the National Education Association, only report bond or loan interest expenditures.

The fiscal structures employed by local school districts to acquire the resources needed to purchase capital facilities vary significantly among the states. Presented in this chapter is a discussion of the unmet capital facility needs and related problems faced by many school districts, the terminology related to the process of facility acquisition, examples of several state capital facility programs, and the outlook for the future. First, however, the fiscal relationship between current expenditures, capital outlay, and interest on school debt per enrolled student, in 2010 constant dollars (CPI adjusted), is presented in Table 16.1 as trend data from Fiscal Years 1990 to 2013.

Arrayed in Figure 16.1 are total expenditures, capital outlay, and interest on school debt per enrolled student are expressed in current dollars. Figure 16.2 contains the same data but have been converted into 2010 constant dollars through use of the consumer price index (CPI). In current dollars, the total expenditures per enrolled student increased from $12,236 in FY 2008, prior to the *Great Recession,* to $12,640 in FY 2013;

	Expenditures per Enrolled Student				% Change of Total Expenditures				% Change of Current Expenditures				% Change of Total Expenditures			
Type and object	1989–90	1998–99	2007–08	2012–13	1989–90	1998–99	2007–08	2012–13	1989–90	1998–99	2007–08	2012–13	1989–90 to 1998–99	1998–99 to 2007–08	1989–90 to 2007–08	1989–90 to 2012–13
[In current dollars]																
Total expenditures	$5,174	$7,533	$11,952	$12,640	1.00	1.00	1.00	1.00	†	†	†	†	**46**	**59**	**131**	**144**
Current expenditures	4,643	6,508	10,297	10,890	0.90	0.86	0.86	0.86	100	100	100	100	40	58	122	135
Salaries	3,045	4,225	6,175	6,530	0.59	0.56	0.52	0.52	66	65	60	60	39	46	103	114
Employee benefits	775	1,078	2,093	2,213	0.15	0.14	0.18	0.18	17	17	20	20	39	94	170	186
Purchased services	383	583	1,001	1,059	0.07	0.08	0.08	0.08	8	9	10	10	52	72	161	177
Supplies	347	507	840	888	0.07	0.07	0.07	0.07	7	8	8	8	46	66	142	156
Tuition and other	93	115	189	200	0.02	0.02	0.02	0.02	2	2	2	2	24	64	104	115
Capital outlay	439	849	1,336	1,413	0.08	0.11	0.11	0.11	†	†	†	†	94	57	205	222
Interest on school debt	93	176	319	337	0.02	0.02	0.03	0.03	†	†	†	†	89	81	242	262
[In constant 2009–10 dollars]																
Total expenditures	$8,832	$9,923	$12,236	$13,533	1.00	1.00	1.00	1.00	†	†	†	†	**12**	**23**	**39**	**53**
Current expenditures	7,925	8,572	10,542	11,659	0.90	0.86	0.86	0.86	100	100	100	100	8	23	33	47
Salaries	5,198	5,565	6,321	6,991	0.59	0.56	0.52	0.52	66	65	60	60	7	14	22	34
Employee benefits	1,323	1,420	2,142	1,236	0.15	0.14	0.18	0.18	17	17	20	20	7	51	62	–7
Purchased services	654	768	1,025	1,134	0.07	0.08	0.08	0.08	8	9	10	10	17	33	57	73
Supplies	592	668	860	951	0.07	0.07	0.07	0.07	7	8	8	8	13	29	45	61
Tuition and other	158	151	193	214	0.02	0.02	0.02	0.02	2	2	2	2	–4	28	22	35
Capital outlay	749	1,119	1,368	1,513	0.08	0.11	0.11	0.11	†	†	†	†	49	22	83	102
Interest on school debt	159	232	326	361	0.02	0.02	0.03	0.03	†	†	†	†	46	41	105	127

† Incomplete or missing data.

Sources: Institute of Education Sciences, *Public School Expenditures* (Washington, DC: National Center for Education Statistics, 2013) and National Education Association, *Rankings of the States (2012) and Estimates of School Statistics (2013)* (Washington, DC: NEA, 2013).

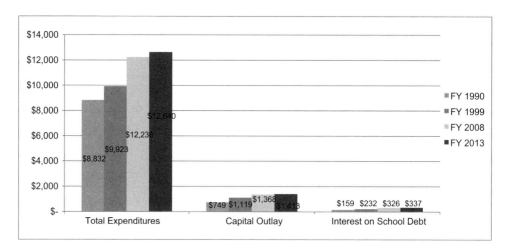

Figure 16.1 Total Expenditures, Capital Outlay, and Interest on School Debt Per Enrolled
Student in Public K–12 Schools, FYs 1990, 1999, 2008, and 2013[1]

[1] Current dollars.

Sources: Adapted from Institute of Education Sciences, *Public School Expenditures,* Figure 1 (Wash-
ington, DC: National Center for Education Statistics, 2013). Updated by authors to include estimated
Total Expenditures, Capital Outlay, and Interest on School Debt obtained from the National Education
Association, *Rankings of the States (2012) and Estimates of School Statistics (2013)* (Washington, DC:
NEA, 2013).

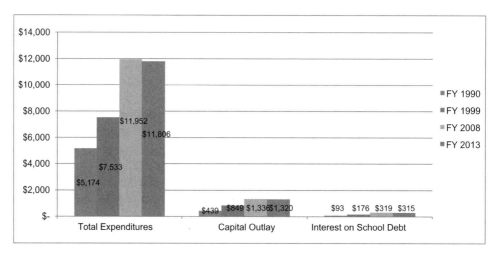

Figure 16.2 Total Expenditures, Capital Outlay, and Interest on School Debt Per Enrolled
Student in Public K–12 Schools, FYs 1990, 1999, 2008, and 2013[1]

[1] Constant 2010 dollars.

Sources: Adapted from Institute of Education Sciences, *Public School Expenditures,* Figure 1 (Wash-
ington, DC: National Center for Education Statistics, 2013). Updated by authors to include estimated
Total Expenditures, Capital Outlay, and Interest on School Debt obtained from the National Education
Association, *Rankings of the States (2012) and Estimates of School Statistics (2013)* (Washington, DC:
NEA, 2013).

however, when converted to constant dollars (FY 2010), the total expenditures per enrolled student declined from $11,952 in FY 2008 to $11,806 in FY 2013. Concurrently, capital outlay and interest on school debt per enrolled student, in current dollars, increased from $1,368 to $1,413, and from $326 to $337, respectively. When converted to constant dollars (FY 2010), total expenditures per enrolled student declined from $11,952 to $11,806 and expenditures for capital outlay and interest on school debt declined from $1,336 to $1,320 and from $319 to $315, respectively.

Despite the alarming increases in unmet capital facility needs that are presented below, capital outlay (constant dollars) per enrolled student declined from $1,336 in FY 2008 to $1,182 in FY 2013, paralleling the decline of total expenditures experienced by the nation's public schools.

UNMET CAPITAL FACILITY NEEDS

In 1989, a national study conducted by the Education Writers Association (EWA) reported that the unmet financial needs for acquisition, replacement, and renovation of capital facilities of public elementary and secondary schools totaled $125 billion.[3] Since the EWA study, estimates of the cost to repair and modernize school facilities nationwide has continued to grow from the $112 billion estimated by the U.S. General Accounting Office (GAO) in their landmark 1995 report, to the National Center for Educational Statistics (NCES) estimate of $127 billion in 1999, to $268.2 billion estimated by the National Education Association in 2000, to the $542 billion estimated by the Center for Green Schools in 2013.

According to the Center for Green Schools, nearly 100,000 elementary and secondary public schools are located across the United States, yet American citizens and public officials lack an understanding of the scale of this infrastructure or that "it will take approximately **$271 billion** to bring school buildings up to working order and comply with laws . . . [including] modernization costs to ensure that our schools meet today's education, safety and health standards . . . [resulting in] a jaw-dropping **$542 billion** [that] would be required."[4]

Adding to the difficulty of meeting the capital needs of the public schools is the competition for resources from the private and often religiously-affiliated organizations seeking public funds for their schools. Once restricted by adherence to the doctrine of a *wall of separation between church and state,* embodied in the First Amendment of the United States Constitution, the courts prohibited public funds from being used to fund religiously affiliated schools; but due to the appointment of conservative justices to the United States Supreme Court by republican presidents,[5] public funding of religiously affiliated schools is now permitted.[6] The proponents of the *Charter School* movement have been clamoring effectively in state capitols for public capital outlay and debt service appropriations throughout the nation, even while public school facilities are crumbling.

FINANCING CAPITAL FACILITIES: LOCAL OPTIONS

Prior to the twentieth century, financing public school facilities was the sole responsibility of local governments in the United States. The schools were an integral part of American frontier life, and the actual construction of buildings often proved to be one of the year's biggest social events.[7] Initially, public school facilities were financed by private donations of sites and materials and erected by volunteer workers. Later, special local property taxes were levied to finance the construction of needed facilities. By the latter part of the nineteenth century, local communities found it necessary to borrow funds, and state legislatures enacted laws which permitted the issuance of bonds for school construction by specific school districts or municipalities.[8] Although the population of the country was burgeoning and the costs of providing public school facilities were increasing rapidly, most states were reluctant to allocate state resources for financing the construction of local public school facilities. While an examination of current public school support programs will show a myriad of state capital outlay and debt service programs, the tradition of financing public school facilities primarily from local resources continues to exist in most states today. In contrast, the Canadian Provinces have implemented shared-cost systems for current expenditures not unlike many state systems in the United States. Unlike the United States, however, the Canadian provinces have assumed primary fiscal responsibility for funding capital outlay and debt service requirements of their local school districts. For example, the Province of Manitoba developed an equalization formula for allocation of funds for capital outlay and debt service that takes into consideration the fiscal capacities of the school districts, their age, and size of school facilities.[9]

With the exception of the limited funds available in several states from state-supported capital outlay and debt service programs and a miniscule amount from the federal government, most local school districts have relatively few options available for obtaining funds to finance the construction of their school facilities. In essence, local school districts are faced with one, or a combination, of the following three choices: current revenues, school building reserve funds, and the acquisition of long-term debt.

Current Revenues

Often referred to as *pay-as-you-go* financing, the ability to finance the construction of school facilities from current revenues is an alternative available only to the large and/or very affluent school districts. Thus, the entire cost of a project or projects is accrued from local tax levies for a limited number of fiscal years, which usually results in sharp increases in local tax rates. According to Brimley et al., for those districts with the available resources, financing the construction of school facilities through current revenue "is an ideal way to finance capital outlays. It is the quickest perhaps the easiest way to getting the necessary resources from the private sector of the economy. It eliminates expenditure of large sums of money for interest, the costs of bond attorney fees, and election costs."[10]

In opposition, there are those who argue that the use of current revenue for financing capital facilities results in the following:

1. Creation of tax friction among taxpayers and governmental agencies;
2. Inability to achieve intergenerational equity through distribution of capital outlay and debt service costs among several generations of students; and
3. Inability to realize the economic advantages from the incurrence of debt during inflationary periods, i.e., the inability to *borrow expensive dollars and repay them with inexpensive dollars.*

Primarily due to the inability of most school districts to finance capital construction through current revenue, the latter argument has prevailed. The use of current revenue to finance the costs of constructing public school facilities has been insignificant when compared to the capital costs financed by the sale of municipal bonds. According to the 21st Century School Fund "capital funds are typically borrowed and repaid over many years, using the annual revenues to repay the debt."[11]

School Building Reserve Funds

Some states permit school districts to accumulate tax funds for the purpose of funding the construction of future school facilities. Such funds, usually referred to as building reserve funds, are kept separate from the school districts' current operating funds and are commonly financed by special tax levies. Generally, state laws stipulate that building reserve funds can only be invested under very controlled conditions and, as a consequence, the interest yield is very modest and fails to keep pace with inflation.

Critics of the building reserve fund option claim that changes in school district leadership and economic downturns often result in diversion of reserve funds to purposes other than those intended when the reserve funds were established. For example, routine maintenance projects become deferred and their necessary expenditures accumulate into substantial unfunded requirements that often are met by exhausting the building reserve funds. Also, critics contend that many of the taxpayers who contribute to the reserve funds will not realize benefits from the capital investment. Most importantly, although reserve funds and current operating funds are usually financed and maintained separately, taxpayers are concerned primarily with the total costs of the school district's budget. In some instances, the higher tax rates required to finance reserve building funds have created taxpayer resistance and have resulted in a reduction of the current operating budget.

On the other hand, there are several advantages to the use of the building reserve fund option. After sufficient funds have been accumulated, the project can be constructed without the delays or expenses associated with gaining voter approval for the issuance of bonds. Debt service charges are avoided and local restrictions on taxing or debt limitations usually do not interfere with the project. Although prohibited by several states, building reserve funds are used by school districts in several states; but nationally, they only provide a small fraction of funds used for the construction of public school facilities.[12]

General Obligation Bonds

The vast majority of public school facilities are constructed through the sale of general obligation bonds by local school districts.[13] School bonds, generically referred to as municipal bonds, are legal papers issued with the government's commitment to use its full taxing and borrowing authority to make timely payments of interest and principal. Such bonds are also called *full faith and credit bonds*.[14] General obligation bonds are recognized as the most secure of all municipal bonds.

Municipal bonds enjoy tax-exempt status from the federal income tax and from state income taxes in most states. In some instances, municipalities have lost the tax-exempt status and had their bonds ruled as *arbitrage bonds*.[15] Also, there is political pressure by the Obama Administration to either eliminate or restrict the tax-exemption percentage that can be claimed by a taxpayer.[16] The tax-exempt status makes the purchase of municipal bonds particularly desirable for investors with high incomes. Probably one of the most desirable features of municipal bonds from the vantage point of the investor is the relative safety of principal. According to Stoever Glass & Company,

> from 1970 through 2000, less than one-half of one percent of all tax exempt municipal bonds defaulted. Over the same period, almost 10 percent of corporate bonds defaulted. In other words, tax free [municipal] bonds remain the surest of sure bets.[17]

As stated above, one type of municipal bond, *general obligation bonds*, is secured by the full faith, the credit, and generally the unlimited taxing power of the issuer. In effect, the borrower promises to use every available means to meet interest payments when due and to return the full face value of a *term bond* to the investors at maturity. However, public school municipal bonds are usually issued in *serial form* where the interest and principal are retired simultaneously at regular intervals. Serial bonds are chronologically arranged so that the bonds comprising the issue mature at regular intervals, usually annually or semiannually. Therefore, balanced debt service can be arranged over the life of the total issue. In contrast, the term bond is rarely used and actually prohibited by several states due to a history of poor management practices. A term bond is used in conjunction with a *sinking fund* and is designed to meet interest payments at regular intervals, while the repayment of the principal is made at the end of the indebtedness period. A sinking fund is designed to receive revenue transfers at regular intervals plus investment earnings in order to accumulate sufficient funds to retire the specified debt. It should be monitored regularly to adjust the revenue transfers.

Normally, municipal bonds, including general obligation bonds, are rated by one of the national rating companies for the purpose of alerting potential purchasers of the relative security of the issue.[18] The rating awarded the school district by the rating company significantly influences the interest charged the issuer.[19] The three largest rating agencies are: Standard & Poor's (S&P), Moody's, and Fitch Group. Moody's, which rates the majority of public school bonds, and Standard & Poor's are based in the United States, while Fitch is dual-headquartered in New York City and London.[20] The three rating companies hold a collective global market share of *roughly 95 percent* with Moody's and Standard & Poor's having approximately 40 percent each, and Fitch around 15 percent.[21]

The constraints that school districts operate under regarding the issuance of general obligation bonds vary considerably among states and even among school districts in some states. Most states have enacted school district debt limitations that prohibit local school districts from exceeding a specified percent of the local tax base, e.g., 10 percent of the total assessed valuation of real and public service corporation property.[22] Restrictive debt limitations have proved particularly troublesome for those states or school districts with limited local tax bases.[23] There is also considerable variation among the states regarding the approval process required prior to the sale of general obligation bonds by the school districts. Some states require a simple majority of those voting at referendum, while other states require considerably more than a simple majority. Oklahoma serves as an example of a state that has a restrictive debt limitation, from 5 to 10 percent of the assessed taxable valuation of property, and a super majority, 60 percent, voter approval required for incurrence of long-term debt.[24]

The lack of uniform property assessment practices resulting in inequitable tax rates plagues some states, while voter-initiated property tax limitations, such as the infamous *Proposition 13* of California,[25] have restricted the sale of school bonds. Nevertheless, despite the many problems inherent in the sale of municipal bonds, this method remains the primary option for many, and the only option for other school districts, to acquire the resources necessary to construct public school facilities in the United States.

During the inflationary periods of the 1970s and early 1980s,[26] municipal bonds, including school bonds, were sold at the highest interest rates during the twentieth century. Local school boards were reluctant to bind their taxpayers to high interest rates for 20 to 25 years. Prudent school boards sold their bonds during that period so that they could refinance them when interest rates abated. Thus, local boards were able to call their long-term bonds bearing the highest interest rates and refund their bonded debts at lower interest rates. Bonds issued for a period of 20 to 25 years usually carry a sliding scale of interest rates, the earlier-maturing bonds bearing a lower interest rate than the longer-maturing bonds. Most municipal bonds are now subject to call, with a small premium, e.g., ten years after the date of issuance. Usually, school bonds containing a callable provision are sold at nearly the same prices as non-callable bonds. However, if bonds are issued callable at any time after their issuance, the issuing body will have to pay a higher interest rate than on non-callable bonds or bonds subject to deferred call at a premium.

The number of years over which a bond issue matures should not exceed the life of the facility for which the bond was issued. This is not a problem for a school building, which has a life span from 40 to 50 years. School bonds are usually issued to mature over a period of 20 to 25 years, because it would be difficult to sell bonds that mature over 40 or 50 years without paying excessive interest rates. However, certain types of equipment, particularly technology purchases, have much shorter life spans and if financed by the sale of bonds,[27] should be sold through separate issues and for much shorter retirement periods. Some school boards purchase school buses by separate bond issues, and such bonds should mature in not more than 12 years. As indicated earlier, it is good fiscal policy, and nearly mandatory,[28] to have school bonds rated by a national rating company such as Moody's, Standard & Poor's Corporation, and the Fitch Group. Arrayed in Table 16.2 are rating scales and their respective explanations for Moody's and Standard & Poor's Corporation. Unfortunately, these rating agencies often will not rate a small bond issue or one issued by a small school district. A marketed bond issue or one with a low rating will be sold at a higher interest rate than a highly rated issue. In order to lower the interest rates for lower-rated or non-rated bonds, some school boards acquire insurance coverage with a municipal bond insurance company such as the Municipal Bond Insurance Association or the American Municipal Bond Assurance Corporation.[29] Such insurance will guarantee to the bond holder the payment of principal and interest on an insured bond issue.

Table 16.2 Rating Scales and Definitions Used by Moody's Investors Service and Standard & Poor's Corporation

Moody's Investors Service	Symbol	Symbol	Standard & Poor's Corporation
Best quality, carrying smallest degree of investment risk; referred to as "gilt edge"	Aaa	AAA	Prime; obligor's capacity to meet its financial commitments on the obligation is extremely strong
High quality; rated lower than Aaa because margins of protection not as large	Aa	AA	Differs from the highest-rated obligations only in small degree; obligor's capacity to meet its financial commitments on the obligation is very strong
Higher medium grade, many favorable investment attributes; some elements of future risk evident	A	A	Somewhat more susceptible to the adverse effects of changes in circumstances and economic conditions than obligations in higher-rated categories; obligor's capacity to meet its financial commitments on the obligation is still strong
Lower medium grade; neither highly protected nor poorly secured; may be unreliable over any great length of time	Baa	BBB	Exhibits adequate protection parameters; adverse economic conditions or changing circumstances are more likely to lead to a weakened capacity of the obligor to meet the financial commitment of the obligation
Judged to have speculative elements; not well safe-guarded as to interest and principal	Ba	BB	Speculative non-investment grade obligation; faces major ongoing uncertainties or exposure to adverse business, financial, or economic conditions which could lead to the obligor's capacity to meet its financial commitment on the obligation
Lacks characteristics of desirable investment	B	B	More vulnerable to nonpayment than obligations rated BB; adverse business, financial, or economic conditions will likely impair the obligor's capacity or willingness to meet its financial commitment on the obligation
Poor standing; issue may be in default	Caa	CCC	Currently vulnerable to nonpayment
Speculative in high degree; marked shortcomings	Ca	CC	Currently highly vulnerable to nonpayment
Lowest rated class; extremely poor prospects of ever attaining any real investment standing	C	C	Bankruptcy petition has been filed or similar action has been taken, but payments on this obligation are being continued.
Default	D	D	Obligation in payment default

Source: Alan W. Steiss, "Marketing Municipal Bonds," *Local Government Finance: Capital Facilities Planning and Debt Administration* (Lanham, Maryland: Lexington Books, Rowman & Littlefield, 1975). Reprinted by permission of Dr. Alan Walter Steiss.

Obviously, premiums for the bond insurance should be analyzed relative to the lower interest rate obtained for the bond sale, but the purchase of bond insurance may be a good fiscal decision.

Private-Public Partnerships

Local school districts that have title to unused facilities or acreage have the potential to enter into agreements with private development firms to generate revenue for construction of school facilities. Such partnerships are more likely to be successful whenever major development is occurring in the area. In the case of high-growth school districts and where permissive legislation exists, impact fees[30] can be levied against developers and the additional revenue dedicated for school construction projects. Some states, including Florida, also have levied impact fees against current residents which have resulted in considerable acrimony.[31]

Sale/Leaseback Agreements

A specific type of private-public partnership is the sale of unused school district facilities and acreage to developers. Contingent upon the sale of the unused facilities and acreage, the private developer agrees to construct or renovate a school building pursuant to certain specifications, while the school district agrees to a long-term lease or purchase arrangement with the developer. The developer borrows funds to construct or renovate the facility and QPEF tax-exempt bonds provide an attractive mechanism. The *Economic Growth and Tax Relief Reconciliation Act of 2001*[32] changed Section 142 of the Internal Revenue Code to allow states to issue tax-exempt bonds for qualified public educational facilities (QPEF). Each state, beginning in 2002, was given a volume cap or allocation equal to the greater of $10 per capita or $5,000,000. The state can allocate the amount of volume cap in such manner as the state determines appropriate. The QPEF bonds can be used to construct, rehabilitate, refurbish, or equip a public school facility. The bond proceeds are loaned to a private, for-profit corporation (developer) who owns the school facility and leases it to a public school. A public-private partnership agreement needs to be entered into between the developer and the public school. The public school leases the school facility from the developer and at the end of the lease term the school facility is transferred to the public school for no additional consideration.

Tax Increment Financing (TIF)

Tax increment financing (TIF) is designed to generate revenue for economically depressed areas within a municipality. Rather than folded into the general fund of the municipality, the revenue gained from real estate development, both commercial and residential, is targeted for the depressed geographical area of the municipality. The new revenues are referred to as *increments* for the life of the TIF, and if dedicated for construction of school facilities, the public schools located in depressed area can receive additional funds for capital outlay.

The rules for tax increment financing, and even its name, vary across the 48 states in which the practice is authorized. The designation usually requires a finding that an area is "blighted" or "underdeveloped" and that development would not take place "but for" the public expenditure or subsidy. It is only a bit of an overstatement to characterize the "blight" and "but for" findings as merely *pro forma* exercises, since specialized consultants can produce the needed evidence in almost all cases. In most states, the requirement for these findings does little to restrict the location of TIF districts.[33]

Qualified Zone Academy Bond (QZAB)

The federal government assumes financial responsibility for the interest on QZAB bonds[34] by awarding tax credits to the bond holder. Qualifying school districts are districts designated as *Enterprise Communities* or *Empowerment Zones*, or have over 35 percent of their students eligible for free and reduced price lunches. These can save up to 50 percent of the cost of construction of a school building by qualifying for funds from the $400 million appropriated by Congress and *pro-rated* to the states by population.

FINANCING CAPITAL FACILITIES: STATE OPTIONS

As discussed previously, prior to the twentieth century, capital facilities for public elementary and secondary education were financed almost exclusively from local resources. Undoubtedly, some school districts experienced difficulty in providing adequate school facilities before 1900,[35] but no state had seen fit to develop a continuing capital facilities assistance program until Alabama took the initiative in 1901 and established an aid plan for rural schools. Although it was not established initially as a capital outlay program, earlier in 1810, Virginia established the Literary Fund to help educate *pauper children*. Later, the Literary Fund was amended in order to loan state funds to local school districts for capital construction.[36] Two years following enactment of the Alabama rural education capital facilities program, Louisiana, by constitutional amendment, enacted a state plan in 1903 for issuance of bonds requiring construction of school facilities in impoverished areas of the state. By 1909, South Carolina was providing state assistance for financing capital facilities serving African-American rural school children, while North Carolina established a modest state loan fund.[37] The following 20 years saw several states implementing matching grants for the purpose of assisting and encouraging consolidation of schools, and in 1927, Delaware took the first major step toward a comprehensive state capital facilities financing program. The Delaware plan required that primary support for the financing of local public school facilities be borne by the state government, with only small contributions required of the local school districts.

During the years of the Great Depression and World War II, a shortage of both local and state resources virtually prohibited local school districts from engaging in extensive building programs. Burdened with the problems of aging facilities, inadequate and insufficient buildings, and a growing desire for more and better school facilities, the limited number of state assistance programs were either woefully inadequate, inequitable, or both. A report by Webber in 1941 indicated that of the 12 states that had established various forms of state-aid programs to assist local school districts to finance their public school facilities, none had implemented programs that could be regarded as equitable. Such programs were crude, inequitable distribution systems in which the principles of equalization were neither recognized nor applied, or else were simple low interest loan devices provided by the states.

Shortly after World War II, attention once again focused on the problem of providing necessary funds for financing the construction of capital facilities for public school children. In 1947, Florida became the first state to develop and adopt a comprehensive plan. The Florida program was based on the concept of determining annually the financial resources needed for each school district to replace buildings that were

Table 16.3 Capital Funding for PK-12 Public Schools

Full State-Funded (60% or Greater)	%	Grants	%	Reimbursements	%	Loans	Low State Aid (Less than 20%)	%
Hawaii	100	New Jersey	57	West Virginia	44	Michigan	Arkansas	18
Wyoming	100	Tennessee	57	Rhode Island	34	Minnesota	Connecticut	17
Alaska	85	Alabama	52	Maryland	32	North Dakota	Georgia	14
Maine	84	New Mexico	52	New Hampshire	31	Virginia	North Carolina	14
Delaware	63	New York	52	Vermont	30		Texas	12
Iowa	60	Ohio	49	Washington	20		Idaho	11
Kansas	60	Kentucky	41	Massachusetts	—		Montana	11
		Arizona	32				Illinois	8
		California	29				Utah	6
		Florida	21				Pennsylvania	4
		Minnesota	20				South Carolina	2
							Mississippi	1
							Colorado	1
							Indiana	0
							Louisiana	0
							Michigan	0
							Missouri	0
							Nebraska	0
							Nevada	0
							North Dakota	0
							Oklahoma	0
							Oregon	0
							South Dakota	0
							Virginia	0
							Wisconsin	0

Source: Based on 21st Century Fund, *State Capital Spending for PK-12 School Facilities* (Washington, DC: 21st Century Fund and NCEF, 2010).

at the end of their normal life expectancies. The Florida plan, initially implemented as full state-funded, evolved into a shared-cost program. Stimulated primarily by the increased demand for school facilities due to the postwar baby boom, several states enacted various forms of state capital facilities assistance plans. By 1947, approximately 25 states had enacted some form of state-aid program, including grants, reimbursement programs, and loans that were designed to provide assistance for local districts to fund school construction programs. After 1950, a still greater effort was made to encourage states to participate in financing the construction of local public school facilities. For many years, school finance experts and proponents of public schools had been urging state legislatures to enact a wide assortment of state capital-outlay programs. Additional impetus was given in 1951 to the drive for increased state funding of public school facilities when the United States Office of Education and the University of California at Berkeley cooperated in a national study of state public school capital-outlay programs. After an analysis of the various state programs, the researchers recommended, in part, that the states should provide additional leadership and financial resources for comprehensive and efficient public school capital-outlay programs.[38]

According to Webb, by 1978–1979, thirty-seven states provided financial support to aid local school districts in funding their capital outlay and debt service needs. As evident from an examination of Table 16.3, several mechanisms in FY 2008 were used by states to assist their local school districts to acquire resources for construction of school facilities. The number of states, thirty-eight, that provided state capital outlay support in FY 2008 was nearly identical to the thirty-seven states identified by Webb nearly three decades earlier. If the states that provide less than 20 percent state funds to their local school districts for capital outlay are discounted, only 50 percent of the states have implemented effective systems to support public school facilities. Each of these mechanisms presented in Table 16.3 is discussed along with their relative advantages and disadvantages.

Full State-Funded

As its name suggests, a full state-funded program requires that 100 percent of the capital outlay and debt-service expenditures for the public schools is borne by the state. Upon examination of Table 16.3, it is apparent that only two states, Hawaii and Wyoming, have implemented fiscal systems that provide 100 percent of the costs for school facilities from state resources. However, five additional states, Alaska, Maine, Delaware, Iowa, and Kansas, provide from the state 60 percent or higher of the costs for capital outlay and debt service.

Advantages cited by proponents of full state-funded programs usually include the following:

1. Absolute fiscal equalization is achieved within the state and the quality of facilities is not a function of the taxpaying abilities of local school districts;
2. State governments normally have access to a greater variety and quantity of resources than do local governments and can avoid the overutilization of a single tax base, i.e., the real property;

3. A state government can develop an allotment mechanism based upon needs, which will provide a higher level of cost-efficiency; and
4. If it were necessary for the state governments to acquire the necessary funds from the issuance of bonds, it is likely that the larger issue would result in overall savings in interest and services charges.

Disadvantages cited by opponents of complete-state-support programs usually include the following:

1. Additional concentrations of power and control of the public schools will become focused at the state level, thereby further alienating local citizens from public schools;
2. The centralization of power would result in uniformity of public school facilities throughout the state, and such facilities would not recognize the unique needs of varying localities. In addition, it is likely that the centralization of power would result in less experimentation and innovation of school facilities and in a high level of mediocrity; and
3. Due to a high level of competition for resources at the state level, the construction of urgently needed public school facilities could be unnecessarily delayed.

Grants: Flat

As its title implies, the flat grant is designed as a fixed amount of funds per unit allocated by the state to local school districts, regardless of their fiscal capacity, to be used to finance local capital construction. Some states annually allocate a fixed amount of funds per ADA or ADM, while other states allocate a fixed amount per state-approved project. Regardless of the unit of need used by the state, the flat grant ignores the variation in fiscal capacity among the state's school districts.

Advantages cited by proponents of the flat grant usually include the following:

1. Control of the local school building program generally remains with the local school district, thus, the building program can be tailored to meet local needs or desires;
2. While usually viewed as non-equalizing, the flat grant does provide some measure of equity since statewide resources are used for funding the flat-grant program. Obviously, the greater the amount of the flat grant provided by the state (in other words, as the flat grant approaches complete state aid), the greater will be the equity provided both pupils and taxpayers;
3. State assistance in the form of a flat grant would reduce dependency of the local school districts on the property tax, thereby freeing local resources for other governmental purposes. In addition, the economic health of local governments would be strengthened and the marketability of municipal bonds for purposes other than education would be enhanced;
4. Since all school districts would be eligible for funds appropriated through a flat grant, the potential for divisive action by high capacity districts would be eliminated; and
5. The flat-grant program can be easily administered due to its simple allocation technique and the ability to accurately anticipate required funds.

Disadvantages cited by opponents of the flat-grant program usually include the following:

1. Most state flat grants only supplement the local funds required to finance the school building program. Consequently, variation in the quality of school facilities among the states' school districts is considerable, coupled with an inequitable tax effort;
2. In those states that annually allocate funds on a percentage basis without consideration of building needs, some school districts receive unneeded funds while others have unfunded capital needs; and
3. The flat grant requires large state appropriations, often resulting in inadequate state support for capital construction.

Grants: Equalization

The primary purpose of the equalization grant is to provide increased pupil and taxpayer equity within the state. In the absence of state support for the construction of public school facilities, students who reside in low capacity school districts are forced to attend school in inadequate facilities, and taxpayers in school districts with low capacity are required to make a significantly greater fiscal effort to construct capital facilities than taxpayers in districts with high capacity. Consequently, equalization grants are designed to allocate revenues per unit of need inversely to the fiscal abilities of the local school districts. The variety of equalization grants in use is extensive, ranging from an annual allocation in the manner of the Strayer-Haig equalization model for current expenses, to a varying percentage of state support based on the local school districts' relative fiscal capacity standard.

Advantages cited by proponents of equalization grants usually include the following:

1. Comparable public school facilities can be provided all school districts without imposition of excessive tax burdens upon low capacity school districts;
2. Since some local contribution is required for participation in most equalization grants-in-aid, the frivolous use of state funds would be curtailed; and
3. Reduced dependency on the local property tax for the construction of school facilities would provide local government with additional resources for other governmental services and/or tax relief. In addition, the economic health of local governments would be strengthened and the marketability of municipal bonds for purposes other than education would be enhanced.

Disadvantages cited by opponents of equalization grants usually include the following:

1. In order to guarantee funds for all school districts in the state, a substantial amount of state resources would have to be dedicated to this purpose, while inadequate appropriations would render the program ineffective; and
2. A statewide system would not necessarily be responsive to the variety of local needs, and local schools initially might experience difficulty in responding to immediate construction needs.

Grants: Percentage-Matching

The percentage-matching grant is designed to provide a fixed percentage of state support for each local (usually state-approved) public school capital-facilities project. The fiscal capacity of the local school district is not taken into consideration, and the total amount of state assistance varies in accordance with the cost of the project.

Advantages usually cited by proponents of percentage-matching grants include the following:

1. Initiation of school construction projects remains the prerogative of local school districts, and the building programs can be tailored to meet the needs and desires of local citizens;
2. The state, through the use of its approval process, can encourage cost-effective construction practices and influence the design and location of school buildings; and
3. State assistance would reduce the dependency of local school districts upon the property tax, thereby freeing local resources for other governmental purposes. In addition, the economic health and the marketability of municipal bonds for purposes other than education would be enhanced.

Disadvantages usually cited by opponents of percentage-matching grants include the following:

1. A percentage-matching grant invariably penalizes local school districts with limited fiscal capacity to support school building programs. Local school districts with high fiscal capacity can obtain sufficient funds to qualify for state-matching funds with relative ease, while districts with less capacity can only obtain the required matching funds through an extraordinary tax effort by their citizens. Of course, if the state's matching percentage were quite high (for instance, 90 percent state to 10 percent local), the dis-equalization effect of the percentage-matching grant would be neutralized and the percentage-matching grant would assume the characteristics of an equalization grant;
2. In order to guarantee funds for all local school districts with qualifying building projects, it would be necessary for the state to appropriate substantial resources. Insufficient appropriations would render the program ineffective; and
3. School districts with sufficient capital facilities would not seek state assistance, and citizens would see little direct benefit from their state taxes.

LOANS

State capital-assistance loan funds have been established to provide direct financial assistance to local school districts. Commonly, states have established a permanent fund, or funds, often through the use of dedicated revenues, for the purpose of providing low-interest loans to local school districts.[39] Unlike the previous state assistance plans, loans provided by the states contain the provision that the funds be repaid at some future date. With some exceptions, loans do not take into consideration the relative fiscal capacities of the local school districts,[40] and as a consequence, do not provide for a high degree of fiscal equalization.[41] Funds available from state loan funds are usually modest, and states have had to either restrict all school districts to a certain amount per approved project or to control the number of eligible school districts by implementing certain qualifying criteria. For example, a school district may have to tax or bond itself at a certain level or fall below a specified measure of fiscal capacity in order to qualify for a state loan. Additionally, state loan funds have been diverted by state legislatures to fund other services during the Great Recession.

Advantages cited by proponents of state loan funds usually include the following:

1. The loan funds provide local school districts with economical mechanisms for borrowing necessary funds due to the modest interest rates charged by the state;
2. Generally, state loans to local school districts are not charged against the constitutional or legislated debt limitation of the state, thereby giving them access to additional resources;
3. The time required to acquire funds from state loan funds is usually considerably less than the time required to acquire funds through the sale of bonds; and
4. The state, through the use of its approval process, can encourage cost-efficient construction practices and influence the design and location of school buildings.

Disadvantages usually cited by opponents of state loan funds include the following:

1. Normally, state loan funds are extremely limited and serve only as a minor resource to the local school district's total building program;
2. During periods of falling state revenue, states often drain revenue from the loan fund;
3. Due to limited funds in most state loan funds, plus the common practice of permitting all school districts equal access to state loans, fiscal equalization is not enhanced.
4. The establishment of modest state loan funds often diverts the attention of the legislature from adequately funding the construction of public school capital facilities; and
5. Local control of school construction may be diluted through use of the state approval process required for those school districts seeking state loans.

Building Authorities and Bond Banks

A unique device designed to help local school districts finance the construction of their school facilities is the school building authority. Building authorities can be designed to function at either the local or state levels of government. The public school building authorities, local and state, and state bond banks are state-established quasi-public corporations that provide alternatives for funding local school facilities. Most school building authorities were developed initially for the purpose of circumventing restrictive debt limitations imposed by state constitutional provisions. In one instance, the Virginia Public School Authority (VPSA), technically a bond bank, was established for the purpose of circumventing voter approval of bond referenda.[42] Displayed in Box 16.2 are definitions for school building authority[43] and school bond bank.

> **BOX 16.2**
>
> ## Definitions for School Building Authority and School Bond Bank
>
> **School Building Authority:** A public or quasi-public corporation authorized by state legislation to function as a separate agency outside the regular government structure to finance, construct, and/or operate revenue-producing enterprises.
>
> **School Bond Bank:** A public or quasi-public corporation authorized by state legislation to issue its own financial bonds and notes which are secured by the purchase of bonds and notes of subordinate governmental agencies.

Since the building authorities are quasi-agencies of government and do not operate schools, the taxing or debt limitations of the local school districts have been ruled inapplicable by some state courts. Other state courts have declined to make debt limitations inapplicable, thereby negating the implementation of building authorities for acquisition and construction of school facilities.[44] Most state authorities were designed so that loan purchase agreements were made with school districts for the acquisition of school facilities; however, recent state authorities have evolved into mechanisms designed to achieve greater efficiency in financing and fiscally equalizing the quality of school facilities among school districts.[45]

Advantages cited by proponents of building authorities usually include the following:

1. Many of the debt and taxing restrictions on local school districts are imposed by state constitutions that are difficult to amend. The use of building authorities and bond banks permits the state to assist local school districts to finance the construction of needed facilities without ratification of a constitutional amendment;
2. Unless prohibited by the federal or state governments, a combination of state, local, and federal current revenues may be used to pay the costs of lease-rental or lease-purchase agreements with the building authorities; and
3. Building authorities and bond banks can be used without acquisition of voter approval, thereby acquiring the necessary facilities and avoiding building delays.

Disadvantages usually cited by opponents of building authorities and bond banks include the following:

1. The enactment of building authorities ignores the need for state appropriations for school facilities and delays adequately financing the construction of public school facilities;
2. Revenue bonds primarily are used to finance building authorities and bond banks, which results in higher interest costs than would be required by general-obligation bonds; and
3. The right of taxpayers and citizens to express their approval or disapproval is circumvented by the use of building authorities.

Reimbursements

Several states provide state revenue to support capital outlay and debt service of their local school districts through reimbursement programs. Instead of providing up-front payments, i.e. grants, to the local school districts, the districts are reimbursed, either fully or partially, for state-approved capital outlay and debt service projects. Reimbursement programs have similar advantages and disadvantages that are attributed to grant programs excluding the following disadvantage.

Reimbursement programs deny the local school districts from investing the grant before payment is made to the contractor and vendors for the capital project.

PERSISTENT FISCAL PROBLEMS IN FINANCING CAPITAL FACILITIES

The National Educational Finance Project[46] made a national survey of the problems of financing school facilities in 1971. Twenty-two years later, 1993, the problems identified still remained. The following is a summary of the findings of the study of school facilities made by that project.[47]

In any general discussion of aid for public school construction throughout the nation, two paramount problems emerge:

1. Many state-aid plans are only token in nature, and several states do not provide local school districts with any financial assistance for school construction; and
2. The federal government has not provided financial support for any general programs for school construction. Even though title for school buildings may legally reside with the state and education has historically and legally been considered a state function, the entire, or a major portion of the, financial burden for providing housing for educational programs and students has been placed upon the shoulders of the local school district in a great number of states.

This general pattern throughout the nation has resulted in a heavy drain upon local fiscal resources as a source of financial support for school construction. Various constitutional limitations and statutory provisions restrict the latitude available to the local school district by imposing constraints such as the following:

1. Unduly restrictive debt and tax-rate limitations in some states and wide variations among the states in these matters;
2. Assessment practices in local districts which do not coincide with statutory or constitutional prescriptions, and wide variations in assessment levels among local districts which result in property tax bases unrelated to the real fiscal capacity (as measured by property value) of several districts;
3. A property tax base which is heavily relied upon for school construction funds is not immediately responsive to changes in the economy as a whole, does not

necessarily coincide with taxpaying capacity, and is regressive in terms of assumption of the burden.

4. Voter reactions to property tax rates which suggest that psychological limits may have been reached and that rates may have reached confiscatory levels in many states;

5. Unduly rigid voter qualifications and provisions which require more than a majority vote for passage, thereby making it extremely difficult to obtain approval in some states;

6. An extremely rapid increase in school construction costs without a uniformly corresponding increase in revenue potential from property taxes;

7. Overdependence on the property tax which is also heavily relied upon to support other local governmental functions;

8. School district geographical boundaries which result in the isolation of commercial and industrial taxable wealth, thereby creating residential areas with low revenue-generating capacity; and

9. Variations in local district facility needs and fiscal abilities which are so extreme that many districts could not meet their needs even if all legal restrictions on local debt and tax rates were removed.[48]

It is obvious that an equitable plan of financing school plant facilities cannot be based exclusively on local school district financing, even if all legal obstacles were eliminated, because of the wide variance among local school districts in their wealth and taxpaying ability. School districts often vary in equalized valuation as much as 10 to 1 in states with large school districts such as county unit states, and variations are much greater in states with many small districts. Therefore, an equitable plan for financing school facilities must involve either full-state financing or an equitable combination of local and state financing. Also, a case can be made for the federal government to contribute to the financing of public school facilities. Unfortunately, the likelihood of significant federal support for capital outlay is improbable at best.

Another 20 years has elapsed since the above analysis was conducted in 1993 and the problems faced by those who desire efficient and effective systems to acquire and maintain public school facilities have not improved. Instead, the situation has deteriorated despite considerable evidence that the private sector alternatives, through tax incentives, vouchers, charters, and on-line programs, are, in the best cases, achieving comparable results recorded by the underfunded traditional public schools. In many cases, the private sector alternatives post results that are inferior to the traditional public schools.[49] According to the Stanford University based CREDO institution,

[Twenty-five] percent of schools had significantly stronger growth than their TPS market counterparts in reading, 56 percent were not significantly different and 19 percent of schools had weaker growth. In math, the results show that 29 percent of charter schools had stronger growth than their [Traditional Public School] (TPS) market counterparts, 40 percent had growth that was not significantly different, and 31 percent had weaker growth.[50]

CHARACTERISTICS OF AN EQUITABLE
CAPITAL-OUTLAY PROGRAM

Characteristics of an equitable capital-outlay program should contain the following:

1. The quality of school facilities available to the pupils of a school district should not be determined by the fiscal capacity of the district. Either the state must fully finance the facilities needed or it must provide equalization grants which substantially equalize the financial resources of the school districts that are available for financing needed facilities. This is one of the principal criteria used to evaluate the equity of a state plan for acquisition of capital facilities and retirement of debt;

2. An equitable measure of need for school facilities should be utilized. The measure of need for school facilities should be based primarily upon the educational program needed. The measure of need should give consideration to at least the following factors:

    a. The school buildings of all school districts depreciate at a rate of about 2 percent per year; therefore, all districts have a depreciation need of at least 2 percent of present replacement cost. The depreciation of equipment is still greater; therefore, the depreciation of buildings and equipment combined is probably about 2 ½ percent per year. Unit depreciation costs can readily be computed on a pupil- or teacher-unit basis;

    b. The measure of need should include pupil growth, projected pupil growth, and capital-outlay needs resulting from a shift in the geographical location of the pupil population within a district;

    c. Different types of educational programs require varying costs per unit. Furthermore, school plants may cost more in some school districts than the state average, due to differences in site costs and other factors. These cost variations should be included in the measure of need; and

    d. Some districts may have issued bonds and provided the needed facilities without waiting for the state to develop an equitable plan of school financing. The debt service on such bonds should be included in the measure of need for such districts.

3. The finance plan should provide for financing school facilities by borrowing and by current revenue. Boards of education should have ample authority to issue bonds for school facilities and utilize annual state grants to pay all or part of the debt service on such bonds. If a district does not have the bonding capacity needed to finance the facilities needed, a state authority should be given the power to issue state bonds on behalf of the district and should utilize all or part of the annual state capital-outlay allotment to the district to pay the debt service on the bonds. School districts should also have the authority to use current annual state allotments for capital outlay and current local revenue in order to reduce the interest costs of excessive borrowing;

4. The school plant program should be carefully planned and projected over a period of years. The state departments of education should provide technical assistance to their local boards of education for this planning process;

5. The state should not exercise unnecessary controls over the plant program of a school district. It is recognized that the state should enforce minimum standards with respect to health and safety, but the state should not establish state plans for school buildings or require a uniform number of square feet per elementary or high school pupil. The need for the school plant originates in the educational program, and local boards of education, while complying with state directives, should be given a large measure of authority to determine the educational program needed in the district. Educational needs vary among the districts of a state, and the same program in every district would not be equitable to the pupils. The school plant should facilitate the educational program needed, not control it; and

6. The plan for financing the school plant should be an annual, continuing plan as contrasted to *ad hoc*, emergency plans.

SUMMARY AND CONCLUSION

The doctrine of local fiscal responsibility for capital facilities has resulted in a backlog of unmet needs and considerable variance in the quality of school facilities throughout the nation.

The proportion of total expenditures for public elementary and secondary education allocated for capital outlay and interest on school indebtedness tends to follow the growth or decline in pupil enrollment.

Local options for funding capital construction commonly include: pay-as-you-go using current revenue; the use of building reserve funds; and the sale of general obligation bonds.

For those states that provide fiscal support for local capital construction, funding options commonly include: complete state support; grants (flat, percentage-matching, and equalization); loans; and building authorities/bond banks.

Persistent problems encountered by local school boards seeking to construct or renovate their capital facilities include: restrictive debt limitations; overburdened property tax bases; high costs of construction; diversion of funds to the private sector; and lack of public support.

Characteristics of equitable state capital-outlay programs include the neutralization of fiscal capacity and fiscal effort of local school districts in order to break the link between fiscal capacity, fiscal effort and quality of school facilities, and the development and use of more accurate measures of capital needs.

Resources for capital construction should include a mix of current and non-revenue funding sources.

Unduly restrictive state controls pursuant to the design of local school facilities should be avoided in order to tailor school buildings to the needs of the local communities.

KEY TERMS

- Capital outlay
- Debt service
- Principal
- Interest
- Tax friction
- Building reserve fund
- General obligation bond
- Municipal bond
- Revenue bond
- Term bond

- Serial bond
- Arbitrage bond
- Sinking fund
- Bond rating
- Sale – leaseback
- Tax increment financing
- Qualifying zone academy bond
- Building authority
- Bond bank

NOTES

1. Expenditures were adjusted for inflation, 2002 dollars, by the consumer price index. National Education Association, *Rankings & Estimates, Ranking 2012 & Estimates 2013* (Washington, DC: NEA, 2013).
2. Ibid., Glossary.
3. Education Writers Association, *Wolves at the Schoolhouse Door* (Washington, DC: Education Writers Association, 1989), p. 4.
4. Center for Green Schools, *State of Our Schools 2013 Report* (Washington, DC: USGBC, 2013).
5. The conservative justices and the republican presidents who nominated them are as follows: Alito-George W. Bush; Kennedy-Reagan; O'Connor-Reagan; Rehnquist-Nixon; Roberts-George W. Bush; Scalia-Reagan; and Thomas-George H.W. Bush.
6. Commencing in 1983 with *Mueller v. Allen*, 463 U.S 388, 103 S. Ct 3062, 77 L. Ed 2d 721, followed in 2000 by *Mitchell v. Helms*, 530 U.S. 793, 120 S. Ct 2530, 147 L. Ed 2d 660 and a series of other cases, the *wall of separation between church and state* has been substantially breached regarding public funding of religiously-affiliated schools.
7. W. Monfort Barr and William Wilkerson, *Financing Public Elementary and Secondary School Facilities in the United States*, Special Study Number Seven, National Education Finance Project (Bloomington, Indiana: Indiana University, 1970), p. 25.
8. Ibid.
9. Manitoba Ministry of Education, *Funding of Schools, 2013–2014* (Winnipeg, Manitoba: Schools' Finance Branch, 2013).
10. Vern Brimley, Jr., Rulon R. Garfield, and Deborah A. Verstegen, *Financing Education in a Climate of Change*, 11th Edn. (Upper Saddle River, New Jersey: Pearson Education, Inc., 2011).
11. 21st Century School Fund, *State Capital Spending on PK-12 School Facilities* (Washington, DC: National Clearinghouse for Educational Facilities, 2010).
12. Glen I. Earthman, *Planning Educational Facilities*, 3rd Edn. (Lanham, Maryland: Rowman & Littlefield Education, 2009).
13. Although seldom available to local school districts, revenue bonds are used by school districts in some states to fund the construction of school facilities. See for example: *Georgia Constitution*, Article VIII, § VI, Para IV; O.C.G.A. § 48-8-110 through § 48-8-121; O.C.G.A.

§ 48-8-140 through § 48-8-142 (Articles 3 and of Chapter 8 of Title 48 of Official Code of Georgia annotated, as amended in 1997) which permits local school districts to dedicate the revenue from a $0.01 sales tax to retire revenue bonds issued for school construction projects.

14. Business Dictionary.Com, *General Obligation Bonds* (Fairfax, Virginia: Web Finance, Inc., 2013).

15. U.S.C., § 148. Arbitrage (a) Arbitrage bond defined . . . the term "arbitrage bond" means any bond issued as part of an issue any portion of the proceeds of which are reasonably expected (at the time of issuance of the bond) to be used directly or indirectly – (1) to acquire higher yielding investments, or (2) to replace funds which were used directly or indirectly to acquire higher yielding investments . . . For purposes of this subsection, a bond shall be treated as an arbitrage bond if the issuer intentionally uses any portion of the proceeds of the issue of which such bond is a part in a manner described in paragraph (1) or (2).

16. Michael A. Fletcher, *Changing Tax Exemption for Municipal Bonds Face Stiff Opposition* (Washington, DC: Washington Post, 2013).

17. Stoever Glass & Company, *The Truth About Tax-Free Municipal Bonds* (New York: Stoever Glass & Company, 2013).

18. One of the most widely used rating companies for school bonds is Moody's Investor Service, which rates each issue on an eight-point continuum from Aaa to C. Other rating companies include, Standard & Poor's Corporation and the Fitch Group.

19. Earthman, *op. cit.*, p. 93

20. The Fitch Group, including Fitch Ratings, Fitch Solutions, and Fitch Learning, is controlled by the French-owned FIMALAC.

21. Christopher Alessi and Roya Wolverson, *The Credit Rating Controversy* (New York: The Council on Foreign Relations, 2012).

22. See for example: *Virginia Constitution*, Article VII, § 10(a).

23. See for example, *Oklahoma Constitution*, Article X, § 26. Indebtedness of political subdivisions – Assent of voters – Limitation of amount – Annual tax.

24. Ibid.

25. Proposition 13, *People's Initiative to Limit Property Taxation*, was an amendment of the Constitution of California enacted during 1978, by means of the initiative process. It was approved by California voters on June 6, 1978.

26. Interest rates for 20-year general obligation bonds approached 12 percent during the mid-1980s. See W.M. Financial Strategies, *Rates Over Time-Interest Rate Trends* (St. Louis, Missouri: WMFS, 2013).

27. It is not recommended to purchase technology-related equipment through the sale of municipal bonds. It is difficult to explain to voters that their debt service payments are for items resting in a landfill.

28. Most municipal bonds are purchased by large investment firms and banks that only purchase rated bonds.

29. American Municipal Bond Assurance Corporation (AMBAC) was founded in 1971 and is headquartered in New York City. The Municipal Bond Insurance Association (MBIA) was founded in 1973 and established its home office in Armonk, New York.

30. In some states, municipalities are permitted to charge fees to property developers for new infrastructure that must be funded due to new property development. Such fees are designed to reduce the additional costs to the community and residents for infrastructure and services, including police, fire, schools, etc.

31. Gregory Burge and Keith Ihlanfeldt, *Chapter 17: Impact Fees in Florida*. Chapter in Timothy S. Chapin, Charles E. Connerly, and Harrison T. Higgins (Eds), *Evaluating Florida's Growth Management Approach* (Farnharm, Surrey, UK: Ashgate Publishing, 2007).

32. Pub.L. 107–16, 115 Stat. 38, June 7, 2001.
33. Richard F. Dye and David F. Merriman, "Tax Increment Financing: A Tool for Local Economic Development" (*Landlines,* Vol. 18, No. 1, January, 2006).
34. *Taxpayer Relief Act of 1997*, Pub.L. 105–34, § 226, H.R. 2014, 111 Stat. 787, enacted August 5, 1997.
35. In 1810, Virginia established the *Literary Fund* to help educate *pauper children*. Later, the *Literary Fund* was amended in order to loan state funds to local school districts for capital construction.
36. Foney G. Mullins, *A History of the Literary Fund as a Funding Source for Free Public Education in the Commonwealth of Virginia* (Unpublished dissertation, Blacksburg, Virginia: Virginia Tech, 2001).
37. North Carolina established a school building loan fund similar in name and structure as the Virginia Literary Fund, see: David C. Thompson, William E. Camp, and G. Kent Stewart, *Capital Outlay as an Educational Equity Issue: A Review of Educational Research and Legal Opinion.* (Research in Rural Education: Vol. 5, No. 3, 1989).
38. A total of 16 specific recommendations were made by the researchers. See Erick Lindman et al., *State Provisions for Financing Public School Capital Outlay Programs* (Washington, DC: U.S. Government Printing Office, 1951), p. 136.
39. See for example, *Virginia Literary Fund, Virginia Constitution*, Art. VIII, § 8.
40. Virginia Board of Education, *Regulations Governing Literary Loan Applications in Virginia* (Richmond, Virginia: Virginia Department of Education, 2013).
41. Some states have combined the techniques of loan funds and reimbursements by implementing loan reimbursements which are designed to assist school districts that cannot make full repayment in a reasonable time period without enacting a burdensome tax effort. In such cases, the state is authorized to cancel the unpaid portion after a certain number of years.
42. *Code of Virginia*, Chapter 11, §§ 22.1–162 et seq.
43. Also referred to as a *School Bonding Authority*.
44. See for example: *Fletcher v. Executive Council,* 207 Iowa 923, 223 N.W. 737 (1929) and *Boswell v. State,* 181 Okla 435, 74 P. 2d 940 (1937).
45. K. Forbis Jordan, Mary P. McKeown, Richard G. Salmon, and L. Dean Webb, *School Business Administration* (Thousand Oaks, CA: Corwin Press, 1985), pp. 273–274.
46. The National Educational Finance Project (NEFP) was a multi-million study funded by the United States Office of Education that addressed funding issues affecting public schools in the United States. The study was managed and conducted primarily at the University of Florida by Roe L. Johns and Kern Alexander. Components of the NEFP were conducted at satellite institutions by other school finance experts. The study commenced in 1968 and continued for five years.
47. Adapted from W. Monfort Barr and K. Forbis Jordan, *Financing Public Education and Secondary School Facilities*, in *Planning to Finance Education*, eds. Roe L. Johns, Kern Alexander, and K. Forbis Jordan (Gainesville, Florida: National Educational Finance Project, 1971), pp. 251–252.
48. Ibid., p. 252.
49. Center for Research on Education Outcomes, *National Charter School Study* (Stanford, California: CREDO, 2013).
50. Ibid., p. 23.

CHAPTER 17

School Budget Development and Administration

TOPICAL OUTLINE OF CHAPTER

- Budget Development in the United States
- Purpose of Budgets
  - Allocation of Authority
  - Comprehensive Fiscal Plan
  - Estimates of Revenue Receipts and Expenditures
  - Balancing Revenue Receipts and Expenditures
  - Basis for Accounting
- School Budgets
- Alternative School Budgets
  - Traditional Function Budget
  - Performance Budget
  - Planning-Programming-Budgeting System (PPBS)
  - Zero-Based Budgeting
  - Site-Based Budgeting
  - Outcome-Focused Budgeting

INTRODUCTION

Historically, the development and administration of budgets coincided with the establishment of popular governments. The budgetary practices of governments in the United States were patterned from the English system where a protracted battle waged for centuries between the monarchy and Parliament regarding the control and distribution of taxes.[1] The authority to develop a budget initially was the prerogative of the monarch and the appointed ministers, but subsequently, this responsibility was transferred to a cabinet ostensibly controlled by Parliament. However, it was not until the *Glorious Revolution of 1688–1689* that the cabinet was granted full authority to prepare the budget and submit it to the House of Commons. It then became the right of English citizens to control public finances through an elected parliament.[2]

The basic budgetary procedures developed by England are now followed in principle by all modern democratic countries. The budget is developed by the executive branch of government and presented to the legislative branch. The legislative branch then approves the proposed budget with such amendments as it deems appropriate and levies the necessary taxes to cover the estimated expenditures. However, before payments can be made, the legislative branch has to appropriate revenue to the administering agencies, which are components of the executive branch of government. A typical example that distinguishes between budget approval and appropriation is provided by Virginia,

> In no event, including school division budgets, shall such preparation, publication and approval be deemed to be an appropriation. No money shall be paid out or become available to be paid out for any contemplated expenditure unless and until there has first been made an annual, semiannual, quarterly or monthly appropriation for such contemplated expenditure by the governing body, except funds appropriated in a county having adopted the county executive form of government, outstanding grants may be carried over for one year without being re-appropriated.[3]

The administration of a budget reflects a process by which the people in a democracy exercise their constitutional right of self-government.

BUDGET DEVELOPMENT IN THE UNITED STATES

Although the precise term, *budget,* is not mentioned in the Constitution of the United States, it is clear that our founding fathers intended that the basic principles of the English budgetary system would be followed. The following constitutional provisions are relevant,

> no Money shall be drawn from the Treasury, but in Consequence of Appropriations made by Law[4] . . . Congress shall have power to lay and collect taxes, duties, imposts and excises, to pay the debts and provide for the common defense and general welfare of the United States; but all duties, imposts and excises shall be uniform throughout the United States.[5] [The President] shall from time to time give to the Congress Information of the State of the Union, and recommend to their Consideration such Measures as he shall judge necessary and expedient . . .[6]

The latter provision was the constitutional origin of the *Presidential Budget Message* to Congress. While the basic principles of budget development and administration under a democratic government were recognized early in the history of the United States, modern budgetary procedures were not implemented until much later.

Alexander Hamilton, first Secretary of Treasury, attempted to present to Congress a national budget containing all federal services but was rebuffed. It was not until 1921 that Congress passed a national budget bill which was signed by President Warren G. Harding[7] and became the foundation of the current budgetary system used by the federal government.[8] Initially, the newly formed Bureau of the Budget was installed in the Department of the Treasury, but in 1939, it was transferred to the Executive Office of the President (EOP). In 1970, during the Nixon administration, the Bureau of Budget was reorganized into the Office of Management and Budget (OMB). While the responsibility for preparation and submission of budgets to Congress lies with the president, Congress provides input and exercises control through legislation.[9]

In regard to the development of state budgetary systems, some states enacted budgetary systems that preceded the one implemented by the federal government. In 1910, Ohio became the first state to authorize the governor to prepare and submit a budget to the state legislature. A.E. Buck assessed the progress of budget development made by states in 1929 and indicated that 1913 marked "the beginning of practical action in the states."[10] By 1920, some budget reform had occurred in 44 states; and by 1929, all states had established a central budget office.[11] The titles of the state offices vary among states, e.g., Department of Planning & Budget (Virginia), Department of Finance & Administration (New Mexico), Department of Finance (California), and Office of Budget, Planning & Policy (Texas); their responsibilities and functions are similar.

PURPOSE OF BUDGETS

The purpose of budgets has evolved in parallel to the changing structure and role of democratic governments. As the power shifted from monarchies to systems of *checks and balances,* typically in the form of tripartite branches of government, i.e., executive, legislative, and judicial, budgets were designed and implemented to reflect power sharing among the governmental branches. While public and common schools were established primarily by the localities, the plenary power for the operation of public schools rests with state governments. According to Ray et al.,

> Subject to constitutional limitations, a state legislature has plenary power with respect to educational policy. It may determine the ends to be achieved and the means to be employed. It may determine the types of schools to be established, the means of this support, the content of their curricula, and the qualifications of their teachers. It may do all of these things with or without the consent of the localities, for, in education, the state is the unit and there are no local rights except those safeguarded by the Constitution. Even local school board members are state officers. This plenary power allows the state to mandate that school districts develop budgets and determine the format, calendar, procedures, and so forth for the budgeting process. The state mandates budget categories. This is also related to the state's mandated system of financial accounting, auditing, and reporting. The budgeting process is also utilized to establish tax rates.[12]

Presented below are the primary purposes of a modern system of budgeting.

Allocation of Authority

Coincident with the demise of a singular branch of government, monarch, or executive branch, and the establishment of the legislative branch, there has been a continuous struggle between the two branches to control both taxation and appropriation of revenue. The judiciary entered the fray and ceded much of the authority to the legislative branch through its interpretation of the federal and state constitutions. Ultimately, the executive branches of government have been limited to the expenditure of appropriated funds for the purposes specified by the legislatures.

Comprehensive Fiscal Plan

While the allocation of authority has been transferred to the legislative branch, considerable tension still exists between the executive and legislative branches, often at the expense of the public.[13] The legislative branch, by not seeking advice, or in some instances, ignoring the input from the executive branch, developed budgets that were inefficient and unwieldy to administer. As a result, most state legislatures now require the executive branches to prepare coordinated and comprehensive budgets for their consideration. The purpose of requiring submission of comprehensive budgets by the executive branch is to ensure equitable and efficient allocation of resources.

Estimates of Revenue Receipts and Expenditures

Without question, one of the most important purposes of the budget process is to accurately project revenue receipts and expenditures for the budgetary and/or project period. An underestimation of either revenue receipts or expenditures can lead to deficit financing, a practice that is prohibited by law in most states. According to Poterba,

> Unlike the federal government, most states are constitutionally prohibited from deficit financing over any prolonged period . . . Most state constitutions prevent state governments from running deficits for any substantial length of time. Anti-deficit provisions take two forms: limitations on projected deficits, and limitations on actual deficits. In all but five states, the governor[s] must submit a balanced budget. Thirty-nine states have constitutional or statutory provisions requiring the[ir] legislatures to pass a balanced budget. After the budget has passed, however, revenues and expenditures may diverge from expectations and lead to an unexpected deficit. States vary in the speed with which they require such deficits to be eradicated. Only nine states allow actual deficits to be carried forward to the next fiscal year. Only six do not require the deficit to be eliminated in the following fiscal year.[14]

In addition to the specter of deficit financing, without accurate forecasts of the flow of revenue receipts and disbursements, it would be difficult, if not impossible, to administer a properly-functioning school district.

Balancing Revenue Receipts and Expenditures

The need to balance expenditures with revenue receipts generates two opposing philosophies. That is, when a budget is out-of-balance, i.e., when the proposed expenditures exceed the projected revenue receipts, it can be balanced by reducing the expenditures or increasing revenue receipts through levying higher tax rates, securing larger and/or additional grants, or a combination of reducing expenditures and increasing revenue. Those who consider themselves as *progressives* generally favor balancing a budget by increasing revenue receipts, while those who consider themselves *conservatives* usually advocate for reducing expenditures. However, whether progressives or conservatives support increasing revenue receipts or decreasing expenditures to bring a budget into balance, it is a much more complex issue; and in most cases, budgets are balanced by application of both alternatives. One of the principal purposes of budgetary practices is to provide a system to maintain revenue receipts and expenditures in reasonable balance.

Basis for Accounting

Orderly fiscal administration is not feasible without an adequate system of financial accounting. Sound budgetary procedures cannot be developed without the aid of financial accounting; and without a budget, accounting is of little benefit to management. Accounting is much more than maintaining a record of revenue receipts and expenditures; it makes it possible to determine whether the funds have been used for the purposes that they were appropriated.

SCHOOL BUDGETS

While similarities and commonalities exist among all budgets, both public and private entities, school budgets have their own distinct characteristics and features that distinguish them from those employed by other public and private agencies. The American Association of School Administrators (AASA) summarized some of the major differences,

> the budget process in public schools has noticeable differences that impact how districts' allocate and prioritize their funds . . . while most public and private organizations and businesses have 35 to 40 percent of their budgets tied to personnel and benefits, the comparable number in public schools is, on average, more than double, between 80 and 85 percent. Further complicating districts' ability to address budget priorities, the remaining 15 percent of their budgets is oftentimes impacted and limited by state, local and federal mandates related to everything from building codes to class size requirements.[15]

The revenue receipts reported in school budgets are derived from three primary sources: state grants, local appropriations,[16] and federal funds. Displayed in Figure 17.1 are the national percentages of revenue receipts by source for FY 2010.[17] However, as discussed previously, there are significant variances, both nationally and within several states,

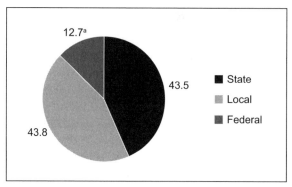

a The federal revenue receipts include ARRA funds.

Figure 17.1 Percent Revenue Receipts by Source, FY 2010

Source: Institute of Education Sciences, *Revenues and Expenditures for Public Elementary and Secondary Education: School Year 2009–10 (Fiscal Year 2010)* (Washington, DC: National Center for Education Statistics, 2012).

regarding the percent of revenue receipts provided by the three governmental agencies. Note that the 12.7 percent revenue receipts reported for the federal government contains a portion of the *American Recovery and Reinvestment Act of 2009*[18] *(ARRA);* normally, the federal government provides revenue receipts that account for approximately 10 percent of the resources for public elementary and secondary education. The National Education Association (NEA) estimated that the percent provided by the federal government for FY 2013 waned to 10.1 percent[19] from the 12.7 percent for FY 2010 reported in Figure 17.1 by the Institute of Education Sciences.[20] Local and state governments were nearly equal financial partners, each contributing between 43 and 44 percent of the revenue receipts for FY 2010.[21] The NEA has estimated that for FY 2013, state governments provided 45.8 percent of the revenue receipts and local governments appropriated 44.2 percent.[22]

BOX 17.1

The Four Categories of Expenditure

Function: The activity for which a service or material object is acquired.

Object: The service or commodity obtained as the result of a specific expenditure.

Project: Expenditures identified to meet a variety of specialized reporting requirements at local, state, and federal levels.

Instructional Level: Expenditures segregated by instructional level.

In the early years, school budgets were divided simply into two sections: revenues and expenditures.[23] Gradually, school budgets evolved into parallel accounting systems where expenditures were reported for function, object, program, and instructional level. Displayed in Box 17.1 are brief definitions of the four categories of expenditures.[24]

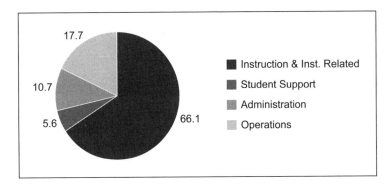

Figure 17.2 Current Expenditures by Major Function, FY 2010

Source: Institute of Education Sciences, *Revenues and Expenditures for Public Elementary and Secondary Education: School Year 2009–10 (Fiscal Year 2010)* (Washington, DC: National Center for Education Statistics, 2012).

In regard to the expenditure of funds by major function,[25] as illustrated in Figure 17.2, the Institute of Education Sciences reported the following percentages: Instruction and Instruction Related (66.1 percent); Student Support (5.6 percent); Administration (10.7 percent); and Operations (17.7 percent). Interestingly, there has been a trend in recent years, school years 2001–2002 to 2009–2010, for the instruction and instruction-related expenditures to increase slightly. According to the Institute for Education Sciences, the percent expended for instruction and instruction-related functions increased from 61.5 in 2001–2002 to 65.9 in 2005–2006 to 66.1 in 2009–2010.

ALTERNATIVE SCHOOL BUDGETS

School districts' budgets are presented and structured into a series of self-balancing sets of accounts known as funds that record cash and other financial resources, together with all related liabilities and residual equities and balances, or changes therein. The federal government authorizes school districts to employ nine separate funds which are described in Box 17.2.[26] Among the nation's 15,525 operating school districts,[27] alternative budgetary systems have been employed. Several of the most prominent alternatives are presented below.

BOX 17.2

Alternative Budgetary Systems

General Fund: This fund is the chief operating fund of the school district. It is used to account for all financial resources of the school district except for those required to be accounted for in another fund.

Special Revenue Funds: These funds account for the proceeds of specific revenue sources (other than trusts or major capital projects) that are legally restricted to expenditure for specified purposes.

Capital Projects Funds: These funds account for financial resources to be used to acquire or construct major capital facilities.

Debt Service Funds: These funds account for the accumulation of resources for, and the payment of, general long-term debt principal and interest.

Permanent Funds: These funds account for resources that are legally restricted to the extent that only earnings, and not principal, may be used for purposes that support the school districts' programs.

Enterprise Funds: These funds account for any activity for which a fee is charged to external users for goods or services.

Internal Service Funds: These funds account for any activity within the school district that provides goods or services to other funds, school district departments, component units, or other governments on a cost-reimbursement basis.

Trust Funds: These funds account for assets held by a school district in a trustee capacity for others and that therefore cannot be used to support the school district's own programs.

Agency Funds: These funds account for funds that are held in a custodial capacity by a school district for individuals, private organizations, or other governments.

Traditional Function Budget

Virtually all school districts initially employed budgets that were structured into a series of functions defined as activities for which services or material objects are acquired. Examples of functions include expenditures for *administration, instruction, operations and maintenance, student transportation, etc.* While both federal and state governments permit local school districts the flexibility to structure their budgets into more sophisticated budgetary systems, school districts commonly are required to report their expenditures pursuant to specified functional expenditures. For example, the Commonwealth of Virginia requires local governing agencies to approve and appropriate projected school expenditures in accordance with the following classifications (functions): instruction, administration, attendance and health, pupil transportation, operation and maintenance, school food services and other non-instructional operations, facilities, debt and fund transfers, technology, and contingency reserves.[28] Local school districts in Virginia are fiscally dependent upon local governing agencies; however, the governing agencies are restricted to approving and appropriating funds in accordance with the budgetary functions.[29]

The traditional budget is often referred to as a *Line-Item Approach* and remains the most popular due to its simplicity and ease of budget control. Proposed expenditures are presented in columns that are parallel to prior year(s) proposed and/or actual expenditures. Greater budgetary control can be achieved through the level of expenditure detail, e.g., fund, function, object, etc., incorporated into the budget. Budgetary control also can be heighted or lessened by the number of required line-items; as the number of line-items increases, greater control is exercised. The traditional budget remains popular due to its simplicity, ease of preparation, historical recordation, and budgetary control. The major disadvantages of traditional budgets are the absence of performance information that justifies further expenditures and the increased tendency to engage in micro-management by untrained and uninformed board members.

Performance Budget

The Organization for Economic Cooperation and Development (OECD) has defined performance budgeting as the linkage between the funds allocated to measurable results. There are three broad types.

Presentational Performance Budgeting simply means that performance information is presented in budget documents or other government documents. The information can refer to targets, or results, or both, and is included as background information for accountability and dialogue with legislators and citizens on public policy issues. The performance information is not intended to play a role in decision making and does not do so.

Performance-Informed Budgeting. Resources are indirectly related to proposed future performance or to past performance. The performance information is important in the budget decision-making process, but does not determine the amount of resources allocated and does not have a predefined weight in the decisions. Performance information is used along with other information in the decision-making process.

Direct Performance Budgeting. Resources are allocated based on results achieved. This form of performance budgeting is used only in specific sectors in a limited number of OECD countries. For example, the number of students who graduate with a Master's degree will determine the following year's funding for the university running the programme.[30]

The *Performance Budgeting Approach* is considered superior to the Traditional Budget described above because it provides administrators with more useful information, including quantitative estimates of costs and a focus on the evaluation of outcomes. Its major weakness is due to the absence of standardized and reliable cost information inherent in governmental organizations.[31]

Planning-Programming-Budgeting System (PPBS)

The Planning-Programming-Budgeting System (PPBS) links expenditures primarily to specific educational programs and secondarily to budgetary objects. A fully developed PPBS aligns expenditures solely on educational programs regardless of objects or organizational units. Program budgeting differs from the approaches previously discussed because it places less emphasis on control and evaluation. Budget requests and reports are summarized in terms of a few broad programs rather than in the great detail of line-item expenditures or organizational units.

According to the Institute of Education Sciences, the PPBS conceptual framework,

> includes the practices of explicitly projecting the long-term costs of programs and evaluating different program alternatives that may be used to reach long-term goals and objectives. The focus on long-range planning is the major advantage of this approach; and advocates believe that if PPBS is employed, schools are more likely to reach their stated goals and objectives. However, several conditions can limit the implementation of this approach, including changes in long-term goals, a lack of consensus regarding the fundamental objectives of the organization, a lack of adequate program and cost data, and the difficulty of administering programs that involve several organizational units. Despite these limitations, program budgeting is often used as a planning device while budget allocations continue to be made in terms of objects and organizational units – a process that has been adopted in many schools throughout the nation. As with performance budgeting, program budgeting information may be used to supplement and support traditional budgets in order to increase their informational value.[32]

Zero-Based Budgeting (ZBB)

Zero-based budgeting is based on the principle that all program activities and services fall to zero at the conclusion of the budgetary period, usually annually, and must be re-justified during the subsequent budget development process. The ZBB budget is segregated into decision units at the program level of the organization and presented to management in the form of decision packages. Each decision package contains prior, current, and future program objectives, costs, outcomes, and rank of importance to the organization. Both objectives and outcomes are presented in measureable terms and are aligned to actual and projected costs. Decision packages are then ranked by their importance in reaching organizational goals and objectives. Therefore, when the proposed budget is presented, it contains a series of budget decisions that are tied to the attainment of the organization's goals and objectives.

ZBB can be used by both private and public organizations; however, it has proven to be more successful in the private sector. Peter Phyrr, while serving as Manager, Staff Control, at Texas Instruments, Inc., Dallas, Texas, developed and then applied ZBB successfully during the late 1960s and 1970s. Subsequently, Jimmy Carter, while serving as Governor of Georgia from 1971–1975, contracted with Phyrr to integrate ZBB into the executive budget process. Later, as President of the United States, 1977–1981, Carter required the adoption of ZBB by the federal government. However, ZBB was eliminated officially in 1981, although vestiges remained in use by several federal agencies until 1994.

School districts in several states have reported adoption and employment of ZBB; but in most cases, due to excessive record-keeping, paperwork, administrative costs, and, most importantly, mandated programs and services, full implementation has not occurred. According to the National Council of State Legislatures (NCSL),

> In recent years, 17 states have used zero-base budgeting in some form and several more have made serious efforts to do so. Fifteen state legislatures considered bills calling for some form of zero-base budgeting in 2009, two did so in 2010, and at

least nine considered legislation in 2011. They include a mix of small and large states: Iowa, Kansas, Rhode Island and South Carolina among the smaller ones, and California, Georgia, Illinois and Ohio among the larger ones. Despite this widespread interest, none of the enabling legislation has been enacted between 2009 and 2011. In analyzing proposals for its legislature, the Illinois Legislative Research Unit found no real evidence of actual application of zero-base budgeting in most of the 17 states that report using it.[33]

Site-Based Budgeting (SBB)

Site-based budgeting is based on the premise that the people charged with the responsibility to deliver or produce the product should have budgetary authority, including personnel decision making.[34] Unlike the previous budgetary approaches that were developed by other private and public organizations, SBB was developed by educators who intended to transfer a portion of decision making from the top of the school district hierarchy to the operational levels of individual schools. Impetus was provided to SBB following the Kentucky *Rose v. Council for Better Education* decision in 1989.[35] As part of the court-ordered remedy, the Kentucky General Assembly mandated a statewide site-based management and budgetary system.

The principals and instructional staff of the schools versus the central staff of the school districts are granted increased authority to make decisions regarding educational programs and services. However, the principals and their staffs remain obligated to the rules and regulations promulgated by the state and local governance structure.

There are several advantages that accrue from implementation of SBB. Those who have the greatest understanding of the needs of the individual schools now have the authority to influence resource allocations. In addition, the decentralization of decision making may widen the pool of participants in the school community while enhancing accountability. SBB also has disadvantages, including the inability to effect meaningful budgetary decisions. This is particularly the case for school districts with limited fiscal resources. And, due to a limited ability to make budgetary decisions, accountability of outcomes is often overstated and it becomes difficult to match outcomes to those assigned responsibility for resource allocation. Extensive pre-employment training is required if SBB is to be successfully implemented, requiring significant expenditures. Finally, in order to gain the support of those affected by employment of SBB, both those who relinquish and those who accept resource allocation authority must agree to the transfer.

Outcome-Focused Budgeting

Since the late 1990s, local, state, and federal officials have been pursuing a broad range of reforms designed to ensure more accountability in the nation's public school system.[36] Consistent with increased accountability, school budgeting has become more *outcome-focused*.[37] Severe reductions in local and state appropriations for public schools and greater competition for resources from other public agencies have exacerbated the fiscal plight of public schools and given greater impetus to the *outcome-focused* movement. The rationale for *outcome-focused budgeting* is based on the notion that linking outcomes to appropriations will lead to improved results, measured primarily by achievement tests. *Outcome-focused budgeting* can be applied to each of the budgeting systems discussed above and is likely to see increased use in the future.

SUMMARY AND CONCLUSION

A brief history of budgeting and its purposes were presented, including allocating authority, fiscal planning, estimating revenues and expenditures, balancing revenues and expenditures, and as a basis for accounting. The national pattern of revenues by source, current expenditures by major function, and commonly established funds were defined. The following budgetary systems employed by school districts were identified: Traditional Function Budget, Performance Budget, Planning-Programming-Budgeting System (PPBS), Zero-Based Budget (ZBB), Site-Based Budget (SBB), and Outcome-Focused Budget.

KEY TERMS

- Budget approval versus appropriation
- Balancing revenue receipts and expenditures
- Traditional function budget
- Performance budget
- Planning-programming-budgeting system
- Zero-based budget
- Site-based budgeting system
- Outcome-focused budget

NOTES

1. G.L. Harris, *King, Parliament and Public Finance in Mediaeval England to 1369* (Oxford, England: Oxford University Press, 1975).
2. Steven C. A. Pincus and James Robinson, *What Really Happened During the Glorious Revolution*. Ninetieth Birthday Celebration for Douglas C. North (St. Louis, Missouri: Washington University, 2010).
3. Code of Virginia, § 15.2-2506 (2013).
4. *United States Constitution*, Article I, § 9.
5. Ibid., § 8.
6. Ibid., Article II, § 3.
7. *Budget and Accounting Act of 1921*, Pub.L. 67–13, 42 U.S.C. 20.
8. C. William Garner, *An Inquiry Into the Feasibility of a National Accounting Policy for Public Schools*. In *Public Budgeting and Finance*, 4th Edn., Eds Robert T. Golembiewski and Jack Rabin (Boca Raton, Florida: CRC Press, 1997).
9. See for example: *The Budget Control Act of 2011*, Pub.L. 112–25, § 365, 125 U.S.C. 240.
10. A. E. Buck, *Public Budgeting* (New York: Harper and Brothers, 1929).

11. York Willbern, *Personnel and Money*. In James W. Fesler (Ed.), *The 50 States and Their Local Governments* (New York: Knopf, 1967).

12. John R. Ray, I. Carl Candoli, and Walter G. Hack, *School Business Administration, A Planning Approach*, 8th Edn. (Boston: Pearson, 2005).

13. See for example, the *Budget Sequestration*, The Budget Control Act of 2011 (Pub.L. 112–25, § 365, 125 U.S.C. 240.

14. James M. Poterba, *State Responses to Fiscal Crisis: The Effects of Budgetary Institutions and Politics* (Los Angeles: UCLA Center for American Politics and Public Policy, 1999).

15. American Association of School Administrators, *AASA White Papers: School Budgets 101.* (Alexandria, Virginia: AASA, 2010).

16. In some states, primarily in the Midwest, local funds are provided by two local governmental agencies, e.g., school districts and counties.

17. Institute of Education Sciences, *Revenues and Expenditures for Public Elementary and Secondary Education: School Year 2009–10 (Fiscal Year 2010)* (Washington, DC: National Center for Education Statistics, 2012).

18. Pub. L. No. 111-5, 123 Stat. 115, 516 (Feb. 19, 2009).

19. National Education Association, *Rankings of the States 2012 and Estimates of School Statistics 2013* (Washington, DC: NEA, 2012).

20. Institute of Education Sciences, *op. cit.*

21. Ibid.

22. National Education Association, *op. cit.*

23. The two sections often were referred to as pages.

24. Institute of Education Sciences, *Financial Accounting for Local and State School Systems: 2009 Edition* (Washington, DC: National Center for Education Statistics, 2009).

25. Several expenditure functions have been consolidated. For example, expenditures reported for operations include operations and maintenance, student transportation, food services, and enterprise operations. Also, it is important to note that the 10.7 percent reported for administration expenditures include central office and building level costs. Usually, building level administration costs are classified in school budgets as instruction expenditures.

26. Institute of Education Sciences, *Financial Accounting, op. cit.*

27. National Education Association, *Rankings (2012) & Estimates of School Statistics (2013)* (Washington, DC: NEA, 2013).

28. Code of Virginia, Article 5, §22.1–93. Approval of annual budget for school purposes; §22.1–94. Appropriations by county, city, or town governing body for public schools.

29. Ibid., §22.1–115. System of accounting; statements of funds available; classification of expenditures.

30. Organization for Economic Cooperation and Development, *Performance Budgeting: A User's Guide: A Policy Brief* (Washington, DC: OECD, March, 2008).

31. Institute of Education Sciences, *op. cit.*

32. Ibid.

33. Legislative Research Unit, *Zero-Based Budgeting in Other States* (Springfield, Illinois: Illinois General Assembly, 2008).

34. Often used in combination with other budgetary approaches.

35. 790 S.W.2d 186, 60 Ed. Law Rep. 1289 (Ky. 1989).

36. Allison Rizzolo, *Accountability and Public Schools* (New York: Public Agenda, 2013).

37. See for example, *No Child Left Behind Act of 2001*. Pub.L. 107–110, 115 Stat. 1425, enacted January 8, 2002.

CHAPTER 18

Risk Management, Student Transportation, and School Food Services*

TOPICAL OUTLINE OF CHAPTER

- Fiscal Considerations
  - Underwriting
  - Deductibles
  - Legal Authority to Purchase Insurance
- Individual Optional Insurance
- Fire Insurance
  - Fire and Casualty Insurers
  - Safeguarding Records
- Student Transportation
  - Purposes of Student Transportation
  - Transportation Service Policies
- School Food Services
  - National School Lunch Program
  - Eligibility Requirements
  - Meal and Nutritional Standards
  - Qualification for Free and Reduced-Price Meals
  - Reimbursement Levels
  - Additional USDA Support, Other Than Cash Reimbursements
  - Foods Distributed by the USDA
  - Children Served (Various Years) from FYs 1947 to 2012
  - Cost of the Federal Food Programs, Including the National School Lunch Program
  - School Food Services Meal Production Programs

---

*Portions of this chapter appeared in *The Economics and Financing of Education,* by Roe L. Johns, Edgar L. Morphet, and Kern Alexander. Copyright 1983, 1975, 1969, 1960 by Kern Alexander.

INTRODUCTION

The primary purpose of *risk management* is to shift to others or share with others the risks that are greater than it is prudent for an institution, person, firm, or agency to bear individually. Central to the conduct of risk management is the acquisition of several types of insurance coverage. In addition, school districts often purchase insurance to provide coverage to individuals for whom a moral obligation is due despite the absence of a legal obligation.

Most school boards have custody of property, cash, and securities that are subject to loss or damage from many causes under varied circumstances. School boards and their employees, in the course of fulfilling their contractual obligations, may cause financial loss or bodily injury to others to whom they are legally or morally responsible. School boards have the legal responsibility in some states and the moral responsibility in all states to *save harmless*[1] their employees for injury done to others during the lawful performance of their duties. The boards have the legal responsibility in some states and the moral responsibility in all states to provide financial protection for their employees who were injured while performing their duties. There is a legal responsibility in some states and a moral responsibility in all states for school boards to provide financial protection for students who were injured while receiving instruction.

FISCAL CONSIDERATIONS

The financial risks of school boards are complex and their moral obligations are numerous; thus, the development of a sound system of risk management involves many considerations. The laws of states vary substantially as follows:

1. Types of insurance coverage and amounts of the coverage for different types of risks that school districts must carry;
2. Types of insurance coverage and amounts of the coverage that are permissible; and
3. Degree of liability of school districts for loss or injury caused to others or suffered by others as a consequence of operating schools.

School districts vary greatly by:

1. Types of potential risks;
2. Financial significance of the risks;
3. Spread of property risks among players;
4. Size of school districts; and
5. Fiscal capacity to withstand loss of assets.

As an example, consider the variance in enrollment among the nation's school districts; in 2012, Alzada Elementary School District, Montana, served two students,[2] while the New York City School District enrolled nearly one million students (993,903).[3] The variance in fiscal capacity among states, as measured by *Personal Income Per Capita* in 2013 (1st Quarter), also was striking. See Table 7.2 for more about variations in fiscal capacity of states. Connecticut was ranked first with $61,361 Personal Income Per Capita and Mississippi last with $33,508, a ratio of 1.8:1.0; or it can be interpreted that Connecticut has nearly twice the fiscal capacity than Mississippi.[4] Within states, the variance among local school districts is even more startling. For example, Texas reported that the *Wealth Per-Pupil in Average Daily Attendance* for School Year 2012–2013 varied from $29,315 for Boles ISD to $13,187,084 for Fort Elliot CISD, yielding an extraordinarily high fiscal capacity ratio of 449.8:1.0,[5] suggesting that Fort Elliot CISD possessed nearly 500 times the fiscal capacity possessed by Boles ISD.

Due to the varied circumstances facing the approximately 15,000 operating school districts[6] in the United States, there is no one system of risk management and accompanying insurance protection that can be implemented universally. Therefore, a risk management program should be tailored to meet the unique requirements of each school district. **The primary purpose of school districts' risk management programs is to obtain maximum coverage at minimum cost.** Insurance coverage can be obtained from one or more of four sources as defined in Box 18.1.

BOX 18.1

Sources of Insurance Coverage for School Districts

- *Commercial:* Commercial insurers are generally for-profit companies that provide a wide range of insurance products. In many instances, commercial insurers operate across state boundaries and sometimes internationally;
- *State:* Several states provide certain types of insurance coverage from state resources;
- *Self-Insurance:* An individual school district that is responsible for certain types of claims from own sources; and
- *Risk-Pool:* A group of school districts that join together and share the risks for certain types of claims.

School buildings and their contents represent major investments by school boards. The loss of a major building, such as the high school that collapsed from heavy snow in Montgomery County, Virginia, February 10, 2010,[7] placed severe fiscal stress on the community to rebuild the high school. Exacerbating the fiscal stress were the several construction projects already under construction faced by the school district.

The financial risks of a school board are very complex and its moral obligations numerous. The development of an adequate insurance program for a school district involves many considerations. The laws of the states vary widely, including:

1. types of insurance coverage and amounts of the coverage for different types of risks that a school district must carry,
2. types of insurance coverage that are permissible, and
3. degree of liability of the board for loss or injury caused to others or suffered by others as a consequence of operating schools.

Boards of education differ greatly in:

1. types of risks that are likely to be incurred,
2. financial magnitude of risks,

3. breath of property risks among school districts, and
4. collective financial ability to bear risks.

No one insurance program is suitable for all school districts. In fact, no single insurance program is equally suitable for any two districts unless it occurs as a rare statistical coincidence. Therefore, the insurance program for each district should be tailored to its specific needs. This requires much study and intelligent planning. As mentioned previously, the purpose in planning the insurance program is to obtain the maximum needed protection at the minimum cost. The principal types of protection needed by boards of education are presented in this chapter.

Commercial insurance is procured from private companies. Several states provide state-financed coverage to their governmental entities, including school districts. Whenever a school district builds up an insurance reserve fund in order to spread its losses from insurable risks over several years, it has implemented self-insurance. Primary emphasis is given in this chapter to the most common coverage, commercial insurance.

Underwriting

The first step in applying for any type of coverage is a process called *underwriting*. During this process, the insurer will assess the value of the items to be insured and the potential risk of a claim of loss, damage, or injury. These factors, combined with the level of coverage provided, will determine the rate the carrier will charge. In general, the greater the value of the thing insured and the greater the risk of the claim, the higher the rate. Historically, the process of underwriting displayed in Box 18.2 evolved from the need to protect the investment from shipping and cargo losses during the seventeenth century.

A carrier may determine that certain risks are too high and decline to issue coverage entirely or only issue coverage on the condition that certain items or causes of loss are excluded from the policy. Most policies will contain exclusions for some causes of loss. It is important to understand your policy and what it does and does not cover.

BOX 18.2

Definitions of Underwriting

- Sign and accept liability under (an insurance policy), thus guaranteeing payment in case loss or damage occurs.
- Accept risk under an insurance policy of a financial institution assuring to buy all unsold shares in an issue of securities.
- (Of a bank (or other financial institution) Engage to buy all the unsold shares in (an issue of new securities).
- Undertake to finance or otherwise support or guarantee (something): *they were willing to underwrite the construction of a ship.*

Source: *The Oxford Pocket Dictionary of Current English* (Oxford University Press, 2009).

Deductibles

Almost every type of policy will contain a provision for deductible amounts. A deductible is the amount the policyholder must pay out of pocket toward a loss before the insurer will begin to pay. For example, an automobile policy may contain a $5,000 deductible for collision damage. This means the owner would have to pay the first $5,000 of the cost of vehicle repair or replacement in any collision claim. The insurance company would then pay the remainder of the costs.

Most policies also contain a provision for limitation of coverage. This is the maximum amount the insurance company is liable for in any covered loss. The company will not pay the balance of claims exceeding this amount. For example, an auto liability policy may have a $50,000 limitation of coverage for property damage liability. If an insured driver causes an accident resulting in $60,000 in property damage, the insurance company would contribute $50,000 for the loss. The school district would then be liable for the remaining $10,000 of the loss.

A policy with a higher deductible will generally have a lower premium because the district is accepting a greater share of the financial responsibility for a loss. Higher limitations of coverage amounts will generally result in lower premiums because the maximum amounts for which the insurer could be liable are greater.

Certain policies that have very high deductibles are often referred to as self-insured retention plans. Under such a policy, the district accepts financial responsibility for the value of most anticipated losses, essentially acting as its own insurer. The purpose of the retention policy is to protect the district from an unexpectedly large number of claims, or an unlikely truly catastrophic claim that could be an extreme financial burden. Premiums for retention policies are generally substantially lower than of those of policies with standard-level deductibles.

The risks covered by a policy, deductible amounts, and limitation of coverage amounts can all be negotiated with a carrier to arrive at a premium a district can afford. A district should be careful when purchasing insurance at extremely low premiums because the policies may not provide adequate coverage.

A school district should generally only purchase insurance coverage within the framework of a formal risk management process. Such a process might include distinct phases to identify potential risks:

1. assess the consequences should they occur;
2. create a solution plan to mitigate the risk and possibly buy insurance protection if it cannot be eliminated completely;
3. implement the plan;
4. monitor the plan's progress; and
5. periodically reassess.

Legal Authority to Purchase Insurance

Purchasing insurance can be a significant expense, particularly for large-scale construction projects. District purchases, including insurance, valued at specified levels or more in the aggregate for a 12-month period are often governed by state law. Most state codes require that such purchases undergo a competitive bidding process pursuant to state law, rules, and regulations.[8]

States often offer guidelines such as the *Financial Accountability System Resource Guide* prepared by the Texas Education Agency that outlines in detail the following purchasing process.

Required, Permitted, and Prohibited Coverage

Required Coverage:

1. Health care coverage for full-time school district employees that is at least comparable to the coverage offered to state of Texas employees;
2. Workers' compensation insurance to cover workers who suffer work-related injuries or illnesses;
3. Medical liability insurance to cover volunteer physicians and registered nurses who administer treatment or medication to students; and
4. Minimum automobile liability insurance which compensates injured parties for accidents caused by drivers covered under the district's policy.

Optional Coverage:

1. Life insurance and annuities to allow employees to provide for beneficiaries when they die or save for retirement or other purposes;
2. Commercial property insurance to protect against damage to district property caused by fire, windstorm, lightning, or other covered perils. Other property-related coverage that typically requires the issuance of a separate policy includes crime, and windstorm insurance for districts in coastal areas;
3. General liability insurance to protect against wrongful acts or omissions, or the negligence of employees resulting in bodily injury or property damage. Volunteers may be included; and
4. Optional auto coverage. Collision and comprehensive auto insurance to protect district owned or regularly used vehicles from accidents in which the driver is at fault and non-traffic-related damage such as theft, hail, or fire. Towing and labor coverage pays towing charges when a car can't be driven.

Prohibited Coverage:

School districts are prohibited from purchasing the following automobile coverage:

1. Medical payments coverage pays medical and funeral expenses of injured occupants of the insured's vehicle, regardless of who was at fault;
2. Personal injury protection (PIP) coverage pays the same as medical payments coverage, plus 80 percent of an occupant's lost income as a result of an accident; and
3. Uninsured/underinsured motorist coverage pays expenses incurred by a vehicle owner or occupants as a result of an accident that was the fault of another driver who did not have insurance or lacked sufficient coverage.

INDIVIDUAL OPTIONAL INSURANCE

It is well advised for college and high school students to acquire individual insurance. According to the Ohio State Bar Association, for approximately $360 annually, college students can obtain insurance to protect themselves and their personal belongings.[9] There are numerous insurance carriers that offer this type of insurance. While states rarely require that colleges offer insurance to all students, several states require their public schools to offer insurance to certain specified students, particularly those students engaged in interscholastic athletics or other high risk activities. Several insurance companies provide individual insurance for high school and grade school students that is not exceptionally expensive. For example, if tackle football is excluded, fulltime coverage including dental accidents can be obtained for approximately $425.00 annually.[10]

FIRE INSURANCE

School buildings and their contents represent major investments by the school board. The loss of a major building and its contents would be a financial disaster to all except the largest school districts unless the building was adequately insured at the time of the loss. The cost of replacing a school plant may be several times the annual revenue receipts of a school district.

Decisions about fire insurance can be some of the most complex and important decisions that a school board will make. Most states require school districts to carry certain types of coverage, including a workers' compensation policy, an employee health plan, and certain minimum liability insurance for district vehicles. Many districts elect to purchase several additional types of coverage, but there are also types of coverage that state law prohibits school districts from purchasing.[11]

A contract (insurance policy) is where the insurer (insurance company) agrees for a fee (insurance premiums) to pay the insured party all or a portion of any loss suffered by accident or death. The losses covered by the policy may include property damage from accident or fire, theft or intentional harm, medical costs and/or lost earnings due to physical injury, long-term or permanent loss of physical capacity, and claims by others due to the insured's alleged negligence.

Fire and Casualty Insurers

Stock Life Companies are formed for the purpose of maximizing profit. Like other companies that own stock, it is managed by boards of directors and its officers chosen by the board. If the company realizes a profit, the stockholders receive dividends; if business is unprofitable, reserves are depleted. Some stock companies issue nonparticipating policies; these companies charge a fixed, definite premium, and the policyholders share through dividends in the profit of the company.[12]

Mutual Companies are classified into four classes: *assessment mutual, advance-premium mutual, factory mutual,* and *specialty and class mutual.* The use of mutual companies to protect the physical assets of school districts is very complex and requires expert advice. While funds can be saved through use of mutual companies, school districts are well advised to seek professional assistance.

A *reciprocal* or *inter-insurance exchange* is a special form of insurance company and is not a *mutual insurance company*, which is generally *incorporated*; rather, it is an *unincorporated association* of subscribing members who exchange contracts of indemnity with each other.[13] A reciprocal or inter-insurance exchange is an insurance carrier without any corporate existence. The school districts pay an advance premium and are also liable for assessments of a stipulated amount. Theoretically, a reciprocal should have the capacity to provide low-cost insurance for its members, i.e., school districts.

State Insurance. Until recently, the success of state retirement systems was the most striking example of the benefits of state insurance. School employees and boards of education were able to buy far more protection for school employees through state retirement systems that could be purchased through commercial insurance companies. While this principle remains the same, several states have shifted from fixed benefits to fixed contributions. As a result, the shift to a fixed contribution system by several states for the purpose of reducing public costs has made the teacher retirement systems much less appealing to school employees.

State insurance for fire and casualty protection remains sound public policy. Few would disagree that a desirable objective of government and sound business management is to purchase the maximum amount of needed protection at the minimum cost, then, the provision for state insurance is prudent public policy. Several states, including Alabama, North Dakota, and South Carolina, have provided state insurance for school buildings for many years at rates which have been 40 percent less than commercial rates, and state insurance fund reserves have been increasing in those states. North Carolina has provided state insurance at 6 percent less than commercial rates and Wisconsin at 50 percent less.

Safeguarding Records

It is impossible to express the value of records in terms of money. Therefore, ordinary insurance coverage is of no value. The only protection for records that can be obtained is to prevent their destruction or loss. Insurance against loss or destruction of records must be obtained by providing appropriate storage space and protection devices for irreplaceable items.

Records are of four principal types:

1. vital records which are irreplaceable and which if reproduced do not have the same value as originals;
2. important records which can be reproduced but at a considerable expense of time and labor;
3. useful records whose loss will cause some inconvenience but which can be readily replaced; and
4. nonessential records which should be destroyed after proper authorization in order to conserve storage space and eliminate a fire hazard.

There are four principal types of protective equipment:

1. vaults;
2. safes;
3. insulated record containers; and
4. electronic storage devices.

Each of these different types of equipment varies considerably in its fire resistance rating, depending on its quality, material, and construction.

The National Fire Protection Association has presented excellent suggestions for safeguarding documentation in its booklet, *Protection of Records*. The following degrees of protection are recommended:

1. *Vital Records* – should have protection which will assure that the records will be preserved even if there is a complete burning-out of the section of the building in which they are located. This degree of protection may be achieved by housing the records in fire-resistant vaults or safes. Six-hour or four-hour vaults or four-hour safes are recommended for most buildings.
2. *Important Records* – should be given the protection recommended for vital records to the greatest possible extent. If it is physically impossible to so protect them, and the building is fire-resistant, important records may be kept in the next best equipment available, but this storage should not be considered as protecting the records against an all-out fire.
3. *Useful Records* – should, as a minimum, be housed in closed steel containers located where they will be least exposed to combustibles, but this should not be regarded as full protection against fire.
4. *Nonessential Records* – require no special protection so far as their value is concerned. Records of this class should be segregated from more valuable records. Any unneeded records should be disposed of in order to eliminate a fire hazard and to save space.[14]

Preservation of records through electronic means has made recordkeeping more secure and less expensive through ease of duplication and placement of records at alternative and remote locations.

STUDENT TRANSPORTATION[15]

Student transportation has become an important item in the school budget. The cost of transportation for the public elementary and secondary schools increased from $35,600,000 in 1925–1926 to more than $415,000,000 in 1958–1959. The number of students transported increased from 1,100,000, representing 31 percent in 1925–1926, to approximately 11,000,000 in 1958–1959 where approximately 36.5 percent of the public school students were transported to school. By 1990–1991, 22,000,000 students were transported, representing 57.3 percent of all students enrolled in public schools and costing $8,700,000,000. Slightly over 25 million students were transported in

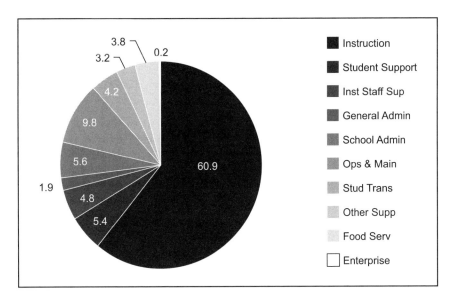

Figure 18.1 Public School Expenditure by Function, FY 2009

2007–2008, or 54.6 percent of all students enrolled in public schools, and costing approximately $21,500,000,000. In FY 1991, student transportation accounted for 3.8 percent of total expenditures, and by FY 2009, the percent of funds expended for student transportation had increased slightly to 4.2 percent. Displayed in Figure 18.1 are national expenditures, by function, for FY 2009. Note that the percent of funds expended for student transportation is relatively modest (4.2 percent), illustrating a pattern that has remained consistent for several years.

Purposes of Student Transportation

Student transportation is essential for the operation of most modern school systems. Transportation is provided for normal students who live beyond a reasonable walking distance, for students who have to transit dangerous and hazardous areas, and for physically disabled children living any distance from school if they need transportation. Transportation is frequently provided for children who live within a reasonable walking distance but who live on routes dangerous for walking.

School buses have become an extension of the classroom in many school systems. The bus can be used to extend the learning experience of students much as a library or laboratory. Therefore, the purpose of school transportation is not only to transport students to and from school but to extend the education experience. Nevertheless, transportation of students is not without costs and can be excessively expensive. It is not good business management to spend more on student transportation than the amount necessary for providing a safe, comfortable, and hygienic service for students who require transportation services. Listed below are suggestions for providing a cost-efficient system that is safe and comfortable.

Transportation Service Policies

Although most states, i.e., state departments of education, distribute student transportation guidelines, regulations, and policies to their individual school districts, it is left to the local school districts to define its transportation service policies before bus routes can be established and time schedules developed.[16] This involves the determination of:

1. how far normal students must live from school in order to be entitled to transportation;
2. whether transportation will be furnished to students who live within the established walking distance but must walk to school on dangerous streets and roads that lack sidewalks;
3. what types of disabled children are entitled to transportation;
4. how far students are required to walk to the main bus line from side roads;
5. whether the bus will stop in front of each student's home on the main route or only at spaced stops limited in number by a required minimum distance between stops;
6. the maximum time that transported students arrive at school before it opens or wait for a bus after school is dismissed; and
7. the maximum speed that buses are permitted to operate.

All of these policies affect student transportation costs, all affect quality of service, and some affect the safety and health of pupils. The problem of the school district is to determine what quality of student transportation service is really needed to enable students to attend school and to protect their health and safety. For example, a school district could establish the following student transportation service policies: all students who want to ride a school bus are entitled to service, buses will give door-to-door service whether on main roads or side roads, no student will spend more than thirty minutes riding a bus to school, no transported student will arrive at school more than five minutes before school opens or wait for a bus more than five minutes after school is dismissed, and buses will not operate at a speed of more than 45 miles per hour. These characteristics represent a high-quality service, but they are expensive and may be difficult to justify to the public.

Further, it is impossible to recommend student transportation service policies that are suitable for all school districts. Variations in climate and traffic patterns and other conditions require variations of service policies among school districts in order to provide equivalent levels of service. Following are some policies that may provide a reasonable quality of service for a school district with an average climate and traffic conditions:

1. Physically normal children living more than one (1) mile from school should be entitled to student transportation;[17]
2. Students with specified disabilities are entitled to public transportation;[18]
3. Students living on roads or streets with heavy traffic and lacking pedestrian sidewalks or paths are entitled to transportation if they live one-half mile or more from school;
4. Buses will not travel on side roads from the main bus routes unless the students live more than three-quarters of a mile from a main route;
5. Secondary students will not spend more than one hour and elementary students not more than 30 minutes in transit to and from school; and

6. Transported students will not arrive at school more than 15 minutes before school opens or wait for a bus for more than 15 minutes after school dismissal.

The Los Angeles Unified School District has published an excellent chart (Figure 18.2) that contains safety rules for those who are transported by school buses.

List of Safety Regulations for Riders of Los Angeles Unified School District Buses

To Parents of School Bus Riders
Responsibility for the safe transportation of school children is a joint effort and must be shared by parents, students and school personnel, as well as school bus drivers and supervisors.

At the Bus Stop
- Show respect for property around the bus stop. Avoid littering or walking on planted areas.
- Students should exit their personal cars prior to the arrival of the bus. Remain at least 12 feet back from the curb.
- Do not run toward the bus. Wait in line until the bus has stopped completely and the door has been opened.
- Board the bus in single file, without pushing. Keep one hand free and use the handrail.

Bus Pass Requirement and Riding
- If you are a middle or senior high school student, you must show the driver your bus pass each time you board the bus.
- While on the bus, you must remain seated, facing forward for the entire trip. Keep your feet and legs out of the center aisle. Keep all parts of your body inside the bus.
- While on the bus, loud conversation is distracting to the driver and unsafe.
- Cell phone usage is for emergency purposes only; driver authorization is required.
- Animals or large hazardous objects are prohibited on the school bus.
- Smoking, eating, fighting, swearing, loud electronic devices, drinking and littering on the bus are not permitted.

Leaving the Bus
- You may get off the bus only at your assigned stop. If you need a different stop in the afternoon, written permission must be obtained from the school administrator and Area Bus Supervisor (ABS).
- Remain seated until the bus comes to a complete stop and the door is opened. Follow the driver's instructions for the unloading sequence. Hold the handrail for balance and safety while walking down the steps. Stay back from the curb as the bus leaves. Stay out of the Danger Zones (please refer to the "Official Notification of Your Child's Transportation Schedule" pamphlet).

Student Behavior on the Bus
- The safe transportation of students requires responsible behavior by all persons who ride school buses. Students who do not follow the regulations or the driver's instructions may be counseled or denied transportation.

Transportation Information
- To the extent feasible and considering traffic conditions, the District will provide transportation for eligible students within a maximum riding time of 90 minutes. The majority of routes and pickup locations are established and will not be changed. Secondary students residing within a five-mile radius or within the magnet school's attendance boundary (whichever is further) will not receive District transportation.

Figure 18.2 List of Safety Regulations for Riders of Los Angeles Unified School District Buses

Source: Los Angeles Unified School District, "Regulations for School Bus Safety," http://transportation.lausd.net/Division_Staff/Regulations_for_School_Bus_Safety. Reprinted by permission of the Los Angeles Unified School District Transportation Services Division.

SCHOOL FOOD SERVICES

It was not until 1904 that Robert Hunter brought the plight of hungry school children to the attention of the nation when he authored *Poverty*.[19] Two years later in 1906, John Spargo reported that several million children in the United States were undernourished and recommended that the nation attack malnourishment through a system of school food services.[20] Prior to the increased interest to address malnourished children during the early years of the twentieth century, several charity-motivated, privately funded school food services programs were initiated during the late 1800s and early 1900s in a number of large cities, including, New York City, Philadelphia, Boston, Milwaukee, Chicago, and Los Angeles.[21]

Good nutrition, particularly in the first three years of life, is important for establishing a good foundation that has implications for a child's future physical and mental health, academic achievement, and economic productivity. Unfortunately, food insecurity is an obstacle that threatens that critical foundation. Displayed in Box 18.3 are statistics concerning food insecurity in the United States. According to the United States Department of Agriculture (USDA), 15.9 million children under age 18 in the United States live in households where they are unable to consistently access enough nutritious food necessary for a healthy life.[22] Although food insecurity is harmful to any individual, it can be particularly devastating among children due to their increased vulnerability and the potential for long-term negative consequences.

BOX 18.3

Food Insecurity in the United States

- 15.9 million children lived in food-insecure households in 2012.
- 20% or more of the child population in 37 states and the District of Columbia lived in food-insecure households in 2011, according to the most recent data available. New Mexico (30.6%) and the District of Columbia (30.0%) had the highest rates of children in households without consistent access to food.
- In 2011, the top five states with the highest rate of food-insecure children under 18 are New Mexico, the District of Columbia, Arizona, Oregon, and Georgia.
- In 2011, the top five states with the lowest rate of food-insecure children under 18 are North Dakota, New Hampshire, Massachusetts, Virginia, and Minnesota.

Eventually, it was the federal government that provided leadership and partial funding that addressed malnourishment of a significant percent of children who were enrolled in our public and nonprofit private schools, including residential child care institutions. In 1946, President Harry S. Truman signed into law the National School Lunch Program (NSLP),[23] named for the influential and long-serving Senator Richard Russell from Georgia. President Truman did so after he read a study that revealed many young men had been rejected from the World War II draft due to medical conditions caused by childhood malnutrition. Since that time, more than 180 million lunches have been served to American children who attend either a public school or a nonprofit private school.

National School Lunch Program[24]

The National School Lunch Program (NSLP) is a federally assisted meal program operating in over 100,000 public and nonprofit private schools, including residential child care institutions. In 1966, President Lyndon Johnson extended the program by offering breakfast to school children. It began as a two-year pilot program for children in rural areas and those living in poorer neighborhoods. It was reported that these children would have to skip breakfast in order to catch the bus for the long ride to school. There were also concerns that the poorer families could not always afford to feed their children breakfast. President Johnson believed that children would do better in school if they had a good breakfast to start their day. The pilot study was such a success that it was decided the program should continue. By 1975, breakfast was being offered to all children in public or nonprofit private schools. This change was made because educators felt that more children were skipping breakfast due to the employment of both parents in the workforce.

In 1968, a summer meals program was offered to low-income children, and breakfast, lunch and afternoon snacks are provided to students each year during the summer break. Any child in need can apply for the program at the end of the school year. Parents that are interested in the summer meals program should contact their local school administration. In 2012, NSLP provided nutritionally balanced, low-cost, or free lunches to more than 31 million children each school day and is administered by the Food and Nutrition Service. At the state level, the NSLP is usually administered by State Education Agencies (SEAs) which operate the program through agreements with school food authorities.

Eligibility Requirements

Generally, public or nonprofit private schools of high school grade or under and public or nonprofit private residential child care institutions are eligible to participate in the NSLP. Participating school districts receive cash subsidies and USDA foods from the U.S. Department of Agriculture (USDA) for each meal served. In return, they must serve lunches that meet federal requirements, and they must offer free or reduced-price lunches to eligible children. School food authorities also are eligible for reimbursement payments for snacks served to children through age 18 if they participate in after school educational or enrichment programs.

Meal and Nutritional Standards

School lunches must meet meal pattern and nutrition standards based on the latest *Dietary Guidelines for Americans*.[25] The current meal pattern increases the availability of fruits, vegetables, and whole grains in the school menu. The meal pattern's dietary specifications set specific calorie limits to ensure age-appropriate meals for grades K–5, 6–8, and 9–12. Other meal enhancements include gradual reductions in the sodium content of the meals (sodium targets must be reached by SY 2014–15, SY 2017–18, and SY 2022–23). While school lunches must meet federal meal requirements, decisions concerning the specific foods served and how the meals are prepared are made by local school food authorities.

Qualification for Free and Reduced-Price Meals

Any child at a participating school may purchase a meal through the National School Lunch Program. Children from families with incomes at or below 130 percent of the poverty level are eligible for *free meals*. Those with incomes between 130 percent and 185 percent of the poverty level are eligible for *reduced-price meals* for which students can be charged no more than 40 cents. (For the period July 1, 2013, through June 30, 2014, 130 percent of the poverty level was $30,615 for a family of four; 185 percent is $43,568.)

Children from families with incomes over 185 percent of poverty pay a full price, although their meals are still partially subsidized. Local school food authorities set their own prices for full-price (paid) meals, but must operate their meal services as nonprofit programs.

Afterschool snacks are provided to children on the same income eligibility basis as school meals. However, programs that operate in areas where at least 50 percent of students are eligible for free or reduced-price meals may serve all their snacks for free.

Reimbursement Levels

Most of the support USDA provides to schools in the National School Lunch Program comes in the form of a cash reimbursement for the number of meals served. The current (July 1, 2014 through June 30, 2015) basic cash reimbursement rates **if** school food authorities served less than 60% free and reduced-price lunches during the second preceding school year are displayed in Box 18.4.

BOX 18.4

Basic Cash Reimbursement Rates

- Free lunches; Reduced-Price Lunches; Paid Lunches
  $2.93; $2.53; $0.28
- Free Snacks; Reduced-Price Snacks; Paid Snacks
  $0.80; $0.40; $0.07

School food authorities that are certified to be in compliance with the updated meal requirements will receive an additional six cents of federal cash reimbursement for each meal served. This bonus will be adjusted for inflation for subsequent years. These above rates exclude the additional six cents. Higher reimbursement rates are also in effect for Alaska and Hawaii, and for schools with high percentages of low-income students.

Additional USDA Support, Other Than Cash Reimbursements

In addition to cash reimbursements, schools are entitled by law to receive USDA foods, called *entitlement* foods, at a value of $0.2325 per meal served in Fiscal Year 2013. Schools can also receive *bonus* USDA foods, contingent upon their availability from surplus agricultural stocks. Through *Team Nutrition,* USDA provides schools with technical training and assistance to help school food service personnel prepare healthy meals, and provide nutrition education to help children understand the link between diet and health.

Foods Distributed by the USDA

States select entitlement foods for their schools from a list of various foods purchased by USDA and offered through the school lunch program. Bonus foods are offered only as they become available through agricultural surplus. The variety of both entitlement and bonus foods provided to schools by the USDA depend upon quantities available and market prices.

Additionally, a very successful project between USDA and the Department of Defense (DoD) has helped provide schools with fresh produce purchased through DoD. USDA has also collaborated with schools to help promote connections with local small farmers who may be able to provide fresh produce.

Children Served (Various Years) from FYs 1947 to 2012

In 1946, the National School Lunch Act created the modern school lunch program, although USDA had provided funds and food to schools for many years prior to 1946. About 7.1 million children were participating in the National School Lunch Program by the end of its first year, 1947. By 1970, 22 million children were participating, and by 1980 the figure was nearly 27 million. In 1990, over 24 million children received school lunches each school day. In FY 2012, more than 31.6 million children received their lunches through the National School Lunch Program. Since the modern program began, more than 224 billion lunches have been served.

Cost of the Federal Food Programs, Including the National School Lunch Program

Figure 18.3 shows the amounts expended for federal food programs, including the National School Lunch Program, in current dollars: $4.4 billion in 1990; in 2000, $7.6 billion; in 2010, $13.7 billion; and in 2012, $14.9 billion. In constant 2012 dollars,[26]

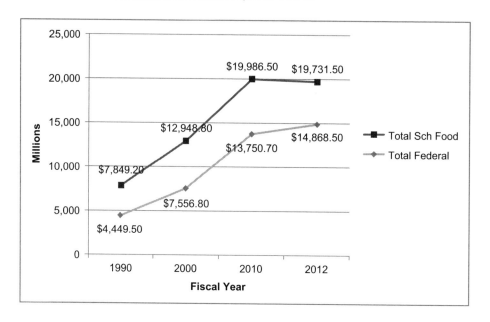

Figure 18.3 Total School Food Services Expenditures and Total Federal Expenditures for Food Services, FYs 1990 to 2012

Source: Institute of Education Sciences, *Revenues and Expenditures for Public Elementary and Secondary Education* (Washington, DC: National Center for Education Statistics, 2013).

NSLP expended $7.7 billion in 1990, $10.1 billion in 2000, $14.4 billion in 2010, and $14.9 billion in 2012. The total current costs for school food services rose from $7.8 billion in 1990 to $12.9 billion in 2000, $20.0 billion in 2010, and $19.7 billion in 2012. When converted to constant 2012 dollars, the total costs for school food services rose from $13.7 billion in 1990, to $17.2 billion in 2000, $21.1 billion in 2010, before falling to $19.7 billion in 2012. The percentages of current disbursements expended for school food services from federal sources declined slightly from 4.2 percent in 1990 to 4.0 percent in 2000, 3.8 percent in 2010, and to 3.7 percent in 2012. Concurrently, the percentages of current disbursements expended for school food services increased slightly from 2.4 percent in 1990, 2.3 percent in 2000, 2.6 percent in 2010, and to 2.8 percent in 2012.

School Food Services Meal Production Programs

Initially, schools provided meals to their students by establishing independent kitchens that implemented their own menus, and they relied on unique, albeit similar procedures for acquisition of goods, services, and equipment. Many of the policies necessary to manage systems of school food services were also independently crafted and implemented. Gradually, due to several pressures, both state and local education agencies began to centralize and standardize the various systems of school food services. A study conducted by Bartlett et al. reported the type of meal production

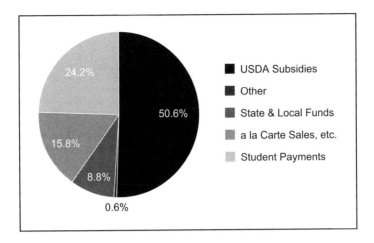

Figure 18.4 Source of Revenue of School Food Authorities.

systems used by School Food Authorities (SFAs) as defined by the mix of the various types of kitchens used by schools in the SFA.[27] Meal production systems included:

1. on-site kitchens only;
2. base/central kitchens only;
3. mostly on-site kitchens; and
4. mostly satellite kitchens.

Also included in the Bartlett study, displayed in Figure 18.4, were the percentages of revenues provided by source.[28] While most school districts continue to provide and manage their own system of school food services, a growing number of school districts are opting to *outsource* the provision of this function. The primary motivation that is driving school districts to seek the services of private providers is to gain increased cost efficiency. Although a shift to outsourcing school food services may initially result in some cost savings, there are disadvantages. The primary disadvantage is that the cost reductions are accrued through reduced employee compensation and benefits. Former employees are replaced or rehired at reduced levels of compensation, thereby negatively affecting personnel morale and experiencing community displeasure.[29]

SUMMARY AND CONCLUSION

The primary purpose of *risk management* is to shift to others or share with others the risks that are greater than it is prudent for an institution, person, firm, or agency to bear individually. Central to the conduct of risk management is the acquisition of several types of insurance coverage. In addition, school districts often purchase insurance to provide coverage to individuals for whom a moral obligation is due despite the absence of a legal obligation. Due to the varied circumstances facing the approximately 15,000 operating school districts in the United States, there is no one system of risk management and accompanying insurance protection that can be implemented universally. Therefore, a risk management program should be tailored to meet the unique requirements of each school district. The primary purpose of school districts' risk management program is to obtain maximum coverage through purchase of appropriate insurance at minimum cost.

Student transportation, while not directly a component of the instructional program of public schools, is an indispensable function of school budgets and has established a record of cost efficiency. Although the percent of students transported has increased over several decades, the percent of the budget allocated to student transportation has remained rather constant at approximately 4.0 percent. Slightly over 25 million students were transported in 2007–2008, or 54.6 percent of all students enrolled in public schools, at a cost of approximately $21.5 billion.

Good nutrition, particularly in the first three years of life, is important for establishing a good foundation that has implications for a child's future physical and mental health, academic achievement, and economic productivity. Unfortunately, food insecurity is an obstacle that threatens that critical foundation. According to the United States Department of Agriculture (USDA), 15.9 million children under age 18 in the United States live in households where they are unable to consistently access enough nutritious food necessary for a healthy life.[30] Eventually, it was the federal government that provided leadership and partial funding that addressed malnourishment of a significant percent of children who were enrolled in our public and nonprofit private schools, including residential child care institutions. In 1946, President Harry S. Truman signed into law the National School Lunch Program (NSLP),[31] the cornerstone of school food services.

KEY TERMS

- Insurance sources
- Underwriting
- Deductible
- Optional insurance
- Fire and casualty

- Transportation service
- Food insecurity
- Free and reduced prices
- Meal production types
- National School Lunch Program

NOTES

1. That is, the school boards assume the liability of their employees.
2. Great Schools, *Montana School Districts* (San Francisco: Great Schools, Inc., 2013). Retrieved from: http://www.greatschools.org/montana/alzada/Alzada-Elementary/
3. Proximity One, *Largest 100 U.S. School Districts* (Proximity One, 2013). Retrieved from: http://proximityone.com/lgsd.htm#info
4. United States Department of Commerce, Bureau of Economic Analysis, *Personal Income Per Capita* (Washington, DC: Survey of Current Business, September, 2013). Retrieved from: http://www.bea.gov/newsreleases/regional/spi/sqpi_newsrelease.htm

5. Texas Education Agency, *Wealth Per Average Daily Attendance* (Austin, Texas: TEA, 2013). Retrieved from: http://www.tea.state.tx.us/index2.aspx?id=8342&menu_id=645&menu_id2=789

6. National Education Association, *Rankings of the States (2012) and Estimates of School Statistics (2013)* (Washington, DC: NEA, 2013). Retrieved from: http://www.nea.org/assets/img/content/NEA_Rankings_And_Estimates-2013_(2).pdf

7. Blacksburg High School, in addition to several other projects that were currently under construction, was integrated into the *Excellence in Education: Realizing Student Success Comprehensive Plan 2008-2014.*

8. See for example: *Code of Virginia*, §2.2-4308.1. *Purchase of owner-controlled insurance in construction projects.*

9. Ohio State Bar Association, *What You Need to Know About Renters' Insurance* (Columbus, Ohio: Ohio State Bar Association, 2013). Retrieved from: https://www.ohiobar.org/forpublic/resources/lawyoucanuse/pages/lawyoucanuse-558.aspx

10. See for example: BCS Insurance Company, Oakbrook Terrace, Illinois. Retrieved from: http://www.bcsins.com/privacy.html.

11. See for example, RCW 48.27.010, Over-insurance prohibited [1984 c 6 § 1; 1947 c 79 § .27.01; Rem. Supp. 1947 § 45.27.01.] Retrieved from: http://apps.leg.wa.gov/rcw/default.aspx?cite=48.27.010http://apps.leg.wa.gov/rcw/default.aspx?cite=48.27.010

12. George E. Rejda and Michael McNamara, *Principles of Risk Management and Insurance* (12th Edition) (New York: Pearson Series in Finance, 2013)

13. See for example: United Services Automobile Association.

14. National Fire Protection Association, *NFPA Catalog* (Customer Contact Center: 11 Tracy Drive, Avon, MA, 2013).

15. Periodically, a group of organizations, including the National Association of State Directors of Pupil Transportation Services, convene and promulgate national school transportation specifications and procedures. The fifteenth national congress on school transportation was held May 16-20, 2010, at the University of Central Missouri, Warrensburg, Missouri. This publication is available from: Missouri Safety Center, University of Central Missouri, Humphreys Suite 201, Warrensburg, MO 64093 Phone: (660) 543-4830 Fax: (660) 543-4482.

16. Assuming that the local school districts have complied with the minimum requirements established by the state.

17. Several states and organizations recommend that children who reside one or more miles from school should be transported. See for example: Washington Department of Education, *School Walk and Bike Routes: A Guide for Planning and Improving Walk and Bike to School Options for Students* (Olympia, Washington: Office of Superintendent of Public Instruction, 2010).

18. *Individuals with Disabilities Education* Act (IDEA) 20 U.S.C. § 1400 et seq., *Americans with Disabilities Act of 1990* (ADA) 42 U.S.C. § 12101 et seq.

19. Robert Hunter, *Poverty* (London: Macmillan, 1904).

20. John Spargo, *The Bitter Cry of Children* (London: Macmillan, 1906).

21. Robert Garvue, Thelma G. Flanagan, and William H Castine, *The National School Food Service and Nutrition Education Finance Project,* Chapter 8, in R.L. Johns, Kern Alexander, and K. Forbis Jordan, *Planning to Finance Education,* Volume 3 (Gainesville, Florida: National Educational Finance Project, 1971).

22. A. Coleman-Jensen, M. Nord, and A. Singh, Household Food Security in the United States in 2012. Table 1B (Washington, DC: USDA ERS, 2013).

23. *The Richard B. Russell National School Lunch Act* (79 P.L. 396, 60 Stat. 230, 1946).

24. USDA, *The National School Lunch Program* (Alexandria, Virginia: Communication Division, USDA, 2013).

25. United States Department of Agriculture, *Dietary Guidelines for Americans, 2015* (Washington, DC: USDA, 2013).

26. Current dollars were converted to constant dollars through use of the Consumer Price Index.

27. Susan Bartlett, Frederic Glantz, and Christopher Logan, *School Lunch and Breakfast Cost Study – II, Executive Summary.* Nutrition Assistance Program Report Series (Washington, DC: United States Department of Agriculture, Food and Nutrition Series, 2008).

28. Ibid.

29. David Thompson, Faith E. Crampton, and R. Craig Wood, *Money and Schools,* 5th Edn. (Larchmont, NY: Eye on Education, 2012).

30. Coleman-Jensen et al., *op. cit.*

31. *The Richard B. Russell National School Lunch Act, op. cit.*

Index

Note: Page numbers followed by 'f' refer to figures and followed by 't' refer to tables.